ENCHIRIDION MILITIS CHRISTIANI

EARLY ENGLISH TEXT SOCIETY

No. 282

1981

I. Albrecht Dürer, The Knight, Death and the Devil

By permission of the National Gallery of Art, Washington D.C.
(Gift of W. R. Russell Allen)

ERASMUS
Enchiridion Militis Christiani

AN ENGLISH VERSION

EDITED BY

ANNE M. O'DONNELL, S.N.D.

Published for
THE EARLY ENGLISH TEXT SOCIETY
by the
OXFORD UNIVERSITY PRESS
1981

Oxford University Press, Walton Street, Oxford OX2 6DP

London Glasgow New York Toronto
Delhi Bombay Calcutta Madras Karachi
Kuala Lumpur Singapore Hong Kong Tokyo
Nairobi Dar es Salaam Cape Town
Melbourne Auckland

and associate companies in
Beirut Berlin Ibadan Mexico City

British Library Cataloguing in Publication Data
Erasmus
  Enchiridion militis Christiani
  1. Christian life
  I. Title   II. O'Donnell, Anne M.
  III. Early English Text Society
  248   BV4501.2   78–40912
  ISBN 0–19–722284–6

*Printed in Great Britain
at the University Press, Oxford
by Eric Buckley
Printer to the University*

DEDICATION

To my first teachers, John J. O'Donnell, Jr. (†1960) and Marie A. O'Donnell, who devoted themselves to the education of their children in the spirit of Erasmus:

Therfore the chefe care of christen men [and women] ought to be applyed to this poynte / that their chyldren streyght waye from the cradle / amongest the very . . . kysses of the parentes / maye receyue and sucke vnder the handes of them whiche are lerned / opynyons and perswasyons mete and worthy of Christe. . . .

Enchiridion, 136/18–23

CONTENTS

PLATES

ACKNOWLEDGEMENTS

THIS edition of the 1534 English translation of Erasmus's *Enchiridion militis Christiani* is the revised version of my doctoral dissertation, which was originally presented in 1972 to Yale University, New Haven, Connecticut. The first stage of my research was supported by a fellowship from the American Association of University Women. This generous grant enabled me to study in Europe during 1969–70, the academic year in which The Netherlands observed the 500th anniversary of Erasmus's birth, and to consult such eminent Erasmians as Abbé Raymond Marcel, Paris; Sir Roger Mynors, Corpus Christi College, Oxford; and Dr. C. Reedijk, the Royal Library, The Hague. A grant from the Folger Shakespeare Library, Washington, D.C., enabled me to continue full-time research in the fall semester of 1970.

The Folger Library has proved to be the home of most of my scholarly labours, but I am also indebted to other libraries for the use of their copies of sixteenth-century Latin and English *Enchiridions*: the Beinecke Library, Yale University; the Library of Congress, Washington, D.C.; the City Library, Rotterdam; the Bodleian Library, Oxford; the University Library, Cambridge; the John Rylands Library, Manchester; the British Library, London.

Among the many who have aided me in this study, I wish to give special acknowledgement to my dissertation director, Professor R. S. Sylvester, whose untimely death is a personal as well as a professional loss to his former students, colleagues, and friends. In addition, I would like to thank: Professor Fred C. Robinson, also of Yale University, for many valuable suggestions regarding sixteenth-century English; Sister Ann Julia Kinnirey, S.N.D., Trinity College, Washington, D.C., for help in evaluating the relative merits of *1533* and *1534* in translating difficult passages of the Latin text; the Revd. Thomas Tighe, S. J., for assistance in translating the Greek in the 1518 *Enchiridion*; Professor E. J. Devereux, of the University of Western Ontario, for light on bibliographical problems in the sixteenth-century English editions of the *Enchiridion*; my typist, Mrs. June Rohrer, who having typed the first version of my Introduction and Commentary was willing to undertake the typing of the revised version; the Catholic University of America for subsidizing typing and xeroxing expenses; Stanley Furmanak, graduate student at Catholic University, for diligent assistance in correcting the page-proofs; Dr. Curt Bühler, of the Pierpont Morgan Library, N.Y. and Professor Norman Blake, of the University of Sheffield, for their exacting review of the bibliographical data; Dr. Pamela Gradon, of the Early English Text Society, for her patient care in reading my typescript and in maintaining our transatlantic correspondence; and finally, the Sisters of Notre Dame de Namur, who have indeed been a supportive community to me in the demanding apostolate of scholarship.

BIBLIOGRAPHY AND ABBREVIATIONS

The bibliography contains only works frequently consulted for Erasmus, the *Enchiridion*, and its possible English translator William Tyndale. Full bibliographical references for other works are given in the footnotes or Commentary. I have used the following abbreviations:

BB   *Bibliotheca Belgica*

DNB   *Dictionary of National Biography*

LP   *Letters and Papers, Foreign and Domestic, of the Reign of Henry VIII*

OED   *Oxford English Dictionary*

OO   *Desiderii Erasmi Roterodami Opera Omnia*

PG   *Patrologia Graeca*

PL   *Patrologia Latina*

STC   Pollard and Redgrave's *Short-Title Catalogue*, 1926 ed.

Allen, *see* Erasmus.

Bainton, Roland H. *Erasmus of Christendom*. New York, 1969. Cited as 'Bainton'.

Béné, Charles. *Erasme et Saint Augustin*. Travaux d'humanisme et renaissance, Prospectus No. 103. Geneva, 1969. Cited as 'Béné'.

Biblia Sacra juxta Vulgatam Clementinam divisionibus, summariis et concordantiis ornata. Tournai, 1956. Cited as 'Vulgate'.

Cassell's New Latin Dictionary: Latin–English, English–Latin. Ed. D. P. Simpson. Rev. edn. New York, 1960.

Devereux, E. J. *A Checklist of English Translations of Erasmus to 1700*. Occasional Publication No. 3. Bodleian Library, Oxford, 1968. Cited as 'Devereux'.

Dictionary of National Biography. Ed. Leslie Stephen and Sidney Lee. 22 vols. New York, 1908–9.

Douai-Rheims, *see The Holy Bible*.

Elton, G. R., ed. *The Reformation: 1520–1559*. The New Cambridge Modern History, vol. 2. Cambridge, 1958.

Erasmus, Desiderius. *Christian Humanism and the Reformation: Selected Writings*. Trans. John C. Olin. Harper Torchbooks. New York, 1965. Cited as 'Olin'.

—— *The Colloquies of Erasmus*. Trans. Craig R. Thompson. Chicago, 1965. Cited as *Colloquies*.

—— *The Correspondence of Erasmus*. Translation of *Opus epistolarum Des. Erasmi Roterodami*. Toronto, 1974– .

—— *Desiderii Erasmi Roterodami Opera Omnia*. Ed. *Joannes Clericus*. 10 vols. Leiden, 1703–6.

——*Douze lettres d'Erasme*. Ed. Roland Crahay and Marie Delcourt. Paris, 1938. Cited as *Douze lettres*.

—— *The Enchiridion*. Trans. Ford Lewis Battles. In *Advocates of Reform from Wyclif to Erasmus*. Ed. Matthew Spinka. The Library of Christian Classics, vol. 14. London, 1953.

—— *Enchiridion: Handbüchlein eines christlichen Streiters*. Trans. Werner Welzig. Graz, 1961.

—— *Enchiridion militis Christiani*. Introduction et Traduction par A. J. Festugière. Bibliothèque des Textes Philosophiques. Paris, 1971. Cited as 'Festugière'.

—— *Enchiridion militis Christiani*. In *Desiderius Erasmus Roterodamus: Ausgewählte Werke*. Ed. Hajo and Annamarie Holborn. 1933; reprinted Munich, 1964. Cited as 'Holborn'.

—— *The Enchiridion of Erasmus*. Trans. Raymond Himelick. A Midland Book. Bloomington, Indiana, 1963. Cited as 'Himelick, *Enchiridion*'.

—— *El Enquiridion o Manual del Caballero Cristiano* . . . Ed. Marcel Bataillon. Traducciones Españolas del Siglo XVI. Madrid, 1932. Cited as 'Bataillon'.

—— *The Epistles of Erasmus from his Earliest Letters to his Fifty-First Year*. Trans. Francis Morgan Nichols. 3 vols. London, 1901–18. Cited as 'Nichols'.

—— *Handbook of the Militant Christian*. Trans. John P. Dolan. Notre Dame, Indiana, 1962.

—— *Opus epistolarum Des. Erasmi Roterodami*. Ed. P. S. Allen *et al*. 12 vols. Oxford, 1906–58. Cited as 'Allen'.

—— *The Praise of Folie*. Trans. Sir Thomas Chaloner. Ed. Clarence H. Miller. EETS 257. London, 1965.

—— *The Praise of Folly*. Trans. Hoyt Hopewell Hudson. New York, 1941. Cited as *Folly*.

—— 'Selections from the Letters—Volz.' In *Erasmus and the Seamless Coat of Jesus*. Translations with Introduction and Notes by Raymond Himelick. Purdue University Studies. Lafayette, Indiana, 1971. Cited as Himelick, 'Letter to Volz'.

Festugière, *see* Erasmus.

Gee, John Archer. 'John Byddell and the First Publication of Erasmus's *Enchiridion* in English.' *ELH*, iv, 1 (1937), 43–59. Cited as Gee, 'John Byddell'.

—— 'Tyndale and the 1533 English *Enchiridion* of Erasmus.' *PMLA*, xlix, 2 (1934), 460–71. Cited as Gee, 'Tyndale'.

Haeghen, Ferdinand van der. *Bibliographie générale des Pays-Bas*. Rééditée M.-T. Lenger, 7 vols. Brussels, 1964–75.

Holborn, *see* Erasmus.

The Holy Bible. Trans. from the Latin Vulgate. Baltimore, 1914. Cited as 'Douai–Rheims'.

Letters and Papers, Foreign and Domestic, of the Reign of Henry VIII. Ed. J. S. Brewer *et al.* 21 vols. London, 1862–1932.

Lewis, Charlton T., and Charles Short, eds. *A Latin Dictionary Founded on Andrews' Edition of Freund's Latin Dictionary, Revised, Enlarged and in Great Part Rewritten.* 1879; reprinted Oxford, 1958.

McConica, James Kelsey. *English Humanists and Reformation Politics: under Henry VIII und Edward VI.* Oxford, 1965. Cited as 'McConica'.

McKerrow, R. B., and F. S. Ferguson. *Title-page Borders used in England & Scotland 1485–1640.* Bibliographical Society, Illustrated Monographs No. 21. London, 1932 [for 1931]. Cited as 'McKerrow and Ferguson'.

More, Thomas. *The vvorkes of Sir Thomas More Knyght . . . wrytten by him in the Englyssh tonge.* London, 1557. Cited as 'More'.

Mozley, J. F. 'The English *Enchiridion* of Erasmus, 1533.' *RES*, xx (1944), 97–107. Cited as 'Mozley'.

New Catholic Encyclopedia . . . 15 vols. New York, 1967.

Nichols, *see* Erasmus.

O'Donnell, Anne M., S.N.D., 'Rhetoric and Style in Erasmus' *Enchiridion Militis Christiani'*, *SP*, lxxvii (1980), 26–49.

Olin, *see* Erasmus.

Patrologiae cursus completus: Series Graeca. Ed. J.-P. Migne. 161 vols. Paris, 1857–66.

Patrologiae cursus completus: Series Latina. Ed. J.-P. Migne. 221 vols. Paris, 1844–65.

Pico della Mirandola, Giovanni. *Opera Ioannis Pici: Mirandule . . .* Strassburg, 1504. Cited as 'Pico'.

Pollard, A. W., and G. R. Redgrave. *A Short-Title Catalogue of Books Printed in England, Scotland, & Ireland . . . 1475–1640.* London, 1926.

—— *A Short-Title Catalogue . . . 1475–1640.* Vol. 2: I–Z. 2nd edn. Eds. W. A. Jackson, F. S. Ferguson, Katharine F. Pantzer. Bibliographical Society Series. London, 1976 (for 1973–5).

Potter, G. R., ed. *The Renaissance: 1493–1520.* The New Cambridge Modern History, vol. 1. Cambridge, 1957.

Tyndale, William. *The New Testament Translated by William Tyndale, 1534 . . .* Ed. N. Hardy Wallis *et al.* Cambridge, 1938. Cited as 'Tyndale's NT'.

—— *William Tyndale's . . . Pentateuch, being a Verbatim Reprint of the Edition of MCCCCCXXX . . .* Ed. J. I. Mombert. New York, 1884. Newly introduced by F. F. Bruce. Carbondale, Illinois, 1967. Cited as 'Tyndale's Pentateuch'.

Vulgate, *see Biblia Sacra. . . .*

Williams, C. H. *William Tyndale.* Leaders of Religion Series. London, 1969. Cited as 'Williams'.

INTRODUCTION

Encomium Enchiridii

THE *Enchiridion militis Christiani* by Erasmus of Rotterdam evoked widespread interest in the sixteenth century as a compendium of humanistic piety. During Erasmus's lifetime alone, the handbook went through more than fifty editions of the Latin original, while during the entire sixteenth century there were ten editions of the English translation. Tudor monarchs obviously considered the *Enchiridion* a book for all seasons since—with only a few emendations—it was acceptable to the religious position of Henry (six editions), Edward (one edition), Mary (two editions), and Elizabeth (one edition).

At first one wonders why the book was so popular, for the text of the *Enchiridion* is repetitive and its tripartite structure is flawed. The sections on the theory of Christian living (Chapters 1–7) and on its practice (Chapters 8–31) are followed by a section on four of the Seven Deadly Sins (Chapters 32–8), a coda which might well have been omitted altogether. Although the author maintains the character and tone of a moral instructor throughout the book, the person addressed varies. Throughout much of the *Enchiridion* Erasmus addresses as 'brother' the courtier friend for whom the book was originally written (44/16, 59/4–5, 90/18, 134/31, 137/27, 168/14).[1] In some instances, however, Erasmus's concern seems to move from the layman to the cleric, perhaps even himself, as Roland H. Bainton[2] suggests.

While this inconsistency in the person addressed may be viewed as a literary flaw, the *Enchiridion*'s 'quality of exhortation' is, according to James Kelsey McConica,[3] one of its most appealing features. Erasmus exhorts his wayward friend with affection, 'Byleue me well brother syngularly beloued in my hert' (44/16–17), and anticipates objections both from his penitent, 'But thou wylt say: it is an harde thynge that thou commaundest: who sayth nay?' (69/20–1), and from other spiritual directors, 'But I heare euen

---

[1] All page and line references in the Introduction and Commentary indicate the 1534 English text.   [2] p. 66.   [3] p. 17.

now, what certayne men (whiche are somwhat well aduised) wyll answere vnto me' (127/25–7). Erasmus reveals his psychological penetration by rehearsing an interior debate between the spirit, 'god is aboue thy father . . . To god thou art bounde for all thynge that thou hast' (81/17–19), and the flesh, 'Excepte thou obey thy father / he wyll disheryte the / thou shalt be called of euery man an vnkynde and vnnaturall chylde . . . ' (81/20–1). Moreover, he demonstrates how an interior discourse ought to be conducted: 'mynisshe ye wronge done of an other man commenly after this maner. He hurte me / but it wyll be sone amended' (202/3–5). Although the *Enchiridion* should be classified as a monologue, its dramatic manner anticipates the dialogue form of Erasmus's maturest work, the *Colloquies*.

Another literary merit of the *Enchiridion* is its use of figurative language. The same love of homely anecdote which moved Erasmus to collect the *Adagia* leads him to illustrate his moral teaching with proverbial lore. The tenuous coexistence between body and soul resembles the mortal impasse between the weaponless forester and the wolf he is holding off by its ears (60/S.4). The man who neglects spiritual goods for material ones recalls Aesop's dog, who dropped his bone while gaping after its reflection in the water (149/19–21). Mythology is transformed into metaphor as Hercules battles with the self-regenerating Hydra of pride (76/11–15) and Ulysses steers a middle course between the Scylla of presumption and the Charybdis of despair (41/24–30). But it is in dealing with the Old Testament that Erasmus's allegorical method, in the tradition of Origen and St. Augustine, finds its proper object. The Israelite's marriage to a tonsured Gentile bride provides a model for the Christian humanist's discriminating study of pagan literature (47/28–31). The sibling rivalry between Esau and Jacob depicts the struggle between 'ryght of law' and 'craft of grace' (73/20). Aaron the high priest and Moses the lawgiver symbolize 'prayer' and 'knowlege of the law of god' (43/15), the two chief weapons of the Christian soldier.

As befits a manual which inculcates a specifically Christian piety, the *Enchiridion* makes its most significant religious contribution in its treatment of the New Testament. Erasmus's standard practice here is direct quotation from the sacred text, as the following anticipation of the *Praise of Folly* demonstrates: 'If any man (sayth Paule) amonge you semeth to be wyse in this worlde / let hym be a foole . . . ' (56/22–3). Unlike his handling of the Old Testament, Erasmus uses a literal approach in his exegesis of the New Testament. The Pauline distinction between 'spirit' and 'flesh', so central to the teaching of the *Enchiridion*, is carefully defined according to the best philological method: 'That the philosophers call reason / y^t calleth Paule somtyme the spyrit / somtyme ye inner man / otherwhyle the lawe of the mynde. That they call affection / he calleth somtyme the flesshe: somtyme ye body: another tyme the vtter man and the lawe of the membres' (71/17–21). The other leading theme of the handbook, the union of all believers in Christ, is given a vivid practical application: 'Thy membre complayneth and grynneth for hunger, and thou spewest vp partryges' (156/11–12). While Erasmus's *philosophia Christi* gives scant attention to the historical Jesus (see the Commentary, 96/19–22 n.), it is permeated by an awareness of his Mystical Body and rooted in his Word. But as McConica notes, the revolutionary aspect of the *Enchiridion*'s exegesis was its assumption that the new scriptural criticism could be practised by a layman.[1]

THE COMPOSITION OF THE *ENCHIRIDION*

While visiting Tournehem in the Pas de Calais during the summer of 1501, Erasmus renewed his friendship with James Batt, tutor of the son of Erasmus's patroness, and with a certain courtier named John. This visit occasioned the genesis of the *Enchiridion*, as Erasmus later recalled in his 'Letter to John Botzheim':

Erat in ea arce quidam amicus mihi Battoque communis. Huic erat vxor singulari pietate praedita, ipse nulli peior quam sibi; homo profusus, scortationibus et adulteriis opertus, alioqui comis ad omnem conuictum. Theologos omnes fortiter contemnebat, vno me excepto. Vxor mire satagebat de salute viri. Haec per Battum mecum agit vt aliqua notarem scripto, quae religionem incuterent homini; sic tamen ne sentiret haec vxoris impulsu geri. Nam erat et in hanc saeuus vsque ad plagas, more videlicet militari. Obsequutus sum, annotaui quaedam ei tempori congrua.[2]

---

[1] p. 18.

[2] Allen, *1*, 19–20. 'There was in this borough a certain friend of Batt's and mine He had an extremely devout wife, but he was his own worst enemy, an extravagant man, openly adulterous, obliging to anyone for every kind of entertainment. He vehemently objected to all theologians, except me. His wife certainly had her hands full with the man's spiritual well-being. Through Batt, she arranged for to me write something to drive religion into the man, but he was not to see his

Erasmus addressed two letters to this courtier friend. The first of these (Ep. 164) now forms the beginning and end of the main text of the Enchiridion (see below, 32/8–28 and 205/31–207/26). The second (Ep. 698), written in 1517, again admonished John in brotherly fashion to mend his ways and congratulated him on a recent honour. Allen tentatively identifies this courtier with John of Trazegnies, who was appointed to the Order of the Golden Fleece in November 1516.[1] Otto Schottenloher identifies him with Johann Poppenreuter, a manufacturer of armaments from Nürnberg.[2] A. J. Festugière discounts this identification primarily because he believes John the German was unmarried, notwithstanding Erasmus's statement to the contrary in the 'Letter to Botzheim'.[3] Whatever his identity, John the German was not converted to a more spiritual way of life by the Enchiridion, as Erasmus explained in the 1518 edition: 'he also not onely hath not withdrawen hym selfe from the courte / but is dayly moche deper drowned therin than he was afore tyme / . . . as he confesseth hym selfe with moche great mysery' (5/33–6/1).

Selecting a more flourishing model of Christian piety, Erasmus dedicated the new edition to Abbot Volz, 'that who so euer shall take any preceptes to lyue well, of Erasmus, sholde haue an example redy at hande of our father Volzius' (29/3–5). Paul Volz (1480–1544)[4] had been elected abbot of the Benedictine community at Hügshofen near Schlettstadt in 1512. His correspondence with Erasmus extended from 1515 until the latter's death in 1536 and includes four letters from Erasmus (Epp. 858, 1075, 1518, 1529) and six letters from Volz (Epp. 368, 372, 1525, 1607, 3069, 3114). Erasmus's criticisms of monastic living in the 'Preface' (Ep. 858) to the Enchiridion (see, for example, 27/13–31) seems to have occasioned doubts in Volz's mind about the validity of his own vocation (Epp. 1075, 1518). Internal strife at Hügshofen (Ep. 1525), the sack of the abbey during the Peasants' Revolt (Ep. 1607),

---

wife's hand in this. For he could be violent on the subject even to assault, just like a soldier. I complied and wrote something suitable for the occasion.' Unless noted otherwise, the translation is my own'.

[1] Allen, 1, 373.
[2] 'Erasmus, Johann Poppenreuter und die Entstehung des Enchiridion Militis Christiani', Archiv für Reformationsgeschichte, xlv, 1 (1954), 109–16, cited by Bainton, p. 76.
[3] Festugière, 1971), pp. 29–34.
[4] Allen, 2, 158–9.

and his own sympathy with the Reformers eventually moved Volz
to leave the monastic life. While the *Enchiridion* had failed to effect
a change of heart in the courtier, it did succeed in making a good
Christian layman out of the abbot.

When Erasmus decided to publish his handbook of moral teaching in February 1503/4,[1] he consciously grafted this work on to
a literary tradition that stemmed back to classical and patristic
times. Cicero in his *De Officiis* (44 B.C.) had written a treatise on
Stoic ethics for his son Marcus Tullius, then a student of Peri-
patetic philosophy in Athens. Erasmus published an annotated
edition of the *De Officiis* in April 1501, a short time before he began
composition of his *Enchiridion*. Although both books are handbooks
of morality written for a specific person, their differences are more
striking than their similarities: Cicero's outlook is social and civic;
Erasmus's, personal and religious. In his 'Letter to James Voecht',
which serves as the editor's preface to the *De Officiis*, Erasmus
anticipated his later use of the double meaning of 'enchiridion',
'handbook' and 'hand-dagger':

> Quos quoniam Plinius Secundus negat vnquam de manibus deponi
> oportere, voluminis magnitudinem quoad licuit contraximus, quo sem-
> per in manibus enchiridii vice gestari et, quod scripsit idem, ad verbum
> edisci possint ... Quapropter te hortor, mi charissime Iacobe, vt hunc
> pugiunculum semper in manibus gestites; breuem quidem illum, sed non
> Vulcaniis armis aut Homericus Achilles aut Aeneas Vergilianus munitior.[2]

Another classical manual of Stoic philosophy actually bore the
title of *Encheiridion*. This was a compendium of the teachings of
the Greek ex-slave Epictetus (A.D. *c.* 50–120),[3] which in name and
in tone of moral exhortation anticipates Erasmus's *Enchiridion*.
Epictetus's works had been translated from Greek into Latin by
the Florentine humanist Angelo Poliziano (1454–94).[4] Although

---

[1] Since the year at Antwerp was calculated from Easter, 'February 1503'
means '1504'. Nichols, *1*, 361 n.

[2] Allen, *1*, 356–7.'Since Pliny the Younger asserts that these [three books of
Cicero's *Offices*] should never be put out of one's hands, we have contracted the
size of the volume as much as possible so that it can always be carried by hand
and, as the same Pliny wrote, learned word for word ... Thus I exhort you, my
dear James, always carry in your hands this little dagger, that short [treatise], no
less fortified [by it] than either Homer's Achilles or Virgil's Aeneas was with
the arms of Vulcan.'

[3] Epictetus, *Encheiridion*, in *The Discourses as Reported by Arrian, The
Manual and Fragments*, trans. W. A. Oldfather, 2 vols. (London, 1926).

[4] See, e.g., Epicteti Stoici En- / CHIRIDION, / E *Graeco interpretatum*

Erasmus became aware of the scholarly achievement of the Italian Renaissance as a schoolboy at Deventer and again as an Augustinian friar at Steyn,[1] it cannot be proved that he had actually read Epictetus's manual. It is certain, however, that he had read Augustine's.[2] In a letter to Batt, Erasmus lists among his personal effects sent separately from England in 1500 'Augustini Enchiridion membranis scriptum'.[3] St. Augustine had written his spiritual handbook in A.D. 421 for the Christian layman, Laurentius. Using the Apostles' Creed for a framework, he expounded his perennial themes: the Trinity, the problem of evil, predestination. One amusing similarity between these two works of Augustine and Erasmus is the authors' common difficulty in curbing their expansiveness.

While the tradition of the moral handbook stems from the pagan classics, the motif of the Christian soldier comes from the Scriptures. St. Paul elaborates the metaphor in his exhortation to the Ephesians:

Stand therefore, having your loins girt about with truth, and having on the breastplate of justice, And your feet shod with the preparation of the gospel of peace: In all things taking the shield of faith, wherewith you may be able to extinguish all the fiery darts of the most wicked one. And take unto you the helmet of salvation, and the sword of the Spirit (which is the word of God) (Eph. 6: 14–17).[4]

Christian iconography and church history give many other examples of the spiritual combat. The figures of Sebastian, George, and Martin of Tours, all three Roman soldiers, were depicted by legend as pierced by the arrows of fellow soldiers, embattled with a dragon like a Christian Perseus, or dividing the military cloak with Christ disguised as a beggar. In the early twelfth century military orders such as the Knights Templar and Knights Hospitaller were founded to combine the practice of poverty, celibacy, and obedience with military service against the Moslems. After the failure of the Crusades, the Knights Templar were disbanded, but the Knights Hospitaller moved their headquarters to Rhodes,

ab Angelo Politiano. / [printer's mark] / PARISIIS, / *Apud Iacobum Bogardum* . . . / 1545. Duke University, Durham, N.C., Rare Book Room D9/E64EN.

[1] Albert Hyma, *The Youth of Erasmus,* 2nd ed., enl. (New York, 1968), pp. 48, 165.

[2] Augustine, *Enchiridion,* in *Confessions and Enchiridion,* trans. Albert C. Outler, The Library of Christian Classics, vol. 7 (Philadelphia, 1955).

[3] Allen, *1,* 285. 'The *Enchiridion* of Augustine written on parchment'.

[4] Douai–Rheims.

where they remained until they were driven to Malta by the Turkish victory in 1522 (four years after Erasmus wrote the 'Letter to Volz'). In 1513 Albrecht Dürer designed the famous copper engraving 'The Knight, Death, and the Devil',[1] possibly inspired by Erasmus's Christian soldier, *Miles Christi*, appropriately enough as *miles* was the technical term for 'knight' in Medieval Latin. Eight years later on hearing the rumour of Luther's alleged assassination, Dürer wrote in his diary:

'O Erasme Roderodame, where wilt thou take thy stand? Look, of what avail is the unjust tyranny of worldly might and the powers of darkness? Hark, thou Knight of Christ . . . , ride forth at the side of Christ our Lord, protect the truth, obtain the crown of the Martyrs![2]

Besides returning to the sources of classical and Christian antiquity in writing the *Enchiridion*, Erasmus drew on contemporary witness. During his first visit to England in the latter half of 1499, Erasmus made the acquaintance of the Oxford reformer John Colet (*c.* 1466–1519), whose lecture notes on St. Paul's Epistle to the Romans and First Epistle to the Corinthians survive from this period.[3] In his 'Letter to Jodocus Jonas on Vitrier and Colet' Erasmus later recalled the powerful attraction of Colet's Oxford lectures: 'In theologica professione nullum omnino gradum nec asequutus erat nec ambierat: tamen nullus erat illic doctor vel theologiae vel iuris, nullus abbas aut alioqui dignitate praeditus quin illum audiret, etiam allatis codicibus'.[4] Besides enthralling his fellow Englishmen, Colet deeply impressed the young Dutchman, who after his return to the Continent undertook his own commentary on Romans. When Erasmus sent Colet a complimentary copy of the *Enchiridion* in 1504, he referred to this earlier work of exegesis: 'Quanquam ante triennium ausus sum nescio quid in epistolam Pauli ad Romanos, absoluique vno quasi impetu quatuor volumina.'[5] Erasmus probably refers to this very commentary at

[1] See frontispiece.

[2] Erwin Panofsky, *Albrecht Dürer* (Princeton, 1943), *I*, 151–2, 198–9.

[3] *An Exposition of St. Paul's Epistle to the Romans*, ed. J. H. Lupton (London, 1873); *An Exposition of St. Paul's First Epistle to the Corinthians*, ed. J. H. Lupton (London, 1874).

[4] Allen, *4*, 515. 'Though he had neither obtained nor sought for any degree in divinity, yet there was no doctor there, either of divinity or law, no abbot or other dignitary but came to hear him and brought his textbooks with him as well', Olin, p. 177.

[5] Allen, *1*, 404. 'Three years ago, indeed, I ventured to do something on Paul's Epistle to the Romans, and at one rush, as it were, finished four volumes', *The*

the end of the *Enchiridion*, when he recommends assiduous reading of St. Paul, 'vpon whome we haue now a good while enforced with great diligence to make a comment or a enarracyon' (206/32–3). The *Enchiridion* itself reveals how thoroughly Erasmus steeped himself in Pauline texts since, after the ninety-odd references to St. Matthew's Gospel, the greatest number of scriptural allusions in the book are to First Corinthians (*c.* sixty examples) and to Romans (*c.* fifty examples).

Before taking up residence in Oxford, Colet had travelled in Italy, drawn especially by the fame of the Florentine Neo-Platonists, Marsilio Ficino and Pico della Mirandola. Either through his English contacts or through his independent reading, Erasmus was influenced by the works of Pico, first published at Bologna in 1496. As I demonstrate in the Commentary to this edition, there is a parallel between the following rules in the *Enchiridion* and the 'Regulae Dirigentes' of Pico:

Erasmus	*Pico*
8th Rule	12th Rule
9th Rule	10th Rule
11th and 12th Rules	7th Rule
11th Rule	5th Rule
13th Rule	8th and 6th Rules
15th Rule	11th Rule
17th Rule	4th Rule
18th Rule	8th Rule
20th Rule	7th and 8th Weapons
21st Rule	4th and 5th Weapons
22nd Rule	6th Weapon
1st Remedy	12th Weapon[1]

Another young Englishman, Thomas More, shared Colet's enthusiasm for the New Learning. About two years after the first publication of the *Enchiridion*, More translated Pico's Twelve Rules and expanded Pico's Twelve Weapons into rhyme-royal stanzas.[2] Since

---

Correspondence of Erasmus: Letters 142 to 297, 1501 to 1514, trans. R. A. B. Mynors and D. F. S. Thomson, annotated by Wallace K. Ferguson (Toronto, 1975), 2, 86.

[1] *Opera Ioannis Pici: Mirandule* . . . (Strassburg, 1504), ff. 111ᵛ–12.
[2] Frederic Seebohm, *The Oxford Reformers* (3rd ed., 1911), pp. 151–9. For

interests converge here, it is difficult to say whether Colet or Erasmus or both influenced More, but when Erasmus came to write his manual of piety, he in turn was very probably influenced by the memory of two contemporary Christian laymen, Giovanni Pico and Thomas More.

LATIN EDITIONS OF THE *ENCHIRIDION*[1]

During Erasmus's lifetime there appeared more than fifty editions of the *Enchiridion* in Latin and over a dozen in various vernaculars. This mighty river of editions began as a freshet in Antwerp with Thierry Martens's publication of the *Enchiridion* in the collection *Lucubratiunculae* in February 1503/4. Some five years later, in 1509, Martens issued a reprint while in 1515 the very same publisher, now established in Louvain, produced the first separate edition of the *Enchiridion*. In the same year (1515) and again in 1516 Mathias Schurer of Strassburg and Valentin Schumann of Leipzig responded to the growing interest in the *Enchiridion* by each bringing out editions.[2]

In 1518 Erasmus himself added to the growing tide of *Enchiridion*s by commissioning John Froben of Basel to issue an edition prefaced by the newly written 'Letter to Volz'. Froben's edition is the ultimate, and perhaps even the actual, source of the English editions of 1533 and 1534. The year 1519 saw a sudden spate of Latin editions, five in all, as well as the first vernacular translation, a Czech version made by the Bohemian Brethren, who recognized in the *philosophia Christi* a spirituality akin to their own ideal of gospel piety and simplicity.[3]

The real inundation of *Enchiridion*s, however, occurred in the early 1520[?]'s: three Latin editions and one German in 1520, six Latin and another German in 1521, eight Latin in 1522, and the high-water mark in 1523 with ten Latin[4] and two Dutch editions.

More's version of Pico see *The vvorkes of Sir Thomas More Knyght . . . wrytten by him in the Englyssh tonge* (London, 1557), pp. 21A–27C. For the possibility that More introduced Erasmus to Pico see R. S. Sylvester, 'A Part of His Own: Thomas More's Literary Personality in His Early Works', *Moreana*, xv and xvi (November 1967), 35.

[1] The bibliographical data discussed in this section are drawn chiefly from *BB*.
[2] Schurer, 1517, seems to be another issue of Schurer, 1516.
[3] P. S. Allen, *The Age of Erasmus* (New York, 1914), pp. 293–4.
[4] Two editions of 1523, Paris (Bonnemere) and Venice (Gregory of Gregorius),

After this the flood abated: two Latin editions in 1524, a French and a German in 1525, one Latin edition each in 1525, 1526, 1527, and 1528, with a Spanish edition in 1527 and in two 1528, three Latin editions and one French in 1529, two Latin and one Italian in 1531, an English editions in 1533 and in 1534, and a Latin edition in 1534/35 and another in 1535.[1]

Ascertaining which of these many post-1518 editions is the source of the Tudor translation is a Herculean labour. By comparing the bibliographical descriptions given in *BB*, those lent me by Sir Roger Mynors of Corpus Christi College, Oxford, and those made by me from editions located in the Bodleian Library, the British Library, the Cambridge University Library, the John Rylands Library in the University of Manchester, and the Rotterdam City Library, I have been able to group the various editions under the following heads:

A

Basel (Froben, 1518)

B

Editions lacking side-notes

C

Editions lacking the 'Letter to Volz'

D

Mainz (Schoeffer, January 1520)

E

Miscellaneous

According to the information given in *BB*, there are surprisingly few editions springing from the stock of Basel, 1518. Of these, Basel (Froben, October 1519) and Louvain (Martens, May 1520) lack the word 'ira' in the 'Letter to Volz'.[2] Thus of the A

are not listed in *BB*, but a copy of each can be found in the City Library, Rotterdam; neither contains margin notes.

[1] Mainz (Schoeffer, 1521) is a German translation, and Leipzig (Lotter, *c.* 1522), a Latin edition of the 'Letter to Volz' only.

[2] Since English *1533* and *1534* both contain 'ire' (18/11), the Tudor translation must have been made from Froben, 1518, or from one of its reprints containing 'ira', see Allen, *3*, 361, 370 n.

stock only Basel (Froben, 1518) and Vienna (Singrenius, 1524) are possible sources of the English translation:

A

Froben, 1518
⋮
Singrenius, 1524[1]

Strassburg (Schurer, January 1519 and Morhard, February 1522) Paris (de Colines, April 1523 and Bonnemere, 1523); Cologne (Cervicornus 1523), and Venice (Gregory of Gregorius, February 1523); all lack side-notes so the B stock is eliminated as a possible source. The C stock does not include the 'Letter to Volz' so Leipzig (Schumann, 1519, 1520, 1521, 1522 and Lotter, c. 1522) and Zwolle Corver, October 1519), also missing side-notes, are also excluded as possible sources of the Tudor translation of the *Enchiridion*.

The D stock is so complex that for greater clarity I have divided it into two sub-heads: Mainz (Schoeffer) and Strassburg (Knobloch). According to *BB*, Mainz (Schoeffer, January 1520) is a reprint of one of the early *Lucubrationes* editions. Nevertheless, this edition must derive from Froben, 1518, at least in part, since it contains the 'Letter to Volz'. The three other Mainz editions (Schoeffer, March 1521, December 1522, and February 1523) are also possible sources of the English translation. W[illem] K[orver?],[2] July 22 [1522?], lacks the poem 'Libellus Loquitur', and is thus eliminated:

D1

Schoeffer, January 1520
⋮
Schoeffer, March 1521
|
Schoeffer, December 1522
|
Schoeffer, February 1523

BB sees a large group of predominantly Strassburg editions springing from the Schoeffer, March 1521, stock, all of which are described as containing side-notes and the 'Letter to Volz':

[1] The dotted line indicates probable derivation; the solid line, *BB*'s affirmation of certain derivation.

[2] Sir Roger Mynors suggested this identification for 'W. K.'.

D2

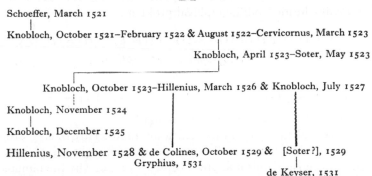

Schoeffer, March 1521
|
Knobloch, October 1521–February 1522 & August 1522–Cervicornus, March 1523
|
Knobloch, April 1523–Soter, May 1523

Knobloch, October 1523–Hillenius, March 1526 & Knobloch, July 1527

Knobloch, November 1524
|
Knobloch, December 1525

Hillenius, November 1528 & de Colines, October 1529 & [Soter?], 1529
Gryphius, 1531 |
de Keyser, 1531

Furthermore, the following copies (which I have been able to examine more closely) all contain 'ira' in the 'Letter to Volz': three in the Beinecke Library, Yale University, namely Strassburg (Knobloch, October 1523, November 1524, December 1525); and four in the Folger Shakespeare Library, Washington, D.C., namely Mainz (Schoeffer, January 1520, March 1521) and Strassburg (Knobloch, October 1521, February 1522). The descent of the D1 and D2 stock from Froben, 1518, and the burgeoning of editions in this group would argue that the source of the English *Enchiridion* is very probably to be found here.

Finally *BB* describes several editions which do not clearly fit into any of the groups named above. Because they contain sidenotes and the 'Letter to Volz', the following editions qualify as possible sources of English *1533* and *1534*: Cologne (Cervicornus, 1519) and Antwerp (Thibault, *c.* 1521, and Hillenius, October 1523). Less probable candidates are Lyons (Jacques Moderne, *c.* 1521) and Paris (Veuve de Gourmont, *c.* 1522), both of which fail to mention the 'noua mireque utilis Praefatio' on their title-pages, unlike English *1533* with its 'newe and meruaylous profytable preface' (see the Commentary, 3/11–14 n.). Cologne (Soter, 1521) and Lyons (Gryphius, 1529) are listed but not described in *BB*. This comparison of bibliographical descriptions has eliminated approximately half of the known Latin editions of the *Enchiridion* from consideration as the exact source of the English translation. At the present time, a critical Latin text of the *Enchiridion* is being prepared for The Hague edition of the *Complete Works of Erasmus* by Abbé Raymond Marcel. Perhaps in the course of his research Abbé

Marcel will be able to furnish us with new weapons for overcoming this Hydra-headed bibliographical problem.

ENGLISH EDITIONS OF THE *ENCHIRIDION*

1. *Bibliographical Descriptions*[1]

1533[2]

1. STC 10479; Devereux No. C42.1; *BB* No. E1107.

[A four-piece border with a floral design]
❡ A booke called in latyn En= / chiridion militis christiani- -[3] / and in englysshe the ma= / nuell of the christen / knyght- - replenys= / shed with moste / holsome pre= / ceptes- - / made / by the famous / clerke Erasmus of / Roterdame- - to the whiche / is added a newe and / meruaylous pro= / fytable pre= / face. /

Colophon: [The same four-piece border as on the title-page] ❡ Here endeth this boke called / Enchiridion or the manuell of / the chrysten knyght- - made by / Erasmus of Roterdame- - in the / whiche boke is conteyned many / goodly lessons very necessary and / profytable for the soules helth / of all true christen people: Im= / printed at London by Wynkyn / de Worde- - for Iohan Byddell- - / otherwyse Salisbury- - the .xv. / daye of Nouembre. And be for / to sell at the sygne of our Lady / of pytie next to Flete bridge. / 1533. / ❡ Cum priuilegio regali.

Collation: 8°. a–c⁸ A–R⁸ S¹⁰.

Contents: a1 [title], a1ᵛ ❡ The booke speaketh. ❡ The printer to the faythfull reder., a2–c7ᵛ [Letter to Volz], c8–c8ᵛ [Table of Contents], A1–S10 [Enchiridion], S10ᵛ [colophon].

Signatures: The first four leaves of each gathering are signed except the title-page, which is unsigned. Of the ten leaves of gathering S, the first five are signed.

---

[1] In the bibliographical descriptions of the title-pages and colophons roman type indicates the original gothic; italic indicates italic in the original; bold face, a heavier gothic type and sans-serif, the roman type of the original. All abbreviations except 'yᵉ' have been expanded.

[2] H. S. Bennett, *English Books & Readers, 1475–1557, Being a Study in the History of the Book Trade from Caxton to the Incorporation of the Stationers' Company* (Cambridge, 1952), p. 249, suggests under no. 10478.1 that there is a 1501 edition with a copy at the Huntington Library, San Marino, California. When he checked the catalogue at my request, however, the Curator of Rare Books failed to find such a copy.

[3] A virgule in the sixteenth-century text is represented by a double dash in these bibliographical descriptions.

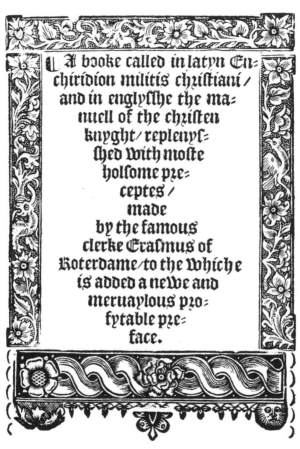

¶ A booke called in latyn En=
chiridion militis christiani /
and in englysshe the ma=
nuell of the christen
knyght / replenys=
shed with moste
holsome pre=
ceptes /
made
by the famous
clerke Erasmus of
Roterdame / to the whiche
is added a newe and
meruaylous pro=
fytable pre=
face.

II. Erasmus, *Enchiridion Militis Christiani*:
Title page of the 1533 English Translation

By permission of the Folger Shakespeare Library

Running titles: None.

Copy used: *A1*, Copy 1 at the Folger Library. The inside cover of this copy bears the label, '*From the library of* | SIR R. LEICESTER HARMSWORTH, BART.' Page a4 bears the signature 'Robt Rush-brooke' and page C2ᵛ, two lines of faint secretary handwriting.

A2, that in the Beinecke Library, Yale University. In this copy single words from the text are written in the margin on fifty-two pages in a post sixteenth-century hand. Pages from a2ᵛ–S10 are numbered, probably by the same hand. S10 is signed:

R S
Reading 1685

This copy also contains: the arms of C. Inglis, M.D.; the book-plate of Sir Thomas Brooke Bart., F.S.A., Armitage Bridge; an engraving of ERASMVS ROTERᵒDAMVS; a woodcut inserted as a frontispiece of the risen Christ dressed as a soldier accompanied by a kneeling cleric.

Copies consulted: One at the Folger Library, and a University Microfilm copy of one at the British Library, G. 11983.

Remarks: Thirty lines per page, five woodcut initials, text and side-notes in gothic type, no catchwords.

1534

2. STC 10480; Devereux No. C42.2; *BB* No. E1108.

[A frame of personified Virtues, McKerrow and Ferguson, No. 29, with printer's mark and 'Iohan Byddell' at the bottom of the frame.]
❡ Enchiridion militis chri / stiani- - whiche may be called in / eng-lysshe, the hansom wea= / pon of a christen knyght- - / replenysshed with ma= / ny goodly and godly / preceptes: made / by the fa= / mous / clerke Erasmus of Ro= / terdame, and newly / corrected and / imprin= / ted. / ∵ / Cum priuilegio regali. /

Colophon: ❡ Here endeth this boke called Enchiri= / dion, or the manuel of the christen knyght / made by Erasmus of Roterdame- - in the / whiche boke is conteyned many goodly les / sons, very necessary and profytable for the sou / les helthe of all true christen people. Im= / prynted at London in Fletestrete, by Wyn= / kyn de Worde, for Iohan Byddell, other= / wyse Salysbury, dwellynge at the sygne / of our lady of pytye, nexte to Flete brydge / where they be for to sell. Newly corrected / and amended, in the yere of our lorde god / M.v.C.xxxiiij. the .xij. daye of February. /

Collation: 8°. a–c⁸ A–Q⁸ r⁸ S¹⁰.

Contents: a1 [title], a1ᵛ ⁅ The booke speaketh. ⁅ The printer to the faythfull reder., a2–c7ᵛ Epystle., c8–c8ᵛ The table., A1–S10 (middle) Enchiridion., S10 (middle) [colophon], S10ᵛ [woodcut of an angel with two cornucopias marked with 'Gratia' and 'Charitas' and two shields with 'Iohan Byddell' and his printer's mark[1]].

Signatures: The first four leaves of each gathering are signed except the title-page, which is unsigned. Of the ten leaves of gathering S, the first five are signed.

Running titles: Epystle. a2–c7ᵛ, The table. c8–c8ᵛ, Enchiridion. A1, Caplo. primo. A1ᵛ–A2, A3ᵛ–A8ᵛ; Caplo .j. A2ᵛ–A3, Caplo .ij. to .xxxviij. B1–S10.

Copies used: *A1*, that in the Folger Library. The inside cover bears the notation in red ink 'Eb.23' and the label '*From the library of* / SIR R. LEICESTER HARMSWORTH, BART.' There are margin notes in secretary handwriting on fifty-five pages (frequently clipped). The last of these handwritten notes, that on S10ᵛ, is in Latin: 'Fata fruetur / Eternam requiem dictitet ille / mihi.' This is a correct transcription of the Latin, but the maxim is difficult to translate because of lack of agreement: *fruetur* is not in the plural to agree with 'Fata', and *fruor* usually governs the ablative not the accusative as in 'Eternam requiem'.

A2, a xerox made from a University Microfilm of a copy at the British Library, 4400. f. 23. In this microfilm b1ᵛ and b2 are missing and have been supplied by a xerox from the original in the British Library.[2]

A3, a xerox of a copy in the John Rylands Library, R 16397.

Remarks: Thirty lines per page, two woodcut initials, running titles, text and side-notes in gothic type, no catchwords.

[1] In spite of this woodcut, the 1534 *Enchiridion* is not listed in Edward Hodnett, *English Woodcuts, 1480–1535*, 2nd edn. (London, 1973).

[2] University Microfilm and the *British Museum General Catalogue of Printed Books* (London, 1960) give the call no. as 4400. f. 23, while E. J. Devereux gives it as C.110. a. 37.

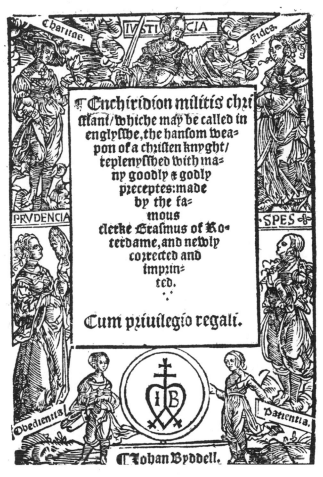

Charitae. IVSTICIA Fides.

PRVDENCIA SPES

¶ Enchiridion militis chri
ſtiani/whiche may be called in
englyſſhe,the hanſom wea=
pon of a chꝛiſten knyght/
replenyſſhed with ma=
ny goodly ⸪ godly
pꝛeceptes:made
by the fa=
mous
clerke Eraſmus of Ro=
terdame,and newly
coꝛrected and
impꝛin=
ted.
⸪

Cum pꝛiuilegio regali.

Obediens Patientia.

¶ Iohan Byddell.

III. Erasmus. *Enchiridion Militis Christiani*
Title page of the 1534 English Translation

By permission of the Folger Shakespeare Library

1538

3. STC 10480.1; Devereux No. C42.3; not in *BB*.

[An architectural border, McKerrow and Ferguson, No. 42, with printer's mark at the bottom of the frame.]

[Printer's ornament: leaf] ENCHIRIDION / militis christiani-- whiche / may be called in englysshe, / the hansom weapon of a / chrysten knyght - -reple= / nyshed with many / goodly and god= / ly preceptes : / made by the / famous / clerke Erasmus of Ro= / terdame, and newly / corrected and / imprin= / ted. / ·.· / Cum priuilegio Regali. /

Colophon: ❡ Here endeth this boke called En= / chiridion, or the manuel of a chrysten / knyght, made by Erasmus of Roter= / dame- - in the whiche boke is contey= / ned many goodly lessons, very neces= / sary and profitable for the soule helth / of all true christen people. Imprynted / at London by Iohan Byddell, dwel= / lynge at the sygne of the Sonne a= / gaynste the Cundyte in Fletestrete, / where they be for to sell. Newly / corrected and amended— in the / yere of our lorde god. M / CCCCC.xxxviij. the / xxx. day of May. / [Printer's ornament: inverted leaf and upright leaf] / [Type ornament with John Byddell's mark.]

Collation: 8°. A–D⁸ G⁸ F⁸ E⁸ H–V⁸.

Contents: A1 [title], A1ᵛ ❡ The boke speaketh. ❡ The prynter to the faythfull reder., A2–C6 Epystle., C6ᵛ–C7 The table, C7ᵛ–V7ᵛ Enchiridion, V8 [colophon], V8ᵛ [blank].

Signatures: The first three leaves of each gathering are signed except the title-page, which is unsigned.

Running titles: Epystle. A2–C6, The table. C6ᵛ–C7, Enchiridion. C7ᵛ, Caplo primo. C8–D6ᵛ, Caplo .ij. to .xxxviij. D7–V7ᵛ.

Copy used: That in the John Rylands Library, R 18285. In this copy pages C7, K8ᵛ, and V8ᵛ have owners' names written in secretary hand. Other pages have 'note,' 'note well', and hand marks written in the margins, all in secretary hand.

Remarks: Thirty-two lines per page, three woodcut initials, running titles, text and side-notes in gothic type, no catchwords.

1541

4. STC 10482; Devereux No. C42.4; *BB* No. E1109.

[An architectural border, McKerrow and Ferguson, No. 42, with printer's mark at the bottom of the frame.]

[Printer's ornament: leaf] ENCHIRIDION / militis christiani, whiche / may be called in Englisshe, / the hansom weapon of a / christen knight, reple= / nished with many / goodly and god= / ly pre- ceptes: / made by the / famous / clerke ERASMVS / OF ROTER= / DAME, and / newly cor= / rected and / imprin= / ted. / CVM PRIVILEGIO / ad imprimendum solum. /

Colophon: [Printer's ornament: hand] HERE endeth this boke called / ENCHIRIDION, or y^e manuell / of a chrysten knyght, made by E= / RASMVS of ROTERDAME / in the which boke is conteyned ma= / ny goodly lessons, very necessary and / profitable for the soule helth of all / true christen people. / IMPRINTED at LONDON / by IOHAN BYDDELL, dwel / lynge at the sygne of the SONNE / agaynst the CVNDYTE in / FLETESTRETE, where / they be for to sel. Newly / corrected and amended. / in the yere of our lorde / god. M.CCCCC / xlj. the .xviij day / of August. / [Printer's ornaments: inverted leaf, (:'), leaf] / [Type ornament and mark as in 1538.]

Collation: 8°. A–V⁸.

Contents: A1 [title], A1ᵛ The booke speaketh. The printer to the faythfull reader., A2–C6 Epistle., C6ᵛ–C7 The table., C7ᵛ–V7ᵛ Enchiridion., V8 [colophon], V8ᵛ [blank].

Signatures: The first three leaves of each gathering are signed except the title-page, which is unsigned.

Running titles: Epistle. (with variant spelling 'Epystle') A2–C6, The table. C6ᵛ–C7, ENCHIRIDION. C7ᵛ, Caplo. primo. C8–D6ᵛ, Caplo .ij. to .xxxviij. D7–V7ᵛ (eleven errors in numbering).

Copy used: That in the Cambridge University Library, Syn. 8. 54. 120. In this copy A1ᵛ is inscribed in ink, 'Presented by F. Seebohm / 1895 /' and in pencil, '189; 95.' C7ᵛ, C8, and V8ᵛ have notes in secretary hand. O1ᵛ and O4ᵛ have notes printed in a post-secretary hand. C6 has the pencil note, 'Aug 15.'

Remarks: Thirty-two lines per page, three woodcut initials, running titles, text and side-notes in gothic type, no catchwords.

1544 A

5. STC 10483; Devereux No. C42.5; *BB* No. E1110.
[An architectural border, McKerrow and Ferguson, No. 42, with printer's mark at the bottom of the frame.]

[Printer's ornament: leaf] ENCHIRI= / dion militis christiani, / whiche may be called in En= / glisshe, the hansome weapon / of a christen knight, reple= / nisshed with many / goodly and god= / ly preceptes: / made by the / famous / clerke / ERASMVS / of Roterdame, and / newly corrected / and imprin= / ted. / [Printer's ornament: leaf] *Cum priuilegio ad im= / primendum solum.* /

Colophon: [Printer's ornament: hand] Here endeth this boke cal= / led Encheridion [sic], or yᵉ manuell / of a chrysten knyght, made by / Erasmus of Roterdame in yᵉ / whiche boke is conteyned ma= / ny goodly lessons, very neces= / sary and profitable for the soule / helthe of all true christen peo= / ple. / [Printer's ornament: leaf] Imprynted at London by / Iohn byddell, dwellyng at the / sygne of the sonne agaynste yᵉ / cundyte in fletstrete, where thei / be for to sel. Newly corrected / and amended. in the / yere of oure lorde / god. M.v.C. / xliiii. the xix / of Nouem / bre. / [Printer's ornaments: inverted leaf, (:), leaf.]

Collation: 8°. A–V⁸.

Contents: A1 [title], A1ᵛ The booke speaketh. The printer to the faithfull reader., A2–C6 Epystle., C6ᵛ–C7 The table., C7ᵛ–V7ᵛ ENCHIRIDION, V8 [colophon], V8ᵛ [blank].

Signatures: The first three leaves of each gathering are signed except the title-page and R3, which are unsigned.

Running titles: *Epystle*. A2–C6, *The table*. C6ᵛ–C7, ENCHIRI-DION C7ᵛ, *Capitulo primo*., *.ij*., *.iij*., *.iiij*., *.V*., *.VI*. to *.XXXVIII*. C8–V7ᵛ (nineteen errors in numbering).

Copy used: That in the Bodleian Library, Vet. A1. f. 46. In this copy A1–A2, A7–A8, C2, V3, V6–V7 are missing. V8 is a fragment and the side-notes on A3–A4 have been partially trimmed away. The British Library copy on University Microfilm, 696. a. 43 (2), has been consulted in these defective places. The Bodleian copy is inscribed with an English and a Latin passage both written in secretary hand on the inside cover.

Remarks: Thirty-two lines per page, three woodcut initials, running titles in italic, text and side-notes in gothic type, no catchwords.

1544 B

6. STC 10484; Devereux No. C42.6;[1] *BB* No. E111.

[An architectural border, McKerrow and Ferguson, No. 42, with printer's mark at the bottom of the frame.]

[Printer's ornament: leaf]: EN= / CHIRIDION MI= / litis christiani, whiche / may be called in Englysshe, the / hansome weapon of a Chrysten / knyght, replenysshed with many / goodly and godly preceptes: / made by the famus [*sic*] clerke / ERASMVS OF / Rotterdame, and / newly corrected / and imprin= / ted. / ❡ CVM PRIVILE= / GIO AD IMPRI= / MENDVM SO= / LVM. /

Colophon: [Printer's ornament: leaf]: **Here en=** / **deth this boke called** En= / chiridion, or the manuell of a / Chrysten knyght, made by / Erasmus of Roterdame in the / which boke is conteyned ma / ny godly lessons, very neces= / sary and profitable for the soule / helth of all true christen peo= / ple. / **Imprynted at London** / in Fletestre [*sic*], at the sygne of y^e / Sonne by Iohnn Byddell. / Newly corrected and amended. / **In the yere of our lorde god.** / M.CCCCC.XLIIII. / The .xix. daye of / Nouembre. / [Printer's ornament: Maltese cross.]

Collation: 8°. A–V⁸.

Contents: A1 [title], A1^v The booke speaketh. The prynter to the faythful reader., A2–C6 Epystel., C6^v–C7 The table., C7^v–V7^v Enchiridion., V8 [colophon], V8^v [blank].

Signatures: The first five leaves of each gathering are signed except the title-page, which is unsigned.

Running titles: Epystel. A2–C6 (with the error "Ehystel', A3), The table. C6^v–C7, Enchiridion. C7^v–V7^v (verso only), Capitulo .I. to .XXXVIII. C8–V7 (recto only).

Copy used: That in the Folger Library, which contains secretary handwriting on the title-page and P6^v.

Copy consulted: A University Microfilm of one in the British Library, C. 25. c. 25.

Remarks: Thirty-two lines per page, three woodcut initials, running titles in roman, text and side-notes in gothic type, catchwords.

---

[1] Devereux, p. 15, suggests a date before June 1545 for this edition.

1548

7. STC 10485; Devereux No. C42.8;[1] *BB* No. E1113.

[An architectural border: McKerrow and Ferguson, No. 55]
❡: ENCHI= / RIDION MI= / LITIS CHRISTI / ani, which may be cal /
led in englyshe yᵉ hansome / weapon of a Chrysten / knyght,
replenyshed with / many goodlye and godlye / preceptes made by
the fa= / mus clearke Erasmus / of Roterdame, and / newly corrected / and impryn / ted. / *Cum priuilegio ad impri- / mendum
solum.* /

Colophon: [Printer's ornament: leaf]: **Here en= / dethe this
booke called** / Enchiridion, or the manuell of a / Chrysten knight,
made by Erasmus / of Roterdame, in the which boke is / conteyned
many godly lessons, ve / ry necessary and profytable for / the soule
helth of al true / christen people. / [Printer's ornaments: leaf,
flower, inverted leaf] / ❡ Imprynted at London in Flete / strete
at the Sygne of the George / next to saynt Dunstons church by /
Wyllyam Powel. In the yere / of our lord God. M.D. / xlviii.
The xxv. / daye of Octo= / ber. / [Printer's ornament: hand] Cum
priuilegio ad impri= / mendum solum. /

Collation: 8°. A–P⁸ Q⁴.

Contents: A1 [title], A1ᵛ ❡ THE BOKE SPEAKETHE. ❡ The
prynter to the faythefull Reader., A2–C1ᵛ Epystell., C2–C2ᵛ The
table., C3–Q3ᵛ Enchiridion., Q4 [colophon], Q4ᵛ [blank].

Signatures: The first five leaves of each gathering are signed except
the title-page, which is unsigned. Of the four leaves of gathering
Q, only the first two are signed.

Running titles: Epystell. A2–C1ᵛ (except for variants 'Epestell',
A6, A8ᵛ, and B2, and 'Epysteil', A4ᵛ and B3), Enchiridion. C2,
The table. C2ᵛ, Capitulo .i. C3, Enchiridion. C3ᵛ–Q3ᵛ (verso only),
Capitulo .i. to .xxxviii. C4–Q3 (recto only).

Copy used: That in the Folger Library, which contains an obliter-
ated owner's name on the title-page and Q4, and worm-holes and
water-stains throughout.

---

[1] No mention is made of C42.7, William Middleton, *c*.1547, because there is
no copy known, Devereux, p. 16.

Copy consulted: A University Microfilm of one in the British Library, 3925. b. 31.

Remarks: Thirty-six lines per page, three woodcut initials and one woodcut ornamental bar on C1ᵛ, running titles in roman, text and side-notes in gothic type, catchwords.

Marian A

8. STC 10481; Devereux No. C42.9; *BB* No. E1114.

[No border]
❧ ENCHIRI / dion militis Christiani, / whiche maye be called in En= / glishe, the hansome weapon / of a Christian Knight, reple= / nished with many goodli and / godly Preceptes, made by the / famous Clarke Erasmus of / Roterdame, and newly / corrected and im= / prynted. / [In a cartouche] Cum priuilegio ad impri= / mendum solum. /

Colophon: ❧ **Imprinted** / at London in Poules / Churchyard at the / sygne of the Bel / by Robert / Toy. / *Cum priuilegio ad Im-primen / dum solum.* /

Collation: 8°. A–V⁸.

Contents: A1 [title], A1ᵛ The boke speaketh. The prynter to the faithful Reader., A2–C5ᵛ Epystle., C6–C6ᵛ The Table., C7–V6ᵛ Enchiridion., V7 [blank], V7ᵛ [colophon], V8–V8ᵛ [blank].

Signatures: The first five leaves of each gathering are signed except the title-page, A4, A5, and C5, which are unsigned. The first leaf of each gathering from E to V is signed only with the capital letter. The number in signature G5 is inverted.

Running titles: Epystle. (with variant spellings: 'Epistel', 'Epystel', 'Epystell') A2–C5ᵛ, The table. C6ᵛ, Enchiridion. C7ᵛ, Capitulo. I. to XXXVIII. C8–V6ᵛ (eight errors in numbering).

Copy used: That in the Bodleian Library, 8° S 308 Art.; this copy lacks V8, for which the University Microfilm of a copy in the British Library, 3925. b. 30, was consulted.

Remarks: Thirty-two lines per page (R8 has thirty-three lines), two woodcut initials, running title in roman, text and side-notes in gothic type, catchwords.

Marian B

9. STC 10486: Devereux No. C42.10;[1] *BB* No. E1115.

[No border]
❡ ENCHIRI / dion militis Christiani, / whiche maye be called in En= / glishe, the hansome weapon / of a Christian Knight, reple= / nished with many goodli and / godly Preceptes, made by the / famous Clarke Erasmus of / Roterdame, and newly / corrected and im= / prynted. / [In a cartouche] Cum priuilegio ad impri= / mendum solum. /

Colophon: ❡ **Imprinted** / at London in Poules / Churchyard at the / syne of the Lambe / by Abraham / Veale. / *Cum priuilegio ad Imprimen* / *dum solum.* /

Collation: 8°. A–V⁸.

Contents: A1 [title], A1ᵛ The boke speaketh. The prynter to the faithful Reader., A2–C5ᵛ Epystle., C6–C6ᵛ The table., C7–V6ᵛ Enchiridion., V7 [blank], V7ᵛ [colophon], V8–V8ᵛ [blank].

Signatures: The first five leaves of each gathering are signed except the title-page and A4, A5, and C5, which are unsigned. The number in G5 is inverted.

Running titles: Epystle. (with variant spellings: 'Epistel', 'Epystel', 'Epystell') A2ᵛ–C5ᵛ, The Table. C6ᵛ, Enchiridion. C7ᵛ, Capitulo. I. to XXXVIII. C8–V6ᵛ (eight errors in numbering).

Copy used: That in the Library of Congress, BV 45009/.L2 E75/ 1550?/Rare BK. Coll.

Copy consulted: A University Microfilm of one in the British Library, 4400. f. 24.

Remarks: Thirty-two lines per page (R8 has thirty-three lines), two woodcut initials, running titles in roman, text and side-notes in gothic type, catchwords.

1576

10. STC 10487; Devereux No. C42.11; not described in *BB*.

[A border composed of arabesques and stylized flowers]
ENCHIRI-- / dion militis Chri-- / stiani, *which may be* / called in

---

[1] In a private letter to me, Professor Devereux affirmed that the Toy and the Veale issues have the same date; 1576, the date given for the Veale issue in his *Checklist*, p. 16, is a typographical error taken from the date of the next edition, STC 10487.

English, the / hansome weapon of a / *Christian Knight*: / Replenished with many good / ly preceptes: made by the / famous Clerke Erasmus / of Roterdame, and newly / corrected and im= / prynted. / 1576. / Imprinted at London in Fleet / streete, by William How / for Abraham Veale. /

Colophon: None.

Collation: 8⁰. A–B⁸ C⁴ D–Y⁸ Z⁴.

Contents: A1 [title], A1ᵛ [blank], A2–C3 The Epistle., C3ᵛ–C4 The Table., C4ᵛ The Booke speaketh. The Printer to the faithfull Reader., D1–Z4ᵛ The hansome weapon of a christian Knight.

Signatures: The first four leaves of each gathering are signed except the title-page and A3, B4, E4, T3, Z3, and Z4, which are unsigned.

Running titles: The Epistle. A2ᵛ–C3 (with variant spelling 'Epistell' and with 'The Table' erroneously given on B8), The Table. C4, The hansome weapon D1ᵛ–Z4ᵛ (verso only), of a christian Knight. D2–Z4 (recto only), (with 'a christian of Knight' erroneously given on Y5, Y6, and Z3).

Copy used: That in the Bodleian Library, Vet. A1 f. 101. This copy has water-stains and many torn edges.

Copies consulted: One in the Folger Library and a University Microfilm of one in the British Library, C. 58. aa. 10.

Remarks: Thirty-three lines per page in the 'Letter to Volz', twenty-eight lines per page in the *Enchiridion*, two woodcut initials, text of the 'Letter to Volz' in small gothic type, text of the *Enchiridion* in larger gothic type, side-notes of the 'Letter to Volz' in small roman type, side-notes of the *Enchiridion* in small gothic type, catchwords. Proper names and foreign words are usually printed in roman type; introductory lines to the 'Letter to Volz' (A2) and to the *Enchiridion* (D) are printed in consecutive lines of roman, italic, and gothic type, running titles in roman.

2. *The English Editions*

The first English translation of the *Enchiridion* was published by Wynkyn de Worde for John Byddell[1] on 15 November 1533,

---

[1] The first six editions of the *Enchiridion* (*1533, 1534, 1538, 1541, 1544A, 1544B*) were printed for or by John Byddell, who specialized in publishing

two months after the birth of the Princess Elizabeth. On 12 February 1534 a second and revised edition appeared, two months before the Act of Royal Supremacy was passed by Parliament.[1] In spite of its approximately nine hundred and fifty variants, the 1534 English *Enchiridion* is closely based on that of 1533. In fact, there is usually a page-by-page correspondence between the two editions except for I2^v to I3^v, where the material-per-page covered by *1534* runs behind that covered by *1533*. Then on page I4, *1534* substitutes an eight-word phrase for a fifty-one-word phrase in *1533*, a concise instead of a verbose translation (see Commentary, 115/18-19 n.). After this substitution, the material-per-page covered by *1534* runs ahead of that covered by *1533* until page I8^v, after which *1534* again generally maintains a page-by-page correspondence with *1533*. The edition of *1538*, not listed in the 1926 *STC* or described in *BB* but included in E. J. Devereux's *Checklist of English Translations of Erasmus to 1700*,[2] reprints *1534* rather than *1533*, as do all editions in this genealogy. Even though *1538* is the first edition to be published after the passage of the Act of Supremacy, its emendations connote but do not, strictly speaking, denote schism: approximately ten variants designating the 'Pope' as 'Bishop of Rome' and one associating Paul with Peter's primacy, 'Peter and Paule ye apostles and capteyns of the churche' (see Appendix, 177/26 n.).[3]

In addition to preserving the anti-papal emendations of *1538*, *1541* introduces five more of its own (see Appendix, notes to 13/24, 13/25-7, 19/30, 138/26, 163/14). Its other emendations argue for obedience to the king and for civil concord (see Appendix,

works of religious controversy until his death c. 1545. See Gee, 'John Byddell', pp. 45, 47.

[1] It seems likely that the date '12 February, 1534' follows the popular method of counting the new year from 1 January. If the publisher of the *Enchiridion* had been following the official method of counting the new year from 25 March, then '12 February, 1534' (i.e. 1535) would indicate that the book appeared ten months after the passage of the Act of Royal Supremacy, surely time enough to make the warranted emendation of 'Pope' to 'Bishop of Rome'. But no such emendation occurs in the second edition, a fact which argues that '12 February, 1534' indicates the two-month interval before the Act of Supremacy. Cf. Sir W. W. Greg, 'Old Style—New Style', *Collected Papers*, ed. J. C. Maxwell (Oxford, 1966), p. 371.

[2] Devereux, p. 15.

[3] See also Douglas H. Parker, 'The English "Enchiridion militis christiani" and Reformation Politics', *Erasmus in English*, v (1972), 16-21.

13/27–30 n.), emphasize the right preaching of the Gospel (see Appendix, 14/25 n.), deny the efficacy of papal pardons (see Appendix, 22/8–9 n.), and remove ten references to monks or friars, the dissolution of the monasteries having by then been completed. The substantive changes or omissions first introduced by *1541* were all followed by the two later Henrician and the Edwardian editions, except for a side-note (see Appendix 206/S.3 n.), which the editors of *1544 B* and *1548* could easily have derived from a casual consultation of an earlier edition.

The next two issues present a challenge since they are undated. Both come from the same press although their colophons differ, the one reading '❡ Imprinted / . . . at the / sygne of the Bel / by Robert / Toy', the other reading '❡ Imprinted / . . . at the / syne of the Lambe / by Abraham / Veale'. Since there is an exact correspondence between *STC* 10481 and 10486 in collation, signatures, and number of lines per page, both were evidently printed from the same type-setting with Toy and Veale each contracting to sell part of the edition. Although the two issues are undated, internal evidence suggests that they were published during the reign of Mary Tudor (1553–8) since most of the anti-Roman emendations introduced in *1538* and *1541* are reversed.

In the first third of the text, *Marian A* and *B* seem to follow the *1541–1548* tradition since they do not restore passages where references to the pope have been simply omitted rather than changed into anti-papal statements (see Appendix, notes to 13/24, 13/25–7, 14/25, 19/30). In other places 'Bishop of Rome' is further emended to 'Pope of Rome', although the editors overlook one 'bysshop of Rome' (see Appendix, 11/18 n.), the plea for civil obedience and concord (see Appendix, 13/27–30 n.), and the repudiation of papal pardons (see Appendix, 22/8–9 n.). In the last two-thirds of the book, however, *Marian A* and *B* restore all the *1534* references to monks and friars, even where the emendations of *1541–1548* are not anti-clerical. Perhaps a cursory glance at *1534* revealed the side-notes 'Monkes' (see Appendix, 124/S.1 n.) and 'Fryers' (see Appendix, 193/S.1 n.) and cautioned the editors to make a closer collation with the pre-Act of Supremacy text. At the very end of the book, however, *Marian A* and *B* again seem to follow the *1541–1548* tradition as several minor variants indicate, for example: 'thrusteth' (*1541–1576*) instead of 'crussheth' (*1533–1538*) (199/31), 'bryngyng' (*1548–1576*) for 'burgynge'

(*1533–1544 A*) and 'burnynge' (*1544 B*) (205/17). Strangely enough, the Elizabethan (1576) edition of the *Enchiridion* follows *Marian A* and *B* in their pro-papal and pro-monastic restorations, but introduces its own Protestant emendations, in which references to the Mass become references to the Communion Service (see Appendix, 113–4 n.). *1576* also restores several side-notes found in *1534* (32/S.2, 42/S.2, 77/S.2) and two lines from the same edition (sig. D1, line 21 and sig. H6, line 5), all omitted by *Marian A* and *B*.

Two sixteenth-century abridgements of the English *Enchiridion*— one made by Miles Coverdale from the 1534 *Enchiridion*, the other a separate anonymous translation edited by John Gough[1]—will not be discussed here or represented in the following genealogical table:

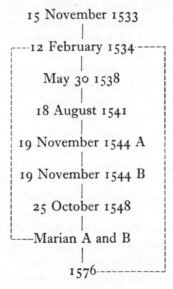

15 November 1533

12 February 1534

May 30 1538

18 August 1541

19 November 1544 A

19 November 1544 B

25 October 1548

Marian A and B

1576

COMPARISON OF THE ENGLISH TEXT WITH THE LATIN ORIGINAL

Since it has not as yet been possible to ascertain which particular Latin edition of the *Enchiridion* was the source of the English translation, I have used the Froben, 1518, edition as the basis of

---

[1] *A shorte Recapitulacion or abrigement of Erasmus Enchiridion*, trans. Myles Coverdale (Antwerp, 1545), *STC* 10488; *A godly boke wherein is contayned certayne fruitfull rules, to be exercised by all Christes souldiers*, ed. John Gough (London, 1561), *STC* 12132.

my comparison of the Latin text with the 1534 copytext and the
1533 variants. In focusing attention on the fidelity of the translation
to the original, I have noted in the Commentary every omission of
more than three Latin words.

These omissions fall into three general categories. The first set
includes clauses containing a Greek word: 'nam Paulino uerbo
[ἀναζωπυρῶμεν] libenter utimur' (see Commentary, 12/7-8 n.)
and 'atque ut uerbo utar Paulino, πειθαρχεῖ' (see Commentary,
24/33 n.). The second set omits repetitive clauses from a series: 'et
dum utrumque male conantur. in utroque claudicant' (see Commentary, 77/24 n.), 'et cum multiplicaueritis orationes uestras, non
exaudiam uos' (see Commentary, 128/28-129/1 n.), and 'bene mereri,
de male merentibus' (see Commentary, 148/18 n.). A subset containing phrases of three words or less illustrates this same habit of
pruning: 'quid auditur' (see Commentary, 12/4 n.), 'Minor Coletae'
(see Commentary, 154/13 n.), and 'si resarcire, resarci' (see Commentary, 203/25 n.). The third set contains clauses which seem to
have been eliminated for substantive rather than stylistic reasons,
but only the first of these excisions seems politically significant:
'et [populi res] quam minima tyrannide premantur' (see Commentary, 13/30 n.), 'in spiritu, hoc est' (see Commentary, 43/30 n.),
'sed hic cibus temporarius erat' (see Commentary, 48/3-4 n.), and
'id genus plurima facinora' (see Commentary, 159/24 n.).

Besides the omissions noted above and in the Commentary, the
English translation differs notably from the Latin in the following
cases. Erasmus himself made two significant interpolations in the
'Letter to Volz' in an edition of his selected correspondence published at Basel in 1529. Perhaps mindful of the Peasants' Revolt in
1524-5, Erasmus attempted to mollify secular rulers in the first
interpolation: 'Etenim si mores aestimemus, vix alios videas crassius
Christianos: de plerisque [principum] loquor, non de omnibus.'[1]

With the Reformation establishing itself in Basel that same year
(1529) and occasioning his remove to Freiburg im Breisgau,
Erasmus in the long second interpolation adopted a somewhat
more conciliatory approach to Roman Catholic monasticism:

Quod si quis Benedicti, Francisci, Augustini vitam et regulas attentius
excutiat, perspiciet illis nihil aliud in votis fuisse quam vt cum spontaneis

---

[1] Allen, 3, 370. 'And indeed, if we are appraising morals, you will scarcely
see other Christians more gross; I am speaking of the majority [of princes], not
of all', trans. Olin, p. 121.

amicis iuxta doctrinam Euangelicam in libertate spiritus viuerent; eos-
que fuisse compulsos vt de vestibus ac cibis caeterisque rebus exter-
nis aliquid praescriberent; nimirum veritos ne, quod fieri solet, plus
tribueretur humanis constitutionibus hominum quam Euangelio. Hor-
rebant diuitias; fugitabant honores etiam ecclesiasticos. Laborabant
manibus, vt non solum ipsi graues non essent cuiquam, sed superesset
vnde subuenirent aliorum inopiae; occupabant montium cacumina,
nidulabantur in locis palustribus, colebant arenas locaque deserta.
Denique tantam hominum multitudinem sine conuiciis, flagris et car-
ceribus moderabantur, sola doctrina, monitis, officiis et vitae exemplis.
Tales erant monachi quos amat laudatque Basilius, quos tuetur Chryso-
stomus: in illos vtcunque quadrabat, quod ad Marcellam scribit diuus
Hieronymus, monachorum et virginum choros esse florem et precio-
sissimum lapidem inter ornamenta Ecclesiae.[1] Hoc elogio dictu mirum
quam hodie sibi blandiantur monachi qualescunque. Verum feremus
vt amplectantur laudem, si simul amplectantur exemplum. Mox enim
vir prudentissimus subiicit formam monachorum, quos eo titulo dignos
censuit. 'Vox quidem' inquit 'dissona, sed vna religio. Tot pene psal-
lentium chori quot gentium diuersitates. Inter haec, quae vel prima
inter Christianos virtus est, nihil arrogant sibi de continentia supercilii.
Humilitatis inter omnes contentio est. Quicunque nouissimus fuerit,
hic primus putatur. In veste nulla discretio, nulla admiratio. Vtcunque placuerit incedere, nec detractionis est nec laudis. Ieiunia quoque
neminem subleuant, nec defertur inediae, nec moderata saturitas con-
demnatur. Suo Domino stat vnusquisque aut cadit.[2] Nemo iudicat
alterum, ne a Domino iudicetur: et quod in plerisque prouinciis fami-
liare est, vt genuino dente se lacerent, hic penitus non habetur.'[3] Hac-
tenus ille formam optimorum monachorum depinxit: eam ad horum
temporum mores conferat qui velit.

Talia fuerunt monachismi primordia, tales patriarchae.[4]

[1] Jerome, *Epistola 46*, PL xxii, 489.   [2] Rom. 14:4.
[3] Jerome, *Epistola 46*, PL xxii. 489-90.
[4] Allen, *3*, 375-6. 'But if anyone examines more attentively the life and
rules of Benedict, Francis, or Augustine, he will observe that what they wished
was only to live with willing friends in liberty of spirit close to the Gospel
teaching; and that they had been forced to prescribe to some extent about
clothing and food and other outward matters, undoubtedly fearful lest more
be attributed, as is often the case, to the human ordinances of men than to the
Gospel. They dreaded wealth, they fled honors, even ecclesiastical ones. They
labored with their hands not only that they themselves might not be a burden
to anyone but that there might be an abundance from which to help others in
need. They occupied mountain peaks, they nested in marshy places, they dwelt
in sandy and abandoned regions. At length they tamed a great multitude of men
without reproaches, scourgings, and prisons but by teaching alone, by counsel,
by service, and by the example of their lives. Such were the monks whom Basil
loves and praises, whom Chrysostom defends; there was complete agreement

Although it is possible that 1529 marks a *terminus ad quem* for the Latin source of the English translation or even that the English translator deliberately omitted these passages (especially the eulogy of good monks), it seems more probable that the translator never even saw these interpolations since Erasmus introduced them into an edition of selected letters and not into the *Enchiridion* itself.

The English translation of the *Enchiridion* is less striking for its omissions from the Latin however than for its myriad additions .In the Commentary I have noted only the most significant of thees: full English translations of elliptical Latin, such as 'tuos', which is translated 'thy frendes and subiectes, or them ouer whom thou bearest offyce, rowme or authorite' (161/14–15); doublets in which native English defines a word newly introduced into the language from Latin, for example, 'speke moost agaynst / and crye out vpon' which introduce 'exagerate' (22/25 and Glossary); internal glosses that add to as well as explain the original context, as in 'holy scripture' (54/34), which defines the armour of the spiritual warfare in a more specific way than would Eph. 6 : 14–17; and finally all side-notes not found in the 1518 Latin edition. I have omitted from the Commentary the forty-odd instances where proper names have been supplied by the translator such as 'kyng *Dauid* the prophete' (39/27-8); all the doublets whose members say virtually the same thing, as in 'so farre disagreyng / and of so sondry opinyons' (8/27-8); all the many glosses which make explicit material that is

among these men, as Saint Jerome writes to Marcella, that the troop of monks and virgins is the flower and the most precious jewel among the ornaments of the Church. It is wonderful to relate how today monks of every kind flatter themselves with this statement. But we shall allow them to embrace the praise if at the same time they embrace the example. Moreover, the most prudent man suggests this image of the monks whom he has judged worthy of that title: "A dissonant voice indeed", he says, "but one religion. Almost as many choruses of psalm singers as different kinds of people. Meanwhile, and this is certainly the very first virtue among Christians, they arrogate nothing to themselves because of the control of their pride. All strive for humility. Whoever shall have been last, this man is considered first. In their dress there is no distinction, no admiration. It is the cause neither of blame nor of praise however one has been pleased to conduct himself. Fasts also exalt no one, nor is deference paid to total abstinence, nor is a moderate satiety condemned. Each one stands or falls in the sight of his Lord [Rom. 14:4]. No one judges another, lest he be judged by the Lord; and what is customary in very many regions, to censure oneself severely, does not entirely prevail here." Thus far this man has painted the picture of the best monks; whoever wishes may compare it with the morals of these times.

Such were the origins of monasticism, such were the patriarchs,' trans. Olin. pp. 129–30.

already implicit in the text, for example, '*to be a faythfull sowdyour* vnto thy captayne Chryste' (35/15–16).

In spite of his frequent use of amplification, however, the English translator is remarkably faithful to the content and intention of the Latin *Enchiridion*. His aim is instruction and clarification, though in some cases he is carried away by the spirit of the text to add vivid examples of his own. He glosses classical names like 'Polycrates', 'whiche euer lyued in prosperyte without any maner trouble' (6/8–9), and 'Labirinthus', 'whiche is a certayne comberous maze' (83/30–1). He allegorizes the pagan classics and the Old Testament, warning the reader against the Siren-lure of secular authors: 'that is to put his hole delectacyon in them / and neuer go farther' (46/10–11) and giving an anagogical meaning to the whiteness of manna: 'by this propertie is signyfied the puryte and clennesse of goddes lawe' (44/30–1). He signals directions to the reader by identifying the speaker: 'answereth the prophete' (129/23), 'sayth Christ there' (157/3), and by repeating the main verb within a series of subordinate clauses: 'Oneles ye wolde thynke . . . *excepte ye do thynke*' (19/3 and 6). Sometimes the English translator spells out the obvious: 'wysshe thou haddest some other mans eyen *to beholde thy selfe withall*' (190/5–6) or even 'Mary Christes mother' (196/22). But more often than not his additions are dramatic, expressing contemporary scorn for the clergy: 'sayeng thou clerke / thou preest / thou monke, that thou art' (159/15–16), or concrete, depicting spiritual sloth and luxury: 'bathed in damaske and rose waters / smoked in pommaunders and with muskballes' (34/28–9). In general, however, the sixteenth-century internal glosses perform the same service for the reader as do the twentieth-century annotations in the commentary.

One specialized form of addition to the English text is the medieval and Renaissance habit of giving two or more words in the vernacular for one in the original. The primary purpose of such doubling is clarification, often through linking an idiomatic expression with a literal translation, such as 'the typ of his tonge' with 'vttermost parte of his lyppes' ('summis labijs') (47/4–5). A striking though not isolated example of the translator's practice is the following sentence which contains six doublets:

Also yf a man *note, or reproue* ('taxet') the *preposterous and wronge* ('praeposterum') iudgement of the commune people / whiche amonge vertues, esteme those to be of *moost great valure and chefest* ('primas') /

whiche be of the lowest sorte: and contrary, whiche also amonge vyces moost sore *hateth and abhorreth* ('detestantis') those whiche be the *smallest and lyghtest* ('leuissima'), and clene cam / whan they be *moost abhominable and greuous* ('atrocissima') (21/29–22/2).

Doublets can also occur in phrases: 'out of our owne flesshe out of the very bowels and inwarde parte of vs' ('ex ipsis uisceribus') (59/33–60/1) and in clauses: 'passe not thy boundes / kepe the within thy lystes' ('tuo te modulo metire') (98/27–8). Sometimes the translator's fertility of invention leads him beyond doublets to triplets: 'shame, rebuke, or abhomynacyon' ('probro') (140/10–11); to quadruplets: 'scisme, diuisyon, debate or stryfe' ('schisma') (155/24–5) and even to quintuplets: 'helthe, welth, sauyng, defence and protection' ('salus') (199/1–2). Not all of the doublets are as rhythmical as these in which the same part of speech is duplicated. Sometimes the English translator yokes a clause to a word, as to the noun 'felon': 'or hym that hath trespased the lawe' ('sontem') (82/4–5) or to the past participle 'amended': 'and whan thou art come agayne to thyselfe' ('resipiscentem') (181/15–16). Although the translator did not possess an Augustan sense of form, the overall effect of his usage of doublets is to translate Erasmus's pointed, staccato Latin into balanced, sonorous English.

One of the most distinctive features of the Tudor translation of the *Enchiridion* is its handling of 'pietas' and 'pius', which together occur over a hundred times in the Latin text and are rendered in approximately fifty different ways in the English. ('Impietas' and 'impius' occur only about twenty times and are rendered in about fifteen different ways.) An obvious reason for the variety of translations is the lack in the sixteenth century of a clear orthographical distinction between 'pity' and 'piety'. Since the latter is found in the text spelled in seven different ways ('piete, pietie, pietye, pite, pitie, pyte, pytie'), internal glosses and doublets are necessary to distinguish between 'compassion' and 'devotion'. A more profound reason for this variety of expression is the richness of the Erasmian concept of 'pietas'. Although his humanistic piety bears a real relation to doctrine or 'fayth and relygyon' (165/34), Erasmus is much more concerned with 'godlynes, and holy lyfe' (49/29). In fact, 'godlynes' occurs as a translation of 'pietas' a dozen times in the work (6/14, 17/27, 19/35, 20/8, 22/16, 23/S.3, 23/26, 26/29, 28/17, 102/16, 144/30, 148/25), more than any other word except 'piety' itself. The English translator spells out the implications of this

'charitable liuing' (50/25): it is 'dewe seruynge god' (131/3; cf.
also 50/21, 102/18–19, 117/30–1, 147/21), 'honouryng of sayntes'
(101/25), 'trewe vertue and . . . pure lyfe' (115/14). In sum, the
'pious' are 'relygyous / obedyent to god / kynde and mercyfull'
(80/29–30), while conversely the 'impious' are 'dispysers of god /
disobedient to god / vnkynde and cruell' (80/30–1). Although the
1533 *Enchiridion* is aware of the relationship of 'good men' (26/4,
87/4, 152/10, 193/4) to their neighbour, it primarily defines
'piety' in terms of obedience to God. When the second edition
appeared in 1534, three God-orientated glosses were removed (see
Commentary, 103/25 n., 105/5 n., 114/1 n.) and a side-note added
which defined 'piety' in terms of submission to human authority:
'Piety is the reuerent loue and honour which the inferiors haue
towarde theyr superiors / whiche is chefly requyrcd / and therfore it
is that perfytenes of a chrysten man' (103/S.1). Certainly 'piety'
includes both obedience to God and to ecclesiastical and civil
rulers, but in early 1534 the King of England was preparing to set
himself up as the ultimate interpreter of God's will.

COMPARISON OF THE 1533 AND 1534 ENGLISH *ENCHIRIDIONS*

As we have aready noted in the general examination of the history
of the English *Enchiridion*, the first edition underwent extensive
revision before its republication in 1534.[1] The nine hundred and
fifty-odd changes reveal certain characteristic features, chief of
which is *1534*'s habit of revising the English translation towards
a more literal fidelity to the Latin original. *1534* displays its
more conservative spirit by removing internal glosses, correcting
verb forms, and occasionally substituting Middle English plural
forms. Contrary to what might be expected, *1534* shows an eye
for concrete images and an ear for flowing rhythms so that many—
though not all—of its revisions are more felicitous than the readings
of *1533*. Moreover, there are a number of revisions where *1534*
is neither better nor worse that *1533*, and even some where both
versions are remarkably good. Finally, *1534* shows certain minor,
idiosyncratic preferences in diction, which are consistent enough
to suggest that the *1534* revisions came from a different pen from
that of the *1533* translator.[2]

---

[1] See p. xxxvii.   [2] See Mozley, pp. 99–100.

Typical of *1534*'s more literal agreement with the Latin text is its removal of about thirty-five internal glosses, predominantly from the last two-thirds of the book. These glosses aimed at defining religious terminology such as 'the flesshe' : 'that is to say / the lettre / or that ye se outwarde' (see Commentary, 50/30 n.), at explicating classical allusions such as 'Adrasta' : 'otherwyse called Nemesis or Rhamnusia / that is to say' (see Commentary, 89/11 n.), and at introducing Latinate vocabulary to the English reader such as 'emulacion (whiche may be called indignacion or disdayne)' (see Commentary, 124/19 n.). Since many of the scriptural and classical allusions are generously glossed in the *1534* side-notes, the removal of these internal glosses is usually no loss to the reader. However, *1534* does sacrifice helpful definitions of 'Iudaismum' : 'supersticion of ceremonyes lyke vnto the iewes' (see Commentary, 119/1–2 n.) and 'mutis . . . elementis' : 'vnfruytfull tradicyons and ceremonyes of the inuencyons of man' (see Commentary, 120/13–14 n.). A concrete stylistic loss comes from the removal of a proverb as a definition of 'praepostera' : 'the carte set before the horse' (see Commentary, 115/25–6 n.).

Besides its deletion of some of *1533*'s additions to the *Enchiridion*, *1534* makes approximately fifty changes in *1533*'s rendering of Latin verb forms. In some cases *1534* corrects the tense, restoring the past sense of 'ignorauimus' : 'knewe not' for 'knowe not' *1533* (93/16), and the present of 'iudicat' : 'iudgeth' for 'supposed' *1533* (197/25). In other cases *1534* corrects the number, giving the plural 'sunt' : 'are' for 'is' *1533* (145/3), and the person, substituting the first person 'I wolde' for 'I woldest' *1533* (188/6). Although *1534* makes some corrections in *1533*'s rendering of verb mood, such as restoring the imperative for 'coniecturam facito' : 'make a coniecture' for 'thou mayst easely coniecte' *1533* (86/24–5), there are relatively few corrections to make in mood because of *1533*'s preference for the subjunctive. In fact, *1534* emends erroneously in several places by translating Latin subjunctives as indicatives, such as 'fiat' : 'is made' for 'shulde be made' *1533* (94/30) and 'cantaueris' : 'haddest songe' for 'shuldest synge' *1533* (108/26). In general, however, the emendations of verbs in *1534* are grammatically correct more often than the readings of *1533* in the ratio of four to one. In keeping with *1534*'s adherence to a more literal rendering of the Latin text is its conservative approach to English morphology with its occasional use of the *en*-plural for nouns, 'eyen' for 'eyes' *1533*,[1] and for person plural present verbs, 'causen' for 'cause' *1533* (93/9).

Sometimes, of course, *1534*'s conservatism obscures meaning, as when it restores the noun-form in 'armaturae uim' without rearranging the word-order: 'Of suche armure . . . haboundaunce' for 'Of suche armure . . . haboundauntly' *1533* (54/24). At other times *1534* prefers correctness to homely and vivid language, as when 'yonge sucklynges' ('infantilibus') replaces 'lytle bodyes' *1533* (136/26) or when 'excellently vnlerned and ignorant' ('egregie indocti') replaces 'starke fooles' *1533* (121/27)—certainly *1534*'s most insensitive emendation! Sometimes, however, *1534*'s literalism actually enhances its style, as when it follows the concrete diction of the Latin 'inculcat': 'stampeth' for 'mengleth' *1533* (126/16) or of 'explodat, exibiletque': 'clap, stampe, and hysse' for 'repreue / refuse / and disalowe' *1533* (148/27). Then, too, *1534* can give the English a vivid turn even when the original Latin is as bland as 'uulgus': 'rascals' for 'comen people' *1533* (138/26) or as 'dimoueri': 'puffed asyde' for 'put asyde' *1533* (148/7).

Besides occasionally improving on *1533* in matters of diction, *1534* also smooths down an intermittent roughness by word-substitution: 'They wyll not *haue* those *whiche* thurst . . . *to* drynke' for 'They wyll not *that* those y^t thurst . . . *do* drinke' *1533* (13/7–8), or by rearrangement: 'he *ought so* greatly to reioyce' for 'he *so ought* greatly to reioyce' *1533* (82/31). At times *1534* even improves on a well-written passage in *1533* by heightening the emphasis: 'how be it forsothe, he loueth not hymself' for 'yet loueth he not hym selfe verily' *1533* (146/6–7) and 'this pleasure and that' for 'this and that pleasure' *1533* (185/14). Surprisingly enough, the emendations of *1534* are stylistically better than the readings of *1533* at a ratio of about two and a half to one.

Although the emendations taken as a whole make the edition of *1534* stylistically better than that of *1533*, there are about eighty instances where the different translations of *1533* and *1534* are both equally good and about twenty-five other instances where *1534* gives a different order to the same words found in *1533*.[2]

---

[1] In the Commentary the Latin original is not given when *1534* uses the conservative plural form *eyen* instead of *1533*'s *eyes*: 38/12, 49/2, 60/12, 74/13, 78/9, 86/9, 91/12, 114/3, 116/28, 117/9, 138/S.2, 151/12, 153/24, 154/20, 187/30, 188/1, 188/8, 188/9, 188/23, 190/6.

[2] In the Commentary the Latin original is not given when *1533* and *1534*

One would need the wisdom of Solomon to adjudicate between 'Socrates fable' and 'The fable of Socrates' *1533* (67/16) or between 'Contrary wyse' and 'On the other syde' *1533* (148/2) for 'Contra', although the latter example demonstrates *1534*'s adherence to a more literal style of translation. Sometimes both *1533* and *1534* are not only adequate but even excellent, as when the English defines inordinate attachment to creatures: 'settyng his herte in them' or 'putting his hole felycite in them' *1533* (98/2–3) or when the English translates freely 'Mihi... religio fuisset' as 'I . . . durst not' or 'I . . . wolde haue ben afrayde' *1533* (111/26).

Among the indifferent emendations are a number so idiosyncratic, so stylistically insignificant that they seem to proceed from an instinctive preference rather than from a conscious choice. *1534* translates the relative pronoun as 'whiche' rather than 'that' (*1533*) sixteen times[1] although inconsistently reversing the emendation three times (101/5, 144/29, 157/17).[2] *1534* changes *1533*'s 'to' into 'vnto' six times.[3] *1534* emends the co-ordinating conjunction between doublets from 'or' (*1533*) to 'and' fifteen times[4] and from 'and' (*1533*) to 'or' once (141/11). *1534* consistently shows an aversion to 'veryly' (*1533*) by replacing it with 'surely' twice (134/30, 157/20), 'truly' four times (33/7, 138/26, 152/15, 207/25), and 'forsothe' nine times.[5] If these emendations are not a deliberate straining at gnats, perhaps they are an instinctive swatting at them!

translate the genitive case in different forms, 67/16, 77/11, 87/22, 91/9, 121/30–122/1 and when *1533* and *1534* give the same words in a different order: 25/10, 27/17–18, 38/13, 51/10, 51/19, 71/26, 82/13, 82/31, 90/1–2, 91/22, 121/21–2, 134/24, 140/20–1, 142/12, 143/S.2, 149/28, 153/12–13, 159/19, 165/12, 169/18, 169/19, 177/27, 185/14, 192/13, 197/23.

[1] In the Commentary the Latin original is not given when 1534 uses 'whiche' instead of *1533*'s 'that' to introduce a relative clause: 27/31, 36/20, 39/9, 59/2, 86/11, 107/26–8 (four times), 110/25, 123/27, 125/5, 135/S.3, 160/28, 175/27, 184/15, 203/19.

[2] In the Commentary the Latin original is not given for these examples.

[3] In the Commentary the Latin original is not given for these changes: 18/3, 57/11, 95/30, 108/14, 123/19, 195/S.1.

[4] *1534* uses 'and' instead of *1533*'s 'or' to join the halves of a doublet in the following instances: 57/2, 59/13, 90/29, 91/28, 100/6, 120/17, 120/21, 121/18, 129/6, 138/17, 138/19, 139/5, 160/15, 171/25, 191/21. Unless *1534* differs from *1533* in other words besides 'and/or', the Latin original of the doublet is not given in the Commentary.

[5] *1533*'s 'veryly' becomes 'forsothe' in *1534* nine times: 136/3, 140/1, 146/6, 182/24, 184/4, 190/9, 192/13, 193/19, 202/16. In the Commentary the Latin original is not given when the only difference between *1533* and *1534* is between 'veryly' and a synonym.

In view of my argument above that only three months elapsed between the publication of the first and the revised editions of the *Enchiridion*, it seems unlikely that the same person would have evolved so different a rationale of translation within so short a time. As will be seen below, William Tyndale, the early Protestant translator of the New Testament, is known to have made a translation of the *Enchiridion* before he went into permanent exile on the Continent. If Tyndale's version were the one published in 1533, he would not have been available to correct the text, and a more linguistically conservative scholar might have been called upon to prepare the second edition in 1534.

THE PROBLEM OF THE ENGLISH TRANSLATOR

Two persons are known to have translated the *Enchiridion* into English in the early sixteenth century, William Tyndale and Thomas Artour.[1] According to E. J. Devereux,[2] Artour's translation may never have been printed; on the other hand, it may be the source of the anonymous translation edited by John Gough and published by William Seres in 1561 as *A godly boke wherein is contayned certayne fruitfull rules, to be exercised by all Christes souldiers*. The latter translation is certainly not dependent on the English *Enchiridion* of 1533 or 1534.

William Tyndale's translation of the *Enchiridion* was made between 1521 and 1523, the same period which saw the publication of Latin *Enchiridion*s reach their high-water mark. During this period Tyndale served as tutor to the children of Sir John Walsh at the manor house of Little Sodbury in Gloucestershire. The schoolmaster was included at the table of Sir John and his wife when the high-ranking churchmen of the district were entertained, 'Amongest whome commonly was talke of learning, as well of Luther and Erasmus Roterodamus, as of opinions in the scripture . . . '[3] When the well-to-do clerics belittled the opinions of their poorer confrère, and these criticisms were relayed to Tyndale, the latter made his defence through Erasmus: 'But then did he translate into Englyshe a booke called as I remember *Enchiridion militis Christiani*. The

---

[1] Thomas Artour, listed as 'Thomas Arthur' (by T[hompson] C[ooper]) in the *DNB*, was a dramatist and Norfolk divine who twice recanted heretical opinions (in 1526 and 1527) before his death in 1532.

[2] Devereux, pp. 15–16.

[3] John Foxe, *Actes and Monuments* . . . (London, 1563), p. 514a.

whiche being translated, deliuered to his maister and Lady. And after they hadde read that booke, those great prelates were no more so often called to the house... '¹ When Tyndale left Little Sodbury for London, he took his translation of the *Enchiridion* with him; but when he sailed for Germany in May 1524, he left several copies behind in the house of Humphrey Monmouth, a London merchant. Four years later Monmouth was arrested for abetting the translation and importation of Tyndale's 1526 New Testament and for possessing other heretical books. In a petition to the King's Council of 19 May 1528, Monmouth explained his disposition of Tyndale's early translations:

The foresaid Sir William [Tindale]² left me an English book, called *Enchiridion*. The which book the Abbes of Dennye desyred yt of me, and I sent yt to her ...
     Another book I had of the same copie: a frier of Grenwich desired yt of me, and I gave yt him. I think my Lord of Rochester [Bishop John Fisher] hath it. I had other two books in English wrytten; the one was called the Pater Noster, an old book ... and the other is called *De libertate Christiana* [the former probably and the latter certainly by Luther] ... And all those books ... laye openly in my house for the space of two yeres or more, that every man might rede on them that would, at their pleasure. I never harde priest, nor fryer, nor lay man find any great fault in them ...
     When I harde my Lord of London [Bishop Cuthbert Tunstall, c. 1526] preach at Pawles Cross, that Sir William Tyndal had translated the N. Testament in English, and was noughtilie translated, that was the first time, that ever I suspected or knew any evil by him. And shortely after, al the lettres and treatyes that he sent me, with dyvers copies of books, that my servant did write, and the sermons that the priest [Tyndale] did make at St. Dunstones, I did burne them in my howse. He that did write them did se it ....³

Meanwhile, the arrival in England of Tyndale's *Obedience of a Christian Man* (Antwerp, October 1528) drew the favourable attention of Thomas Cromwell and Henry VIII,⁴ who sent their agent Stephen Vaughan to Antwerp with a safe conduct for

¹ Ibid.
² Name inserted by Gee; other bracketed material is taken from Gee's footnotes.
³ *Letters and Papers, Foreign and Domestic, of the Reign of Henry VIII*, ed. J. S. Brewer *et al.* (London, 1862–1932), iv, No. 4282. Quoted by Gee, 'Tyndale', p. 463.
⁴ Williams, p. 36.

Tyndale.[1] Though refusing to return to England, Tyndale continued to meet Vaughan, who forwarded copies of *An answere vnto
sir Thomas Mores dialoge*[2] and *The exposition of the fyrste epistle of
seynt Ihon*.[3] After 1531 Tyndale went back into hiding to work
on the revised edition of his New Testament, which appeared
in November 1534. In this same year Tyndale moved into the
residence of the English merchants at Antwerp from which he was
betrayed to the Imperial government in May 1535. In spite of
some efforts to persuade the English government to intervene,[4]
Tyndale was condemned to death as a heretic and executed at
Vilvoorde near Brussels on 6 October 1536.

The *Enchiridion*, with its critical though moderate religious
position, might well have recommended itself for publication as
part of Cromwell's campaign to justify the possible break with
Rome.[5] But if Tyndale was indeed the translator of the 1533
Enchiridion, how did his manuscript reach the publisher? Even
though Monmouth had burned *c*.1527 all the copies of Tyndale's
writings then in his possession, it is possible that an unreturned
copy of Tyndale's English *Enchiridion* found its way into Cromwell's
hands. This is the opinion of Gee[6] and of Devereux,[7] though actual
evidence is lacking. On the other hand, it is possible that Vaughan
had sent Cromwell a copy of the translation from Tyndale as he
had done with the *Answer to More* and the *Exposition of 1 John*.
This is McConica's opinion,[8] although Vaughan's correspondence
contains no mention of Tyndale's *Enchiridion*. In short, the
external evidence for Tyndale's authorship of the 1533 English
Enchiridion is insufficient to lead us out of the labyrinth.

In my examination of the internal evidence for Tyndale's
authorship, I have compared the more than 550 scriptural references in the *Enchiridion* with their counterpart in Tyndale's known
biblical translations, the New Testament (1526; rev. ed., 1534)

---

[1] Cf. 'Stephen Vaughan to Henry VIII, Barrugh, January 26, 1531', *LP*, v,
No. 65, i.
[2] Cf. 'Vaughan to Cromwell, Antwerp, March 25, 1531', *LP*, v, No. 153, and
'Vaughan to Henry VIII, Antwerp, 1531', *LP*, v, No. 201.
[3] Cf. 'Vaughan to Cromwell, Antwerp, November 14, 1531', *LP*, v, No. 533.
[4] Cf. 'Vaughan to Cromwell, April 13, 1536', *LP*, x, No. 663.
[5] Gee, 'John Byddell', pp. 54, 58.   [6] 'Tyndale', pp. 467–8.
[7] E. J. Devereux, 'Some Lost Translations of Erasmus', *The Library*, 5th
series, xvii (1962), 257.
[8] McConica, p. 145.

and the Pentateuch (1530). Of the total, less than a tenth were remarkable enough to be given special mention in the Commentary, and of this tenth the similarities are outweighed by the dissimilarities at a ratio of four to six. Among the similarities are: 'one tytle or pricke' and 'tytle' (see Commentary, 45/9–10 n.), 'paynted sepulchers' and 'paynted tombes' (see Commentary, 39/26 n.), 'tuters or scholemaisters' and 'scholemaster' (see Commentary, 125/14–15 n.), 'cast in their tethes' and 'cast in their tethe' (see Commentary, 117/23–5 n.). Three characteristically Tyndalian phrases appear verbatim in the *Enchiridion*: 'fylthy lucre', the first recorded usage of which occurs in Tyndale's 1526 New Testament (see Commentary, 12/28 n., 115/6 n.), 'iote, or tytle' (see Commentary, 49/5–6 n.),[1] and 'wycked mammon', which occurs in *Wicked Mammon* (1528) (see the Commentary, 99/8 n.). Although not found among the scriptural references, another point of identification with Tyndale's known practice is the English *Enchiridion*'s habit of translating 'parens' as 'father' (55/25, 81/17, 124/18, 207/19) and, more unusually, 'parentes' as 'father and mother' (62/33, 146/17–18, 186/18) or 'progenytours' (84/18).[2] In view of the suggestion that the reviser of *1534* was a different person from the translator of *1533*, it is perhaps significant to note that *1534* twice emends 'father and mother' to 'parentes' (81/6, 136/21).

Among the dissimilarities between the *Enchiridion* and Tyndale's scriptural translations, the most noteworthy are the differences in handling 'charity' and 'love', 'church' and 'congregation'. In his *Dialogue Concerning Tyndale*, More objects to the equivocal word 'love' as opposed to the unequivocal 'charity': 'But now whereas charite signifieth in english mens eares, not euery common loue, but a good vertuous and wel ordred loue, he y^t wyl studiously flee fro ye name of good loue, and alway speke of loue, and alway leaue out good: I would surely say y^t he meaneth nought.'[3] The English *Enchiridion*, however, consistently uses 'charity' where Tyndale's New Testament uses 'love' (see Commentary, notes to 7/29–30, 12/2–3, 39/10–11, 123/13–15, 125/32–4, 134/13, 155/32–156/2, 164/11). More also took exception to Tyndale's substitution of 'congregation', with its Lutheran connotations, for 'church', with its Catholic associations, because: 'it shoulde seme to englishe men, either that Christ in the

---

[1] The first recorded usage of 'iote' also occurs in Tyndale's 1526 New Testament.

[2] Mozley, p. 101.

[3] More, p. 221 G–H.

ghospell had neuer spoken of the churche, or els that the churche wer but such a congregacion as thei might haue occasion to saye, that a congregacion of suche some heretikes were the church y^t god spake of.'[1] Here too, the English *Enchiridion* adopts the traditional terminology and uses 'church' where Tyndale's New Testament uses 'congregation' (see Commentary, 165/31–2 n., 180/15–16 n., 189/20–1 n.). In other cases of dissimilarity, the New Testament frequently displays a stylistic advance over the *Enchiridion* by avoiding circumlocutions. The *Enchiridion* had translated 'ius primogenitorum' as 'the right that perteyned to hym by inherytaunce / in y^t he was the elder brother' (see Commentary, 73/16–17 n.); Tyndale's *Pentateuch* renders this succinctly as 'byrthrighte'. Where the translation of 'pietas' was so problematic in the *Enchiridion* as to evoke fifty different forms of translation, Tyndale's New Testament gives simply 'godlines' (see Commentary, 102/18–19 n., 126/6–8 n.).

The internal evidence for Tyndale's authorship of the 1533 *Enchiridion* is no more conclusive than the external evidence. There is a disappointing lack of correspondence between the scriptural references in the *Enchiridion* and in Tyndale's known biblical translations. The chief reason for this discrepancy is the fact that the English *Enchiridion* translates quotations from the Latin Vulgate while Tyndale's New Testament is based on Erasmus's Greek text. For the same reason the scriptural references in the *Enchiridion* (1533 and 1534), ironically enough, correspond more frequently with the Douai–Rheims version (1582 and 1609–10) that with Tyndale's (1526 and 1534). Since Tyndale's known translation of the *Enchiridion* was made *c.*1522, four years before the publication of the New Testament, his *Enchiridion* is the product of an earlier stage of his development both theologically and stylistically. Because of its traditional use of 'charity' and 'church', its circumlocutions and doublets, the English *Enchiridion* published in 1533 may represent Tyndale's apprentice-work as a translator. This stylistic study of the *Enchiridion* has been limited to a comparison with Tyndale's New Testament and Pentateuch; an examination of all his polemical writings in conjunction with my present work of editing Tyndale's *Answer to More* may reveal further points of similarity.

[1] More, p. 222 C.

A NOTE ON THE TEXTS

This edition of the 1534 English translation of the *Enchiridion militis Christiani*[1] is based on the copy in the Folger Shakespeare Library, Washington, D.C. I have also used a University Microfilm xerox of the British Library copy and consulted a copy at the John Rylands Library, Manchester. The Latin notes are based on the Froben 1518 edition in the Beinecke Library, Yale University.

Signature marks enclosed in square brackets have been inserted into the text of this edition of the *Enchiridion* to indicate the beginning of a new page in the 1534 text. The spelling is given as in the 1534 original. Abbreviations, except *y^e* and *y^t*, have been silently expanded. Abbreviations occurring in the English edition of 1533 and the Latin edition of 1518 have also been expanded, but quotations from other works mentioned in the Introduction and Commentary give the original spelling exactly. In order to conform to modern usage, capital W and Y are silently substituted for these lower-case letters, and capital U is rendered as V. Capitals have also been provided at the beginning and periods at the end of the side-notes. The original punctuation has been generally retained, although *1533* variants have been recorded when *1533* punctuates better than *1534* or when both need emending. Neither *1533* nor *1534* has a consistent policy for hyphenization so compound words have been rendered in the form in which they are most usually found mid-line. The modern single hyphen has been substituted throughout the Text (though not in the Bibliographical Descriptions) for *1533*'s and *1534*'s double hyphen.

[1] I have chosen the 1534 version as my copy-text because it was the first of the nine editions of this version that was available to sixteenth-century readers and because I have been unable to establish that Tyndale was the author of the earlier edition.

ENCHIRIDION MILITIS CHRISTIANI

℃ Enchiridion militis chri
stiani / whiche may be called in
englysshe, the hansom weapon of a christen knyght /
replenysshed with ma-
ny goodly and godly
preceptes: made
by the fa-
mous
clerke Erasmus of Ro-
terdame, and newly
corrected and
imprin-
ted.
∴

Cum priuilegio regali.

❡ The booke speaketh.

TO please all sortes of men I do not passe
To please the good and lerned is a fayre thyng
Yea, and these bothe, were more than couenant was
5 And more than I loke for. Who so the lernyng
Of Christ dothe sauour / if he lyke well althyng
I seke no further / Christe is myne Apollo
Onely strengthyng me to speake this that I do.

❡ The printer to the faythfull reder.

10 THe mortall worlde, a felde is of batayle
    Whiche is the cause y^t stryfe dothe neuer fayle
Agaynst man / by warrynge of the flesshe
    With the dyuell / that alway fyghteth fresshe
The spyrite to oppresse by false enuy
15   The whiche conflycte is contynually
Durynge his lyfe / and lyke to lese the felde
    But he be armed with weapon and shelde
Suche as behoueth to a christen knyght
    Where god echone, by his Christ choseth ryght
20 Soole capitayne / and his standarde to bere
    Who knoweth it not / than this wyll teche hym here
In his breuyer / poynarde / or manuell
    The loue shewyng of hygh Emanuell
In gyuyng vs suche harneys of werre
25   Erasmus is the onely furbyssher
Scouryng the harneys, cankred and aduste
    Whiche neglygence had so sore fret with ruste
Than champyon receyue, as thyne by ryght
    The manuell of the trewe christen knyght.

30   ❡ Finis.

[a2]   Epystle.
                    ❧ Erasmus Roterdame sendeth
                   gretyng to the reuerende father
                   in Christ (and lorde) the lorde
                    Paule Volzius / the moste   5
                     religyous abbot of the
                        monastery the
                          whiche is
                          comenly
                       called Hughes   10
                          courte.

ALl be it moste vertuous father, that the lytell booke / to the
whiche I haue gyuen this name or tytle Enchiridion militis christiani /
whiche many a day a go I made for my selfe only / and for a certayne
frende of myne beyng vtterly vnlerned / hath begon to myslyke and   15
displease me the lesse / for as moche as I do se that it is alowed of
you and other vertuous and lerned men suche as you be / of whome
(as ye are in dede endued with godly lernynge / and also with lerned
godlynesse) I knowe nothynge to be approued / but [a2v] that
whiche is bothe holy and also clerkly: yet it hath begon well nyghe   20
also to please and lyke me nowe / whan I se it (after that it hath ben so
often tymes printed) yet styll to be desyred, and greatly called for /
as if it were a newe werke made of late: if so be the printers do not
lye to flatter me withall. But agayne there is an other thyng whiche
often tymes greueth me in my mynde / that a certayne wel lerned   25
frende of myne longe ago sayde, very properly and sharply check-
ynge me / that there was more holynesse sene in the lytell booke /
than in the hole authoure and maker therof. In dede he spake these
wordes in his iestyng bourdyngly / but wolde to god he had not
spoken so trewly, as he bourded bytterly. And that greueth me so   30
moche the more bycause y\e same thynge hath chaunsed to come
lykewyse to passe in hym, for the chaungyng of whose maners
principally I toke vpon me this labour and trauayle / for he also
not onely hath not withdrawen hym selfe from the courte / but is
dayly moche deper drowned therin than he was afore tyme / for   35
what good purpose I can not tell / but as he confesseth hym selfe with

Against l. 36–p. 6, l. 1: Trouble or aduersitie correcteth some.

moche great mysery. And yet for all that I do not greatly petie my frende / bycause that peraduenture [a3] aduersyte of fortune may teche hym ones to repent hym selfe, and to amende / seyng that he wolde not folow and do after my counsayle and admonycions.
5 And veryly thoughe I, enforsynge me to the same thyng and purpose / haue ben turned and tossed with so many chaunces and tempestes / that Vlixes a man lyuyng euer in trouble (which Homer speketh of) myght be counted in comparyson to me euen Polycrates / whiche euer lyued in prosperyte without any maner trouble. I do not
10 vtterly repente me of my labour / seynge it hath moued and prouoked so many vnto the study of godly vertue: nor I my selfe am not vtterly to be blamed and rebuked although my lyuynge be not in all poyntes agreyng to myne owne preceptes and counsayles. It is some parte of godlynesse whan one with all his herte desyreth
15 and is wyllyng to be made good and vertuous: nor suche a mynde so well intendynge I suppose is not to be caste away / although his purpose be not euer luckely perfourmed. To this we ought to endeuoyre our selfe all our lyfe longe / and no doute but by the reason that we so often tymes shal attempt it / ones at the laste
20 we shall attayne it. Also he hath dispatched a good pece of a dout-full iourney whiche hath [a3v] lerned wel of the iourney the way. Therfore am I nothing moued with ye mockes of certayne persons which dispyse this lytle boke / as nothing erudite and clerkly / sayeng that it myght haue ben made of a chylde that lerned his
25 A / b / c / bycause it entreateth nothynge of Dunces questyons: as though nothyng without those coude be done with lernynge. I do not care if it be not so quick, so it be godly: let it not make them instructe and redy to disputacyons in scholes / so that it make them apte to kepe Christes peace. Let it not be profytable or helpyng for
30 ye disputacyon in diuynite / so it make for a diuyne lyfe. For what good shulde it do to entreate of that thyng that euery man entre-medleth with? Who hath not in handlyng questions of diuynite / or what els do all our swarmes of schole men? There be almost as many commentaryes vpon the mayster of the sentence as be names
35 of diuynes. There is neyther mesure nor nombre of summularies / whiche after the maner of potycaries myngle often tymes sondry thynges togyther / and make of olde thynges newe / of newe thynges

Against ll. 8–9: Fortunate Policrates.

24 lerned] lerneth 1533

olde / of one thynge many / of many thynges one. Howe can it be that these great volumes instructe vs to lyue well and after a christen maner / whiche a man [a4] in all his lyfe can not haue layser ones to loke ouer. In lyke maner as if a phisycien shulde prescribe vnto him that lyeth sicke in parell of deth, to rede Iacobus de partibus / 5 or suche other huge volumes / sayeng that there he shulde fynde remedy for his disease: but in the meane tyme the pacyent dyeth / wantynge presente remedy wherwith he myght be holpen. In suche a fugytyue lyfe it is necessary to haue a redy medycyne at the hande. Howe many volumes haue they made of restytucion / of confessyon / 10 of sclaunder / and other thynges innumerable? And though they boulte and serche out by pecemeale euery thyng by it selfe / and so diffyne euery thynge as if they mistrusted all other mens wyttes / ye as though they mistrusted yᵉ goodnesse and mercy of god / whyles they do prescribe how he ought to punyssh and rewarde euery 15 facte eyther good or badde: yet they agre not amongest them selues / nor yet somtymes do open the thing playnly / if a man wolde loke nere vpon it / so moche dyuersyte bothe of wyttes and circum- staunces is there. Moreouer althoughe it were so that they had determyned all thynges well and trewly / yet besydes this that they 20 handle and treate of these thynges after a barbarous and vn- pleasaunt fassyon / [a4v] there is not one amongest a thousande that can haue any layser to rede ouer these volumes: Or who is able to beare aboute with hym Secundam secunde / the werke of saynte Thomas? And yet there is no man but he ought to vse a good lyfe / 25 to the whiche Christe wolde that the waye shulde be playne and open for euery man / and that not by inexplicable crokes of disputa- cions / not able to be resolued / but by a trewe and a sincere faythe and charyte not fayned / whom hope doth folowe whiche is neuer asshamed. And fynally lette the great doctours / whiche muste nedes 30 be but fewe in comparyson to al other men / study and besy them selfe in those great volumes. And yet neuer the lesse the vnlerned and rude multytude whiche Christe dyed for ought to be prouyded for: and he hath taught a great porcyon of christyan vertue whiche hath inflamed men vnto the loue therof. The wyse kynge whan he 35 dyd teache his sonne trewe wysdome / toke moche more payne in

Against ll. 23–4: The great volumes.
Against ll. 30–2: The theology appertayneth to fewe men / but the saluacion appertayneth to all.

2 instructe] *1533*; iustructe *1534*

exhorting hym thervnto, than in teachyng hym / as who shulde
say that to loue wysdom were in a maner to haue attayned it. It is
a great shame and rebuke bothe for lawyers and also phisycions,
that they haue of a set purpose / and for the nones / made their arte
5 [a5] and science full of diffyculty / and harde to be attayned or
come by / to thentent that bothe their gaynes and auauntage myght
be the more plentyfull / and their glory and prayse amonge the
vnlerned people the greater: but it is a moche more shamefull
thyng to do the same in the philosophy of Christ. But rather con-
10 trary wise we ought to endeuer our selues with all our strengthes
to make it so easy as can be / and playne to euery man. Nor let not
this be our study to apere lerned our selues / but to alure very many
to a christen mans lyfe. Preparacyon and ordynaunce is made nowe
for warre to be made agaynst the turkes / whiche for what so euer
15 purpose it is begon / we ought to praye, not that it maye turne to
y⁰ profyte of a fewe certayne persons / but that it may be to y⁰ comen
and generall profyte of all men. But what thinke you shulde come of
it / if to suche of them as shall be ouercomen (for I do not suppose
yᵗ they shall all be kylled with weapons) we shall lay the werkes of
20 Occam / Durandus / Duns / Gabriell / Aluaros / or any such schole
men, for thentent to bring them in mynde to take Christes profession vpon them? What shall they ymagyn and thynke in their
myndes (for surely euyn they, though they be naught els, are
men [a5v] and haue wyt and reasone) whan they shall here those
25 thorny and combrous inextricable subtyll ymagynacions of instantes /
of formalytes / of quiddites / of relacion: namely whan they shall
se these great doctours and teachers of religyon and holynesse so
farre disagreyng / and of so sondry opinyons amonge them selfe yᵗ
often tymes they dispute and reason so longe one with another /
30 vntyll they chaunge colour, and be pale / and reuyle one another
spytting eche at other and fynally dealynge buffettes and blowes
eche to other. Whan they shall se y⁰ blacke freres fyght and skolde

Against ll. 1-4: Those be noted that of purpose make the faculty whiche
they professe obscure and harde.
Against ll. 13-14: The warre agaynst the turkes.
Against ll. 28-9: The dyscorde amonge dyuynes.

---

3 and also] and *1533*

Side-note 1: of purpose make the faculty whiche they professe obscure and
harde] yelde tharte wherin they be conuersant defycile by study *1533*

for their Thomas / and than the gray freres matched with them, defendying on yᵉ other partye their subtyle and feruent hote doctours / which they call seraphicos / some spekyng as reals / some as nominals. Whan they shall also se the thyng to be of so gret diffyculte yᵗ they can neuer discusse suffyciently with what wordes 5 they may speke of Christ: as though one dyd deale or had to do with a waywarde spyrit whiche he had reysed vp vnto his owne distructyon / if he dyd fayle neuer so lytle in the prescript wordes of coniuryng / and not rather with our moste mercyfull sauyour / whiche desyreth nothyng els of vs but a pure lyfe and a symple. 10 I beseche the for the loue of god shew me [a6] what shal we bring aboute with all these reckenynges / specially if our maners and our lyfe be lyke to the proude doctryne and lernyng? and if they shall se and well perceyue our ambycion and desyrousnesse of honoure by our gorgyousnesse / more than euer any tyrant dyd vse: our 15 auaryce and couetousnesse by our bribyng and pollyng / our lecherousnes by the defyling of maydens and wyues / our cruelnes by thoppressions done of vs, with what face or how for shame shal we offre to them the doctryne of Christ whiche is farre away contrary to all these thynges. The best way and most effectuell to ouer- 20 come and wyn the turkes / shulde be if they shal perceyue yᵗ thyng which Christ taught and expressed in his lyuing, to shyne in vs. If they shal perceyue yᵗ we do not hyghly gape for their empyres / do not desire their golde and good / do not couet their possessyon / but that we seke nothynge els but only their soules helth and the 25 glory of god. This is that right trewe and effectuous diuynite / the which in tyme passed subdued vnto Christ arrogant and proude phylosophers / and also the myghty and inuincible princes. And if we thus do / than shal Christ euer be present and helpe vs. For trewly it is not mete nor conuenient to declare our selues christen 30 men by this profe or token / if [a6v] we kyll very many / but rather if we saue very many: not if we sende thousandes of hethen people to hell / but if we make many infydels faythful: not if we cruelly curse and excomunycate them / but if we with deuout prayers and with all our hertes desyre their helth, and pray vnto god to sende 35 them better myndes. If this be not our entent it shall soner come to

Against ll. 13–15: The lyfe vsed amongest christen people.
Against ll. 20–2: With what artylery chiefely the turkes ought to be ouercom.
Against ll. 29–31: The parte of a chrysten man is to saue and not to dystroy.

17 wyues /] *1533*; wyues *1534*　　　18 thoppressions] yᵉ oppressions *1533*

passe y^t we shall degenerate and turne in to turkes our selues / than
that we shal cause them to become christen men. And although y^e
chaunce of warre / whiche is euer doutfull and vncertayne / shulde
fall so luckely to vs y^t we had goten the victory / so shulde it be
5 brought to passe that the popes domynion and his cardynals myght
be enlarged / but not the kyngdome of Christe / whiche fynally
florissheth and is in prosperyte / if faythe, loue, peace, and chastyte
be quicke and stronge. Whiche thyng I trust shalbe brought to passe
by ye good gouernaunce and prouisyon of the pope Leo the tenth /
10 vnlesse the great trouble and rage of worldly besynesse plucke him
from his very good purpose another waye. Christ dothe professe to
be primate and heed hymselfe in the heuenly kyngdom / which
neuer dothe florisshe but whan celestyall thinges be aduaunced.
Nor Christ dyd not dye for this purpose, that goodes of the [a7]
15 worlde / that rychesse / that armure / and the rest of rufflyng fassyon of ye worlde, shulde be nowe in the handes and rule of certayne
preestes / whiche thynges were wonte to be in the handes of the
gentiles / or at the leest amongest lay princes / not moche differyng
from gentyles. But in my mynde it were ye best / before we shulde
20 trye with them in batayle, to attempte them with epystels and
some lytell bookes : but with what maner of epystels ? Not with
thretnyng pystels, or with bokes full of tyranny / but with those
whiche myght shewe fatherly charyte / and resemble the very herte
and mynde of Peter and Paule / and whiche shulde not onely pre-
25 tende and shewe outwardly the tytle of ye apostels / but which also
shuld sauour and taste of the effycacy and strength of the apostels.
Not bycause I do not knowe that all the trewe fountayne and
vayne of Christes philosophy is hydde in the gospell and the
epystels of the apostels : But the straunge maner of phrase / and
30 often tymes the troublous spekynge of dyuers croked fygures and
tropes be of so great diffyculte / that often tymes we our selfe also
muste labour ryght sore, before we can perceyue them. Therfore
in myne oppinyon the best were that some, bothe well lerned men
and good of [a7v] lyuing, shuld haue this offyce assyned and put

Against ll. 6–7: The kyngdom of Christe.
Against ll. 27–9: The difficultie of holy scrypture.

16 shulde] *om.* *1533*
Side-note 1: kyngdom] royalme *1533*; kyugdom *1534*
Side-note 2: of] of the *1533*

vnto them / to make a collectyon and to gather the somme of
Christes phylosophy out of the pure fountayne of the gospell / and
the epystels and moste approued interpretours / and so playnly,
that yet it myght be clerkly and erudyte / and so breuely, that it
myght also be playne. Those thynges whiche concerne faythe or 5
byleue / let them be contayned in a fewe artycles. Those also that
appertayne to the maner of lyuynge, lette them be shewed and
taught in fewe wordes / and that after suche fassyon, that they
may perceyue the yoke of Christe to be pleasaunt and easy /
and not greuous and paynfull: so that they maye perceyue that 10
they haue goten fathers and not tyrantes / feders, and not robbers,
pyllers nor pollers / and that they be called to their soule helthe /
and not compelled to seruytude. Vndouted they also be men /
neyther their hertes be of so harde yron or adamante / but that
they may be molyfyed and wonne with benefites and kyndnesse / 15
wherwith euen very wylde beestes be woxen gentle and tame. And
the moste effectuous thynge is the trewe veryte of Chryste. But
lette the pope also commaunde them whome he appoynteth to this
besynesse / that they ne[a8]uer swarue nor go from the trewe
patron and example of Christe / nor in any place haue any respecte 20
to the carnall affectes and desyres of men. And suche a thynge my
mynde was aboute to bringe to passe as well as I coulde / whan I
made this booke of Enchiridion. I dyd se the comen people of
christendome / not onely in effecte / but also in opinyons to be
corrupted. I consydred the moste parte of those whiche professe 25
them selues to be pastours and doctours, to abuse the tytles of
Christ to their propre aduauntage. And yet wyll I make no mencyon
of those men, after whose wyll and pleasure the worlde is ruled and
tourned vp and downe / whose vyces though they be neuer so manyfest / a man maye scarsely ones wynche. And in suche great derke- 30
nesse, in suche great troublous rufflynge of the worlde, in so great
dyuersyte of mens opynions / whyther shulde we rather flye for
socour than to the very great and sure anker of Christes doctryne /
whiche is the gospell? Who beyng a good man in dede, dothe
not se and lamente this meruaylous corrupte worlde? Whan was 35
there euer more tyranny? Whan dyd auaryce reigne more largely,

Against ll. 5–7: The breueness of Christes doctryne.
Against ll. 13–14: The turkes be men.
Against ll. 23–4: The corruptnes of the worlde.
Against ll. 33–4: The sure anker.

and lesse punysshed? Whan were cerymonyes at any tyme more in
estymacion? [a8v] Whan dyd our iniquyte so largely flowe with
more lyberty? Whan was euer charyte so colde? What is brought /
what is redde / what is decreed or determyned, but it tasteth and
5 sauoureth of ambycion and lucre? Oh howe infortunate were we if
Christe had not lefte some sparkes of his doctryne vnto vs / and as
it were lyuely and euerlastynge vaynes of his godly mynde. Hereto
therfore we must enforce our selfe to know these sparkes / leauyng
the coles of mens fantasyes. Let vs seke these vaynes vntyll we
10 fynde fresshe water whiche springeth in to euerlastyng lyfe. We
delue and dygge the grounde meruaylously depe for to plucke out
rychesse / whiche nouryssheth vyce: And shall we not labour than
the ryche erthe of Christe, to get out that thyng whiche is our
soules helth? There was neuer no storme of vyces that dyd so
15 ouercome and quenche the heate of charyte / but it myght be
restored agayne at this flynt stone. Christ is a stone / but this stone
hath sparkes of celestyall fyre / and vaynes of lyuely water. In tyme
passed Abraham in euery lande did dygge pyttes and holes / serchynge in euery place the vaynes of lyuely water: but those same
20 beyng stopped vp agayne by the phylistyens with erthe / Isaac and
his seruauntes [b1] dyd delue agayne / and not beynge onely content
to restore the olde / dyd also make newe. But than the philistians
dyd scolde and chyde / yet he dyd not cease from dyggynge. And
in this our tyme we haue philistians, whiche do preferre the naughty
25 erth to the lyuely fountayns / euen those whiche be worldly wyse /
and haue theyr respect to erthly thinges: and wrynge and wraste goddes doctryne and his gospel to theyr carnall affections / makynge it
serue to theyr ambicion / bolstryng vp therwith theyr fylthy lucre
and tyranny. And yf now any Isaac or any of his family sholde dyg
30 and fynde some trewe and pure vayne / by and by they brable and
crye agaynst hym: perceyuynge ryght well that that vayne shall hurte

Against ll. 8–10: In thynges confused / we must haue recourse to the euan-
gyles.
Against l. 16: i. Corin. x.
Against ll. 17–18: Gene. xvj.
Against ll. 20–1: Gene. xxvj.
Against ll. 24–5: The Philistyans of our tyme.

24 philistians] phylistyans *1533*; philistiaus *1534*   31 shall] shulde
1533
Side-note 1: the] *1533*; / he *1534*   euangyles] euagyles *1533*

theyr aduauntage / shall hurte theyr ambycyon / although it make
neuer so moche for the glory of Chryst: streyghtways they cast in
naughty erth / and with a corrupte interpretacyon, they stoppe vp
the vayne / and dryue awaye the dygger: or at the leest they make
it so muddy with claye and fylthynesse: that who so euer drynketh 5
therof, shall drawe vnto hym more slyme and naughtynesse, than
he shall good lycour. They wyll not haue those whiche thurst and
desyre ryghtousnesse to drynke of the pure lycour: but they bring
them vnto [b1v] theyr olde worne and al to troden cesternes / whiche
haue broken stones and morter / but water they haue none. But 10
yet for all this, the very true chyldren of Isaac, that is, the true
worshyppers of Chryste, must not be weryed and dryuen awaye
from this labour: for veryly euen they whiche thrust naughty
erthe in to the fountayne of the gospell / wolde be counted the very
worshyppers of Chryste. So that in dede nothynge now a dayes 15
is more peryllous, than to teache trewly Chrystes lernynge. So
greatly haue the philistians preuayled, fyghtynge for theyr erth /
prechyng erthly thynges for celestyall: and mennes inuencyons for
gods commaundementes: that is to say / not techyng those thynges
whiche make for ye glory of Christ / but those thinges whiche be 20
for theyr owne aduauntage. Whiche be pardons / composicions /
and suche lyke pelfare. And this they do so moche more peryllously,
bycause they cloke their couetousnesse with the tytles and names
of great prynces / of the pope of Rome / ye of Christ also hymselfe.
But there is no man that dothe more for the popes profyte or 25
besynesse, than he that techeth Chrystes lernynge purely and
truly / wherof he is the chefe techer. There is no man that dothe
more good to princes, or deserueth more of [b2] them, than he
whiche endeuereth hymself that the people may be welthy and in
prosperite. But some of the flocke of schole men, wyll here speke 30
agaynst me / sayinge, it is easy to any man to gyue general preceptes,
what is to be desyred, and what is to be eschewed: but what shal be
answered than to those that aske counseyle for so many fortunes
and chaunces? Fyrst I answere, that there be mo dyuers kyndes of
suche worldly besynesse, than that any lyuyng person can gyue 35

Against l. 7: Hiere. ij.
Against ll. 19–20: The marchantes of pardons.
Against l. 35–p. 14, l. 3: A man can make no certeyn answer to euery thynge.

---

1 shall] shulde *1533*   7 haue] that *1533*   whiche] y^t *1533*   8 to]
do *1533*   11 is] be *1533*   22 this] these *1533*

dyrecte and sure answere to eche one of them. Secondaryly, there is suche dyuersite of circumstaunces / whiche yf a man do not knowe / it is not well possyble to make an answere. In conclusion, I doute greatly, whether they them selues haue any sure answere, that they may make: seynge they dyffer in so many thynges amongest them selues: And they also whiche amongest them be of the wyser sorte, do not thus answere: This ye shall do / this ye shall not do / but of this maner. This in myne opinyon were the better / this I suppose to be intollerable. But yf we haue that symple and bryght eye whiche the gospel speketh of / yf the house of oure mynde haue in it the candell of pure faythe, set vpon a candelstycke / all these tryfles shall easely be put away, and [b2v] auoyded as it were clowdes or mystes. If we haue the rule and patrone of Christes charite / to it we may apply and make mete all other thynges ryght easely. But what wyll ye do whan this rule dothe not agre with those thynges / whiche hath be communly vsed, so many hondreth yeres: and which be ordeyned and stablysshed by the lawes of prynces: for this thyng chaunceth very ofte. Ye must not condempne that thynge whiche prynces do, in executynge theyr offyce / but agayne do not corrupte and defyle the heuenly philosophy with mens dedes. Let Chryst contynue and abyde / as he is in dede / a very centre or myddle poynte vnmoued / hauyng certayne circles goyng rounde aboute hym: moue not the marke out of his owne place. Those whiche be in the fyrst circle nexte to the centre (that is to say nexte to Chryst) as preestes / bysshops / cardynalles / popes / and suche, to whome it belongeth to folowe the lambe whether so euer he shall go / let them enbrace and holde fast that moost pure parte / and so farre forth as they may / let them communycate and plentuously gyue the same vnto theyr nexte neyghbours. In the seconde circle / let all temporall and ley princes be / which in kepyng warre and making lawes / after a certeyn maner do seruyce to Christ [b3] eyther whan with ryghtfull batayle they dryue away theyr ennemyes / and defende and mayntayne the publyke peace,

Against l. 11: The lyght of faythe.
Against ll. 21–2: Chryst is the centre.
Against l. 22: iij. Circles.
Against ll. 24–5: The fyrst of men of the churche.
Against ll. 29–30: The seconde of prynces.

6 they] those *1533*   6–7 of the wyser sorte] more wyse than other *1533*
9 intollerable] tollerable *1533*   30 let] *om. 1533*

and tranquilite of the commune welth: or els whan with punysshment accordyng to ye lawes / they punyssh malefactours and euyll
doers. And yet bycause they can not chose but of necessite be
occupyed, and besyed in suche thynges as be ioyned, with the
most vyle dregges and fylth of the erth / and with the besynesse of 5
the worlde: it is ieopardous lest they fall somwhat further of, from
ye centre and marke / lest they make somtymes warre for theyr
owne pleasure / and not for the commune welth: lest vnder ye pretext
of iustyce they vse cruelte vpon those, whome they myght reforme
with mercy: lest vnder the tytle of lordshyp they pyll and poll those 10
people, whose goodes they ought to defende. And moreouer, as
Chryst lyke ye fountayne of euerlastyng fyre / dothe drawe next vnto
hym the ordre of preestes / and maketh them of lyke nature / that
is to say / pure and clene from all corrupcyon of worldly dregges and
fylthynesse: So in lyke case, it is the offyce of preestes / and specy- 15
ally of ye hyghest / so moche as they can, to call and drawe vnto
them those that be prynces, and haue power and authorite. And yf
it fortune at any tyme, that warre do ryse sodeynly in [b3v] any
place / let the bysshoppes endeuoyre them selues, so moche as in
them is / eyther to ende the stryues and varyaunces without shed- 20
ynge of blode: or yf that can not be brought to passe / by reason of
the great stormes of worldly besynesse / yet let them so do, that as
lytell blode as may be be shedde / and that the warre may shortly be
brought to an ende. ⊄ In tymes past the bysshoppes authorite had
place euen in iuste punysshmentes / and hathe goten dyuerse tymes 25
(as saynt Augustyn playnly in his epystle dothe testyfye) the malefac-
tour from the handes of temporall iudges. For some thynges there
be so necessary vnto the ordre of the commune welthe that partly
yet Chryste dyd dissymule at them / and partly he put them from
hym / and partly neyther approuynge nor disalowyng them, dyd in 30
a maner wynke and loke besyde them. He wolde not knowe the
money of Cesar, nor the scripture vpon it. The trybute he commaunded to be payde yf it were due and dette / as though it lytell

Against ll. 13–14: The offyce of Sacerdotes.
Against l. 26: Augustyne.
Against l. 32–p. 16, l. 1: What thynges and how farforth they apertayn to the
heedes of the chyrche.

6 fall somwhat further of] do fall further *1533*   7 lest] as leste *1533*
make] shulde make *1533*   9 vse] shulde vse *1533*   10 pyll] shulde
pyll *1533*   24 ⊄] *om. 1533*

pertayned to hym / so that god had his duty. The woman taken and founde in adultery, he neyther condempned, neyther openly absolued / but onely dyd bydde her, that she sholde no more do so. Of those whiche were condempned of Pylate / whose blode [b4] he
5 entremyngled amongest theyr sacryfyces / he neyther sayd, it was well done, nor euyll / but onely thretened euery man, that they sholde be punysshed with a lyke destructyon, yf they dyd not amende. More ouer, whan he was desyred to deuyde the enherytaunce bytwene yᵉ two bretherne / he playnly refused it, as an vnworthy thing, for
10 him to gyue iudgement of such grosse maters / whiche dyd teche thynges heuenly. And also of the other parte, there be certeyn thynges whiche he openly abhorred / as yᵉ couetous pharisees / the ypocrytes / the proude ryche folkes / saying vnto them. Wo be vnto you. He neuer rebuked the apostles more sharply than whan they
15 wolde have ben auenged / or whan they were ambycyous. Whan they asked hym, whether they sholde commaunde fyre to be sent downe from heuen to burne vp the cite from whens they were shyt forth / he answered and sayd to them. Ye knowe not of what spirit ye are. Whan Peter was about to call hym vnto yᵉ worlde from
20 his passyon suffring / he called him an aduersary. Whan they contended about yᵉ preeminence, whiche of them sholde be yᵉ best / how often and how many wayes doth he call them backe to a contrary mynde? And other thynges there be whiche he techeth and commaundeth openly [b4v] to be obserued: as not to resyst
25 euyll / to do good to thyne ennemyes / to vse mekenes of mynde / and other lyke. These must be departed in sonder / and euery of them set in ordre in his owne place. Let vs not therfore strayght wayes make Chryste an auctour of all thynges whiche be done by prynces and temporall offycers / nor defende it (as we call it) to be
30 done by gods lawe. They deale and meddle with many thinges whiche be lowe and grosse / not all togyder of the very purenes of a chrysten man: yet they be not to be rebuked, in as moche as they be necessary to the mayntenaunce of ordre to be obserued. Nor we be not by the mynistryng of theyr offyce made good / all be it,
35 that by them it is caused, that we be lesse euyll / and that they

Against ll. 12–14: What thynges chryste openly rebuked.
Against ll. 22–4: What thynges christ teacheth openly.
Against ll. 26–8: Princes lawes ar of the mean sort of thinges.

17 to burne] to haue burned _1533_   19 to call] to haue called _1533_
21 yᵉ preeminence] preeminence _1533_

whiche be euyll do lesse hurte and noyaunce to the commune
welthe. And therfore they also ought to haue theyr honour, bycause
they do somwhat serue the iustyce of god, and the publyke and
commune tranquillite / without the whiche, somtyme those thynges
be troubled and vexed, whiche belonge to godly holynesse. They 5
must be honoured whan they do theyr office: and yf somtymes they
vse theyr power for theyr owne pleasure or profyte / yet peraduenture it were the best to suffre them / leest more hurte sholde [b5]
spryng therof: for there appereth an ymage, or rather a shadowe of
the diuyne iustyce in them / whiche iustyce yet ought to shyne more 10
euydently, and more purely in the lyuyng and lawes of preestes. An
ymage dothe of an other maner shewe in a myrrour of glasse, than
it doth in yron. And in the thyrde circle must all the commune
people be, as the moost grosse parte of all this worlde: but not yet
so grosse, but that they pertayne vnto the mistycal body of Chryst: 15
for the eyen be not onely membres of the body / but also the legges /
the fete, and the preuy partes. And those whiche be in the thyrde
circle, we ought so to suffre in their infyrmytye / that as moche as
is possyble, we do call them vnto those thynges whiche be more
approued of Chryste. For in the mystycall body, he that but late 20
was the fote, may be the eye. And lyke as the prynces, yf they be
not all ye best / must not with chydyng be exasperate / lest (as saynt
Augustyne saythe) whan they be moued, they styrre vp more peryllous tragedyes / so ye weyke people, lyke as Chryste suffred his
apostles, and nourysshed them / muste be suffred / and after a 25
fatherly maner cherysshed, vntyll they wexe more aged, and
stronge in Chryst. For godlynesse also hath his infancie / it hath
meane age / it hath full [b5v] strengthe and perfyte age. Yet all
men after theyr degre must endeuoyre them selfe to attayne and
comme vnto Chryste. The elementes haue euery one his propre 30
place / but the fyre whiche hath the highest place by lytell and
lytell draweth all the other vnto hym / and so moche as he can,
tourneth them in to his nature. The clere water, he tourneth in to
the ayre / and the ayre claryfyed, he transfourmeth in to his owne
nature. Saynt Paule dothe in many thynges suffre and pardon the 35
Corynthyans / but in the meane season puttyng difference bytwene

Against ll. 7–8: Euyll rulers must be suffred.
Against ll. 12–13: The thyrde circle.
Against ll. 24–5: The weyke must be forborne.
Against ll. 32–4: The chaunge of one element in to an other.

those thynges whiche he dyd profer in the name of his lorde, vnto
them that were perfyte / and those thynges whiche he dyd pardon,
that were wrytten in his owne name, vnto them that were yet weyke
and yonge in Chryste: but euer on this trust, that they sholde pro-
5 fyte and go forwarde to more strength and perfectyon. And also he
trauaylleth agayne, to brynge forth the Galathyans vntyll Chryste
be fassyoned in them. Now yf any man wyll thynke this cyrcle to be
more conuenyent for prynces / I wyll not stryue greatly with hym.
But what so euer is without the thyrde cyrcle, is at all tymes, and in
10 all poyntes to be hated, and refused: as ambycyon, and de[b6]-
syre of money / lechery / ire / vengeaunce / enuy / backbytyng / and
suche other pestylences / whiche than onely be made incurable /
whan they disguysed with the viser and cloke of holynesse and vertue do crepe in to the cyrcle afore spoken: that is / whan vnder the
15 pretexte of executynge the lawe and iustyce, we vse our tyranny.
Whan by the occasyon of relygyon, we prouyde for great lucre.
Whan vnder the tytle of defendyng the churche, we hunte for
worldly power, and authoryte: and whan so euer those thynges be
commaunded, as thynges pertaynynge vnto Chryst / whiche be
20 disagreynge moche from his lernynge. Therfore, the marke muste
be set before euery man, whiche they ought to shote at: and there is
but one marke / whiche is Chryste, and his moost pure lernynge. If
thou sette forth a worldly marke, in the stede of a celestyall marke /
than shall there be nothyng whervnto a man ought iustly enforce
25 hym selfe / whiche laboureth to profyte and go forwarde. Euery
man ought to enforce hym selfe, to that whiche is best, and moost
perfyte / that at the leest, we may attayne and comme to the meane
thynges. And there is no cause why we sholde put awaye any
kynde, or maner of lyuynge from this marke. [b6v] The perfection
30 of Chryst consisteth onely in the affectes / and not in the maner or
kynde of lyuynge: it consysteth in the myndes / and not in the
garmentes / or in meates and drynkes. There be amonge the monkes
whiche be scarse able to be put in ye thyrde circle / and yet I speke of
those whiche be good / but yet weyke, and not perfyte. There be
35 amongest these that haue had two wyues, whiche Chryste thynketh
worthy for the first circle. Nor yet in the meane tyme I do no

Against ll. 18–20: The marke may not be chaunged.
Against ll. 26–8: Al must labour to perfytnesse.

3 vnto] to *1533*

wronge to any maner of lyuyng, or professyon / though I propone,
and set forth afore euery man, that thyng whiche is best, and moost
perfyte: Oneles ye wolde thynke Plato to haue done iniury against
all citees / bicause in his boke of the gouernynge of a cite, or a
commune welth / he fayned suche example of a commune welth / 5
as yet neuer any man coude se. Or excepte ye do thynke that Quintilian hath hurt the hole ordre of oratours / bycause he fayned suche
an example of an oratour, as yet neuer was. And though thou be
farre from the princypall and chefe patron Chryste / thou art not
yet therfore cast awaye / but extymulate and moued to go forwarde 10
and profyte. Art thou nere the marke? than art thou monysshed
and counseyled to approche more nere: for there was neuer yet
any [b7] man that went so farre forward / but that he might haue
gone moche more nere the marke. There is no kynde of lyuyng, but
it hathe some peryllous poyntes annexed vnto it / to cause men to 15
degenerate from the truth. And who so euer sheweth those ieopardous and daungerous poyntes / dothe not derogate or mynysshe
the honour of the ordre / nor speke agaynst it / but rather is for the
profyte therof. As the felicite of prynces, is in daunger to fall in to
tyrannye, is in daunger and ieopardy of folysshnes and flatering. 20
Now who so euer sheweth those daungers to be eschewed / dothe
deserue thankes of the ordre of prynces. Nor he dothe not speke
agaynst theyr maiesty / wherin they glorye / whiche dothe shewe
in what thynges theyr very maiesty dothe consyste / whiche also
dothe put them in remembraunce, wherto they were sworne, whan 25
they toke theyr authorite: what is theyr dutye vnto theyr people /
and what they ought to do vnto theyr officers. The heedes and
rulers of the churche, haue in a maner affynite with two pestylent
vyces / auaryce, and ambycyon: whiche well perceyuynge saynt
Peter, the chefe pastour nexte vnto Chryste / dothe monysshe the 30
bysshoppes to fede theyr flocke / and not to pyll, poll, and fley them:
Nor that they [b7v] sholde not fede them, bycause of any fylthy
aduauntage / but of theyr free and redy wyll: nor that they sholde
vse them selfe as lordes vpon them / but that by the example of
lyfe, they sholde prouoke them to godlynesse, rather than by 35
thretenynge and power. Dothe he than speke agaynst the ordre of

Against ll. 19–20: The commune vyces of prynces.
Against ll. 27–8: Bysshoppes and other.
Against l. 30: i. Petri. v.

---

1 propone] propounde *1533*   18 the honour] thonour *1533*

preestes, whiche dothe shewe by what meanes, and how the bysshops may trewly be great, myghty, and ryche? More ouer, the
kynde of relygyous men, is accompanyed moost communly (besydes
other enormytees) with supersticyon, pryde, ypocrysye, and back-
5 bytyng. He dothe not streyght condempne theyr maner of lyuynge /
whiche dothe shewe and admonysshe them, in what thynges moost
trewe relygyon dothe stande, or rest: and how moche the trewe
godlynesse of a chrysten man, is awaye from pryde: and how farre
trewe charite is from all faynynge and disceyte: how moche back-
10 bytyng and sclaundryng and venymousnesse of tonge, is contrary
to pure and trewe holynesse. And specyally, yf he shewe what is to
be eschewed, after suche sobre and discrete maner, that he do
neyther name any man, nor touche any ordre. What thynge is that
in this mortall lyfe so fortunate and prosperous, but it hathe some
15 pestylent thynges annexed [b8] vnto it? Therfore, lyke as he dothe
not noye the helthe of the body, but helpeth it, who so euer sheweth
what thynges corrupteth helthe, and what thynges preserueth it:
so he dothe not disswade men from religyon / but exhorteth them
rather vnto it / whiche sheweth the corruptous infectyons therof,
20 and also the remedyes. For I am enformed, that there be dyuerse
whiche so iudgeth of this boke, as though the preceptes therof,
dyd withdrawe and tourne away mennes myndes from the lyfe of
relygyous men, bycause they do not so moche prayse and alowe
ceremonyes, neyther yet mannes constytucyons, as some wolde:
25 whiche in dede ouer moche regarde them. And there can be
nothynge so circumspectly spoken, but that therof lewde and euyll
persones done take occasyon, eyther of quarellynge, or elles of
synnynge: So that it is daungerfull now a dayes to any man to teche
any thynge well. If a man sholde disswade frome suche warre and
30 batayle, whiche nowe of longe tyme hathe ben vsed, worse than
was euer any amongest the gentyles, for thynges of no valure / he
sholde be noted by and by of the pykequarelles, to be one of those

Against ll. 2–4: To which vyces the commune sorte of monkes be prone.
Against l. 5: A sentence.
Against l. 13: A sentence.
Against ll. 20–1: The quarell of some persons.
Against ll. 28–9: Nothing is fre from the cauelacion of lewde persons.

14 it] *om.* 1533
Side note 5: persons] 1533; petsons 1534

whiche thynken, that no warre is lawfull for [b8v] a chrysten man.
For these whiche were the bryngers vp and auctours of this
sentence / we haue made heretykes / bycause a pope / I wote not
who / dothe seme to approue and alowe warre. And yet he is not
suspected nor noted of heresy / whiche dothe prouoke and styrre 5
vp men to batayle / and bloweth the trumpet thervnto for euery
tryfelynge mater / agaynst the doctryne bothe of Chryst and of his
apostles. If a man admonysshe, that this is a dede trewly belongynge
to the successour of an apostle, to brynge the turkes vnto religion
with Chrystes helpe / rather than with warre: anone he is suspected, 10
as though he affyrmed not to be lawfull for chrysten men to withstande the turkes / whan they inuade vs. If a man shewe and prayse
the temperaunce that was in the apostles / and speke any thynge
agaynst the greate superfluyte that is vsed now adayes / there be
that note hym for a fauourer of the Ebionytes. And yf a man exhorte 15
diligently / that these which be maryed / sholde rather be ioyned
togyder by the consentes and agreynge of theyr myndes / than by
the enbrasynges of theyr bodyes / and so purely to vse matrymony /
that as moche as myght be, it were made lyke to virginite: he is
anone suspected to thynke that euery acte of ma[ci]trymony were 20
synne and vnlawfull / as the marcionytes dyd. If a man do admonysshe, that in exercyse and disputacyons, specyally of dyuynite,
there sholde be no ambicious pertynacy to ouercomme his felowe,
in defendynge his owne opinyons / nor no ambicyon to shewe what
they can do in commune places: he is wrongfully accused, as though 25
he dyd condempne vtterly all schole lernynge. For saynt Augustyne
whan he gyueth warnynge to the logycyens, that they sholde beware of lust to braule and chyde / dothe not condempne logyke /
but sheweth the pestylence therof, that it myght be eschewed. Also
yf a man note, or reproue the preposterous and wronge iudgement 30
of the commune people / whiche amonge vertues, esteme those to
be of moost great valure and chefest / whiche be of the lowest sorte:
and contrary, whiche also amonge vyces moost sore hateth and

Against l. 6: Batayle.
Against l. 12: Pouerte.
Against ll. 29–31: The subuerted iudgemente of vertues and vyces.

1 whiche thynken] whiche that thynketh *1533*   14–15 there be that note
hym for] he shulde be noted as *1533*   15 exhorte] dyd exhorte *1533*
19 is] shulde be *1533*   20 thynke] *1533*; thyuke *1534*   26 For] Nor
1533   30 yf a man note, or reproue] he dothe not disprayse vertue nor
prayse vyce / whiche sheweth *1533*   33 contrary, whiche also] om. *1533*

abhorreth those whiche be the smallest and lyghtest, and clene
cam / whan they be moost abhominable and greuous. Anone he is
accused, as though he sholde fauour those vices whiche he sheweth
to be more greuous than other / and as though he sholde con-
5 dempne those good dedes and benefytes, to whome he preferreth
other more holy and better. As if a man dyd ad[ciiv]monysshe and
gyue vs warnynge / that it is more sure to trust vnto good dedes,
than to trust to the popes pardon / yet he dothe not forsothe condempne ye popes pardons / but preferreth that, whiche by Chrystes
10 lernynge and doctryne, is of more certeynte. Also yf a man do
teche those for to do better whiche tary at home, and prouyde for
theyr wyfe and chyldren / than those whiche go to se Rome, Hierusalem, or saynt Iames: and that money whiche they sholde spende
in that longe and peryllous iourney, to be better and more deuoutly
15 spente vpon poore folkes /   yet condempneth not he their good
entent / but preferreth that whiche is more nere to very godlynesse.
And this is a thynge, not onely vsed now in our tyme, but also in
tymes here tofore past: to abhorre some vices, as though there
were none other / fawnynge vpon the rest, as they were no vyces at
20 all / whan in very dede, they be more detestable, than those whiche
we so hate and abhorre. Saynt Augustyne dothe complayne in his
epystles, that lasciuiousnesse of the flesshe, is onely imputed vnto
the preestes of Affryke as a vyce / and that the vyce of couetousnesse, and dronkenesse be taken well nygh for a prayse. This spe-
25 cyally we speke moost agaynst / and crye out vpon, and exagerate
[c2] for an exceding abhomynable facte / yf one touche the body of
Chryste with the same handes, wherwith he hath touched the body
of an harlot. And there be some ouer ragyng bolde, that be not
afrayde openly to affyrme, that it is lesse synne for a woman to
30 commytte carnal acte with a brute beest, than to lye with a preest.
Nowe he that somthynge rebuketh theyr vnshamefastnes / dothe
not therfore fauour the naughtynesse of preestes / but sheweth that
they regarde not those offences, whiche be a greate deale more to

Against l. 8: Pardons.
Against ll. 12–13: They whiche go to Hierusalem do no gret thynge.
Against ll. 21–3: Onely voluptuousnesse is abhorred in sacerdotes.

1–2 whiche be the smallest and lyghtest, and clene cam / whan they be moost
abhominable and greuous] moste small fautes and tryfles / and so contrary wyse
1533   22 lasciuiousnesse] lastimyousnesse *1533*   28 an harlot] a
harlotte *1533*

be cryed out vpon. But if a preest be a dycer, a fyghter, a brauler, al vnlerned, drowned and wrapped in temporall besynesse, all gyuen to the euyll seruyce of euyll prynces: yet agaynst hym they crye nothynge at all, whiche all togyder worldly, and polluted / dothe handle and entremeddle with holy mysteryes. Whan a preest is a 5 flaterer, or a pyke quarell / whiche with his bytter tongue, and false lyes, dothe hurte the names of those whiche neuer offended hym / but rather hathe done hym pleasures / why do we not now crye out? Oh what an horryble synne is this, to receyue thy lorde god / whiche suffred his passyon for synners, with that tongue 10 whiche is full of poyson of hell / and with that mouth wherwith [c2v] thou kyllest and sleest an innocent? But this euyll and vngracyousnesse we set so lytell by, that in a maner those men are euen praysed for it / whiche professe them selues to be the moost relygyous amongest relygyous men. There is no man that denyeth 15 but they be to be reprehended and sore rebuked / whiche nourysshe and kepe at home concubynes / to the euyll example of all the commune people: but yet these other euyll vices be more hateful to god. Nor he doth therfore say that butter is naught, which sayth that hony is better, and more to be preferred: Nor yet dothe not 20 approue the feuer, that counseyleth the phrenesy more to be auoyded. And it is harde to tell and expresse, how great infection of maners and disposicyon, dothe sprynge of these peruerse and wronge iudgementes. There be dyuers thynges now a dayes receyued in to the ordre of vertues / whiche rather haue the vyser 25 and apparaunce of godlynesse, than the nature and strength of it: in so moche that oneles we loke well vnto them, and take good hede of them, they do quenche and vtterly destroye vertue. If it had ben but a lytell pestylence of religyon, whiche in ceremonyes dothe lye couered / Paule wold neuer so sharply haue spoken against 30 them in al his epystles. And yet do not we [c3] condempne in any place ceremonyes, that be moderatly obserued / but that all holynesse shold be ascrybed vnto them / we can not suffre. Saynt Augustyne dyd prohibyte those of the clergye, whiche were in

Against ll. 1–3: A sacerdote beyng a dycer or fyghter.
Against ll. 5–6: A sacerdote pyke quarell.
Against ll. 24–5: Certayn thinges haue onely an outwarde shew of godlynesse.
Against ll. 31–3: Ceremonyes be of the mean sorte.
Against l. 34: A rule of saynt Augustyne.

30 dothe lye couered] do lye couerte *1533*   33 shold *om. 1533*

house with hym, to vse any notable vesture / but yf they wolde be commended of the people / that they shold rather bringe that to passe by theyr maners and vertuous lyuyng, than by any sondry fassion of rayment. But now a dayes it is a worlde for to se what
5 newe and wonderful fassions of apparayle and vesture there be. But yet I speke not agaynst that: but this I meruayle of / that those thynges are so ouer moche regarded and set by/whiche peraduenture myght by ryght be reprehended. And agayne that those thynges be so lytell regarded / whiche we sholde onely beholde and regarde. I
10 do not rayle agaynst the grey freres and blacke monkes, that they make moche of theyr owne rule / but bycause certayne of them regarde more theyr owne rules, than they do the gospell: whiche thyng wold to god were not founde in the most parte of them. I do not speke agaynst this / that some eate fysshe / some lyue with
15 herbes / other with egges / but I admonysshe those to erre, and to be farre out of the waye / whiche wyll of these thynges iustifye them selues [c3v] after the maner of the iewes/thynkynge them selues better / and preferrynge them selues to other, for suche tryfles of mennes inuencyon / and take it for no defaute at all, to hurte an
20 other mannes good name with false lyes. Of the dyuersite of meate and drynke, Chryst neuer commaunded any thyng/nor the apostles: But Paule often tymes dyd disswade vs from it. Chryste curseth bytter sclaundrynge / whiche also all the apostles dothe detest and abhorre: and yet that not withstandynge, we wyll appere religyous
25 in suche vsing of meates / and in hurtynge mennes fame, we be bolde and hardy. I praye you, thynke you that he, whiche dothe admonysshe these bothe in generall, not touchynge any man / and also louyngly / dothe hurte religyon? Who is so madde, that he wolde be accompted eloquent, for shewynge and bryngynge to
30 lyght, the vyces that belongen to monkes? But these peraduenture feare, leest theyr couentes and bretherne, wolde be lesse obedyent / and leest also there wolde not so many desyre to be shauen in to theyr ordre. Yet veryly, no man is more obedyent to his heed, than he whiche enspyred with the holy goost, is free and at liberte.
35 True and very charite, taketh all thynges well in worthe / and suffreth all thynges / refuseth [c4] nothynge / is obedyent vnto rulers /

Against ll. 5–6: The rules of men.
Against ll. 20–1: Dyuersyte of meates.

---

14 this] that *1533*   16 these] those *1533*   17 selues²] selfe *1533*
18 selues] selfe *1533*   32 wolde] do *1533*

not onely to those that be sobre and gentyll / but also to those that be sharpe and rough. But yet rulers must be wyse of this, that they do not tourne the obedience of other men, in to theyr owne tyranny / and that they had leuer thcrfore to haue them supersticious, than holy and vertuous / wherby they myght be more obedyent at euery 5 becke. They haue pleasure to be called fathers: but what carnall father is there, yᵗ wolde haue his chyldren euer infantes and yonge, bycause he might vse his power vpon them at his owne pleasure? And of the other parte / all those that purpose to protyte in the liberte of Chryste / of this they must beware / leest as saynt Paule 10 dothe admonysshe, they make theyr liberte a cloke or couer to theyr carnall lyuing. Or as saynt Peter techeth / with theyr liberte, they make a couer and a cloke to malyciousnesse. And be it, that one or two do abuse this liberte / yet it is not right forthwith, that al other therfore sholde be euer kepte in supersticiousnes and 15 bondage of ceremonyes, lyke vnto yᵉ iewes. And who soeuer wyl marke it / shall perceyue that amongest these relygyous men, no man causeth yᵉ ceremonies to be more straytly obserued, than they, whiche vnder the preceptes therof, be as [c4v] kynges ouer other / and seruauntes to theyr owne bellyes, rather than to Christ. More 20 ouer, they nede not to be afrayde, lest suche kynde of essenes be not ynough spred abrode in so greate diuersite of mens natures / wherby it is caused that nothyng is so vnreasonable, but diuers and many wyl loue and desyre it / although their selues ought more to desyre that they had true professours of religion, rather than many. 25 But wolde to god that it were prouyded and ordeyned by a lawe, that no man shold be taken in suche snares afore he were.xxx. yeres of age / before he somthing knewe him selfe, or knewe what the nature and vertue of true religyon is. But these whiche lyke vnto the pharisees, doynge theyr owne besynesse / and prouydyng for 30 theyr owne profyte, wander about to make nouysses bothe by see and lande, shall neuer fayle of yonge men lackyng experience, whome

Against ll. 2–3: The inferyors obedyence may not be abused.
Against ll. 20–2: The more religious a man is / the lesse he yeldeth to ceremonyes.
Against ll. 29–30: Math. xxiij.

10 of this . . . beware] this . . . beware of *1533*   11 couer] couert *1533*
13 be it] if *1533*   15 sholde be euer kepte] be euer kept *1533*   19 be as
kynges ouer other] doth bere rule *1533*   20 seruauntes to theyr owne
bellyes] serue their bellyes *1533*   to Christ] Christ *1533*   21 to be]
be *1533*

they may alure in to their veyles and nettes / and also deceyue. There be a great nombre of fooles and symple soules in euery place. But I desyre euen with all my herte / and I doubte not but so do all that be very good men / that the relygyon of ye gospell myght
5 be so pleasaunt to euery man, that they beyng contented therwith / sholde not desyre the relygyon of blacke monkes or grey freres. And I doubte not [c5] but so wolde saynt Benedicte and Frauncys them selues. Moyses dyd reioyce that his owne honour was defaced and dymmed with the glory of Chryst: and so sholde those other be
10 glad / yf for the loue of Chrystes lawe, we set nothynge by mannes constitucyons. I wolde that all christen men dyd so lyue / that these whiche now be called onely religyous / sholde appere lytell religyous / whiche thyng euen at this daye is of trewth, and that in many: for why sholde I dissymule that thynge that is so manyfest?
15 And yet in the olde tyme, the begynnyng of the monastical lyfe, was nothing els but a goyng asyde in to a secrete place from the cruelnesse of ydolaters. And anone after the maner of lyuynge of relygyous men whiche folowed them, was nothyng els but a reformacyon and callyng agayn to Chryste: for the courtes of
20 prynces in the olde tyme, shewed and declared theyr christendom in their tytles, rather than in theyr lyuyng. The bysshoppes anone after, were corrupt with ambicyon and couetousnesse: and the commune people also faynted and woxen colde, from that charite, whiche was in the primytyue churche: and for this purpose dyd
25 saynt Benet seke a solytary lyfe / and than after hym Barnard / and after that dyuerse other dyd assocyate them selues [c5v] togyder / for this entent onely / that they myght vse the pure and symple lyfe of chrysten men. Than after in processe of tyme, whan theyr rychesse and ceremonyes dyd encrease / their trewe godlynesse and
30 symplenesse dyd abbate and decrease. And now although we se men of relygyon to be ouermoche out of good ordre / and to vse maners lyke vnto gentyles / yet is the worlde fylled with newe institucions and kyndes of religyon / as though they sholde not fall to the same

Against l. 3: Nota.
Against ll. 8–9: Al thinges gyue place to the glory of Chryste.
Against ll. 15–7: The fyrst begynnynge of monkes in olde tyme.
Against ll. 29–30: From whence ceremonyes came.

---

4 myght] shulde *1533*   11 dyd] shulde *1533*   20 and declared
theyr christendom] them christened *1533*
Side-note 1: *om. 1533*

poynt here after, that other haue done afore them. In tymes passed
(as I sayd) a relygyous lyfe was nothynge but a solytary lyfe. And
now these be called religious, which be al togyder drowned in
worldly besynesse / vayngo playnly certayne tyranny in worldly
maters. And yet these, for theyr apparayle and tytle (I can not 5
tell what) doth chalenge suche holynesse to them selues / that they
accompte all other in comparison no christen men at al. Why do we
make so strayte and narowe Chrystes relygyon, whiche he wolde
haue so large? If we be moued with magnyfycall and hyghe termes /
I praye you, what thynge elles is a Cytye but a greate monastery? 10
Monkes be obedyent to theyr abbot and gouernoures / the cytezyns
obey the bysshoppes and cu[c6]rates / whome Chryst hym selfe
made rulers, and not the authorite of man. The monkes lyue in
ydlenesse / and be fedde of other mennes liberalite / possessynge
that amongest them selfe in commune, whiche they neuer laboured 15
or swet for (yet speke I nothynge of them that be vycyous). The
cytezyns bestowe that whiche they haue goten with theyr greate
labour and trauayle, to them that haue nede / euery man as he is of
habylite and power. Now as concernynge the vowe of chastite, I
dare not be bolde to expresse what difference is betwyxte the 20
religyous man vnmaryed / and the chaste matrymony of the other.
And to be shorte / he shall not veray greatly lacke those thre vowes
of mannes inuencyon / that dothe kepe and obserue purely and
syncerely that fyrste onely vowe, whiche we all, solempnely make
vnto Chryste / and not vnto man / whan we receyue our baptysme. 25
And yf we compare those that be euyll of one kynde / with those that
be euyll of the other / without doubte the temporall men be moche
better. But if we compare those whiche be good of ye one sorte /
with those that be good of the other, there is lytell difference, yf
there be any at all: sauynge that those appere to be more relygyous 30
[c6v] whiche kepe theyr relygyon and dutye with lesse coaction.
The rest is therfore, that no man folysshly stande in his owne
conceyte, neyther for his dyuersite of lyuyng from other men / nor

Against ll. 3–4: Monkes most worldly.
Against ll. 9–10: A Cyte is a great monasterye.
Against ll. 13–14: Obedyence / pouerty / chastity.

6 them] their *1533*   7 accompte] do accompte *1533*   compari-
son] comparison of them selues *1533*   15 them selfe] theym *1533*
17–18 greate labour and trauayle] laboure and great trauayle *1533*   31 whiche]
that *1533*

despyse or condempne the rule or ordre of other mennes lyuing.
But in euery kynde of lyuynge, let this be our commune study / that
euery man accordyng to his power, endeuoyre hym selfe to attayne
vnto the marke of Chryste / whiche is set open to al men / and that
5 euery man do exhorte other to it / and also helpe other / neyther
enuyenge them that ouer ronne vs in this course / nor disdaynynge
them that be weyke, and can not yet ouer take vs. In conclusion,
whan every man hath done that he can, let hym not be lyke vnto the
pharisey / whome the gospell maketh mencyon of / whiche dothe
10 boste his good dedes vnto god, saying. I fast twyse in the weke / I
paye all my tythes, and suche forth. But after Christes counseyle,
let him speke from the herte, and to hymselfe / and not to other,
sayinge: I am an vnprofytable seruaunt / for I haue done no more
than I ought to do. There is no man that better trusteth / than he
15 that so dystrusteth. There is no man further from true relygyon /
than he that thynketh hym selfe to be very relygyous. Nor Chrystes
godly[c7]nesse, is neuer at worse poynt / than whan that thyng,
whiche is worldly, is writhen vnto Chryst / and the authorite of man,
is preferred vnto the authorite of god. We must all hange of that
20 heed, yf we wyll be true chrysten men. More ouer, who so euer is
obedyent to a man, whiche dothe perswade and call hym vnto
Chryste / he is obedyent vnto Chryste / and not vnto man. And
who so euer doth tollerate and suffre those men whiche be subtyle,
cruell, and ymperyous / teachyng that thyng whiche maketh not
25 for religyon / but for theyr tyrannye: he vseth the pacyence mete for
a christen man / so that these thynges whiche they commaunde, be
not vtterly wycked and contrary to Chrystes doctryne: for than it
shall be conuenient to haue that answere of thapostles at hande:
we must rather be obedient vnto god, than to any man. But we
30 haue longe ago passed the measure and quantite of an epystle / so
greatly the tyme disceyueth vs / whyles we comon and talke moost
pleasauntly with our well beloued frende. This boke is sent vnto you
in Frobenius prynte, as though it were newe borne agayne / moche
more ornate, and better corrected, than it was before. I haue put

Against ll. 2–3: No kynde of lyfe ought to be reproued.
Against ll. 7–9: The confydence in our selfes is most pernycious.
Against ll. 22–3: How farre prelates must be obeyed.

18 worldly] wordly *1533*
Side-note 2: selfes] selfe *1533*

vnto it certayne fragmentes of myne olde study in tymes passed.
Me thought [c7v] it moost conuenyent to dedycate this edicyon
(suche as it is) vnto you / that who so euer shall take any preceptes
to lyue well, of Erasmus, sholde haue an example redy at hande of
our father Volzius. Our lorde preserue you good father / the honour 5
and worshyp of all religion. I praye you counseyle Sapidus / that he
be wyse, that is, that he go forth as he hath begon: and to Wynphelingus ye shall speke also / that he prepare al his armure , to
fyght shortly with the turkes / for as moche as he hath kepte warre
longe ynough with kepers of concubynes. And I haue great hope 10
and trust to se hym ones a bysshop, and to ryde vpon a mule / and
to be set hygh in honour, with a myter and crosse. But in ernest,
I praye you commaunde me hertely bothe vnto them and vnto
Ruserus, and the rest of my frendes: and in your deuoute prayers
made to god, I praye you remembre Erasmus / and pray for his 15
soules helth. At Basyle the euen of the Assumpcyon of our Lady /
in the yere of our lorde god M.CCCCC. and .xviij.

13 commaunde] commend *1533*

The table.
❧ Here foloweth the table of
this present booke.

1 The table.] om. 1533   5 Capitulo] capitulo 1533   7 Caplo.]
cap. 1533   9–10 the apparent] apparent 1533   10–32 Capi., Ca.] cap.
1533   25 Of certayne] Here foloweth 1533   a good chrysten man] a
christen man 1533   28 eyght] eygth 1533   31 enleuenth] enleueth 1533

❡ Finis   25

1–7 -teenth] -tenth *1533*   1–10 Capi.] cap. *1533*   12 Ca.] ca. *1533*
14–24 Capi., Ca.] cap. *1533*

Enchiridion.

⁋ A compendyous treatyse of the
sowdyour of Chryst / called Enchiridion. Whiche Erasmus
5   of Roterdame wrote vnto
a certayne courtyer / a
frende of his.

THou hast desyred me with feruent study syngular beloued
brother in Chryst / that I sholde descrybe for the compendyously /
10 a certeyn craft of vertuous lyuing / by whose helpe thou myghtest
attayne a vertuous mynde / accordyng to a true chrysten man. For
thou sayst, that thou art, and hast ben, a greate whyle wery of the
pastyme of the courte : and doest compasse in thy mynde, by what
meanes thou myghtest escape egipt with all her bothe vyces and
15 pleasures / and be prepared happely with the capteyn Moyses, vnto
the iourney of vertue. The more I loue the / the gladder I am of this
thyne so holy a purpose : which I trust (ye without our helpe) he
that hath vouched safe to styre it up in the / shal make prosperous,
and brynge to good effect. Notwithstandynge yet haue I very
20 gladly, and wyllyngly accomplysshed thy desyre, partly bicause
thou art [A1v] so greate a frende of myne / partly also bycause thou
requyrest so charitable thynges. Now enforce thy selfe, and do thyne
endeuoyre / that neyther thou mayst seme to haue desyred my
seruyce and dutye in vayne : neyther I to haue satysfyed thy mynde
25 without any fruyte. Ye let vs bothe indifferently beseche the
benygne spiryte of Iesu / that he bothe put holsome thynges in my
mynde, whyle I wryte : and make the same to the of strengthe and
effycacye.

⁋ We must watche and loke aboute vs euer more, whyle we be in
30 this lyfe.   Caplo. j.

THe first poynt is / we must nedes haue in mynde continually,
that ye lyfe of mortall men, is nothynge but a certeyn perpetuall

Against ll. 13–15: Egypt betokeneth synfull lyuyng.
Against ll. 16–17: The lande of promyssyon signyfyeth pure lyfe.
Against l. 32–p. 33, l. 2: The lyfe of man is but a warfare / sayth Iob. vii.

1 Enchiridion.] om. 1533   24 neyther] or els 1533

exercise of warre: as Iob wytnesseth, a warryour proued to ye vttermost, and neuer ouercomme. And that the most parte of men, be
ouermoche deceyued/whose myndes this worlde as a iugler holdeth
occupyed with delicyous and flateryng pleasures / whiche also departing from warre, as though they had conquered all theyr enne- 5
myes / make holyday out of season / and gyue themselfe to rest out
of tyme / none otherwyse truly, than in a very assured peace. It is
a meruaylous thyng to be[A2]holde, how without care and circum-
spection we lyue / how ydelly we slepe / now vpon the one syde / and
now vpon ye other / whan without ceasyng we are beseged with so 10
great a nombre of armed vices / sought and hunted for with so great
craft / inuaded dayly with so great lyeng awayt. Behold ouer thy heed
wycked deuyls that neuer slepe / but kepe watche for our destruc-
tion/armed against vs with a thousand deceites / with a thousand
craftes of noysaunces / whiche enforce from on hygh to wounde our 15
myndes with wepons brenning and dipped in deedly poyson, than
the which wepons neyther Hercules nor Cephalus had euer a surer
darte / except they be receyued with ye sure and impenetrable
shelde of fayth. Than agayn on ye ryght hand, and on the left hand /
afore and behynde, this worlde stryueth against vs / which after 20
the saying of saint Iohn, is set al on vice and myschefe. And therfore is to Chryste, bothe contrary and hated. Neyther is it one
maner of fyght. For somtyme with gonnes of aduersite / as one
ragynge with open warre / he shaketh the walles of the soule: Somtyme with great promesses (but yet most vayne) he prouoketh to 25
treason: and somtyme by vndermining he steleth on vs vnware, to
catche vs among the ydle and careles men. Last of all, vndernethe /
the slypper serpent, the [A2v] fyrst breker of peace, father of
vnquietnes / otherwhyles hyd in the grene grasse, lurkyng in his
caues, wrapped togyder in an hondred rounde rolles, ceaseth not to 30
watche and lye in a wayte bynethe in the hele of our woman / whome
he ones poysoned. By the woman is vnderstande the carnall parte of

Against ll. 3–4: The comparacyon of the worlde to a iugler.
Against ll. 6–7: Peace peace / and yet is there no peacce at all.
Against ll. 12–14: Dyuers enemyes from aboue.
Against ll. 19–20: Enemyes at hande.
Against ll. 28–9: Enemyes of hell.

4–5 departing from warre] *om.* 1533   6–7 and gyue themselfe to rest
out of tyme] *om.* 1533   7 truly] veryly *1533*   18 with] *om.* 1533
21–2 therfore] *1533*; thefore *1534*   22 is to Chryste] to Chhryst *1533*
23–4 as one ragynge with] ragyng / as with *1533*   30 an hondred] a
hondred *1533*

a man / otherwyse called sensualite. This is our Eue, by whom y^e
most crafty serpent dothe entyce and drawe our myndes to
mortall and deedly pleasures. And furthermore, as though it were
but a tryfle, y^t so great a company of ennemyes sholde assawte vs
5 on euery syde: we bere about with vs, where so euer we go, in the
very secrete partes of the mynde, an ennemye nerer than one of
acqueyntaunce / or one of housholde. And as nothynge is more inwarde / so nothyng is more peryllous. This is the olde and erthly
Adam / which by acqueyntaunce and customable familiarite, is more
10 nere to vs than a citezyn / and is in al maner studyes and pastymes to
vs more contrary, than any mortal ennemy: whom thou canst kepe
of with no bulwarke / neyther is it lawfull to expell hym out of thy
pauilyon. This felowe must be watched with an hondred eyes / leest
perauenture he set open the castel or cite of god, for deuyls to entre
15 in. Seynge therfore we be vexed with so fereful and cruel warre /
and that [A3] we haue to do or stryue with so many ennemyes /
whiche haue conspyred and sworne our deth / whiche be so besy /
so appoynted / so false and expert: Ought not we mad men on the
other syde to arme our selfe / and take our wepons in our handes to
20 kepe watche and haue all thynges suspecte? But we as though all
thynges were at rest and peace, slepe so fast that we rowte agayne /
and gyue our selfe to ydelnes, to pleasure / and as the commune
prouerbe is / gyue our myndes to reuelyng and makyng good chere /
as though our lyfe were a feestynge or bankettynge / suche as the
25 grekes vsed / and not warfare. For in the stede of tentes and pauyl-
yons, we tumble and walter in our beddes: and in the stede of sallets
and harde armure, we be crowned with roses and fresshe floures,
bathed in damaske and rose waters / smoked in pommaunders and
with muskballes / chaungyng poyntes of warre with ryot and
30 ydelnes / and in the stede of wepons belongyng to ye warre we
handle and take vnto vs the vnhardy harpe / as who say, this peace
were not of all warres ye moost shamefull. For who so euer is at
one with vices / hath broken the truce made bytwene him and god,
in tyme of baptysme. And thou oh madde man cryest peace peace /
35 whan thou hast god thyne ennemy / whiche onely is peace, and the
author [A3v] of peace / and he hymselfe with open mouth cryeth

Against ll. 1–3: Eue signyfyeth affeccyons.
Against ll. 9–11: Olde erthly Adam betokeneth appetytes or affeccions.

---

24 bankettynge] backettyng *1533*   31 who say] *om. 1533*   33 the
truce] truce *1533*

the contrary by ye mouth of his prophete / saying. There is no peace
to synners or wicked persones, whiche loue not god. And there
is none other condicyon of peace with hym, excepte that we (as longe
as we warre in the fortresse of this body) with deedly hate, and
with al our might, kepe batayle and fyght agaynst vyces. For yf we 5
be at one with them / we shal haue hym, whiche onely, beyng our
frende, may make vs blyssed / and beynge our foo, may destroye
vs / our double ennemy, bothe bycause we stande on their syde,
whiche onely can neuer agre with god (for how can lyght and
darknes agree) and also bycause we as men moost vnkynde, abyde 10
not by the promesse that we made to him / and wickedly breke the
appoyntment whiche was made with protestacyon and holy ceremonyes. Oh thou chrysten man, remembrest thou not whan thou
were professed and consecrate with the holy mysteryes of y^e
fountayne of lyfe / how thou boundest thy selfe to be a faythfull 15
sowdyour vnto thy captayne Chryste: to whome thou owest thy
lyfe twyse / bothe bycause he gaue it the / and also bycause he
restored it agayne to the / to whome thou owest more than thou
art able to paye? Commeth it not to thy mynde, how whan thou
[A4] were bounde with his sacramentes, as with holy gyftes / thou 20
were sworne with wordes for the nones, to take the parte of so
courteys an Emperour / and that thou dydest curse and banne
thyne owne heed / desyrynge vengeaunce to fall vpon thyne owne
selfe / yf thou dydest not abyde by thy promesse? For what entent
was the sygne of the crosse printed in thy foreheed, but that as 25
long as thou lyuest, thou sholdest fyght vnder his standarde? For
what entent were thou anoynted with his holy oyle / but that thou
for euer sholdest wrastle and fyght agaynst vyces? What shame, and
how great abomynacyon is it accounted with all men, yf a man forsake his kynge, or chefe lorde? Why settest thou so lyght than by thy 30
capteyn Chryst? neyther kepte downe with the feare of hym /

Against ll. 1–3: There is no peace to wicked persones.
Against ll. 13–16: In tyme of Baptysme we professe with protestacion to fyght
euer vnder the standard of christ.
Against ll. 26–7: Badges and sygnes of baptysm.

1 There] there *1533, 1534*   5 with] *1533*, wtih *1534*   kepe batayle
and] sholde*1533*   6–8 we shal haue hym . . . our double ennemy, bothe]
we shall haue him twyse our ennemy / . . . bothe *1533*   7 beynge] yf he
be *1533*   8 bycause] bycause that *1533*   10 also] also that *1533*
11–12 and wickedly breke the appoyntment whiche was made] but vniustly
haue broken thappoyntment made bytwene hym and vs *1533*

seynge he is god / nor refraynynge for the loue of hym / seynge for
thy sake he was made man? ye and seynge thou vsurpest his name,
thou oughtest to remembre what thou hast promysed hym. Why
departest thou awaye from hym lyke a false forsworne man / and
5 goest vnto thyne ennemye / frome whense he ones redemed the,
with the raunsome of his precyous blode? Why doest thou so ofte
a renegate warre and fyght vnder the standarde of his [A4v]
aduersary? With what face presumest thou to set vp contrary baners
against thy king, whiche for thy sake bestowed his owne lyfe? Who
10 so euer is not on his part / as he saith himself Luc.xj. standeth against
hym. And he y^t gadereth not with him, scatereth abrode. Thou
warrest not onely with fylthy tytle or quarell / but also for a myserable rewarde. Wylt thou heare who so euer thou be, y^t art a
seruaunt or soudyour to the worlde / what shalbe thy mede? Paule
15 the standarde berer in the warre of Christ answereth y^e. The
rewarde (saith he) of synne is deth. And who wold take vpon hym to
fight in a iust and an honest cause, yf he were sure to dye but
bodyly onely: and thou fyghtest in a wronge and also a fylthy
quarell, to obtayne for thy rewarde, the dethe of thy soule. In these
20 mad warres whiche man maketh agaynst man / eyther thrugh beestly
furye / or thrugh wretched and myserable necessite / seest thou not,
yf at any tyme the greatnes of ye praye promysed, or hoped for / or
comforte of the captayne / or the cruelnes of the ennemyes / or
shame of cowardnes cast in theyr tethes / or in conclusyon, yf
25 desyre of prayse hath prycked and stered vp the sowdyours myndes:
with what courage, and how lusty stomackes they fynyssh, what so
euer labour remayneth? how lytel they [A5] regarde theyr lyues?
With how great fyersnes they renne vpon theyr ennemyes: wel is
him that may go formest? And I beseche the how moche worth is
30 ye rewarde, whiche those wretched men go about to gete, with so
great ieopardies and diligence? Which is nothing els, but to haue
prayse of a wretched man theyr capteyn / and that they myght be
gloryfyed with a rude and homely songe / suche as are vsed to be

Against ll. 3–4: The name of Chryste ought to put vs in remembraunce.
Against ll. 15–16: The guerdon of synne.
Against ll. 29–30: Comparacyon of rewardes.

1 the loue of hym] loue *1533*   10 Luc.] Luce. *1533*   13–14 a seruaunt]
seruaunt *1533*   20 whiche] that *1533*   21 thrugh wretched and]
for *1533*   26 how ... they fynyssh] with what ... fynysshe they
1533   28 they renne] ronne they *1533*   29 moche worth] smal *1533*
31 Which is nothing els] Veryly *1533*   33 gloryfyed] praysed *1533*

made in ye tyme of warre / to haue happely their names wryten in a
harpers bederoll, to gete a garlande of grasse, or oken leues / or at
the moost, to bryng home a lytel more vauntage, or wynnyng with
them. We on ye other syde clene contrary, be kendled neycher
with shame nor hope of reward / and yet he beholdeth vs whyle we 5
fyght, y^t shall quyte our payne, yf we wynne the felde. But what
reward setteth forth ye chefe ruler of our game, for them y^t wynne
the maystry: veryly not mules, as Achylles dyd in Homere / not
tripodas / that is to say / meate bordes with .iij. fete / as Eneas dyd
in Virgil: but suche as the eye neuer sawe / ne ye eare neuer herde, 10
neyther coude synke in to the hert of man. And these rewardes
he gyueth in ye meane season to his (whyles they be yet fyght-
ing) as solaces, and thinges to comfort them in their labours and
trauayles. And what afterward? [A5v] certes blissed immortalite.
How beit in games of sporte / as rennynge, wrastlyng and lepyng, in 15
whiche the chefest parte of rewarde, is prayse: euen they which be
ouercom / haue lykewyse theyr rewardes assygned vnto them. But
our mater is tryed with great and doutfull peryll / neyther we fyght
for prayse, but for lyfe. And as reward of most valure is set before
hym that quiteth hym selfe moost manfully: so payne most ter- 20
ryble is appoynted for hym y^t gyueth backe. Heuen is promysed to
hym that fyghteth lustely. And why is not the quick courage of a
gentyll stomacke enflamed with the hope of so blessed a rewarde:
namely whan he promyseth / whiche as he can not dye / euen so he
can not deceyue. Al thynges be done in the syght of god, whiche al 25
thynges beholdeth: we haue al the company of heuen beholders of
our conflict? And how are we not moued at the lestway euen for
very shame? He shall prayse our vertue and diligence / of whome to
be lauded is very felicite. Why seke we not this prayse / ye with the
losse of our lyues? It is a cowardfull mynde y^t wyl be quickened 30
with no maner of reward. The veryest hertles coward in the
worlde / for feare of peryls oft tyme taketh courage to hym. And in
worldly batayles, though thyne aduersary be neuer [A6] so cruell /
yet rageth he but on thy goodes and body onely. What more than
that coude cruell Achilles do to Hector? But here the immortall 35

Against ll. 25–6: God beholdeth vs.
Against ll. 34–5: Achylles slewe Hector.

8 verily] *om. 1533*   14 afterward] here after *1533*   14–15 How beit]
But *1533*; how beit *1534*   15 and] *om. 1533*   16 euen] *om. 1533*
19 set before] profred to *1533*

parte of the, is assawted: and thy carkas is not drawen aboute the
sepulcre as Hectors was: but thy body and soule are togyther cast
downe in to hell. There the greatest calamite or hurt is, that a
sworde shall separate the soule from the body: here is taken from
5 thy soule ye lyfe / which is god hym selfe. It is natural for ye body
to dye: whiche yf no man kyll / yet must it nedely dye. But thy
soule to dye, is extreme mysery. With how great cautel voyde we
the woundes of the body / with how great diligence cure we them /
and set we so litel of the woundes of the soule? Our hertes
10 aryseth and grudgeth at the remembraunce of deth of the body, as
at a terryble or outragyous thing, bycause it is seen with bodily
eyen. The soule to dye, bycause no man seeth, and fewe byleueth /
therfore very fewe feare it. And yet is this deth more cruell, than
the other: Euen as moche as the soule passeth the body / and god
15 excelleth the soule. ❡ Wylte thou that I shewe the certayne coniectures, examples, or tokens, wherby thou mayst perceyue the syckens
and deth of the soule? Thy stomacke dygesteth yll / it kepeth no
meate: thou perceyuest by and by [A6v] thy body to be out of temper.
And breade is not so naturall meate for thy body / as the worde of
20 god is meate for thy soule. Yf that seme bitter / yf thy mynde ryse
against it / why doutest thou yet, but y^t the mouth of thy soule is
out of taste / and infected with some disease. Yf thy memory, the
stomacke of thy soule, kepe not ye lernynge of god / yf by contynual
meditacion thou digestest not / yf whan it is digested / thou sendest
25 it not to al partes by operacyon / thou hast an euydent token that
thy soule is acrased. Whan thy knees for weyknes bowe vnder the /
and moche worke to drawe thy lymmes after the / thou perceyuest
playnly thy body to be euyll at ease. And doest thou not perceyue the
sycknes of thy soule / whan he grudgeth and is weyke and faynt to
30 all dedes of pite / whan he hath no strengthe to suffre pacyently, the
leest rebuke in the worlde / and is troubled, and angry with the
losse of a halfpeny. After that the syght is departed from the eyes /
and the eares cease to heare. After that all the body hath lost his

Against ll. 10–13: The deth of the body semeth terryble / the deth of the soule
is not perceyued.
Against ll. 17–18: The token of a sycke soule.

2 was] om. *1533*   are togyther] is *1533*   12 eyen] eyes *1533*   13 yet
is this deth more cruell, than] is this dethe more cruell yet than *1533*   14 pas-
seth] dothe passe *1533*   15 ❡ om. *1533*   19 for thy body] to thy body
1533

felynge: no man douteth than, but the soule is departed. Whan the
eyes of thy herte be waxen dym / in so moche that thou canst not se
the most clerest light / whiche is trouth. Whan thou hearest not
with thy inwarde eares the voyce of god. Whan thou lackest all thy
[A7] inwarde felyng and perceyuyng of the knowlege of god /   5
thynkest thou that thy soule is alyue? Thou seest thy brother
vngoodly entreated / thy mynde is nothynge moued / so thy mater
be in good case. Why feleth thy soule nothynge here? Certaynly
bycause he is deed. Why deed? bycause her lyfe is awaye / whiche is
god. For veryly where god is / ther is charite, loue, and compassyon   10
of thy neyghbour: for god is that charite. For yf thou were a
quycke member / how coude any part of thy body ake / thou not
sorowyng / no not ones felyng or perceyuyng it. Take a more
euident token. Thou hast deceyued thy frende / thou hast commytted
adultery, thy soule hath caught a deedly wounde / and yet it   15
greueth the not / in so moche that thou ioyest, as it were of gret
wynnynge / and bostest thy selfe, of that thou shamefully hast
commytted: byleue surely that thy soule lyeth deed. Thy body is not
alyue, yf he fele not the prycking of a pyn. And is thy soule alyue
whiche lacketh the felyng of so great a wounde? Thou hearest some   20
man vse lewde and presumptuous communycacyon / wordes of
backbytyng / vnchaste and fylthy / ragyng furyously agaynst his
neyghbour: thynke not ye soule of that man to be alyue. There
lyeth a rotten carkas in the sepulcre of y^t stomak, fro whens
[A7v] suche stenche aryseth, and infecteth euery man that commeth   25
nygh. Chryst called the pharysees paynted sepulcres. Why so?
bycause they bare deed soules aboute with them. And kyng Dauid
the prophete sayth. Theyr throte is a sepulcre wyde open / they
spake deceytfully with theyr tonges. The bodyes of holy people be
the temples of the holy goost. And lewde mennes bodyes be the   30
sepulcres of deed corpses / that the interpretacions of the gram-
maryens to them myght well be applyed Soma quasi Sima. It is
called a body, bycause it is the buryall / that is to say, the graue of
the soule. The brest is the sepulcre / the mouth and the throte is

Against ll. 9–10: God is lyfe of the soule.
Against ll. 13–14: Felynge is a token of lyfe.
Against ll. 29–31: The bodyes of good men be the temples of the holy goost.
Against ll. 32–3: The body is the buryal or graue.

3 trouth] vertue or trouth *1533*   9 whiche] that *1533*   16 as it were]
as it it were *1533*   28 Theyr] theyr *1533, 1534*   32 It] it *1533, 1534*

the gapying of the sepulcre / and the body destytute of the soule, is not so deed as is the soule, whan she is forsaken of almyghty god / neyther any corpse stynketh in the nose of man so sore / as the stenche of a soule buryed .iiij. dayes, offendeth the nose of god and
5 all sayntes. Therfore conclude / whan so euer deed wordes procede out of thy herte / it must nedes be, that a deed corpse lyeth buryed within. For whan (accordyng to the gospell) the mouth speketh of the haboundaunce of the hert / no doubte he wolde speke the lyuely wordes of god / yf there were lyfe present / that is to wyte, god.
10 In an other place of the gos[A8]pell / the disciples saye to Chryst. Mayster whether shall we go / thou hast y[e] wordes of lyfe? Why so I praye the/the wordes of lyfe? Certaynly, for bycause they spronge out of that soule, from whome the godhede, whiche restored vs agayn to lyfe immortal, neuer departed so moche as one moment.
15 The phisycyan easeth thy body somtyme whan thou art diseased. Good and holy men somtymes haue called y[e] body deed, to lyfe agayn. But a deed soule, nothing but god onely, of his free and syngular power restoreth to lyfe agayn / ye and he restoreth her not agayne, yf she beyng deed, haue ones forsaken the body. More
20 ouer, of the bodyly deth, is the felyng lytel, or none at al. But of the soule, is the feling eternal. And though also the soule in that case, be more than deed/yet as touchynge the felyng of eternal deth, she is euer immortall. Therfore, seynge we must nedes fyght with so straunge and meruailous ieopardy / what dulnes, what neclygence,
25 what folysshnes is that of our mynde / whome fere of so great myschefe sharpeneth not? And agayn on y[e] contrary parte, there is no cause wherfore, eyther the greatnes of peryll, or elles the multytude, the violence, the subtyltye of thyne aduersaryes, sholde abate the courage of y[e] mynde. It commeth to thy mynde [A8v]
30 how greuous an aduersary thou hast. Remembre also on the other syde, how present, how redy at hande thou hast helpe and socour. Agaynst the, be innumerable / ye but he that taketh thy parte / hymself alone is more of power, than all they. Yf god be on our syde / what mater is it who be agaynst vs. Yf he stay the / who shall
35 cast y[e] downe. But thou must be enflamed in al thy hert and brenne

Against ll. 27–9: Many causes why a christen man ought to be of good conforte / and to haue confidence.

9 haboundaunce] aboundaunce *1533*   14 that soule] the soule *1533*
15 so moche as] not yet *1533*   32 present,] present *1533, 1534*
Side-note 1: causes] canses *1533, 1534*

in feruent desyre of victory. Let it comme to thy remembraunce, that thou stryuest not / nor hast not to do with a fresshe sowdyour and a newe aduersary / but with hym that was many yeres ago discomfited, ouerthrowen, spoyled, and ledde captyue, in triumphe of vs / but than in Chryst our heed / by whose myght no doubte, 5 he shall be subdued agayne in vs also. Take hede therfore that thou be a membre of the body, and thou shalt be able to do al thynges in the power of ye heed. In thy selfe thou art very weyke / in hym thou art valyaunt / and nothynge is there, that thou art not able to do. Wherfore the ende of our warre, is not doutfull / bycause the victory 10 dependeth not of fortune / but is put holly in ye handes of god / and by hym in our handes. No man is here that hath not ouercomme / but he that wolde not. The benignite of our protectour neuer fayled man. If thou take hede to [B1] answere and to do thy parte agayn / thou art sure of the victory : for he shal fyght for the / 15 and his liberalite shall be imputed to the for meryte. Thou must thanke hym all togyder for the victory / whiche fyrst of all hym-selfe alone beyng immaculate / pure and clene from synne / op-pressed the tyranny of synne. But this victory shal not come with-out thyne owne diligence also / for he that sayd / haue confydence, 20 I haue ouercomen the worlde / wold haue the to be of a good comfort / but not careles and necligent. On this maner in conclusyon, in his strength / and by hym we shall ouercome, if by his ensample we shall fyght as he fought : wherfore thou muste so kepe a meane course / as it were bytwene Scilla, and Charibdis / that neyther 25 trustyng to moche, and bearyng the ouer bolde vpon the grace of god, thou be carelesse and rechelesse / neyther yet so mystrustyng in thy selfe / feared with the difficulties of the warre / do cast from the courage / boldnesse or confydence of mynde togyder with harneys and wepons also. 30

C Of the wepons to be vsed in the
warre of a chrysten man. Ca. ij.

ANd I suppose that nothynge perteyneth so moche to the discyplyne of [B1v] this warre as that thou surely know and

Against ll. 2–4: Our enemy was ouercom many yeres agone.
Against ll. 8–10: No man is stronge in his owne strengthe.
Against ll. 25–9: Scilla is a ieopardous place in the see of cecyle. Charibdis is a swalowe or whyrlepole in the same see.

34 as that] than that *1533*

presently haue recorded, and exercysed in thy mynde alwaye, with
what kynde of armure or wepons thou oughtest to fyght / and
agaynst what enemyes thou must encounter and iust. More ouer
that thy wepons be alway redy at hande / leest thyne so subtyle an
5 enemy shulde take the sleper and vnarmed. In these worldly warres
a man may be often tymes at rest / as in the depe of the wynter / or
in tyme of truce: but we as longe as we kepe warre in this body /
may departe from our harneys, and wepons no ceason / no not (as
ye sayeng is) one fynger brede. We must euer stande afore the
10 tentes and make watche / for our aduersary is neuer ydle: but whan
he is most calme and styll / whan he fayneth to flee or to make
truce / euen than most of al he ymagyneth gyle: and thou hast
neuer more nede to kepe watche than whan he maketh countenaunce or semblaunce of peace. Thou hast neuer lesse nede to
15 feare / than whan he assaulteth the with open warre. Therfore let
thy first care be, that thy mynde be not vnarmed. We arme our
body bycause we wold haue no nede to feare the dagger or priuy
murderer of the thefe. Shall we not arme our mynde lykewise / that
he might be in sauegarde? Our enemyes be armed to distroye
20 [B2] vs / dothe it greue vs to take our wepons of defence y^t we
perysshe not? They watche to kyll / shall nat we watche to be out of
daunger? But of the armure and wepons of a christen man, we
shall make specyal mencion whan we come to the places conuenyent.
In ye meane ceason, to speke breuely who so euer wyl assayle with
25 batayle the seuen nacyons that be called / Cananei / Cethei / Amorrei /
Pherezei / Gergezei / Euei / and Iebuzei / y^t is to say / who so euer
wyl take vpon hym to fyght agaynst the hole hoost of vices / of the
which seuen be counted as chefe capitaynes / must prouyde hym
of two specyall wepons / prayer and knowlege / otherwyse called
30 lernynge. Paule wolde we shulde be euer armed / whiche byddeth
vs pray continually without stop. Prayer pure and perfyte lyfteth
vp thyne affectyon to heuen / a toure beyonde thyne enemyes reache.
Lernynge or knowlege fenseth or armeth the mynde with holsom
preceptes and honest opinyons / and putteth the euer in remem-
35 braunce of vertue / so that neyther can be lackyng to ye other.
These twayne cleueth so togyder lyke frendes / the one euer

Against ll. 9–11: A chrysten man shold neuer cease from warre.
Against ll. 23–6: The .vij. nacyons inhabyted the lande of behest or promis-
sion / promysed to Abraham and his ofsprynge.
Again ll. 29–31: Prayer and knowlege be the chefe armour of a chrysten man.

requyring the others helpe. The one maketh intercessyon and prayeth. The other sheweth what is to be desyred, and what thou oughtest to pray. To pray [B2v] feruently / and (as Iames exhorteth vs) without doutyng or mystrustyng, fayth and hope bringeth to passe. To pray in the name of Iesu / whiche is nothyng els but to 5 desyre thinges holsom for thy soule helth onely / lernyng or doctryne techeth the. Said not Christ to the sonnes of zebedei ye knowe not what ye aske? But prayer verily is the more excellent / as she that communeth and talketh famyliarly with almyghty god. Yet for all that is doctryne no lesse necessary. And I can not tell, whether y^t 10 thou fledde from Egypt, myghtest without great ieopardy commyt thyselfe to so long a iourney so harde and full of diffyculte / without the capteyns Aaron and Moyses. Aaron whiche was charged with thynges dedycate to the seruyce of goddes temple / betokeneth prayer. By Moyses is fygured the knowlege of the law of god. And 15 as knowlege of god, ought not to be vnperfyte: so prayer shulde not be faynte / slacke / without courage or quycknesse. Moyses with the wepons of prayer, fought agaynst his enemyes / but had his handes lyfted vp to heuen / whiche whan he let downe / the israelites had the worse. Thou happely whan thou prayest consydrest only, how 20 moche of thy psalmes thou hast mombled vp / and thynkest moche bablyng to be the strength, and vertue of [B3] prayer: whiche is chefely the vyce of them whiche (as infantes) cleue to the lytterall sence / and are not yet growen vp to the rypenesse of the spyrite. But here what Christ techeth vs in Mathewe / sayeng. 25 Whan ye pray speke nat moche / as the ethneys and gentyles do / for they thynke their prayers to be accepted bycause of moche bablyng. Counterfayte them not therfore / for your father knoweth wherof ye haue nede before ye desyre it of hym. And Paule to the Corinthes dispyseth .x. thousande wordes babled with mouthe / in 30 comparison of fyue, spoken in knowlege. Moyses opened not his lyppes / and yet god sayd to hym: why cryest thou so to me. It is not the noyse of thy lyppes / but the feruent dsyre of thy mynde / whiche (as it were a very shyrle voyce) beateth the eares of god. Let this therfore be a customable thynge with the that as soone as 35

Against ll. 6–8: The sonnes of zebedei be Iames the more / and Iohnn the Euangelyst.
Against ll. 13–15: Aaron signyfyeth prayer. Moyses betokeneth knowlege.

9 communeth] commeth *1533*

thyne enemye aryseth agaynst the / and the vyces whiche thou hast forsaken trouble the / thou than without taryeng with sure confydence and trust lyfte vp thy mynde to heuen / from whence helpe shall come to the / and thyder also lyfte vp thy handes. The
5 surest thynge of all is to be occupied in dedes of pytie / that thy dedes may be referred and applyed / not to worldy besynes / but vnto Christ. Yet leest [B3v] thou shuldest dispyse the helpe of knowlege / consyder one thynge. Before tyme it was ynough for the israelytes to flee and escape from their enemyes / but they were
10 neuer so bolde as to prouoke the Amalachytes / and to trye with them hande for hande, before they were refresshed with manna from heuen / and water rennynge out of the harde rocke. The noble warryour Dauid refresshed and made strong with these cates / set naught by the hole hoost of his aduersaryes / sayeng. Oh
15 good lorde thou hast set a table of meate before me, to defende me agaynst al men that trouble me. Byleue me well brother syngularly beloued in my hert / there is none so great violence of thy foes / that is to saye / none so great temptacion, whiche feruent study or meditacion of holy scripture / is not able to put abacke / nor any so
20 greuous aduersite, which it maketh not easy. And lest I shulde seme to be somwhat to bolde an interpretour (though I coude defende my selfe with great authorite) what thyng I pray the coude more properly haue signifyed the knowlege of the secrete lawe of god than dyd manna? For first in that it sprange not out of ye erth /
25 but rayned downe from heuen: By this propertie thou perceyuest ye difference bytwene the doctryne of god, and the [B4] doctryne of man. For al holy scripture came by diuyne inspiracyon and from god the author. In that it is small or lytle in quantite / is signified the humilite / lowlynes or homlynesse of the style vnder rude
30 wordes including great mystery. That it is whyte, by this propertie is signyfied the puryte and clennesse of goddes lawe. For there is no doctryne of man, whiche is not defyled with some blacke spot of errour / only the doctryne of Christ is euerywhere bright / euery where pure and clene. That it is somwhat harde and some deale

Against ll. 2–7: Pite is not taken for compassion / but for the honouryng and worshyppynge of god with charite or loue ordynate / as Chryst taught vs to loue.
Against ll. 12–16: Manna is a hony dewe wherwith the chyldren of Israhel were fed .xl. yeres / and it is sygnyfyed knowledge / and also by water lykewyse.

33 is] om. 1533

rough and sharpe / betokeneth secrete misteryes hydde in the litteral sence. If thou handle the vtter syde and if I may so call it the codde / what is more harde or vnsauery? They tasted but the vtter rynde of manna / whiche sayd to Christ / this is an hard sayeng / and who may abyde the heryng therof. But get out the spirituall 5 sence / and nothyng is more sweter nor more full of pleasure and swete iuce. More ouer manna is in the ebrewe tonge as moche to say, as what is this? Whiche questyon agreeth well to holy scripture / which hath nothyng in it ydle or in vayne / no not one tytle or pricke / vnworthy to be serched / vnworthy to be pondred / vnworthy 10 of this sayeng / what is this? It is a comen vse vnto the holy goost to signifye [B4v] by water ye knowlege of the lawe of god. Thou redest of ye water of comfort by whose bankes Dauid reioyseth to haue be nourysshed vp: thou redest of ye waters whiche wysdom conueyeth in to the toppes of euery waye: thou redest of the 15 mystical ryuer in to the whiche Ezechiel entred / and coude not wade ouer: thou redest of the welles that Abraham digged / whiche whan they were stopped of the philistiens ysaac repared agayne. Thou redest of .xij. fountaynes at whiche ye israelytes after they had walked through .xl. mansions / and began than to be wery and 20 faynte / rested and refresshed themselfe and made them strong to the long iourney of desert. Thou also redest in the gospell of the well wheruppon Christ sate weryed in his iourney. Thou redest of the water of Siloe / whyther he sendeth the blynde to recouer his syght. Thou redest of ye water poured in to the basen to wasshe the apos- 25 tels fete. And bicause it nedeth not to reherse all places in this significacyon / ofte mencion is made in scripture of welles / fount- aynes / and ryuers / by whiche is signyfied nothyng els, but that we ought to enquyre and serche diligently for misteryes hydde in scripture. What signyfyeth water hydde in ye vaynes of the erth 30 but mystery couered or hyd in the litterall sence? What [B5] mean- eth the same conueyed abrode but mistery opened and expouned? Whiche beyng spred and dilated bothe wyde and brode / to the edyfyeng of ye herers / what cause is there why it myght not be called a ryuer? Wherfore if thou dedycate thy selfe holly to the 35 study of scripture, and exercise thy mynde day and nyght in y^e

Against ll. 24-6: Siloe is a poole within Ierusalem at the fote of the mount Syon.

---

4 an hard] a harde *1533*   27 welles /] welles *1533, 1534*   29 mis- teryes] the mysteryes *1533*

lawe of god / no feare shall trouble the / neyther by day nor night:
but thou shalte agaynst all assautes of thyne enemyes, be armed
and exercised also. And I disalowe it not vtterly, if a man for a
season (to begyn withall) do exercyse and sporte hymselfe in werkes
5 of poetes and philosophers, whiche were gentyles / as in his A b c.
or introductory to a more perfyte thynge / so that he taste of them
measurably / and whyles youth shal gyue hym leue / and euen as
though a man toke them in his waye / but not abyde and tary vpon
them styll / and to wexe olde and dye in them / as he were bounde
10 to the rockes of Syrenes / that is to put his hole delectacyon in
them / and neuer go farther. For holy Basilius to suche pastyme
exhorteth yonge men / whom he hymselfe had induced to y^e
conuersacion of christen people. And our Augustyn calleth backe
agayne his frende Licentius, to passe the tyme with the muses /
15 neyther Ierom repenteth hym selfe, that he hath loued a [B5v]
woman taken prisoner in warre. Cyprian is commended, bycause
he garnysshed the temple of god, with the spoyles of the Egipcians.
But in no case wolde I that thou with the gentyles lernynge /
shuldest also souke the gentyles vyces and conuersacion. For if thou
20 do not / thou shalte fynde many thynges helping to honest lyuyng /
neyther is it to be refused what so euer an author (ye though he be a
gentyle) teacheth well. For Moyses verily though he were neuer so
famylyer with god / yet dispysed he not the counsayle of his father
in lawe Ietro. Those scyences fassyon and quycken a childes wytte /
25 and maketh hym apte afore hande meruaylously to the vnderstandyng of holy scripture: whervnto sodaynly and irreuerently to
presume with handes and fete vnwasshed / is in maner a certayne
kynde of sacrilege. And Ierom checketh ye shamelesse pertnesse of
them, whiche streyghtway from seculer or worldly scyence, dare
30 take in hande to medle or interprete holy scripture. But how moche
shamefuller do they whiche neuer tasted other science / and yet at
the fyrst dare do the same thynge? But as the scripture is not
moche fruytful if thou stande and stycke styll in the lettre: In lyke

Against ll. 4–15: Sirenes were iij. ladyes dwelling in an yland / whiche with
swetnes of songe drewe vnto them who so euer sailed by / and after killed them.
But Vlixes returning fro the siege of Troye hauynge that waye a necessari iourney stopped his maryners eres with wexe / and bounde himselfe to the mast / so
herde he their songe auoydynge all ieopardye /

31 other] orher 1533

Side-note 1: them.] them *1533*, *1534*

maner the poetry of Homere, and Virgyll shal not profyte a lytell /
if thou remembre [B6] that it must be vnderstande in the sence
allegory / whiche thing no man wyll denye, that hath assayed or
tasted of the lernyng of olde antiquitees neuer so lytell / ye with the
typ of his tonge / or vttermost parte of his lyppes. As for the poetes, 5
which write vnclenly / I wolde counsayle the not ones to touche
them / or at the leestway, not to loke farre in them : except thou can
the better abhorre vices whan they be discrybed to the / and in
comparacions of fylthy thynges the more feruently loue thinges
honest. Of the philosophers, my mynde is that thou folowe them that 10
were of Platoes secte / bycause bothe in very many sentences / and
moche more in their style and maner of spekynge / they come very
nygh to the fygure and propertie of speche vsed of the prophetes
and in the gospels. And to make an ende shortly / it shall be profytable to taste of al maner of lernynge of the gentyles / if it so be done 15
as I shewed before / bothe in yeres accordyng and measurably /
more ouer with cautele and iudgement discretly / furthermore
with spede, and after the maner of a man that entendeth but to
passe ouer ye countre onely / and not to dwel or inhabyte. In conclusion (whiche thynge is chefest of all) if euery thyng be applyed 20
and referred to Christ. For so shal althyng be clene to them y^t
be clene [B6v] whan on the other syde to them that be vnclene
nothynge is clene. And it shall be no rebuke to the / if after the
ensample of Salomon, thou nourysshe vp at home in thy house .lx.
quenes .lxxx. souereyn ladyes and damoysels innumerable of 25
secular wysdome. So that the wysdome of god be aboue al other /
thy best beloued / thy doue / thy swete hert / which onely semeth
beautifull. And an israelyte loueth a straunger and a barbarous
damsell / ouercome with her beautie : but fyrst he shaueth of her
heere and pareth her nayles / and maketh her of an alyen an 30
israelyte. And the prophete Ozee maryed an harlot / and of her

Against ll. 22–30: As Salomon had .lx. queenes lxxx. concubynes and damoyselles innumerable / yet one chefe quene / whome all the rest honored. So may we
of all sciences haue authours inumerable / yf holy scrypture be chefe of all other
for the honestyng of her.

Against l. 31–p. 48, l. 6 (Referring to p. 47, ll. 28–31): The Israelyte
myght take to wife a straunger taken in warre so that her nayles were fyrste
pared and her heare shauen : So may chrysten men honour god with gentyles
lernyng / yf we cut of that is superfluous.

17 furthermore] farthermore *1533*   21 shal althyng] all shall *1533*
28 israelyte] *1533*; israeryte *1534*

had children not for himselfe / but for ye lorde of sabaoth: and the holy fornycacion of the prophete, augmented the housholde of god. The ebrewes after they had forsaken Egypt / lyued with lyght and pure whyte breed for a season / but it was not suffycient to so
5 great a iourney. Therfore that breed lothed at ones / thou must make as good spede as can be, vnto manna of celestyall wisdome the whiche shal nourysshe the haboundantly and strength the vntyll thou obtayne thy purpose / and wynne by victory the rewarde y^t neuer shall cease: but thou muste euer remembre in the meane
10 season / y^t holy scripture may not be touched but with [B7] clene and wasshen handes / that is to vnderstande / but with high purenesse of mynde / lest that, whiche of it selfe is a preseruatyue or tryacle / by thyne owne faute turne to y^e in to poyson / and lest manna to the, begyn to putrifye / except y^t thou conuey or sende it in
15 to the inwarde partes of thy mynde and affectyon / and leest happyly it shulde fortune to the as it dyd to Oza / whiche feared not to set his prophane and vnclene handes to the Arke of god enclynyng on ye one syde, and with sodeyn deth was punysshed for his leude seruyce. The fyrst poynt is, that thou haue good opinyon of the holy
20 scriptures / and that thou esteme them of no lesse valure and dignite: than they are worthy to be estemed: and that they came out of the secrete closet of the mynde of god. Thou shalt perceyue, that thou art inspired of god moued inwardly / rapt and in an vnspecable maner altered and chaunged in to an other maner
25 fygure or shap / if thou wylt come religiously / if with reuerence and mekely: thou shalte se the pleasures / delycates / or deynties of the blissed spouse. Thou shalt se the precyous iowels of ryche Salomon / thou shalt se ye secrete treasure of eternall wisdom. But beware that thou breke not malepertly in to the secrete closet: the
30 dore is lowe / beware leest thou stryke the dore [B7v] with thy

Against ll. 7–10 (Referring to ll. 3–6): The light and pure whyte breed betokeneth the gentiles lyuing. Manna betokeneth the wysdom of god.

Against ll. 11–21: Dauid entended to translate the ark of god out of the hous of Amynadab / whiche was in Gaboa / they put the ark vppon a cart / Oza with his bretherne wayted on it on eyther side / as the ark enclyned and bowed / Oza set his hande to stay it / and was smytten with sodeyne dethe for his presumpcyon.

Facing ll. 22–3 (Referring to ll. 19–21): Scriptur must be had in great reuerence.

16 set] set to *1533*   24 in to] to *1533*   25 wylt] shalte *1533*
28 wisdom.] wysdom: *1533*; wisdom? *1534*

heed / and be fayne to lepe backe agayn. Thynke on this wise, nothing that thou seest with thyne eyen / nothyng that thou handlest with thy fyngers, to be in dede the same thing whiche it apereth / so surely as these thynges be true in holy scripture: so y^t if heuen and erth shuld perysshe / yet of ye wordes of god not one iote, 5 or tytle shal perissh / but al shalbe fulfilled. Though men lye / though men erre / yet the veryte of god neyther disceyueth nor is disceyued. Of ye interpretours of scripture / chose them aboue al other y^t go farthest from the lettre / which chefely next after Paule be Origene / Ambrose / Ierom and Augustyne. For I se the diuines of later 10 tyme stycke very moche in ye lettre / and with good wyll gyue more study to subtyle and disceytfull argumentes / than to serche out ye misteryes / as though Paule hath not sayd truly our lawe to be spirituall. I haue herd some men myselfe, which stode so greatly in their owne conceyte with the fantasticall tradycions / ymagy- 15 nacions and inuencyons of man / y^t they dispysed ye interpretacion of olde doctours, that were nigh to Christ and his apostles, bothe in tyme and lyuyng also: and accompte them as dremes / ye and mayster Dunce gaue them suche confydence: that notwithstanding they neuer ones redde the holy scripture / yet thought 20 they them [B8] selfe to be perfyte diuynes / which persones, though they speke thynges neuer so crafty and subtile: yet whether they speke thynges worthy of ye holy goost, and the meke spyrite of Christ or not / let other men iudge. But if thou haddest leuer to be somwhat lusty and quicke of spyrite / than to be armed to 25 contencion / that is to say / to brawlyng or scolding. If thou seke rather to haue thy soule made fatte / than thy wyt to be vainly delyted / study and rede ouer chefly ye olde doctours and expositors / whose godlynes, and holy lyfe is more proued and knowen / whose religion to god is more to be pondred and loked vpon, 30 whose lerning is more plenteous and sage also, whose style is neyther bare ne rude, and interpretacion more agreable to ye holy misteryes. And I say not this, bycause I dispise these newe diuynes: but bycause I set more by thinges more profytable / and more apt for the purpose. And also the spyrit of god hath a certayn tonge or 35

Against ll. 3–5: Fayth must be gyuen to holy scripture.
Against ll. 8–9: The chefe interpretours of holy scripture.
Against ll. 19–20: Mayster doctour Dunce.
Against l. 35–p. 50, l. 1: The spekynge of scripture.

2 eyen] eyes *1533*   22 they²] *1533*; thy *1534*

speche apropriate to him selfe: he hath his fygures / similitudes / parables / comparisons / prouerbes and redils, which thou must obserue and marke dilygently / if thou shuldest vnderstande them. The wisdom of god stutteth and lyspeth as it were a diligent
5 mother, fassyoneth her wordes acording to our infancie and feblenes. She gyueth mylke to them that be infantes in Christ / weake [B8v] meate to feble stomackes. Thou therfore make spede thou were a man / make haste to perfyte and stronge meate / and prepare a mannes stomacke. She stoupeth downe and boweth her
10 self to thy humilite and lownes. Aryse than the contrary wyse / and ascende to her heyght and excellencye. It is lyke a monstre and vnnatural, to be euer a childe. He is to hertles, that neuer ceaseth to be feble and weake. The recording of one verse shall be more sauery in thy mouth / and shall nourysshe the better, if thou breke
15 the codde, and taste of the swetnes which is within / than if thou shuldest synge the hole psalter / vnderstande onely after the litterall sence. Wherof verily I gyue admonycion a great deale the rather / bycause I knowe by experyence, that this errour hath not infected the ley people onely / but also the myndes of them whiche professe
20 and shewe outwarde in their habyte and name or tytle / perfyte religion / in so moche that they thinke the very seruyce of god, to be put chefely in this one thynge / if they shall saye ouer euery day as moche as they can of the psalmes scarse vnderstande ye in the litterall sence. Neyther I thynke, any other thyng to be the cause,
25 why we se ye charitable liuing of our monkes and cloysterers so to fayle euery where / to be so colde / so slacke / so faynte and [C1] so to vanysshe away, than that they contynue all theyr lyfe, and wexe olde in the lettre: and neuer enforce to comme to the spiritual knowlege of scriptur. Neyther heare they Chryste cryenge in the
30 gospell / the flesshe profyteth nothyng at all. It is the spiryte that quickeneth or giueth lyf. They heare not Paule, affermynge with his mayster / the lettre kylleth / it is the spiryte that gyueth lyfe.

Against ll. 16–17: Redynge without vnderstandynge.
Against ll. 24–6: The charitable lyuynge of monkes.
Against l. 30–p. 51, l. 2: The flesshe is called in scrypture what so euer is vysyble or perceyued outward with any sensyble power.

10 the contrary wyse] vpon the other syde *1533*   24 cause] *1533*; tause
1534   25 so] *om. 1533*   26 slacke] slacked *1533*   27 than] but
1533   30 the flesshe] the flesshe / that is to say / the lettre / or that ye se
outwarde *1533*   nothyng] not 1533   spiryte] spiryte within *1533*   32 the
lettre] y^t the lettre *1533*   it is] and it is *1533*   that gyueth] gyueth *1533*

And agayne, we knowe (sayth he) that the lawe is spirituall / and
not carnall. Spirituall thynges must be compared with spirituall
thynges. In tyme passed, the father of al spiritual gyftes, wolde be
honoured in the mountayne: but now he wyll be honoured in the
spirytc. How be it, I despyse not the feblenesse of them, whiche for 5
lacke of knowlege and vnderstandyng, doth that thynge whiche
onely they be able to do / pronouncyng the mystical psalmes with
pure fayth, without dissimulacyon or ypocrysye: but rather as in
charmes and enchauntementes of magyke, certayne wordes not
vnderstande / no not of them whiche pronounce them, be yet 10
byleued to be of vertue and strengthe: euen so the wordes of god /
though they be not perfytly vnderstande: neuerthelesse we must
trust that they be profytable to them, that eyther saye them, or
heare them with per[Civ]fyte fayth / with pure affection and mynde.
And that the aungels, whiche are present and dothe vnderstande, be 15
prouoked to helpe them. And Paule despyseth not them whiche
saye psalmes with theyr mouth / or whiche speke with tonges:
but he exhorteth them to folowe more perfyte gyftes. Vnto whiche
yf there be any that can not attayne / through the defaute not of the
mynde / but at the leest of nature: let hym not barke agaynst them, 20
whiche enforce to better thynges. And after the precept of Paule /
let not hym whiche eateth, despyse hym whiche eateth not / neyther
he that eateth not / iudge him that eateth. Neuerthelesse I wyll not
haue the, whiche art endewed with so happy a wytte, to be slowe,
and to tary longe in the bareyn lettre: but to make spede vnto more 25
secrete mysteryes / and to helpe the contynuall endeuoyre and
enforcement of thyne industrye, and wyll with often prayers:
vntyll he open to the, the booke clapsed with seuen clapses, whiche
hath the key of Dauyd / whiche also shitteth, and no man openeth

---

Against ll. 3-6 (Referring to p. 50, l. 30): The spiryte is called what so euer
is perceyued inwardly with the eye of the soule.
Against ll. 7-8 (Referring to ll. 5-8): A similitude of mekenes of them
whiche lack capacite.

6-7 that thynge whiche onely they] y^t they onely *1533*   10 be yet]
yet be *1533*   17 or whiche speke] whiche speketh *1533*   tonges] tonges
that thynge they vnderstande not *1533*   18 them] them to leue theyr
infancy / and *1533*   19 there be any that] a man *1533*   through the defaute not] not through the defaute *1533*   19-20 the mynde] a corrupte
mynde *1533*   20 at the leest of nature] for lacke of capacite *1533*   21 enforce to] enforce *1533*   28 seuen clapses] .vij. claspes *1533*   29 whiche]
the which *1533*

Side-note 1: eye] *1533*; eve *1534*

the preuytees of the father / whiche neuer man knewe but his sone /
and he to whome his sone hathe vouched saufe to dysclose them.
But whether gothe our style asyde / myne entent was to descrybe
the forme of [C2] lyuynge, not of lernynge. But I tourned out of
5 the waye thus farre, whyle I laboured to shewe the a mete shoppe,
from whens thou oughtest to fetche newe armure, and wepons
belongynge to thy newe warre. Therfore, to comme to our purpose
agayne / yf thou shalte pyke and chose out of the bookes of the
gentyles, of euery thynge the best. And also, yf thou by the example
10 of the bee / fleynge rounde aboute by the gardynes of olde authours,
shalte sucke out onely the holsome and swete iuce (the poyson
refused and left behynde) thy mynde shall be better apparaylled a
great deale / and armed vnto the commune lyfe or conuersacyon /
in whiche we lyue one with an other in honest maner. For the
15 philosophers and lerned men of the gentyles, in theyr warre vse
certeyn wepons and armure not to be despysed. Neuerthelesse,
what so euer thynge of honestye, or trouth thou fyndest any where /
thynke that to be Chrystes. But that dyuyne armure, and (to
speke as the poetes do) that harneys of Vulcanus making / which
20 with no wepons can be persed / is fette onely out of the armory of
holy scripture / where our noble capteyn Dauid, layde vp all his
ordynaunce of warre for his sowdyours, with whiche they sholde
fyght afarre and [C2v] at hande agaynst the incircumcised philistiens. With this harneys was clothed, neyther Achilles / of whom
25 Homere wryteth, neyther Eneas / of whome Virgyll speketh /
though they be so fayned. Of which, ye one with ire / ye other with
loue, was ouercom shamefully. And it is not spoken without reason,
that those wepons be not forged in the werkhouse of man / but in
the werkhouse or forge, that is commen to Vulcanus and Pallas /
30 otherwyse called Mynerue. For poetes, the fayners of goddes, make
Vulcanus lorde of fyre / and Mynerua lady of wytte, facultyes,
scyences, and craftes. Whiche thynge I iudge to be done in very
dede (as thou mayst easely perceyue) whan fyre of ye loue of

Against ll. 19–20: The artyllery of Vulcanus.
Against ll. 24–5: Achylles ouercome with yre. Eneas / ouercom with loue.
Against ll. 29–30: Poetes the fayners of goddes.

---

6 newe] thy newe *1533*   7 thy newe] the newe *1533*   9 the ex-
ample] thexample *1533*   22 sowdyours,] sowdyours *1533*, sowdyours.
1534   29 Vulcanus] Vulcan *1533*   30 make] maketh *1533*   31 Vul-
canus] Vulcan *1533*   33 fyre] the fyre *1533*   ye loue] loue *1533*

Side-note 1: artyllery] Artyllery *1533*, artyllery *1534*

god, hath armed thy wyt / endued with honest faculties, so strongly /
that yf al ye worlde shold fall on thy heed / yet sholde not the
stroke put the to feare. But fyrst thou must cast away the harnes of
proude Saule: whiche rather ladeth a man, than bc any thynge
necessary or profytable. And combred Dauyd, redy to fyght with   5
Golias, and holpe him not at al. More ouer, from the banke of the
broke of holy scripture, thou muste gather fyue stones: whiche
pcraducnture, be the fyue wordes of Paule / whiche he speketh in
knowlege. Than take a slynge in thy ryght hande / [C3] with
these wepons, is ouerthrowen our onely ennemy the father of   10
pryde, sathan / whome at the last, with what wepons dyd our heed
Chryste Iesu ouercomme? dyd not he smyte the foreheed of our
aduersary, as it had ben with stones, fette out of ye broke / whan he
answered hym in tyme of temptacyon with wordes of scripture?
Wylt thou heare the instrumentes or artillary of chrysten mens   15
warre? And the zele of hym (saith scripture) shall take harneys,
and shall harneys his creature to auenge his enemyes. He wyll put
on iustyce for his brest plate / and take for his helmet, sure and
true iudgement / he wyl take a shelde of equite impenetrable, or that
can not be persed / yea and he wyll sharpe or fascion cruel wrath   20
in to a spere. Thou redest also in Esaie, he is armed with iustyce /
as with an habergyon, and a salet of helth vpon his heed / he is
clothed with the vestures of vengeaunce / and couered as it were with
a cloke of zele. Now if thou list to go to the storehouse of Paule, that
valyaunt capteyn / certeynly thou shalt also fynde there the armure   25
of warre / not carnal thynges / but valyaunt in god to destroye
fortresses and counseyles / and euery hygh thing, that exalteth

Against ll. 1–8: Kynge Saule armed Dauyd to fyght against golias with heuy
and comberous harneys / puttyng on hym a salet of bras / and cote of mayle /
but Dauid put it of / and gatherd v stones out of a broke / and with a slyng hyt
Golyas in the forhed with a stone / and slew him.
Against ll. 10–24: When Sathan wold haue had chryst to turne stones in to
bred Christ answered with scripture / sayeng: man lyueth not onely by bred /
but by euery worde that procedeth of the mouthe of god / than he wold haue
had christ to fall fro the pynacle. Christ answered with scripture / sayenge / a
man sholde not attempt his lord god. Than the deuil bad christ honoure hym.
Christe answered / a man must honor his lord god / and serue hym onely.
Against l. 25–p. 54, l. 2: If zeale be in knowlege / it is good / and yf not / it
is euyll. As the pharyseys for zele of theyr traditions persecuted Chryst and the
apostels.

Side-note 1: cote] a cote *1533* Side-note 2: than] then *1533* Than] then *1533*
Side-note 3: the apostels] thapostelles *1533*

himself agaynst the doctryne of god. Thou shalt fynde there the
armure of god / by the whiche thou mayst resyst in [C3v] a wofull
daye. Thou shalt fynde the harneys of iustyce on the ryght hande/
and on the lefte, thou shalte fynde the defence of thy sydes, verite /
5 and the hawbergyon of iustyce, the bukler of fayth / wherwith thou
mayst quenche al the hote and fyery wepons of thy cruell aduersarye.
Thou shalte fynde also the helmet of helth, and the swore of the
spiryte / whiche is the worde of god: with whiche all, yf a man be
diligently couered and fenced / he may boldly withoute feare,
10 brynge forth the bolde sayinge of Paule. Who shall separate vs
from the loue of god? shall tribulacyon? shall straytnes or difficultye? shall hunger? shall nakednes? shall peryll? shall perse-
cucyon? shall a sworde? Beholde how myghty ennemyes, and how
moche feared of all men, he setteth at nought. But heare also a
15 certayne greater thynge / for it foloweth. But in all thynges we
haue ouercomme, by his helpe, whiche loued vs. And I am assured
(sayth he) that neyther deth nor lyfe / nor aungels / neyther principates / neyther vertues / neyther present thynges / neyther thynges
to comme / neyther strengthe / neyther hyghnes / neyther lownesse /
20 nor none other creature, shall or may separate vs, from the loue of
god / whiche is in Chryst Iesu. O happy truste [C4] and confydence /
whiche the wepons or armure of lyght gyueth to Paule / that is by
interpretacyon a lytell man / whiche calleth hymself the refuse or
outcast of the worlde. Of suche armure therfore haboundaunce shall
25 holy scripture mynister to the / yf thou wylte occupy thy tyme in it
with all thy myght: so that thou shalt not nede our counseyle or ad-
monycyons. Neuerthelesse, seynge it is thy mynde / leest I sholde
seme, not to haue obeyed thy request / I haue forged for the this
lytell treatyse called Enchiridion / that is to saye / a certayn lytell
30 dagger / whome neuer lay out of thy hande / no not whan thou art at
meate / or in thy chambre. In so moche, that yf at any tyme thou
shalt be compelled to make a pilgrymage in these worldly occupa-
cyons / and shalte be accombred to beare aboute with the, the hole
and complete armure and harneys of holy scripture: yet commytte
35 not, that the suttell lyer in wayte at any season sholde comme vpon
the, and fynde the vtterly vnarmed. But at the leest, let it not greue
the, to haue with the this lytel hanger / whiche shall not be heuy to
beare / nor vnprofytable for thy defence. For it is very lytell / yet yf

---

8 whiche²] the whiche *1533*   be] shall be *1533*   18 vertues] virtutes
1533   24 haboundaunce] haboundauntly *1533*

thou vse it wysely / and couple with it, the buckler of fayth / thou shalte easely withstande the [C4v] fyerse and ragyng assawte of thyne ennemye: so that thou shalte receyue no deedly wounde. But now it is tymc that I begyn to gyue the a certayne rule of the vse of these wepons / whiche yf thou shalt put in execucyon or practyse / I 5 trust it wyll comme to passe / that our capytayne Iesus Chryst, shall translate the a conquerour, out of this lytell castell or garryson, in to his great cite Ierusalem with triumphe / where is no rage at all of any batayle: but eternall quietnes / perfyte peace / assured tranquillite. Where as in the meane season all hope and confydence 10 of saufgarde, is put in armure and wepon.

℩ That the fyrst poynt of wysdome, is
to knowe thy selfe / and of two maner wysdomes / the true wysdom
and the apparent. Ca. iij.   15

THat excellent good thynge desyred and sought for of al men, is peace or quietnes: vnto whiche the louers of this worlde also referre al theyr study / but they seke a false peace / and shote at a wronge marke. The same peace, the philosophers also promysed vnto the folowers of theyr doctrynes / but yet falsly / for Chryst 20 onely gyueth it / the worlde gyueth it not. To [C5] comme to this quietnes / the only waye or meanes is, yf we make warre against our selfe / yf we fyght strongly agaynst oure owne vyces. For with these ennemyes, god whiche is our peace, is at varyaunce, and that with deedly hate / seyng he is naturally vertue it selfe, and father 25 and lorde of al vertue. And where as a fylthy puddle or a synke gathered togyder of all kynde of vices / is named of the Stoikes (whiche are the moost feruent defenders of vertue) folysshnes: and in our scripture the same is called malyce. In lyke maner vertue or goodnes lackynge in no poynt / of bothe partes, is called wysdome. 30

Against ll. 21–2: A man must fyght agaynst hym selfe.
Against ll. 23–4: God is our peace and felicite.
Against l. 27–p. 56, l. 2: Stoicy were phylosophers / as Socrates / and Plato / with theyr folowers whiche put felicitie in trewe pleasure / in vertue onely / and within the conscyence without any outwarde pleasure or rychesse.

2 easely] be able to *1533*   3 receyue] haue *1533*   10 Where as] but
where as *1533*   20 doctrynes] conclusions *1533*   22 is, yf] is (yf *1533*,
is. yf *1534*   warre] warre) *1533*   24 and that] *om. 1533*   28 defenders]
deferders *1533, 1534*

But (after the saying of the wyse man) doth not wysdom ouercomme malyce? The father and heed of malyce, is the ruler of darknes Beliall: whose steppes who so euer foloweth, walketh in the nyght, and shall comme to eternall nyght. On the other syde, the grounde
5 of wysdome, and in dede wysdome it selfe, is Chryst Iesus / whiche is the very lyght, and bryghtnes of the glory of his father / puttynge away by hym selfe onely, the nyght of the folysshnes of ye worlde. Whiche (wytnessing Paule) as he was made redempcion and iustificacyon to vs that be borne agayne in hym. Euen lyke
10 wyse was made also our wysdome. We (sayth Paule) preche [C5v] Chryste crucifyed / whiche to the iewes, is an occasyon of stumblyng and fallyng / and to ye gentyles folyshnes. But to ye elected, bothe of the iewes, and also of ye gentyles, we preche Chryst, the vertue or strength of god, and the wysdom of god / by whose wysdom
15 thrugh his ensample, we may beare away the victory of our ennemy malyce / yf we shal be wyse in hym, in whome also we shal be conquerours. Make moche of this wysdom, and take her in thyne armes. Worldly wysdom set at nought / which with false tytle, and vnder the name of wysdome, bosteth and sheweth her selfe gay to
20 foles / whan after Paule there is no greater folyshnes with god, than worldly wysdom / a thynge that must be forgete in dede agayn of hym that wyll be wyse in dede. If any man (sayth Paule) amonge you semeth to be wyse in this worlde / let hym be a foole, yt he may be wyse / for the wysdome of this worlde, is folysshnes with god.
25 And a lytell afore Paule sayth, for it is wryten. I wyl destroy the wysdome of wyse men / and the prudence of prudent men, I wyl reproue. Where is the wyse man? Where is ye subtile lawyer? Where is the sercher of this worlde? Hath not god made the wysdom of this worlde folyshnes? And I doute not but euen now with greate

Against ll. 3–10 (Referring to p. 55, ll. 28–30): Folyshnes is mysery. Wysdome is felicitie. Fooles also be wretches / and vnhappy. Wyse men also be happy and fortunate. Fylthynesse is folysshenes. Vertue is wysdom.
Against ll. 17–18: Worldly wysdome is very folysshnes.
Against ll. 22–4: He must be a foole in this worlde / that wyll be wyse in god.
Against l. 25–p. 57, l. 1: The serchers were the Phylosophers whiche serched for worldly wisdom / yet coude they attayn no wysdom to saue the soule of man / vntyll chryst cam.

---

6 the very lyght] very lyght *1533*   bryghtnes] the bryghtnes *1533*
8 Whiche] The whiche 1533   11–12 stumblyng and fallyng] vnite *1533*
19 the name of wysdome] a fayned colour of honeste *1533*   25 for it is
wryten.] it is wryten? *1533*

hate, these folysshe wyse men [C6] barke against the / and these
blynde capteyns and guydes of blynde men, crye out and rore
agaynst the / sayinge, that thou art deceyued, that thou dotest, and
art madde as a bedlem man / bycause thou entendest to departe
vnto Chrystwarde. These be in name onely chrysten men: but in 5
very dede, they are bothe mockers, and also ennemyes of Chrystes
doctryne. Take hede and beware that theyr folysshe bablynge
moue the not: whose miserable blyndnes ought rather to be wepte,
sorowed, and mourned / than to be counterfeyted, or folowed. Oh
what folysshe kynde of wysdom, and clene out of ordre, is this, in 10
tryfles and thinges of no value / ye vnto fylthynes onely to be clere
wytted, ware, and experte: but in those thynges whiche onely make
for our sauegarde or helthe: not to haue moche more vnderstandynge, than a brute beest? Paule wolde we sholde be wyse but in
goodnes / and chyldren in euyll. These men be wyse to all iniquite: 15
but they haue no lernynge to do good. And for as moche as that
facoundyous and greke poete Hesiodus, counteth hym good for
nothynge: whiche neyther is wyse of hym selfe / neyther yet wyll
folowe, and do after hym that gyueth hym good counseyle. Of what
degre than shall they be counted, whiche [C6v] whan they them 20
selfe be moost shamefully deceyued / yet neuer seace to trouble, to
laugh, to scorne, and put in feare them whiche al redy be comme to
their wyttes agayne? But shal not ye mocker be mocked? He that
dwelleth in heuen, shall mocke them agayn / and our lorde shall
laugh them to scorne. Thou redest in the boke of Sapyence / they 25
shall se veryly, and shall despyse him / but god shall mocke them.
To be mocked of lewde men / is as it were a prayse. And no doubte,
it is a blessed thynge to folowe our heed Chryste, and his apostles /
and a fearful thynge truly to be mocked of god. I also (sayth
wysdome) wyll laugh whan ye perysshe / and mocke you whan that 30

Against ll. 1–7: Many be christen men in name onely / but the very chrysten
men be they whiche kepe and obserue inwardly chrystes preceptes. A true
christen man must dispise the folishnes of worldly men.
    Again ll. 8–20: He is good for nothyng sayth Hesiodus which neyther hathe
wysdom / nor yet wyll lerne it. To haue knowledge is best of all. To be wyllyng
to lerne / and obedient to the truth / is also a good thynge. To lack knowledge /
is a very euyll thynge. To disdayn to lerne is worse / but to withstande and re-
pugne agaynst the truthe to them whiche teache the truthe / is worst of all / and
farthest from grace.

2 capteyns and guydes] capteyns or guydes *1533*   11 vnto] to *1533*
30 wysdome] the wysdom *1533*

thing hath hapned to you which ye feared : that is to say / whan they
awaked out of theyr dreames, and comme agayn to themself, whan
it is to late / shall say. These be they whome we haue had in dery-
syon and reprofe / we for lacke of vnderstanding haue counted
5 their lyues to be madnes / and their ende to be without honour.
This wysdom is beestly : and as Iames sayth, diabolyke, and of the
deuyll / and is an ennemy to god / whose ende is destruction. For
always after this wysdom, foloweth as a waytynge seruaunt or hand-
mayde myscheuous presumpcion / after presumpcyon, foloweth
10 blyndnes of mynde / [C7] after blyndnes of mynde, foloweth
feruent rage and tyranny of affections and appetytes / after the
tyranny of affections, foloweth the hole hepe of al vices, and liberte
to do what he lysteth. Than foloweth custome / after custome
foloweth moost wretched dulnes or insencibilite of mynde / a
15 dasynge of the wyttes, for lacke of capacite. By whiche meanes it
commeth to passe at length / that euyl men perceyue not themself
to synne. And whyles they be in suche insencibilite, without any
felyng or perceyuyng of themselfe / bodily deth commeth sodeynly
on them : and after it, foloweth ye seconde deth / whiche is deth
20 euerlastyng. Thou seest how ye mother of extreme mischefe, is
worldly wysdom. But of the wysdom of Chryst, whiche ye worlde
thinketh folyshnes / this wyse thou redest. Al good thinges came
to men by hepes with her / and inestimable honestie by the handes
of her. And I reioysed in all thynges, bycause this wysdom
25 went before me / and I was not ware, that she was mother of al
good thynges. This wysdom bryngeth with her as companyons,
sobrenes, and mekenes. Mekenes disposeth and maketh vs apte
to receyue the spiryte of god. For in the lowly, humble and
meke persone, he reioyseth to rest. And whan ye spiryt hath
30 replenysshed our myndes with his seuenfolde grace / than [C7v]
forthwithall springeth that plenteous erbage of all vertue, with
those blissed fruytes : of whiche ye chefe, is the secrete ioye of a

---

Against ll. 3–7 : Euyll men say / ye good men / as ye lyue now / so liued suche
and suche pope holy foles / and this cam of them / and so we trust to se happen
of you.
Against ll. 8–10 : Note how one vyce bryngeth in an other.
Against ll. 20–1 : The wysdome of Christe.

---

2 dreames] dreame *1533*   13 lysteth.] lysteth *1533*   custome²]
om. 1533.   15–16 meanes it commeth to passe at length] it is caused *1533*
20 extreme] thextreme *1533*   30 than] thau *1533*

clere conscience: a ioye knowen of none, but onely of suche, to whome it hath chaunced to taste of it: whiche ioye neuer vanyssheth awaye / nor fadeth with the ioyes of this worlde: but encreaseth and groweth to eternal gladnes and myrth. This wysdom my brother (after the counseyle of Iames) must thou requyre of god, with feruent and brennyng desyre. And after the counseyle of the wise man, dygge her out of the veynes of holy scripture / as it were treasure hyd in ye erth. The chefe parte of this wysdom is, that thou sholdest knowe thy selfe. Whiche worde, to haue descended from heuen, the antiquite byleued: and so moche hath that sayinge pleased great auctours / that they iudged all plenty of wysdom, to be shortly comprehended in this lytell sentence / that is to wyte / yf a man knowe himselfe. But let the weyght and authorite of this doctryne and teachynge be of no valure with vs / excepte it agre with our lernyng. The mystical louer in canticis, threteneth his spouse / and byddeth her to gete her selfe out of ye dores / except she knowe her selfe / saying. O thou beauteful amonge al women / yf thou knowe not thy selfe / go out [C8] of the dores, and walke after the steppes of thy flocke and sorte. Therfore let no man presumptuously take vpon hym this so great a thynge / to thynke that he knoweth him selfe well ynough. I am not sure whether any man knoweth his body vnto ye vttermost / and than how can a man knowe the state of his mynde surely ynough? Paule, whom god so loued, that he sawe the mysteryes, ye of the thyrde heuen / yet durst he not iudge hymself. Whiche thyng doutles he wolde haue ben bolde to do / yf he had knowen himselfe surely ynough. If so spiritual a man, whiche discerneth al thinges, and is himselfe to be iudged of no man / was not surely ynough knowen to himself: how do we carnal men presume? In conclusion, let hym seme to be a very vnprofytable sowdyour / whiche surely ynough neyther knoweth his owne company / neyther his ennemyes hoost. But so it is, y^t one chrysten man hath not warre with an other: but with hymself. And veryly a great hoost of aduersaries spring out of our owne flesshe out

5

10

15

20

25

30

Against l. 31–p. 60, l. 3: Thou mayste rede of Iason and dyuers other / howe they sowed serpentes tethe / and how of theym sprange gyantes / which fought among them self / and slew eche other.

1 a ioye knowen of none] which ioye is knowen of none *1533*   2 whiche ioye] Ioye *1533*   neuer] that neuer *1533*   13 weyght and authorite] weyght or authorite *1533*   14 doctryne and teachynge] conclusyon and doctryne *1533*   24 ye] *om. 1533*   29 do] shold *1533*   30 knoweth] knewe *1533*

of the very bowels and inwarde parte of vs: lykewyse as it is red in
certeyn poetes tales, of the bretherne gendred of the erth. And
there is so lytell dyfference bytwene our ennemy, and our frende /
and so harde to knowe the one fro the other / that there is [C8v]
5 great ieopardy, lest we somwhat recheles or neclygent, defende our
ennemy, in stede of our frende / or hurte our frende, in stede of
our ennemy. The noble capteyn Iosue was in doute of an aungell of
lyght / saying. Art thou on our parte / or of our enemyes parte? Therfore seyng that thou hast taken vpon the, warre agaynst thy selfe /
10 and the chefe hope and comfort of victory, is yf thou knowe thy selfe
to the vttermost: I wyll paynte a certayne ymage of thy selfe / as
it were in a table / and set it before thyne eyen: that thou mayst
perfytly knowe, what thou art inwarde / and within thy skynne.

☞ Of the outward and inward man. Ca. iiij.

15 A Man is than a certeyn monstrous beest / compact togyder of
partes, two or thre of great dyuersite. Of a soule, as of a certeyn
goodly thynge: and of a body, as it were a brute or dombe beest.
For certeynly, we so greatly excell not al other kyndes of brute
beestes in perfytnes of body / but that we in al his natural gyftes,
are founde to them inferyours: as concernyng ye soule veryly, we
20 be so receyuable of ye diuyne nature: that we may surmount
aboue the nature of aungels / and be vnyt, knyt, and made one with
god. Yf thy body had not ben added [D1] to the / thou haddest ben
a celestial or godly thyng. Yf this mynde had not ben graffed in the /
playnly thou haddest ben a brute beest. These two natures by-
25 twene them self so dyuerse: that excellent werkman had coupled
togyder with blessed concorde. But the serpent the ennemy of

Against ll. 15-16: A man is a certeyn monstrous beest.
Against ll. 23-4: God is the authour of peace.
Against ll. 25-6: The serpente is the maker of debate.
Against l. 27-p. 61, l. 15: He holdeth the wolf by the eares / this prouerbe we
vse vpon them whiche be in such combrance fro whens they can in no wyse ryd
them selfe. The prouerbe this wise sprong. A certen man walked in a forest /
vpon whom came a wolfe / and he coude make no other shyfte but toke him by
the eares / whiche were so shorte that it was harde to hold them: yet durst he
not let them go nor laye hande on his wepons for fere of bytyng / but held fast
and cryed for helpe.

8 saying.] saying 1533,1534   12 eyen] eyes 1533   14 iiij.] 1533,
1534   20 as concernyng ye soule] In our myndes 1533   21 receyuable
of ye diuyne nature] celestial and of godly capacite 1533

Side-note 4: vpon^1] on 1533   sprong.] sprong 1533, 1534

peace, put them asonder agayn with vnhappy discorde: so y^t now
they neyther can be seperate, without very great turment and
payne / neyther lyue ioyned togyder, without contynual warre.
And playnly after the commun saying, eche in the other holdeth
the wolfc by ye eares: and eyther may say very well, and accor- 5
dyngly to the other, that proper and pleasaunt verse of Catullus.
I neyther can lyue with the nor without the. Suche ruffeling, wrang-
lynge, and trouble they make bytwene them selfe with comberous
debate: as thynges dyuerse / whiche in dede are but one. The body
veryly, as he hymselfe is vysyble / so delyteth he in thynges 10
vysyble. As he is mortall / so foloweth he thynges temporall. As he
is heuy / so synketh he downwarde. On the other parte / the soule
myndfull of her celestyall nature, enforceth vpwarde with great
violence, and with a terrible hest stryueth and wrastleth with the
heuy burthen of the erthly body. She despyseth ye thinges that 15
are seen / for she knoweth them to be [D iv] transytory / she seketh
true thynges, whiche be permanent and euer abydyng: and bycause
she is immortall and also celestiall, she loueth thynges immortal and
celestial / and reioyseth in thynges of lyke nature / excepte she be
vtterly drowned in the fylth of the body: and by his contagyousnes 20
be gone out of kynde from her natyue gentylnesse. And veryly,
neyther Prometheus, so moche spoken of amonge poetes, sowed this
discorde in vs, a porcyon of euery beest mynglyng to our mynde:
neyther our primatyue and first makyng gaue it / that is to say / it
spronge not in vs naturally / or god gaue it not to vs in our first 25
creacyon: but synne hath euyll corrupted and decayed that, whiche
was well created / sowyng the poyson of dissencion bytwene them
that were honestly agreed. For before y^t tyme, bothe the mynde
ruled the body without besynes: and the body obeyed without
grudgyng. Now is it clene contrary. The ordre bytwene them is so 30
troubled, the affections or appetytes of the body stryue to go

Against ll. 21–7: Poetes fayne prometheus to haue made men of claye / and
thrugh help of Pallas to put lyfe in them / and a porcion of euery beest / as the
fyersnes of the lyon / the wylynes of the foxe / the fearefulnes of the hare / and
so of other bestes.

12 parte] party _1533_   15 ye thinges] these thinges _1533_   17 whiche]
of substaunce which _1533_   19 in] with _1533_   20 his contagyousnes]
contagiousnes of hym _1533_   21 be gone] hath gone _1533_   23 myngl-
yng] myxed _1533_   25 god] nature _1533_   26 creacyon] creacion or
natiuite _1533_   corrupted] corrupte _1533_

before reason: and reason is in a maner compelled to enclyne and folowe the iudgement of the body. Thou mayst compare therfore a man properly to a communaltie / where is debate and parte takyng in it selfe. Whiche communaltie, for as moche as it is made of sondry
5 kyndes of [D2] men gadered togyder / which be of dyuerse and contrary appetytes. It can not be auoyded, but that moche stryfe shal ryse therin / and partes taken oftentymes / oneles the chefe rule and authorite be in one. And he hym selfe be suche a felowe, as wyll commaunde nothynge, but that whiche shall be holsome,
10 and profitable for the commune welthe. And for that cause it must nedes be / that he whiche is moost wyse, sholde moost beare rule. And he nedes must obey that leest perceyueth or vnderstandeth. Now there is nothynge more folysshe, than the rascall or vyle communaltye. And therfore ought they to obey the offycers and
15 rulers / and beare no rule nor offyce them selfe. The noble estates, or suche men which be moost auncyent of age / ought to be herde: but so that it lye onely in the kynges arbytrement to make statutes and lawes / whome it is mete to be aduertysed, to be put in remembraunce, or counseyled now and than. But it is not mete that he
20 sholde be compelled / or that any man sholde maystry, or rule hym. And fynally, the kynge obeyeth no man, but the lawe onely. The lawe muste be correspondent to the orygynall decree of nature, or the fyrste example of honestye. Wherfore yf this ordre subuerted, the vnruly communes, and that ragyng [D2v] dregges of the cite,
25 stryue to go before the senyours or eldermen: or yf ye chefe lordes despyse the commaundement of ye kyng / than aryseth perylous sedicyon, or dyuysyon in our commune welth / ye and excepte the prouisyon, decree or authorite of god socour / all the mater weyeth and enclyneth to extreme myschefe, and to vtter destruction. In man
30 reason beareth ye rowme of a kyng. Thou mayst accompt for the chefe lordes certeyn affections, and them of the body: but yet not all thinges so beastly. Of the whiche kynde, is naturall reuerence towarde the father and mother / loue to thy brethern / a benyuolent

Against ll. 1–4: Man is compared to a comon welthe or realme / where is a kynge / lordes / and the comon people.
Against ll. 21–2: The kynge obeyeth the lawe onely.
Against ll. 29–30: Reason is kyng in a man.
Against ll. 31–2: The lordes be certayn gentyl affections.

3–4 in it selfe] among them selfe *1533*   8 as that *1533*   25 stryue]
shall stryue *1533*   or eldermen] *om.*] *1533*   26 despyse]
shall despyse *1533*

mynde towarde thy frendes and louers / compassyon vpon them that be vexed with aduersite, or combred with sycknes / feare of infamy, sclaunder, or losse of thy good name, desyre of honest reputacyon, and suche other lyke. But suche affections or passyons which be very greatly disagreyng from the decrees of reason / and whiche be 5 cast downe, and must bow euen to the vylenes of brute beestes: thynke and reken those, to be as it were the most raskal and vile sort of ye commune people. Of which kynde and sort be lechery, ryot, enuy, and suche like diseases / which al without excepcion, must be kept vnder with prison and punyshment, as vyle and bonde 10 seruauntes, that they may rendre to their mayster, their [D3] taske and worke appoynted to them, yf they can: but yf not, at the lest y^t they may do no harme. Whiche thynges Plato perceyuyng by inspiracyon of god / wrote in his booke called Timeus, how ye sones of goddes had forged in man, to their owne lykenes, two 15 kyndes of soules: the one kynde spiritual and immortal / the other as it were mortall / in daunger to dyuerse perturbacions or mocions of vnquietnes. Of whiche the fyrst is voluptuousnes (as he sayeth) the bayte wherby men are allured and brought to vngracyousnes or myschefe. The next is sorowe or grefe, whiche letteth men / and 20 dryueth them from vertue or goodnes. After that feare and presumptuous boldnes / two mad counseylours: whome accompanyeth indurate wroth, the desyre of vengeaunce. More ouer, flatering hope, with beestly ymaginacion and knowlege not gouerned of reason / and worldly loue, that layeth handes violently on al thynges. 25 These be almost the wordes of Plato / and it was not vnknowen to him, the felicite of this lyfe, to be put in refraynyng suche perturbacions. For he wryteth in the same worke, that they shall lyue iustly and blessedly / that haue ouercomme these appetytes: and that they shall lyue vniustly and myserably, that were ouercomme of 30 ye same. And for the soule, whiche is lyke vnto the [D3v] nature of god / that is to saye / for reason, as for a kyng, he appoynted a place

Against ll. 4–5: The comoners be vyle appetytes.
Against ll. 18–20: Foure affections of the mynde / Ioye / sorowe / hope / and feare.

---

10 with prison and punyshment] in preson / and with punyshment *1533*
11 may rendre] rendre *1533*   13 may do] do *1533*   14 Timeus]
Timens *1533*   27 refraynyng] refraynyng of *1533*   28 that they
shall] them for to *1533*   29 that haue] whiche sholde haue *1533*   30 that
they shall] them for to *1533*   were] sholde be *1533*   31 for the] to that
1533   32 for¹] vnto *1533*   for²] vnto *1533*

in the brayne, as in the chefe toure of our cite: and as thou mayst se, the hyghest parte of our body, and nexte to heuen, and most farre fro the nature of beestes / as a thynge veryly, whiche is bothe of a very thynne bone / and neyther lade with grosse synewes nor
5 flesshe / but surely furnysshed and appoynted within and also without, with powers of knowlege / that no debate myght ryse in our commune welthe / but that he by them, as by reporters, sholde immedyatly perceyue it. But as touchynge the partes of the mortall soule / that is to wyte / the affectyons or appetytes, as euery one is /
10 eyther obedyent, or els grudgeth agaynst reason: so he remoued them fro hym. For bytwene the necke and the mydryffe, he set that parte of the soule / wherin is conteyned boldnes / wrath or anger / a sedycyous affection veryly and full of debate / whiche nedes must be refrayned: but he is not very brutysshe or beestly /
15 and therfore he separated hym in a meane space from the hyghest and lowest / leest yf he had ben to nygh to eyther of them / he wolde eyther haue troubled the kynges quietnes / or else corrupte with the contagyousnes of them of the lowest sortes, sholde with them also con[D4]spyre agaynst hym. Last of all, that power whiche
20 desyreth the voluptuous pleasure of meate and drynke / wherby also we be moued to bodyly lust / he banysshed vtterly awaye far fro the kynges palays, downe alowe bynethe the mydryffe in to the lyuer and the paunche / that as it were a certeyn wylde beest vntamed / he sholde there stable and dwell at the racke: for bycause that power
25 is accustomed to reyse vp mocyons moost violent / and to be dis- obedyent to the commaundementes of the kynge. What beestly- nesse, ye and what rebellyon is in the lowest porcyon of this power / at the leestwaye the preuy partes of thy body may teche the, in whiche parte chefely, this power of concupiscence rageth and
30 tyranny reygneth / whiche also of al membres onely euer among maketh rebellyon with vnclenly mocions / the kyng cryenge the contrary / and that in vayne. Thou seest than euydently, how that

Against ll. 1–2: Reason dwelleth in the braynes as in the palays.
Against ll. 11–12: The power wherin is contayned wrathe and hate.
Against ll. 21–2: The power wherin is contayned desyre.

---

3 beestes] a beest *1533*   6 no debate] thrugh the shewyng of them no debate *1533*   myght] sholde *1533*   7 but that he by them, as by report- ers] whiche he *1533*   sholde] sholde not *1533*   8 perceyue it] perceyue *1533*   9 one] one of them *1533*   15 separated] separate *1533*
Side-note 1: braynes] brayne *1533*

this noble beest man / so goodly a thynge aboue: playnly and without any excepcyon, endeth in an vnreasonable or brute beest. But
that noble counseylour, whiche sytteth lyke a kyng or a ruler in his
hygh toure: hauynge alway in remembraunce his owne begynnynge,
thynketh no fylthy nor lowe thynge. And he hath wherby he may 5
be knowen from [D4v] other, a scepter of yuorye / bycause he doth
commaunde nothynge but y^t whiche is ryght and good / in whose
top wryteth Homere to syt an egle / bycause that reason mountyng
vp to celestiall thynges / beholdeth from aboue those thynges that
be on the grounde disdeynfully / as it were with egles eyes. In 10
conclusion, he is crowned with a crowne of golde. For golde in the
mystycal lettres moost communly betokeneth wysdom. And the
circle betokeneth, that the wysdom of the kyng sholde be perfyte
and pure in euery parte. These be the very gyftes or vertues
properly belongyng to kynges. Fyrst that they be very wyse, that 15
they do nothynge amysse by meanes of errour and lacke of true
knowlege. And than suche thynges as they knowe to be good
and ryght / those onely to wyll and purpose to do: that they do
nothyng agaynst the decree or iudgement of reason inordynatly,
frowardly, and corruptly. And who so euer lacketh any of these 20
two poyntes / counte hym to be, not a kynge / that is to saye, a ruler /
but a robber.

⦅ Of the diuersite of affections. Ca. v.

OVr kynge Reason may be oppressed veryly / yet bycause of y^e
eternal lawe which god hath grauen in him, he can not [D5] be 25
corrupted, but that he shal grudge and cal backe. To whome yf
the resydue of the communaltie wyll obey / he shall neuer commyt
any thynge at all, eyther to be repented or of any ieopardye: but all
thynges shal be admynystred with great moderacyon / with moche
quietnes and tranquillite. But as touchyng affections / veryly Stoici 30
and Peripotetici vary somwhat / though bothe agree in this, that we

Against ll. 4–5: The ornamentes of a kynge.
Against ll. 26–31: We ought to lyue after reason / and not after affections.
Perypoteticy wyll that affections sholde be refrained / only thynkynge them
necessary to prouoke and to stirre a man to vertue.

8 syt] set 1533   16 nothynge] not 1533   meanes] reason 1533
28 ieopardye] 1533; ieopadye 1534   29 moderacyon] moderacyon
discretly 1533

ought to lyue after reason / and not after affections. But Stoici wyll, whan we haue vsed for a season (as it were a scholemayster to teche vs our fyrst prynciples) the affections, whiche immedyatly are stered vp of the sensuall powers / and be comme to the iudgement
5 and true examynacyon, what is to be ensewed or chosen / and what to be eschewed or forsaken / that than we vtterly dampne and forsake them. For than are they (as they saye) not onely no profyte to veray wysdom / but also hurtful and noyous. And therfore they wil, that a perfyt wyse man sholde lacke all suche mocions / as
10 diseases or sycknesses of the mynde / and with moche ado some which be more gentyll graunte to a wyse man these first mocions / preuentyng reason, whiche they call fantasyes or ymaginacyons. Peripotetici teche the affections not to be destroyed vtterly / but to be refrayned: and that the vse of [D5v] them, is not vtterly
15 to be refused / for bycause they thynke them to be gyuen of nature / as a prycke or a spurre, to styre a man to vertue. As wrath maketh a man bolde and hardy / and is a mater of fortitude. Enuy is a great cause of polycy / and in lykewyse of the other. Socrates in a certayne booke that Plato made, called Phedo / semeth to agre
20 with Stoici: where he thynketh philosophy to be nothing els but a meditacion or practisyng of deth / that is to saye, that the mynde withdrawe her self as moche as she can from corporal and sensyble thynges / and conuey her self to those thinges, whiche be perceyued with reason onely / and not of the sensyble powers. First of al

Against ll. 2–14. Stoicy be the folowers of plato which put felicite and blessednes in the inward constancy of the mynde onely / yf a man were so armed with all vertues / that he myght be wounded with no darte of aduersitie or fortune / sayeng also / no outward goodes of fortune nor outward gyftes of nature be required necessaryly vnto felycyte: but the testimony of conscience inwarde to be sufficyent.

Against l. 15–p. 67, l. 10 (Referring to p. 66, ll. 13–18): Perypotetici be Arystoteles folowers / whiche say / a man apareiled with al kinde of vertue and with a pure conscience to be a good man / yet not happye or blessed / for they wyll beatitude to reste in the act and outward practise of vertue in profiting the comon wele. Therfore (say they) rychesse / frendes / strength of body / helth / eloquence / and suche lyke / to be required necessaryly / without whiche a man can not profyte an other / yet wolde they not suche thynges to be desyred for loue of the thynges them self: but to proufyte the comon welth and for the conuersacyon of mankynde.

4 be] now be *1533*   the iudgement] iudgement *1533*   10–12 and with moche ado some which be more gentyll graunte . . . preuentyng] ye and scarsely they graunte . . . more gentyl preuentyng *1533*

Side-note 2: wele] welth *1533*

therfore, thou must beholde and consyder diligently, al the mocions, mouynges, or steryng of thy mynde / and haue them surely knowen. Farthermore, thou must vnderstande, no mocyons to be so violent, but they may be eyther refrayned of reason, or els turned to vertue. Notwithstanding I heare euerywhere this contagyous 5 opinyon / that some sholde say, they be constrayned to vices. And on ye other syde many for lacke of knowlege of them selfe, folowe suche mocyons as the sayings or decrees of reason: in so moch that what so euer wrath, or enuy doth counseyle or moue them to do / that they call the zeale of god. [D6] And as thou seest one 10 commune welth to be more vnquiet than another: so is one man more enclyned or prone to vertue, than an other. Whiche difference commeth not of the dyuersite of myndes / but eyther of the influence of celestyall bodyes / or els of our progenytours / or els of the bryngyng vp in youth / or of ye complexion of the body. 15 Socrates fable, of carters and horses, good and badde / is none olde wyues tale: for thou mayst se some to be borne of so moderate, softe, quiet and gentyl disposicyon / so easy to be handled / to be turned and wynded / that without besynes, they may be enduced to vertue / and renneth forwarde by theyr owne courage without any 20 spurryng. To some clene contrary thou mayst perceyue to haue happened: a body rebellyous as a wylde and kycking horse: in so moche y^t he which tameth him / shal haue ynough to do and swete apace / and yet scarse with a very rough byt / scarse with a waster and sharpe spurres, can subdue his fiersnes. If any suche one hath 25 hapned to the / let neuer ye rather thy herte fayle the / but so moche the more feruently set vpon it, thynking on this wyse: not the waye of vertue to be stopped or shutte vp from the: but a larger mater of vertue to be offred vnto the. But and yf so be, that nature hath endued ye with a gentyll mynde / [D6v] thou art not therfore 30 streyghtway better than an other man / but happyer / and yet agayn on that maner wyse art thou more happy / that thou art also more bounde. How be it, what is he y^t is endued with so happy gyftes of nature / whiche hath not haboundauntly thynges ynough to wrestle withal. Therfore in what parte shal be perceiued most 35 rage or rebellion to be: in that parte reason our kynge must watche

Against ll. 11–12: Some man is more prone to vertue than som.
Against ll. 21–3: The rebellyon of nature is to be imputed to no man.

___

16 Socrates fable] The fable of Socrates *1533*   25 and] and with *1533*
27 not] not that *1533*   28 to be] is *1533*   32 that²] so that *1533*

diligently. There be certeyn vices appropriate to euery countree / as to breake promesse, is famylyar to some: to some ryot or prodigalite: to some bodyly lust or pleasure of the flesshe / and this happeneth to them by ye disposycyon of theyr countrees. Some vices
5 accompany the complexion of the body / as appetite and lust for the company of women and the desyre of pleasures and wanton sportes accompany the sanguyne men. Wrath, fyersnes, cursed spekyng foloweth the coleryke men. Grosnes of mynde / lacke of actiuite / sluggishnes of body, and to be giuen to moche slepe, foloweth the flu-
10 matyke man. Enuy, inwarde heuynes, bytternes, to be solytary, selfe mynded, soleyn, and chorlysshe, foloweth the melancolyke persone. Some vices abate and encrease after the age of man / as in youth, lust of ye body, wastful expences, and rashnes, or folysshe hardynes. In [D7] olde age, nyggishnes, or to moche sauyng, waywardnes and
15 auarice. Some vices ther be which shold seme appropriate to kynde as fyersnes to the man / vanite to the woman, and desyre of wreke, or to be reuenged. It fortuneth now and than, that nature (as it were to make amendes) recompenseth the disease or sycknes of the mynde / with an other certeyn contrary good gyfte or propertye.
20 One man is somwhat prone or enclyned to pleasure of worldly pastymes / but nothyng angry / nothyng enuyous at all. An other is chaste, but somwhat proude or hygh mynded, somwhat hasty, somwhat to gredy vpon the worlde. And there be whiche be vexed with certeyn wonderfull and fatall vices / with thefte, sacrylege,
25 and homicyde: whiche truly thou must withstande with al thy might / against whose assaulte must be cast a certeyn brasen wall of sure purpose. On the other syde, some affections be so nygh neyghbours to vertue / that it is ieopardous leest we sholde be deceyued, the diuersitye is so daungerous and doutfull. These
30 affections are to be corrected and amended / and may be turned very well to that vertue whiche they most nygh resemble. There is some

Against ll. 1–2: Some vyces folowe the countrees.
Against ll. 5–6: Some vyces folow the complexcyon of the body.
Against ll. 12–13: Vyces folowynge the age.
Against ll. 14–15: Vices appropried to kynd.
Against ll. 17–20: An yll dysease of the mynde is somtyme recompensed with an other good gyft in properte.
Against ll. 28–30: Let the vices whiche drawe nere vnto vertue be corrected.

---

10 Enuy,] Enuy *1533, 1534*
18 the disease] one disease *1533*
Side-note 5: yll] euyll *1533*

man (bycause of example) whiche is soone set a fyre / is hote / at
ones prouoked to anger with the leest thyng in ye worlde / [D7v]
let hym refrayne and sobre his mynde / and he shall be bolde and
couragyous / nothynge faynt herted or fearfull / he shall be free of
speche, without dissimulacion. There is an other man somwhat 5
holding, or to moche sauyng: let hym put to reason / and he shal be
called thryfty and a good husbande. He that is somwhat flateryng /
shal be with moderacyon curteys and pleasaunt. He that is obstynate,
may be constant. Solempnes, may be turned to grauite. And he
that hath to moche of folysshe toys, may be a good companyon. 10
And after the same maner of other lyghter diseases of the mynde.
We must beware of this onely, y^t we cloke not the vice of nature,
with ye name of vertue / callyng heuynes of mynde grauite / crudelite iustice / enuy zeale / fylthy nyggishnes thryfte / flatering good
felowshyp / knauery or rybaldry, vrbanite or mery spekyng. The 15
onely waye therfore to felicite, is fyrst that thou knowe thy selfe.
Secondly, that thou do nothing after affections / but in all thynges
after the iudgement of reason. Let reason be sounde and pure and
without corrupcyon: let not his mouth be out of taste / that is to
say / let hym beholde honest thynges. But thou wylt say: it is an 20
harde thynge that thou commaundest: who sayth nay? And veryly
the sayinge of Plato is true: what so [D8] euer thynges be fayre
and honest / the same be harde and trauaylfull to obteyne. Nothyng
is more harde, than y^t a man sholde ouercomme hym selfe. But than
is there no greater rewarde, than is felicite. Iheronymus spake that 25
thynge excellently, as he dothe all other thynges: nothyng is more
happy, than a chrysten man / to whome is promysed ye kyngdom
of heuen. Nothyng is in greater peryll, than he whiche euery houre is
in ieopardy of his lyfe. Nothyng is more stronge, than he that ouercommeth the deuyll, Nothyng is more weyke, than he that is ouer- 30
comme of the flesshe. If thou ponder thyne owne strengthe onely /
nothing is harder, than to subdue the flesshe vnto the spiryt. If thou
shalt loke on god thy helper / nothynge is more easy. Now therfore,

Against ll. 11–12: Put not the name of vertue to any maner of vyce.
Against l. 15 (Referring to l. 16): Know thy self.
Against ll. 18–19: Do all thynges after the iugement of reason.
Against ll. 25–6: The sayeng of saynt Ierome.

---

9 And he] And *1533*   11 lyghter] somwhat easyer *1533*   14 iustice /]
iustice *1533, 1534*   17 Secondly] more ouer *1533*   33 Now therfore]
Than now therfore *1533*

conceyue thou with all thy myght and with a feruent mynde, the purpose and professyon of perfyte lyfe. And whan thou hast grounded thy selfe vpon a sure purpose / set vpon it, and go to it lustely: mannes mynde neuer purposed any thynge feruently, 5 that he was not able to bryng to passe. It is a greate parte of a chrysten lyfe / to desyre with full purpose, and with all his herte, to be a chrysten man. That thynge whiche at the first syght or metyng / at the first acqueyntaunce or commynge to / shall [D8v] seme impossible to be conquered or wonne, in proces of tyme, shall be 10 gentyl ynough, and with vse easy: yea and at lengthe through custome, shall be very pleasaunt. It is a very proper saying of Hesiodus. The waye of vertue is harde at the begynnynge / but after thou hast crepte vp to the top, there remayneth for the very sure quietnes. No beest is so wylde, whiche wexeth not tame by 15 the crafte of man. And shall there be no crafte to tame the mynde, of the tamer of all thynges? That thou myght be hole in thy body / thou canst stedfastly purpose, and commaunde thy selfe for certeyn yeres, to abstayne from drynkynge of wyne / to forbeare the flesshe, and company of women: whiche thynges the phisician beyng 20 a man, prescribed to the. And to lyue quietly al thy lyfe, canst thou not rule thyne affections / no not a fewe monethes? Whiche thyng god that is thy creatour and maker commaundeth the to do? To saue thy body from sycknes: there is nothyng whiche thou doest not? To delyuer thy body and thy soule also, from eternal 25 deth / doest thou not these thynges whiche infydeles ethnicy and gentyles haue done?

¶ Of the inwarde and outwarde man:
and of the two partes of man / proued by holy scripture. Caplo. vj. [E1]

30 CErtaynly I am ashamed in christen mens behalfe / of whome
the moost parte folowe as they were brute beestes their affectyons

---

Against ll. 5–7: To be willyng to be a christen man is a great part of christendome.
Against ll. 12–13: The waye of vertue in proces waxeth easye.

---

1 thou] *om.* *1533*   2 perfyte lyfe] the perfyte lyfe *1533*   10–11 yea
and at lengthe through custome] in conclusion with custome it *1533*   15 shall
there be] is there *1533*   16 the tamer] hym that is yᵉ tamer *1533*

and sensuall appetytes / and in this kynde of warre are so rude and vnexercised / that they do not as moche as knowe the diuersitie bytwene reason, and affections or passyons. They suppose y^t thing onely, to be ye man whiche they se and fele / ye and they thynke nothyng to bc besyde the thynges whiche offre themselfe to ye 5 sensyble wyttes whan it is nothyng lesse than so. What so euer they greatly coueyte / y^t they thynke to be ryght: they call peace, certayn and assured bondage / whyle reason oppressed, and blynded foloweth whyder so euer ye appetyte or affection calleth without resistence. This is y^t myserable peace, whiche Christ the authour of 10 very peace that hath made both one, came to breke / stering vp holsom warre bytwene the father and the sonne / bytwene the husbande and the wyfe / bytwene those thynges whiche filthy concorde had yuell coupled togyther. Now than let the authoritie of the philosophers be of lytell weyght / excepte those same thynges 15 be all taught in holy scripture / though not with the same wordes. That the philosophers call reason / y^t calleth Paule somtyme the spyrit / somtyme y^e inner man / otherwhyle [E$_{IV}$] thc lawe of the mynde. That they call affection / he calleth somtyme the flesshe: somtyme y^e body: another tyme the vtter man and the lawe of the 20 membres. Walke (sayth Paule) in the spiryte / and ye shal not accomplysshe the desyres and lustes of the flesshe / for the flesshe desyreth contrary to the spyryte / and the spiryte contrary to the flesshe / that ye can not do what so euer thinges ye wolde. And in an other place. If ye shall lyue after ye flesshe ye shall dye. 25 If ye walkyng in the spiryt shal mortifye the dedes of the flesshe /

Against ll. 1–18: Cryst in math. sayth he came to make not peace: but diuisyon / to set the father agaynst the sonne / the sonne agaynst his father / the wyfe agaynste her husbande / the husband against his wife and so forthe. The hystorye meaneth that at somtyme and in some places the husbande sholde accepte the faythe of christ only and folow his holsom doctryne / and the wyfe shold persecute hym / somtyme the wyfe shoulde folowe christe and the husbande persecute her / and in lykewise the sonne his father / and the father the sone.
    Against ll. 19–21 (Referring to ll. 17–19): Reason / the spirite / the inner man / the lawe of the mynde / be one thynge with Paule.
    Against ll. 22–5 (Referring ll. 19–21): Affection / the flesh / the body / the vtter man / the lawe of the membres / be one thynge with Paule.

---

11 hath made both one] knyt two in one *1533*   12 holsom] a holsom *1533*   26 ye walkyng in the spiryt shal] ye shal walkyng in the spiryte *1533*
    Side-note 1: math.] *1533*; math *1534*

ye shal lyue. Certayn this is a newe chaunge of thinges / that peace shuld be sought in warre / and warre in peace: in deth lyfe / and in lyfe deth: in bondage liberty / in liberty bondage. For Paule writeth in an other place. I chastise my body and bring hym in to seruytude.
5 Here also the liberty. If ye be led with the spiryt / ye be not subiect to ye lawe. And we haue not (sayth he) receyued agayne the spiryte of bondage in feare / but the spiryte / whiche hath elected vs to be ye chyldren of god. He sayth in an other place. I se an other lawe in my membres repugnynge agaynst the lawe of my mynde / sub-
10 duyng me to the lawe of synne whiche lawe is in my membres. Thou redest with him also of the vtter man whiche is corrupte / and of the inner man whiche [E2] is renewed daye by daye. Plato put two soules to be in one man. Paule in one man maketh two men so coupled togyder / that neyther without other can be eyther
15 in heuen or hell: and agayne so separated that the deth of the one must be ye lyfe of the other. To the same (as I suppose) pertayn those thynges whiche he wrote to the Chorintes. The fyrst man was made in to a lyuynge soule. The laste Adam was made in to a spiryte quyckenynge: but that is not fyrst whiche is spirituall / but
20 that whiche is lyuynge: than foloweth that whiche is spirytuall. The fyrst man came of the erthe, hym selfe terrestryall. The seconde came from heuen, and he hym selfe celestyall. And bycause it shulde more euydently appere these thynges to pertayne not onely to Christ and Adam / but to vs al: he added sayeng. As was the man
25 of the erth / suche are terrestryall and erthly persons. As is the celestial man / suche are the celestial persons. Therfore as we haue borne the ymage of the erthly man: euen so nowe let vs beare the ymage of the celestyall man. For this I say bretherne, that flesshe and blode shall not possesse the kyngdom of heuen / nor corrupcion
30 shall possesse incorrupcion. Thou perceyuest playnly how in this place he calleth Adam made of erth, that thing which [E2v] in another place he calleth the flesshe, and the vtter man whiche is

Against ll. 1–3: Peace / lyfe / lybertie of soule / is the warre. Dethe / bondage of the body.
Against l. 14: A double man.
Against ll. 18–19: The last adam is Christe.
Against l. 32–p. 73, l. 1 (Referring to p. 73, l. 8): Iacob fygureth the spiryt. Esau the fleshe.

3 in bondage liberty /] in bondage liberty *1533*, *1534*   6 spiryte] *1533*;
spityte *1534*   14 eyther] outher *1533*; yether *1534*   15 separated] separate *1533*   16 must] sholde *1533*   ye lyfe] lyfe *1533*   17 Chorintes.]
Chorintes *1533*, *1534*

corrupte. And this same thynge certaynly is also the body of deth / wherwith Paule agreued cryed out. Oh wretched man y^t I am / who shal delyuer me from this body of deth? In conclusyon Paule declaring ye most dyuers fruite of the flesshe and of the spyrite / writeth in an other place / sayeng. He that soweth in his flesshe, shal also 5 repe or mowe of his flessh corrupcion: but he that soweth in ye spiryt shall repe or mowe of the spiryte lyfe eternal. This is ye olde debate of two twynnes Iacob and Esau / whiche before they were brought forth in to light, wrastled within the cloysters of the mothers belly / and Esau verily caught from Iacob the preemynence 10 of byrth / and was first borne: but Iacob preuented him agayne of his fathers blessing. That whiche is carnall cometh fyrst / but the spirituall thyng is euer best. The one was reed / hygh coloured and rough with heere: the other smothe. The one vnquiet and an hunter: the other reioysed in domestycall quietnes. And 15 ye one also for hunger solde the right that perteyned to hym by inherytaunce / in y^t he was the elder brother: whyle he enticed with a vyle prest and rewarde of voluptuousnes / fell from his natyue lybertie, in to the bondage of synne. [E3] The other procured by craft of grace that whiche belonged not to hym by ryght of law. 20 Bitwene these two brethern though bothe were borne of one bely / and at one tyme / yet was there neuer ioyned perfyte concorde. For Esau hateth Iacob / Iacob for his parte though he quyteth not hate for hate / yet he fleeth and hath euer Esau suspected / neyther dare come within his daunger. To the lykewyse, what so euer thyng 25

Against ll. 2–19: Iacob and Esau / the sones of Isac and Rebecca foughte in theyr mothers bely / she counseyled with god / and he answered / Of them shal spryng two contrary peple which sholde euer be at warre / but the elder shold serue the yonger. Esau was fyrst borne / and Iacob folowed / holdyng Esau fast by the fote. Afterwarde / Esau beyng an hungred / solde to Iacob his inheritaunce for a messe of potage. Whan Isac was olde / he bad Esau to kyll some venyson / that I myght eate of it and blysse the ere I dye.

Against l. 20–p. 74, l. 12: But by the deuyce and meanes of the mother: Iacob stale awaye his fathers blessyng / and was made lorde of his brother. Than came Esau waylyng to haue a blessynge / then answered the father. I haue made hym thy lorde. After that / Iacob sawe our lorde face to face. In good men the spiryt whiche is fygured by Iacob / ruleth / and the body obeyeth. In euyll men the flesshe / whiche is signifyed by Esau / ruleth of hym the Empyre or dominion of the spyryte.

---

2 out.] out *1533, 1534* Oh wretched man] Oh wretche *1533*   5 also]
om. 1533   10 belly /] *1533*; belly. *1537*

Side-note 1 : an hungred] a hungred *1534*

affection counsayleth or persuadeth: let it be suspected, for the
doutfull credence of the counsaylour. Iacob onely sawe the lorde:
Esau as one delytynge in blode lyueth by the sworde. To conclude
whan the mother asked counsayle of the lorde, he answered, the
5 elder shalbe seruaunt to ye yonger. And Isaac the father added:
thou Esau shalt do seruyce to thy brother. And the tyme shall come
whan thou shalt shake of and lose his yoke from thy necke. The
lorde prophecieth of good and obedyent persons / the father of
yuell and disobedyent persons. The one declareth what ought to
10 be done of al men: the other tolde afore hande what ye most parte
wolde do. Paule wylleth that the wyfe be obedyent to her husbande:
for better is (sayth scripture) the iniquite of the man / than the
goodnes of ye woman. Our Eue is carnal affection / whose eyen y^e
subtyle and crafty ser[E3v]pent daily troubleth and vexeth with
15 temptacyon / and she ones corrupted gothe forthe and ceaseth not
to prouoke and entyce the man also thrugh consent to be parte taker
of the iniquite or mischeuous dede. But what redest thou of the
newe woman / of her I meane that is obedyent to her husbande / I
wyl put hatred bytwene the (meanyng the serpent and the woman)
20 and bytwene her generacion and thyne / she shal trede downe thy
heed / and thou shalte lay awayte to her hele. The serpent was
caste downe on his brest / the dethe of Christ weakened his vyolence /
he now only lyeth awayte to her hele priuely. But the woman
thrugh grace of fayth, chaunged as it were in to a man, boldly tredeth
25 down his venymous heed. Grace is encreased / and the tyranny of

Against ll. 14–18 (Referring to ll. 23–5): The woman here signyfyeth a carnall
person / whiche (chaunged by grace of fayth) foloweth the biddyng of the spyryte in euery thynge.

Against ll. 20–1 (Referring to ll. 17–18): The woman fygureth affection. The
man   reson.

Against l. 22–p. 75, l. 10: Abraham had a sonne by his seruaunt Agar /
whose name was Ismaell / and an other by his wyfe Sara / whom he callid Isaac.
Ismael was moche elder than Isaac / and in playeng togyther mysentreated
Isaac / wherwith sara displeased / bad Abraham / put awaye thy seruaunt Agar
with her son also / which Abraham was loth to do / but god commaunded him to
obey his wyues request.

1–2 suspected, for the doutfull credence of the counsaylour. Iacob] suspected.
For the doutfull credence of the counseylour Iacob *1533*   5 And] but
1533   Isaac the father] the father Isaac *1533*   13 eyen] eyes *1533*   15 she]
she is *1533*   corrupted] corrupte *1533*   22 weakened] weyked *1533*
     Side-note 2: affection.] affection *1533, 1534*
     Side-note 3: wyues] *1533*; wynes *1534*

the flesshe is dimynysshed. Whan sara was mynisshed and decayed / than dyd Abraham (god beynge the authour) growe and encrease. And than she called hym not husbande but lorde / neyther yet coude she optayne to haue a childe before she was dried vp and woxen barayn. What I pray the brought she forth at the last to her 5 lorde Abraham now in her olde days / ye and past childe bearing? Verily Isaac that is to say ioy. For as sone as affections be woxed olde and are weake in a man / than at the last springeth vp y^t blissed tranquilite [E4] of an innocent mynde / with sure quietnes of the spirit / as it were a continual feest. And as the fader let not his 10 wife haue her plesure without aduysement: euen so hath he the sportyng of the children togyder suspecte / I mene of Isaac with Ismaell. Sara wold not y^t the childe of a bondwoman and the childe of a fre woman, shuld haue conuersacion togyder at y^t age: but that Ismael (while as yet youth is feruent) shulde be banysshed out 15 of presence / lest vnder a colour of pastyme he myght entyce and drawe vnto his owne maners, Isaac yet yonge and tender of age. Now was Sara an olde wyfe and now had brought forth Isaac / yet mistrusteth Abraham, except the answer of god had aproued his wyues counsayle. He is not sure of the woman vntyll he herde of 20 god: in al thynges that Sara hath sayd to y^e / here her voyce. O happy olde age of them, in whom so mortifyed is the carnall man made of the erth, that he in nothynge besyeth the spiryte. Whiche agrement, whether in al thinges perfyte may happen to any man in this lyfe or no / verily I dare not affyrme: peraduenture 25 it were not expedyent. For euen vnto Paule was gyuen vnquietnesse and trouble of the flesshe, ye messenger of sathan to vex him with- all. And at ye thyrde tyme whan he desyred the lorde to haue ye messenger taken from him. [E4v] Than had he none other answer but only this. Paule my grace is sufficient for the. For strength is 30 wrought and made perfyte in weaknes. In dede this is a newe kynde of remedy. Paule leest he shulde be proude, is tempted with

Against ll. 15–16: Let youth flee the occasyon of synne.
Against ll. 25–7: Trouble of the flesshe is expedyent to the exercyse of vertue and custodye of humilitie.

---

3 called] calleth *1533*   5 woxen barayn] bareyn *1533*   7 be] haue *1533*   woxed] wexed *1533*   8 weake] weyked *1533*   y^t blissed] the blissed *1533*   11 hath he] hath *1533*   13 y^t the childe] ye chylde *1533*   28 whan] *om. 1533*   the lorde] *om. 1533*   28–9 ye messenger] y^t messenger *1533*   29 him.] him *1533, 1534*   answer] answere of god *1533*

pride, y^t he myght be stronge in Christ, he is compelled to be weake in hymselfe. For he bare the treasure of celestyal reuelacions in a vessel of erth: that the excellencye shulde depende of ye might of god / and not of himselfe. Whiche one example of the apostle
5 putteth vs in remembraunce and warneth vs of many thynges. First of al y^t whan we be assaulted of vyces / immediatly we must gyue our selfe to prayer / and often tymes desyre helpe of god. More ouer that temptacions to perfyte men are not perilous: but also are very expedyent to the contynuance and preseruyng of vertue.
10 Last of al we be admonysshed y^t whan all other thynges are full tamed, than the vice of vaynglory euen in the chefe tyme of vertues, layeth awaite: and that this vice is as it were Hidra whom Hercules fought withal, a quycke monstre long of lyfe and fruitful / by reason of her own woundes / which at ye last ende whan all labours
15 be ouercome can scarse be distroyed. Neuerthelesse contynuall and importunate labour ouercometh althing. In the meane tyme whyle thy mynde rageth and is [E5] vexed with vehement perturbacions / by al maner meanes thrust togyder / pull and drawe downe / holde and bynde fast this Protheus with tough bandes, whyle he goth
20 aboute to chaunge himselfe in to al wonderful thinges / in to fyre / in to ye shap of some terrible wylde beest, and in to a rennyng ryuer, and neuer leaue him vntyll he come agayn in to his owne natural lykenes and shap. What is so lyke Protheus, as is the affections and appetites of fooles, whiche drawe them somtyme in to
25 beestly and bodyly lust / somtyme in to mad ire or wrath / otherwhyle in to poyson, enuy and straunge fassyons of vyces? Agreeth

Against ll. 5–6: When thou art tempted / fal to prayer.
Against ll. 9–17: Hydra was a serpente with many heddes / of whiche one was immortal / with her foght Hercules / and whan he smote of one hed .vij. sprange for it. At the laste he fought with a burnyng sword and so sered he theyr neckes / that they coud no more spring.
Against ll. 18–25: Protheus / that is to say / affeccyon muste be holden downe. Protheus is a god which chaungeth hym to all maner facyons. He is a grete prophesier but he wyl tell nothyng without compulsyon.

---

2 For] om. *1533*   4 the apostle] thapostle *1533*   7 prayer /
and often tymes desyre] prayer agayne / and desyre *1533*   10 we be
admonysshed y^t] om. *1533*   12 that] om. *1533*   is] to be *1533*
18 pull and drawe] drawe *1533*   19 bynde fast] bynde *1533*   20 wonderful thinges] maner monstres and affections of thynges *1533*   22 and neuer
leaue him] om. *1533*   26 poyson,] poyson *1533*, *1534*
Side-note 3: holden] holde *1533*

it not wel that the excellent connyng poete Virgil sayd: than shal
dyuers similitudes and fassyons of wylde beestes delude and mocke /
for sodaynly he wyll be a fearfull swyne and foule tygre / and a
dragon ful of scales / and a lyonesse with a reed maane / or shal
counterfayte the quicke sounde of the flame of fyre. But here haue 5
in remembraunce what foloweth. The more he chaungeth hym self
in to al maner of similitudes / the more my sonne (sayth Virgil)
strayne thy tough bandes. And also bycause we shall not nede to
returne agayne to fables of poetes / thou shalt by thensample of
the holy patriarke Iacob lerne to endure and to wrastle lustely all 10
nyght vnto y[e] mornyng of goddes helpe [E5v] begyn to gyue lyght.
And thou shalt say / I wyll not let the departe excepte thou shalt
haue gyuen me thy blessyng first. But what rewarde of his victory
and great vertue that myghty and excellent stronge wrastler
obtayned / it is certaynly very profytable to here. Fyrst of all god 15
blyssed hym in that same place. For euermore after that the
temptacyon is ouercome / a certayne synguler encrease of diuyne
grace is added vnto a man / wherby he shuld be an other tyme
moche more surely armed than he was before agaynst thassaulte of
his enemye. Furthermore by touchyng the thigh the synewe of the 20
conquerour wyddred and shronke / and he began to halte on the one
fote. God curseth them by the mouth of his prophete whiche halt
on bothe their fete / that is to say / them whiche wyll bothe lyue
carnally / and please god also. But they be happy in whome carnall
affectyons be so mortifyed / that they beare and lene moste of 25
all to the ryght fote / that is / to the spiryte. Fynally his name was
chaunged: of Iacob he was made Israel / and of a besy wrastler a
quyet persone. After thou haste chastysed thy flesshe / and crucifyed

Against ll. 1–11: Vyrgyll reherseth of arestew which had lost his bestes / and
counselled with his mother Cirene a goddes how he might restore them agayne /
she sent him to protheus and taught a craft to bind hym vntyll he had tolde the
truthe. Than taught protheus howe of a deed and putrified oxe they might be
restored again.
Against ll. 12–18: Iacob wrestled with an aungell all nyght. Whom in the
morning he wold not let go tyll he had blessyed hym in the same place. The
aungell smot his thigh and the synewes shranke / so that Iacob halted on the one
leg after that.

---

1 than] there *1533*   11 of goddes helpe] of the helpe of **god** *1533*
19 thassaulte] the assaulte *1533*   20 Furthermore by] Farthermore **thrugh**
1533   the thigh] of y[e] thigh *1533*   21 wyddred] wexed wyddred *1533*
28 After] After that *1533*   flesshe] flesshe or thy body *1533*
Side-note 2: tyll] vytyll *1533*

it with vyces and concupyscences / than shall tranquyllyte and
quyetnesse without all trouble come vnto the / that thou mayste [E6]
be at leyser to beholde the lorde / that thou mayste taste and fele
that the lorde is plesaunt and swete / for that thyng is signyfyed by
5 Israell. God is not sene in fyre or in the whorle wynde and troublous
rage of temptacyon / but after the tempest of the dyuell (if so be
thou shalt endure perseuerantly) foloweth the hyssyng of a thynne
ayre or wynde of spirituall consolacion. After that ayre hath
brethed quyetly vpon the / than applye thyne inwarde eyen / and
10 thou shalte be Israel / and shalt say with hym. I haue sene my
lorde / and my soule is made hole. Thou shalte se hym that sayde:
no flesshe shall se me. Consyder thy selfe dilygently / if thou
be flesshe / thou shalte not se god: if thou se hym not / thy soule
shall not be made hole. Take hede therfore that thou be a spiryte.

15   ℂ Of thre partes of man / the spiryte /
          the soule / and the flesshe. Caplo. vij.

THese thynges afore written were euen a great deale more than
suffycyent: neuerthelesse that thou mayste be somwhat more
sensybly knowen vnto thy selfe / I wyll reherse compendyously
20 the dyuysyon of man / after the discrypcyon of Orygene / for he
foloweth Paule [E6v] makyng thre partes / the spiryte / the soule
and the flesshe / whiche thre partes Paule ioyned togyder / writyng
to the Thessalonicences. That your spiryte (sayth he) your soule
and your body may be kepte clene and vncorrupte / that ye be not
25 blamed or accused at the comyng of our lord Iesu Christ. And
Esaias (leuing out the lowest parte) maketh mencion of two / sayeng
my soule shall desyre and longe for the in the nyght / ye and in my

Against ll. 3–4 (Referring to ll. 6–8): God appereth after a greate tempest.
Against ll. 5–14: He hathe walked .xl. dayes and xl. nightes vnto the mounte
of Oreb / where he prayed in a caue. A voice bad hym come forthe and stande
afore god / and then came a greate wynde / than a quaking / than fire / and god
not in the fire. Than folowed the hissyng of a thynne ayre / and than appered
god to Elyas.
Against ll. 17–19: Origene in his first boke vpon the Epistle of paule to the
romains maketh this diuision.

1 it] hym 1533   5 or in] neyther in 1533   9 eyen] eyes 1533
12 me] me / that is to say / no carnall man 1533   17 were euen] had ben and
that 1533   21 makyng] maketh 1533
Side-note 2: Oreb] Orell 1533, 1534

spiryt and my hert strynges I wyll wake in the mornynges for to
please the. Also Daniell sayth / let the spirytes and soules of good
men laude god. Out of the which places of scripture Origene
gathereth not agaynst reason the thre porcions of man / that is to
wete / yᵉ body / otherwyse called the flesshe / thc most vile parte of 5
vs / wherin the malycious serpent through originall trespace, hath
written the lawe of synne / wherwithall we be prouoked to filthynes:
and also if wc bc ouercom we be coupled and made one with
the dyuell. Than the spiryt, wherin we represent yᵉ similitude of the
nature of god / in which also our most blyssed maker after the original 10
paterne and example of his owne mynde hath grauen the eternal
lawe of honestie with his fynger / that is with his spirit the holy
goost. By this parte we be knyt to god / and made [E7] one with
him. In the thirde place and in the myddes bytwene these two
he putteth the soule / whiche is part taker of the sensyble wyttes 15
and natural mocions. She as one in a sedicious and wrangling
commun welth must nedely ioyne her selfe to yᵉ one parte or the
other / she is troubled of bothe partes / she is at her libertie to
whether part she wyl enclyne. If she forsake the flesshe and conuey
her selfe to the partes of the spiryt / she her selfe shal be spiritual 20
also. But and if she cast her selfe down to thappetites of the body
she shall growe out of kynde in to the maner of yᵉ body. This is it
that Paule ment writyng to the Chorintes. Remembre ye not that he
yᵗ ioyneth hym selfe to an harlot is made one body with her: but
he that cleueth to the lord / is one spirit with him. He calleth the 25
harlot the frayle and weake parte of the man. This is that plesaunt
and flatering woman of whom thou redest in the seconde chapiter
of prouerbes on this wyse. That thou mayst be delyuered from a
straunge woman and from a woman of an other countre / whiche
maketh her wordes swete and plesaunt / and forsaketh her husbande 30

Against l. 4 (Referring to l. 5): The flesshe.
Against l. 8 (Referring to l. 9): The spiryte.
Against ll. 16–29: Thou must remembre the soule and the spiryte to be
one substaunce / but in the soule be many powers / as wyt / wyll / memory:
but the spiryte is the most pure and fardest fro corrupcion / the most high
and diuine porcion of our soule. Capax of god immediatly / wherein god hathe
grauen the lawe of honesty / that is to saye / the law naturall after the symylytude
of the eternall lawe of his owne mynde.

4 porcions] peticions *1533*   16 as one] is *1533*   21 thappetites]
yᵉ appetites *1533*

Side-note 3: wyt /] wit *1533*; wyt *1534*

to whom she was maryed in her youth / and hath forgotten the
promesse she made to her lorde god: her hous boweth downe to
deth and her path is to hell. Who so euer gothe [E7v] in to hell /
shall neuer returne: nor shall attayne the path of lyfe. And in the
5 .vj. chap. That thou mayst kepe the from an yuell woman / and from
the flateryng tonge of a straunge woman / let not thy hert melte on
her beautye / be not thou disceyued with her beckes / for the pryce
of an harlot is scarce worthe a pece of breed: but the woman
taketh awaye the precyous soule of the man. Dyd he not whan he
10 made mencion of the harlot / the herte and the soule, expresse by
name thre partes of man. Agayn in the .ix. chapiter. A folysshe
woman euer bablyng and full of wordes / swymmynge in pleasures /
and hath no lernyng at al / sytteth in the dores of her house vpon
a stole in an high place of the cyte to call them that passe by the
15 waye and be goynge in their iourney / who so euer is a chylde / let
hym turne in to me: and she said vnto a foole and an hertles person:
water that is stolen is plesaunter / and breed that is hyd priuely, is
sweter. And he was not ware that there be gyauntes / and their
gestes be in the bottom of hell. For who so euer shall be coupled to
20 her / he shall discende in to hell. And who so euer shall departe from
her / shalbe saued. I beseche the with what colours coude more
workmanly haue ben paynted and set out eyther the venymous
entycemen[E8]tes and wanton pleasures of the poysoned flesshe /
prouokyng and temptyng the soule to fylthynesse of synne / or els
25 the importunytie of the same, cryenge and stryuyng agaynst the
spiryte / or the wretched ende that foloweth whan she dothe ouercome the spiryte. To conclude therfore / the spiryte maketh vs
goddes / the flesshe maketh vs beestes: the soule maketh vs men:
the spiryte maketh vs relygyous / obedyent to god / kynde and
30 mercyfull. The flesshe maketh vs dispysers of god / disobedyent to
god / vnkynde and cruell. The soule maketh vs indyfferent / that
is to say / neyther good nor badde. The spyryte desyreth celestyal
thynges: the flesshe desyreth delycate and plesaunt thynges. The
soule desyreth necessary thynges: the spiryte caryeth vs vp to
35 heuen: the flesshe thrusteth vs downe to hell. To the soule nothyng
is imputed: what so euer is carnall or springeth of the flesshe, that
is fylthy: what so euer is spirytuall procedyng of the spiryte / that

1 hath forgotten] hath forgete *1533*   11 man] the man *1533*   22 ben]
be *1533*   36 imputed] imputed / that is to saye / it dothe neyther good
nor harme *1533*

is pure / perfyte and godly: what so euer is naturall and procedeth
of the soule / is a meane and indifferent thyng / neyther good nor
badde. Wylt thou more playnly haue the dyuersytie of these thre
partes shewed vnto the as it were with a mannes fynger? certaynly
I wyll assaye. [E8v] Thou art vnder the reuerent feare of thy 5
parentes: thou louest thy brother / thy chyldren and thy frende: it
is not of so great vertue to do these thynges, as it is abhomynable not
to do them. Foi why shuldest thou not beyng a christen man do that
thing whiche the gentyles by the techyng of nature do / ye whiche
brute beestes do? That thynge that is naturall shal not be imputed 10
vnto meryte. But thou arte come in to suche a strayte case, y^t
eyther the reuerence towarde thy father must be dispised / ye inward loue toward thy children must be subdued / the benyuolence to
thy frende set at naught / or god must be offended. What wilt thou
now do? The soule standeth in the myddes bytwene two wayes: the 15
flessh cryeth vpon her on thone syde / the spiryte on the other
syde. The spiryte sayth / god is aboue thy father / thou art bounde
to thy father but for thy body only. To god thou art bounde for
all thynge that thou hast. The flesshe putteth the in remembraunce /
sayeng. Excepte thou obey thy father / he wyll disheryte the / 20
thou shalt be called of euery man an vnkynde and vnnaturall chylde /
loke to thy profite / haue respecte to thy good name and fame. God
eyther dothe not se / or els dissymuleth and wetyngly loketh besyde
it / or at ye leest wyll be sone pacifyed agayn. [F1] Now thy soule
douteth / nowe she wauereth hyther and thyder: to whether of 25
eyther parte she tourne her selfe / euen that same shall she be
what so euer that is she goth vnto. If she obey y^t harlot the flesshe
(the spiryte dispysed) she shal be one body with the flesshe. But
and if she lyfte vp her selfe and ascende to the spiryte (the
flesshe set at naught) she shalbe transposed and chaunged in to 30
the nature of the spiryte. After this maner accustome to examyne
thyselfe prudently. The errour of those men is excedyng great
which oftentymes wenen that thing to be perfyte vertue and

Against ll. 5–6: That whiche is naturall / deserueth no rewarde.
Against ll. 25–6: The soule doubteth.

5–6 art vnder the reuerent feare of thy parentes] doest reuerence to thy father
and mother *1533*   10 imputed] *1533*; impured *1534*   16 thone] y^e
one *1533*   26 euen that] That *1533*   27 what so euer that is] that that
thynge is *1533*   goth] went *1533*   y^t harlot] the harlot / that is to say *1533*
30 in to] to *1533*   33 wenen] weneth *1533*

goodnesse whiche is but of nature, and no vertue at al. Certayne affections somwhat honest in apperance / and as they were disgysed with vysers of vertue / disceyuen neclygent persons. The iudge is hasty and cruell agaynst the felon, or hym that hath tres-
5 pased the lawe: he semeth to hymselfe constant, and of grauyte, vncorrupt, and a man of good conscyence. Wylte thou haue this man discussed? If he fauour his owne mynde to moche, and folowe a certayne naturall rygorousnes without any grefe or sorow of mynde / peraduenture with some pleasure or delectacyon: yet not
10 leanyng from the offyce and duty of a iudge / let hym not forthwith stande to moche in his owne conceyte. It is an indifferent thyng [FIV] that he dothe. But if he abuse the lawe for priuate hate or lucre: now is it carnall that he dothe / and he commytteth murder. But and if he fele great sorow in his mynde / bycause he is compelled
15 to distroye and kyll him / whom he had leuer haue amended and saued: and also enioyne punysshment accordynge to the trespace, with suche a mynde / with suche sorowe of herte / as the father commaundeth his syngulerly beloued sonne to be cutte / launced / or seared: of this maner shall it be spirituall that he dothe. The most
20 parte of men through pronesse of nature and some specyall propertie / eyther reioyce or abhorre certayne thynges. Some there be whom bodily lust tykleth not at al: let not them by and by ascribe that vnto vertue, which is an indifferent thing. For not to lacke bodyly lust / but to ouercome bodily lust, is the office of vertue.
25 An other man hath a pleasure to fast / a pleasure to be at masse / a pleasure to be moche at churche and to say a great deale of psalmodye: examyne after this rule that thynge whiche he doth. If he regarde the commune fame or aduauntage / it smelleth of yᵉ flesshe and not of the spiryt. If he do folowe but his owne inclynacyon (for he
30 dothe that whiche pleaseth his owne mynde) than he hath not, wherof he ought so greatly [F2] to reioyce / but rather wherof he ought to feare. Beholde a ieopardous thyng vnto thy selfe. Thou prayest and iudgest hym that prayeth not. Thou fastest / and con-

Against ll. 2–3: Some affections be disguysed with visers of vertue.
Against ll. 4–5: An example of the iudge.
Against ll. 20–2: Some men reioice naturally with some certayne thynges.
Against ll. 25–6 (Referring to l. 27): The rule of true pitie.
Against ll. 33–p. 83, l. 1: Let a christen man marke this well

3 disceyuen] deceyueth *1533*   8 or sorow] *om. 1533*   13 is it] it is *1533*   15 haue] *om. 1533*   16 and also enioyne] Also yf he enioyne *1533*   31 ought so] so ought *1533*

dempnest hym that fasteth not. Who so euer dothe not that thou doest / thou thynkest thy selfe better than he: beware leest thy faste pertayne to thy flesshe. Thy brother hath nede of thy helpe / thou in the meane space momblest vp thy prayers vnto god / and wylt not be knowen of thy brothers necessyte. God shall abhorre 5 these prayers: for how shall god here the whyle thou prayest / whan thou whiche art a man canste not fynde in thy herte to here an other man. Perceyue also an other thing. Thou louest thy wyfe for this cause onely that she is thy wyfe? Thou doest no great thynge / for this thynge is commune as well to infydeles as to 10 the. Or els thou louest her for none other thynge but bycause she is to the pleasaunt and delectable. Thy loue nowe draweth to thy flesshwarde. But thou louest her for this thynge chefely / bycause thou hast perceyued in her the ymage of Christ / whiche is godly reuerence / modesty / sobrenesse / chastyte: and nowe louest not 15 her in her selfe but in Christ / ye rather Christe in her. After this maner thou louest spirytually. [F2v] Notwithstandynge we shall say more of these thynges in their places.

⟨ Certayne generall rules of true
chrysten lyuynge. Ca. viij.   20

NOw for bycause we haue opened as me semeth ye way (howe so euer we haue done it) and haue prepared as it were certayne stuffe and mater vnto the thyng whiche was purposed, we muste haste to that whiche remayneth / leest it shulde not be an Enchiridion / that is to saye / a lytell treatyse hansom to be caryed in a mannes hande / 25 but rather a great volume / we wyll enforce to gyue certen rules / as they were certayne poyntes of wrastlyng / by whose gydyng and conueyaunce / as it were by the gydyng of ye threde of Dedalus, men may easely plunge vp out of the blynde errours of this worlde / as out of Labirinthus / whiche is a certayne com- 30 berous maze / and come vnto the pure and clere lyght of spirituall lyuyng. None other science is there whiche hath not her rules. And shall the crafte of blissed lyuing onely / be without the helpe of all maner preceptes? There is without fayle a certayne crafte of

Against ll. 13–14: The chaste loue towarde thy wyfe.
Against l. 24: Enchiridion.
Against l. 34–p. 84, l. 1: Lerne the crafte of vertue.

4 vp] in *1533*   23 purposed,] purposed. *1533, 1534*

vertuous lyuynge and a discyplyne / in whiche who so euer exercyse
themselfe manfully / them [F3] shall fauoure that holy spiryte /
whiche is the promoter and bringer forwarde of all holy enforcement
and godly purposes. But who so euer sayth / departe from vs we wyll
5 not haue ye knowlege of thy wayes: these men the mercy of god
refuseth / bycause they fyrste haue refused knowlege. These rules
shall be taken partly of the persone of god / of the persone of the
dyuell / and of our persone / partly of the thynges / that is to say /
of vertues and vyces / and of thynges to them annexed / partely of
10 the mater or stuffe wherof vertues or vices be wrought. They shall
profyte synglerly agaynst thre yuels, the remanentes of orygynall
synne. For though baptysme haue wyped away the spotte / yet there
cleaueth styll in vs a certayne thyng of the olde disease left behynde /
bothe for the custody of humylyte / and also for the mater and
15 encrease of vertue. These yuels be blyndnesse / the flesshe and
infyrmytie or weaknesse. Blyndnesse with the myst of ignoraunce
dymmeth the iudgement of reason. For partly the synne of our
first progenytours, hath not a lytel dusked that so pure a lyght of
the countenaunce / resemblaunce or similitude of god / which our
20 creatour hath shewed vpon vs. And moche more corrupte bryngynge vp / leude company / frowarde affectyons / derk [F3v]-
nesse of vices / custome of synne hath so cancred it / that of y^e
lawe grauen in vs of god scarse any sygnes or tokens dothe apere.
Than as I began / blyndnes causeth that we in the election of
25 thinges be as good as halfe blynded and disceyued with errour / in
the stede of the best, folowyng the worste / preferryng thynges of
lesse valure, before thynges of greater price. The flesshe troubleth y^e
affection so moche / y^t euen though we knowe what is best / yet loue
we ye contrary. Infirmyte and weaknesse maketh vs that we beyng
30 ouercome, eyther with tedyousnes or with temptacion / forsake the
vertue whiche we had ones gotten and attayned. Blyndnes hurteth
the iudgement: the flesshe corrupteth the wyll: infirmyte weaketh
constancye. The fyrst poynte therfore is, that thou can discerne
thynges to be refused, from thynges to be accept: and therfore

Against l. 20: Nota.
Against l. 34–p. 85, l. 1: Euyll must be knowen and had in hate.

6 rules] rulers *1533*   8 the thynges] thynges *1533*   10 wrought.]
wrought *1533, 1534*   11 yuels, the remanentes] euyl thynges remaynyng *1533*   14 bothe] bothe partly *1533*   15 These yuels] These *1533*
20 vs.] vs *1533, 1534*   21 vp /] vp *1533, 1534*   34 accept:] accepte:
1533, accept. *1534*

blyndnes must be taken away: leest we stomble or stager in y^e
election of thynges. The next is / that thou hate the yuell as sone as
it is ones knowen / and loue that whiche is honest and good: and
in this thynge the flesshe must be ouercome / leest contrary to y^e
iudgement of the mynde, we shulde loue swete and delectable 5
thynges in the stede of holsom thynges. The thyrde is / that we
contynue in these thynges which [F4] we began well: and therfore
the weaknes must be vnderact / leest we forsake the way of vertue
with greater shame, than if we had ben neuer aboute to walke or
enter therin. Ignoraunce must be remedied / that thou mayst se 10
which way to go. The flesh must be tamed, leest she lede the asyde
out of the hyghway / ones knowen in to bypathes. Weaknesse must
be comforted / leest whan thou hast entred in to the streyght way,
thou shuldest eyther faynte or stoppe or turne backe agayne / or
leest after thou hast ones set thy hande to ye plow thou shuldest 15
loke backwarde / but must reioyce as a stronge gyaunt to haste the
way / euer stretchyng forth thy self to those thinges which be afore
the, without remembraunce of those thynges which be behynde the /
vntyll thou mayst lay hande on the reward apoynted, and on y^e
crowne promised to them y^t contynue. Vnto these thre thynges 20
therfore, we shall aplye certayn rules accordyng to our lytel
power.

⸿ Agaynst the yuell of ignoraunce
the fyrst rule. Caplo. ix.

BVt in as moche as faythe is ye onely gate vnto Christ / the 25
fyrst rule must be that thou iudge very wel bothe of him and also
of scripture, gyuen by his spiryt / and [F4v] that thou byleue not
with mouth onely / not fayntly / not neclygently / not doutfully / as
the commune raskall of christen men do: but let it be set faste and
immouable thrughout all thy brest / not one iote to be contayned in 30
them, that apertayneth not greatly vnto thy helthe. Let it moue the
nothing at all, that thou seest a gret parte of men so lyue / as though
heuen and hell were some maner tales of olde wyues / to feare or

Against ll. 7–8: Perceiueraunce must be had.
Against ll. 25–6 (Referring to l. 27): We must iudge wel of scripture.
Against ll. 30–1: Counterfayte not euyll persons.

1 taken] take *1533*   15 thou shuldest] sholdest *1533*   16 must]
sholdest *1533*   33 were] were but *1533*   maner] maner of *1533*

flater yong chyldren withall: but byleue thou surely / and make
no haste. Though the hole worlde shulde be madde at ones /
though the elementes shulde be chaunged / though the aungels
shulde rebell: yet verite can not lye / it can not but come whiche god
5 tolde before shulde come. If thou byleue he is god / thou muste by-
leu nedes that he is true also. On this wyse, thinke without wauer-
ing / nothyng to be so true / nothynge to be so sure / and without
doute of these thinges, whiche thou herest with thyne eares / which
thou presently beholdest with thyne eyen / whiche thou handlest
10 with thy handes / as these are whiche thou redest in ye scriptures /
whiche god of heuen / that is to say verite gaue by inspiracion /
whiche the holy prophetes brought forth / and the bloode of so
many martyrs hath approued: vnto whiche now so ma[F5]ny hundred yeres the consent of all good men hath agreed and set their
15 seales: whiche Christ here beyng in flesshe bothe taught in his
doctryne and expresly represented or counterfayted in his maners
and lyuynge. Vnto whiche also myracles beare wytnes / whiche
the dyuels confesse / and so moche byleue / that they quake and
tremble for feare. Last of al, whiche be so agreable vnto the equyte
20 of nature / whiche so agree bytwene themselfe / and be euery
where lyke themselfe / whiche so rauyssheth the myndes of them
that attende / so moueth and chaungeth them. If these so great
tokens agre vnto them alone / what the dyuels madnesse is it to doute
in the faythe? At the leestway of thynges passed, make a coniec-
25 ture of thinges to come. Howe many and howe great thynges also /
howe incredyble to be spoken dyd the prophetes tell before of
Christ: whiche of these thynges came not to passe? shal he in other
thynges disceyue whiche in them disceyued not? In conclusyon the
prophetes lyed not / and shall Christ the lorde of prophetes lye? If
30 with this and suche other lyke cogytacyons, thou often styrre vp the
flame of fayth / and than feruently desyre of god to encrease thy
fayth, I shall meruayle if thou canst be any longe tyme an yuell
man. For who is all togy[F5v]der so vnhappy and full of myschefe
but that he wolde departe from vyces / if so be he vtterly byleued

Against ll. 1–2: Probacions of christen fayth.

6 On] and on *1533*   8 these thinges] the thinges *1533*   9 eyen] eyes
1533   10 these] those *1533*   are] thynges be true *1533*   11 whiche
god] that god *1533*   17–18 whiche the dyuels] the deuylles *1533*   24 At
the leestway of] ye of those *1533*   24–5 make a coniecture of thinges to
come] thou mayst easely coniecte what shall folowe *1533*   25 howe great]
great *1533*   34 but] *om. 1533*   he wolde departe] wolde not departe *1533*

that with these momentany pleasures / besyde the vnhappy vexacyon of conscyence and mynde / is purchased also eternall punysshmentes. On the other syde / if he surely byleued, for this temporall
and lytell worldly vexacyon, to be gyuen vnto good men an hundred
folde ioye of pure conscyence, and at the laste, lyfe immortall.   5

❡ The seconde rule. Caplo. x.

LEt the fyrst poynte be therfore that thou doute in no wyse of
ye promyses of god. The next yt thou go vnto the way of lyfe / not
slouthfully / not fearfully: but with sure purpose / with all thy hert /
with a confydent mynde / and (if I may so say) with suche mynde 10
as he hath that wolde rather fyght than drinke: so that thou be
redy at all houres for Christes sake to lese bothe lyfe and goodes. A
slouthful man wyll and wyl not. The kyngdom of heuen is not goten
of neclygent and recheles persons / but playnly reioyseth to suffre
vyolence: And vyolent persons violently obtayne it. Suffre not 15
the affection of them whom thou louest syngularly to holde the
backe hastyng thyder[F6]warde: let not the pleasures of this worlde
call the backe agayne: let not the care of thy housholde be any
hyndraunce to the. The chayne of worldly besynesse must be cut
asonder / for surely it can not otherwise be losed. Egypt must be 20
forsaken in suche maner, that thou turne not agayne in thy mynde
at any tyme vnto ye flesshe pottes. Sodoma must be forsaken vtterly
hastely, ye and at ones: it is not lauful to loke backe. The woman
loked backe, and she was turned in to ye ymage of a stone. The man
hath no leyser any where to abyde in the regyon / but is commaun- 25

Against ll. 8–11: We must entre in to the waye of helthe or saluacion boldly /
and with a ioconde courage.
Against ll. 17–24: Egypte sygnyfyeth bondage / affliccion / vices / and blyndnes. The Israelytes being a hongred in deserte / wysshed to go back agayne to
Egipt / sayeng to Moyses / how happy were we whan we onto thore by the pottes
of flesh.
Against l. 25–p. 88, l. 11: Loth was commaunded to departe hastelye out of
Sodoma / and not to loke backe / his wyfe loked backe / and was turned in to
a salt stone. So we may neither with the Israelytes desyre to go back agayne to
the pleasure of Egypt of vices and synne: neyther with the wyfe of Loth may
looke backe again to our old conuersacion.

1 vnhappy] *1533*; vphappy *1534*   4 gyuen vnto] rewarded or recompensed to *1533*   5 conscyence] conscyence presently *1533*   13 kyngdom]
1533; kyndom *1534*   21 in suche maner] in suche a maner *1533*
22 flesshe pottes] pottes of the flesshe *1533*   24 and] *om. 1533*   25 hath]
had *1533*   the regyon] any region *1533*   is] was *1533*

Side-note 3: So] so *1533, 1534*

ded to haste in to the mountayne / onelesse he had leuer perysshe.
The prophete cryeth out that we shulde flee out of the myddes of
Babylon. The departyng of yᵉ israelytes from Egypt, is called flyght
or ronnyng awaye. We be commaunded to flee out of Babylon
5 hastely / and not to remoue a lytell and a lytell slowly. Thou
mayst se the moste parte of men prolonge the tyme / and with
very slowe purpose go aboute to flee from vyces. Whan I haue
ones rydde my selfe out of suche and suche maters / saye they / ye
whan I haue brought that and that besynes to passe. Oh foole,
10 what and if god this same day take agayne thy soule from the?
Perceyuest thou not one besynes to ryse of [F6v] an other / and one
vyce to call in an other. Why rather doest thou not to daye that
thynge whiche the soner thou doest / the easyer shall it be done:
Be dylygent some other where: in this mater to do rasshly, to ronne
15 heedlonge, and sodaynly, is chefe of all and moste profytable.
Regarde not nor ponder howe moche thou forsakest: beyng sure
that Christ onely shal be suffycyent for all thynges. Onely be bolde
to commyt thy selfe to hym with all thyne hert. Se thou mistrust
thyne owne selfe. Aduenture to put vnto hym al the gouernaunce
20 of thy selfe. Trust to thy selfe no longer: but with full confydence
cast thy selfe from thy selfe to hym / and he shall receyue the. Commytte thy care and thought to the lorde / and he shall nourysshe the
vp / that thou mayst synge the songe of yᵉ same prophete. The lorde
is my gouernour / and I shall lacke nothynge. In a place of pasture he
25 hath set me / by the water syde of comforte he hath brought vp me:
he hath conuerted my soule. Be not mynded to parte thy self in to
two: to the worlde and to Chryste. Thou cannest not serue two
maysters: there is no felowshyp bytwene god and Belial. God can
not awaye with them whiche halte on both their legges: his stomake
30 abhorreth them whiche be ney[F7]ther hote nor colde / but luke
warme. God is a very ialouse louer of soules: he wyll possesse onely
and all togyder that thyng whiche he redemed with his bloode. He

1 onelesse] oneles that *1533*   perysshe] to haue perysshed *1533*
11 Perceyuest] perceyuest *1533, 1534*   15 chefe] chefest *1533*   16 beyng]
but be *1533*   17 that] *om. 1533*   18 Se] set *1533*   mistrust] mystruste
in *1533*

can not suffre the felowshyp of the dyuell whome he ones ouer-
came by his dethe. There be but two wayes onely. The one whiche
by folowyng ye affectyons ledeth to perdycion. The other whiche
through mortyfyeng of the flesshe: ledeth to lyfe. Why doutest
thou in thyselfe: There is no thyrde way. In to one of these two, 5
thou must nedes entre / wylt thou or wylt thou not. What so euer
thou arte / or of what degree / thou muste nedes entre in to
this strayte way / in whiche fewe mortall men walke. But this waye
Christe hym selfe hath trode / and haue troden sythe the worlde
began, who so eure pleased god. This is doutlesse ye ineuitable 10
necessite of the goddesse Adrasta. It can not be chosen, but y^t thou
must be crucyfied with Christ as touchyng the worlde / if thou
purpose to lyue with Chryst. Why lyke fooles flater we our selfe.
Why in so weyghty a mater disceyue we our selfe? One saith / I am
not of the clergye or a spiritual man / I am of ye worlde / I can not 15
but vse the worlde. An other thynketh / though I be a preest yet am
I no monke / let hym loke vpon it. [F7v] And the monke also hath
founde a thing to flater himselfe withal / though I be a monke
sayth he, yet am I not of so strayte an ordre as suche and such. An
other sayth. I am a yong man / I am a gentle man / I am ryche / I 20
am a courtier / and to be short a prince / those thynges pertayne
not to me whiche were spoken to thapostles. Oh wretche than aperteyneth it nothyng to the y^t thou shuldest lyue in Christ? If thou
be in ye worlde / in Christ thou art not. If thou call ye skye / the
erthe / the see / and this commune ayre the worlde: so is there no 25
man whiche is not in the worlde. But and if thou call the worlde
ambicion / desyre of honour / promocion or authoryte / pleasures /

Against ll. 2–3: Two wayes onely / the one of saluacion / the other of
perdicion.
Against ll. 8–17: Adrasta nemesis or Rhamnusia is a goddes whiche punyssheth insolency / she forbiddeth that any man loke to hyghe / if any so do / he
escapeth not / vnpunysshed / thoughe it be neuer so late / yf any be to ful of
insolencye / we say / take hede / Rhamnusia seeth the well ynoughe.
Against ll. 19–22: Euery man putteth to an other the lyfe of Christe and
sayenges of his apostels.
Against l. 25: The worlde.

2 by his] with *1533*   3 folowyng] obedyence of *1533*   9 and]
1533; aud *1534*   sythe] synce *1533*   11 Adrasta] Adrasta / otherwyse
called Nemesis or Rhamnusia / that is to say *1533*   12 must] *om. 1533*
19 sayth he] *om. 1533*   20 ryche /] *1533*; ryche *1534*   22 than] then
1533   27 ambicion] ambicyon / y^t is to say *1533*   pleasures]
yf thou call ye worlde pleasures *1533*

couetousnesse / bodyly lust: certaynly so arte thou worldly, a christen man thou arte not. Christ spake indifferently to al men: who so euer wolde not take his crosse and folowe hym / coude be no mete man for hym / or be his discyple. To dye with Chryste as 5 touchynge the flesshe, is nothyng to the / if to lyue by his spiryte pertayneth nothyng to the. To be crucifyed as touching the world, pertayneth nothyng to the / if to lyue godly or in god pertayne nothing to the. To be buried togyder with Christ belongeth nothing to the / if to aryse agayn to eternal glory, belonge nothing to 10 the. The humilite / pouerte / tri[F8]bulacion / vyle reputacyon / the laborous agonyes and sorowes of Christ, pertayne nothyng at all vnto the: if the kyngdome of hym pertayne nothyng vnto the. What can be more leude than to thynke the rewarde to be commune as well to the as to other: and yet neuerthelesse to put the labours 15 wherby the rewarde is obtayned, from the to a certayne fewe persons. What can be more wanton or nyce than to desyre to reygne with the heed: and yet wyll take no payne with him? Therfore my brother loke not so greatly what other men do / and in comparyson of them flatter or please thy selfe. To dye as 20 touching synne, to dye as touching carnall desyres, to dye as touchynge the worlde, is a certayne harde thyng, and knowen to very fewe / ye though they be monkes / and yet is this the commune and generall professyon of all christen men. This thynge a great whyle agone thou hast sworne and holyly promysed in ye tyme of 25 baptysme. Than which vow, what other thing can ther be eyther more holy, or religyous? eyther we must perysshe / or els without excepcion, we must go this way to helth, whether we be kynges or poore plow men. Notwithstanding though it fortune not to al men to attayne the perfyte counterfaytyng and folowyng of the 30 heed / yet al must enforce with fete and [F8v] handes to come therto. He hath a great parte of a christen man / whiche with all his herte / with a sure and stedfaste purpose, hath determyned to be a christen man.

Against ll. 4–5 (Referring to ll. 12–16): The rewarde is gyuen to hym that laboreth.
Against l. 23: Monkes.

---

1 so arte thou worldly] yf thou be worldly *1533*   1–2 a christen man thou arte not] thou art not a chrysten man *1533*   16 wanton or nyce] a wanton thyng *1533*   17 wyll] wilt thou *1533*   27–8 kynges or poore plow men] knyghtes or plowe men *1533*   29 and] or *1533*   31 man] mans lyuynge *1533*

❡ The thyrde rule. Caplo. xj.

BVt leest that thyng feare the from the waye of vertue, bycause it semeth sharpe and greuous / partly bycause thou must forsake worldly commodites, partly bycause thou must fyght continually agaynst thre very cruell enemyes / the flesshe / yᵉ dyuell and the 5 worlde: set this thirde rule before the alway. Beare thyselfe in hande that all the fearful thinges and fantasies, which apere forthwith vnto the, as it were in yᵉ first entring of hel: ought to be counted for a thing of naught / by thexample of Virgils Eneas. For certaynly if thou shalt consider the very thynge somwhat groundly and sted- 10 fastly (settyng at naught these aparent thinges which begyle thyne eyen) thou shalt perceyue that none other way is more commodious than the way of Christ. Though thou account this thyng not at all, that this way onely leadeth to eternall lyfe / ye and though thou haue no respecte vnto the rewarde. For (I beseche the) what kynde 15 of lyuynge after the commune course of the worlde, is there [G1] that thou canst chose, in which thou shalt not beare / and suffre many thinges haboundantly, bothe carefull and greuous? Who is he, that knoweth not the lyfe of courtyers to be full of greuous laboure, and wretched myserye: excepte it be eyther he, that neuer proued 20 it, or certaynly a very naturall foole? Oh immortall god, what bondage muste be suffred there, how longe, and how vngoodly, euen vnto the lyues ende? What a comberous besynesse is there, in sekynge, in purchasynge the prynces loue and fauoure. A man must flatter to obtayne the fauour of all suche as may eyther hynder 25 or further one. The countenaunces must now and than be fayned and newe fassyoned. The iniuryes of the greater men, must be whyspered and muttered with sylence secretely. Consequently, what kynde of euyll lyfe can he ymagyned / wherof the lyfe of warryours is not full? Of eyther lyfe mayst thou be a very good 30

Against ll. 9–15: Eneas in the .vi. boke of Virgil went downe in to hell / accompanyed with the prophetesse Sybyl. In the first entree appered many fantasyes and wonderful monsters / not so peryllous in dede as they apperyd.

Again ll. 28–9: The lyfe of warryours.

9 Virgils] Virgilius *1533*   11 begyle] begiled *1533*   12 eyen] eyes *1533*
15 (I] I *1533*;)I *1534*   17 shalt] shal *1533*   18 many thinges] thynges
ynough *1533*   22 muste be suffred there, how longe, and how vngoodly]
howe longe and how ungoodly muste there be suffred *1533*   24 fauoure]
grace *1533*   28 and] or *1533*   30 mayst] than mayste *1533*

wytnesse / whiche hast lerned bothe, at thyne owne peryll. And as
touchynge the marchaunt man, what is it that he eyther dothe not,
or suffreth not, fleynge pouertye by se, by lande, through fyre
and water? In matrymony, what a mountayne of housholde cares
5 be there? What mysery feale not they there, whiche proueth and
[Giv] hath experyence therof. In bearyng of offices, how moche
vexacion? how moche labour? and how moche peryl is there?
Whiche waye so euer thou turne thy selfe: an huge company of
incommodytees meteth the. The very lyfe of mortal men of it selfe,
10 without addicion of any other thyng, is combred and tangled with
a thousand myseries: which be commune and indifferent, as well
to good as bad. They al shall growe in to a great heape of merytes
vnto the, yf they shall fynde the in the way of Christ. If not,
they shall be ye more greuous / more ouer fruytlesse / and yet
15 must neuerthelesse be suffred. Who so euer be sowdyours of this
worlde / fyrst how many yeres do they pante / blowe / sweate / and
canuasse the worlde / tourmentynge them selfe with thought and
care? more ouer, for how transytorye, and thynges of naught?
Laste of all, in how doutfull hope? Adde to this, that there is no
20 rest, or easement of myseryes / in so moche that the lenger they
haue laboured, with the more grefe they do labour. And whan all
is paste, what shall the ende be of so tedyous and laborous a lyfe?
veryly eternall punysshment. Go now and with this lyfe compare
the waye of vertue / whiche at the fyrst seaseth to be sharpe / in
25 processe is made easyer / is made plea[G2]saunt and delectable /
by whiche waye also we go with very sure hope to eternall felicite.
Were it not the vttermoste madnesse, to haue leuer with equall
laboure to purchase eternall dethe, rather than lyfe immortall?
Yet are these worldely men moche madder than so / whiche chose
30 with extreme laboure, to go to laboure euerlastynge: rather than

Against ll. 1–2: The lyfe of marchauntes.
Against ll. 4–5: The misery of matrymony.
Again ll. 6–7: In bearynge of offyces.
Again ll. 11–12: A chrysten man obteyneth meryte in euery thynge.
Against l. 30–p. 93, l. 13 (Referring to p. 93, ll. 11–12): Ticius / bycause he wolde haue ioyned with Appollos mother / was caste of apollo down to
hell / where vulters gnawe his herte / euer encreasynge agayne. The meanyng of
the fable is this / he was a great man and coude not be contented but wold haue
more: and aduaunced hym selfe to more honour / and wold haue put Apollo

2 it] om. 1533   6 therof] of it 1533   20 lenger] more 1533   21 with
the more grefe they do labour] the greuouser is the payne 1533   24 sharpe]
tedyous 1533   29 whiche] that they whiche 1533

with meane labours, to go to immortall quyetnesse. More ouer, yf the waye of pietie or obedyence to god, were moche more laboryous, than the waye of the worlde: yet here the greuousnesse of the laboure, is swaged with the hope of rewarde / and the comforte of god is not lackynge, whiche tourneth the bytternesse of the gall in 5 to the swetnesse of hony. There one care calleth in an other / of one sorowe spryngeth an other / no quyetnesse is there at all. The laboui and affliction withoutforth / the greuous cares and thoughtes withinforth, causen the very easementes to be sharpe and bytter. These thynges so to be, was not vnknowen to the poetes of the 10 gentyles. Whiche by the punysshment of Ticius / Ixion / Tantalus / Sisiphus / and of Pentheus / paynted and descryued the myscrablc, and greuous lyfe of lewde and wretched persones. Whose also [G2v] is that late confessyon in the boke of Sapyence. We be weryed in the waye of iniquite and perdicyon / we haue walked 15 harde wayes / but ye waye of god we knewe not. What coude be eyther fylthyer or more laboryous, than the seruytude of Egypte? What coude be greuouser, than the captyuite of Babylon? What more intollerable, than the yoke of Pharao and of Nabugodonosor? But what sayth Chryste? take my yoke vpon your neckes: and ye 20 shall fynde rest vnto your soules? My yoke (saith he) is pleasaunt / and my burthen lyght. To speke breuely / no pleasure is lackynge, where is not lackyng a quiet conscyence. No mysery is there lackynge, where an vnhappy conscyence crucyfyeth the mynde. These thynges must be taken, as of moost certaynte. But and yf thou yet 25

out of his contre / whiche signyfyed by his mother / but Apollo subdued hym and spoyled hym of his possessyons / so that afterward he lyued in care and mysery among the lowest sort / and coude not obtayne any further honour. Yxion was cast of Iuno (lady of honour) into hell / where he ronneth round and contynually compasseth for honor / but he coude not obtayn. Sysyphus rolleth a stone from the hyll fote to the top / than slydeth the stone / and he dyscendeth to fetche hym vp agayne. Ambytion is euer at the hyl foote. He is neuer so hyghe: but that he hathe one hyll more to clym. He seeth one thynge more whiche he coueyteth. Tantalus standeth styl in hell in a ryuer of wyne / euer athurst / and al maner of fruytes aboute hym / and yet he is euer hungry / neither is suffred to drynke or eate. Couetous men dare not vse theyr goodes: but be hungry and thirsty for more. Pentheus was turned in to an hart / and eaten of his owne dogges / and he dyd non other thinge all his lyfe but hunte and folowe dogges / so he consumed hym selfe and his substaunce like a fole wretchedly and beestly.

---

2 moche] so moche *1533*   4 the hope] hope *1533*   9 causen] cause *1533*
13–14 Whose also is that] of whome is also the *1533*   16 knewe] knowe *1533*

Side-note 5: ryuer] *1533*; ryner *1534*

doute, go aske of them whiche in tyme passed haue ben conuerted
out of the myddle of Babylon vnto the lorde: and by experyence
of them at the leestway byleue, nothynge to be more troublous and
greuous than vices: nothyng to be more easy or of quycker spede,
5 than not to be drowned in besynesse / nothynge more cherefull
and more confortable, than is vertue. Neuerthelesse go to, let it be
that the wages be lyke / and that the labours be lyke also / yet for
all that, how greatly [G3] ought a man to desyre to warre vnder the
standarde of Chryst / rather than vnder the banners of the deuyll.
10 Ye how moche leuer were it, to be vexed, or to suffre affliction
with Chryst / than to swymme in pleasures with the deuyl. More
ouer, ought not a man with wynde and wether, with shyppe sayle,
and swyftnes of horses, to flye from a lorde, not very fylthy onely,
but also very cruell and disceytfull: whiche requireth so cruell
15 seruyce, and so strayte a taske / whiche promyseth agayne thynges
so vncertayne, so caduke, so transytory, so soone vadynge and
vanysshynge awaye. Of the whiche self thynges, yet disceyueth he
the wretches, and that not seldome. Or though he perfourme his
promesse ones / yet an other tyme, whan it pleaseth hym, he taketh
20 them awaye agayne / so that the sorowe and thought for the losse
of thynges ones possessed, is moche more than was the greuous
labour in purchasyng them. The marchaunt man, after he hath
myngled togyder bothe ryght and wronge, for the entent of encreasynge his goodes / after he hath put his honest reputacyon of
25 good reporte, that is spronge of hym, his lyfe, his soule in a thousande ieopardyes / be it that the chaunce of fortune happe aryght,
what other thynge with all his [G3v] trauayle hathe he at lengthe
prepared for hym selfe, yf he kepe his goodes, than the mater of
myserable care / yf he lese them, than a perpetuall tourment. But
30 yf fortune chaunce amysse, what remayneth but that he is made

Against ll. 25-6: The troublous care of a marchaunt.

---

6 confortable] comfortable *1533*　　14 but also] but *1533*　　16 so soone]
whiche so sone *1533*　　16-17 vadynge and vanysshynge] fade and vanysshe
1533　　17 self] very same *1533*　　22 The marchaunt man, after he] After
that the merchaunt man *1533*　　26 be it] if it so be than *1533*　　27-8 what
other thynge . . . hathe he at lengthe prepared] at the later ende . . . what other
thynge hath he prepared *1533*　　27 hathe] hath *1533*; hafhe *1534*　　28-9 yf
he kepe his goodes, than the mater of myserable care / yf he lese them, than
a perpetuall tourment] more than the mater of myserable care if he kepe his
goodes / if he lese them a perpetuall tourment *1533*　　29-30 But yf] If *1533*
30 is] shulde be *1533*

Side-note 1: a marchaunt] a marchauntes *1533*

twyse a wretche, wrapped in double mysery / bothe bycause he is
disappoynted of the thyng, wheron his hope hanged / and also
bycause he can not remembre so greate labour spente in waste,
without moche sorowe of herte and grefe of mynde. No man hathe
enforced with sure purpose to comme to good lyuynge or con- 5
uersacyon, whiche hath not attayned it. Chryste as he is not
mocked / so mocketh he not. Remembre also that thynge, whan
thou flyest from the worlde vnto Chryste / yf the worlde haue any
commodytees or pleasures, that thou forsakest them not: but
chaungest tryfles with thynges of more value. Who wyll not be 10
very glad to chaunge syluer for golde / flynte for precyous stone?
Thy frendes be displeased? What than / thou shalte fynde more
pleasaunte and better companyons. Thou shalt lacke outwarde
pleasures of thy body: but thou shalte enioye the inwarde pleasures
of the mynde / whiche be better / purer / and more certayne. 15
Thy good must be dymynysshed? neuerthelesse that ry[G4] chesse
encreaseth, whiche neyther mothes destroye, nor theues take
awaye. Thou ceasest to be of pryce in the worlde: but thou for all
that, arte well beloued of Chryste. Thou pleasest the fewer:
but yet the better. Thy body waxeth leane: but thy mynde waxeth 20
fatte. The beautye of thy skynne vanyssheth awaye: but the beauty
of thy mynde appereth bryght. And in lyke maner, yf thou wylte
ronne through out all other thynges: thou shalt perceyue nothynge
of all these apparant good thinges, to be forsaken in this worlde /
that is not recompensed largely, with greater aduauntage, and more 25
excellent a greate waye. But yf there be any thynges, whiche though
they can not be desyred without vyce: yet without vyce may be
possessed (of whiche kynde of thynges, is the good estymacyon of
the people / fauoure of the communaltye / loue, or to be in conceyte /
authorytc / frendco / honoure dewe vnto vertewe) for the moost 30
parte it chaunseth, that all these be gyuen without serchynge for /
to them that aboue all thynge seke the kyngdome of heuen. Whiche

Against ll. 25–6: Many thynges may be receyued and possessed / but not
desyred.

---

1 bothe] partly *1533*   2 and also] besyde that *1533*   4 moche]
moche bothe *1533*   4–5 hathe enforced] enforseth *1533*   7 mocketh he not] neyther he mocketh any man *1533*   also that] an other *1533*
8 from] out of *1533*   16 that] these *1533*   17 encreaseth] encrease
1533   mothes] the mouthes *1533*   22–3 wylte ronne through out] shalte
reken *1533*   23–4 nothynge of all] nothynge not of all *1533*   30 vnto]
to *1533*   31 these] these thinges *1533*

selfe thynge Chryste promysed, and god performed to Salomon.
Fortune for the moost parte, foloweth them that flye from her / and
flyeth from them that fo[G4v]lowe her. Certaynly what so euer
shall happen to them that loue: nothynge can be but prosperous,
5 vnto whome losse is tourned to aduauntage, tourment, vexacyon
or aduersytye to solace, rebukes to laude, punysshment to pleasure
and conforte, bytter thynges to swete, euyll thynges to good.
Doutest thou than to entre in to this waye, and forsake that other
waye / seynge there is so vnequall comparyson / ye none at all / of
10 god vnto the deuyll / of hope to hope / of rewarde to rewarde / of
labour to labour / of solace to solace?

⁋ The fourth rule. Caplo. xij.

BVt that thou mayst haste and make spede vnto felicite with a
more sure course / let this be vnto the, the fourth rule / that thou
15 haue Chryste alwaye in thy syght, as the onely marke of all thy lyuynge and conuersacyon / vnto whome onely thou sholdest dyrect al
thyne enforcementes / all thy pastymes and purposes / al thy rest
and quietnesse / and also thy besynesse. And thynke thou not
Christ to be a voyce or a sounde without signyfycacyon: but thynke
20 hym to be nothynge els, saue charite, symplicite, innocencye,
pacience, clennesse / and shortly, what so euer Chryste [G5]
taught. Vnderstande well also, that the deuyll is none other thynge,
but what so euer calleth away from suche thynges as Chryste taught.
He directeth his iourney to Christ, whiche is caryed to vertue onely.
25 And he becommeth bonde to the deuyll, whiche gyueth hym selfe
to vyces. Let thyne eye therfore be pure / and all thy body shall
be bryght and full of lyght. Let thyne eye loke vnto Chryste all
onely, as vnto onely and very felicite / so that thou loue nothynge /
meruayle at nothyng / desyre nothynge, but eyther Chryste, or for
30 Chryst. Hate nothyng, abhorre nothyng, flye nothynge, nothynge
auoyde, but onely synne, or elles for synnes sake. By this meanes it

Against ll. 13–15: Let Chryste be thy marke and ensample of liuyng.
Against l. 19: What christ is.
Against ll. 22–3: What the deuyll is.

2 flye] flyeth *1533*   7 and conforte] *om. 1533*   swete] swetnesse *1533*
12 Caplo.] cap. *1533*   19 a sounde] sounde *1533*   20 symplicite, in-
nocencye] symplycite / or innocency *1533*   29–30 or for Chryst] or els
for Christe *1533*   30 Hate] Also that thou hate *1533*

wyll comme to passe, that what so euer thou shalt do, whether thou
slepe, whether thou wake, whether thou eate, whether thou drynke /
and to conclude, that thy very sportes and pastymes / yea (I wyll
speke more boldly) that some vices of the lyghter sorte, in to whiche
we fall now and than, whyle we haste to vertue / all the hole shal 5
growe and tourne in the, vnto a great heape of rewardes. But and
yf thyne eye shall not be pure: but loke any other warde than
vnto Chryste / yea thoughe thou do certayne thynges, whiche be
good or honest of them selfe / [G5v] yet shall they be vnfruytfull,
or peraduenture very peryllous and hurtfull. For it is a great faute 10
to do a good thynge not well. And therfore that man that hasteth
the streyght waye vnto the marke of very felicite / what so euer
thynges shall comme and mete hym by ye waye: so farforth ought
he eyther refuse or receyue them, as they eyther further or hinder
his iourney. Of whiche thynges there be thre orders or thre degrees. 15
Certayne thynges verily, be in suche maner fylthy: that they can
not be honest / as to auenge wronge / to wysshe euyll to another.
These thinges ought alway to be had in hate / ye though thou
sholdest haue neuer so great aduauntage to commyt them / or
neuer so great punysshment, if thou dyddest them not. For nothyng 20
can hurt a good man, but fylthynes onely. Certeyn thinges on
thother syde be in suche maner honest: that they cannot be
fylthy. Of whiche kynde be, to wyll or wysshe all men good / to
helpe thy frendes with honest meanes / to hate vices / to reioyce
with vertuous communycacion. Certeyn thinges veryly be in- 25
different or bytwene bothe / of theyr owne nature neyther good nor
bad / honest nor fylthy: as helth, beaute, strength, facoundiousnes,
connyng, and suche other. Of this last kynde of thynges therfore
nothing ought [G6] to be desyred, for it selfe: neyther ought to
be vsurped more or lesse / but as farforth as they make and be 30
necessary to ye chefe marke / I meane to folowe Christes lyuyng.
The very philosophers haue certayne markes also vnperfyt and
indifferent / in whiche a man ought not to stande styll nor tary /

Against ll. 14–15: Howe ferforthe thynges profered vnsought for ought to be
refused.
Against ll. 17–18: (Referring to l. 15): Thre orders of thynges.
Against ll. 21–2: Thynges honest.
Against ll. 25–6: Thynges indifferent.

16 in] of *1533*   fylthy] fylthe *1533*
Side-note 4: *om. 1533*

whiche also a man may conueniently vse / referring them to a better purpose / but not enioye them, and tary vpon them / settyng his herte in them. Notwithstanding those meane and indifferent thynges, do not all after one maner and equally, eyther further or
5 hynder them that be goyng vnto Christ. Therfore they must be receiued or refused, after as eche of them is more or lesse of value vnto thi purpose. Knowlege helpeth more vnto pietie than beautye, or strengthe of body, or ryches. And though all lernyng may be applyed to Chryst: yet some helpeth more compendyously than
10 some. Of this ende and purpose se thou measure ye profitablenes or vnprofitablenes of all meane thynges. Thou louest lernyng: it is very well, yf thou do it for Chrystes sake. But yf thou loue it therfore onely, bicause thou woldest knowe it: than makest thou a stop and a restyng place there, from whens thou oughtest to haue made
15 a step to clymbe further. But if thou desyre sciences, that thou by their helpe, migh[G6v]test more clerely beholde Christ, hyd in the secretes of scripture / and whan thou knowest hym, loue hym / whan thou knowest and louest hym, teche, declare, and open hym to other men / and profyte, or take fruyte of him thyself: than prepare
20 thyself vnto study of scyences. But no further, than thou mayst thynke them profytable to good lyuyng. If thou haue confidence in thy selfe, and trust to haue great aduauntage in Chryste: go forth lyke a marchaunt venterer, bolde to walke as a straunger somwhat further / ye in the lernynge of gentyles / and apply the rychesse or
25 treasure of the egypciens, vnto the honestynge of the temple of god. But and yf thou feare greater losse than thou hopest of aduauntage: than returne agayn to our fyrst rule. Knowe thy selfe, and passe not thy boundes / kepe the within thy lystes. It is better to haue lesse knowlege, and more loue: than moche to knowe, and not to
30 loue. Knowlege therfore hath the maystrye or chefe rowme amonge meane thinges. After that is helth / the gyftes of nature / eloquence /

Against ll. 7–9: Pietie signifyeth seruyce / honour / reuerence / obedyence due to god.
Against ll. 14–16 (Referring to l. 11): Science must be loued for Christes sake.
Against ll. 25–8: How ferforth the letters of the gentyles be to be red / loke in the seconde chapitre what this meaneth.

2 but] and *1533*   enioye] to enioy *1533*   2–3 settyng his herte] putting his hole felycite *1533*   14 a restyng place] taryeng *1533*   19 profyte, or take fruyte of him thyself] in thy selfe enioye hym *1533*   23 lyke a marchaunt venterer, bolde] boldly as an aduenterous merchaunt *1533*   29 more] more of *1533*   moche to knowe] to haue more of knowlege *1533*   30 amonge] amongest *1533*

beaute / strength / dignite / fauour / authorite / prosperite / good reputacyon / kynne / frendes / stuffe of housholde. Euery one of these thynges, as it helpeth moost and nyghest waye vnto vertue: so shall it moost chefely be applyed, in case they be [G7] offred vnto vs hastyng in our way. If not than we may not for 5 cause of them turne asyde from our iourney purposed. Money is chaunced vnto the / yf it let nothyng to good lyuynge / mynyster it / make frendes with ye wycked mammon. But yf thou feare the losse of vertue and of good mynde: despyse that aduauntage, full of domage and losse / and folowe thou euen Crates of Thebes, 10 flynge thy greuous and comberous packe in to the see / rather than it sholde holde the backe from Chryste. That thynge mayst thou do the easylyer: yf (as I haue sayd) thou shalte custome thy selfe to meruayle at none of those thinges, whiche be without the (that is to say) whiche pertayne not vnto the inner man. For by that meanes 15 it wyll comme to passe, that thou canst neyther wax proude or forgete thy self, yf these thynges fortune vnto the, neyther thou shalt be vexed in thy mynde, yf they sholde eyther be denyed the, or taken from the: for as moche as thou puttest thy hole felicite in Chryste onely. But and yf it chaunce they comme vnto ye besydes 20 thyne owne labour / be thou the more diligent and circumspect / and not the more carelesse: this wyse thynkynge, that a mater to exercise thy selfe vertuously on, is gyuen to the of god / but yet not without ieopardy and daunger. But yf thou [G7v] haue the benignite of fortune suspected, counterfeyte Prometheus / do not 25

Against ll. 6–7: Money shuld this wyse be loued.

Against ll. 9–16: Crates of the cite of Thebes cast a gret sum of golde in to the see / sayeng hence ye mischeuous richesse / better it is that I drowne you / than you me. He supposed that he coude not possesse rychesse and vertue bothe togyther.

Against l. 24, p. 100, l. 10. Dycause Prometheus had made a man of cley and with fire stolen from heuen put lyfe in to hym: Iupyter sent Pandor a woman with a boxe ful of al kindes of disesis to him / but prometheus was prouidid and refusid it / but his broder Epimetheus receiued it and opened it / and than all maner of sycknesses flewe abrode. Prometheus taught rude men ciuyle and honest maner / yet wolde he bere no rule amongest them / but fled to solitarynes / thynkyng al kyndes of mysery to be in berynge rule / but his broder Epymetheus toke the misery vpon hym.

6–7 is chaunced] chaunsed *1533*   8–9 the losse] losse *1533*   9 of good] good *1533*   11 flynge] flyeng *1533*   21 thou the] *om. 1533*   22 and not the more carelesse] hauyng no lesse care than thou haddest before *1533* this wyse thynkynge] haue in mynde *1533*

Side-note 1: shuld] suhlde *1533*

receyue the disceytfull boxe / and go lyght and naked vnto that,
which is onely very felicite. Certaynly who so euer with great
thought and care desyre money as a precyous thynge / and count
the chefe socour of lyfe to be therin / thynkyng them selfe happy,
5 as longe as it is safe / callyng them selfe wretches whan it is lost:
those men no doubte haue made and feyned vnto them selfe many
goddes. Thou hast set vp thy money and made it equall vnto
Chryst / if it can make the happy or vnhappy. That I haue spoken
of money, vnderstande the same lykewyse of honours, voluptuous-
10 nesse, helthe, yea and of the very lyfe of the body. We must enforce
to comme to our onely marke, whiche is Chryste, so feruently,
that we sholde haue no leyser to care for any of these thynges:
eyther whan they be gyuen vs / or elles whan they be taken from vs.
For the tyme is shorte, as sayth Paule. Hence forwarde sayth he,
15 they that vse the worlde / must be as they used it not. This mynde
I knowe well the worlde laugheth to scorne, as folysshe and
mad: neuerthelesse it hath pleased god by this folysshnesse to saue
them that byleue. And the folysshnesse of god, is wyser than man.
After this rule thou shalt ex[G8]amyn / yea what so euer thou doest.
20 Thou exercysest a crafte? it is very well done, yf thou do it without fraude. But whervnto lokest thou? to fynde thy housholde?
But for what entent to fynde thy housholde? to wyn thy housholde
to Chryst? thou ronnest wel. Thou fastest / verily a good werke, as
it appereth outward. But vnto what ende referrest thou thy fast /
25 to spare thy vytayles, or that thou mayst be counted the more holy?
Thyne eye is wycked, corrupt, and not pure. Peraduenture thou
fastest, lest thou sholde fall in to some disease or sycknesse. Why
fearest thou sycknesse? leest it wolde take the from the vse of voluptuous pleasures. Thyne eye is vicyous and fawty. But thou desyrest
30 helth, bycause thou mayst be able to study. To what purpose I
beseche the referrest thou thy study? to gete ye a benefyce withall?
With what mynde desyrest thou a benefyce? veryly, to lyue at
thyne owne pleasure / not at Chrystes. Thou hast myssed the marke,
whiche a chrysten man ought to haue euerywhere prefixed before
35 his eyes. Thou takest meate y^t thou myghtest be strong in thy
body / and thou wilt haue thy body strong, that thou mightest be

Against ll. 20–1: Whan labour is profytable.
Against ll. 23–4: Whan fastynge is supersticious.

6 and] or *1533*   17 hath pleased] pleaseth *1533*   24 fast] selfe
1533   26 wycked] wanton *1533*   29 vicyous and fawty] corrupt *1533*

sufficyent vnto holy exercises and watche. Thou hast hyt the marke. But thou takest hede to thy helth and lyuynge, leest thou sholdest [G8v] be more euyll fauoured or deformed / leest thou sholdest not be stronge ynough vnto bodyly lust / thou hast fallen from Chryst, makyng vnto the an other god. There be that honour 5 certeyn sayntes with certeyn ceremonyes. One saluteth Christofer euery daye / but not excepte he beholde his ymage. Whether loketh he? veryly to this poynte. He hath borne hym selfe in hande that he shal be all that day sure from euyl deth. An other worshyppeth one Rochus / but why? bycause he byleueth that he wyl kepe awaye 10 the pestylence from his body. An other mombleth certayne prayers to Barbara or George / lest he shold fall in to his ennemyes handes. This man fasteth to saint Apolyne, leest his tethe shold ake. That man visiteth ye ymage of holy Iob / bycause he wolde be with-out scabbes. Some assygne and name a certayne porcion of their 15 wynnyng to poore men / lest their marchaundyse sholde perysshe by shyp wrake. A taper is lyght before Hieron, to the entent that thynge whiche is lost, may be had agayne. In conclusyon, after this maner, loke how many thinges be, whiche we eyther feare, or coueyte: so many sayntes haue we made gouernours of the same 20 thynges. Whiche same sayntes also be dyuerse to dyuerse nacyons: so that Paule [H1] dothe the same thyng among the frensshe men, that Hieron dothe with our countrey men the almayns / and neyther Iames, nor Iohan can do that thynge euery where, whiche they do in this or y^t place. Whiche honouryng of sayntes trewly / 25 except it be referred from ye respect of corporal commodytees or incommodytees vnto Chryst / is not for a chrysten man / in so

Against ll. 4–5: The supersticious honouring of sayntes.
Against l. 6: Christopher.
Against l. 10: Rochus.
Against l. 11: Barbara.
Against l. 12: George.
Against l. 13: Appolyne.
Against l. 14: Iob.
Against l. 17: Hieron.

1 Thou] thou *1533, 1534*   2 takest hede to] prouydest for *1533* thy] *om. 1533*   lyuynge] good lyuing *1533*   5 that] whiche *1533* 14 wolde] shulde *1533*   15 a certayne] certayne *1533*   17 Hieron] saynt Hierom *1533*   the entent] thentent *1533*   19 maner] same maner *1533*   19–20 feare, or coueyte] fauour or els loue *1533*   21 also] *om.* *1533* to dyuerse nacyons] in dyuers natures *1533*   24 euery where] in euery where *1533*

moche y^t it is not farre from ye supersticiousnesse of them, whiche
in tyme passed vowed ye tenth parte of their goodes to Hercules /
to thentent they myght waxe ryche. Or a cocke to Esculapius, that
they myght be recouered of theyr diseases. Or whiche sacryfyced
5 a bull to Neptunus, that they myght haue good passage by see,
and prosperous saylyng. The names be chaunged / but veryly they
haue bothe one ende and entent. Thou prayest god, that thou mayst
not dye to soone / or whyle thou art yong: and prayest not rather
that he wolde gyue to the a good mynde, that in what so euer place
10 deth shold comme vpon the, he myght not fynde the vnprepared.
Thou thynkest not of chaungynge thy lyfe / and prayest god thou
myghtest not dye. What prayest thou for than? certeynly that
thou myghtest synne as long as is possyble. Thou desyrest ryches:
and can not vse ryches. Doest not thou than desyre thyne [H1v]
15 owne confusyon? Thou desyrest helth, and canst not vse helth / is
not now thy godlynes made deuyllysshe and wycked? In this place
I am sure some of our holy relygyous men, wyll crye out agaynst
me, with open mouthes / whiche thynke lucre to be to the honouring
of god / and (as the same Paule sayth) with certayne swete benedic-
20 tions, deceyue the myndes of innocent persones, seruyng theyr
owne belyes / and not Iesu Chryste. Than wyll they saye / forbyd-
dest thou worshyppyng of sayntes, in whome god is honoured? I
veryly disprayse not them so greatly, which do these thynges of a
certayne symple and chyldysshe supersticyon, for lacke of instruc-
25 tion, or capacite of wytte / as I do them, whiche sekyng theyr owne
aduauntage, prayseth and magnyfyeth those thynges for most
great and perfyte holynesse / whiche peraduenture be tollerable
and may be suffred / and for theyr owne profyte and aduauntage,
cherysshe and mayntayne the ignoraunce of the people, (whiche
30 neyther I my selfe do vtterly despyse) but I can not suffre that they
sholde accompte thynges to be hyghest and moost chefe, which of

Against ll. 3–4: A cocke to Esculapius.
Against ll. 5–6: A bull to Neptunus.
Against ll. 7–8: Thou prayest for longe lyfe.
Against ll. 23–5: They accompte the honouryng of sainctes for absolute
piete.

10 myght] shulde *1533*   16 godlynes made deuyllysshe and wycked]
honouryng of god dishonouryng of god *1533*   17 relygyous] *om. 1533*
20–1 seruyng theyr owne belyes] whyle they obey and serue their bely *1533*
22 worshyppyng] worshyp — *1533*   23 these] those *1533*   of a] with
1533   27 whiche] whiche thynges *1533*   30 vtterly] *om. 1533*

them selfe be neyther good nor bad / and those to be greatest and of moost value, whiche be smallest and of leest value. I wyll prayse it and be content, that they de[H2]syre theyr lyues helth of Rochus, whome they so greatly honour / so that they consecrate that lyfe vnto Chryste. But I wyll prayse them more, yf they wolde praye 5 for nothyng els, but that with the hate of vices, the loue of vertues myght be encreased. And as touchyng to lyue or to dye, let them put it in to the handes of god / and let them saye with Paule / whether we lyue, whether we dye / to god and at goddes pleasure we lyue or dye. It shall be a perfyte thyng, yf they desyre to be dissolued 10 from the body, and to be with Christ, yf they put their glory and ioye in diseases or sycknes / in losse or other domages of fortune, bycause they be accompted worthy, euen after this maner to be made lyke or confyrmable vnto theyr heed. To do therfore suche maner thynges: is not so moche to be rebuked, as it is peryllous to 15 abyde styll and cleue to them. I suffre and permyt infirmite and weyknes: but with Paule I shewe a more excellent waye. If thou shalte examyne thy studyes, and all thy actes by this rule, and shalt not stande any where in meane thinges, tyl thou comme euen vnto Christ: thou shalte neyther go out of thy waye at any tyme / neyther 20 shalt do or suffre any thyng in all thy lyfe, whiche shall not turne and be vnto the a mater of pietie. [H2v]

❡ The fyfth rule. Caplo. xiij.

LEt vs adde also the fyfth rule as an ayder vnto this foresaid fourth rule, that thou put perfyte pietie in this thyng onely: yf 25 thou shalte enforce alwaye from thynges visyble, whiche almost euery one be imperfyte, or els indifferent, to ascende to thynges inuysyble, after the dyuysyon of a man aboue rehersed. This precepte

Against ll. 17–22: Piety is the reuerent love and honour which the inferiors haue towarde theyr superiors / whiche is chefly requyred / and therfore it is that perfytenes of a chrysten man.
Against l. 25: Perfite pietie.

1 those] those thynged 1533   3 theyr lyues] om. 1533   4 so that] if 1533   that lyfe] it 1533   5 them] it 1533   13 bycause] yᵗ 1533 be] might be 1533   13–14 euen after this maner to be made] whiche euen in this worlde shulde be 1533   15 maner] maner of 1533   16 and permyt] om. 1533   22 pietie] seruynge and honourynge god 1533   23 Caplo.] capi. 1533   25 pietie] pity / that is to saye the honouryng of god 1533
Side-note 1: om. 1533

is appertaynyng to the mater so necessarily / that whether it be
through neclygence, or els for lacke of knowlege therof / the most
parte of chrysten men, in stede of true honourers of god, are but
playne superstycyous / and in all other thynges, saue in the name
5 of chrysten men onely, vary not greatly from the superstycyon
of the gentyles. Let vs ymagyn therfore two worldes / the
one intellygyble, the other vysyble. The intelligible, whiche also
we may call the angelycall worlde / wherin god is with blessed
myndes. The visyble worlde / the circles of heuen / the planettes
10 and sterres / with all that included is in them. Than let vs ymagyn
man as a certayne thyrde worlde / parte taker of bothe the other : of
the visyble worlde yf thou beholde his body / of the inuysyble
worlde yf thou consyder his soule. In the vysyble worlde, bycause
[H3] we be but straungers, we ought neuer rest / but what thynge
15 so euer offreth it selfe to the sencyble powers / that must we vnder
a certayne apte comparyson or symylytude, apply eyther to the
angelycall worlde / or els (whiche is more profytable) vnto maners,
and to that parte of man whiche is corespondent to the angelyke
worlde. What this visyble sonne is in the visible worlde, that is the
20 dyuyne mynde in the intellygyble worlde / and in that parte of the,
whiche is of that same nature / that is to saye, in the spiryte. Loke
what the moone is in the visyble worlde / that in the inuysyble worlde
is the congregacyon of aungels, and of blessed soules, called the
triumphant churche / and that in the is the spiryte. What so euer
25 heuens aboue worketh in the erthe vnder them / that same dothe god
in the soule. The sonne gothe downe, aryseth / rageth in heate / is
temperate / quyckeneth / bryngeth forth / maketh rype / draweth
to hym / maketh subtyle and thynne / purgeth / hardeneth / molly-
fyeth / illumyneth / clereth / cheryssheth, and comforteth. Therfore
30 what so euer thou beholdest in hym / yea what so euer thou seest in
this grosser worlde of the elementes (whiche many haue separated
from the heuens aboue and circles of the fyr[H3v]mament) in

Against l. 5 : Two worldes.
Against ll. 21-2 (Referring to ll. 19-20) : The sonne is the dyuyne mynde of
god.

2 els] *om. 1533*   therof] of it *1533*   9 circles] cyrcle *1533*
10 them] them as the foure elementes *1533*   15 powers] powers / that is to
say to the fyue wyttes *1533*   16 eyther] *om. 15333*   17 more]
most *1533*   19 worlde²] worlde / that is to say to the soule of man *1533*
20 mynde] mynde / that is to say god *1533*   31 this grosser] the grosse parte
of this *1533*

conclusion, what so euer thou consyderest in the grosser parte of thy selfe: accustome to applye it to god, and to the inuysyble porcyon of thy selfe. So shall it comme to passe, that what so euer thynge shall any where offer it selfe to any of the sensyble wyttes: that same thynge shall be to the an occasyon of pietye. Whan it 5 delyteth thy corporall eyes, as ofte as this vysyble sonne spredeth hym selfe on the erth with newe lyght: by and by call to remembraunce, how greate the pleasure is of the inhabytauntes of heuen / vnto whome the eternall sonne euer spryngeth and aryseth / but neuer goth downe. How greate are the ioyes of that pure mynde, 10 whervpon the lyght of god alwayes shyneth and casteth his beames. Thus by occasyon of the vysyble creature praye with the wordes of Paule / that he whiche commaunded lyght to shyne out of darknesse, may shyne in thy herte / to gyue lyght and knowlege of the glorye of god in the face of Iesu Chryste. Repete suche lyke places 15 of holy scripture, in whiche here and there the grace of the spiryte of god, is compared to lyght. The nyght semeth tedyous to the and darke / thynke on a soule destytute of the lyght of god, and darke with vices. Yea and yf thou canst perceyue any [H4] darknesse of nyght in the: praye that the sonne of iustyce may aryse vnto the. 20 This wyse thynke, and surely byleue, that the thynges inuysyble are so excellent, so pure and so perfyte / that the visyble thynges in comparyson of them, are scarse very shadowes, representyng to the eyes a small and a thynne simylytude of them. Therfore in these outwarde and corporal thynges, what so euer thy sensyble wyttes 25 eyther desyre or abhorre: it shal be mete y^t the spiryt moche more loue or hate the same in inward and incorporall thynges. The goodly beaute of thy body pleaseth thyne eyes: thinke than how honest a thynge is the beaute of the soule. A deformed vysage semeth an

Against ll. 4–5: The occasyon of pietie.
Against ll. 11–17: The glory of god appered in the face of moyses / but we behold the glory of god in the face of Iesus Chryste. The grace of god is called lyght / and nyght is compared to synne.
Against l. 28–p. 106, l. 2: What so euer is perceyued in the body / that same is to be vnderstande in the mynde.

---

5 pietye] pity / to honour god *1533*
inuysible whiche thou seest not *1533*
thynges] thinges whiche be sene *1533*
warde *1533*   26 mete] a gret deale meter *1533*
27 same] same thynge *1533*

21 the thynges inuysyble] thinges
22 and] *om. 1533*   the visyble
24–5 these outwarde and] this out-
moche more] *om. 1533*

Side-note 2: to] *1533*; is *1534*

vnplesaunt thyng: remember how odious a thing is a mynde defyled with vyces. And of all other thinges do lykewyse. For as the soule hath certeyn beaute wherwith one whyle she pleaseth god / and a deformite wherwith an other whyle she pleaseth ye deuyll / lyke
5 pleasyng lyke: so hath she also her youth, her age, sycknes, helth, deth, lyfe, pouerte, ryches, ioye, sorowe, warre, peace, colde, heate, thurste, drynke, hunger, meate. To conclude shortly, what so euer is felt in the body / that same is to be vnderstande in the soule. Therfore in this thynge resteth the iourney to the spirytuall and
10 pure lyfe / yf by [H4v] a lytell and lytell we shall accustome to withdrawe our selfe from these thynges whiche be not trewly in very dede: but partely appere to be, that they be not / as fylthy and voluptuous pleasure / honour of this worlde, partely vanysshe awaye, and haste to retourne to naught / and shall be rauysshed and
15 caryed to these thynges, whiche in dede are eternall, immutable, and pure. Whiche thynge Socrates sawe full well / a philosopher not so moche in tonge and wordes, as in lyuyng and dedes. For he sayth, that so onely, shall the soule departe happely from her body at the last ende: yf aforehande she haue dylygently through true know-
20 lege recorded and practised deth, and also haue longe tyme before, by the despysynge of thynges corporall / and by the contemplacyon and loue of thynges spirytuall, vsed her selfe to be as it were in a maner absent from the body. Neyther that crosse, vnto whiche Chryste calleth and exhorteth vs / neyther that deth in whiche
25 Paule wylleth vs to dye with our heed / as also the prophete sayth, for thy sake we be slayne all the daye longe / we be accompted as shepe appoynted to be kylled / neyther that whiche the apostle wryteth in other termes, sayenge / seke those thynges that be aboue / not whiche [H5] be on the erthe, Taste and haue perceyuaunce of
30 thynges aboue / meaneth or is any other thynge, than that we, vnto thynges corporall sholde be dull and made as though we were insensyble and vtterly without capacite. So that the lesse fealynge we haue in thynges of the body: so moche the more swetnesse we myght fynde in thynges pertaynynge to the spiryte. And myght
35 begyn to lyue so moche the trewlyer inwardly in the spiryte / the lesse we lyued outwardly in the body. In conclusyon to speke more

Against ll. 12–13: The nature of filthy pleasure.
Against ll. 23–4: What is the crosse of christ.

4–5 lyke pleasyng lyke] as lyke vnto lyke *1533*   8 felt] fylthy *1533*
22 loue] louyng *1533*   23 that] the *1533*   30 or is] it *1533*

playnly / so moche the lesse sholde moue vs thynges caduke and transytorye / the more acquaynted we were with thynges eternall. So moche the lesse sholde we regarde the shadowes of thynges: the more we haue begon to loke vp vpon the very true thynges. This rule therfore must be had euer redy at hande / that we in no wyse 5 stande styll any where in temporall thynges: but that we ryse thence, makynge as it were a steppe vnto the loue of spirituall thynges, by matchyng the one with the other. Or els in comparyson of thynges whiche are inuysyble, that we begyn to despyse that, whiche is vysyble. The disease of thy body wyll be the easyer, yf 10 thou woldest thynke it to be a remedy for thy soule. [H5v] Thou sholdest care the lesse for the helthe of thy body: yf thou woldest tourne all thy care, to defende and mayntayne the helthe of the mynde. The deth of the body putteth the in feare / the deth of the soule is moche more to be feared. Thou abhorrest ye poyson which 15 thou seest with thyne eyes / bycause it bryngeth myschefe to the body / moche more is the poyson to be abhorred which sleeth the soule. Cicuta is a poyson to ye body / but voluptuousnes is a moche more redy poyson to the soule. Thou quakest and tremblest for feare / thy heare standeth vpryght, thou art spechelesse, thy spirytes 20 forsaken the, and thou waxest pale, fearyng leest the lyghtnynge, whiche appereth out of the clowdes sholde smyte the: but how moche more is it to be feared, leest there comme on the, the inuy- syble lyghtnynge of the wrathe of god / whiche sayth. Go ye cursed persones in to eternall fyre? The beaute of the body rauyssheth the / 25 why rather louest thou not feruently that fayrnesse whiche is not seen? Translate thy loue in to that beaute whiche is perpetuall / whiche is celestial / whiche is without corrupcyon / and the dis- cretelyer shalte thou loue the caduke and transytory shappe of the body. Thou prayest that thy felde may be watred with rayne [H6] 30 lest it drye vp / praye rather that god wyll vouchesafe to water thy mynde, leest it waxe bareyn from the fruyte of vertues. Thou restorest and encreasest agayne with great care, the waste of thy

Against ll. 17–18: Cicuta is a poyson erbe.
Against l. 33–p. 108, l. 15: The mysterye in all thynges must be loked vpon. Holy scrypture is Sylenus of Alcybyades. Sylenus be ymages made with ioyntes / so that they may be opened contaynynge outwarde the symylytude of a

4 the very] the the very *1533*   18 a poyson] poyson *1533*   to] of *1533*
18–19 a moche more] moche more and *1533*   23 comme] shulde come *1533*
23–4 inuysyble] inuysybe *1533*   26 whiche] y^t *1533*   27 whiche] that
1533   28 whiche^1] that *1533*   whiche^2] that *1533*

money: the greatest care of all oughtest thou haue, to restore agayne
the losse of the mynde. Thou hast a respecte longe afore hande to
age / leest any thynge sholde be lackyng to thy body: and sholdest
thou not prouyde, that nothynge be lackynge to the mynde? And
5 this veryly ought to be done in those thynges, whiche dayly meteth
our sensyble wyttes / and as euery thynge is of a dyuerse kynde / euen
so dyuersly dothe moue vs with hope / feare / loue / hate / sorowe and
ioye. The same thynge must be obserued in all maner of lernyng,
whiche include in them selfe a playne sence and a mystery / euen
10 as they were made of a body and a soule / that the lytterall sence
lytell regarded, thou loke chefely to the mystery. Of whiche maner
are the lettres of all poetes and philosophers, chefely the folowers of
Plato. But moost of al holy scripture / whiche beynge in a maner lyke
vnto Silenus of Alcibiades / vnder a rude and folysshe couerynge,
15 include pure diuyne and godly thynges. For els yf thou shalte rede
without ye allegory, the ymage [H6v] of Adam fourmed of moyst
cley, and the soule brethed in to hym / Eue taken out of the rybbe /
the eatynge of the tree forbydden / the serpent entysynge to eate /
god walkynge at the ayre / whan they knewe they had synned / how
20 they hydde them selfe / the aungell set at the dores with a tournynge sworde, leest after they were eiecte / the waye to them sholde
be open to comme agayne shortly. If thou sholdest rede the hole
hystorye of the makynge of the worlde / yf thou sholdest rede (I
saye) superfycyally these thynges / sekynge no further than apper-
25 eth outwardly / I can not perceyue what other greate thynge thou
shalt do, than yf thou haddest songe of the ymage of cley made by
Prometheus / or of the fyre stolen from heuen by deceyte and put
in to the ymage, gaue lyfe to the cley. Yea peraduenture a poetes
fable in the allegory, shall be redde with somwhat more fruyte, than

fole or an ape or suche like tryfles / and whan they are opened / sodenly apereth
some excellent or meruaylous thynge. Vnto suche thinges alcibiades a noble
man of Athenes compared the phylosopher Socrates / for Socrates was so
simple outward and so excellent inwarde.

Against l. 28–p. 109, l. 5: The fable of the gyauntes / A great nombre of
gyauntes buylded mountayne vpon mountayne to pluck Iupyter out of heuen /
but Iupiter vndermyned theyr mountaynes and slewe them with lyghtnynge.

---

8 obserued] obserued and kepte *1533*   11 loke] shuldest loke *1533*
14 vnto] to *1533*   17 Eue] and Eue *1533*   taken] plucked *1533*   18 the
eatynge of the tree forbydden] howe they were forbyd the tree of knowlege of
good and yuell *1533*   23 sholdest] *om. 1533*   26 haddest songe]
shuldest synge *1533*   27 the fyre] fyre *1533*   deceyte] subtyltie *1533*
28 gaue] to gyue *1533*

a narracyon of holy bokes / yf thou rest in the rynde or vtter parte.
If whan thou redest the fable of the gyauntes / it warneth and
putteth the in remembraunce, that thou stryue not with god, and
thynges more myghty than thou / or that thou oughtest to abstayne
from such studyes, as nature abhorreth / and that thou sholdest 5
sette thy mynde vnto [H7] these thynges (yf soo be they be honest)
whervnto thou art moost apte naturally. That thou tangle not thy
selfe with matrymony / yf chastite be morc agreable to thy maners.
Agayne that thou bynde not thy selfe to chastyte / yf thou seme
more apte to maryage. For most communly those thynges comme 10
euyll to passe, whiche thou prouest agaynst nature. If the cuppe of
Cyrces teche, that men with voluptuousnes, as with wytchecrafte
fall out of their mynde, and be chaunged vtterly fro men vnto
beestes. If thyrsty Tantalus teche the, that it is a very myserable
thynge for a man, to syt gapyngc vpon his rychesse heaped togyder, 15
and dare not vse them. The stone of Siciphus, that ambicyon is
laboryous and myserable. If the labours of Hercules putteth the in
remembraunce that heuen must be opteyned with honest labours
and enforcementes infatygable: lernest thou not that thynge in the
fable, whiche philosophers teache, and also dyuynes, the maysters 20
of good lyuyng. But yf (without allegory) thou shalte rede the infantes wrestlyng in theyr mothers bely, thinherytaunce of the elder
brother solde for a messe of potage / the blessynge of the father
preuented and taken away by fraude. Golye smytten with the
slynge of Da[H7ᵛ]uid / and the heare of Sampson shauen: it is not 25
of so greate valure, as yf thou sholdest rede the feynyng of some
poete. What difference is there, whether thou rede the boke of
kynges, or of the iudges in the olde testament / or els the history of
Titus Liuius / so that thou haue respect to the allegorye in nere
nother? For in that historye arc many thynges, whiche may amende 30

Against ll. 10–14: Circes was a woman which by enchauntment turned men
to dyuers fascions of bestes / with poisons or drenches.
Against l. 14: Tantalus.
Against l. 15 (Referring to l. 16): Sysyphus.
Against ll. 17–18: The labours of Hercules.
Against ll. 20–1: Without allegory / scripture is bareyn.
Against ll. 26–9 (Referring to l. 30–p. 110 l. 3): Many vngoodly thynges in
scrypture / as they appere outwarde.

20 philosophers] yᵉ philosophers *1533*   the maysters] maisters *1533*
29 so that] so *1533*   30 that historye] the one / that is to say Titus Liuyus
1533   are] be *1533*   may] wolde *1533*
    Side-note 6: Many] *1533*; Mauy *1534*

the commune maners: in the other are some thynges / ye vngoodly,
as they seme at the first lokyng on / whiche also yf they be vnderstande superficially, may hurt good maners. As the theft of Dauid /
and adultery bought with homicide. The vehement loue of Samp-
5 son. How the doughters of Lot lay with theyr father by stelthe /
and were conceyued / and a thousande other lyke maters. Therfore
the flesshe of scriptur euery where despised, but chefely of the
olde testament: it shall be mete and conuenyent to serche out the
mystery of the spiryte. Manna to the shall haue suche taste as thou
10 bringest with the in thy mouth. But in openynge of mysteryes,
thou mayst not folowe the coniectures of thyne owne mynde / but
the rule must be knowen and a certayne crafte / whiche one Dionisius teacheth in a boke entyteled De diuinis nominibus / that is to
saye / of the names of god: and saynt [H8] Augustyne in a certayne
15 warke called Doctrina christiana / that is to saye / the doctryne of
a christen man. The apostle Paule after Chryste, opened certayne
fountaynes of allegoryes / whome Origene folowed / and in that parte
of diuynite obtayned doubtlesse the chefe rowme and maystrye.
But oure dyuynes eyther set naught by the allegorye / or handle
20 it very dreamyngly and vnfruytfully: yet are they in subtyltye of
disputacyon equall, or rather superyours to olde dyuynes. But in
treatynge of this crafte / that is to saye, in pure, apte, and fruytfull
handlyng the allegorye, not ones to be compared with them / and
that specyally, as I gesse, for two causes. The one, bycause the
25 mysterye can be but colde and barayne / whiche is not kendled with
the fyre of eloquence / and tempred with certayne swetnesse of
spekynge / in which our elders were passynge excellent / and we not
ones taste of it. An other cause is / for so moche as they contented

---

Against ll. 3–5: Dauyd commytted adulterye with Barsabe / and caused Vrye
her husbande to be slayne.
Against ll. 10–12: The misteries must be handeled with craft.
Against l. 17: Allegoryes.
Against l. 19: Our diuynes.

---

1 are] be *1533*   3 may] shulde *1533*   4–5 The vehement loue of
Sampson.] *om. 1533*   6 were conceyued] conceyued *1533*   7 scriptur]
the scripture *1533*   euery where despised, but] dispysed *1533*   17 alle-
goryes] allegorye *1533*   24 causes] caused *1533*   bycause] that
1533   25 colde] weake *1533*   whiche] that *1533*   kendled] fortyfyed
1533   26 the fyre] strengthe *1533*   28 so moche as] *om. 1533*   con-
tented] content *1533*
          Side-note 3: Allegoryes] Allegory *1533*

with Arystotle onely / expell from scholes the secte of Plato and
Pictagoras / and yet saynt Augustyne preferreth these later / not
onely bycause they haue many sentences moche agreable to our
religyon / but also bycause the very maner of open and clere
speche / whiche they vse (as we [H8ᵛ] haue sayd) full of allegoryes / 5
draweth very nygh to the style of holy scripture. No meruayle
therfore though they haue more commodiously handled the allegoryes of the worde of god / whiche with plenteous oracyon were
able to encrease and dylate / to coloure and garnysshe any maner
thynge neuer so bareyn, symple, or homely / and also beynge moost 10
experte and connynge of all antiquite, had practysed and exercysed
longe before in the poetes and bookes of Plato / that thynge whiche
they sholde do after in diuyne mysteryes. I had leuer that thou
sholdest rede the commentaryes of those men / for I wolde instructe
and induce the, not vnto contencyons of argumentes / but rather 15
vnto a pure mynde. But and yf thou can not attayne the mystery /
remembre yet that some thynge lyeth hyd whiche though it be not
knowen / yet veryly to haue trust to obtayne it, shall be better than
to rest in the letter which kylleth. And that se thou do not onely in
the olde testament / but also in the newe. The gospell hath her 20
flesshe / she hath also her spiryte. For though the vayle be pulled
from the face of Moyses / neuerthelesse yet vnto this day Paule
seeth per speculum and in enigmate / that is through a glasse
vnperfytly and obscurely. And Chryst hymselfe [I1] sayth in his
gospell of Iohan. The flesshe profyteth nothynge at all / it is the 25
spiryte that gyueth lyfe. I veryly durst not haue sayd it profyteth not at all / it had ben ynough for me to say, the flesshe
profyteth somwhat / but moche more yᵉ spiryte. But nowe
veryte hym selfe hath sayd, it profyteth not at all. And so greatly
it profyteth not / that after the mynde of Paule it is but dethe / 30

Against ll. 1–2: Arystotle only is redde nowe a dayes.
Against ll. 8–11: Olde dyuynes with helpe of eloquence handeled the Allego-
ryes wel fauouredly.
Against ll. 20–1: The gospell hath her fleshe and spirite.

5 we] I *1533*   sayd] sayde before *1533*   9 dylate /] delate *1533*;
dylate *1534*   10 and] whiche men *1533*   12 the poetes] poetes *1533*
15 contencyons] contencion *1533*   23 seeth] saythe *1533*   speculum and]
speculum *1533*   that is through] not the thynge selfe and clerely / but the
ymage or symylitude of the very thynge as it were in *1533*   24 And]
and as *1533*   26 durst not] wolde haue ben afrayde to *1533*   27 had]
shold haue *1533*   for me] om. *1533*

excepte it be referred to the spiryte. Yet at the leest way vnto this thynge is the flesshe profytable: for that she ledeth our infir-mytie as it were with certayne greces or steppes vnto the spiryte. The body without the spiryte can haue no beynge: the spiryte of 5 the body hath no nede. Wherfore if after the doctryne of Chryst, the spiryte be so great and excellent a thyng / that he onely gyueth lyfe: hyther, to this poynte muste our iourney be / that in all maner letters / in all our actes, we haue respecte to the spiryte / and not to the flesshe. And if a man wolde take hede, 10 he shulde sone perceyue: that this thyng onely is it, whervnto exhorteth vs amonge the prophetes specially Esaias: amonge the apostels Paule / whiche almoste in euery epystle, playeth this parte and cryeth, that we shulde haue no confidence in the flesshe / and that in the spiryte is lyfe, lybertye, [I1ᵛ] lyght, adopcion: and those 15 noble fruytes so greatly to be desyred whiche he nombreth. The flesshe euery where he dispyseth, condempneth, and casteth of. Take hede and thou shalte perceyue that our mayster Christ dothe the same thyng here and there / whyles in pullyng the asse out of the pytte / in restoringe the syght to the blynde / in rubbynge the eares 20 of corne / in vnwasshen handes / in the feestes of synners / in the parable of the pharysee and the publycane / in fastynges / in the carnall bretherne / in the reioysynge of the iewes that they were the chyldren of Abraham / in offryng of gyftes in the temple / in prayynge / in dilatyng their philateirs / and in many lyke places, he 25 dispyseth the flesshe of the lawe / and superstycion of them, whiche had leuer be iewes openly in the syght of man, than priuely in the syght of god. And whan he sayd to the woman of Samary / byleue me that yᵉ houre shall come, whan ye shall honour the father, neyther in this mountayne / neyther in Ierusalem. But the houre 30 shall be and now is / whan the very true worshyppers shall worshyp the father in spiryte and verite. For surely the father requyreth such to honour hym. The father is a spiryte / and they whiche honour hym must honoure in spiryte and [I2] verite. He signy-fyed the same thynge in dede, whan at the maryage he turned the 35 water of the colde and vnsauery lettre, in to wyne of the spiryte /

Against ll. 15–16: Adopycyon is inherytaunce / not by byrthe / but by election.
Against ll. 23–7: Phylateyrs were papers whiche the phariseys ware on hygh in theyr forheedes / hauynge the ten commaundementes wryten in them.

---

1 vnto] in *1533*   11–12 the apostels] thapostles *1533*   16 casteth of] counseyleth from her *1533*   24 dilatyng] delatyng of *1533*

makynge dronke the spirytuall soules / euen vnto the contempte and dispysynge of their lyfe. And leest thou shuldest thynke it a great thing, that Christ dispysed these thynges, whiche nowe I haue rehersed / ye he dispysed the eatyng of his owne flesshe and drinkynge of his owne bloode / excepte it were done spirytually. To 5 whome thynkest thou spake he these thynges: the flesshe profyteth nothynge at all / it is the spiryte that quyckneth and gyueth lyfe? veryly not to them whiche with saynt Iohans gospell, or an agnus dei hangynge aboute their neckes, thynke themselfe sure from al maner of harme / and suppose that thynge to be the very 10 perfyte religyon of a christen man: but to them to whome he opened ye hygh mistery of eatynge his owne body. If so great a thyng be of no valure / ye if it be pernycious or perylous: what cause is there wherfore we shulde haue confidence in any other carnal thinges, exc?pt ye spiryt be present? Thou peraduenture 15 sayest masse dayly, and lyuest at thyne owne plesure / and art not ones moued with thy neyghbours hurtes / no no more than if they pertayned [I2^v] nothynge at all to the: thou art yet in the flesshe of the sacrament. But and if whyle thou sayest, thou enforcest to be the very same thynge whiche is signyfyed by receyuyng that 20 sacrament / that is to say / to be one spiryte with the spiryte of Christe / to be one body with the body of Christ / to be a quicke membre of the churche / if thou loue nothing but in Christ / if thou thynke all thy goodes to be commune to all men / if the incommodytes of all men greue the euen as thyne owne: than no doute thou 25 sayest masse with great fruyte / and that bycause thou doest it spirytually. If thou perceyue that thou art in maner transfygured and chaunged in to Chryste / and that thou lyuest now lesse and lesse in thyne owne selfe / gyue thankes to the spiryte which onely quyckeneth and gyueth lyfe. Many ben wont to nombre howe 30 many masses they haue ben at euery daye / and hauynge confidence in this thynge as of moste valure (as though nowe they were no farther bounde to Christe) as soone as they be departed out of ye churche returne to their olde maners agayne. That they enbrace

Against ll. 8–9: Saynt Iohnns gospel hangyng at theyr neckes.
Against ll. 32–4 (Referring to p. 114, l. 1): Pietie is the honour and seruice whiche we owe to god.

27 in maner] in a maner *1533*
Side-note 2: *om. 1533*

the flesshe of pite / I disprayse not: that they there stoppe I prayse
not. Let that be perfourmed in the, whiche is there represented to
thyne eyen. There is re[I3]presented to the, the dethe of thy heed:
discusse thy selfe withinforthe / and (as the sayeng is) in thy
5 bosome, howe nygh thou art deed to the worlde. For if thou be
possessed holly with wrath, ambycion, couetousnes, enuy / ye
though thou touche the aulter/yet art thou farre from masse. Christ
was slayne for the / slee thou therfore these beestes. Sacrifyse thy
self to hym, whiche for thy sake sacrifysed hym selfe to his
10 father. If thou ones thynke not on these thynges / and hast confydence in the other: god hateth thy carnall and grosse religyon.
Thou arte baptysed / thynke not forthwith that thou art a christen
man. Thy mynde all togyder sauoureth nothynge but this worlde:
thou art in the syght of the worlde a christen man / but secrete and
15 before god thou art more hethen than any hethen man. Why so?
for thou hast the body of the sacrament, and art without the spiryt
whiche onely profyteth. Thy body is wasshed / what mater maketh
y^t, whyle thy mynde remayneth styll defyled and stayned? The
body is touched with salte / what than, whan thy mynde is yet
20 vnsauery? Thy body is anoynted / but thy mynde is vnanoynted.
But if thou be buryed with Christe withinforthe / and studyest
to walke with hym in the new lyfe: [I3^v] I than knowe y^e for
a christen man. Thou art sprincled with holy water / what good
dothe that / if so be thou wype not awaye the inwarde fylth from
25 the mynde. Thou honourest sayntes / and art ioyous and glad to
touche their relykes: but thou dispysest the chefe relykes whiche
they left behynde them / that is to vnderstande / the examples of
pure lyuynge. There is no honour more pleasaunt to Mary, than if
thou woldest counterfayte her humylite. No religyon is more accep-
30 table to sayntes or more appropriate, than if thou dyddest labour to
represent and folowe their vertues. Wylte thou deserue the loue and
fauour of Peter or of Paule? counterfayte the ones faythe, and the
others charyte / and thou shalt do a greater thing than if thou

Against ll. 1–3: Let it be performed in the that is represented in the masse.
Against ll. 22–3: Sprynclynge of holy water.
Against ll. 25–6: Touchynge of relykes.
Against ll. 27–8: The true honoryng of saintes.

1 pite] pite / that is to say of pure lyfe or seruyce of god *1533*   3 eyen]
eyes *1533*   18 stayned] inquinate *1533*   The] Thy *1533*   25 the
mynde] thy mynde *1533*   27 that is to vnderstande] that is to be vnderstande *1533*   29 woldest] sholdest *1533*   30 dyddest] woldest *1533*

shuldest ron to Rome .x. tymes. Wylt thou worshyp saynt Fraunces
singularly? thou art hye mynded / thou art a great louer of money /
thou art stubburne and selfe wylled / full of contencion / wyse in
thyne owne opinyon: gyue this to the saynt / swage thy mynde /
and by the example of saynte Fraunces be more sobre, humble, or 5
meke / dispyse fylthy lucre / and be desyrous of rychesse of the
mynde / put awaye stryuynge and debates with thy neyghbours / and
with goodnes, ouercome yuell. The saynt [I4] setteth more by this
honour, than if thou shuldest set before hym a thousande brennyng
tapers. Thou thynkest it a specyall thyng to be put in thy graue, 10
wrapped in the cowle or habyte of saynt Fraunces? Trust me lyke
vesture shall profyte ye nothynge at all whan thou art deed / if
thy lyuynge and maners be founde vnlyke whan thou were a lyue.
And though the sure example of all trewe vertue and of pure lyfe,
is fette of Christe moste commodyously: neuer the lesse if the 15
worshyppynge of Chryste in his sayntes delyte the so greatly / se
that thou counterfayte Christ in his sayntes / and for the honoure of
euery one of his sayntes, study and laboure to put awaye one vyce /
or els to enbrace one vertue. If this be done inwardly / than wyll I
not reproue those thynges whiche be doone outwardly. Thou hast 20
in great reuerence the asshes of Paule? I dampne it not / if thy
relygyon be perfyte in euery poynte. But if thou haue in reuerence
the deed asshes or pouder of his body / and settest no store by his
quycke ymage yet speakyng / and as it were brethynge / whiche
remayneth in his doctryne: is not thy relygyon preposterous and 25
out of ordre? Honourest thou the bones of Paule hyd in a shryne /
[I4v] and honourest thou not ye mynde of Paule hydde in his

Against l. 14: Pietie.
Against ll. 17–18: Let vs counterfeyt Christe in his sayntes.
Against l. 27–p. 116, l. 1: Let vs honour the quycke ymage of Paule.

14 of pure] pure *1533*   15 is fette] shewynge how thou sholdest honour god
in euery thynge is fette *1533*   commodyously] commodyously in suche maner /
that in no wyse thou canst be deceyued *1533*   18 euery one of his sayntes,
study and laboure to] euery saynt loke thou *1533*   18–19 one vyce / or els
to enbrace one vertue] all vyces / vyce by vyce / so that thou sacryfyse to euery
saynt syngularly some one vyce syngularly / or else study to enbrace and counterfayte some one syngular vertue in euery saynt / suche as thou perceyuest to haue
reigned moost chefely in euery saynt / syngularly of them whiche thou worshyppest so specyally *1533*   19 If this be done inwardly] If this shall comme to
passe *1533*   26 ordre] ordre / and accordynge to the commune prouerbe /
the carte set before the horse *1533*   a shryne] the shryne *1533*

Side-note 1: *om. 1533*

writynges? Magnifyest thou a pece of his carkas shynynge through
a glasse / and regardest not thou the hole mynde of Paule shynynge through his letters? Thou worshyppest the asshes, in whose
presence now and than the deformytees and diseases of bodyes be
5 taken awaye / why rather honourest thou not his doctryne / wherwith the deformytees and diseases of soules are cured and reme-
dyed? Let the vnfaythfull meruayle at these myracles and sygnes
for whome they be wrought: but thou that art a faythfull man
enbrace his bokes / that as thou doutest not, but that god can do all
10 thinges / euen so thou mayst lerne to loue hym aboue al thynges.
Thou honourest the ymage of the bodyly countenaunce of Christ
formed in stone or tree / or els portrayed with colours: with moche
greater reuerence is to be honoured the ymage of his mynde /
whiche by workmanshyp of the holy goost, is fygured and expressed
15 in the gospels. Neuer any Apelles so expresly fassyoned with pensell
the proporcyons and fygure of the body, as in the wordes and
doctryne of euery man apereth the ymage of the mynde / namely in
Chryste / whiche whan he was very simplicite and pure verite / no
discorde / no vnlykenesse at [I5] all coude be bytwene the fyrste
20 and chefe paterne of his diuyne mynde, and the ymage of his
doctryne and lernyng from thence deducted and deryued. As
nothynge is more lyke the father of heuen than his sonne / whiche
is the worde, the wisdom and knowlege of the father / springyng
forthe of his most secrete hert: so is nothyng more lyke vnto
25 Christ than the worde / the doctryne and teachyng of Christ /
gyuen forthe out of the priuy partes of his most holy brest. And
ponderest thou not this ymage? honourest it not? lokest thou not
substancially with deuoute eyen vpon it? enbrasest it not in thy
herte? hast thou of thy lorde and mayster relykes so holy / so
30 full of vertue and strength / and settyng them at naught / sekest
thou thinges moche more alienate, straunger and farther of? Thou
beholdest a cote or a sudorye, that is sayde to haue ben Christes /

Against l. 7: Nota.
Against ll. 11–13: The very ymage of Christe is expresly paynted in the gos-
pell.
Against ll. 14–15: Appelles was the moost cunnynge paynter that euer was.

10 mayst] myghtest *1533*   16 wordes] oracyon *1533*   19 vnlykenesse]
vnlyke thynge *1533*   21 deducted and deryued] deducte and deryuate *1533*
28 eyen] eyes *1533*
Side-note 1: *om. 1333*

astonyed therat, as though thy wyttes were rauysshed: and art thou
in a dreme or slumber whan thou redest the diuyne oracles or
answeres of Christe? Thou byleuest it to be a great thyng, ye a
greater than ye greatest, that thou possessest at home a lytell pece
of the crosse: but y^t is nothyng to be compared to this / if thou 5
beare shrined in thy hert ye mystery of the crosse. Or els if suche
thynges make a man [I5^v] religyous and deuout / what can be
more religious that y^o iewes / of whiche very many (though they
were neuer so wycked) yet with their eyen sawe Iesu Christ lyuyng
bodyly / herde hym with their eares / with their handes handled 10
hym? What is more happy than Iudas, which with his mouth
kyssed ye diuyne mouth of Christ? So moche doth ye flesshe without the spirit profyte nothing at all / that it shulde not ones haue
profited the holy virgin his mother, y^t she of her owne flesshe
begate hym / excepte she in her spiryt had conceyued his spiryte 15
also. This is a very gret thing / but here a greater. While thapostels
enioyed ye corporal presence and felyshyp of Christe / redest thou
not howe weake / how childysshe they were / how grosse and without capacite: who wold desyre any other thing vnto the most perfite
helth of his soule, than so longe familiarite and conuersacyon 20
togyder with hym y^t was bothe god and man? Yet after so many
myracles shewed / after ye doctryne of his owne mouth taught and
declared to them / after sure and euydent tokens y^t he was rysen
agayne / dyd he not at ye last hour, whan he shulde be receyued
vp in to heuen, cast in their tethes their vnstabylite in the faythe? 25
What was than the cause? verily the flesshe of Christ dyd let: and
thence is it y^t he saythe: except I [I6] go away, the holy goost
wyll not come / it is expedyent for you y^t I departe. The corporal
presence of Christ is vnprofytable vnto helth: and dare we in any
corporal thyng besyde that, put perfyte pyte / y^t is to say, the loue 30
and honour of god? Paule sawe Christ in flessh / what supposest
thou to be a greater thing than y^t / yet setteth he naught by it, sayeng. Though (saythe he) we haue knowen Christ carnally / nowe we
do not so. Why knewe he him not carnally? for he had profyted and

Against ll. 3–4: The honoryng of the crosse.
Against ll. 17–19: The very apostels / as longe as Chryst was present wauered
in the faythe.

---

1 rauysshed] rapte *1533*   2 slumber] a slumber *1533*   9 eyen]
eyes *1533*   16 While thapostels] The apostles *1533*   31 flessh] his
humanite *1533*

ascended vnto more perfyt gyftes of the spiryt. I vse peraduenture
mo wordes in disputyng these thynges, than shulde be mete for
him whiche gyueth rules. Neuerthelesse I do it ye more dilygently
(and not without a great cause) for y^t in very dede I do perceyue
5 this errour to be the commen pestilence of al christendom: which
bringeth and occasioneth euen for this cause ye greter mischefe /
for as moche as in semblaunce and apparence it is nexte vnto pyte.
For there are no vices more perylous than they whiche counterfayte vertue. For besydes this y^t good men may lightly fal into
10 them / ther are none with more difficulty cured, bycause the
commune people vnlerned thynken our religion to be violate,
whan such thynges are rebuked. Let incontynent al the worlde
cry out agaynst me / let certayn prechers, such as are [16^v] wont to
crye out in their pulpettes, barke whiche with right good wyll synge
15 these thinges inwardly in their own stomackes, lokyng verily not
vnto Christ / but vnto their owne aduauntage. Through whose
eyther superstycion without lernynge / or fayned holynes, I am
compelled oftentymes to shewe and declare, that I in no wyse rebuke
or checke ye corporal ceremonyes of christen men, and the deuout
20 myndes of simple persons: namely in suche thinges that are
approued by authorite of the churche. For they are now and than
partly sygnes of pyte, and partly helpers thervnto. And bycause
they are somwhat necessary to yonge infantes in Christ, tyll they
waxe elder, and growe vp vnto a perfyt man: therfor it is not mete
25 they shulde be disdayned of them whiche are perfyte / leest by
their example the weake persone shulde take harme. That thou
doest I approue / so the ende be not amysse. More ouer if thou stop
not there, whence thou oughtest to ascende to thynges more nere
to helth. But to worship Christ with visible thynges in stede of
30 inuysible, and in them to put the hyghest poynt of religyon / and
for them to stande in thyne owne conceyte / to condempne other
men / to set thy hole mynde vpon them / and also to dye in them /
and (to speke shortly) to be with[17]drawen from Christe, with
the very same thynges whiche be ordeyned for thentent onely that
35 they shulde helpe vnto Christ: this is verily to departe from the

Against ll. 18–19: The vse of ceremonyes.

6 euen for this cause] yea for this causeth *1533*   7 pyte] godly loue or
holynes *1533*   10 ther are none] none are *1533*   11 thynken] thynketh
1533   19 the deuout] deuout *1533*   33 to be] that thou be *1533*
34 thentent] the entent *1533*

lawe of the gospell whiche is spirytuall / and to fall in to a certayne
iewysshnesse: whiche thyng peraduenture is of no lesse ieopardye,
than if without suche superstycion thou shuldest be infecte with
great and manyfest vyces of the mynde. This is forsoth the more
deedly disease. Be it, but ye other is worse to be cured. Howe 5
moche euery where sweateth the chefe defender of the spiryte
Paule, to call away ye iewes from the confydence of dedes and ceremonyes / and to promote them vnto those thynges whiche are
spirytuall: and nowe I se the communaltie of christen men to be returned hyther agayne. But what sayd I the communaltie? that myght 10
be yet suffred, had not this errour inuaded and caught a great parte
bothe of preestes and doctours: and to be shorte the flockes of them
almost through out, whiche professe in tytle and habyte a spirytuall
lyfe. If they whiche shulde be the very salte be vnsauery / wherwithall shall other be seasoned? I am asshamed to reherse with 15
what supersticion the most parte of them, obserue certayne ceremonyes of mennes inuencyons / yet not instytute for [I7^v] such
purpose / howe odiously they requyre them of other men? What
confidence without mystrust they haue in them: howe indiscretly
they iudge other men: howe ernestly they defende them. To these 20
their dedes they thynke heuen to be due / in whiche if they be ones
roted, at ones they thynke them selfe Paules and Antonyes. They
begyn, O good lorde / with what grauyte / with howe great authorite
to correcte other mens lyues / after the rule of fooles and vndiscrete
persons (as sayth Terens) so that they thynke nothynge well done, 25
but y^t they do them selfe. But for all that, whan they be woxen olde
syres in their maner of lyuyng thou shalt se that as yet they sauour
or taste of Christ nothyng at all: but to be beestly swymmynge in
certayne chorlisshe vices, in their lyuyng and pastyme frowarde,
and scarse can suffre and forbeare their owne selfe / in charyte colde, 30
in wrath feruent, in hate as tough as white lether, in their tonges
venymous and full of poyson, excercysyng and puttyng forthe of
their malyce conquerours and not able to be ouercome, redy to

---

Against ll. 10–12: The communaltie is turned to the confydence of ceremonyes.
Against ll. 18–19: Supersticious persones are touched.
Against ll. 21–3: Paule and Antony were hermytes of passynge holy conuer-
sacyon.
Against ll. 24–5: The defenders of ceremonies.

1–2 to fall in to a certayne iewysshnesse] fall in to certeyn supersticion of
ceremonyes lyke vnto the iewes 1533

stryue for euery lyfell tryfle, and so farre from the perfection of
Christ / that they be not ones endued with these commune vertues /
whiche the very ethnytes or hethen men haue [I8] lerned / eyther
by reason gyuen to them of nature / or by vse of lyuyng, or by the
5 preceptes of philosophers. Thou shalte also se them in spirytuall
thynges clene without capacyte / fyerse that no man shall knowe
howe to entreate or handle them / full of stryfe and contencyon /
gredy vpon voluptuous pleasure / at the worde of god redy to spewe /
kynde to no man / mysdemynge other men / flaterynge their owne
10 selues. It is come to this poynte nowe at laste with the labours of so
many yeres / that thou shuldest be of all men the worste / and yet
thynke thy selfe the best? that in stede of a christen man, thou
shuldest be a playne iewe / doynge seruyce vnto dombe elementes
onely? that thou shuldest haue thy glory and ioye / not in secrete
15 before god / but openly afore the worlde? But if thou haste walked
in the spiryt and not in the flesshe: where be the fruytes of the
spiryte? Where is charyte? Where is that cherefulnesse and ioyous
myrthe of a pure mynde? Where is tranquillite and peace towardes all
men? Where is pacyence? Where is perseueraunce of softe mynde /
20 wherwith thou lokest daye by daye contynually for the amendement
euen of thyne enemyes? Where is curtesy and gentylnesse / Where
is frenesse of hert / [I8ᵛ] Where is mekenesse, fydelyte, discrecyon,
measure or sobrenesse, temperaunce, and chastyte? Where is the
ymage of Christ in thy maners? I am sayest thou no keper of hoores,
25 no thefe, no violatour of holy thinges / I kepe my professyon. But
what other thynge is this, than I am not lyke other men, extor-
cyoners, adulterers / ye and I faste twyse a weke? I had leauer haue
a publycane humbly and lowly askynge mercy, than this kynde of
pharysees rehersynge their good dedes. But what is thy profes-
30 syon? is it I pray the that thou shuldest not performe that thynge
thou promysed longe ago whan thou were baptysed / whiche was
that thou woldest be a christen man / that is to saye / a spiritual
person / and not a carnall iewe, whiche for the tradycions of man
woldest transgresse the commaundementes of god? Is not the lyfe of

---

Against ll. 24–5: The ypocrysy of relygyous persones.

13 be] be but *1533*   13–14 doynge seruyce vnto dombe elementes onely]
obseruyng onely vnfruytfull tradicyons and ceremonyes of the inuencyons of
man *1533*   15 worlde] *1533*; worde *1534*   if] and yf *1533*   17 and]
or *1533*   21 and] or *1533*   26 this] this to saye *1533*   27 a weke]
in a weke *1533*   28 humbly] humble *1533*   34 woldest] sholdest *1533*

a christen man spirytuall? Here Paule speakynge to the Romaynes.
No dampnacion is to them that are graffed in Christe Iesu / whiche
walke not carnally or after the flesshe: for the lawe of the spiryte of
lyfe in Christ Iesu hath delyuered me from the lawe of synne and
dethe: for that thing whiche was impossyble for the lawe to do or 5
bringe to passe, whiche was weake by reason of the flesshe / that
same [K1] god made good / sendyng his sone in the symilitude of
flesshe, prone to synne / and of synne condempned synne in the
flesshe / that the iustyfyeng of the lawe, myght be fulfylled in vs,
whiche walke not after the flesshe, but after the spirit. For they 10
that be in the flesshe, be wyse in thynges perteynyng to the
flesshe: but they whiche be in ye spiryt, perceyue those thynges
that perteyne to ye spiryt. The wysdome of the flesshe is deth / and
the wysdom of the spirit is lyfe and peace: for the wysdom of y^e
flesshe, is an ennemy to god, bycause she is not obedyent to the 15
lawe of god / nor yet can be. They y^t be in the flesshe they can
not please god. What coude be spoken more largely? What more
playnly? neuerthelesse many men subtyle and crafty to flater and
fauour their owne vices: but prone and redy without aduysement
to checke other mens / thynke these thynges to pertayne to them- 20
selfe nothyng at al: and Paule spake of walking carnally, or after the
flesshe / that referre they to adulters onely, and kepers of quenes:
what he spake of wysdome of the flesshe, which is ennemy to god /
that they turned to them which haue lerned humanite / or (as they
call it) seculer sciences. In eyther other they set vp their creestes / 25
and clap their handes for ioye / bothe y^t they neyther be adulters /
and in all scyences excellent[K1^v]ly vnlerned and ignorant. But to
lyue in the spiryt: they dreme to be none other thyng than to do as
they them selues do. Whiche persones, yf they wolde as diligently
obserue the tong of Paule, as they manfully despise the tong of 30

Against ll. 21–2: The exposicyon and mynde of some clerkes.
Against ll. 29–30: The flesshe and the spyryt after Paule.

5–6 that thing whiche was impossyble for the lawe to do or bringe to passe,
whiche was weake by reason of the flesshe] y^t which the lawe weyked by
reason of the flesshe coude not performe or make good *1533*   13 The
wysdome] for wysdom *1533*   14 the wysdom^1] wysdom *1533*   18 flater
and] flater or *1533*   21–2 and Paule spake . . . that referre they] and that
Paule spake . . . they referre *1533*   23 what] that *1533*   24 that they
turned] they turned it *1533*   24–5 as they call it] that they call *1533*
27 excellently vnlerned and ignorant] starke fooles *1533*   But] More ouer
1533   30 manfully] maliciously *1533*   30–p. 122, l. 1 the tong of Tully]
Tullys *1533*

Tully: they sholde soone perceyue, that the apostle calleth the flesshe, that thyng that is visyble / and the spiryte, that thyng y^t is inuisyble. For he techeth euery where that thynges visyble, ought to serue to thinges inuisyble: and not contrary wyse, inuisyble thynges
5 to serue thynges visyble. Thou of a preposterous ordre, applyest Chryst to those thynges whiche were mete to be applyed vnto Christ. Requirest thou of me recorde, that this worde flesshe perteyneth not onely to fylthy and superfluous lust of the body? holde and vnderstande, that thyng whiche ye sayd apostle (doynge that
10 same which he in all places doth) wryteth to the Colocenses. Let no man mysleade you for the nones, in ye humilite and religion of aungels, whiche thynges he neuer sawe, walkyng in vayne / inflate with the ymaginacyon of the flesshe / and not holdyng the heed / that is to say Christ / of whome all ye body mynystred,
15 nourysshed, compacte and set togyder by couples and ioyntes, groweth in to ye encrease of god. And lest thou sholdest doubte any thynge that he spake of them [K2] which hauyng confidence in certeyn corporal ceremonyes, barke agaynst ye spiritual purposes of other men: take hede what foloweth. Yf ye be deed with Christ / ab
20 elementis huius mundi / from tradicions, ceremonyes and inuencions of men: why haue ye yet suche decrees among you / as though ye lyued vnto the worlde? And anone after, callyng vs from the same thinges he sayth: yf ye be rysen vp agayn with Christ/seke those thynges that are aboue where Chryst sytteth on ye ryght hande of
25 god. Be expert and wyse in those thinges y^t be aboue/and not on ye erth. More ouer gyuyng preceptes of ye spiritual lyfe / what exhorteth he vs to do at the last: whether y^t we sholde vse suche or suche ceremonyes? Whether we sholde be this or that wyse arayed? that we sholde lyue with this or y^t meates? that we sholde saye
30 customably any certeyn nombre of psalmes: he made mencion of no suche thynges: what than? Mortifye (said he) your membres whiche be on the erth / fornicacyon, vnclennes, bodyly lust, euyl concupiscence, and auaryce, which is the seruice of ydols. And a litel after. Now put from you al suche thynges, wrath, indignacyon,
35 malyce: and agayn, spoylyng your self of ye olde man with al his

Against ll. 31-3: Mortifie the membres on the erthe.

14-15 body mynystred, nourysshed, compacte and set togyder by couples and ioyntes] body by couples and ioyntes mynystred vp and compacte *1533*
23 he] *om. 1533*   28 Whether] whether y^t *1533*   34 after] after that *1533*

actes, puttyng on you the newe man, whiche is renewed in knowlege of god, after ye ymage of hym [K2^v] whiche made hym. But
who is the olde man? veryly Adam / he that was made of the erth /
whose conuersacion is in erth / not in heuen. By the erth vnderstande what so euer is visyble / and therfore temporall and transy- 5
tory. Who is that newe man? veryly the celestial man y^t descended
from heuen, Chryst. And by heuen vnderstande what so euer is
inuisyble / and therfore eternal and euerlastyng. At the last, leest we
sholde be mynded to purchase the fauour of god, after ye maner of
the iewes with certeyn obseruaunces / as with ceremonyes magicall: 10
he techeth that our dedes are pleasaunt and alowed of god / so long
as they are referred vnto charite / and also sprynge therof / sayinge.
Aboue al these thynges kepe charite the bonde of perfection / and
let the peace of god reioyse as an ouercommer in your hertes / in
which also ye be called in one body. I wyll gyue the a more playne 15
token, and euydent probacion: that this worde flesshe signifieth
not the lust of the body onely. Paule nameth often the flesshe / often
the spiryt / wrytyng to a certeyn people named Galatas / whiche
he called not onely from lust of the body vnto chaste lyuynge:
but enforceth to withdrawe them from the sect of ye iewes, and 20
confidence of workes / in to whiche they were enduced by false
apostles. In this [K3] place therfore, nombryng the dedes of the
flesshe / marke what vyces he reherseth. The dedes of the flesshe
(sayth he) be manyfest / whiche are fornycacyon / vnclenlynes /
vnshamefastnes / lechery / worshyppyng of ydolles / wytch- 25
crafte / preuy hate / discorde, otherwyse called contencyon, or
stryfe / emulacyon which may be called indignacyon or disdayne /
ire otherwyse called wrath / scoldyng / discencyon / that is to say /
dyuersite in maynteynyng of opynyons, sectes / or maynteynyng
of quarelles / enuy / homycyde / dronkennesse / excesse in eatynge / 30
and suche lyke. And not longe after he sayth: yf we lyue in the
spiryte / let vs walke in y^e spiryt. After that, as declaryng and
vtteryng a pestylence contrary to the spiryt / he addeth: let vs not
be made desyrous of vayne glory, prouokynge one the other / and

Against l. 3: The olde man.
Against ll. 32-4: Vayne glorye is a pestylence contrary to the spirite.

___

10 as with] as *1533*   14 an ouercommer] a victor *1533*   19 vnto]
to *1533*   21 workes] worke *1533*   25 vnshamefastnes] to be shameles
1533   27 which] that *1533*

enuyenge one an other. The tree is knowen by the fruite. As vnto this that thou omyttest not watche / fasting / sylence / orysons / and suche other lyke obseruaunces: I passe not theron / I wyl not byleue that thou art in the spiryt: excepte I may se the fruytes of
5   thy spiryte. Why may I not affyrme the to be in ye flesshe, whan after almoost an hondreth yeres exercyse of these thynges / yet in the I fynde the dedes of the flesshe: enuyousnesse more than is in any [K3^v] woman / contynuall wrath and fyersnes, as in a man of warre: scoldynge / lust and pleasure insaciable / malicious cursing /
10 backbyting with tong more venymous than the poyson of a serpent / an hygh mynde / stubburnnes / lyght of thy promesse / vanite / faynyng / flaterynge? Thou iudgest thy brother in his meate / drynke or rayment: but Paule iudgeth the of thy dedes. Dothe that separate the from worldly and carnall men / that thou
15 art in lyghter causes veryly, but yet with the same vices infected? Is he more fylthy / whiche for his enherytaunce taken from hym or it came to his handes, for whiche his doughter defyled / for hurt done to his father / for some offyce / for his prynces fauour: conceyueth wrath / hatred / emulacyon and disdayne: than thou whiche
20 (I am ashamed to tell) for how lytel a tryfle / yea for nothynge, doest all the same thynges moche more malyciously? The lyghter occasyon to synne lyghteth not / but aggrauateth ye synne. Neyther it maketh mater in how lytel or great a thyng thou synne / so it be done with lyke affection. And yet is there difference veryly: for so
25 moche the greuouser dothe euery man trespace / the lesse the occasyon is / wherwith he is pulled awaye from honestye. I speke not now of those monkes or religious persones, whose [K4] maners euen the hole worlde abhorreth: but of them whome ye commune people honoureth not as men, but as aungels. Whiche
30 selfe same, notwithstanding ought not to be displeased with these wordes: whiche rebuketh ye vices, and noteth not the persones. But and yf they be good men / let them also be glad to be warned of what so euer man it be / in those thynges whiche perteynen to helth. Neyther it is vnknowen to me, that amonges them are very many,
35 which holpen with lernyng and wytte, haue tasted the mysteryes of y^e spiryt. But (as Liuius saith) it fortuneth almost euery where:

Against l. 27: Monkes.

_____

1-2 As vnto this that] That *1533*   5 thy] the *1533*   6 an hondreth] a
hondreth *1533*   17 for whiche] for *1533*   19 and disdayne] (whiche may
be called indignacion or disdayne) *1533*   33 perteynen] perteyneth *1533*

that the greater parte ouercommeth the better. Notwithstandyng (yf it be lawfull to confesse the trouth) se we not all the moost strayte kynde of monkes, to put the chefe poynte of relygyon, eyther in ceremonyes, or in a certeyn maner or forme of saying, whiche they call their diuyne seruice / or in certeyn dedes of ye 5 body? Whiche monkes yf a man sholde examyne and appose of spirituall thinges, he sholde scarse fynde any at all that walked not in the flesshe. And here of commeth this so great infyrmytye of myndes / tremblyng for feare, where is no feare / and therin sure and carelesse, where is moost peryll of all. Here of commeth that per- 10 petuall infancye in Chryst (to speke no greuouslyer) [K4^v] that we preposterous estemers of thinges make moost of those whiche by them selfe are of no value, those set at nought, whiche onely are sufficyent, euer lyuyng vnder tuters or scholemaisters / euer in bon- dage, neuer aduaunsynge our selfe vp to the lyberty of the spiryte, 15 neuer growyng vp to the large stature of charite. Whan Paule cryeth to a certayne people called Galathas / stande fast / be not ye locked agayne vnder ye yoke of bondage. And in an other place, and so was the lawe our tutor or scholemayster in Chryst / that of fayth we myght be iustifyed. But seynge that fayth is comme / now be 20 we no more vnder a tutor or scholemaister: for euery one of you (saith he) is the veray sone of god through fayth whiche he hath in Chryste Iesu. And not moche after he sayth / and we also whan we were lytell ones, were in seruyce and bondage vnder the cere- monyes and lawe of this worlde. But whan the tyme was fully 25 expyred / god sent his sone made of a woman / made vnder the lawe, to redeme them whiche were vnder the lawe / that we by adopcyon sholde be his sones. And for bycause ye be the sones of god / god hath sente the spiryt of his sone in to your hertes / cryong Abba pater (as a man wolde saye, dade father). And so is 30 he not now a seruaunt / but [K5] a sone to god. And agayn in an other place. Bretherne ye be called in to lybertye / let not your lybertye be an occasyon vnto you to lyue in the flesshe: but in charite of the spiryte serue one an other. For all the lawe is ful- fylled in one saying. Loue thy neyghbour as thy self. But and yf ye 35

Against ll. 12–14: Preposterous / is settynge behynd that that shuld be before.

___

5 whiche] that *1533*   certeyn dedes] a labour *1533*   9 sure]
suertye *1533*   12 those] suche thynges *1533*   18–19 and so was the lawe]
the lawe was *1533*   20 myght] sholde *1533*   30 father).] father) *1533*,
1534

byte and eate one the other / take hede leest ye be consumed one of an other. And agayne to the Romaynes. Ye haue not receyued the spiryte of bondage agayne in feare / but the spiryte that maketh you the sones of god by adopcyon / in whome we crye dade father.
5 Vnto the same also pertayneth that he wryteth to Timothe / saying. Exercyse thy selfe vnder the dedes of pietie: for bodyly exercyse is good but for a small thynge / pietie is good vnto all maner thynges. And to the Corynthes. God is a spiryte / and where the spiryte is / there is lybertye. But why reherse I one or two
10 places. Paule is all togyder at this poynte / that the flesshe, whiche is full of contencion, mought be despysed / and that he myght settle vs in the spiryte, whiche is the authour of charite and lyberty. For these companyons be euer inseparable on the one syde / the flesshe, bondage, vnquietnesse, contencyon or stryfe. And on the
15 other syde, the spiryte, peace, loue, lybertye. [K5ᵛ] These thynges euery where Paule stampeth in to vs. And seke we a better mayster of our religyon / namely whan all diuyne scripture agreeth to hym? This was the greatest commaundement in the lawe of Moyses. This Chryste iterateth and fynyssheth in the gospell, and for
20 this cause chefely was he borne, for this cause dyed he, to teche vs not to counterfeyte yᵉ iewes, but to loue. After the last souper made the euen before his passyon / how dylygently / how tenderly / and how affectuously gaue he charge to his discyples / not of meate / not of drynke / but of charite to be kepte one
25 towardes an other. What other thyng techeth he? What other thynge desyreth his disciple Iohan, than that we loue one an other? Paule euery where (as I haue sayd) commendeth charite / but specyally wrytynge vnto the Corynthes he preferreth charite, bothe before myracles and prophecyes / and also before the tonges of aungelles.
30 And saye not thou by and by, that charite is, to be ofte at the churche, to croche downe before the ymages of sayntes, to lyght tapers or waxe candelles, to saye many lady psalters, or saynt Katherynes knottes. God hath no nede of these thynges. Paule calleth charite, to edyfye thy neyghbour / to compte that we al be
35 mem[K6]bres of one body / to thynke that we all are but one in

Against ll. 21–2: To loue / is the gretest commaundement.
Against ll. 24–5: Chryste last of all warneth vs of charitie.
Against ll. 33–4: What is true charitie.

6 saying.] sayenge. *1533*; saying *1534*   10 places] places / whan *1533*
11 mought] sholde *1533*   16 stampeth in to vs] mengleth with other sayinges *1533*

Chryst / to reioyse in god of thy neyghboures welthe, euen as thou
doest of thyne owne. To remedy his incommodytees or losses, as
thyne owne. Yf any brother erre, or go out of the ryght waye: to
warne hym / to monysshe hym / to tell hym his faute mekely,
sobrely, and curteysly / to teche the ignoraunt, to lyfte vp hym 5
that is fallen, to comforte and courage hym that is in heuynesse, to
helpe him y^t laboureth, to socour the nedy. In conclusyon to referre
all riches and substaunce / al thy study / all thy cares to this poynte /
that thou in Chryste sholdest helpe as moche as thy power extendeth to. That as he neyther was borne for hym selfe / nor lyued to 10
his owne pleasure / neyther dyed for hym selfe but dedycate hym
selfe hoolly to our profytes: euen so sholde we apply our selfe /
and awayte vpon the commodytees of our bretherne / and not our
owne. Whiche thyng yf it were vsed / nothyng sholde be eyther
more pleasaunt or elles easy, than the lyfe of religyous persones / 15
whiche we se now clene contrarye / greuous almoost euery where
and laboryous / and also full of superstycyon / lyke vnto the iewes /
neyther pure from any vyces of the laye people / and in many sondry
thynges moche more [K6^v] defyled. Whiche kynde of men saynt
Augustyne (of whome many glorye and reioyce as of the authour 20
and founder of theyr lyuynge) yf he now myght lyue agayn /
certaynly wolde not ones knowe / and wolde crye out / sayinge that
he wolde approue nothyng lesse than this kynde of lyfe / and that
he had instytuted an ordre and maner of lyuynge / not after the
superstycyon of the iewes / but after the rule of the apostles. But 25
I heare euen now, what certayne men (whiche are somwhat well
aduised) wyll answere vnto me. A man must take hede in lytel and
small thynges / leest a lytell and a lytell he sholde fall in to greater
vyces. I heare it ryght well / and I alow the saying. Neuertheles
thou oughtest to take hede a greate deale more, that thou so cleue 30
not to these lytell and small thinges, that thou sholdest fall clene
from the moost chefe and greatest thynges. There is the ieopardye
more euydent / but here more greuouse. So flee Scilla, that thou
fall not in to Charibdis. To obserue these lytell thynges, is holsome
veryly: but to cleue vtterly vnto them, is veray ieopardous. Paule 35

Against ll. 15–17: The lyfe of relygyous men is greuous and tedyous.
Against ll. 20–3: Saynt Augustyne wold not knowe monkes and chanons of
his owne relygyon yf he were now alyue.
Against ll. 29–31: Howe ferforth we oughte to cleaue to the small thynges.
Against ll. 33–5: Scilla and Caribdys / loke what they meane at the ende of
the fyrst chapytre.

forbyddeth not the to vse the lawe and ceremonyes: but he wyll
not hym to be bounde to the lawe and ceremonyes, whiche is free
in Christ. He con[K7]dempneth not the lawe of dedes: yf so be
a man vse it lawfully. Without these thynges peraduenture thou
5 shalt not be a chrysten man / but they make the not a christen man.
They wyll helpe vnto pietie and godlynesse / euen so yet yf thou
vse them for that purpose. But and yf thou shalte begyn to enioye
them / to put thy trust and confydence in them / at ones they
vtterly destroye all the lyuyng of a chrysten man. The apostle
10 setteth nought by the dedes of Abraham / whiche to haue ben
veray perfyte, no man doubteth: and hast thou confydence in
thyne? God disdeyneth certeyn sacrifices called victime / the
sabbots and certeyn holy days called Neomenye, of his people the
iewes / of whiche thynges he hymselfe was the authour and com-
15 maunder: and darest thou compare thyne owne obseruaunces,
with the preceptes of the lawe of god? Yet here god redy to spue
at them, and sore agreued with them. For what entent (sayth he)
offre ye to me, the multytude of your victimes? I am full. As for
holocaustes of wethers / talowe or inwarde suet and fatte of beestes /
20 blode of calues / of lambes and gotes, I wolde not haue. Whan ye
comme before my presence, who hath requyred these thynges of
your handes, that ye myght walke in my hou[K7ᵛ]ses? Offre ye no
more sacryfyce in vayne / your ensence is abhomynacyon to me / I
wyll not suffre the feest of the Neomenye and sabbot daye / with
25 other feest dayes. The companyes of you are infected with iniquite /
my soule hathe hated your kalendas, and your solempne feestes.
These thynges be greuous vnto me / I was euen sycke to abyde them.
And whan ye put forth your handes: I wyll tourne myne eyes from

Against ll. 4–5: Corporal thynges helpe to pietie.
Against ll. 10–18: Vyctyma was the sacrifyce of a beest / wherof he that
offered dyd eate perte / and part went to thuse of the prestes / the call / the
kydneys / and the fat aboute them was burned to god. That same sacryfyce for
certayn consyderacions is also called hostia.
Against ll. 19–22: Holocaustes that is / the hole beest sacrificed to god / no
man hauyng parte therof.
Against ll. 23–5: Sabbot daye was euery seuenth daye / as our sondaye.
Against ll. 26–7: Neomenye were holydays at the newe of the mone.
Against l. 28–p. 129, l. 1: Kalendas / that same that neomenyes be.

---

3 so be] om. 1533   14 the authour] authour 1533   14–15 commaunder]
commauuder 1533   17 sore] om. 1533   18 your] om. 1533   24 suffre]
suffre any more 1533

Side-note 1: thynges] thyn thynges 1533

you. Whan he reherseth the obseruaunces and maners of holy feestes
and sacryfyce, more ouer the multyplyenge of prayers: noteth he
not them as though he poynted them with his fynger / whiche
measure theyr relygyon with a certayne nombre of psalmes and
prayers? Marke also an other thynge, how meruaylously the facun-   5
dyous prophete expresseth, heapyng togyder the disdayne and
indignacyon of god: so that he now coude suffre neyther with
eares, neyther eyes. What thynges (I besechc the)? veryly tho thinges
whiche he hymself had ordeyned to be kepte so religiously / whiche
also were obserued so reuerently, so many yeres of holy kynges and   10
prophetes. And these thynges abhorreth he as yet in ye carnall
lawe. And trustest thou in ceremonies made at home in thine owne
house / now in the lawe of the spiryt? God [K8] in an other place
byddeth the same prophete to crye incessantly, and to put out his
brest after the maner of a trumpe / as in an ernest mater, and worthy   15
to be rebuked sharply / and suche a mater as vnneth coude be
opteyned of these men but with moche ado. Me (sayth he) they
seke from day to day / and knowe they wyll my wayes / as a people
that hath done iustice / and hath not forsaken the iudgement of
their god. They aske me for the iudgementes of iustyce / and desyre   20
to drawe nygh to god: why haue we fasted (saye they) and thou
hast not loked vpon vs and meked our soules / and thou woldest
not knowe it. Lo in ye day of your fast (answereth the prophete)
your owne wyll is founde in you / and ye seke out al your detters. Lo
vnto stryfe and contencyon ye fast / and ye smyte with your fyst   25
cruelly. Faste ye not as ye haue fasted vnto this day / that your
crye myght be herde on hygh. Is this the fast that I haue chosen /
that a man sholde vexe and trouble hym selfe for one daye / eyther
that a man sholde bowe his heed as a hoke or cyrcle / and to cast
vpon hym sacke clothe and asshes? Wylte thou call this a fast, or a   30
daye acceptable vnto god? But what shall we saye this to be: dothe
god condempne that thynge, whiche he hym selfe commaunded?
Naye forsothe. [K8v] What then? But to cleue and stycke fast in
the flesshe of the lawe / and to haue confydence of a thynge of

Against l. 5: Esayas.
Against ll. 20–1: The Iewysshe fast.

---

5 prayers] prayers / whiche they call dayly seruyce *1533*   6 and] or *1533*
29 bowe] bowe downe *1533*   29–30 cast vpon] strawe vndernethe *1533*
Side-note 2: *om. 1533*

nothynge / that is it veryly whiche he hateth deedly. Therfore he
sheweth what he wolde haue added in eyther place. Be ye wasshen
(sayth he) and made clene / take away your euyll cogitacions and
thoughtes out of my syght. Whan thou hearest the euyll thoughtes
5 rehersed / toucheth he not euydently the spiryte and the inwarde
man? The eyes of god seeth not outwarde / but in secrete / neyther
he iudgeth after the syght of the eyes / neyther rebuketh after the
hearyng of the eares. God knoweth not yᵉ folysshe virgyns, smothe
and gay outwarde / empty of good workes inwarde. He knoweth
10 not them whiche say with lyppes Mayster maister. More ouer he
putteth vs in remembraunce yᵗ the vse of yᵉ spirituall lyfe standeth
not so greatly in ceremonyes, as in yᵉ charite of thy neyghbour.
Seke (saith he) iudgement or iustice / socour him that is oppressed /
gyue true iudgement and ryght to hym that is fatherles and motherles
15 or frendles / defende the wydowe / suche lyke thinges dyd he knyt
to the other place / where he speketh of fastyng. Is not this rather
(sayth he) that faste whiche I haue chosen? Teare and cancell
cruell obligacyons / vnbynde yᵉ burthens whiche make [L1] them
stowpe to the grounde that beare them: let them that be brused go
20 free and breake a sonder all burthen. Breake thy breed to hungry.
The nedy and them whiche haue no place of habytacion / lede in to
thy house. Whan thou seest a naked man clothe hym / and dispyse
not thyne owne flesshe. What shall a christen man do than? shall he
dispyse the commaundementes of the churche? Shall he set at
25 naught yᵉ honest tradycions of fore fathers? Shall he condempne
godly and holy customes? Nay, if he be weake and as a begynner,
he shall obserue them as thynges necessary. But and if he be
stronge and perfyte: so moche the rather shall he obserue them /
leest with his knowlege he shulde hurte his brother whiche is yet
30 weake: leest he also shulde kyll hym for whome Christ dyed. We
may not omytte these thynges: but of necessyte we must do other
thynges. Corporall dedes be not condempned / but spirytuall are
preferred. This visyble honouring of god is not condempned / but
god is not pleased sauyng with inuysible pyte and seruyce. God is a
35 spiryt and is moued and styrred with inuysible sacryfyce. It is a great

Against ll. 9–10: The vse of spirytuall lyfe.
Against l. 17: Esayas.
Against ll. 25–6: The tradicions of our elders.

---

2 what] that *1533*   wasshen] wasshed *1533*   3 sayth] sayd *1533*
17 whiche] *om. 1533*   Teare and] loose or *1533*   21 haue] hath *1533*

shame for christen men not to knowe that thyng whiche a certayne
poete beyng a gentyle knewe ryght well / whiche gyuyng a pre[LIV]-
cept of dewe seruynge god saythe: If god be a mynde as scrypture
sheweth vs / se thou honoure hym chefely with a pure mynde.
Lette vs not dispyse the authour though he be an hethen man, or 5
without degre of schole / the sentence becometh ye a ryght great
diuyne. And (as I very well haue perceyued) is lykewyse vnderstande
of fewe, as it is redde of many. The sentence veryly is this / lyke
reioysen in lyke. Thou thynkest god to be moued greatly with
an oxe kylled and sacryfyced / or with the vapoure or smoke of 10
frankensence / as though he were a body. God is a mynde / and without doute a mynde moste pure / moste subtyle and perfyte: therfore
ought he to be honoured moste chyfely with a pure mynde. Thou
thynkest a tapre lyghted to be a sacrifyce: but a sacryfyce to god
(saythe Dauid) is a wofull or a sorowfull spyrite. And thoughe he 15
hath dyspysed the bloode of gotes and calues / yet wyll not he
dispyse a herte contryte and humble. If thou do that thynge whiche
is gyuen to the eyen of men / moche rather take hede that that thyng
be not away whiche the eyen of god requyre. Thy body is couered
with a coule or habite / what is that to the purpose if thy mynde 20
beare a seculer vesture? If thy vtter man be cloked in [L2] a cloke
whyte as snowe / lette the vestymentes of the inner man be also
whyte as snowe. Thou kepest sylence outwarde: moche more
procure that thy mynde be quyet within. In the visyble temple
thou bowest downe the knees of thy body: that is nothyng worthe, 25
if in the temple of thy brest thou stande vpright agaynste god. Thou
honourest the tree of the crosse / moche more folowe the mistery of
ye crosse. Thou kepest the fastyng day and absteynest from those
thinges whiche defyle not a man: and why absteynest thou not
from fylthy talkynge / whiche polluteth thyne owne conscience 30
and other mens also? Meate is withdrawen from the body / but
whye glutteth thy soule her selfe with coddes, draffe, and suche
lyke, whiche are meate mete for swyne? Thou makest the churche

Against ll. 15–17: Inwarde thynges be represented by inwarde thinges.

4 thou] that thou *1533*   5 though he be] beyng eyther *1533*   8 The
sentence] The intellectyon of the sentence *1533*   9 in] with *1533*   11–12
without doute a] veryly *1533*   14 thynkest] thynkest that *1533*   to be a]
is *1533*   18 that] om. *1533*   19 be not] not to be *1533*   22 the inner
man] thy inner maner *1533*   22–3 be also whyte as snowe] be white as snowe
also agreable to the same *1533*   25 worthe] worthy *1533*   30 fylthy]
fylthy *1533*   32 coddes, draffe] coddes of beenes / peson *1533*

of stone gay with goodly ornamentes / thou honourest holy places: what is that to the purpose, if the temple of thy herte / whose walles the prophete Ezechyell bored thorowe, be prophanat or polluted with ye abhomynacions of Egypt? Thou kepest the sabbot

5 day outwarde / and within all thynges be vnquiet thrugh ye rage and tombling of vices togider. Thy body commytteth no adultry, but thou art couetous: now is thy mynde a fornycatour. Thou syngest or prayest [L2v] with thy bodily tonge / but take hede within what thy mynde sayth. With thy mouth thou blyssest /and

10 with thy hert thou cursest. In thy body thou arte closed within a strayte celle / and in thy cogytacion thou wandrest throughout all the worlde. Thou herest the worde of god with thy corporall eares / rather here it within. What saythe the prophete? Except ye here within / your soule shall mourne and wepe. Ye and what redest thou

15 in ye gospell: that they whiche se may not se / and they whiche here maye not here. And agayne the prophete sayth / with your eare ye shall here and ye shall not perceyue: blissed be they therfore whiche here the worde of god within. Happy are they to whom god speaketh within / and their soules shall be saued. This eare to

20 enclyne Dauyd commaundeth that noble doughter of the kyng, whose beautye and godlynesse is all togyther within in golden hemmes. Fynally what auayleth it if thou do not those yuell thynges outwarde / whiche with affection thou desyrest and coueytest inwarde? What auayleth it to do good dedes outwarde /

25 vnto whiche within are commytted thynges clene contrary? Is it so great a thyng if thou go to Hierusalem in thy body / whan within thyne own selfe is both Sodome, Egipt, [L3] and Babylon? It is no great thynge to haue troden ye steppes of Christ with thy bodyly heles / but it is a great thynge to folowe the steppes of

30 Christ in affectyon. If it be a very great thynge to haue touched the sepulcre of Christe / shall it not be also a very great thynge to haue expressed the mistery of his buryeng? Thou accusest and vtterest thy synnes to a preest / whiche is a man: take hede how thou accusest and vtterest them before god. For to accuse them afore hym,

Against ll. 5–6: The sabot day the day of rest.
Again ll. 28–9: Pylgrymages vnto holy places.
Against l. 32: Confession.

3 thorowe] through *1533*   15 they whiche se may not se] whan they se they shulde not se *1533*   15–16 they whiche here maye] whan they here they shulde *1533*   20 Dauyd commaundeth] is commaunded *1533*   21 god-lynesse] goodlynesse *1533*

is to hate them inwardly. Thou byleuest perchaunce all thy synnes
and offences to be washen awaye at ones with a lytell paper or
parchement sealed with wexe / with a lytell money or ymages of
wexe offred / with a lytle pylgrymage goyng. Thou arte vtterly disceyued and cleane out of the way. The wounde is receyued in- 5
wardly: the medycyne therfore must nedes be layde to within.
Thyne affection is corrupt / thou hast loued that whiche was worthy
of hate / and hated that which ought to haue ben beloued. Swete was
to the sower / and bytter was swete. I regarde not what thou shewe
outwarde. But and if cleane contrary thou shalte begynne to hate, to 10
flye, to abhorre that whiche thou lately louedest / if y^t waxe swete to
thyne appetyte, whiche lately had the taste of [L3v] gall: of this
wyse at ye last I perceyue and take a token of helth. Magdaleyne
loued moche / and many synnes were forgyuen her. The more thou
louest Christ, ye more thou shalt hate vices. For ye hate of synne, 15
foloweth the loue of pyte, as ye shadowe foloweth the body. I had
leuer haue the hate ones thy vycyous maners within and in dede /
than to defye them before a preest ten tymes in worde. Therfore
(as I haue rehersed certayne thynges for loue of ensample) in the
hole spectacle and syght of this vysyble worlde / in the olde lawe / 20
in the newe lawe / in all the commaundementes of the churche /
fynally in thy selfe and in all besynesse apertaynyng to man, withoutforth is there a certayn flessh / and within a spiryt. In which
thynges if we shall not make a preposterous ordre / neyther in
thynges whiche are sene shal put very great confydence / but euen 25
as they do helpe to better thynges / and shal always haue respecte
to the spiryte and to the thynges whiche be of charite: than shal
we waxe not heuy as men in sorowe and payne (as these men be)
not feble, euer chyldren (as it is a prouerbe) not beestly and dry bones
(as sayth the prophete) without lyfe / drousye and forgetfull, as 30
men diseased of the lethargy / not dull hauyng no quicknesse / not
brawlers and scolders / not enuyous and [L4] whysperars or back-
byters / but excellent in Christe / large in charyte / stronge and
stable bothe in prosperyte and aduersyte / lokyng besyde small
thynges and enforsyng vp to thinges of most profyte / full of 35

Against ll. 19–20: In all besynes the spyryte is within.
Against ll. 26–7: What thynges folow charitie.
Against ll. 33–4: Prosperitie and aduersitie.

2 washen] wasshed *1533*   20 worlde] *1533*; worde *1534*   27 and
to the thynges whiche be] to thinges *1533*   28 these] those *1533*

myrthe / full also of knowlege. Whiche knowlege who so euer
refuseth / him doth that noble lorde of all knowlege refuse. For
veryly ignoraunce or lacke of experyence / whome for the most
parte accompanyeth dulnesse of lernyng / and that gentlewoman
5 whome the grekes call Philautia / y^t is to say loue of thy selfe /
onely bringeth to passe (as Esayas sayth) y^t we put confidence in
thynges of nothyng / and speke vanytes / that we conceyue labour
and bring forth iniquite / and that we alwayes be fearfull and vyle
bonde seruauntes vnto the ceremones of ye iewes. Of whiche maner
10 persons Paule speking sayth / I beare them recorde that the zele of
god they haue / but not acording to knowlege. But what knewe
they not? verily y^t thende of ye lawe is Christ / and Christ veryly
is a spyrit / he is also charyte. But Esayas more plainly discribeth the
miserable and vnprofytable bondage of these men in the flesshe.
15 Therfore saythe he my people be ledde in captyuyte, bycause they
had no knowlege / and the nobles of them perisshed for hunger / and
the multytude of them dryed [L4v] away for thurste. It is no
meruayle that the comen people be seruauntes to the elementes and
princyples of this worlde : as they whiche are vnlerned / neyther haue
20 wysdome more than they borow of other mennes heedes. It is more
to be meruayled that they whiche are as chefe of Christes religion :
in the same captiuyte perisshe for hunger / and wydder away for
thurst. Why perysshe they for hunger? Bycause they haue not
lerned of Christ to breake barly loues / they lycke onely rounde
25 aboute the rough and sharpe codde or huske / they sucke out no
mary or swete lycoure. And whye wydder they so awaye for
thurst? for bycause they haue not lerned of Moyses to fette water
out of the spyrytuall rocke / neyther haue drunke of the ryuers of
the water of lyfe / whiche flowe, issue, or spring out of the bely of
30 Christ. And this surely was spoken of ye spiryt / not of the flesshe.
Thou therfore my brother / leest with soroufull labours thou
shuldest not moche preuayle / but that with meane exercyse
thou mayste shortly waxe bygge in Christ and lusty / dyligently enbrasyng this rule / mynde not to crepe on the grounde with vncleane

Against l. 11–12: Chryste is the ende of the law.

2 him] them *1533*   5 Philautia] Philancia *1533*   11 acording to]
after *1533*   18 elementes] lawe *1533*   24 lycke onely] only lycke *1533*
28 rocke] rocke of stone *1533*   29 flowe, issue, or spring] floweth / issueth /
or springeth *1533*   30 this surely was spoken] that was spoken verely *1533*
33 thou mayste] myghtest *1533*   33–4 enbrasyng] enbrace *1533*   34 mynde not
to crepe on the grounde with] and crepe not alwaye on the grounde with the *1533*

beestes / but alwayes sustayned with those wynges whiche Plato
beleueth to spring euer a fresshe / through the [L5] heate of loue
in the mynde: lyfte vp thy selfe as it were by certayne steppes of
the ladder of Iacob / from the body to the spiryte / from the
visyble worlde vnto the inuysyble / from the letter to the mystery /   5
from thynges sencyble to thynges intelligyble / from thynges grosse
and compounde vnto thynges syngle and pure. Who so euer after
this maner shall approche and drawe nere to the lorde / the lorde of
his parte shall agayne approche and drawe nyghe to hym. And if
thou for thy parte shalte endeuoyre to aryse out of the darknesse   10
and troubles of the sensual powers: he wyll come agaynst the
plesauntly and for they profyte / out of this lyght inaccessyble /
and out of that noble scylence incogytable. In whiche, not onely
all rage of sensuall powers / but also simylytudes or ymagyna-
cyons of all the intellygyble powers dothe cease and kepe   15
scylence.

⦅ The syxth rule. Caplo. xiiij.

ANd for as moche as in sodayn writyng / one thyng calleth
another to remembraunce / I wyll now adde the syxth rule / whiche
is in a maner of kynrede to them that go before: a rule for all men   20
as necessary vnto helthe, as it is of fewe re[L5v]garded. That rule
is thus / that the mynde of hym whiche enforseth and laboureth to
Christ warde / vary as moche as is possyble bothe from the dedes
and also opynyons of the comen ley people: and that the ensample
of pyte be not fette of any other saue of Christe onely. For he is   25
the onely chefe patron / the only and chefe ensample or fourme of

Against ll. 3–5 (Referring to ll. 1–2): By the wynges of loue we must flee vp
to the spirite.
Against ll. 10–12: Inaccessable is that whiche no man can attayne.
Against ll. 12–15: Incogytable / whiche can not be comprehended with
mannes reason.
Against ll. 22–3: Thou must vary from the comon people.
Against ll. 24–5: The ensample of pitie.

---

3 mynde] mynde of men *1533*   by] with *1533*   12 this] his *1533*
17 Caplo.] capi. *1533*   24 the ensample] thensample *1533*

Side-note 1: flee] flye *1533*   Side-note 2: Inaccessable] Incessable *1533*
that whiche] to vnderstonde that *1533*   Side-note 3: whiche] that *1533*

lyuyng: from whome who so euer wryeth one ynche or nayle brede,
he gothe besydes the ryght pathe and ronneth out of yᵉ way. Wherfore Plato with grauyte forsoth as he doth many thynges, in his
bookes of the gouernaunce of a cytie or comen welthe / denyeth
5 any man to be able to defende vertue constantly, whiche hath not
instructed his mynde with sure and vndouted opinyons of fylthynesse and of honesty. But howe moche more peryllous is it if false
opynyons of the thynges whiche pertayne to helthe, synke in to
the depe botome of thy mynde. Therfore he thynketh that this
10 thynge shulde be cared for and loked vpon chefely / that the gouernours them selfe whome it behoueth to lacke all maner of vnclenly-
nesse / graue in their owne myndes very good opinyons of thynges
to be ensued and eschewed / that is to saye of good and yuell / of
vyces and of vertues / and that [L6] they haue them very assured /
15 al doute layde a parte, as certayne lawes very holy and goodly.
For what so euer thyng cleaueth in the mynde surely rooted with
stedfaste byleue: that euery man declareth in his maners and conuersacyon. Therfore the chefe care of christen men ought to be
applyed to this poynte / that their chyldren streyght waye from the
20 cradle / amongest the very flatterynges of the noryses, and kysses of
the parentes / maye receyue and sucke vnder the handes of them
whiche are lerned / opynyons and perswasyons mete and worthy of
Christe: bycause that nothyng eyther synketh deper or cleaueth
faster in the mynde, than that, whiche (as Fabyus saythe) in the
25 yonge and tendre yeres is poured in. Let be a farre of from the
eares of yonge sucklynges wanton songes of loue / whiche christen
men synge at home and where so euer they ryde or go / moche more
fylthy than euer yᵉ comen people of the hethen men wolde suffre
to be had in vse. Let them not here their mother wayle and wringe
30 her handes, for a lytell losse of worldly goodes / nor for the losse of
her suster here her crye out alas that euer she was borne / to be
brought to this wretchydnesse that she shulde thus be lost / lefte

Against ll. 18–20: The bringyng vp of chrysten mens children.

2 he] *om. 1533*   ronneth] rometh *1533*   3 forsoth] veryly *1533*
8 synke] shulde synke *1533*   9 Therfore] For that consyderacion therfore
1533   20–21 and kysses of the parentes] whyles the father and mother
kysse them *1533*   26 yonge sucklynges] lytle bodyes *1533*   27 home]
whom *1533*   31 here] let them here *1533*   31–2 to be brought to
this wretchydnesse that she shulde thus be lost] seyng that she is but a wretche
a woman loste or cast awaye *1533*

Side-note 1: chrysten] 1533; cstrysten *1534*

alone desolate and destytute. [L6v] Let not them here their father
rebukyng and vpbraydyng hym of cowardnes whiche hath not
recompensed iniury or wronge with double: neyther yet laudynge
them whiche haue gathered togyder great habundaunce of
worldly substaunce / by what soeuer maner it were. The disposycion 5
of man is frayle and prone to vyces: he catcheth mischeuous ensample at ones, none otherwyse than towe catcheth fyre if it be put
to. Howe be it this selfe same thynge is to be done in euery age /
that all the errours of the ley people myght be plucked out agayne
of the mynde by the harde rootes / and in their places he planted 10
holsome opynyons / and so myght be roborate, that with no vyolence they coulde be shake or plucked a sondre. Whiche thynge
who soeuer hath done, shal easely and without besynesse by his owne
accorde folowe vertue / and shall accompte them that do otherwyse,
worthy to be lamented and pityed / and not to be counterfayted or 15
folowed. Vnto this thing pertayneth that not vndiscrete sayeng of
Socrates (thoughe it were rebuked of Arystotle) that vertue was
nothynge els but the knowlege of thinges to be ensued and folowed /
and of thynges to be eschewed or fledde. Not but that Socrates
sawe ye difference bytwene [L7] knowlege of honesty and the loue 20
of the same. But as Demosthenes answered pronuncyacion to be
the first, the seconde, and also the thyrde poynt of eloquence /
signyfyeng that to be ye chefe parte / in so moche that he thought
eloquence to rest al togyther in that thynge onely. In lykewyse
Socrates disputyng with Prothagoras / proueth by argumentes, 25
knowlege in all vertue to beare suche roume / that vyces can no
other whence procede than of false opinyons. For certaynly brother
bothe he that loueth Christe / and he also that loueth voluptuousnesse, money, false honoure, dothe folowe that thing whiche is
eyther of them swete, good, and beautyfull. But the one slydeth 30
through ignoraunce / in stede of a swete thyng enbrasyng a thynge

Against ll. 14–17: (Referring to ll. 18–20): Vertue is the knowledge of thynges
to be auoyded and of thynges to be desyred and loued.
Against ll. 27–9: Synne spryngeth of false opynyons.

---

2 cowardnes] cowarnesse *1533*   not] *1533*; uot *1534*   7 towe
catcheth] thou catchest *1533*   10 of] from *1533*   be] myght be *1533*
12 shake] shaken *1533*   15 counterfayted] counterfayte *1533*   29 money]
many *1533*   30 eyther] to eyther *1533*

out of measure soure / flyeng as a soure thyng whiche is swetest
of all. Also folowynge that thyng for good and for lucre,
whiche is naught els but domage and losse / and fearynge
that thynge for losse / whiche is chefe gaynes or aduauntage:
5 and iudgyng that thynge to be fayre, whiche is foule /
and wenyng or trowyng that to be shamfull, whiche onely
is glorious and praysefull. In conclusyon if a man were surely
and inwardly brought in byleue / and if also it were dygested
in to the substaunce [L7v] of his mynde, as meate in to the
10 substaunce of the body / that onely vertue were best / most
swete / most fayre / moste honest / most profytable: and on the
other syde, fylthynesse only to be an yuell thing / a paynfull
tourment or punysshment / a foule thyng / shamfull / full of
domage or losse: and dyd measure these thynges not by the opin-
15 yon of the comen people / but by the very nature of the thynges:
it coulde not be (suche perswasyon or byleue endurynge) that he
shulde stycke faste or cleaue longe tyme in yuell thynges. For nowe
longe ago the comen people is founde to be the moste mischeuous
authour and capitayne bothe of lyuyng and also of iudgement:
20 neyther was the worlde euer in so good state and condycion, but
that the worst thinges haue pleased the most parte. Beware leest
thou this wyse thynke / no man is there that dothe not this / myne
elders before me haue walked in these steppes / of this oppynyon is
suche a man / so great a phylosopher / so great a diuyne. This is the
25 custome and maner of lyuynge of kynges / this wise lyue great men /
this done bothe bysshoppes and popes / these trewly be no rascals.
Lette not these great names moue the one ynche. I measure or iudge
not the comen or rascall sorte by ye roume, [L8] estate, or degree:

Against ll. 18–20: The comen people is the worst auctor or institutor of lyuyng.
Against l. 27–p. 139, l. 19: Plato wylleth that we shulde imagen a certen
nombre of men to be bounde with theyr hedes vpryght / so that they could not
ones stire / before them a wall / a caue at theyr backes hygher then theyr hedes /
without that a fyre / and that all thynges sholde come to and fro bytwene the
fire and the caues mouthe / that the shadowes of all thynges myght appere vpon
the wall before them / so shuld they se nothing but shadowes. So be the ignorant
and unlerned peple bounden with the bondes of affections that they neuer se
the truth with eyen of reason. The flocke of good men is but small.

———

1 whiche] that which *1533*   17 or] and *1533*   19 and] or *1533*
21 thinges haue] hath *1533*   26 trewly be no rascals] veryly ben no
comen people *1533*

Side-note 1: auctor] anctor *1533, 1534*   Side-note 2: eyen] eyes *1533*

but by the mynde and stomacke. Who so euer in the famous caue of Plato bounde with the bondes of their owne affectyons / wonder at the vayne ymages and shadowes of thynges in stede of very true thynges / they be the comen people. Shulde he not do preposterously and out of ordre if a man wolde go aboute to trye not the 5 stone by the ruler or squyre / but the ruler by the stone? And were it not moche more vnreasonable if a man wolde go about to bowe and tourne / not the maners of men to Christ / but Christ to the lyuyng of men? Thynke it not therfore well or aright, bycause that great men or bycause that moste men do it / but this wyse onely 10 shall it be well and ryght what so euer is doone / if it agre to the rule of Chryste. Ye and therfore ought a thynge to be suspected : bycause it pleaseth the moste parte. It is a small flocke and euer shalbe / to whom is plesaunt the symplycite or playnesse, the pouertye, the veryte of Chryste. It is a small flocke veryly but a blyssed / as vnto 15 whome onely is due the kyngdome of heuen. Strayte is the waye of vertue, and of very fewe troden on / but none other leadeth to lyfe. To conclude / whether dothe a wyse buylder fetche his ensample of the most comen [L8v] and vsed or of the best werke? Paynters set afore them none but the best tables or paterns of ymagerye. Our 20 ensample is Christ / in whom onely be al rules of blyssed lyuing / him may we counterfayte without excepcion. But in good and vertuous men, it shall be mete y^t thou call to an ensample euery thynge / so farre forthe as it shall agre with ye first ensample of Christ. As touchynge the comen sorte of christen men, thinke thus : 25 y^t they were neuer more corrupt / no not amongest the gentiles, as moche as concerneth the opinyons of their maners. More ouer as touchynge their faythe what opinyons they haue aduyse them. This surely is doutlesse and to be abydden by, y^t fayth without maners worthy of faythe, preuayleth nothynge / in so moche also 30 that it groweth to an heape of dampnacyon. Serche the hystories of antyquite / to them compare ye maners that be nowe adayes. Whan was vertue and trewe honesty more dispysed? Whan was so had in price richesse goten not regarded whence? In what worlde at any

Against ll. 25–7 : The comen people of Chrysten men be moost corrupte.
Against ll. 31–3 : The maner of the world now a dayes.

5 and] or *1533*   10 moste] the moste *1533*   16 onely is due] doutlesse is due onely *1533*   20 paterns] patrons *1533*   23 an ensample] ensample *1533*   27 moche as concerneth] appertaynyng to *1533*   28 haue] hane *1533*   29 y^t] om. *1533*   31 an heape] a heape *1533*

tyme was trewer y^t sayeng of Horacius? forsoth that lady money gyueth a wyfe with dowery, credence, frendshyppe, noblenesse, noble kynne, and also beautye. And agayne this sayeng of the same Horace / noblenes and [M1] vertue, excepte a man haue good with-
5 all, is vyler than a russhe or a strawe. Who redeth not now in good ernest that bytyng mocke of the same poete? Oh cytezyns cytezyns / fyrst seke money / after seke vertue. Whan was ryot or excesse more immoderate than now? Whan was adultery, and all other kyndes of vnchaste lyuynge, eyther more appert in ye syght of
10 euery man / or more vnpunysshed / or elles lesse had in shame, rebuke, or abhomynacyon? Whyle princes fauour theyr owne vices in other, and euery man accompteth that moost comly and beautefull to be done, what so euer is vsed and take vp amonge courtyers. To whome semeth not pouertye extreme euyll, and
15 vttermost shame and rebuke? In tyme past, kepers of queenes, fylthy nyggardes, gloryous or gorgyous persons, louers and regard-ers of money, were cast in the tethe with rebukefull and sclaun-derous scoffynges and iestynges / and that by authorite. And also in comedyes, tragedyes, and other commune playes of the gentyles,
20 a great clappynge of handes and a showte was made of ye ley people for ioye / whan vices were craftyly and properly rebuked and checked: at the whiche same vices now a dayes beynge euyll praysed, there is made a showte and clappynge of [M1v] handes for ioye, euen of the nobles and estates of chrysten men. The athenes in theyr com-
25 mune house appoynted for disgysynges and enterludes / coude not forbeare ne suffre a iester in playeng a certeyn tragedy of Euripides / to synge the wordes of a certayne couetous man, which preferred

Against ll. 1–2: Horace the poete.
Against ll. 15–16: The lybertie of olde tyme.
Against l. 26–p. 141, l. 15 (Referring to p. 141, l. 16): Whan the im-bassadors of kyng philyp had offred to Phosion great gyftes / and had exhorted hym to receiue them / sayenge: Thoughe you may spare them well ynoughe: yet shall they be necessarye for your childeren / to whom it shal be hard to opteyn to com to suche honor as you are in. Phosion answered / yf my children shal be lyke me / this same possessyon shall fynde theym whiche hathe brought me to so great honor / yf they shulde be vnlyke me: I wyll not that theyr ryot be norys-shed and augmented at my cost.

1 forsoth] veryly *1533*   5 now] *om. 1533*   12 other] other men suf-frynge them vnpunysshed *1533*   15 past] paste against *1533*   18 and that by] ye with *1533*   20–21 of ye ley people for ioye] for ioy of the ley people *1533*
Side-note 3: so great] se grete *1533*

money onely before all other commodytees and pleasure of mannes
lyfe: and they wolde playnly haue clapped out of the play / yea and
violently cast out of the house the player with al the fable, had not
the poete by and by arysynge vp desyred them to tary a lytell and
beholde to what poynte that so great a wonderer of money sholde 5
comme. How many ensamples be there in the gentyles, hystoryes of
them, whiche of the commune welthe well gouerned and mynystred / brought nothinge in to theyr poore housholde but an honest
opynyon or reputacyon. Whiche set more by fidelite, than money /
by chastite, than by lyfe. Whome neyther prosperite coude make 10
proude, wylde or wanton/ neyther aduersite coude ouercomme and
make heuy herted. Whiche regarded honest ieopardies and daungers
before voluptuousnesse and pleasures. Whiche contented onely
with ye conscience of pure lyfe / desired neyther honours neither
rychesse / nor any other commodytees of fortune. And to ouerhyp 15
and make no rehersall [M2] of the holynesse of Phocion / of the
pouerte of Fabricius more excellent than ryches: of the stronge
and couragyous mynde of Camillus / of the strayte and indifferent
iustyce of Brutus / of the chastite of Pithagoras/ of the temperaunce
of Socrates / of the sounde and constant vertue of Cato: and a 20
thousand most goodly beames of al sortes of vertues, whiche are
red euerywhere in thystoryes of the lacedemonyes, of ye perces, of
the athenes, and of the romayns, to our great shame veryly. Holy
Aurelius Augustyne, as he hym selfe wytnesseth in the commentaryes of his owne confessions, longe tyme before he put Chryst on 25
hym, despised money / counted honours for naught / was not
moued with glory, prayse, or fame / and to voluptuousnes kepte the

Against l. 16–p. 142, l. 8 (Referring to ll. 17–20): Fabricius was a noble man
of Rome / whome no man coulde make to posses rychesse / or receiue gyftes /
or to vse crafte or fraude agaynst his enemyes in tyme of mortall warre.
Camyllus was so constaunt of mynde that no fortune coulde moue hym / nor
no iniury could make hym vnkynde to the comune welth. Brute slew his owne
sones bycause they conspyred agaynst the comune welthe. Pythagoras was the
auctor of chast liuyng. Socrates sayd that he knewe well hym selfe to be vnlerned /
and he neuer laughed / and yet was he mery.

3–4 had not the poete . . . desyred] except the poete . . . had desired *1533*
5 of] at *1533*   6 gentyles, hystoryes] hystories of gentyles *1533*   11 or]
and *1533*   16–17 of the pouerte] of pouerty *1533*   24 hym selfe] of
hym selfe *1533*

Side-note 1: fortune] tortune *1533*

brydell so strayte, that he than a yonge man, was content with one
lytell wenche / to whome he kepte also promesse and fayth of mariage.
Suche ensamples among courtyers / amonge men of the churche, I
wyll also say amongest religyous persones, shall not a man lyghtly
5 fynde. Or yf any suche shall be, by and by he shall be poynted,
wondred, or mocked at, as it were an asse amonge apes / he shall
be called with one voyce of al men a doting foole, a grosheed / an
ypocryte, in nothyng experte, melancoly mad / and shall not be
iudged to be a man. [M2v] So we christen men honour the doctryne
10 of Chryst, so counterfayte we it, that euery where now adays nothyng
is accompted more folysshe, more vyle, more worthy to be ashamed
of, than to be a chrysten man in dede / with all herte and mynde.
As though that eyther Chryst in vayne had ben conuersaunt in erth /
or that chrystendom were some other thing now, than in tyme
15 past / or dyd not indifferently appertayne to all men. I wyll therfore
that thou from these men vary with al thy mynde / and esteme the
valure of euery thing by the communyon or felawshyp of Chryst
onely. Who thynketh it not euery where to be an excellent thyng
and worthy to be nombred among ye chefe of al good thynges / yf a
20 man descende of a worshipful stocke and of honourable ancestours,
whiche thyng they call noblenesse? Let it not moue ye one whyt,
whan thou hearest the wyse men of this worlde / men of sadnesse
endued with great authorite / so ernestly disputyng of the degrees
of their genelogies or lynage / hauing their foreheed and vpper
25 browes drawen togyder with very great grauite, as it were a mater
of meruaylous difficulte / yea and with great enforcement bryngyng
forth playne tryfles. Nor let it moue the whan thou seest other so
hygh mynded, for ye noble actes of theyr [M3] grandfathers or
great grandfathers / that they thynke other in comparison of them
30 selfe scarse to be men. But thou laughyng at ye errour of these men,

Against ll. 9–11 (Referring to p. 141, l. 23–p. 142, l. 2): The contynence
of saynte Augustyne.
Against ll. 14–16: To be a very christen man / is accompted euery where a
very vyle thynge.
Against ll. 19–20: The vanitie of noble men.
Against l. 30–p. 143, l. 4: Democrytus laughed at what so euer thyng was
don in the lyfe of mortal men / it semyd to hym so folysh a thyng.

5 yf] els if *1533*   7 grosheed /] grosseheed / *1533*; grosheed *1534*
11 worthy] *om. 1533*   12 herte and mynde] the mynde and herte *1533*
15 dyd not . . . appertayne] as it . . . pertayned not *1533*   19 worthy] *om.*
1533   26 meruaylous] a meruaylous *1533*   29 they] *om. 1533*

after ye maner of Democritus, shalte compte (as trewe it is in dede) that the onely and moost perfyte noblenesse, is to be regenerate in Chryst / and to be graffed and planted in the body of him / to be one body and one spiryt with god. Let other men be kynges sones: to the, let it be the greatest honour that can be, that thou art called, 5 and art so in dede, the sone of god. Let them stande in theyr owne conceytes, bycause they are dayly conuersaunt in great prynces courtes: chose thou rather to be with Dauyd vyle abiecte in the house of god. Take hede what maner felowes Chryst chose / feble persones / fooles / vyle as touchynge this worlde. In Adam we be all 10 borne of lowe degre: In Chryst we be all one. Very noblenesse is to despyse this vayne noblenesse: very noblenesse is to be seruaunt to Chryste. Thynke them to be thyne ancestours, whose vertues thou bothe louest and counterfaytest. Also harke what the true estemer of noblenesse sayd in the gospell agaynst the iewes, 15 whiche bosted them selfe to be of the generacyon of Abraham: a man veryly, not excellent onely, not ryche onely, not the conquer-our [M3v] of kynges onely / but also for his dyuyne vertues lauded of god hym self. Who wolde not thynke this to be a noble thynge and worthy, wherof a man myght reioyce? Harke yet what they 20 herde: ye are (sayd Chryst) of your father the deuyll / and the dedes of your father ye do. And heare also Paule how he estemeth gentyll blode / accordyng to his maysters rule. Not al they (sayth he) whiche be of the circumcysyon of israel, be israelites / neyther al they that be of the sede of Abraham, be the sones of Abraham. It is 25 a lowe degre and shamefull, to serue fylthynesse / and to haue no kynrede with Chryst / whiche knowlegeth kynrede with no man, but with suche as fulfylleth the wyl of his father in heuen. He is with moche shame a bastarde, whiche hath the deyull to his father / and veryly who so euer dothe the dedes of the deuyl, hath the deuyll 30 to his father / and veryly who so euer dothe the dedes of the deuyl, hath the deuyll to his father / excepte Chryste lyed. But the trewth can not lye. The hyghest degre that can be, is to be the sone and heyre of god/the brother and coheyre with Chryst. What theyr badges

Against ll. 5-6: The chefest noblenes is to be the sone of god.
Against ll. 22-3: Here may you se howe Paule estemeth noble blode.

---

5 the greatest] greatest *1533*   9 chose] choseth *1533*   10 be all] all are *1533*   11 be all one] are all one thyng neyther hygh ne lowe of degre one more than another *1533*   24 the circumcysyon] cyrcumcisyon *1533*
Side-note 2: Here may you se] You may se here *1533*

and cognisaunces meane, let them loke. The badges of Chryste
be commune to all men / and yet moost honourable, whiche be the
crosse / the crowne of thorne, the nayles, the spere, the sygnes or
tokens, whiche Paule reioyseth to beare [M4] in his body. Of noble-
5 nesse therfore thou seest how moche otherwyse I wolde haue the to
iudge and thynke, than the ley people ymagyn. Who calleth not him
blyssed, ryche, and happy among the commune people, whiche hath
heaped togyder at home a greate deale of golde? But iudge thou hym
to be blyssed ynough / ye that he onely is blyssed, whiche posses-
10 seth Chryst / very felicite / and of all thynges the best. Iudge hym
happy whiche hath bought that noble and precyous margaryte of pure
mynde, with the losse eyther of all his goodes, or his body also /
whiche hathe founde the treasour of wysdome precyouser than all
rychesse. Whiche to be made ryche, hathe bought of Chryst that is
15 most ryche, golde puryfyed and proued with fyre. What thynges
than be these whiche the commune people wonder at / as golde,
precyous stones, lyuelode? in a wronge name they be ryches / in
the true name they be very thornes, whiche choke the sede of the
worde of god / accordyng to the parable of ye gospell. They be
20 packes or fardels with whiche who so euer be laden, they neyther
can folowe poore Chryst by the strayte waye, neyther enter by the
lowe dore in to the kyngdom of heuen. Thynke not thy selfe better
by one heare, yf thou sholdest passe in rychesse [M4v] eyther
Mydas or Cresus / but thynke thy selfe more bounde, more tangled,
25 more laden. He hath haboundantly ynough, that can manfully
despyse suche thynges. He is prouyded for sufficyently, to whom
Chryst promysed nothyng sholde be lackyng. He shall not be an
hongred, to whose mouth manna of ye worde of god semeth pleasaunt. He shall not be naked, y^t hath put Chryst vpon him. Thinke
30 this onely to be a losse as ofte as any thyng of godlynesse is mynys-
shed / and any thyng of vices is encreased. Thynke it a greate lucre

Against ll. 1–2: The badges of true noblenes.
Against ll. 7–8: Riche men be not blessed.
Against l. 16: What is riches.
Against ll. 24–5: Mydas and Cresus were two ryche kynges.
Against ll. 30–1: There is no domage in the losse of ryches.

---

1 loke] take hede *1533*   2 yet] the *1533*   16 wonder] wondreth
1533   20 they] *om. 1533*   21 the strayte] strayte *1533*   25 manfully]
vtterly *1533*   29 y^t] which *1533*

Side-note 5: of] ef *1533*

or aduauntage, whan thy mynde through encrease of vertue is
waxen better. Thynke thou lackest nothyng, as longe as thou
possessest hym in whome are al thinges. But what is this whiche
wretches call pleasure? surely it is nothing lesse than y^t it is called.
What is it than? Pure madnes it is / and playnly (as grekes be wont 5
to say) ye laughter of Aiax, swete poyson, pleasaunt myschefe.
True and onely pleasure, is the inward ioy of a pure conscyence.
The moost noble and deyntyest dysshe that can be, is ye study of
holy scripture. The moost delectable songes, be the psalmes endyted
of the holy goost. The moost pleasaunt felyshyp, is the communyon 10
of all sayntes. The hyest deyntyes of al, is the fruicion and enioying
of the very truthe. [M5] Pourge now thy eyen, pourge thy eares,
pourge thy mouth / and Chryst shal begyn to waxe swete and
pleasaunt to the. Who tasted ones sauerly: ye if, milesij sibarite / if
al incontynent ryottours and epicuryens / shortly, if the vniuersite 15
of ymagyners and deuysers of pleasures sholde heape togyder al
their flaterynge subtyltees and deynty dysshes / in comparison of
hym onely, they shall seme to prouoke the to spue. That is not by
and by swete, whiche is sauery / but that which is sauery to a hole
man. If water haue the taste of wyne to hym whiche burneth in a 20
hote feuer, no man wyll call that pleasure but a disease. Thou art
deceyued yf thou byleue not, that very teres be moche more pleasaunt to deuout and holy men, than be to wycked men laughynges,
mockinges, gestynges or scoffynges. If thou also byleue not
fastynge to be sweter to the one, than to ye other plouers / quayles / 25
fesauntes / partriches, pyke, troute, porpas, or the fresshe sturgen.
And the moderate bordes of thone apoynted with erbes and frutes to
be moche more delycate, than the costly and disdaynfull feestes of y^e
other. Fynally the true plesure is, for ye loue of Chryst, not to be ones
moued with false apparant plesures. Beholde now how moche the 30

Against ll. 6–26: Aiax in his madnes hanged vp two great swyne / supposyng
the one to haue been Agamenon / the other Vlyxes / his two mortal enemyes.
Than with moche laughter he raged against them / castyng many iniuryes in
theyr teth / but whan he was com to his wittes agayne / he kylled hym self for
shame and sorow / so bicause of voluptuous pleasure / foloweth mischefe / it
may be well called the laughter of Aiax. Milesii Sibarite were people whiche
lyued delycately. Epicure put felicitie in voluptuousnes. That is swete whiche
sauoureth to a hole man.

3 are] is *1533*   14 Who] whiche *1533*   21 feuer, no man] feuer no /
man *1533*   pleasure] a plesure *1533*   22 very] the very *1533*   28–9 y^e
other] thother *1533*   30 plesures.] pleasures. *1533*; plesures *1534*

worlde abuseth the names of loue and hate. Whan a folysshe [M5v] yong man is clere out of his wytte and mad for a wenches sake: that ye commune people call loue / and yet is there no veryer hate in the world. True loue euen with his owne losse, desyreth to se vnto an
5 other mannes profyte. Whervnto loketh he, saue vnto his owne pleasure? Therfore he loueth not her, but hymselfe: how be it forsothe, he loueth not hymself. For no man can loue an other, except he loue hymselfe first / ye and except he loue hymselfe aryght. No man can hate any man at all, excepte he fyrst hate hym selfe. Neuerthe-
10 lesse somtyme to loue well, is to hate well / and to hate well, is to loue well. Who so euer therfore for his lytell pleasure (as he supposeth it) layeth awayte and goth about to begyle a mayden with flaterynges and gyftes / with fayre promesses / to plucke from her the best thynge she hath / that is to wyte, her perfytnesse, her chastite,
15 her symplicite, her innocency, her good mynde, and her good name / whether semeth this man to hate, or to loue? Certeynly there is no hate more cruel than is this hate. Whan the folysshe father and mother fauour the vices of their chyldren: the commune saying is / how tenderly loue they theyr chyldren? But I pray the / how cruelly
20 hate they theyr chyldren, whiche (whyle they folowe their owne affections) [M6] regarde not at all the welth of theyr chyldren? What other thynge wyssheth to vs our moost hatefull ennemy ye deuyll, that that we here synnyng vnpunisshed, sholde fall in to eternall punysshment. They call hym an easy mayster and a mercy-
25 full prynce, whiche at certayne greuous offences eyther wynketh or sheweth fauour / that the more vnpunysshed men do synne / the more boldly and at large they may synne. But what other thynge threteneth god by his prophete to them, whome he iudgeth vnworthy of his mercy. And shal I not (saith he) loke vpon your
30 doughters whan they commyt fornycacyon / nor your doughters in lawe, whan they commyt adultery? Vnto Dauid what promysed he. I wyll (sayth he) with a rodde vysyte theyr iniquytees / and with whyppes, theyr synnes / but I wyll not scater my mercy from theym.

Against l. 2: Folisshe loue.
Against ll. 17-18: Tendernes towardes theyr chyldren.

---

3 call] calleth *1533*   6 how be it forsothe, he loueth not hymself] yet loueth he not hym selfe verily *1533*   13 flaterynges] flateryng *1533* 22 thynge] *om. 1533*   25-6 wynketh or sheweth fauour] wynke or fauoure them *1533*   26 do] *om. 1533*.   27 may] might *1533*   29 And shal I . . . loke vpon your] I wyll . . . vysyte their *1533*   30 your] their *1533*   32 vysyte] loke vpon *1533*   33 scater] take *1533*

Thou seest how all thynges are renewed in Chryst / and how the names of thynges are chaunged. Who so euer loue hym selfe otherwyse than well / hateth hymself deedly. Who so euer is euyll mercyfull towarde hymselfe, is a tyraunt moost cruell. To care well, is not to regarde. To hurte well, is to do good. To destroye well, is to saue. Thou shalt care well for thy selfe, yf thou shalte despyse the desyres of the flesshe. [M6v] If in good maner thou shalt rage agaynst vyces / thou shalte do to the man a good turne. If thou shalt kyll the synner, thou shalt saue the man. If thou shalt destroye that man hath made / thou shalte restore that god hath made. Comme of now and let vs go further. What thynketh the errour of the people power, wyckednesse, manhode, and cowardnesse to be? Call they not hym myghty, whiche can lyghtly hurte whome hym lyst? al be it, it is a very odyous power, to be able to hurte / for in that are they resembled to noysome wormes and scorpyons / and to the deuyll hym selfe / that is to wyte, in doynge harme. Onely god is myghty in dede / whiche neyther can hurt yf he wolde / neyther yet wolde yf he coude / for his nature is to do good. But this myghty felowe how dothe he I beseche the hurt a man? He shall take away thy money? he shall beate thy body? he shall robbe the of thy lyfe? If he do it to hym that serueth god well / he hath done a good dede, in stede of an euyll. But and yf he haue done it to an euyll man / this hath mynystred the occasyon veryly / but he hath hurt hym selfe, for no man is hurt but of hym selfe. No man gothe aboute to hurt an other, excepte the same man hath moche more greuously hurte hym selfe a[M7]forehande. Thou enforsest to hurte me in my money or goodes? Now hast thou through the losse of charite hurte thy selfe moost greuously. Thou canst not fasten a wounde in me / but yf thou haue fyrst receyued a wounde more greuous. Thou canst not take from me the lyfe of my body / oneless thou haue slayne thyne owne soule before. But Paule, whiche to do wronge was a man very weyke and feble / to suffre wronge moost valyaunt and stronge / reioyseth he not that he coude do all thynge in Chryst? They call hym euery where manly and bolde, whiche fyerse and of impotent mynde / for the leest displeasure that can be, rageth, setheth, or boyleth in wrathe / and

---

3 is] be *1533*   14 al be it, it is] though it be *1533*   16 to the deuyll] to to the dyuell *1533*   23 this] the one *1533*   the occasyon] an occasyon *1533*   24 he] the other *1533*   29 fyrst] *om. 1533*   30 more] moche more *1533*   33 he not that] that *1533*   35 fyerse] beyng fyerse *1533*

acquyteth a shrewde worde with a shrewde worde / a checke with
a checke / one euyll tourne with an other. Contrary wyse, who so
euer receyuynge wronge maketh nothynge a do / but dissymuleth
as no suche thynge were done / hym they call a cowarde / a dastarde,
5 hertlesse, mete for nothyng. But yet what is farder of from the
greatnes and valyauntnes of stomacke, than with a lytell worde to
be puffed asyde from the quietnes and constancye of the mynde /
and to be so vnable to set at nought an other mannes folysshnes /
that thou sholdest thinke thy selfe to be no [M7v] man, excepte thou
10 dyddest ouercomme one shrewde tourne with an other? But how
moche more manfull is it, with an excellent and large stomacke to
be able to despyse all maner iniuryes / and more ouer, for an euyll
dede, to recompence a good? I wolde not call hym a bolde man,
whiche durste ieopard on his ennemy / which scaleth castell or
15 towne walles / whiche (his lyfe not regarded) putteth hym selfe in
al maner ieopardies / a thing commune almost to al warryoures.
But who so euer can ouercomme his owne hert / who so euer can
wyl them good, whiche dothe hym harme / praye for them, whiche
curse hym: to this man is due the propre name of a bolde and
20 stronge man, and of an excellent mynde. Let vs also discusse an other
thyng / what the worlde calleth prayse, rebuke, and shame. Thou
art praysed / for what cause, and of whome? if for fylthy thynges
and of fylthy persones / this veryly is a false prayse and a true
rebuke. Thou art dispraysed / thou art mocked, or laughed at / for
25 what cause, and of whome? for godlynesse and innocency / and that
of euyll men: this is not a rebuke / no there is no truer prayse. Be it
forsothe that euen the hole worlde clap, stampe, and hysse at it / yet
can it not be but gloryous, and of greate prayse that Christ appro-
ueth. And though [M8] all mortall men agre, consent, and alowe it /

Against ll. 14–15: A bolde man and a stronge in dede.
Against l. 24: True prayse.

2 Contrary wyse] On the other syde *1533*   3 receyuynge] whan he hath
receyued *1533*   4 dastarde,] dastarde *1533*, *1534*   5 But yet] ye
but *1533*   farder of from] more contrary to *1533*   6 and valyauntnes of
stomacke] of the mynde *1533*   7 puffed] put *1533*   quietnes] quyet *1533*
mynde] spyryte *1533*   10 dyddest] shuldest *1533*   11 stomacke]
mynde *1533*   14 scaleth] scale *1533*   17 can] coulde *1533*   hert]
mynde *1533*   can] coulde *1533*   20 an excellent] excellent *1533*
27 forsothe that euen the hole worlde clap, stampe, and hysse at it] ye all the
worlde repreue / refuse / and disalowe it *1533*   29 all mortall men] what
soeuer is in the worlde *1533*   alowe it] alowe *1533*

cryenge with a showte, that is a noble dede / yet can it not be but shamefull that displeaseth god. They call it wisdom euery where to gete good stoutly / whan it is goten, to mayntayne it lustely / and to prouyde longe before, for the tyme to comme politykly. For so we heare them saye euery where, and in good ernest of them 5 whiche in shorte tyme gate substaunce somwhat haboundantly / he is a thryfty man, ware and wyse, circumspecte and prouydent. Thus sayth the worlde, whiche is bothe a lyer hym selfe, and also his father. But what sayth verite? Foole sayth he / I wyll fette agayne this nyght thy soule from the. He had fylled his barnes with 10 corne / he had stuffed his store houses with prouysyon of all vytayles / and had layde vp at home haboundauntly of money ynough: he thought nothynge was to be done more. Thus had he done / not bycause he entended as a nedy keper to syt abrode on his rychesse heaped togyder / as the poetes fayne the dragon to 15 haue kept the golden flece (whiche thing men do almost euery where) but he entended to haue spente ioyously / and yet doth the gospell call this man a foole. For what is more folyssh / what is more grosse ymaginacyon, or more [M8v] fondnesse, than to gape at the shadowes / and lose the very thinges / a thing whiche we be 20 wonte to laugh at in the famous dogge of ysope. And in the maners of chrysten men, is it not more to be laughed at / or rather to be wept at. He may be compted a rude and vnexperte marchaunt, that knewe not this sayinge of Therence: To refuse money at a season, is somtyme a great aduauntage / or who so euer wolde 25 receyue a lytel aduauntage in hande, whan he knewe great losse sholde folowe. How moche more folysshnesse and vnaduysed-nesse is it, with so great care to make prouysyon for this shadow-isshe lyfe, euery houre redy to fayle, notwithstandynge that god wolde mynystre sufficyently, wherwith it sholde be susteyned / and 30 for the lyfe to comme to prouyde nothyng at all. Whiche we must

Against ll. 2–3: Wysdome of the worlde.
Against ll. 20–4: Whyle we gape at shadowes / we lose the very thynges / as the dogge of ysope / whiche while he gapid at the shadow lost his bone in the water.

---

2 it] *om. 1533* 4 politykly] *om. 1533* 28 with so great care to make prouysyon] to make prouysion with so great care *1533* 28–9 shadow-isshe lyfe] presente lyfe whiche is but a shadow *1533* 29–30 notwithstand-ynge that god wolde mynystre sufficyently, wherwith it sholde be susteyned] namely whan god (if we byleue yᵉ gospel) wyll minyster althing necessary for this lyfe / if we haue confydence in hym *1533* 31 prouyde nothyng] make no prouysion *1533*

lede alway full of mysery and wretchednes / yf prouysyon be not made now aforehande with greate diligence. Heare an other errour / they call hym perelesse polityke, and in all thynges expert / whiche harkenyng for all maner tydynges, knoweth what is done
5 through out all the worlde / what is the chaunce of marchaundyse / what the kyng of Englande entendeth / what newe thing is done at Rome / what is chaunced in Fraunce / how the danes and the scytes lyue / [N1] what maters great princes haue in counsayle. To make an ende shortly / who so euer can babble with al kyndes of men of
10 all maner busynes / hym they say to be wyse. But what can be farder from the thought of a wise man / or nere to ye nature of a foole than to serche for those thynges which be done aferre of, and pertayne to ye nothyng at al? and not so moch as ones verily to thinke on those thynges whiche are done in thyne owne brest and
15 pertayne to the onely. Thou tellest me of the trouble and besynes of Englande / tel me rather what trouble maketh in thy brest wrathe, enuy, bodyly lust, ambycion / howe nygh these be brought in to subiection / what hope is of victory / howe moche of this hoost is put to flyght / how reason is decked or appoynted. In these thynges
20 if thou shalte be watchyng and haue a quycke eare and also an eye / if thou shalte smell / if thou shalte be circumspecte / I wyll call the polityke and pereles: and that thing whiche the world is wont to cast agaynst vs, I wyll whorle agayne at hym. He is not wyse at all, whiche is not wise for his owne profyte. After this maner if thou
25 shalt examyne all the cares of mortall men / their ioyes, hopes, feares, studies, their myndes or iudgementes / thou shalt fynde all thyng full of errour whyle they call good yuel / and [N1v] yuell good / whyle they make swete soure and soure swete: make light darknes / and darknesse lyght. And this sorte of men is the more
30 parte by a great deale / whiche notwithstandyng thou must at one tyme bothe defye, that thou woldest not to be lyke vnto them: and also pyte that thou mayst desyre to haue them lyke vnto the. And (to vse the wordes of saint Augustyn) than is it mete bothe to wepe

Against ll. 4–5: To herken for tydynges oute of all countreys is rebuked.

---

1 alway] away *1533*   9 who so euer] who euer *1533*   23 whorle] horle *1533*   30 whiche notwithstandyng] Notwithstandyng *1533*   30-1 at one tyme] euen at ones *1533*   31 that thou woldest not to be lyke vnto them] them and set no store of them / leest thou sholdest be mynded to be lyke them *1533*   32 that thou mayst desyre to] them so that thou woldest fayne *1533*

for them whiche are worthy to be laughed at / and to laugh at them which are worthy to be wept for. Be not in yuell thynges conformable to this worlde, but be reformed in the newe wytte / that thou mayste approue not tho thynges whiche men wonder at / but what is the wyll of god / whiche is good, well pleasynge and perfyte. 5 Thou art very nygh ieopardy and no doute fallest sodaynly from the true way, if thou shalte begyn to loke aboute the what ye most parte of men do / and to herken what they thynke or ymagyn. Thou whiche art the chylde of lyfe and of lyght also, suffre y^t the deed men bury their deed : lette the blynde capitaynes of blynde 10 men go awaye togyther in to the dyche. Se thou ones moue not the eyen of thy herte any whyder, from the fyrste patron and chefe ensample Christ. Thou shalte not go out of the waye / if thou fo-[N2]lowe the gydynge of verite. Thou shalte not stumble in darknesse, if thou walke after lyght : if this lyght shyne before the thou 15 shalt separate coloured good thinges from good thynges in dede / and yuell thynges in dede from apparant yuell thynges : thou shalte abhorre and not counterfayte the blyndenesse of the commune people ragynge and chafynge them selfe after the maner of the ebbynge and flowyng of the see at the moste vayne illusyons and 20 worldly thynges / with certayne corresyes of affectyons of wrathe, enuye, loue, hate, hope, feare, ioy, sorowe / ragyng more vnquietly than any Euripus. The Bragmanyes / Cynikis / Stoikes be wonte to defende their dogmies and doctryne styfly with tothe and nayle : and euen the hole worlde repugnynge / all men cryeng and bark- 25 ynge agaynst them / yet holde they styfly y^t thing, whervnto they ones haue gyuen sure credence. Be thou bolde lykewyse to fasten surely in thy mynde ye decrees of thy secte. Be bolde without mystrust / and with all that thou canst make, to folow the mynde of thyne authour / departyng from all contrary opynyons and sectes. 30

Against ll. 15–30 (Referring to l. 23) : Eurypus is a certayne place in the see / where the flood chaungeth seuen tymes in a day / and as oft a nyght / so that no shyp can saile against the streme. Bragmanyes were people of a certayne yle in Indea / with whom all thinges were commune / and they liued perfitly / dyspysynge riches / possessions / and all worldly thynges. Cinikes be the folowers of dyogenes the philosopher / whiche chorlysshly checketh the vices of men.

2–3 conformable] confirmable *1533*   9 Thou ... also, suffre] but suffre thou ... also *1533*   9–10 the deed men] deed men *1533*   10 their deed] theyr deed bodies *1533*   lette] and let *1533*   12 eyen] eyes *1533* 13 Christ] of Chryste *1533*   15 if this lyght shyne ... thou] the lyght shynynge ... yf thou *1533*   24 dogmies and doctryne] pryncyples *1533*

❡ Here folowen opynyons mete
for a christen man. Caplo. xv. [N2v]

LEt this excellent lernyng and paradoxes of the true christen
faythe be sure and stedfast with the / that no christen man may
5 thynke that he is borne for him selfe / neyther ought to haue the
mynde to lyue to himselfe: but what so euer he hath / what so
euer he is / that all togyther lette hym ascribe not to himselfe, but
vnto god the authour therof, and of whom it came / all his goodes
let hym thynke to be commune to all men. The charite of a
10 christen man knoweth no propertie: let hym loue good men in
Christe / yuell men for Christes sake / whiche so loued vs fyrste
whan we were yet his enemyes / that he bestowed hymselfe on vs
all togyder for our redemptyon. Let hym enbrace the one bycause
they be good, the other neuertheles to make them good. He may
15 hate no man at all / no more truly than a faythfull phisicyon hateth
a sycke man. Let hym be an enemy onely vnto vyces. The greater
the disease is / the greater care wyll pure charite haue therto. He is
an adulter / he hath commytted sacrylege / he is a turke. Lette a
christen man defye the adulter, not yᵉ man / let hym dispyse the
20 commytter of sacrylege, not the man / let hym kyll the turke, not the
man / let hym fynde the meanes that the yuell man maye perysshe
whome he [N3] made hymselfe, but so that the man be saued whom
god made. Let hym wyll well, wyssh well, and do well to all men
vnfaynedly. Neyther hurte them whiche haue deserued it: and do
25 good to them whiche haue not deserued it. Let hym be glad of all
mennes commodytees as well as of his owne / and also be sory for
all mens harmes none otherwyse than for his owne. For veryly this
is that whiche the apostle commaundeth. To wepe with them that
wepe, to ioye with them that ioyen. Ye let hym take an other mannes
30 harme greuouser than his owne: and of his brothers welth be
gladder than of his owne. It is not a christen mans parte to thinke

Against ll. 8–10: A christen man is not borne for hym selfe / eyther to folowe
his owne pleasure.
Against ll. 18–20: We must defye and abhorre the vyces / but not the man.

2 man.] 1533; man 1534   Caplo.] Capl. 1533   6 hath /] hath 1533, 1534
14 may] shall 1533   15 truly] veryly 1533   17 care] cure 1533
haue] put 1533   21 maye] om. 1533   22 whome] suche as 1533
made hymselfe, but so that] hathe made hym selfe to be / but let 1533
23 wyll well,] wyll well 1533, 1534   24 and] but 1533   28 the apostle]
thapostle 1533   29 wepe,] wepe / 1533; wepe 1534   take] rather take 1533

on this wise: what haue I to do with this felowe / I know not whether
he be blacke or whyte / he is vnknowen to me / he is a straunger
to me / he neuer dyd ought for me / he hath hurt me somtyme,
but dyd me neuer good. Thynke none of these thynges. Remembre
onely for what deseruynge what thynges Chryste hath doone to the,   5
who wolde haue his kyndnesse towarde the to be recompensed, not
in hym selfe / but in thy neyghbour. Onely se of what thynges he
hath nede / and what thou art able to do for hym. Thynke this
thyng onely / he is my brother in the lorde / coheyre in Chryste /
a [N3v] membre of the same body / redemed with one blode / a   10
felowe in ye commune fayth / called vnto ye very same grace and
felicite of the lyfe to come. As the apostle sayd, one body and one
spiryt euen as ye be called in one hope of your calling, one lorde, and
one faith, one baptisme, one god and father of al whiche is aboue all
and euerywhere / and in all vs. How can he be a straunger to whom   15
thou art coupled with so manyfolde bondes of vnite? Amonge y^e
gentyles let those circumstaunces of the rethoricyens be of some
valure and weyght, eyther vnto beniuolence or vnto maliuolence /
he is a citezyn of ye same cyte / he is of aliaunce / he is my
cosyn / he is my famyliar frende / he is my fathers frende / he hath   20
well deserued / he is kynde / borne of an honest stocke/ ryche or
otherwise. In Christ al these thynges eyther be nothyng / or after y^e
mynde of Paule be al one / and the very selfe same thing. Let this
one thyng be euer present before thyne eyen / and it is ynough / he
is my flessh, he is my brother in Christ. What soeuer is bestowed   25
vpon any membre reboundeth it not to al ye body, and from thence
in to ye heed? We all be membres eche one of an other. Membres
cleuyng togyder make a body. The heed of ye body is Iesus Christ /
ye heed of Christ is god. It is done to the, it is done to euery one / it
is done to [N4] Chriate, it is done to god: what so euer is done to   30
any one membre which so euer it be / whether it be well done or
yuell. All these thynges are one / God / Christe / the body / and
the membres. That sayeng hath no place conuenyently amonge

2 whyte /] white 1533; whyte 1534   4 good.] good 1533, 1534
5 what thynges] can those thynges whiche 1533   5-6 to the, who wolde
haue his kyndnesse towarde the to be recompensed] for ye which wolde his
kyndnes done to the / sholde be recompensed 1533   9 the lorde /] our
lorde 1533; the lorde 1534   12-13 As ... euen as] euen as ... as 1533
17 the rethoricyens] rethoricyens 1533   some] no lytel 1533   24 one
thyng] om. 1533   eyen] eyes 1533   it is ynough] let this suffyse the
1533

christen men / lyke with lyke. And y^t sayeng vnlykenesse is the
mother of hate. For vnto what purpose pertaynen wordes of dis-
centyon where so great vnite is. It sauoureth not of christen faythe
that communly a courtyer to a towne dweller: one of the countrey
5 to an inhabyter of the cyte: a man of hygh degree, to an other of
lowe degree: an offycer, to hym that is offycelesse: the ryche to
the poore: a man of honour, to a vyle person: the myghty to
the weake: the italyen to the germayne: the frenche man to the
englysshman: the englysshe to the scotte: the gramaryen to the
10 diuyne: the logycyner to the gramaryen: the phisicien to the man
of lawe: the lerned to the vnlerned: the eloquent to hym that is not
facounde and lacketh vtteraunce: the syngle to the maryed: the
yonge to the olde: the clerke to the ley man: the preest to the monke:
the Carmelytes to the Iacobytes: and that (leest I reherse all dyuer-
15 sytees) in a very tryfle vnlyke to vnlyke / is somwhat parcyall and
vnkynde. Where is charyte whiche [N4v] loueth euen her enemy?
Whan the surname chaunged / whan the colour of the vesture a
lytell altered / whan ye gyrdle or the shoo and lyke fantasies of men
make me hated vnto the? Why rather leaue we not these childysshe
20 tryfles / and accustome to haue before our eyen that whiche perteyneth to the very thyng: wherof Paule warneth vs in many places /
that all we in Christ the heed be membres of one body / endued
with lyfe by one spiryte (if so be we lyue in hym) so that we
shulde neyther enuy the happyer membres / and shulde gladly
25 socour and ayde the weake membres: that we might perceyue and
vnderstande our selfe to haue receyued a good turne, whan we
haue done any benefyte to our neyghbour: and that we our selfe
be hurte, whan hurte is done to our brother / neyther shulde any
man study priuately for hymselfe: but euery man for his owne
30 parte shulde bestowe in commen that thynge whiche he hath receyued of god / that all thynges might redounde and rebounde
thyder agayne, from whence they spronge / that is to wete, from the

Against ll. 17–21: Charite is not in them which hate an other man bycause
his vesture or garmente is a lytell altered and chaunged.
    Against ll. 30–2: Let euery man bestowe in comen what soeuer he receyued of
god.

1 y^t] the other 1533   vnlykenesse] dyuersite 1533   1–2 the mother]
mother 1533   16 her] his 1533   20 eyen] eyes 1533   22 the
heed] our heed 1533   25–6 and vnderstande] om. 1533   26 our selfe
to] y^t we our selfe 1533   28–9 neyther shulde any man] and that we myght
vnderstande how no man ought to 1533

heed. This veryly is the thynge whiche Paule writeth to the Corynthes / sayeng. As the body is one and hath many membres / and all
the membres of the body though they be many / yet be they but
one body: euen so lykewyse is [N5]Christ. For in one spiryt we be
al baptised to make one body / whether we be iewes or gentyles / 5
whether we be bonde or free / and all we haue dronke of one
spiryte (for the body sayth Paule) is not one membre but many.
If y⁰ fote shal say / I am not the hande / I am not of the body:
is he therfore not of the body? if the eare shall say / I am not the
eye / I am not of yᵉ body: is he therfore not of the body? if all the 10
body shulde be the eye / where is than the heryng: if all the body
were the herynge / where than shulde be y⁰ smellyng. But nowe
god hath put the membres euery one of them in the body / as it
pleased him. For if al were but one membre / where were yᵉ body?
But now veryly ben there many membres / yet but one body. The 15
eye can not say to the hande. I haue no nede of thy helpe / or agayn
the heed to the fete / ye be not to me necessary. But moche rather
those membres of yᵉ body whiche seme to be yᵉ weaker, are more
necessary: and to those whiche we thynke to be the vyler membres
of yᵉ body, we gyue more habundaunt honour. And those whiche 20
be our vnhonest membres haue more haboundaunt honesty / for
our honest membres haue nede of nothyng. But god hath tempred
and ordred the body, gyuyng plenteous honour to that parte
whiche lacked / bicause there [N5v] shuld be no scisme, diuisyon,
debate or stryfe in the body / but that the membres shulde care one 25
for an other indifferently. But it is ye whiche are the body of
Christe, and membres one dependyng of an other. He writeth lyke
thynges to the Romayns. For as we (saythe he) in one body haue
many membres / and all membres haue not one offyce. Euen so we
beynge many are but one body in Christ. And euery one the mem- 30
bres one of an other, hauynge gyftes dyuers after the grace whiche is
gyuen to vs. And agayne to the Ephesiens doynge trouthe (saythe
he) in charyte / let vs by all maner thynges growe in hym whiche is
the heed / that is to wete Christ, in whom the hole body compact
and knyt by euery ioynte mynistryng one to an other accordyng to 35

16 hande.] hand *1533*; hande *1534*   17 moche rather] *om. 1533*
18 more] moche more *1533*   24 scisme] *om. 1533*   28 For as we
(saythe he) . . . haue] saying . . . we haue *1533*   30 And euery one the membres one of an other] but syngularly we be membres eche one of another *1533*
32 doynge trouthe] workyng verite *1533*   33 by] in *1533*   34 the hole]
all the *1533*   35 mynistryng one] wherby one parte mynystreth *1533*

the acte and workyng of euery parte in his measure / maketh yᵉ
encrease of the body for the edifyeng of hym selfe in charyte. And
in an other place he byddeth euery man to beare one anothers
burden / bycause we be membres one of another. Loke than whether
5 they pertayne vnto this body whom thou herest speakyng euery
where after this maner / it is my good / it came to me by inherytaunce / I possesse it by ryght and not by fraude / why shall not I
vse it and abuse it after myne own mynde? Why [N6] shulde I gyue
them of it any deale at al to whome I owe nothyng? I spyll, I waste,
10 I distroy / that whiche peryssheth is myne owne / it maketh no
mater to other. Thy membre complayneth and grynneth for hunger,
and thou spewest vp partryges. Thy naked brother shyuereth for
colde / and with the so great plenty of rayment is corrupte with
mothes and longe lyeng. One nightes disyng hath lost the a thousande
15 peces of golde / whyle in the meane season some wretched wenche
(nede compellyng her) hath set forthe her chastyte to sell / and is
become a commune harlot / and thus peryssheth the soule for whom
Christ hath bestowed his lyfe. Thou sayest agayn: what is that to me.
I entreate yᵗ whiche is myne after myne owne fassyon: and after
20 all this with this so corrupt a mynde, thynkest thou thy self to be a
christen man / which art not ones a man verily? Thou herest in yᵉ
presence of a great multytude the good name or fame of this or that
man to be hurt / thou holdest thy peace, or peraduenture reioysest
and art wel content with yᵉ backbyter. Thou sayste I wolde haue
25 reproued him if those thinges whiche were spoken had pertayned to
me / but I haue nothing ado with hym which was there sclaundred.
Than to conclude, thou hast nothynge ado with the body / [N6v] if
thou haue nothyng ado with the membre / neyther hast thou aught
ado with the heed / veryly if the body nothyng apertayne to the. A man
30 (say they now a dayes) with vyolence may defende and put abacke
violence: what the emperours lawes permyt I passe not theron.
This I meruayle, how these voyces came in to the maners of christen men / I haue hurt hym, but I was prouoked / I had leuer hurt
than be hurt. Be it, mans lawes may not punysshe yᵗ whiche they

Against ll. 1–2: Euery membre hath his occupacyon necessarye to the
profite of the soule.

1 acte and workyng of euery parte in his measure] operacion and vertue
whiche spryngeth of the heed and capacite of euery membre / in receyuynge
1533   9 waste,] waste / *1533*; waste *1534*   11 other] other men *1533*
19 myne] myne owne *1533*   20 a mynde] mynde *1533*   34 may not
punysshe] punisshe not *1533*

haue permytted. But what wyll the Emperour Christe do, if thou
begyle his lawe which is written in Mathewe? I commaunde you
(sayth Christ there) not ones to withstande harme: but if a man shal
gyue the a blowe on ye right cheke / offre to hym also ye other.
And who so euer wyll stryue with the in the lawe / and take from   5
the thy cote / yelde vp to him also thy cloke or mantell. And who
so euer shall compell the to go with hym one myle / go with hym
two mo other. Loue your enemyes / and do good to them whiche
hate you / and pray for them whiche persecute you and pyke
maters agaynst you / that ye maye be the sonnes of your father   10
whiche is in heuen / whiche maketh ye sonne to ryse vpon good
and yuell / and sendeth rayne vpon iust and iniust. Thou answerest /
he spake not this to me / he spake [N7] it to his apostels / he spake
it to perfyte persons. Herdest thou not howe he sayd, that ye may be
ye sonnes of your father? if thou care not to be the sonne of god /   15
that lawe perteyneth not to the. Neuerthelesse he is not good
verily that wolde not be perfite. Harke also an other thyng: if thou
desyre no rewarde / the commaundement belongeth not to the: for
it foloweth. If ye loue them whiche loue you / what rewarde shall
ye haue: as who shulde say none: for surely to do this thynge is   20
not vertue: but not to do it, is myschefe. There is dette of neyther
syde where is iuste recompence made of bothe sydes. Here thou
Paule the great counsaylour and interpretour of Christes lawe.
Blysse (saythe he) them that persecute you / blysse them / and
curse them in no wyse / rendringe to no man yuell for yuell. If it   25
maye be as moche as in you is / hauynge rest and peace with all men /
not defendyng your selfe my best beloued bretherne / but gyue
place and withstande ye not wrathe: for it is wrytten. Vengeaunce
shall be reserued to me, and I wyll quyte them saythe our lorde.
But if thyne enemye shall be hungrye / gyue to hym meate: if he   30
be athurste / gyue to hym drinke: for if thou do this / thou shalt
heape coles of fyre vpon his heed. Be not [N7v] ouercome of yuell /
but ouercome yuell in goodnesse. What shall than folowe sayest

Against ll. 2–3: Desyre not vengeaunce.
Against ll. 15–16: This is spoken to all chrysten men.

---

17 that] whiche *1533*   20 surely] veryly *1533*   this thynge] these
thinges (y^t is to saye / to loue them that loueth the) *1533*   21 myschefe] an
euyll thynge *1533*   22 thou] *om. 1533*   23 the great counsaylour and
interpretour] bothe a great wyse man and connynge and an interpretour also *1533*
32 heed] heed / that is to say / thou shalt make hym to loue feruently *1533*

thou, if I shall with my softnesse nourissh vp the knappishsnes or
malyce and frowarde audacyte of an other man / and in suffryng an
olde iniury prouoke a newe? If thou can without thyne owne yuell
eyther auoyde or put by yuell / no man forbyddeth the to do it : but
5 if not / loke thou saye not it is better to do than to suffre. Amende
thyne enemye if thou can / eyther ladynge hym with benefytes / or
ouercomyng him with mekenesse. If that helpe not / it is better that
the one perysshe than bothe: it is better that thou waxe ryche with the
lucre and aduauntage of pacyence / than that whyle eyther to other
10 rendreth yuel / bothe be made yuell. Let this therfore be a decre
amonge christen men / to compare with al men in loue, in mekenesse,
and in benefytes, or doyng good: but in stryuyng, hate, or backbytyng, in rebukes and iniurye / to gyue place euen to them that be
of lowest degree / and that with good wyll. But he is vnworthy to
15 whome a good turne shulde be done / or an yuell forgyuen / yet
is it mete for the to do it / and Christe is worthy for whose sake it
is doone. I wyll neyther (saye they) hurte any man neyther suffre
my selfe to be hurte: yet whan thou arte [N8] hurt / se thou forgyue
the trespace with all thy herte / prouydynge alwayes that nothyng
20 be whiche any man shulde remytte or forgyue vnto the. Be as ware
and dylygent in auoydynge that none offence or trespace procede
from the / as thou art easy and redy to remytte an other mans. The
greater man thou art / so moche the more submytte thy selfe / that
thou in charyte aplye thy selfe to all men. If thou come of a noble
25 stocke / maners worthy of Christe shall not dishonour, but honour
yᵉ noblenesse of thy byrth. If thou be connyng and wel lerned / so
moche the more soberly suffre and amende the ignoraunce of yᵉ
vnlerned. The more is commytted and lente to the / the more art
thou bounde to thy brother. Thou art ryche / remembre thou art
30 the dispenser, not the lorde: take hede circumspectly howe thou
entreatest the commune good. Byleuest thou yᵗ propriete was prohy-
byte and voluntary pouertie enioyned to monkes onely? Thou art

Against ll. 6-8: To a chrysten man it is better to suffre than to doo.
Against ll. 10-11: The decree of chrysten men.
Against ll. 23-4: Offences must be forgyuen.
Against l. 25: A gentylman.
Against l. 26: A connyng man.
Against l. 29: A ryche man.
Against l. 32-p. 159, l. 1: Pouerte is not enioyned to monkes onely.

27 suffre] 1533; fuffre 1534   31 propriete] proprete or impropriacyon 1533
Side-note 1: better] bet-1533

disceyued / both pertayne to all christen men. The lawe punyssheth the if thou take away any thyng of an other mans: it punissheth not if thou withdrawe thyne owne from thy nedy brother. But Christ wyll punysshe bothe. If thou be an offycer / let not the honour make the more fyerse / but let the charge make the [N8v] more dylygent and 5 fuller of care. I beare (sayst thou) no offyce of the churche / I am not a shepherd or a bysshop. Let vs graunt that / but also thou art not a christen man: loke thou of whence thou arte, if thou be not of the churche. So greatly Chryste is commen in to contempt to the worlde / that they thynke it a goodly and excellent thyng to haue 10 nothynge to do with hym: and that so moche ye more euery man shulde be dispysed the more coupled he were to hym. Hercst thou not dayly of the ley persons in their furye the names of a clerke / of a preest / of a monke, to be cast in our tethes in stede of a sharpe and cruell rebuke / sayeng thou clerke / thou preest / thou monke, 15 that thou art: and y^t is done vtterly with none other mynde / with none other voyce than if they shulde cast in our tethes incest or sacrylege. I veryly meruayle why they also cast not in our tethes baptysme / why also they obiecte not agaynst vs with the sarazyns the name of Christ as an obprobrious thyng. If they sayd an yuel 20 clerke / an vnworthy preest / or an vnrelygyous monke / in y^t they myght be suffred as men whiche note the maners of the persones, and not dispyse the professyon of vertue. But who so euer counteth to their glory and prayse ye deflouryng of virgyns / good [O1] taken away in warre / money eyther won or lost at dyce, or other 25 chaunce / and haue nothynge to lay agaynst an other man more spytefull or obprobryous, or more to be ashamed of / than the names of a monke or a preest. Certaynly it is easy to coniecture what these, in name onely chrysten men iudge of Chryst. There is not one lorde of the bysshops, and an other of the temporall 30 offycers: but bothe be vnder one / and to the same, bothe must giue accomptes. If thou loke any otherwhere, saue vnto hym onely / eyther whan thou receyuest thoffyce, or whan thou mynistrest

Against ll. 16–17: Incest is to medell with theyr owne kynne.
Against ll. 19–21 (Referring to l. 18): Sacrylege / is to vyolate persones sacred to god / or to rob churches.

1 pertayne] perteyne indifferently *1533*   6 beare . . . no] beare not . no *1533*   7 graunt] graunt you *1533*   thou art not] art thou not *1533*
8 loke] consyder *1533*   17 voyce] voyce or pronouncynge *1533*   19 they obiecte not] obiect they not *1533*   24 to their glory and prayse] prayse in them self *1533*

it / it maketh no mater though the worlde call the not a symonyake /
he surely wyll punysshe the as a symonyake. If thou labour and
make meanes to obtayne a commune offyce / not to profyte in
commune / but to prouyde for thyne owne welthe pryuatly / and to
5 aduenge thy selfe of them, to whome thou owest a grudge / thy
offyce is brybery or robbery afore god. Thou huntest after theues /
not that he sholde receyue his owne that is robbed / but leest it
sholde not be with the whiche is with the theues. How moche
difference I pray the, is there bytwene the theues and the / excepte
10 peraduenture that they be the robbers of marchauntes / and thou the
robber of robbours. In conclusyon, excepte thou [O1v] beare thyne
offyce with this mynde / that thou be redy / and that with the losse,
I wyll not saye of thy goodes, but of thy lyfe, to defende that whiche
is ryght / Chryst wyll not approue thy admynystracyon. I wyll adde
15 also an other thynge of the mynde, and iudgement of Plato. No
man is worthy of an offyce, whiche is gladly in an offyce. If thou
be a prynce / beware leest these peryllous wytches, the voyces of
flatterers enchaunt or bewytche the. Thou art a lorde / ouer the
lawes thou art free / what so euer thou doest is honest / to the is
20 lawfull what so euer thou lyst. Those thynges pertayne not to the,
whiche are preached dayly of preestes to the commune people. Ye
but thynke thou rather whiche is true, that there is one mayster ouer
all men / and he is Chryste Iesus / to whome thou oughtest to be as
lyke as is possyble / to whome thou oughtest to confyrme thy selfe
25 in all thynges / as vnto hym certaynly whose authorite or rowme
thou bearest. No man ought to folow his doctryne more straytly
than thou / of whome he wyll aske accomptes more straytly than of
other. Thynke not forthwith that to be ryght whiche thou wylte /
but onely wyll thou whiche is ryght. What so euer may be fylthy to
30 any man in the worlde / se thou [O2] thynke not that an honest
thynge to the / but in no wyse permytte to thy selfe any thyng,
whiche is vsed to be forgyuen and pardoned amonge the commune

Against l. 2: A symonyake.
Against ll. 10–11: A prety note for sheryffes and other offycers.
Against ll. 17–19: He is worthy to be an officer whiche is in offyce agaynst his
wyll.
Against ll. 22–3: Chryst is lorde bothe of laye men and also of preestes.
Against ll. 31–2: Desyre but that whiche is ryght.

---

15 and] or *1533*   18 enchaunt] do enchaunt *1533*   28 forthwith]
streyghtwaye *1533*   whiche thou] that thou *1533*   30 se] se that *1533*
31 but] but se thou *1533*

sort. That whiche in other men is but a small trespace / thynke in thy selfe to be a greate outragyous excesse. Let not thy rychesse greater than the rychesse of the commune people, bringe vnto the honour, reuerence and dignite, fauour, and authorite: but let thy maners better than the maners of the commune people vtterly 5 deserue them. Suffre not the commune people to wonder at those thynges in the, wherwith are prouoked and entysed the very same myscheuous dedes, which thou punysshest dayly. Take away this wondryng and prayse of rychesse / and where be theues / where be oppressours of the commune welth / where be commytters of 10 sacrylege / where be errant theues and robbers or reuers? take away wondryng at voluptuousnes / and where be rauisshers of women / where be adulters? As often as thou wylt appere somwhat according after thy degre among thy frendes and subiectes, or them ouer whom thou bearest offyce, rowme or authorite / open not thy 15 rychesse and treasure to the eyen of folysshe persones. Whan thou wylt seme somwhat welthy, shewe not in bost the ryottous example of expence, and [O2v] voluptuousnes. Fyrst of all let them lerne in the to despyse suche thynges / let them lerne to honour vertue, to haue measure in pryce, to reioyce in temperaunce, to gyue honour 20 to sobre lowlynesse or mekenesse. Let none of those thynges be seen in thy maners and conuersacyon / whiche thyne authorite punyssheth in the maners and conuersacyon of the people. Thou shalt bannysshe euyll dedes in the best wyse, yf men shall not se rychesse and voluptuousnes / the mater and grounde of euyl dedes 25 to be magnifyed in the. Thou shalt not despyse in comparyson of thy selfe any man / no not the vylest of the lowest degree / for commune and indifferent is the pryce wherwith ye bothe were redemed. Let not the noyse of ambicyon / neyther fyersnes / neyther wepons / nor men of the garde defende the from contempte / but 30 purenesse of lyuyng, grauyte, maners vncorrupte and sounde from all maner vices of the commune people. Nothyng forbyddeth (in bearynge rule) to kepe the chefe rowme / and yet in charite to discerne no rowme. Thynke bearyng of roume or rule to be this /

Against ll. 6–7: The honesty of good maners.
Against ll. 32–3: The rule of crysten prynces.

2 outragyous] outrage or *1533*   3 the rychesse of the commune people]
the comen peoples *1533*   5 the maners of the commune people] the
comen peoples *1533*   15 open not] set not open *1533*   34 roume[2]]
1533, rowne *1534*

not to excell and go before other men in habundaunce of rychesse /
but to profyte al men as moche as is possyble. Tourne not to thyne
owne profyte thynges whiche are commune / but bestowe those [O3]
thynges whiche be thyne owne / and thyne owne selfe all togyder
5 vpon the commune welthe. The commune people oweth very many
thynges to the / but thou owest all thynges to them. Though thyne
eares be compelled to suffre names of ambycyon / as moost myghty /
moost christened / holynesse, and maiesty / yet let thy mynde
not be a knowen of them / but referre al these thinges vnto
10 Chryst, to whome onely they agre. Let the cryme of treson agaynst
thyne owne person (whiche other with great wordes make an
haynous offence) be counted of the a very trifle. He violateth y^e
maiesty of a prynce in dede / whiche in the prynces name dothe any
thyng cruelly, violently, myscheuously contrary to ryght. Let no
15 mans iniury moue the lesse than y^t whiche pertayneth to y^e
pryuatly. Remembre thou art a commune persone / and that thou
oughtest not to thinke but of that which is commune. If thou haue
any courage with the and redynesse of wytte / consyder with thy selfe
not how great a man thou art / but how great a charge thou bearest
20 on thy backe: and the more in ieopardye thou art, so moche the
lesse fauour thyselfe / fetchyng ensample of mynystryng thyne
offyce, not of thy predecessours, or els of flaterers / but of Chryst:
for what is more vnreasonable, than that [O3v] a chrysten prynce
sholde set before hym for an ensample, Hanyball, great Alexander,
25 Cesar, or Pompey / in ye whiche same persones whan he can not
attayne some certayne vertues / he shall counterfayte those thinges
moste chefely, whiche onely were to be refused and auoyded. Let it
not forthwithall be taken for an ensample yf Cesar haue done
any thyng lauded in hystoryes / but yf he haue done any thyng
30 whiche varyeth not from the doctryne of our lorde Iesu Christ / or
els be suche, that though it be not worthy to be counterfayted, yet
may it be applyed to ye study or exercise of vertue. Let not an hole
empyre be of so great valure to the, that thou woldest wytyngly
ones bowe from the ryght: put of that rather than thou sholdest put
35 of Chryste. Doubte not Chryste hath to make the amendes for them-

Against ll. 12–13: The maiestie of a Prynce.
Against ll. 21–2: The maner and forme of bering rule must be fet of
Christe.

16 commune] publyke *1533*   17 that which is commune] comen maters
1533   31 els] *om. 1533*

pyre refused, a ferre better thynge than the empyre. Nothynge is so
comly, so excellent, so gloryous vnto kynges as to drawe as nygh as
is possyble vnto the symylytude of the hyest kynge Iesu / whiche
as he was the greatest, so was he also the best. But that he was the
greatest that dissymuled he, and hyd secrete here in erth: that he 5
was the best / that had he leuer we sholde perceyue and fele /
bycause he had leuer we sholde counterfayte that. He [O4] denyed
his kyngdom to be of this worlde, whan he was lorde of heuen and
erth also. But the prynces of the gentyles vse domynyon vpon them.
A chrysten man exercyseth no power ouer his, but charite / and he 10
whiche is the chefest, thynketh hym selfe to be mynyster vnto all
men / not mayster or lorde. Wherfore I meruayle the more a great
deale, how these ambicyous names of power and dominion were
brought in, euen vnto the very popes and bysshops / and that our
diuynes be not ashamed no lesse vndiscretly than ambicyously to be 15
called euery where our maysters / whan Chryste forbade his disciples,
that they sholde not suffre to be called eyther lordes or maisters
for we must remembre that one is in heuen bothe lorde and mayster Chryste Iesus / whiche is also heed vnto vs all. Apostle, shepherde, bysshop, be names of offyce, or seruyce / not of dominyon 20
and rule. Pope, abbot, be names of loue / not of power. But why
entre I in to that great see of yᵉ commune errours? vnto what
so euer kynde of men he shal turne hymself / a very spiritual
man shall se many thynges whiche he may laugh at / and mo
which he ought to wepe at / he shal se very many opin- 25
yons to farre corrupt and varyeng from the doctryne of Chryst
bothe farre and wyde. Of the whiche a great [O4v] parte spryngeth
there hence, that we haue brought euen in to christendom a certayne
worlde / and that whiche is redde of the worlde among the olde
diuynes / men of small lernyng now adays referre to them whiche 30
be not monkes. The worlde in the gospell with the apostles / with
saynt Augustyne, Ambrose, and Hierome, be called infydeles /

Against ll. 1-2: What is comly for prynces.
Against ll. 3-4: Chryste is the greatest / he is also the best.
Against ll. 13-15: The clergy is touched of ambicion and vayne tytles of
names.
Against ll. 19-20: The names of offyce.

1 a ferre better thynge] ferre better *1533*   19-20 shepherde, bysshop] a
sheparde a bysshop *1533*   21 Pope, abbot] A pope / an abbot *1533*   25 wepe
at /] *1533*; wepe at *1534*   32 infydeles /] infydels *1533*; infydeles. *1534*

straungers from the fayth / the ennemyes of the crosse of Chryst /
blasphemers of god. They that are suche care for tomorow and for
the tyme to comme / for who so euer mystrusteth Christ, neyther
byleue on hym / they be they which fyght and stryue for rychesse,
5 for rule, for worldly pleasure, as men whiche blynded with delusyons
of sencyble thynges, set theyr myndes and hole affections vpon
apparent good thynges, in stede of very good thinges. This worlde
hath not knowen Chryste the very and true lyght. This worlde is all
togyder set on myschefe / loueth hym selfe / lyueth to hym selfe /
10 studyeth for hym selfe and for his owne pleasure / and all for lacke
he hath not put vpon hym Christ, whiche is very and true charite.
From this worlde separated Chryst not his apostles onely / but all
men, who so euer and as many as he iudged worthy of hym. After
what maner than and fassyon I praye you, do we myngle with
15 christen[O5]dom this worlde euery where in holy scripture condempned? and with the vayne name of the worlde, fauoure, flatter,
and mayntayne our owne vyces? Many doctours and teachers
augment this pestylence / whiche corruptyng the worde of god (as
Paule sayth) wresten and fassyonen his holy scripture accordynge to
20 the maners of euery tyme / whan it were more conuenyent that the
maners sholde be adressed and amended by the rule of his scripture.
And no myscheuouser kynde of flatteryng veryly is there / than
whan with the wordes of the gospel and of the prophetes we flatter
the diseases of the mynde, and cure them not. A prynce heareth
25 al power is of god: forthwith (as the prouerbe sayth) his combe
ryseth. Why hath ye scripture made the hygh or swellynge in
mynde, rather than circumspecte and carefull? Thynkest thou
that god hath commytted to the an empyre to be gouerned / and
thinkest thou not that the same wyll requyre of the a strayte reken-
30 ynge of the ordryng therof? The couetous man heareth it to be
forbyd vnto chrysten men to haue two cotes at ones. The diuyne
interpreteth the second cote to be what so euer sholde be superfluous and more than ynough for the necessite of nature, and
sholde apertayne to the disease [O5v] of couetousnesse: that is
35 very well (sayth the grosse felowe) for I yet lacke very many thynges.

Against ll. 24–5: All power is of god.
Against ll. 31–2: Thou shalte not haue two cotes.

1–2 Chryst / blasfemers of god. They] Christe. Blasfemers of god / they
1533; Chryst. Blasfemers of god, they *1534*   5 delusyons] delyces *1533*
24 and] 1533; anb *1534*

The naturall wyse man, and colde from charite heareth this to be
the ordre of charite / that thou sholdest regarde and set more of
thyne owne money, than of an other mans / of thyne owne lyf, than
of an other mans / of thyne owne fame, than of an other mans. I
wyl therfore sayth he gyue nothynge, leest peraduenture I sholde 5
lacke my selfe. I wyll not defende another mans good fame or
good name / lest myne owne be spotted therby. I wyl forsake my
brother in ieopardy / leest I my selfe sholde fall in peryll also. To
speke shortly, I wyl lyue all togyder to my selfe, that no incom-
modite comme to me for any other mannes cause. We haue also 10
lerned, yf holy men haue done any thyng not to be counterfayted or
folowed, to take that onely of them and drawe it in to the ensample of
lyuynge. Adulterers and murderers flateren and clawen them selues
with the example of Dauyd. Suche as gapeth after worldly rychesse,
lay agaynst vs for their excuse ryche Abraham. Princes whiche 15
counte it but a sporte or pastyme euery where to corrupte and
defyle virgyns / nombre and reken vp, to cloke theyr vyce, the
quenes and concubynes of Salomon. They whose bely is theyr god /
[O6] layeth for theyr excuse the dronkennesse of Noe. Incestes
whiche pollute their owne kynswomen / cloke and couer their fylthy- 20
nes with thensample of Loth / whiche lay with his owne doughters.
Why tourne we our eyen from Chryst to these men? I dare be bolde
to say that it ought not to be counterfayted and folowed / no not so
moche as in the prophetes or Chrystes apostles veryly, yf any thynge
swarue or wrye from the doctryne of Chryst. But yf it delyte men 25
so greatly to counterfayte holy synners / I do not gaynsaye them /
so that they counterfayte them hole and all togyder. Thou hast
folowed Dauyd in adultery / moche more folowe hym in repentaunce.
Thou hast counterfayted Mary Magdaleyne a synner / counterfayte her also louyng moche / counterfayte her wepynge / counter- 30
fayte her castynge her selfe downe at the fete of Iesu. Thou hast
persecuted the churche of god, as Paule dyd / thou hast forsworne
thy selfe as Peter dyd: Se lykewyse that thou stretche forth thy
necke for the fayth and relygyon of Chryste, after the ensample of
Paule / and that thou feare not the crosse no more than Peter. For this 35

Against ll. 2–3: A new order of charitie.
Against ll. 26–8: Nothynge oughte to be counterfeyted whiche varye from
Christe.

---

12 to take that onely] y^t onely to take *1533*   it] *om. 1533*   18 and] *om.*
1533   26 gaynsaye] agaynst saye *1533*

cause god suffreth euen greate and ryght excellent men also to
fall in to certayne vyces / that we whan we haue fallen, sholde [O6v]
not despayre: but with this condicyon / yf that we, as we haue ben
theyr felowes in synnyng and doyng amysse / euen so wyll be theyr
5 companyons and parteners in the amendynge of our synnes and
mysdedes. Now do we greatly prayse and magnifye that same
thynge whiche was not to be counterfayted and folowed / and certayne thynges whiche were well done of them / we do depraue and
corrupte / after the maner of spyders suckynge out the poyson
10 onely / yf any be therin / or els tournynge euen the holsome iuce
also in to poyson to our selues. What dothe Abrahams ensample
belonge to the / whiche makest of thy money thy god? Bycause he
was enryched with encrease of catell (god makynge his substaunce
and goodes prosperously to multyplye) and that in the olde lawe,
15 which was but carnal: shall it therfore be lawfull to the whiche art
a chrysten man / by ryght or wronge / by hoke or croke / from
whence so euer it be / to heape togyther the rychesse of Cresus,
whiche thou mightest eyther euyll spende and lewdly waste / or
elles (whiche is a greate deale worse) hyde and burye moost couet-
20 ously, depe in the grounde. How lytell Abraham dyd set his
mynde vpon his goodes and rychesse / whiche came to hym haboundantly [O7] by theyr owne accorde / euen this thynge may be
an euydent taken and profe, that without delay at the voyce of god
commaundyng hym, he brought forth his onely sone to be slayne.
25 How moche thynkest thou despysed he his droues of oxen, whiche
despysed euen his owne sone? And thynkest thou whiche dream-
est nothynge els but of fylthy lucre and aduauntage / whiche
praysest and settest by nothyng but onely money / whiche art redy
as soone as there chaunce any hope of lucre / be it neuer so lytell /
30 eyther to deceyue thy brother / or to set Chryst at naught / that
there is any symylytude or lyke thynge bytwene the and Abraham?
The symple and innocent wenches the doughters of Loth, whan
they beheld all the regyon rounde about on euery parte brennynge

Against ll. 6–7: We turne good thynges to euyll.
Against ll. 11–12: A coueytous man foloweth not Abraham.
Against l. 17: Cresus.
Against ll. 28–9: Redy to deceyue thy brother for money.

17–18 the rychesse of Cresus, whiche] rychesse as moche as euer kyng Cresus
had (whose exceding great ryches is come into a comen prouerbe) whiche
rychesse ones gotten 1533

and flamynge with fyre / and supposed that it which was than in
syght afore their eyen had ben all yᵉ hole worlde / and that no man
was preserued from that so large and wastfull fyre: but onely
theyr selues / lay pryuely and by stelthe with theyr owne father / not
of a fylthy, but vertuous and holy purpose / that is to wyte, leest 5
none yssue of mankynde sholde haue remayned after them / and
that whan this precepte of god (growe and multyply) was as yet
in full vygour and strengthe. And darest [O7v] thou compare thy
fylthy and prodigyous voluptuousnes and lechery, with the dede of
these wenches? Nay I wolde not doute to counte thy matrymony 10
not so good as theyr incest commytted with theyr father / yf in
matrymony thou doest not study for yssue / but to satysfye thyne
owne voluptuous appetyte or lust. ❡ Dauyd after so many excellent
and noble ensamples of vertue and good lyuyng shewed, fell ones
in to adultery, by occasyon and oportunyte gyuen hym: and shall 15
it be lawfull therfore to the streyghtwaye at thy lybertye, to roll,
walter and tomble from house to house in other mennes beddes all
thy lyfe longe? Peter ones for feare of dethe denyed his mayster
Chryste / for whose sake afterwarde he dyed with good wyll: Shall
it be lawfull thynkest thou to the to forswere thy selfe for euery 20
tryfle? Paule synned not purposely and for the nones / but fell
through ignoraunce: whan he was warned and taught / he repented
forthwith, and came in to the right waye. Thou bothe ware and
wyse / and seynge what thou doest / wytyngly and wyllyngly contyn-
uest from youth to age in vyces and synnes / and yet by the 25
ensample of Paule strokest thou thyne owne heed. Mathewe beynge
commaunded but with [O8] one worde / without any taryeng / at
ones vtterly forsoke all his offyce of receyuyng custome or tollage:
but thou art so sworne and maryed to thy money, that neyther so
many ensamples of holy men, neyther the gospelles so often herde / 30
nor so many preachynges can deuorce or plucke the from it. The
bysshoppes saye vnto me / saynt Augustyne (as it is redde) had
two soueraygne ladyes or concubynes: yea but he than was an

Against l. 10–12: The wedlocke of some men is worse than the incest of
lothes doughters.
    Against ll. 14–16: The mysdedes or synnes of holy men we passe farre nowe
adayes / and that many wayes.
    Against l. 33–p. 168, l. 2: Saynt Austyn is excused / he had but one at ones.

---

13 ❡] om. *1533*   20 thou] thou than *1533*   to forswere] for that cause /
to forsweare *1533*   30 so often] of often *1533*

hethen man / and we be nourysshed vp in chrystendome: he was
yonge / and our heedes be hoore for age. A worshypfull comparyson / bycause that he beynge yonge / and also an hethen man, to
auoyde the snares of matrymony, had a lytell wenche, in stede of a
5 wyfe / and yet to her whiche was not his wyfe, kepte he the promesse
of wedlocke. Shall it be therfore the lesse shame for vs christen
men beynge olde, beynge preestes, yea beyng bysshoppes, to be all
togyder spotted and fyled in euery puddle one after an other of
bodyly lustes? Farewele good maners whan we haue gyuen to vices
10 the names of vertues / and haue begon to be more wyly and subtyle in defendynge our vyces / than diligent to amende them / moost
specyally whan we haue lerned to nourysshe, to vnderset, and to
strengthe our [O8v] frowarde opinyons / with the helpe and ayde
of holy scripture. Thou therfore my moste swete brother (the
15 commune people al togyder set at naught with theyr bothe opinyons
and dedes) purely and holly hasten ye vnto the christen secte.
What so euer in this lyfe apereth to thy sensyble powers, eyther to
be hated or loued / all y^t for the loue of pite and vertuous lyfe indifferently despysed / let Chryst onely to the be sufficient / the onely
20 auctour bothe of true iudgynge, and also of blessed lyuyng. And
this veryly the worlde thynketh to be pure folysshnes and madnes:
neuerthelesse by this folisshnes it pleaseth god to saue them
whiche on hym byleue. And he is happely a foole, that is wyse in
Chryste: and he is wofully wyse, y^t is folysshe in Chryste. But
25 hearest thou, as I wolde haue the to vary strongly from ye commune people / so I wold not that thou shewyng a poynt of currishnes, sholdest euerywhere barke agaynst ye opinyons and dedes
of other men / and with authorite condempne them / prattle
odyously agaynst al men / furyously preche agaynst ye lyuyng of
30 euery persone leest thou purchace to thy selfe two euyls togyder.
The one that thou sholdest fall in to hate of all men: the other, that
whan thou art hated thou sholdest do good to no man. But be thou
all thynges to all men / [P1] to wynne all men to Chryst, as moche
as may be (pite not offended). So shape and fassyon thy self to al
35 men outwardly / that within thy purpose remayne sure, stedfast
and vnmoued. Withoutforth, let gentylnes, courteys language,

Against ll. 25–7: A man may not barke euery where agaynst the dedes of other
men.

---

31 the other] thother *1533*

softnes, profitablenes allure and entyce thy brother / whome it is
mete with fayre meanes to be induced to Chryst / and not to be
feared with cruelnesse. In conclusion, that which is in thy brest
is not so greatly to be rored forth with cruel wordes, as to be declared and vttrcd with honest maners. And agayn thou oughtest 5
not so to fauour the infirmite of yᵉ commune people, yᵗ thou durst
not at a tyme strongly defende the verite: with humanite men
must be amended / and not deceyued.

⟪ The seuenth rule. Caplo. xvj.

MOre ouer yf thrugh infancye and feblenes of myndc wc can 10
not as yet attayne to these spirituall thynges / we ought neuerthelesse to study not the sluggyssher one deale / that at the leest we
may drawe as nygh as is possyble. How be it, the very and compendyous way to felicite is / yf at ones we shall turne oure hole
mynde to the contemplacyon and beholdynge of celestyall thynges 15
so feruently / yᵗ as the body bryngeth [Pɪv] with hym his shadow /
euen so the loue of Chryst, the loue of eternal thinges and honest
may bryng with hym naturally, the lothsomnes of thynges caduke
and transytory, and that hate of thynges fylthy. For eyther necessaryly foloweth the other: and yᵉ one with yᵉ other eyther augment- 20
eth or mynyssheth. As moche as thou shalt profyte in yᵉ loue of
Christ, so moche shalt thou hate yᵉ worlde. The more thou shalt
loue and set by thynges inuisyble, the more vyle shall waxe thinges
vayne and momentany. We must therfore do euen that same in the
disciplyne of vertue, whiche Fabius counseyleth to be done in 25
scyences or facultees of lernynge / that we at ones, prece vp to the
best. Whiche thing yet yf through our owne faute wyll not comme
to passe: the nexte of all is, that we at the least may by certayne
naturall prudence abstayne from great vices / and kepe our selfe (as
moche as may be) hole and sounde to the benefycence of god. For 30
as that body is nere vnto helthe / whiche (though it be wasted) is

Against ll. 10-12: We must styll be clymmyng / ye though we dispayre to
attayn to the top.

_____

13 may] *om. 1533*   18 may bryng] bringeth *1533*   thynges caduke
and transytory] caduke and transytory thynges *1533*   19 thynges fylthy]
fylthy thynges *1533*   eyther] eyther other *1533*
     Side-note 1: attayn] atteyn *1533*, attayu *1534*

free yet and out of the daunger of noysome humours: euen so is
that mynde more receyuable of yᵉ benefyte of god / whiche is not
yet inquynate or defyled with greuous offences / though she lacke
yet true and perfyte vertue. If we be to weyke to folowe the apostles,
5 to folowe the martyrs, [P2] to folowe the virgyns / at the leestway
let vs not commytte that the Ethnykes or hethen men sholde seme
to ouer ronne vs in this playne or lystes. Of the whiche very many,
whan they neyther knewe god, whome they sholde drede / neyther
byleued any hell, whome they sholde feare: yet determyned
10 they, that a man ought by all craftes to auoyde and eschewe
fylthynesse for the thynge it selfe. In so moche, that many of
them chose rather to suffre the losse of fame, losse of goodes /
in conclusyon to suffre losse of lyfe, than to departe from
honestye. If synne it selfe be suche a maner thynge / that for
15 no commodytees or incommodytees proffered to man, it
ought to be commytted: certaynly yf neyther the iustyce
of god feare vs / neyther his beneficence discourage vs, and
moue vs to the contrarye / yf no hope of immortalite or feare
of eternall payne call vs abacke / or elles yf the veray naturall
20 fylthynesse of synne withdrawe vs not / whiche coude withdrawe the myndes of the veray gentyles, at the leestwaye let a
thousande incommodytees whiche accompany the synner in this
lyfe, put a chrysten man in feare, as infamy, losse or waste of goodes,
pouerty, the contempte and hate of good men, grefe of mynde,
25 vnquyetnesse and tourment of [P2v] conscyence moost myserable
of all / whiche though many feale not now presently / eyther bycause
they be blynded with dulnes of youth / or made dronke with the
voluptuousnes and pleasure of synne / yet shal they feale it here
after: and playnly the later it happeneth / so moche the more vn-
30 happely shall they feale it. Wherfore yonge men most specially
must be warned and exhorted, that they wolde rather byleue so
many authors, that this is the very nature and properte of synne in
dede, that with myserable and wofull experyence lerne it in them

Against ll. 5–7: If thou can not counterfeyt holy sayntes / be not yet inferior
to hethen men.
Against ll. 21–3: Ponder in thy mynde the incommodyties of synne.

2 receyuable] capax *1533, which adds the side-note* Capax apte to receyue
(*om. 1534*). *See n.*   16 ought] *1533;* oughr *1534*   31 must] sholde *1533*
32 this is the very nature and properte of synne] the very nature and properte
of synne were thus *1533*

selfe. And that they wolde not contamynate nor defyle theyr lyfe, before they knewe surely what lyfe ment. Yf Christ be to ye vyle, to whome thou art so costly / at ye leestway for thyne owne sake refrayne thy selfe from fylthy thynges. And though it be very perylous to tary anywhyle in this state / as bytwene thre wayes (as it is in ye 5 prouerbe) neuerthelesse vnto them whiche can not as yet clym vp to the pure, perfyte and excellent vertue / it shal not be a lytel profitable to be in the ciuyle or moral vertues, rather than to ronne hedlong in to all kynde of vices and vnclenlynes. Here is not ye restyng place and quiet hauen of felicite / but from hence is a 10 shorter iourney and an easyer stayre vp to felicite. In the meane season for all that, we [P3] must praye god, that he wyll vouchsafe to plucke vs vp to better thynges.

❡ The eyght rule. Caplo. xvij.

IF the storme of temptacion shal ryse agaynst the somwhat 15 thycke and greuously / begyn not forthwithall to be discontent with thyself, as though for that cause god eyther cared not for the / or fauoured the not / or y^t thou sholdest be but an easye christen man / or els the lesse perfyte: but rather gyue thankes to god, bycause he instructeth the as one which shal be his heyre in tyme to 20 comme / bycause he beateth or scourgeth y^e as his most singular beloued sone / and proueth the as his assured frende. It is a very great token, a man to be reiecte from the mercy of god whan he is vexed with no temptacyons. Let comme to thy mynde the apostle Paule, whiche obteyned to be admytted and receyued vnto the 25 mysteryes of the thyrde heuen / yet was he beaten of the aungell of sathan. Let comme to remembraunce the frende of god Iob: remembre Ierom, Benedict, Frauncys, and with these innumerable other holy fathers vexed and troubled of very great vices. Yf that which thou suffrest be commen to so greate men / be commen to so many 30 men, as well as to the : what [P3v] cause is there wherfore thou sholdest be smytte out of countenaunce / sholdest be abasshed or fall in to despayre ? enforce rather and stryue that thou mayst ouercomme as

---

Against ll. 8–10: Heare that is in cyuyll or morall vertues.
Against ll. 25–6: Temptacyon is a sygne that god loueth vs.

---

25 and receyued vnto] or let in euen in to *1533*

they dyd / god shall not forsake the / but with temptacion shall cause encrease, that thou mayst be able to endure.

ℂ The nynth rule. Caplo. xviij.

AS expert capteyns are wont to cause whan all thinges are quiet
5 at rest and at peace / that the watche neuerthelesse be dewly kept: lykewyse se thou y^t thou haue alway thy mynde watchyng and circumspecte against the sodeyn assaute of thyne enemy (for he euer compasseth rounde about, sekyng whom he myght deuour) that thou mayst be the more redy, as soone as he assauteth the, to put hym
10 backe manfully, to confounde hym, and forthwith to trede vnderfote ye heed of the pestyferous and poyson serpent. For he is neuer ouercome, eyther more easly, or more surely and perfytly, than by that meanes. Therfore it is a very wise poynt, to dasshe the yong chyldren of babilon (as soone as they be borne) against the stone,
15 whiche is Chryst / or they growe stronge and greate.

ℂ The tenth rule. Caplo. xix. [P4]

BVt the tempter is put backe most of all by this meanes, yf thou shalt eyther vehemently hate, abhorre and defye, and in a maner spyt at hym streyghtway, whan so euer he entyceth and moueth the
20 with any temptacyon: or els yf thou pray feruently / or gete thy selfe to some holy occupacyon / settyng thyne hole mynde thervnto: or yf thou make answere to the tempter with wordes fet out of holy scripture, as I haue warned the before. In whiche thynge veryly it shall not profyte meanly agaynst all kynde of temptacion, to haue
25 some certayne sentences prepared and redy / specyally those with whiche thou hast felte thy mynde to be moued and stered vehemently.

Against ll. 5–6: We must euer kepe watche.
Against ll. 7–9: Let temptacion be hold downe at the begynnynge whyle it is fresshe.
Against ll. 12–15: The chyldren of babylon sygnyfyeth subgestyon or temptacion / or the fyrst mocyons to syn.
Against ll. 17–18: Remedyes against temptacion.

2 cause] make *1533*   13 meanes.] *1533*; meanes *1534*   17 meanes,] meanes / *1533*; means. *1534*

Side-note 2: hold] holden *1533*
Side-note 3: babylon] *1533*; babylou *1534*

⟪ The .xj. rule. Caplo. xx.

TWo daungers chefely folowe good men / one leest in temptacyon they gyue vp theyr holde. An other leest after the victory, in
theyr consolacyon and spirituall ioye, they waxe wanton, and
stande in theyr owne conceyte / or elles please them selfe. Therfore 5
that thou mayst be sure, not onely from the nyght feare, but also
from the deuyll of myddaye: loke whan thyne ennemy stereth the
vnto fylthy thynges, that thou beholde not thyne [P4v] owne
feblenes or weyknes / but remembre onely that thou canst do all
thynges in Chryste / whiche sayd not to his apostles onely / but to 10
the also and to all his membres, euen the very lowest. Haue confidence, for I haue ouercomme yᵉ worlde. Agayn whan so euer,
eyther after thyne ennemy is ouercomme / or in doyng some holy
worke / thou shalt fele thy mynde inwardly to be comforted with
certeyn preuy delectacions: than beware diligently yᵗ thou ascrybe 15
nothing therof vnto thyne owne merites / but thanke onely the free
benefycence of god for all togyder / and holde downe and refrayne
thy selfe with the wordes of Paule / sayinge. What hast thou, that
thou hast not receyued? Yf thou haue receyued it / why reioycest
thou as though thou haddest not receyued it? And so agaynst this 20
double myschefe, shall there be a double remedy / yf thou in the
conflict mystrustyng thyne owne strength doest flee for socour vnto
thy heed Chryst / puttynge the hole trust of conquerynge in the
benyuolence of hym onely. And yf also in the spirytuall conforte
and consolacyon thou immedyately gyue thankes to hym for his 25
benefyte / humbly knowynge and confessynge thyne vnworthynesse.

⟪ The .xij. rule Caplo. xxj. [P5]

WHan thou fyghtest with thyne ennemyes, thynke it not ynough
for the to auoyde his stroke / or put it backe / excepte thou also

Against ll. 2–4 (Referring to l. 6): The night feare / is feare leest we sholde
be ouercome.
Against ll. 5–6 (Referring to l. 7): The deuyll of myddaye is pryde.
Against ll. 7–8 (Referring to ll. 9–10): Remembre thou arte able to do all
thynges in Chryste.

11 euen] euen vnto 1533
Side-note 1: feare¹] 1533; fayry 1534

take ye wepon from hym manfully / and laye therwith agayne at the owner / kyllynge hym with his owne sworde. That shall comme to passe on this wyse. Yf whan thou art prouoked vnto euyll thou do not onely abstayne from synne: but therof doest take vnto the an

5 occasyon of vertue. And as poetes elegantly fayne that Hercules dyd growe and was also hardened in courage through the daungers that Iuno put vnto hym of displeasure: thou lykewyse gyue also attendaunce, that by the instigacions of thyne ennemy, not onely thou be not ye worse, but rather be made moche better. Thou art

10 stered vnto bodyly lust / knowe thy weyknes / and also lay apart somwhat the more of lawful pleasures / and adde some encrease vnto chaste and holy occupacions. Thou art prycked vnto couetousnes and nyggysshe kepyng: encrease almes dedes. Thou art moued vnto vayne glory: so moche the more humble thy selfe in al

15 thinges. And thus shall it be brought aboute, that euery temptacyon may be a certeyn renewing of thy holy purpose / and an encrease of pite and vertuous lyuyng. And veryly other meanes is there none at all of so great ver[P5v]tue and strengthe to vaynquysshe and ouerthrowe our ennemy: for he shal be afrayde to prouoke the a fresshe/

20 leest he whiche reioyseth to be the begynner and chefe capteyn of wyckednesse, sholde mynystre an occasyon of pite / vertue and godlynesse.

❡ The .xiij. rule. Caplo. xxij.

BVt alway take hede that thou fyght with this mynde and hope /
25 as though that shold be the last fyght that euer thou shalte haue, yf thou gete the ouer hande. For it may be that the benignite of god wyll gyue and graunte this rewarde vnto thy vertue and noble acte: that thyne ennemy ones ouercomme to his shame / shall neuer afterward comme vpon the agayn. A thyng whiche we rede to haue

30 happened to dyuerse holy men. Neyther byleueth Orygene agaynst reason / that whan chrysten men ouercomme: than is the power of theyr ennemyes mynisshed / whyles ye aduersary ones put backe manfully / is neuer suffred to returne again to make a fresshe bataile. Be bolde therfore in the conflict to hope for per-

---

Against ll. 6–7 (Referring to ll. 4–5): Of temptacion take euer an occasion of vertue.
Against ll. 15–17: Let temptacyons be euer the renewyng of thy holy purpose.

---

26 be] be veryly *1533*

petual peace. But agayn after thou hast ouercomme / so behaue thy selfe, as though thou sholdest go agayne to fyght streyghtwaye / for after one temptacyon, we must [P6] loke euer for an other: we may neuer departe from our harneys and wepons: we may neuer forsake our standing: we may neuer leaue of watche, as longe as we 5 warre in the garryson of this body. Euery man must haue alway that sayinge of the prophete in his herte / I wyll kepe my standynge.

❡ The .xiiij. rule. Caplo. xxiij.

WE must take very good hede that we despyse not any vyce as lyght. For no ennemy ouercommeth oftener, than he which is not 10 set of. In which thing I perceyue not a fewe men to be greatly deceyued: for they deceyue themself, whyle they fauour themself in one or two vices / whiche euery man after his own appetite thinketh to be venial / and al other greuously abhorreth. A great parte of them whiche the commune people calleth perfyte and 15 vncorrupt / gretly defyeth theft, extorcion, murder, adultery, in- cest: but single fornicacion and moderate vse of voluptuous plesures as a smal trespace they refuse not all. Some one man beyng vnto all other thynges vncorrupte ynough: is somwhat a good drynker / is in ryot and expenses somwhat wastefull. An other is 20 somwhat liberal of his tonge. An other is combred with vanite, vainglory and [P6v] bostynge. At the last what vyce shall we lacke, yf euery man after this maner shall fauour his owne vyce? It is an euydent token, that those men whiche fauour any vice at all, sholde not truly possesse ye other vertues: but rather some ymages 25 of vertues, whiche eyther nature or bryngyng vp / fynally very custom hath graffed in ye myndes of the very gentyles. But he y^t with christen hatred abhorreth any one vice, must nedes abhorre al. For he whose mynde true charite hath ones possessed, hateth in- differently the hole host of euyll thynges, and flatereth not hymself 30 so moche as in venial synnes, leest he myght fall a lytell and a lytel from the smallest to the greatest. And whyle he is neclygent in lyght thynges myght fall from the chefest thynges of all. And

Against ll. 1–2: After one bataile we must loke for another.
Against ll. 12–13: Some men fauer theyr owne vyces.
Against ll. 22–3 (Referring to ll. 25–6): The Images of vertue.

14 abhorreth] abhorre *1533*   27 y^t] whiche *1533*

though thou as yet canst not plucke vp by the rotes the hole generacion of vices: neuerthelesse somwhat of our euyl propertes must
be plucked awaye day by day / and somthynge added to good
maners. After y^t maner diminissheth or augmenteth ye great hepe
5 of Hesiodus.

❡ The .xv. rule. Caplo. xxiiij.

IF the labour whiche thou must take in the conflict of temptacyon, shall feare the / this shall be a remedy. Se thou com[P7]pare
not the grefe of the fight with the plesure of the synne: but matche
10 me the present bytternes of the fight, with ye bytternes of the synne
hereafter whiche foloweth hym that is ouerthrowen, and than set
the present swetnes of the synne whiche entyseth the, with the
pleasure of the victory hereafter / and with the tranquillite of mynde
whiche foloweth him that fyghteth lustely: and anone thou shalt
15 perceyue how vnequall a comparyson there shall be. But in this
thyng they which be but lytel circumspect are deceyued, bycause
they compare the displeasure of the fyght, with the pleasure of the
synne / and consyder not what foloweth the one and the other. For
there foloweth him whiche is ouercomme, grefe bothe more payn-
20 full a great deale, and also of longer contynuaunce: than he sholde
haue had in tyme of fyght / yf he had wonne ye victory. And
lykewyse there foloweth the conquerours more pleasure by a great
deale and of longer enduraunce: than was the pleasure whiche
caryed him in to synne that was ouercomme. Whiche thynge he
25 shall lyghtly iudge / that hath had the profe of bothe. But no man
that is chrystened ought to be so outryght a cowarde, though he
were dayly subdued of temptacyon: but that he sholde ones at the
leest do his endeuoyre to proue what [P7v] thynge it is to ouercomme temptacyon. Whiche thyng the oftener he shall do / the
30 pleasaunter shall the victory be made vnto him.

❡ The .xvj. rule. Caplo. xxv.

BVt yf at any tyme it shal fortune the to receyue a deedly

Against ll. 1–3: Dayly must somwhat of our euylles be take awaye / and of
good thynges be added.
Against ll. 6–8: The bytternes of the fyght must be compared with the
payne whiche foloweth the synne.
Against ll. 26–7: Proue somtyme what it shal be to ouercome.

wounde / beware leest by and by (thy shelde cast away and wepons forsaken) thou yelde thy self to thyne ennemyes handes. Whiche thynge I haue perceyued to happen vnto many / whose myndes naturally are somwhat feble and softe without resistence / y^t after they were ones ouerthrowen / they seaced to wrastle any more / but 5 permitted and gaue themselfe al togyder vnto affections / neuer thinking any more to recouer theyr liberty agayne. To to moche perilous is this weyknes of spiryte / whiche now and than, though it be not coupled with the worst wyttes in the worlde / yet is it wonte to brynge to that poynt which is worst of al / to despera- 10 cion veryly. Against this weyknes therfore thy mynde must be aforehande armed with this rule / that after we haue fallen in to synne not onely we sholde not despayre, but counterfayte bolde men of warre / whome not seldome shame of rebuke and grefe of the wounde receyued, not onely putteth not to [P8] flyght, but 15 sharpeneth and refressheth agayn to fight more fyersly than they dyd before. In lyke case also, after that we have ben brought in to deedly synne / let vs haste anone to comme agayn to our selfe, and to take a good hert to vs / and to repayre agayne the re- buke and shame of the fall, with newe courage and lustynesse of 20 vertue. Thou shalt heale one wounde sooner than many: thou shalt easlyer cure a fresshe wounde, that y^t whiche is now olde and putrifyed. Conforte thy selfe with that famous verse whiche Demo- stenes is sayd to haue vsed. A man that fleeth, wyll yet fyght agayne. Call to remembraunce Dauid the prophete, Salomon the kyng, 25 Peter a capteyn of the churche, Paule the apostle / so great lyghtes of holynesse, in to what great synnes for al that they fell. Whiche al peraduenture euen for this cause god suffred to fall / leest thou whan thou haddest fallen sholdest despeyre. Ryse vp agayn ther- fore vpon thy fete, but that quyckly, and with a lusty courage / and 30 go to it a fresshe, bothe fyerser and also more circumspect. It happeneth somtyme that deedly offences growe to good men in to an heape of pite / whyle they loue more feruently, whiche erred moost shamefully.

Against ll. 4–5: Dispayre not / thoughe thou be ouercome.
Against ll. 16–18: A fall somtyme courageth a man to wrastell more strongly.

---

21 vertue] strengthe *1533*   27 they fell] fell they *1533*   33 an heape] a heape *1533*   pite] vertuous lyuynge *1533*

⸪ The .xvij. rule. Caplo. xxvj. [P8v]

BVt agaynst sondry and dyuerse assautes of the tempter thine ennemy / sondry and dyuerse remedyes are very mete and conuenyent. Neuerthelesse the onely and chefe remedy, whiche of all
5 remedyes is of most efficacye and strength agaynst all kyndes, eyther of aduersite, or els temptacion : is the crosse of Chryst. The whiche selfe same, is bothe an ensample to them that go out of the waye, and a refresshyng to them that labour / and also armure or harneys to them yᵗ fyght. This alone, is to be cast agaynst all maner
10 wepons and dartes of our most wycked ennemy. And therfore it is necessary to be exercised diligently therin / not after the commune maner / as some men repete dayly the hystory of the passion of Chryst / or honour the ymage of the crosse / or with a thousande signes of it arme all theyr body rounde on euery syde / or kepe some
15 pece of that holy tree layde vp at home in theyr house / or at certeyn houres so call to remembraunce Chrystes punysshment / that they may haue compassyon and wepe for hym with natural affection / as they wolde for a man that is very iuste, and suffreth great wronge vnworthyly. This is not the true fruyte of that tree : neuerthelesse,
20 let it in yᵉ meane season be the mylke of yᵉ soules, whiche be yonglynges and weyke in Christ. But clyme [Q1] thou vp in to yᵉ date tree, that thou mayste take holde of the trewe fruytes therof. These be the chefe, if we whiche be membres, shall endeuoyre our selfe to be semblable vnto our heed in mortifyeng our affectyons /
25 whiche be our membres vpon the erthe / whiche thynge vnto vs ought not onely to be nothynge bytter / but also very plesaunt, and feruently to be desyred / if so be the spiryte of Christ lyue in vs. For who loueth trewly and hertyly that person, to whom he reioyseth to be as vnlyke as may be / and in lyuyng and conuersacion
30 cleane contrary ? Not withstandyng that that thou mayest with yᵉ more profyte, in thy mynde recorde the mistery of the crosse : it shalbe houefull that euery man prepare vnto hym selfe a certayne

Against ll. 4–5 (Referring to l. 6): The crosse of Chryste.
Against ll. 17–21 : The very frute of the crosse is mortifyenge of our membres / that is to saye of our passions and affectyons bodyly.
Against ll. 22–3 : The date tree / the tree of vyctorye.

---

9 alone] is a thynge *1533*   21–2 yᵉ date tree] the date tree / that is to saye the tre of vyctorie *1533*   26 not] *om. 1533*   30 that] *om. 1533*   with] *om. 1533*
Side-note 3 : *om. 1533*

way and godly crafte of fyghtyng and therin dilygently exercyse /
that as sone as nede shall requyre it may be redy at hande. Suche
may ye crafte be / y^t in crucifyeng of euery one of thyne affectyons,
thou mayste applye that parte of the crosse whiche moste specially
therto agreeth. For there is not at all any maner eyther temptacion 5
eyther aduersyte, whiche hath not his propre remedy in the crosse.
As whan thou art tyckled with ambycion of this worlde / whan
thou arte ashamed to be had in derision and to be set at naught: [Q1v]
consydre thou than oh most vyle membre howe great Christe thy
heed is / and vnto what vylenesse he humbled hym selfe for thy 10
sake. Whan the yuell of enuy inuadeth thy mynde / remembre how
kyndly, howe louingly he bestowed himselfe euerywhyt vnto our
vse and profyte / how good he is euen vnto the worste. Whan thou
art moued with gluttony / haue in mynde howe he dranke gall with
eysell. Whan thou art tempted with filthy pleasure / call to remem- 15
braunce howe farre from al maner of pleasure the hole lyfe of thy
heed was / and howe full of incommodytes, vexacyon, and grefe.
Whan yre prouoketh the / lette hym come immedyatly to thy mynde,
whiche lyke a lambe before the shearer helde his peace and opened
not his mouthe. If pouertye wring the yuell / or couetousnesse dis- 20
quyet the / anone let hym be rolled in thy mynde that is the lorde of
all thynges / and yet was made so poore and nedy for thy sake, that
he had not whervpon to rest his heed. And after the same maner if
thou shalt do in al other temptacions also / not onely it shall not be
greuous to haue oppressed thyne affectyons, but surely plesaunt 25
and delectable / for bycause thou shalte perceyue that thou by this
meanes art conformed and shapen lyke vnto thy heed / and that thou
[Q2] doest as it were recompence hym for his infynyte sorowes /
whiche for thy sake he suffred vnto the vttermoste.

❦ The .xviij. rule. Caplo. xxvij.   30

ANd veryly this maner of remedye / though it alone of all remedyes be most present and redy, moste sure and quicke in werkynge
to them whiche be meanly entred in the waye of lyuyng: neuer the
lesse to the weaker sorte these thynges also shall somwhat profyte.

Against ll. 6–8: Affections are this wyse crucyfyed.
Against l. 9: Nota.

3 crucifyeng] certifyeng *1533*   one of] *om. 1533*   5 maner] *om. 1533*
9 oh] *om. 1533*   30 Caplo.] capi. *1533*

If whan affectyon moueth vnto iniquyte / than atones they call
before the eyen of the mynde howe filthy, howe abhomynable,
howe mischeuous a thynge synne is: on the other syde howe great is
the dignyte of man. In tryfles and maters suche as skylleth not if all
5 the worlde knewe / we take some delyberacyon and aduysement
with our selfe. In this mater of all maters moste weyghty and
worthy to be pondred / before y^t with consent as with our owne
hande writyng we bynde our selfe to the fende / shall we not reken
and accompte with our mynde of howe noble a craftes man we
10 were made / in howe excellent estate we are set / with howe exce-
dynge great pryce we are bought / vnto howe great felycyte we are
[Q2v] called? and that man is that gentle and noble creature for
whose sake only god hath forged the meruaylous buyldyng of this
worlde / that he is of the company of aungels, the sonne of god, the
15 heyre of immortalyte, a membre of Christe, a membre of the
churche / that our bodyes be ye temple of the holy goost / our
myndes the ymages and also ye secret habytacions of the deite.
And on the other syde y^t synne is the moste fylthy pestylence and
consumpcyon bothe of the mynde and of the body also / for bothe
20 of them through innocencye springeth anewe into their owne naturall kynde / and through contagyon of synne bothe putrifye and
rotte euen in this worlde. Synne is that deedly poyson of the
moste filthy serpent / the prest wages of the dyuell / and of that
seruyce whiche is not most filthy only, but also moste myser-
25 able. After thou hast consydred this and suche lyke with thy selfe /
pondre wysely and take sure aduysement and delyberacion whether
it shulde be wysely doone or no, for an apparaunt momentanye
and poysoned lytell shorte pleasure of synne / to fall from so great
dignyte, in to so vyle and wretched estate / from whence thou
30 cannest not rydde and delyuer thy selfe by thyne owne power and
helpe. [Q3]

☖ The nyntenth rule. Caplo. xxviij.

FVrthermore compare togyder those two capitaynes by them
selfe moste contrary and vnlyke, god and the dyuell / of whiche the
35 one thou makest thyne enemy whan thou synnest / and the other

Against ll. 1–3: Considre the filthynes of synne and the dignitie of man.

---

18 the other] thother *1533*   23 wages] wagest *1533*   32 Caplo.]
capi. *1533*

thy lorde and mayster. Throughe innocencye and grace thou art
called into the nombre of the frendes of god / arte electe vnto the
ryght tytle and inherytaunce of the sonnes of god. By synne veryly
thou arte made both the bonde seruaunt and sonne of the dyuell.
The one of them is that eternall fountayne and origynall patron 5
and trewe ensample of very and sure beauty / of very trewe
pleasure / of most perfyte goodnesse minystryng hym selfe to all
thynges. The other is father of all myschefe / of extreme filthy-
nesse / of vttermost infelycite. Remembre the benefytes and goodnesse of thone done to the / and the yuell dedes of the other. With 10
what goodnesse hath the one made the? With what mercy redemed
the? With what lybertie and fredom endued the? With what tender-
nesse dayly suffreth he and sustayneth the a wretched synner /
paciently abydyng and lokyng for amendement? With what ioy
and gladnesse dothe he receyue the amended / and whan thou art 15
come agayne [Q3v] to thyselfe? Contrary to all these thynges with
howe naturall hate and enuy longe ago dyd yᵉ dyuell laye wayte to
thy helth? Into what greuous and combrous vexacion hath he cast
the / and also what other thyng ymagyneth he dayly but to drawe
all mankynde with hym in to eternall mischefe. All these thynges on 20
this syde and that syde well and substancyally wayed and pondred/
thus thynke with thy selfe: shal I vnmyndfull of myne origynall
begynnyng from whence I came / vnmyndfull of so great and manyfolde benefytes / for so small a morsell of fayned and false pleasure /
vnkyndely departe from so noble / from so louynge, from so bene- 25
fyciall a father / and shall mancypate and make my selfe bonde
wyllyngly vnto a most fylthy and a moste cruell mayster? Shall I
not at the leest waye make good to the one that thynge whiche I
wolde perfourme to a vyle man / whiche had shewde kyndenesse,
or done me any good? Shall I not flye from the other / whiche wolde 30
flye from a man that coueyted or were aboute to do me hurte?

❡ The twenteth rule. Caplo. xxix. [Q4]

ANd veryly the rewardes be no lesse vnegall than the capytaynes
and gyuers of them be contrary and vnlyke. For what is more

Against ll. 6–9: We must haue in mynde the benefycence of god / and the
malifycence or noysaunce of the deuyll.
Against ll. 33–4: The rewarde of vertue is heuen.

25 noble /] noble *1533, 1534*   32 Caplo.] capitulo *1533*

vnegall than eternall dethe and immortall lyfe? than without ende to
enioye euerlastynge felycite and blyssednesse, in the company and
felowshyp of the heuenly cytezins: and without ende to be tour-
mented and punysshed with extreme vengeaunge, in the moste vn-
5 happy and wretched companye of dampned soules? And who so
euer douteth of this thynge, he is not so moche as a man veryly /
and therfore he is no christen man. And who so euer thynketh not
on this / nor hath it in remembraunce, is euen madder than madnesse
it selfe. Moreouer and besydes all this / vertue and wyckednesse
10 hath in the meane season euen in this lyfe their frutes very moche
vnlyke / for of the one is reaped assured tranquillyte and quietnesse
of mynde / and that blissed ioy of pure and cleane conscience / of
whiche ioy who so euer shal ones haue a taste / there is nothyng in all
this worlde so precyous, nothyng so plesaunt / wherwith he wolde
15 be gladde or desyrous to chaunge it. Contrary wyse there foloweth
the other / that is to say wickednesse / a thousande other yuels / but
moste specyally that moste wretched [Q4v] tourment and vexacyon
of vncleane conscience. That is that hundredfolde rewarde of
spyrytuall ioye whiche Christ promysed in the gospell / as a certayne
20 ernest or taste of eternall felycyte. These be those meruaylous
rewardes that the apostle speaketh of, whiche eye neyther sawe or
eare hath herde / neyther hath sonke in to the herte of any man /
whiche god hath prepared for them that loue hym in this lyfe /
forsothe whan in the meane season, the worme of wycked men
25 dyeth not / and they suffre their hell paynes here euen in this worlde.
Neyther any other thyng is that flame in whiche is turmented the
ryche glutton of whom is made mencyon in the gospell: neyther any
other thinges be those punysshmentes of them in hell of whome the
poetes write so many thynges / saue a perpetuall grefe, vnquietnes
30 or gnawyng of the mynde whiche acompanyeth ye custome of synne.
He that wyll therfore, let hym set asyde the rewardes of the lyfe to
come / whiche be so dyuers and vnlike: yet in this lyfe vertue hath
anexed to her wherfore she habundantly ought to be desyred / and
vyce hath copled vnto hym for whose sake he ought to be abhorred.

Against ll. 9–10: The fruites of pytie in this worlde.
Against ll. 26–7: The frute of synne in this worlde.

---

3 felowshyp] felowwip *1533*   12 conscience] *1533*; constience *1534*
12–13 of whiche] whiche *1533*   13 a taste] tasted *1533*   14 nothyng]
nor nothynge *1533*   21 the apostle] thapostle *1533*   or] nor *1533*
23–4 hym in this lyfe / forsothe] hym / and verily in this lyfe *1533*

❡ The .xxj. rule. Caplo. xxx. [Q5]

MOre ouer consyder howe full of grefe and mysery how shorte
and transitory is this presente lyfe / howe on euery syde dethe
lyeth in awayte agaynste vs, howe euerywhere he catcheth vs
sodaynly and vnware. And whan no man is sure no not of one   5
moment of lyfe / howe great peryll it is to prolonge and contynue
that kynde of lyfe / in whiche (as it often fortuneth) it sodayne dethe
shulde take the, thou were but loste and vndone for euer.

❡ The .xxij. rule. Caplo. xxxj.

BEsydes all this, impenytency or obduracyon of mynde is to be   10
feared, of all myschefes the extreme and worste. Namely if a man
wolde pondre this one thyng onely of so many / howe fewe there be
whiche trewly and with all their hertes come to them selfe agayne /
and be cleane conuerted from synne / and with due repentaunce
reconcyled to god agayne: specially of them whiche haue drawen   15
alonge the lynes of iniquyte, euen vnto the last ende of their lyfe.
Slypper veryly and easy is the fall or discense in to fylthynesse / but
to retourne backe agayne therhence / and to scape vp vnto spirytuall lyght / this is a worke, this is a laboure. Therfore thou [Q5v]
admonisshed and warned euen by yᵉ chaunce of Esopes gote /   20
before thou discende in to the pytte of synne / remembre that there
is not so easy comyng backe agayne.

Against l. 20–p. 184, l. 15: The foxe and the gote discended bothe in to a
pyt to drynke / and whan they had dronke / they could not get out agayn. The
foxe bad the gote to stand vp agaynst the wall / and the foxe lepte vpon his
backe / and so vp / promisyng afore to pull vp the gote after. The gote desyred
the foxe to fulfyll his promesse and to helpe hym vp. The fox answerd: ha
gote gote / yf thou haddest had as moche wyt in thy hed as thou hast heare in
thy berde, thou woldest not haue entred in except thou haddest knowen howe to
come out.

---

1 Caplo.] capi. *1533*   9 rule.] *1533*; rule *1534*   Caplo.] capi. *1533*
16 lynes] lyues *1533*   19 Therfore] Therfore at the leestway *1533*
20 admonisshed] being monisshed *1533*   euen] *om. 1533*

Side-note 1: drynke / and] drynke / *1533*   ha gote] a gote *1533*

⟨ Remedyes agaynst certayne synnes
and specyall vyces / and first agaynst
bodyly luste. Caplo. xxxij.

HItherto haue we forsothe opende and declared (how so euer it
5 be done) commen remedyes agaynst all kynde of vyces. Nowe we
shal assay to gyue also certayn speciall and pertyculer remedyes /
howe and by what meanes thou oughtest withstande euery vyce
and synne / and fyrste of all howe thou mayste resyst the luste of
the body. Than yᵉ whiche yuell, there is none other that soner in-
10 uadeth vs / neyther sharper assayleth or vexeth vs / nor extendeth
larger nor draweth mo vnto their vtter distructyon. If at any tyme
therfore fylthy lust shall styrre thy mynde / with these wepons and
armour, remembre forthwith to mete hym. Fyrst thynke howe
vnclenly / howe filthy / how vnworthy for any man what so euer he
15 be, yᵗ plesure is whiche assymuleth and maketh vs which be a
diuyne worke, egall not to beestes only / but also vnto fylthy swyne,
to gotes, to dogges, and of all brute beestes / vnto yᵉ most brute.
Ye which [Q6] farderforth casteth downe farre vnder the condycion
and state of beestes, vs whiche be apoynted vnto yᵉ company of
20 angels and feloushyp of yᵉ deite. Let come to thy mynde also howe
momentany the same is / howe vnpure / how euer hauing more
aloes than hony. And on the contrary syde howe noble a thyng the
soule is / howe worshypfull a thing yᵉ body of a man is / as I haue
rehersed in the rules aboue. What yᵉ dyuels peuysshnesse is it than
25 for so lytle, so vnclenly tycklyng of momentany plesures to defyle
at one tyme bothe soule and body with vngoodly maners? to prophane and vnhalowe yᵗ temple whiche Christ hath consecrate to
him selfe with his bloode? Consydre yᵗ also what an hepe of mischeuous incommodytes that flatryng plesaunt pestylence bringeth
30 with him. First of al it pulleth from yᵉ thy good fame / a possession
faraway most precious / for yᵉ rumour of no vyce stynketh more
carenly than yᵉ name of lechery. It consumeth thy patrimony / it
kylleth atones both the strength and also the beautie of yᵉ body / it

Against ll. 19–20: Wepons against bodyly lust.
Against ll. 21–3: Aloes is a bytter thyng / and is put for bytternes.
Against ll. 28–9: The incommodities of bodyly lust.

---

3 Caplo.] capi. *1533*   4 forsothe] verily *1533*   15 which] yᵗ *1533*
22 hony] of hony *1533*   27 vnhalowe] pollute *1533*   29 bringeth]
brinketh *1533*   32 than] that *1533*

decayeth and gretly hurteth helth / it engendreth diseases innumerable and then filthy / it disfygureth ye flour of youth long before
ye day / it hasteth or accelerateth ryueled and yuell fauoured age / it
taketh away the quycknesse and strength of the wytte / it dulleth
[Q6v] the syght of the mynde / and graffeth in a man as it were a   5
beestly mynde / it withdraweth atones from all honest studyes
and pastymes / and plungeth and sowseth a man euerywhyt in the
podle and myre be he neuer so excellent / that nowe he hath lust to
thynke on nothynge, but y^t whiche is sluttisshe, vyle, and filthy. And
it taketh awaye the vse of reason whiche was the natyue property   10
of man / it maketh youthe madde, peuysshe, and sclaundrous / and
age odyous, fylthy, and wretched. Bewyse therfore and on this
wyse reken with thyselfe name by name / this pleasure and that
came so yuel to passe / brought with her so moch losse, so moche
disworshyp / dishonour and dishonesty / so moch tedyousnesse,   15
labour and discase: and shal I nowe a foole most naturall deuoure
the hoke wetyngly? shal I agayne commytte that thynge wherof I
shulde repent of fresshe? And lykewyse refrayne thy selfe by the
ensample of other men / whiche thou hast knowen to haue folowed
voluptuous pleasures fylthyly and vnfortunatly. On thother syde,   20
corage and bolde thyselfe vnto chastyte by the ensamples of so many
yonge men / of so many yonge and tendre virgynes norysshed vp
delycately and in pleasures. And (the cyrcumstances compared
togyder) lay agaynst [Q7] thy selfe thy sluggyshnesse / whye thou at
the last shuldest not be able to do y^t thyng whiche suche and suche,   25
of that kynde or sexe / of that age, so borne, so brought vp were
and yet be able to do? Loue as moche as they dyd / and thou shalte
be able to do no lesse than they dyd. Thynke howe honest, howe
plesaunt, howe lusty and florysshyng a thyng is purenesse of body
and of mynde / she moste of all maketh vs acquaynted and famylyer   30
with angels / and apte to receyue the holy goost. For veryly that
noble spiryte the louer of purenesse, so greatly flyeth backe from
no vyce atall as from vnclenlynes / he resteth and sporteth hym
nowhere so moche as in pure virgyns myndes. Set before thyne
eyen howe vngoodly it is, howe altogyder a mad thing to loue / to   35

Against ll. 20–1: Refrayne thy self by the ensample of other men.
Against l. 36–p. 186, l. 1: The vngoodly office of louers.

---

13 pleasure and that] and that pleasure _1533_   15 disworshyp /] _1533_; dis-
worship _1534_   21 the ensamples] thensamples _1533_   25 shuldest]
shulde _1533_   32 flyeth] fleeth _1533_

waxe pale, to be made leane, to wepe, to flatter / and shamfully
to submyt thy selfe vnto a stynkyng harlot most fylthy and rotten /
to gape and synge all nyght at her chambre wyndowe / to be made to
the lure and be obedyent at a becke / nor dare do any thing except
5 she nod or wagge her heed / to suffre a folysshe woman to reigne
ouer the, to chyde the / to lay vnkyndnesse one agaynst ye other, to
fall out / to be made at one agayne / to gyue thy selfe wyllynge vnto
a queene / that she myght mocke / [Q7v] knocke, mangle, and spoyle
the. Where is I beseche the amonge all these thynges the name of
10 a man? Where is thy berde? Where is that noble mynde created
vnto moste beautyfull and noble thynges? Consydre also an other
thynge with thy selfe / howe great a flocke of myscheues, voluptuousnesse (if she be lette in) is wonte to bringe with her. Other vyces
peraduenture haue some acquayntaunce with certayne vertues /
15 fylthy luste hath none atall / but is anexed and alwaye coupled with
those synnes that be greatest and most in nombre. Let it be but a
tryfle or a lyght mater to folowe queenes / yet is it a greuous thynge
not to regarde thy father and mother / to set at naught thy frendes /
to consume thy fathers good in waste / to plucke awaye from other
20 men / to forsweare thy selfe / to drinke all nyght / to robbe / to vse
wytchcrafte / to fyght / to commyt murdre / to blaspheme. In to
whiche all and greuouser than these, the lady pleasure wyll drawe
the heedlonge, after thou ones hast ceassed to be thyne owne man /
and haste put thy wretched heed vnder her gyrdle. Pondre more
25 ouer howe this lyfe vanyssheth away faster than smoke / lesse of
substaunce than a shadowe / and howe many snares dethe pytcheth
for vs / layeng a[Q8]wayte in euery place and at all seasons. Here
and at this poynte it shall profyte syngularly to call to remembraunce, and that name by name / if that sodayne dethe hath taken
30 awaye any somtyme of thyne acquayntaunce, of thy famylyer frendes /
of thy companyons / or els of them whiche were yonger than thou:
and moste specyally of them whiche in tyme passed thou hast had
felowes of fylthy pastyme. And lerne of an other mannes peryll to be
more ware and cyrcumspecte. Remembre how delyciously they lyued /
35 but howe bytterly they departed. Howe late they waxed wyse / howe
late they beganne to hate their mortyferous and deedly pleasures.

Against l. 30 (Referring to l. 29): Sodayn deth.
Against l. 37–l. 1, p. 187: The straytnes of the extreme iudgement.

6 other,] other *1533, 1534*   8 knocke] kocke *1533*   14 peraduenture]
1533; peaduenture *1534*

Lette come to remembraunce the sharpenesse of the extreme
iudgement / and the terryble lyghtenyng of that fearfull sentence
neuer to be reuoked / sendyng wycked men in to eternall fyre / and
that this pleasure of an hour, shorte and lytell / must be punysshed
with eternall turmentes. In this place wey dylygently in a payre of 5
balaunces / howe vnegall a chaunge it is, for the moste fylthy and
very shorte delectacyon of luste / bothe to lose in this lyfe the ioye
of the mynde beyng moche sweter and more excellent / and in the
lyfe to come to be spoyled of ioyes [Q8v] euerlastyng. Moreouer
with so shadowlyke and lytle vayne pleasure to purchace sorowes 10
neuer to be ended. Fynally if it seme an harde thyng to dispyse y^t
so small delectacyon for Christes sake / remembre what paynes he
toke vpon hym for the tendre loue he bare to the. And besyde the
comen iniuryes of mans lyfe / how moche of his holy bloode shedde
he / howe shamfull, howe bytter dethe suffred he / and all for the. 15
And thou of all those thynges vnmyndfull, crucyfyest agayne the
sonne of god / iteratyng a fresshe those madde pleasures whiche
caused and compelled thy heed and lorde vnto so cruell tourmentes.
Than acordyng to ye rule aboue rehersed / call to mynde howe
moche of benefytes he heaped on the / whan as yet thou haddest 20
deserued nothyng atall: for the whiche although no suffycient or
lyke recompence can be made of thy parte, no for the leest / yet
desyreth he agayne none other thanke but that thou after his ensample, shuldest refrayne thy mynde from deedly and mortall
pleasures / and tourne the vnto the loue of hyghest goodnesse and 25
of infynyte pleasure and beautye. Compare togyther those two
Venus, and two cupydes of Plato / that is to saye honest loue and
fylthy loue / holy pleasure and [r1] vnclenly pastyme / compare
togyder the vnlyke mater of eyther other, compare ye natures / compare the rewardes. And in all temptacyons / but namely whan thou 30
art styrred to fylthy lust / set to the before thyne eyen thy good
aungell whiche is thy keper and contynuall beholder and wytnes of

Against ll. 6–9: The ioyes of pure mynde is moche sweter than is the plesure
of synne.
Against ll. 19–20: The benefites of god.
Against ll. 24–7: Venus is the goddesse of loue and she is put for loue. Cupido
is the god of loue / and is also put for loue.
Against ll. 29–30: Here is a good note for euery chrysten man.

11 an harde] a harde *1533*   22 no] *om. 1533*   25 hyghest] infynyte
1533   26 pleasure] pleasures *1533*   those] these *1533*   26–7 two
Venus] two / Venus *1533, 1534*   31 eyen] eyes *1533*

al thynges thou doest or thynkest / and god euer lokyng on / vnto
whose eyen al thynges are open, whiche sytteth aboue the heuens
and beholdeth ye secrete places of the erth. And wylt not thou be
afrayde before the aungell present and euen harde by the / before god,
5 and all the company of heuen loking on and abhorryng, to commytte
a thyng so abhomynable and filthy, that it wolde shame y^e to do
the same in the presence of one vyle man? This thyng I wolde thou
shuldest thynke as it is in dede. And if it were so y^t thou haddest
eyen moche sharper of syght than hath a beest called lynxe / or
10 moche clerer than hath the egle / yet with these eyen in ye most
clerest lyght that coude be, coudest thou not beholde more surely
that thyng whiche a man dothe before the, than all the priuy and
secrete partes of thy mynde be open vnto the syght of god and of
his aungels. This also counte in thy mynde, whan thou art ouer-
15 come of bodyly lust, of two thynges the one must folowe / eyther that
voluptu[r1v]ousnes ones tasted, shal so enchaunt and derken thy
mynde / that thou must go from fylthynesse to fylthynesse, vntyll
thou clene blynded shalt be brought in sensum reprobum / that is to
say / into a leude and reproued iudgement: and so made obstynate
20 and sturdy in yuell, cannest not / no truly not than yelde vp filthy
pleasure whan she hath forsaken the. Whiche thing we se to haue
happened to very many / that whan the body is wasted / whan
beauty is wydred and vanisshed / whan the bloode is colde / whan
strength fayleth / and the eyen waxe dym / yet styll continually
25 they ytche without ceassing. And with greater myschefe are nowe
become filthy spekers, than before tyme they were vnshamefull
lyuers / than whiche thyng, what can be more abhomynable and
monstrous? The other is if peraduenture it shall happen y^e by the
specyall fauour of god to come agayne to thy selfe. Than must that
30 shorte and fugityue pleasure be purged with very great sorowe of
mynde / with mighty and stronge labour / with contynual stremes
of teares. How moche more wisdom therfore is it not to receyue at
al the poyson of carnall plesure / than eyther to be brought in to so
vncurable blyndnesse / or els to recompence so lytell / and that also
false pleasure with so great greuaunce and dolorous [r2] payne?

Against ll. 9–11: Lynx is a beest of moost purest syght amonge all beestes.
Against ll. 13–15 (Referring to l. 19): Obstinacy of a frowarde mynde springeth of bodyly lust.

2 eyen] eyes *1533*   6 wolde] woldest *1533*   9 eyen] eyes *1533*   10 eyen]
eyes *1533*   24 eyen] eyes *1533*   26 become] *om. 1533*   were] haue ben *1533*

More ouer thou mayste take also many thynges of the circumstaunce of thyne owne person / which myght call the backe from voluptuous pleasure. Thou art a preest / remembre that thou art al togyder consecrate to thynges pertaynynge vnto god . What a mischeuous dede / howe vngoodly, howe vnmete, and howe vnworthy 5 it shulde be, to touche the rotten and stynkyng flesshe of an hore, with that mouth wherwith thou receyuest that precious body so greatly to be honoured / and to handell lothsome and abhomynable fylth with the same handes wherwithall (euen the aungelles mynystrynge to the and assystynge the) thou executest that ineffable and 10 incomprehensyble mysterye. Howe these thynges agre not, to be made one body and one spiryte with god / and to be made one body with an hoore. If thou be lerned / so moche the nobler and lyker vnto god is thy mynde / and so moche the more vnworthye of this shame and rebuke. If thou be a gentylman / if thou be a 15 prynce / the more aperte and open the abhomynacyon is: the greuouser occasyon gyueth it vnto other inferyours to folowe the same. If thou be maryed / remembre what an honest thynge is a bedde vndefyled. And gyue dylygence [r2v] (as moch as infirmite shal suffre) that thy wedlocke may counterfayte the moste holy 20 maryage of Christe and his churche / whose ymage it beareth: that is to wete / that thy mariage may be clene bareyn in vnclenlynes / and plentyous in procreacion. For in no kynde of lyuyng can it be but very fylthy to serue and be bounde to vnclenly lustes. If thou be a yong man, take good hede besyly that thou 25 pollute not vnaduysedly the floure of thy youthe / whiche wyll neuer spring agayne: and that thou cast not away vpon a thyng moste fylthy, thy best and very golden yeres, which flye away most swyftly / and neuer returne agayne. Beware also leest now through the ignoraunce and neglygence of youthe, thou commytte that thyng 30 whiche shulde grudge the here after by all thy hole lyfe / the conscience of thy misdedes euer persecutyng the with those most bytter, moste greuous and sharpe stynges / whiche whan plesure

Against l. 3: A preest.
Against ll. 12–13: If thou be lerned.
Against l. 15: A gentylman.
Against ll. 18–19: A maryed man.
Against l. 24 (Referring to l. 25): A yonge man.
Against ll. 32–3: Fylthy plesure leueth behynde her stynge in our myndes.

---

1 also] *om. 1533*   32 those] those his *1533*

departeth, she leueth in our myndes. If thou be a woman, this
kynde nothyng more becometh than chastyte, than shame, and
feare of dishonesty. If thou be a man / so moche the more art thou
mete and worthy of greater thinges / and vnmete and vnworthy of
5 these so leude thinges. If thou be olde, wysshe thou haddest some
other mans eyen to beholde thy selfe with[r3]all / that thou myghtest se howe yuell voluptuousnesse shulde become the: whiche in
youthe veryly is myserable and muste be bridled / but in an olde
foole forsoth wonderfull and monstrous, and also euen vnto the very
10 folowers of pleasure, a iestynge and mockyng stocke. Among all
monsters none is more wonderfull than fylthy lust in age. Oh dotypol / oh to moche forgetful of thy selfe, at the leestway behold at
a glasse the hoore heares and whyte snowe of thy heed / thy forheed
forowed with wrincles / and thy careyn face moste lyke vnto a deed
15 corps: and now at the last ende, whan thou art come euen vnto
the pittes brinke, care for other thynges more agreable vnto thy
yeres: at the leestway, y^t which became the to haue done before
tyme (reason mouyng the) do now / thy yeres putting the in remembraunce or rather compellyng the. Euen now plesure herselfe
20 casteth the of / sayeng neyther I nowe am comly vnto the / neyther
yet thou mete or apte vnto me. Thou hast playde ynough / thou
hast eaten ynough / thou hast dronke ynough / it is tyme for the to
departe: why holdest thou yet so fast and art so gredy on plesures
of this lyfe, whan very lyfe her selfe forsaketh the. Now is ye tyme
25 for that mystycall concubyne Abysac, that ones she may begyn to
rest in thy bo[r3v]some / let her with holy rage of loue heate thy
mynde / and in her enbrasynges kepe thou warme and comforte
thy colde membres.

Against l. 1: A woman.
Against l. 3: A man.
Against l. 5: An olde man.
Against ll. 10–12: Agaynst the lechery of old men and women.
Against ll. 15–25: Dauyd was so olde that he coulde get no heate in his lymmes /
than brought the Israelytes vnto Dauyd Abisac a fayre yonge mayde whiche
lay with hym and kept hym warme / he knewe her not / she remayned a pure
mayde. By her is sygnyfyed wysdom / a thyng moost mete for age / all fylthynes
and vnclennes layde aparte.

---

1 leueth] leueth behynde her *1533*   6 eyen] eyes *1533*   8 muste]
to *1533*   9 forsoth] veryly *1533*   24 is y^e] it is *1533*   27 in her
enbrasynges kepe thou] with the enbrasynges of her kepe the *1533*

Side-note 4: women] womeu *1533*

**C A shorte recapitulacyon of remedyes
agaynst the flame of lust. Capi. xxxiij.**

FInally to make a shorte and compendyous conclusyon / these be
the moste speciall thinges whiche wyll make the sure from pleasures
and entysynges of ye flesshe. First of all circumspecte and diligent 5
auoydynge of all occasyons. Whiche precepte thoughe it be mete to
be obserued also in other thinges, bycause that he whiche loueth
perylles is worthy in them to perisshe: yet these be moste chefely
those Syrenes whiche almoste neuer man at all hath escaped /
saue he whiche hath kepte farre of. Secondly moderacyon of 10
eatynge and drinkyng and of slepe. Temperaunce and abstynence
from pleasures / ye from suche as be lawful and permytted. The
regarde of thyne owne deth / and the contemplacion of the deth of
Christ. And those thinges also wyll helpe if thou shalt lyue with
suche as be chaste and vncorrupted. If thou shalte eschewe as a 15
certayne pestylence the communycacion of corrupte and wanton
persons. If thou shalte flye ydle solytarynesse and sluggysshe [r4]
ydlenesse. If thou shalt exercise thy mynde strongly in the medy-
tacyon of celestyall thynges, and in honest studyes. But specyally
if thou shalte consecrate thy selfe with all thy myght vnto the 20
inuestygacyon and serchynge of mysteryes of holy scripture. If
thou shalte pray bothe often and purely / most of all whan temptacyon inuadeth and assawteth the.

**C Agaynst the entysynges and prouo-
kynges vnto auaryce. Capi. xxxiiij.**   25

IF thou shalt perceyue that thou art eyther by nature any thynge
enclyned to ye vyce of auaryce / or styrred by the dyuyll: call to
remembraunce (acordyng to the rules aboue rehersed) ye dignyte
of thy condycion or state / whiche for this thynge onely was created /
for this redemed, that thou euer shuldest enioye that infynyte good 30
thynge god / for god hath forged all the hole buyldyng of this

Against ll. 4-5 (Referring to l. 6): Auoydynge occasyons.
Against ll. 8-9: Syrenes be mere maydens.
Against l. 26: Auaryce.

---

8 in them to perisshe] to perisshe therin *1533*   17 If] yf *1533*; It *1534*
flye] flee *1533*   21 and] or *1533*   22 often] ofte *1533*   29 was]
wast *1533*

worlde that all thynges shulde obey vnto thy vse and necessyte.
Howe fylthy than, and of howe strayte and narow a mynde is it, not
to vse but so greatly to wonder at thynges dombe and moste vyle?
take away the errour of men / what shall golde and syluer be but
5 reed erth and whyte? Shalt thou beyng the disciple [r4v] of poore
Christ, and called to a better possessyon / wonder at that as a certayn great and excellent thyng, whiche no philosopher of the
gentyles dyd not set at naught? not to possesse richesse, but to
dispyse rychesse is a noble thynge. But the communalte, of christen
10 men by name onely, crye out agaynst me / and be glad to disceyue
them selfe moste craftily. Very necessite (say they) compelleth vs to
gader good togyder / wherof, if there shulde be none at all / than
coude we not forsothe ones lyue : if it shulde be thynne and poore /
than shulde we lyue in moche mysery without pleasure. But and if it
15 be somwhat clene and honest / and somwhat plenteous withall / it
bringeth many commodytees to man. The good lyking of body is well
sene vnto / prouysion is made for our chyldren / we lende and profyte
our frendes / we are delyuered from contempte and be the more
set by : in conclusion also a man shal haue ye better name whan he
20 is somwhat welthy. Of a great many thousandes of chrysten men
thou canst scarce fynde one or two y^t dothe not both say and thynke
these thinges. Neuer the lesse to answere these men vnto bothe
partes. First of al bycause they cloke their couetousnes with the
name of necessite / I wyll lay agaynst them the parable rehersed in
25 the gospell, of the lylies and of the byrdes [r5] lyuynge from day to
day without farther prouysion / whose ensample Christ exhorteth
vs to counterfayte. I wyll lay agaynst them that the same Christ
wolde not ones suffre so moche as a scrippe to be caryed aboute of
his discyples. I wyll lay agaynst them, y^t he commaundeth vs (all
30 other thinges layde aparte) before all thynges to seke the kyngdome
of heuen : and promyseth that all thynges shalbe cast and gyuen to
vs. Whan at any tyme had not they thinges necessary to mayntayne
lyfe withal sufficiently / whiche with all their hertes haue gyuen

Against ll. 7–8: To dyspyse ryches is a noble thynge.
Against ll. 14–24: Chryste in the gospell of Mathew / leest his disciples shuld
care for meat / drynke / or clothes / bad them to beholde the lilies how they
were clothed / and the byrdes how they were fed / sayeng: if your father of
heuen make prouision for so vyle thynges / moche more ye can not lacke whom
he loueth so syngulerly.

5 beyng] be *1533*   13 forsothe ones lyue] ones lyue veryly *1533*
22 these thinges] the same *1533*

themselfe to vertue and to the true lyfe of a christen man? And how small a thyng is that whiche nature requyreth of vs? but thou measurest necessite not by ye nedes of nature / but by ye boundes of couetousnes. But vnto good men, euen that is ynough that scarsely contenteth nature. How be it verily I do not so greatly set of these which forsake at one choppe their hole substaunce euerywhyt, that they might the more shamfully begge of other. It is none offence to possesse money / but to loue and set store by money, that is a vice and cosyn to synne. If ryches flowe vnto the / vse the offyce of a good dispenser: but and if it ebbe and go away / be not consumed with thought / as though thou were robbed of a great thynge / but rather reioyce [r5v] that thou art delyuered of a perylous fardell. Notwithstandyng he whiche consumeth the chefe study and pastyme of his lyfe in heapynge vp rychesse togyder / whiche gapeth at them as a certayne excellent or noble thyng, and hyghly to be desyred / and layeth them vp in store / that he may haue ynoughe to serue hym for longe tyme / ye though he shulde lyue euen to the age of Nestor: this man peraduenture may well be called a good marchaunt / but that he is a good christen man forsothe I wolde not saye whiche hangeth all togyder of hym selfe / and hath distruste of the promesses of Christe / whose goodnesse, it is easy to wete / shall not fayle a good man puttyng his trust in him / seyng that he so liberally bothe fedeth and clotheth the poore sparowes. But let vs nowe caste a comptes of the commodytees, whiche rychesse is byleued to bring with hym. Fyrst of all euen by the commune consent of the gentyle philosophers: amonge the good thynges whiche are called Bona vtilia / that is to say / good profytable thynges, rychesse hath the lowest place. And whan all other thynges (after the dyuisyon of Epictetus) are without man / excepte onely vertue of the mynde: yet nothynge is so moche without vs as money is / nothynge bringeth [r6] so lytell commodyte. For what so euer there is anywhere of golde / what so euer there is of precyous stones / if thou alone haddest it euery deale in thy possessyon, shall thy mynde be therfore the better by the valure of one heare?

Against l. 6: Fryers.
Against ll. 18–19: Nestor lyued thre hundred yeres.
Against ll. 26–7: Richesse among profitable thinges optayn the lowest rowme.
Against ll. 33–4: Rychesse helpeth nothyng to vertue.

19–20 but that he is a good christen man forsothe I wolde not saye whiche]
but veryly I wolde not say that he were a very good christen man / that _1533_

shalt thou be the wyser? shalte thou be the connynger? shalte thou
be anywhyt the more in good helth of body? shall it make the more
stronge and lusty? more fayre and beautyous? more yonge? No
trewly. But you wyll say that it purchaseth pleasures / truthe it is: but
5 they be deedly pleasures: it getteth a man honour / but what honoure
I praye you? veryly false honoure / whiche they gyue, that prayseth nothing / setteth by nothyng but onely folysshe thynges / and
of whom to be praysed, is wel nere to be dispraysed. Trewe honour
is, to be lauded of them whiche are commendable and prayse
10 worthy them selues. The hyghest honoure that can be, is to haue
pleased Chryste. Trewe honour is, the rewarde not of rychesse / but
of vertue. The folysshe people gyueth the roume and place / gaseth
vpon the / and gyueth the honoure and reuerence. O foole, they
wonder at thyne apparayle, and honoureth it / and not the: why
15 doest thou not discende in to thyne owne conscyence / and consyder
the myserable [r6v] pouerte of thy mynde? Whiche if the commune
people sawe / than wolde they iudge the as myserable and wretched,
as they now call the happy and blyssed. But good getteth frendes.
I graunt / but yet fayned and false frendes: neyther getteth it
20 frendes to the but to it selfe. And certaynly the riche man is in this
poynt of all men moste vnfortunate and wretched / bycause he can
not so moche as discerne or knowe his true frendes and louers
from other. One hateth hym priuely and secretly in herte and
mynde as an harde nygarde. An other hath enuy at him bycause he
25 passeth him in ryches. Another lokyng to his owne profyte and
auauntage, flatreth hym / and holdeth vp his ye and his nay / and
smyleth vpon hym / to the ende that he may scrape and get some
thing from him. He that before his face is moste louyng and kynde,
wyssheth and prayeth for his quycke and hasty deth. There is none
30 that loueth hym so hertily and entyerly / but that he had leuer haue
hym deed than alyue. No man is so famylyer with hym, y^t wyll tell
hym the truthe. But be it in case there were one specyall frende
amonge a thousande that loued a ryche man hertyly without any
maner of faynynge / yet can not the ryche man but haue in suspicion
35 and mystrust euery man. He iudgeth all men to be vultures [r7]

Against ll. 4–5: To false pleasures and vayne honours they helpe somwhat.
Against ll. 11–13: Honour is the rewarde of vertue / and not of rychesse.
Against ll. 18–20: Rychesse getteth frendes / but those false and fayned.

31 y^t] y^t he *1533*   33 thousande] *1533*; thousaude *1534*

and rauenous byrdes gapyng for carayn: he thynketh all men to be flyes flyeng to hym, to sucke out some profyte of hym to them-selues. What so euer commodite therfore riches semeth to bring / it for ye most parte, or els al togyder is but coloured and disceytfull / it is shadowelyke and full of delusyon/aperyng otherwyse than it is 5 in very dede. But they bring very many thinges whiche are yuell in dede / and taketh away very many of these thynges whiche are good in very dede. Therfore if thou wylt lay acomptes well and perfytly of y^t whiche is wonne / and that whiche is lost: doutles thou shalt fynde that they neuer do bring so moche of commodytees / but y^t 10 they drawe with them to to moche more of incommodytes and dis-plesures. With howe paynfull and sore labours are they gotten / and with howe great ieopardyes? With howe great thought and care be they kept? With howe great heuynesse and sorow are they lost? for whiche causes Christ calleth them very thornes, bycause 15 they rent, teare, and plucke in sonder all the tranquyllite and quyet-nesse of the mynde, with a thousande cares / than the whiche tran-quillite of mynde, nothyng is to man more swete and plesaunt / and they neuer quenche thurst and desyre of them selfe / but kendleth and encreaseth it more and more. They driue a [r7v] man heed- 20 longe in to al mischefe. Neyther flatter thou thy selfe in vayne / sayeng nothyng forbyddeth, but y^t a man at one tyme may be bothe ryche and good. Remembre what verite saythe / y^t it is more easy for a camell to crepe thrugh the eye of a nedle, than a ryche man to entre in to the kyngdome of heuen. And playnly without excepcion 25 true is y^t sayeng of saynt Ierome: A ryche man to be eyther vniust hymselfe, or ye heyre of an vniust man. Great ryches can neuer be eyther goten or els kept without synne. Remembre of how moche better rychesse they robbe the. For he hateth the very taste and smell of vertue / he hateth all honest craftes, who so euer setteth 30 his hert vpon golde. More ouer the vyce of auaryce onely is called ydolatry of Paule. Neyther with any other vyce at al Christ hath

Against ll. 15–16: Wherfore christ compareth rychesse vnto thornes.
Against ll. 23–4: It is harde for a riche man to be a good man.
Against l. 31–p. 196, l. 2: Auaryce is called ydolatry. Mammon is the deuyl whiche tempteth and styrreth to couetousnes.

2–3 to themselues] for themselues 1533   15 very] yea 1533   21 thou] om. 1533   23 y^t] that 1533, ye 1534
Side-note 1: vnto] to 1533

lesse acquayntance, neyther yᵉ self same person can please god
and mammon also.

℄ The recapitulacion of the remedyes a-
gaynst the vyce of auaryce. Cap. xxxv.

5   THou shalt lyghtly therfore cease to wonder at money if thou
wilt ponder and wey diligently very good thynges with those yᵗ be
false and apparant good / if paynted and coloured commodytes,
with those that [r8] be very commodytees in dede. If thou wylt
lerne with thyne inner eyen to behold and to loue that noble good
10 thyng whiche is infynyte / whiche onely, whan it is present / ye
though al other thynges shulde be lacking, haboundantly dothe
satisfye the mynde of man / whiche is wyder and larger of capacite
than yᵗ it can be suffysed with all the good thynges of this worlde. If
thou shalte ofte call agayn before thyne eyen in what condicyon and
15 state thou were, whan the erthe first receyued yᵉ whan thou were
first borne: lykewise in what state yᵉ same shal receyue the agayn
whan thou dyest. If euer shalbe present in thy memory yᵗ famous
foole of whome is made mencion in yᵉ gospel: to whom it is said.
This night I wyl fet again thy soule from the: and these thynges
20 whiche thou hast gadred togyder, whose shall they than be? If thou
shalt turne thy mynde from the corrupt maners of yᵉ commen
sorte vnto yᵉ pouerty of Mary Christes mother / vnto the pouerty
of thapostels / of yᵉ martyrs / and most of all of Christ thy heed.
And set before the that fearfull worde Ve, yᵗ is interpretate / wo be
25 to you: whiche Christ so menasseth and threteneth vnto the ryche
men of this worlde.
before) take and holde this with toth and nayle / yᵗ to be honour

℄ Agaynst ambycion or desyre of honour and authorite. Capi. xxxvj. [r8v]

IF at any tyme ambicion shal combre and vexe thy mynde thrugh
30 her enchauntementes / with these remedies thou shalt arme thyself
before hande without taryeng (according to yᵉ rules which I gaue

Against ll. 12–13: The mynde of man is of great capacytie / god onely fylleth it.
Against ll. 14–15: Naked we came and naked we shall go.
Against l. 32–p. 197, l. 1: Honour spryngeth of vertue onely.

---

4 Cap.] Ca. *1533*   23 thapostels] the apostles *1533*

only whiche springeth of true vertue / which selfe same neuerthelesse a man must somtyme refuse / euen as taught vs both with
doctryne and ensample our mayster Iesus Christ. And this to be
the chefe honour and onely honour whiche a christen man shulde
desyre and wysshe for, to be praysed not of men / but of god / for 5
whom he commendeth (as sayth the apostle) that man is perfyte
and worthy of honour in dede. But if honour be gyuen of man for
an vngoodly and vnhonest thynge / and so of vngoodly persons : this
is not honoure but great dishonesty, shame and rebuke. If for any
meane and indifferent thyng / as for beauty, strength, ryches, kynne : 10
yet verily shall it not be called truly honour / for no man deserueth
honoure with y^t thyng wherof he deserueth not to be praysed. If
for an honest thyng in dede it shall be honour : yet he whiche
deserueth it shall not desyre it / but veryly shalbe content with y^e
very vertue and conscyence of his good dede. Beholde therfore how 15
folysshe and howe worthy to be laughed at these ho[Si]nours be /
for whose desire the commune people so greatly burne and rage.
Fyrst of all, of whome are they gyuen ? Truly of them with whome
is no difference bytwene honesty and dishonesty. Wherfore are
they gyuen ? very ofte for meane thynges / now and than for fylthy 20
thynges. To whome ? to hym whiche is vnworthy. Who so euer
therfore gyueth honour, he dothe it, or for feare / and than is he
agayne to be feared, or for profyte / and than he mocketh the : or
bycause he is astonyed at thynges of naught, and worthy of no
honour / and than he is to be pytyed : or bycause he iudgeth the to 25
be indued with suche thynges as honour is gyuen vnto of dutye /
wherin yf he be disceyued / gyue dylygence that thou mayst be,
that he supposeth the to be. But and yf he hyt aryght / referre all
thyne honoure vnto hym, to whome thou art in dette / yea for all
those thynges wheruunto the honour is gyuen. As thou oughtest 30
not to ascrybe vnto thy selfe the vertue : so is it vnsyttynge to take

Against ll. 4–5: It is an honest thynge to be lauded of god.
Against ll. 11–12: Honour gyuen of vnhonest persones.
Against ll. 18–19: Honour gyuen of comen people.

---

22 he dothe it, or for] eyther he doth it for *1533*   23 agayne to be feared]
to be feared agayne *1533*   or for profyte] or bycause thou woldest do hym a
good turne *1533*   25 iudgeth] supposed *1533*   26 vnto] *om. 1533*
29 thyne honoure] the honour y^t is offred the *1533*   in dette] bounde *1533*
31 to ascrybe vnto thy selfe] ascrybe to thyne owne selfe *1533*

vpon the, the honour therof. Besydes this, what is greater madnesse,
than to esteme the valure of thy selfe by the opynyons of folysshe
men / in whose handes it lyeth to take away agayne whan so euer
they lyst, the very same honour whiche they gyue / and dishonest the
5 [Siv] whiche was euen now honested. Therfore nothynge can be
more folysshe, than eyther to reioyce for suche honours whan they
happen / or to be sory or mourne whan they be taken away / which
not to be true honours, thou shalte perceyue at the leestway by this
probacion and argument / for so moche as they be commen to the
10 worst and lewdest persones of all. Yea they chaunce almoost to none
more plentuously: than to them whiche of trewe honours be moost
vnworthy. Remembre how blyssed is the quyetnesse of a meane lyfe,
bothe pryuate, (that is to saye, charged with no commune besynesse) and also separated and remoued out of the waye from all
15 noyse, haunte, or prece. On the other syde, consyder how full of
pryckes, how full of cares, of peryls, of sorowes, is the lyfe of great
men. What difficultye it is, not to forgete thy selfe, in prosperite /
how hard it is for a man standyng in a slypper place not to fal / how
greuous the fal is from on hygh. And remembre that all honour is
20 coupled with great charge / and how strayte the iudgement of the
hygh iudge shal be against them whiche here in vsurpyng of honours, preferre them selfe afore other men. For surely, who so euer
shall humble and submyt hym selfe / hym as an innocent or harme-
lesse persone, mercy [S2] shal socour. But who so euer exalteth
25 him selfe as a perfyte man / the same persone excludeth from hym
selfe the helpe and socour of grace. Let euer the ensample of
Christ thy heed stycke fast in thy mynde. What thyng as touchyng
to ye worlde, was more vyle, more despysed, or lesse honoured,
than he? How forsoke he honours, whan they were proffered
30 hym / whiche was greater than any honour? How set he no store
of honours, whan he rode vpon an asse? How condempned he
them, whan he was clothed in pall, and crowned with thorne? How
vngloryous or vyle a dethe chose he? But whome the worlde despysed, hym the father gloryfyed. Let thy glory be in ye crosse of

Against ll. 2–3: To whome honour chaunceth most comenly.
Against ll. 12–13: The quietnes of a priuate life.
Against ll. 24–7: Let it not exalt thy mynde bycause thou bearest rule ouer
other men.

2 the opynyons] thopinyons *1533*   14 also separated] seperate *1533*
17 What] and what *1533*   19 on] an *1533*

Chryste / in whome also is thy helthe, welth, sauyng, defence and protection. What good shall worldly honours do to the, yf god cast the awaye and despyse the / and the aungels lothe, abhorre, and defye the.

❧ Agaynst elacion, otherwyse called pryde   5
or swellyng of the mynde. Caplo. xxxvij.

THou shalt not swell in thy mynde, yf (according to the commune prouerbe vsed of euery man) thou woldest knowe thyselfe : that is, what so euer great thing, what so euer goodly or beautyfull thyng, [S2v] what so euer excellent thyng is in the / thou accompt that to be   10 the gyfte of god / and not thy good. On the other syde / yf what so euer is lowe or vyle / what so euer is foule or fylthy / what so euer is shrewde or euyl, thou ascrybe that all togyder vnto thyne owne self. If thou remembre in how moche fylthe thou were conceyued / in how moche borne / how naked / how nedy / how brutysshe /   15 howe wretched / howe myserably thou crepest in to this lyght. If thou remembre in to how many diseases or sycknes on euery syde / vnto how many chaunces / vnto how many encombraunces, greues, and troubles this wretched body is daungered. And agayne how lytel a thyng were able shortly to consume and bryng to naught   20 this cruell and vnruly gyaunt / swellyng with so myghty a spiryt. Pondre also this, what maner thyng that is wherof thou takest vpon the. If it be a meane, or an indifferent thynge / it is folysshnes : yf a fylthy thynge / it is madnes : yf an honest thynge / it is vnkyndnes. Remembre also nothynge to be a more sure document, or profe of   25 starke folysshnes, and lacke of vnderstandyng / than yf a man stande greatly in his owne conceyte. And agayne that no kynde of foly is more vncurable. If thy mynde begyn to aryse and waxe great, by-[S3]cause a vyle man submytteth hym selfe to the : thynke how moche greater and myghtyer god hangeth ouer thyne heed / which   30 crussheth downe euery proude necke erecte streyght vp / and bryngeth euery hyll vnto a playne / whiche spared not / no veryly not so moche as the aungell whan he was fallen in to pryde. And

Against l. 8: Know thy selfe.
Against ll. 22–4: Perceiue wherof thou standest so greatly in thyne owne conceyte.

6 Caplo.] capi. *1533*

these thynges also shall be good, though they be of a lyghter sort,
yf thou woldest compare thy selfe alwaye with excellenter persones.
Thou lykest thy selfe, bycause of a lytel beaute of thy body: compare thy selfe to them whiche in beaute be farre before the. A lytel
5 connyng maketh the to set vp thy fethers: turne thyne eyen vnto
them, in comparyson of whom thou mayst seme to haue lerned
nothyng at al. Moreouer if thou wilt accompt not how moche of
good thynges thou hast: but how moche thou lackest. And with
Paule forgetfull of those thynges whiche be behynde the: woldest
10 stretche forth thy selfe to tho thynges whiche remayne afore the.
Furthermore, that also shal not be an vnwyse thyng / yf whan the
wynde of pryde dothe blowe / by and by we turne our very euyll
thinges into a remedy / as it were expelling one poyson with an other.
That thynge shall this wyse comme to passe / if whan any greate
15 vyce or deformite of body / whan [S3v] any notable domage, eyther
fortune hath gyuen, or foly hath brought to vs, whiche myght
gnawe vs vehemently by the stomacke: we set that before our eyen /
and by thensample of the pecocke we beholde our selfe chefely in
that parte of vs, in whiche we be moost deformed / and so shall thy
20 fethers fall forthwith, and thy pryde abate. Beyonde al these
(besydes that none other vyce is more hated vnto god) remembre
also that arrogancye, pryde, and presumpcyon is notably hated, and
had in derision euerywhere amonge men: whan contrary wyse lowlynesse and mekenesse / bothe purchaseth the fauour of god / and
25 knytteth vnto the, the benyuolence of man. Therfore to speke compendyously / two thynges chefely shall refrayne the from pryde / yf
thou consyder what thou art in thy selfe / fylthy in thy byrth / a
bubble (suche as ryseth in the water) throughout all thy lyfe /
wormes meate in thy dethe / and what Chryste was made for the.

30   ¶Agaynst wrathe and desyre of
                   vengeaunce. Caplo. xxxviij.

WHan feruent sorowe of the mynde styrreth the vp vnto vengeaunce / remembre wrath to be nothing lesse [S4] than that whiche

Against ll. 13–14: Consydre thyn owne vyces and deformities.
Against ll. 21–2: Arrogancy / presumpcion / or pertynacy / is a hated vyce.
Against ll. 32–3: Wrathe is a chyldysshe thynge.

1 be of a lyghter sort] seme somwhat as they were tryfles *1533*   25 knyt-
teth] kutteth *1533*   28 bubble] burble *1533*   31 Caplo.] capi. *1533*

it falsely counterfayteth / that is to wyte, fortitude, or manful-
nesse. For nothynge is so chyldysshe / so weyke / nothynge so feble
and of so vyle a mynde, as to reioyce in vengeaunce. Thou woldest
be counted a man of great stomacke / and therfore thou suffrest
not iniury to be vnauenged: but in conclusyon by this meanes thou 5
vtterest thy chyldysshnesse / sayinge thou canst not rule thyne
owne mynde, whiche is the very property and offyce of a man. How
moche manlyer, how moche excellenter is it, to set an other mans
foly at naught, than to counterfayte it? But he hath hurte the / he is
proude and fyerse / he scorneth the. The fylthyer he is, so moche 10
the more beware leest thou be made lyke him. What the deuyls madnesse is it, that thou to auenge another mans lewdnesse, woldest be
made the lewder thy selfe. If thou despyse the rebuke / all men shall
perceyue that it was done to one vnworthy therof: but and yf thou
be moued thou shalt make his quarell whiche dyd the wronge moche 15
ye better. Furthermore take ye thyng as it is / if any wronge be
receyued / that is not eased one whyt with vengeaunce, but augmented. For in conclusyon, what ende shall there be of iniuryes
on bothe sydes, yf euery man go forth and procede to reuenge [S4v]
his owne grefe? Ennemyes encrease on bothe partes / the sorowe 20
waxeth fresshe and rawe agayn / and the longer it endureth, the
more vncurable it is. But with softnes and with suffraunce is healed
now and than / yea euen he whiche dyd the wronge / and after he is
commen to hym selfe agayne / of an ennemy is made a very trusty
and faythfull frende. But the very same hurt whiche by vengeaunce 25
thou coueytest to put from the, reboundeth backe agayne vpon the /
and not without encrease of harme. And that also shall be a souer-
ayne remedy agaynst wrathe / yf (accordynge to the diuysyon of
thynges aboue rehersed) thou woldest consyder, that one man can
not hurt an other yf he wolde not / saue in those thynges onely, 30
whiche be outwarde goodes / whiche so greatly pertayne not vnto
man. For the very good thynges of the mynde, god onely is able
to take awaye / whiche he is not wont to do, but vnto vnkynde
persons / and onely he can gyue them / whiche thynge he hath not
vsed to do, vnto cruell and furyous persons. No chrysten man ther- 35
fore is hurte but of hym selfe. Iniury hurteth no man but the
worker therof. These thynges also helpe (though they be not weyghty)

Against ll. 8–9: Regarde lytell an other mannes foly.

---

29 woldest] shuldest 1533 30 yf he wolde not] onlesse he wyll hym
selfe 1533 34 thynge] *om.* 1533

R

that thou shalte not folowe the sorowe of thy mynde. If the circumstaunces of retho[S5] riciens well gathered togyder, thou bothe
make lyght of thyne owne harmes / and also mynisshe ye wronge
done of an other man commenly after this maner. He hurte me /
5 but it wyll be sone amended. More ouer he is a chylde / he is of
thynges vnexperte / he is a yonge man / it is a woman / he dyd it
through an other mans motyon or counsayle / he dyd it vnware, or
whan he had wel dronke / it is mete that I forgyue hym. And on the
othersyde, he hath hurt me greuously. Certayne, but he is my
10 father, my brother, my mayster, my frende, my wyfe / it is acordynge
that this grefe shulde be forgyuen / eyther for the loue, or els for
the authorite of the person.Or els thou shalt set one thyng agaynst
an other / and recompence ye iniury with other good benefites,
done of hym vnto the. Or with thyne offences done to hym afore
15 season, shalt accounte it euen / and so make quyte. This man
hath hurt me forsoth / but other tymes how oft hath he done me
good. It cometh of an vnlyberal mynde to forget ye good benefytes,
and only to remembre a lytle wronge or displeasure. Now he hath
offended me / but howe often offended of me. I wyll forgyue hym /
20 that he in lykewise by myne ensample maye pardon me, if I an
other tyme trespace agaynst hym. Fynally it shal be a [S5v] remedy
of moche greter vertue and of stronge operacyon, if in the mysdoyng
of an other man agaynst the thou dydest thinke in thy selfe / what
thynges, howe greuous, and how ofte thou hast synned agaynst god /
25 howe many maner of wayes thou art in dette to hym: as moche as
thou shalt remyt vnto thy brother which is in thy dette / so moche
shall god forgyue vnto the. This waye of forgyuynge other mennes
dettes hath he taught vs whiche is himselfe a creditour / he wyll not
refuse the lawe which he himselfe made. To be absolued or losed
30 from thy synnes thou rennest to Rome / saylest to saynt Iames /
byest perdons moste large. I dysprayse not veryly that thyng whiche
thou doest: but whan all is done, there is no redyer waye / no surer
meanes wherby (if thou haue offended) thou mightest come to fauour
agayne and be reconcyled to god / than if thou whan thou art offen-
35 ded / be reconcyled agayne vnto thy brother: forgyue a lytel trespace
vnto thy neyghbour (for it is but small what so euer one man tres-
paseth agaynst an other) that Christe may forgyue the so many

Against ll. 25–6: Forgyue thy dettour.

thousande offences. But it is harde (thou sayest) to subdue the
mynde whan he begynneth to waxe hote. Remembrest thou not,
howe moche harder thynges Chryste suffred for the. [S6] What
were thou whan he for thy sake bestowed his precyous lyfe? Were
thou not his enemy? With what softnesse suffereth he the, dayly 5
repetyng thyne olde synnes? Last of all, howe mekely suffred he the
vttermost rebukes, bondes, strypes / fynally dethe moste shamefull?
Why, why bostest thou thy selfe of the heed / if thou care not to be
in ye body? Thou shalt not be a membre of Christ except thou
folowe ye steppes of Christ. But he is vnworthy to be forgyuen. 10
Ye, were thou worthy whome god shulde forgyue? In thyne owne
selfe thou wylt haue mercy exercysed / and agaynst thy brother wylt
thou vse exteme and cruell iustyce? Is it so great a thyng if thou,
beyng a synner thy selfe, shuldest forgyue a synner / whan Christ
prayed his father for them which crucifyed him? Is it an harde 15
thyng not to stryke thy brother, whom thou art also commaunded
to loue? Is it an harde thyng not to pay agayne an yuell dede / for
whiche except thou woldest recompence a good, thou shalt not be
y^t towarde thy felowe whiche Christ was towarde his seruaunt?
Fynally if this man be vnworthy to whom for an yuell turne a good 20
shulde be recompenced / yet art thou worthy to do it: Christ is
worthy for whose sake it is done. But in suffring an olde displeasure
I call and [S6v] prouoke a new: he wyll do iniury agayne if he shulde
escape vnpunysshed for this, if without offence thou canst auoyde /
auoyde it: if thou canst ease or remedy it, ease it. If thou canst 25
heale a mad man, heale hym / if not let him perisshe himself alone
rather than with the. This man whiche thynketh him selfe to haue
done harme, thinke thou worthy to be pityed / and not to be punysshed. Wylt thou be angry to thy commendacion and laude? be angry with ye vice, not with ye man. But the more thou art enclined by 30
nature to this kynde of vyce / so moche the more diligently arme thyselfe longe before hande / and ones for altogyder print sure in thy
mynde this decre or purpose: y^t thou neyther saye nor do any thing
at any tyme while thou art angry: bileue not thyself whan thou art

Against ll. 1–2: By the ensample of chryst swage thy mynde.
Against ll. 10–11: We must perdon the vnworthy.
Against ll. 29–30: Be angry and agreued with the vice.

---

11 Ye] Euen so *1533*   thou worthy] not thou vnworthy *1533*
19 whiche] y^t *1533*   23 and prouoke] in *1533*   30 man.] man *1533*,
1534

moued. Haue suspected what so euer y^t sodeyn mocion or rage of ye mynde diffineth or iudgeth / ye though it be honest. Remembre none other difference to be bitwene a frantik person and him y^t rageth in ire, than is bytwene a short madnes that dureth but a season, and a
5 continual perseuerant madnes. Cal to minde how many thynges in angre thou hast said or done worthy to be repented / which now though in vayne thou woldest fayne were chaunged. Therfore whan y^t wrath waxeth hote and boyleth: if thou can not streight-way [S7] saue and delyuer thy selfe al togyder from anger / at the
10 leestway comme thus ferforth to thy selfe and sobrenesse, that thou remembre thy selfe, not to be well aduysed, or in thy ryght mynde. To remembre this, is a great parte of helth. On this wyse reason with thy selfe / now veryly so am I mynded / but anone here-after I shall be of an other mynde moche contrary / why sholde I in
15 the meane season say agaynst my frende (whyle I am moued) that thynge whiche hereafter whan I am peased, and my malyce ceased I coude not chaunge? Why sholde I now do in my malyce or anger that thyng whiche whan I am sobred and comme to my selfe agayne, I sholde greatly sorowe and repent? Why rather shold not
20 reason / why sholde not pytie / at the last why sholde not Chryst optayne that of me now / whiche a lytel pause of tyme shall shortly here after optayne. To no man (I suppose) hath nature gyuen so moche of blacke colour, but at the leestwaye he myght so ferforth rule hymselfe. But it shal be a very good thing for ye thus instructed
25 to harden thy mynde with reason / with contynuaunce and custome that thou coudest not be moued at all. It shall be a perfyte thyng / yf thou hauyng indignacyon onely at the vyce / for a displeasure or rebuke done to the / shalte rendre [S7v] agayne a dede of charite. To conclude, euen naturall temperaunce, whiche ought to be in
30 euery man / requyreth that thou sholdest not suffre affections to rule the vtterly. Not to be wrothe at all / is a thynge moost lyke vnto god / and therfore moost comly and beautefull. To ouercomme euyll with goodnesse / malyce with kyndnesse / is to counterfayte the perfyte charite of Chryst Iesu. To holde wrathe vnder and
35 kepe hym backe with a brydell / is the propertye of a wyse man. To folowe the appetyte of wrathe / is not a poynt of a man veryly / but playnly of beestes / and that of wylde beestes. But yf thou woldest knowe now moche vncomly it were to a man to be ouer-

Against ll. 2–3: Say nor do any thynge yf thou be angry.
Against ll. 25–6: The mynde must be hardened agaynst wrathe.

com with wrath / loke whan thou art sobre, that thou marke the
countenaunce of an angry person / or els whan thou thy selfe arte
angry / go vnto a glasse. Whan thyne eyen so burne flamyng in
fyre / whan thy chekes be pale / whan thy mouth is drawen awrye /
thy lyppes fome / all thy membres quake / whan thy voyce soundeth 5
so malycyously / neyther thy gestures be of one fassyon / who
wolde iudge the to be a man? Thou perceyuest now my most
swetest frende, how large a see is open all abrode to dispute of other
vices after this same maner. But we in the myddes of our [S8] course
wyll stryke sayle, leuyng the rest to thy discrecyon. Neyther truly 10
was it my mynde or purpose (for that sholde be an infynyte worke)
as I began / euen so to disswade the from euery vyce / vyce by vyce /
as it were with sondry declamacions / and to bolde and courage the
to the contrary vertues. This onely was my desyre (whiche I thought
suffycyent for the) to shewe a certeyn maner and crafte of a newe 15
kynde of warre / how thou myghtest arme thy selfe agaynst the
euylles of the olde lyfe burgynge forth agayne and spryngynge a
fresshe. Therfore as we haue done in one or two thynges (bycause
of ensample) so must thou thy selfe do partly in euery thynge / one
by one. But moste of all in the thynges whervnto thou shalt per- 20
ceyue thy selfe to be stered or instygate peculyarly / whether it be
through vyce of nature, custome, or euyll bryngyng vp / agaynst
these thynges some certayne decrees must be wrytten in the table
of thy mynde / and they must be renewed now and than / leest they
sholde fayle, or be forgoten through disuse / as agaynst the vices 25
of backbytyng / fylthy spekyng, enuy, gule, and other like. These
be the onely ennemyes of Chrystes sowdyours / agaynst whose
assawte, the mynde must be armed longe aforehande with prayer /
[S8v] with noble sayinges of wyse men / with the doctryne of holy
scripture / with ensample of deuoute and holy men / and specyally 30
of Chryste. Though I doubte not but that the redyng of holy
scripture shal mynystre all these thynges to the haboundauntly /
neuerthelesse charite, whiche one brother oweth to another, hath

Against ll. 1-3: Beholde thyne owne countenance whan thou art angry.
Against ll. 13-15: Declamacions.
        Sermons.
        Orations.
        Prechynges.
Against ll. 23-4: Certen decrees must be wryten in our myndes.

10 truly] certayne *1533*   11 mynde or purpose] mynde / purpose / or
intencyon *1533*   24 renewed] remeued *1533*

moued and exhorted me, that at the leestway with this sodeyn and
hasty writynges, I sholde further and helpe thy holy purpose, as
moche as lyeth in me. A thynge whiche I haue done somwhat the
rather, bycause I somwhat feared, leest thou sholdest fall in to that
5 superstycyous kynde of religyous men / whiche partly awaytyng on
their owne aduauntage / partly with great zele / but not accordyng
to knowlege / walke rounde aboute bothe by see and lande / and if
anywhere they gete a man, recouerynge from vyces vnto vertue /
hym streyghtway with moost importune and lewde exhortacions,
10 thretenynges, and flaterynges they enforce to thrust in to the ordre
of monkes, euen as though without a cowle there were no chrystendome. Furthermore whan they haue fylled his brest with pure
scrupulosite and doutes insoluble / than they bynde hym to certayne
tradicions founde by man / and playnly thrust the wretched persone
15 heedlonge in [S9] to a certayne bondage of ceremonies, lyke vnto
the maner of the iewes / and teche hym to tremble and feare / but
not to loue. The ordre of monkshyp is not pytie / but a kynde of
lyuyng, to euery man after the disposicyon of his body and his mynde
also / eyther profytable or vnprofytable / whervnto veryly as I do
20 not courage the / so lykewyse I counseyle not from it. This thyng
onely I warne the of / that thou put pytie neyther in meate, nor in
rayment or habyte / nor in any visyble thynge / but in those thynges
whiche haue ben declared and shewed the afore: and in what so
euer persones thou shalt fynde or perceyue the true ymage of Chryst /
25 with them couple thy selfe. More ouer whan suche men be
lackyng, whose conuersacion sholde make the better / withdrawe
thy selfe as moche as thou mayst from the company of man / and
call the holy prophete Chryst and the apostles vnto communi-
cacion / but specially make Paule of famylyar acquaytaunce with
30 the. This felowe must be had euer in thy bosom to be redde and
studyed, bothe nyght and daye: fynally and to be lerned without
the boke worde by worde / vpon whome we haue now a good while
enforced with great diligence to make a comment or a enarracyon /
a bolde dede truly. But notwithstandyng we trustyng in the [S9v]
35 helpe of god / wyll endeuoyre our selfe besyly, leest after Origene,
Ambrose and Augustyne / leest after so many newe interpretours,

Against ll. 4–5: Why he wrote this boke somwhat quycklyer and with more
spede.
Against ll. 12–13: Relygyous men.
Against ll. 16–17: The order of monkes.
Against ll. 26–7: What companyons a man shuld chose to lyue withall.

we sholde seme to haue taken this labour vpon vs / vtterly eyther without a cause, or without fruyte. And also that certayne besy and vnquiet pyckquarelles / whiche thynken it perfyte religyon to knowe nothynge at all of good lernyng / may vnderstande and well perceyue, that where as we in youth haue embrased and made moche of the 5 pure lernyng of olde auctours / and also haue gotten (and that not without great swette and watche) a meane vnderstandyng of bothe the tonges greke and latyn. We haue not in so doyng loked vnto a vayne and folysshe fame / or vnto the chyldysshe pastyme and pleasure of our mynde / but that we recorded longe before to 10 adorne and garnysshe the lordes temple with the rychesse of other straunge nacyons and countrees, to the vttermost of our power. Whiche temple some men with their ignoraunce and barbarousnes, hath ouermoche dishonested / that by the reason of suche rychesse, excellent wyttes myght also be inflamed vnto the loue of holy 15 scripture. But this so gret a thynge a fewe dayes layde aparte / we haue taken vpon vs this labour for thy sake / that vnto the (as it were with a fyn[S1o]ger) we myght shewe the waye whiche ledeth streyght vnto Chryste. And I beseche Iesu, the father of this holy purpose (as I hope) that he wolde vouchsafe benygnly to fauoure 20 thy holsome enforcementes / yea that he wolde in chaungyng of the, encrease his grace / and make the perfyte / that thou myghtest quykly waxe bygge and stronge in hym / and spryng vp vnto a per-fyte man. In whome also fare thou well brother and frende / alwayes truly beloued to my hert / but now moche more than euer before, 25 bothe dere and pleasaunt. At the towne of saynt Andomers / the yere of Chrystes byrthe. M.ccccc.j.

❧ Here endeth this boke called Enchiridion, or the manuel of the christen knyght made by Erasmus of Roterdame / in the whiche boke is conteyned many goodly lessons, very necessary and profy- 30 table for the soules helthe of all true christen people. Imprynted at London in Fletestrete, by Wynkyn de Worde, for Iohan Byddell, otherwyse Salysbury, dwellynge at the sygne of our lady of pytye, nexte to Flete brydge where they be for to sell. Newly corrected and amended, in the yere of our lorde god M.v.C.xxxiiij. the .xij. 35 daye of February.

Against ll. 8–9: Good lernyng profiteth vnto pitie.

10 recorded] were mynded *1533*   25 truly] verily *1533*   to] in *1533*
27 M.ccccc.j] 1501 *1533*

COMMENTARY

THE notes which follow are not offered as a complete commentary, but attempt to provide an extended treatment of the relationship between the two English editions (*STC* 10480 and 10479) and the 1518 Latin edition. Throughout the Commentary the English and Latin texts are designated by the abbreviations 'Eng.' and 'Lt.' respectively. English additions to the Latin text have been noted when longer than five or six words. When the copytext (1534) differs from the first edition (1533) the Latin text is given and the variation discussed when relevant. In general, I have exercised restraint in noting wordy translations, doublets, and internal glosses, reserving comment for the more significant of these (see the Introduction, pp. xlii–xliv). In preparing these notes, I have been especially indebted to John C. Olin's translation of the 'Letter to Volz' (an exact and fairly literal translation) and Raymond Himelick's translation of the *Enchiridion* (an accurate but less literal translation). I have also consulted Himelick's translation of the 'Letter to Volz' and A. J. Festugière's French translation of the preface and main text of the *Enchiridion*.

Unless noted to the contrary, quotations in the Commentary from classical authors are taken from the Loeb editions and quotations from patristic authors from Migne's *Patrologia*. Quotations from the Latin works of Erasmus—with the exception of P. S. Allen's edition of the letters (1906–58)—are taken from the Leiden edition of Erasmus' *Opera Omnia* (1703–6). Every scriptural reference, whether a paraphrase (in which case the chapter and verse is preceded by 'Cf.') or a direct quotation (in which case 'Cf.' is omitted) is based on the Latin Vulgate (Tournai, 1956). Each quotation has been checked against the Douai–Rheims version and against Tyndale's New Testament (1526 and 1534) or Pentateuch (1530) for possible verbal similarities between Tyndale's known translations and this attributed translation.

3/2–4 The title-page gives both the Lt. title and an Eng. translation.

3/3 *hansom*: According to the *OED* (*s.v.* 1. b.), Tyndale was the first to use this sense (ready at hand) in 1530: *Prol. Lev.* in *Doct. Treat.* (1848) 428, 'Beware of allegories; for there is not a more handsome or apt thing to beguile withal than an allegory.'

3/5–6 *ma-* | *ny . . . godly*: moste holsome 1533, *salu-* | *berrimis*.

3/7–8 *made by*: autore.

3/8–10 *the fa-* | *mous clerke*: *Des.* in Lt.

3/10–11 The title-page of the Rylands copy of *1534* reads 'Ro-* | *terodame, newly*' where the British Library copy has 'Ro-* | *terdame, and newly*'.

3/11–14 *newly . . . imprin-* / *ted*: The Lt. adds instead: *Cui accessit noua* / *mireque utilis Praefatio,* which *1533* translates: 'to the whiche / is added a newe and / meruaylous pro- / fytable pre- / face'. Both *1533* and *1534* omit to mention the other works of Erasmus included in the 1518 Lt.: *Et Ba* / *silij in Esaiam commentariolus,* / *eodem interprete.* / *Cum alijs quorum Catalogum* / *pagellae sequentis Elenchus* / *indicabit.*

3/16 *Cum priuilegio regali*: Not in *1533* or the Lt. John Archer Gee notes A. W. Reed's assertion that the phrase *cum priuilegio regali* was the equivalent of a Tudor copyright law, but that the government was not averse to having the phrase misunderstood as an indication of official backing. See Reed, *Early Tudor Drama* (London, 1926), pp. 176–80, cited by Gee, 'John Byddell', p. 57 n. If the government did intend the phrase to be so misunderstood, the equivocation might indicate the growing intensity of Cromwell's propaganda campaign as the passage of the Act of Royal Supremacy became more imminent. See the Introduction, p. li.

4 The Lt. gives a table of contents listing eleven works of Erasmus besides the 'Letter to Volz' and the *Enchiridion*. 'LIBELLVS LOQVI-TVR', the original of the first poem, is found at the end of the 'Letter to Volz' in the Lt. Neither *1533* nor *1534* gives the Gk. motto printed above the Lt. poem Ἀρχὴν ἁπάντων καὶ τέλος ποιοῦ θεὸν (Make God the beginning and end of everything).

4/2–8 For this poem see *The Poems of Desiderius Erasmus,* ed. Cornelius Reedijk (Leiden, 1956), pp. 170–1. Reedijk suggests as the date the spring of 1489, when Erasmus still resided in the monastery at Steyn. The poem was first published, together with the *Enchiridion,* in *Lucubratiunculae aliquot* (Antwerp, February 15, 1503/4). For the date of publication, see the Introduction, p. xviii n. 1. The Lt. elegiac distychs are rendered in Eng. rhyme royal, though not as concretely as they might have been. The *laudes* (commendations) and *conuicia* (insults) are dropped and there is no specific reference to the mystical Helicon.

4/10–29 The second poem, written in ten pentameter couplets, is not found in the Lt. The grammatical relationships between the various clauses are not well delineated; 'Soole capitayne' (4/20), for example, seems to be in apposition with 'Christ' (4/19). The form 'breuyer' (4/22) is not found in the OED and there is no Lt. original to indicate the Eng. meaning. For the probable meaning, see the Glossary. 4/22 *manuell*: The first use of the sense 'a handbook' recorded in the OED (*s.v.* B. 1. b.) is taken from the title of the first edition (1533) of the English *Enchiridion,* 'A booke called in latyn Enchiridion militis christiani, and in englysshe the manuell of the christen knyght . . made by . . Erasmus'.

5/2 The Lt. gives Erasmus's first name *Des*[iderius], which the Eng. omits.

5/5–11 *Paule . . . courte*: See the Introduction, pp. xvii–xviii.

5/15 *frende*: See the Introduction, pp. xvi–xvii; *vnlerned*: ἀναλφαβήτῳ (not knowing one's ABC). Festugière notes that the person for whom the *Enchiridion* was written must have known at least Latin or else he could not have been able to read the handbook at all (p. 30). Since Erasmus uses a Greek word for 'vnlerned', perhaps the humanist meant to indicate that his friend knew no Greek.

6/6 *haue* . . . *tossed*: *meus exercuit Genius* (my guardian spirit has harassed [me]).

6/8 *Polycrates*: Tyrant of Samos from *c*.540–522 BC. In order to escape the envy of the gods at his uninterrupted good fortune, Polycrates was advised to do away with his dearest possession. When he cast his emerald signet-ring into the sea, the ring was recovered by a fisherman and returned to the king. His good fortune deserted him later when he was captured by trickery and crucified in Asia Minor (Herodotus, *3*, 40–3 and 122–5).

6/8–9 *whiche* . . . *trouble*: Internal gloss. See the Introduction, p. xliii.

6/18–19 *no doute* . . . *we*: Not in Lt.

6/24–5 *a chylde* . . . *A* | *b* | *c*: The Eng. paraphrases the Lt. *elementario*; *1533* uses the present 'lerneth' and *1534*, the past 'lerned'.

6/25 *Dunces questyons*: John Duns Scotus (*c*.1266–1308) lectured at Oxford, Paris, and Cologne. Because of the precision of his philosophical distinctions, Duns Scotus is called the *Doctor Subtilis*. First applied in a purely denotative sense to the followers of Scotus, 'dunce' came to connote a dimwitted opponent of the New Learning and dullard in general (*OED s.v.*). Tyndale first witnesses to this development in 153[1]: *Answ. to More* Wks. (1573) 278/1, 'Remember ye not how . . the old barkyng curres, Dunces disciples & lyke draffe called Scotistes, the children of darkenesse, raged in euery pulpit agaynst Greke Latin and Hebrue'.

6/28 *to disputacyons in scholes*: *ad palestram Sorbonicam* (wrestling or rhetorical exercises, as in the Sorbonne). The Eng. translator generalizes the place-reference, removing Erasmus's scornful allusion to his own university studies in Paris.

6/32 *questions*: *Quaestiones disputatae* formed one of the major educational methods of medieval scholasticism. Arising out of the need to come to terms with conflicting authorities on a text, the disputation took the following form: the master's presentation of the question, a senior student's answers to the objections proposed by other students, the master's recapitulation of the discussion and presentation of his own solution. The method of disputation was strongly influenced by Aristotle's *Posterior Analytics* and was most successfully demonstrated in Aquinas's *Summa Theologiae*.

6/34 *mayster of the sentence*: The *Book of Sentences* of Peter Lombard (*c*.1095–1160) became a leading textbook in the universities. All seven theologians mentioned below wrote commentaries on it: Ockham, Durandus, Scotus, Biel, Alvaro, Aquinas, and Bonaventure. See below, 7/24–5 n., 8/20 n. and 9/3–4 n. Thomas More, writing to Martin Dorp, described Lombard as one 'from whose *Sentences*, as from a Trojan horse, that whole army of problems, rushed forth . . .' (*St. Thomas More: Selected Letters*, ed. Elizabeth Frances Rogers (New Haven, 1961), p. 36).

6/35 *summularies*: According to the *OED* (*s.v.* 1.) a 'summulary' is the writer of a *summula* or a small compendious treatise of a science. See the Glossary.

7/5 *Iacobus de partibus*: Jacques Despars (1380–1458), canon of Notre Dame at Paris, published an edition of Avicenna's works in 1498 at Lyons (Allen, *3*, 363 n.).

7/14 *god*: *CHRISTI*. The Eng. frequently translates *Christ* as *God*, thus to a certain extent changing Erasmus's Christological emphasis to a theological one. See also 9/26, 23/19, 29/15.

7/15 *do prescribe*: ῥητῶς *praescribunt* (they expressly prescribe). The Gk. adverb is translated by the emphatic form of the verb. See the Glossary for 'do'.

7/24–5 *Secundam secunde* . . . *Thomas*: The most important work of St. Thomas Aquinas (*c.*1225–74) is the *Summa Theologiae*, which is divided into three main topics: Part I, God; Part II, The Advance of the Rational Creature to God; Part III, Christ, the Mediator between God and Man. Part II is subdivided into *Prima Secundae*, which treats of human acts in general, and *Secunda Secundae*, which deals with the virtues of faith, hope, charity, prudence, justice, fortitude and temperance.

7/27–8 *by inexplicable crokes of disputacions*: *inexplicabilibus disputationum labirynthis*. In translation the Eng. 'crokes' loses the Lt. metaphor found in *labirynthis*; *not able to be resolued*: Not in Lt.

7/29–30 *whom hope* . . . *asshamed*: Cf. Rom. 5: 5. Compare 'charyte not fayned' with Tyndale's 'love vnfayned'. For More's objection to this translation, see the Introduction, p. lii.

7/32–3 *the vnlerned* . . . *dyed for*: Cf. 1 Cor. 8: 11.

7/35–6 *The wyse kynge* . . . *wysdome*: Cf. Prov. 1–7.

8/1–4 Sidenote 1, *of purpose make the faculty whiche they professe obscure and harde*: yelde tharte wherin they be conuersant defycile by study *1533*, *artem quam profitentur, studio reddunt difficilem.*

8/3 *and also*: and *1533*, *ac* (and, and also).

8/9 *philosophy of Christ*: Erasmus's most succinct statement on the *philosophia Christi* is found in the *Paraclesis*, the preface to his 1516 edition of the Greek and Latin New Testament: *Hoc Philosophiae genus in affectibus situm verius, quam in syllogismis, vita est magis quam disputatio, afflatus potius quam eruditio, transformatio magis quam ratio* (*OO*, *5*, 141E–F); ('In this kind of philosophy, located as it is more truly in the disposition of the mind than in syllogisms, life means more than debate, inspiration is preferable to erudition, transformation is a more important matter than intellectual comprehension' (Olin, p. 100)).

8/14 *warre* . . . *agaynst the turkes*: Western Christendom had been threatened by Islam ever since the Turks conquered Constantinople in 1453. Several futile attempts to organize a crusade had been made, but in 1521 the Turks captured Belgrade, in 1522 Rhodes, and in 1526 Budapest. The Moslem advance was not to be halted until the Christian victory at Lepanto in 1571.

8/20 *Occam . . . Aluaros*: The principle of economy, which aims at reducing the number of philosophical entities to a bare minimum, is called 'Ockham's razor' after William of Ockham (*c*.1285–1347). The Dominican Durandus of Saint Pourçain (*c*.1275–1334) taught at the University of Paris, where he opposed the system of Thomas Aquinas. For Duns Scotus, see above, 6/25 n. Gabriel Biel (*c*.1410–95) taught theology at Tübingen in the tradition of Scotus and Ockham. See Heiko Augustinus Oberman, *The Harvest of Medieval Theology: Gabriel Biel and Late Medieval Nominalism* (Cambridge, Mass., 1963). Alvaro Pelayo (*c*.1275–*c*.1349) taught canon and civil law in Bologna.

8/21–2 *for thentent . . . vpon them*: *ut CHRISTVM amplectantur* (that they might embrace Christ). The Lt. clause is warmer in tone than the Eng.

8/25–6 *of instantes . . . relacion*: In scholastic philosophy an 'instant' is a particular point of time seen in relation to a specific event. A 'formality' is the distinctive characteristic by which something is defined. A 'quiddity' is the specific nature of a thing; see the Glossary. 'Relation' is that aspect of a thing by which it is seen in comparison or contrast with another thing (*OED s.v.* 3.).

8/32 *blacke freres*: *Praedicatores*, the Order of Preachers, so called because of their black mantles. The order was founded in 1216 by St. Dominic (*c*.1170–1221).

9/1 *Thomas*: After this the Eng. omits *cominus atque eminus* (hand to hand and at a distance), a Bruegel-like image; *gray freres*: *Minoritas*, the Order of Friars Minors, so called because of their grey habits. Founded in 1209 by St. Francis of Assisi (1182–1226), the order aimed at simplicity and poverty of life.

9/2 *on ye other partye*: *iunctis umbonibus* (with joined shields), another Bruegel-like detail.

9/2–3 *feruent hote doctours*: The gloss on *seraphicos* subtly suggests that it is not heavenly love which makes these Franciscans 'feruent hote'. Strictly speaking, however, the title 'Seraphic Doctor' refers to St. Bonaventure (*c*.1217–74), who as minister general renewed his order by his teachings on mysticism and on the ideals of St. Francis of Assisi. Erasmus later satirized the honorific titles of scholastic theologians: 'Here they rise to the height of theological majesty, sounding in the ears of the audience those august titles of Illustrious Doctor, Subtle Doctor, Supersubtle Doctor, Seraphic Doctor, Holy Doctor, Invincible Doctor' (*Folly*, p. 91).

9/3–4 *reals . . . nominals*: Realists, of whom Aquinas was the most notable representative, affirmed the objective existence of abstract concepts.

Nominalists, on the other hand, regarded abstract concepts as mere names without any corresponding reality. Ockham was an exponent of this school of scholastic thought.

9/26 *god*: *CHRISTI.*

10/6–7 Sidenote 1, *kyngdom*: royalme *1533*, kyugdom *1534, regnum.*

10/6–8 *kyngdome . . . stronge*: Cf. Gal. 5: 22.

10/9 *Leo the tenth*: Giovanni de' Medici (1475–1521) was elected to succeed Julius II in 1513. The correspondence between Erasmus and Leo X extends from 1501, when Leo was still Cardinal de' Medici, to 1521 and includes six letters from Erasmus (Ep. 335, 384, 446, 566, 1007, 1143), five letters from Leo (Ep. 338, 518, 519, 864, 1180) and four letters concerning Erasmus or Leo (Ep. 162, 339, 466, 517).

10/11–12 *Christ . . . kyngdom*: Cf. John 18: 36 7.

10/12 *primate*: *uindicem* (protector). This affirmation of Christ's primacy obviates the conflict between Pope and King as Head of the Church in England.

10/15–16 *rufflyng fassyon*: *Tragoedia.*

10/16 *shulde be*: be *1533*, *sit.*

10/26 *effycacy and strength*: ἐνέργειαν (activity, action).

10/28 *vayne*: According to the *OED* (*s.v.* II. 6.), a 'vein' is a small natural channel within the earth through which water flows.

10/31 *tropes*: The first use of the word 'trope' recorded in the *OED* (*s.v.* 1.) occurred in 1533: *Supper of Lord*, Cv, attributed to Tyndale, 'If ye be so sworne to the litterall sense in this matter, that ye will not in these wordes of Christe, Thys is my bodye, &c., admitte in so playne a speache anye troope'.

11/5–7 Sidenote 1, *breuenes*: The translator's choice of 'briefness' or 'conciseness' (*OED*, *s.v.* 2) uses an abstract Eng. word to translate a concrete Lt. one: *Compendium*, 'a shortening, an abbreviation'.

11/9 *yoke . . . easy*: Cf. Matt. 11: 30.

11/11 *feders: pastores.* See the Glossary.

11/24 *effecte*: *affectibus.* The Eng. translates erroneously here since the point of the passage depends on the contrast between *affectibus* (passions) and *opinionibus* (opinions).

11/28–9 *is ruled and tourned*: ἄγονται καὶ φέρονται (are brought and carried).

11/30 *a man . . . wynche*: *uix licet ingemiscere* (it is scarcely permitted to groan over). The Eng. translator shifts the meaning of the Lt. from feeling to action.

11/33–4 Sidenote 4, *The sure anker*: ἱερὰ ἄγκυρα (the holy anchor).

12/2–3 *Whan* ... *colde*: Cf. Matt. 24: 12. Tyndale's NT has: 'And because iniquite shall have the vpper hande, the love of many shall abate.' The *Enchiridion* gives 'charyte' for Tyndale's 'love'. See the Introduction, p. lii.

12/4 *what is redde*: After this the Eng. omits *quid auditur* (what is heard); see the Introduction, p. xl.

12/7–8 *Hereto* ... *sparkes*: Cf. 2 Tim. 1: 6; *to know*: ἀναζωπυρῶμεν (rekindle). The Eng. mistranslates the Gk., then omits *nam Paulino uerbo libenter utimur* (for we gladly use the Pauline word). See the Introduction, p. xl. J. F. Mozley suggests (p. 99), somewhat implausibly, that 'know' is a misprint for 'blow'.

12/9–10 *Let* ... *lyfe*: John 4: 14.

12/12 *rychesse / whiche nouryssheth vyce*: Internal gloss on *uiciorum* ... *alimenta* (the food of vices).

12/16 *Christ* ... *stone*: 1 Cor. 10: 4.

12/18–19 *Abraham* ... *water*: Cf. Gen. 21: 30. Both the Eng. and the Lt. sidenotes incorrectly cite 'Gen. 16', either a typographical error for 'XXI' or a confusion with the next sidenote, 'XXVI' instead of 'XXI'.

12/20–3 *Isaac* ... *dyggynge*: Cf. Gen. 26: 15 ff.

12/24 *philistians*: Erasmus describes the Philistines as 'worldly wyse' (12/25), ambitious and avaricious (12/28) in preaching 'pardons / composicions / and suche lyke pelfare' (13/21–2) under the authority of 'great prynces' and 'the pope of Rome' (13/24). Given the controversy over indulgences that had been raging since Luther published his Ninety-Five Theses ten months before, Erasmus here seems to refer to the unsound preaching of Johann Tetzel, O.P., on the applications of indulgences to the dead, the ambition and simony of Albert of Brandenburg, pluralist archbishop of Magdeburg and Mainz, and the grandiose expenditure of Leo X on the rebuilding of St. Peter's. Conversely 'Isaac or any of his family' (12/29) would refer to Luther and his protests against church abuses.

12/24 *naughty*: The first use of this sense (bad, inferior) recorded in the *OED* (*s.v.* 4.) occurred in 1526: Tyndale, *Wks.* (Parker Soc.) I. 510, 'As this is a naughty argument, so is the other'.

12/25–6 *euen* ... *thinges*: Cf. Phil. 3: 19.

12/28 *fylthy lucre*: The first use of this phrase recorded in the *OED* (FILTHY 4. b.) is found in 1526–34 in Tyndale's NT, Titus 1: 11, 'Teachinge thinges which they ought not, because of filthy lucre'. See the Introduction, p. lii.

12/31–13/1 *shall hurte* ... *shall hurte*: shulde hurte ... shulde hurt *1533*, *offecturam* ... *offecturam*. *1534* translates the Lt. infinitive with the indicative; *1533* with the subjunctive.

13/7–8 *They wyll not . . . drynke*: They wyll not that those y^t thurst
. . . do drinke *1533*, *Nolunt sitientes . . . bibere*. For a comparison of the
style of *1533* and *1534*, see the Introduction, p. xlvii.

13/7–10 *They . . . none*: Jer. 2: 13.

13/11 *is*: be *1533*, *est*.

13/14–15 *the very worshyppers of Chryste*: Internal gloss for *inter hos*
(among those).

13/21 *composicions*: According to the *OED* (*s.v.* III. 25.) a 'composition'
is an agreement for the payment of a sum of money in lieu of the dis-
charge of some obligation. See the Glossary.

13/22 *pelfare*: 'Tyndale's translation of *cauponationes*. *Huckstering* would
be a reasonably close present-day equivalent' (Himelick, 'Letter to
Volz', p. 131 n. 14). *And this*: And these *1533*, *Idque*.

13/30 *prosperite*: After this the Eng. omits *et* [*populi res*] *quam minima
tyrannide premantur* (and that they [the people] may be repressed with the
least tyranny). See the Introduction, p. xl. It is debatable whether or
not the reference to repression was omitted in deference to the political
situation in 1533–4. Repressive measures such as Submission of the
Clergy (1532), the Act in Restraint of Appeals to Rome (1533), and the
Act of Supremacy (1534) affected primarily the upper clergy or prominent
laymen such as ex-Chancellor More, and not the common people.

14/6 *they*: those *1533*, *qui*.

14/6–7 *of the wyser sorte*: more wyse than other *1533*, *in hoc genere
cordatiores* (in this class more prudent).

14/9 *intollerable*: tollerable *1533*, *tolerabile*. *1534* incorrectly emends
1533, perhaps for the sake of contrast with 'better' (14/8).

14/9–11 *But . . . candelstycke*: Cf. Matt. 6: 22 and 5: 15.

14/26–7 *folowe . . . go*: Cf. Apoc. 14: 4 and Augustine, *De Sancta Vir-
ginitate*, *PL*, xl, 410–11.

14/30 *let . . . be*: be *1533*, *habeat*. *1534* translates the subjunctive more
clearly than *1533*.

15/6 *lest they fall somwhat further of*: leste they do fall further *1533*,
prolabantur longius.

15/7 *lest they make . . . warre*: as leste they shulde make . . . warre *1533*,
Ne bellum . . . gerant.

15/8–9 *lest . . . they vse cruelte*: leste . . . they shulde vse crueltye *1533*,
Ne . . . seuiant.

15/10 *lest . . . they pyll*: leste . . . they shulde pyll *1533*, *Ne . . . expilent*.
Throughout this passage *1534* softens the strident accuracy of *1533* into
a more rhythmical prose; *pyll and poll*: The first use of this phrase
recorded in the *OED* (*s.v.* PILL *v.*^I III. 9.) occurred in 1528: Tyndale,

Obed. Chr. Man Prol., Wks. (1573) 105, 'They haue no such authoritie of God so to pylle and polle as they do'.

15/19 *bysshoppes*: *Pontifices* (popes), an incorrect translation, perhaps to downgrade the papacy, perhaps to agree with the example given in 15/24.

15/26 *Augustyn . . . epystle*: *Epistola 133 and 134*, *PL*, xxxiii, 509–10 and 510–12.

15/31–16/1 *He . . . duty*: Cf. Matt. 22: 17–21.

16/1 *so that . . . duty*: *modo detur deo quod illi debetur* (provided that God were given what was due to Him).

16/1–3 *The woman . . . do so*: Cf. John 8: 3–11.

16/4–7 *Of those . . . amende*: Cf. Luke 13: 1–3.

16/8–11 *whan . . . heuenly*: Cf. Luke 12: 13–14.

16/12–14 *couetous . . . you*: Cf. Matt. 23: 13 ff., Luke 6: 24.

16/15–19 *Whan . . . are*: Cf. Luke 9: 54–5. The *Enchiridion*'s translation reads better than Tyndale's, 'ye wote not what maner sprete ye are of'.

16/17 *to burne vp*: to haue burned vp *1533*, *exureret*.

16/19 *was about to call*: was about to haue called *1533*, *reuocare conantem*. *1534* uses the correct sequence of tenses.

16/19–20 *Whan . . . aduersary*: Cf. Matt. 16: 22–3.

16/20–3 *Whan . . . mynde*: Cf. Mark 9: 33–5.

16/24–6 *as not . . . lyke*: Cf. Matt. 5: 39–44.

17/16–17 *for the eyen . . . partes*: Cf. 1 Cor. 12: 14–17.

17/21–4 *And . . . tragedyes*: I have not been able to discover the exact source of this saying attributed to Augustine; indeed the pragmatic advice against exasperating wicked rulers seems out of harmony with his political philosophy. A more typical statement on the theological reasons for obeying even unjust rulers can be found in his *Enarratio in Psalmum 124* [Vulgate numbering], *PL*, xxxvii, 1653.

17/22 *not all yᵉ best*: *impij*. The Eng. uses circumlocution in dealing with the sins of princes.

17/30–3 *elementes . . . nature*: Empedocles (5th c. BC) first proposed the theory that all matter is composed of a mixture of four primary substances. Earth, the heaviest element, stands at the centre of the universe with concentric spheres of the progressively lighter elements, water, air, and fire, filling the space between our planet and the moon. Contrary to Empedocles, Aristotle taught that the four elements could be transformed into one another but in a cyclical manner rather than the hierarchical pattern depicted here. Cf. *Meteorologica* 1: 2–3; *De Generatione et Corruptione* 2: 4. The comparison of the transforming power of Christ

(17/24 ff.) to that of fire is reminiscent of the Stoic teaching on God or Nature as a creative fire which generates the universe out of itself and into which human souls as well as the other elements are periodically absorbed. Cf. Diogenes Laertius, 'Zeno', *Lives of Eminent Philosophers* 7: 137, 156–7.

17/35–18/5 *Paule . . . perfectyon*: Cf. 1 Cor. 7: 6–12 and 3: 1–2.

18/5–7 *And also . . . them*: Cf. Gal. 4: 19. Both the Eng. *Enchiridion* and Tyndale's NT translate *parturio* as 'travail' in preference to 'labour'.

18/8 *with hym*: In a 1529 edition of selected letters, Erasmus here interpolated a sentence qualifying his censure of the morals of princes. See the Introduction, p. xl.

18/35 *that haue had two wyues*: e.g., Thomas More. Erasmus takes a position here contrary to the early Christian writer Tertullian, who forbad remarriage after the death of the spouse (*De Monogamia, PL,* ii, 980–1, 993–7).

19/1 *propone*: propounde *1533, proponitur. 1534* provides the more conservative form of the word. See the Glossary for 'propounde'.

19/6 *excepte ye do thynke*: Not in Lt. See the Introduction, p. xliii.

19/6–8 *Quintilian . . . oratour*: The *Institutio Oratoria* (*c.*95 AD) discusses the preparatory and professional education of an orator, the formal structure of a speech, its style, figures of speech and delivery, and the moral character of the orator.

19/30–6 *dothe monysshe . . . power*: Cf. 1 Pet. 5: 2–3.

20/5 Sidenote 2: Not in Lt.

20/13 Sidenote 3, *A sentence*: γνώμη (a maxim).

20/14 *it*: om. *1533, cui.*

20/22–5 *dyd withdrawe . . . regarde them*: quoniam minus tribuunt ceremonijs, quam uellent quidam, qui plus nimio tribuunt, nec ita multum humanis constitutionibus, hominum animos alienent a uita monastica. The Eng. deftly handles the involved Lt. clausal sequence.

20/32 *pyhequarellos*: 'Piokquarrelo' fito tho oontont bottor than a literal translation of *sycophantis* (informers, tricksters, deceivers). The first use of this sense (quarrelsome persons) recorded in the *OED* (*s.v.* 1.) occurred in 1530: Tyndale, *Pract. Prelates* Wks. (Parker Soc.) II. 264, 'He hath been all his life a pick-quarrel'.

21/1 *whiche thynken*: whiche that thynketh *1533, sentiat.* The plural form in *1534* agrees with 'those' rather than 'one' (20/32).

21/3–4 *a pope / I wote not who*: Giuliano della Rovere (1443–1513). Allen records only one letter from Julius II to Erasmus (Ep. 187A), permitting him to hold a benefice *in absentia* and in spite of his illegitimate birth. For Erasmus's alleged authorship of the diatribe against Julius, see

J. Kelley Sowards, *The Julius exclusis of Erasmus*, trans. Paul Pascal (Bloomington, Ind., 1968), pp. 7–14.

21/5 *of heresy*: Not in Lt.

21/14–15 *there be that note hym for*: he shulde be noted as *1533, non desunt a quibus notetur*.

21/15 *Ebionytes*: A Jewish-Christian sect of the first to fourth centuries whose ascetic practices included strict poverty and vegetarianism; *exhorte*: dyd exhorte *1533, adhortetur*. *1534* correctly supplies the present tense.

21/19–20 *is . . . suspected*: shulde be . . . suspected *1533, in suspicionem uocatur* (indicative).

21/21 *marcionytes*: A heretical Christian sect of the second century which held that celibacy was necessary for salvation.

21/24–5 *ambicyon . . . in commune places*: *theatrica illa . . . ambitio* (that theatrical ambition). The Eng. mistranslates the Lt. or, at least, loses some of the pointedness of Erasmus's criticism of the vanity of scholars.

21/26 *For*: Nor *1533, enim*.

21/26–7 *Augustyne . . . logycyens*: *De Doctrina Christiana, PL*, xxxiv, 57–8.

21/30 *yf a man note, or reproue*: he dothe not disprayse vertue nor prayse vyce / whiche sheweth *1533, Si quis . . . taxet*. *1534* adheres more closely to the Lt.

21/33 *contrary, whiche also*: om. *1533*; *contra, Item*.

22/1–2 *whiche be . . . greuous*: moste small fautes and tryfles / and so contrary wyse *1533, quae leuissima sunt mala, cum sint atrocissima, ac retrorsum*. *1533* omits the translation of *cum . . . atrocissima*, which *1534* supplies; *ac retrorsum* is translated by *1533* as 'and so contrary wyse' and by *1534* as 'and clene cam'. See the Glossary for 'clene cam'.

22/6–10 *As if . . . certeynte*: Erasmus expresses the critical view of pardons common in the late Middle Ages. See, for example, the hostile portrait of the Pardoner, 'Prologue and Tale', *The Works of Geoffrey Chaucer*, ed. F. N. Robinson, 2nd edn. (Boston, 1957), pp. 148–55, and the preference given to good works over pardons by William Langland, *Piers Plowman: The Prologue and Passus I–VII of the B text as found in Bodleian MS. Laud Misc. 581*, ed. J. A. W. Bennett, Clarendon Medieval and Tudor Series (Oxford, 1972), Passus VII, ll. 167–74 and nn. 176 ff. Luther's protest against papal indulgences grows out of the same tradition. See Thesis 41: 'Papal indulgences must be preached with caution, lest people erroneously think that they are preferable to other good works of love', (*Career of the Reformer, 1*, ed. Harold J. Grimm, in *Luther's Works*, ed. Helmut T. Lehmann (Philadelphia, 1957), *31, 29*).

22/10–13 *Also . . . saynt Iames*: Although he himself had made pilgrimages to Walsingham and Canterbury, Erasmus opposed religious devotions which prevented people from fulfilling the duties of their state in life. Cf. Menedemus ('stay-at-home') in 'A Pilgrimage for Religion's Sake': 'From here to one place and another, observing what my children and my wife are doing, careful that everything be in order. These are my Roman stations' (*Colloquies*, p. 312); *saynt Iames*: Santiago de Compostela in northwest Spain, a place of pilgrimage since the ninth century, alleged to contain the tomb of St. James the Great.

22/21–2 *Augustyne* . . . *epystles*: *Epistola 22, PL*, xxxiii, 91.

22/25 *we speke* . . . *exagerate*: *exaggeramus, terque quaterque* (we enlarge upon three and four times). See the Introduction, p. xlii and the Glossary for 'exagerate'.

22/26–8 *yf one* . . . *harlot*: Cf. 1 Cor. 6: 15–16.

22/28 *ouer ragyng bolde*: *nimium tragice* (exceedingly tragically). See above, 21/24–5 n. for another instance of Erasmus's aversion to theatricality of manner.

23/6 *pyke quarell*: *sycophanta*. See above, 20/32 n.

23/9–10 *thy lorde god*: *corpus illius*.

23/10 *whiche* . . . *synners*: Cf. Rom. 5: 6.

23/15 *There* . . . *denyeth*: *Quis neget?* The Lt. places this clause as a rhetorical question after 'commune people' (23/18) for greater dramatic effect.

23/19 *to god*: *CHRISTO*. See above, 7/14.

23/30 *dothe lye couered*: do lye couerte *1533*, *latuisset* (singular).

23/32 *all*: *puppim ac proram* (*quod dici solet*) (the stern and bow—as is customarily said). See *Adagia*, I. i. 8 (*OO, 2*, 28E).

23/33 *shold be ascrybed*: be ascrybed *1533*, *constitui* (to be established).

23/34–24/4 *Augustyne* . . . *rayment*: *Regula ad Servos Dei, PL*, xxxii, 1380.

24/4 *it is a worlde for to se*: Not in Lt.

24/10 *blacke monkes*: *Benedictini*, the Order of St. Benedict (480–c.546), had as its goal retirement from active ministry to liturgical prayer and work within the monastery community.

24/14 *this*: that *1533*. The direct object is not expressed in the Lt.

24/16 *these*: those *1533*, *his* (these).

24/17–18 *thynkynge them selues better | and preferrynge them selues to other*: . . . them selfe . . . them selfe *1533*, *se caeteris anteponunt*.

24/32 *wolde* . . . *desyre*: do . . . desyre *1533*, *ambiant. 1534* with the subjunctive is correct; *to be shauen*: *cooptari* (to be chosen). The Eng. strikes a more anti-monastic note than the Lt.

24/33 *no man . . . heed*: Cf. Tit. 3: 1; *to his heed*: Not in Lt. After this phrase the Eng. omits *atque ut uerbo utar Paulino*, πειθαρχεῖ (and as I should use the Pauline word, 'to obey authority'). See the Introduction, p. xl.

24/35–6 *True . . . nothynge*: Cf. 1 Cor. 13: 7.

24/36–25/2 *obedyent . . . rough*: 1 Pet. 2: 18.

25/10–12 *Paule . . . lyuing*: Cf. Gal. 5: 13.

25/11 *couer*: couert *1533*, *praetextum*. See the Glossary for 'couert'.

25/12–13 *Peter . . . malyciousnesse*: Cf. 1 Pet. 2: 16.

25/13 *And be it*: And if *1533*, *Quod si*.

25/15 *sholde be . . . kepte*: be . . . kept *1533*, *continere* (to keep).

25/15–16 *in supersticiousnes . . . ceremonyes*: Internal gloss on *Iudaismo*.

25/18 *causeth . . . obserued*: *arctius astringere laqueos ceremoniarum* (binds more tightly the snares of ceremonies). The Lt. is more concrete and figurative than the Eng.

25/19 *preceptes*: *praetextu* (cover), an error in the Eng.; *be as kynges ouer other*: doth bere rule *1533*, *regnant*.

25/20 *seruauntes . . . Christ*: Cf. Rom. 16: 18; *seruauntes to theyr owne bellyes*: serue their bellyes *1533*, *uentri suo uiuunt* (live for their stomachs); *to Christ*: Christ *1533*, *CHRISTO*.

25/21 *to be afrayde*: be a frayde *1533*, *metuant; essenes*: A Jewish sect which flourished *c.*150 BC–70 AD. The main group lived on the west shore of the Dead Sea and practised community of goods and celibacy.

25/26–9 *But . . . true religyon is*: Cf. Allen, 2, 309.

25/30–2 *pharisees . . . lande*: Cf. Matt. 23: 15.

26/1 *in to their veyles and nettes*: *in nassam* (snare, net). While not an exact translation of *nassa*, 'veyle' connotes the monastic life against which Erasmus is here warning the reader.

26/3 Sidenote 1: Not in Lt.

26/4–5 *myght be*: shulde be *1533*, *esse*.

26/7 *Benedicte*: For St. Benedict, see above, 24/10 n.; *Frauncys*: For St. Francis, see above, 9/1 n.

26/11 *dyd so lyue*: shulde so lyue *1533*, *ita uiuere*.

26/17 *anone after*: *Mox*; 'after' is an adverb modified by 'anone', not a preposition introducing 'the manner'. The phrase is used again below, 26/21–2.

26/20 *shewed . . . christendom*: shewed them christened *1533*, *erant Christianae*.

26/23 *commune people . . . charite*: Cf. Matt. 24: 12.

26/25 *Benet*: For St. Benedict, see above, 24/10 n. *Barnard*: Because of the affective quality of his mystical writings, St. Bernard (1090–1153) is called the *Doctor Mellifluus*.

26/26–7 *dyd assocyate . . . vse*: Free rendering of *Conspiratum est a paucis non in aliud, quam in* (It was agreed by a few not in any other thing than in).

26/28 *men*: In his 1529 edition of selected letters, Erasmus here inserted a paragraph praising the monks of former days. See the Introduction, pp. xl–xlii.

27/6 *to them selues*: to their selues *1533, sibi.*

27/7 *accompte*: do accompte *1533, habeant*; *in comparison*: in comparison of them selues *1533, prae se.*

27/15 *amongest them selfe*: amongest theym *1533*, not in Lt.

28/7–9 Sidenote 2, *confydence in our selfes*: confydence in our selfe *1533, fiducia sui* (self-confidence).

28/8–11 *the pharisey . . . forth*: Luke 18: 12. *I paye all my tythes*: Not in Lt. Compare with Tyndale's NT, in which the first clauses are exactly alike and the second clauses different: 'I fast twyse in the weke. I geve tythe of all that I possesse.'

28/13–14 *I am . . . to do*: Cf. Luke 17: 10.

28/19–20 *We must all hange of that heed*: *caput conspiremus* (Let us agree with the Head [Christ]). In his phrase 'unite under that one head', Olin (p. 132) gives a closer rendering of the Lt. than does the Tudor translator since 'hange of' means 'depend confidently on' (*OED*, HANG 13. b.).

28/26–7 *be not vtterly . . . Chrystes doctryne*: *calamitosum faciant tantum, non etiam impium*. Roland Crahay and Marie Delcourt interpret *calamitosum faciant* as *calamitosae sint* (are only destructive but not wicked) (*Douze lettres*, p. 106 n.).

28/29 *we must . . . man*: Cf. Acts 5: 29.

28/32 *is sent vnto you*: *in tuum sinum aduolat* (flies into your heart). The Lt. phrase is warmer in tone than the Eng.

28/33 *Frobenius*: John Froben (*c.*1460–1527). His correspondence with Erasmus covers the years 1516 to 1518 with five letters from Erasmus (Ep. 602, 629, 635, 795, 885) and two from Froben (Ep. 419, 801).

29/1 *certayne fragmentes*: One of Colet's replies to Erasmus's *Disputatiuncula* (Ep. 110) and the preface to *Basilij in Esaiam Commentariolus* (Ep. 229) (Allen, 3, 377 n.).

29/6–7 *Sapidus / that he be wyse*: *Sapidum . . . sapiat*. The pun on Sapidus's name is more obvious in the Lt. After studying in Paris, Sapidus, or John Witz, settled in Schlettstadt, where he belonged to the same literary circle as Volz, Wimpfeling, and Rhenanus, fellow editor and early biographer of Erasmus. Because of his sympathy with the reformers, Sapidus moved to Strassburg in 1526 and resided there until his death in 1561. The letters include two from Erasmus (Ep. 364, 1110) and five from Sapidus (Ep. 323, 353, 354, 399, 1251), the most important of which is Erasmus's discussion (Ep. 1110) of the *Antibarbari* dedicated to Sapidus.

29/7–8 *Wynphelingus*: James Wimpfeling (1450–1528). His correspondence with Erasmus extends from 1511 to 1524 and includes three letters from Erasmus (Ep. 305, 385, 1517) and four letters from Wimpfeling (Ep. 224, 302, 382, 1067).

29/8 *al his armure*: τὴν πανοπλίαν.

29/9–10 *warre . . . concubynes*: A reference to Wimpfeling's treatise, *De Integritate*, published at Strassburg in 1505 (Allen, *3*, 377 n.).

29/13 *commaunde*: commend *1533, saluere*. 'Command' (*OED s.v.* IV. 17.) meaning 'commend' became obsolete in the early sixteenth century. See the Glossary.

29/14 *Ruserus*: John Ruser worked for Mathias Schurer's press in Strassburg. He died on 28 October 1518, little more than a month after Erasmus composed the 'Letter to Volz'. Erasmus wrote him two letters in 1517 (Ep. 606, 633).

29/15 *to god*: *CHRISTO Opt. max.* See above, 7/14.

30–1. The Lt. does not give a table of contents for the chapters of the *Enchiridion*.

32/2–4 *A compendyous treatyse . . . called Enchiridion. Whiche*: Not in Lt. The Eng. gives a wordy translation of the Lt. title.

32/8–28 *THou hast . . . effycacye*: The first part of Erasmus's original letter to John the German. See the Introduction, p. xvii.

32/14–15 *egipt . . . pleasures*: Cf. Origen, *De Principiis, PG,* xi, 391–2.

32/17–19 *which . . . effect*: Cf. Phil. 1: 6.

32/24 *neyther*: or els *1533, uel.*

32/32–33/1 *yᵉ lyfe . . . Iob*: Cf. Job 7: 1.

33/4–5 *departing from warre*: om. *1533*, not in Lt.

33/6–7 *and gyue . . . tyme*: om. *1533*, doublet for 'make holyday out of season', *intempestiuas agunt ferias.* Sidenote 2, *Peace . . . all*: Cf. Jer. 6: 14 and 8: 11.

33/17 *Hercules . . . Cephalus*: Hercules dipped his arrows in the blood of the Hydra (Second Labour) to make the wounds they gave incurable, no matter how slight. The Greek hero Cephalus possessed a spear which never missed its target; with it Cephalus accidentally killed his wife Procris as she spied on his hunting party. Cf. Ovid, *Metamorphoses* 7: 672–865.

33/18–19 *with y^e ... shelde*: the ... shelde *1533, scuto; ye sure ... fayth*: Cf. Eph. 6: 16.

33/20–1 *worlde ... myschefe*: Cf. 1 John 5: 19.

33/22 *is^1*: om. *1533*, not in Lt.

33/23–4 *as one ragynge with*: ragyng / as with *1533, uelut ... saeuiens*.

33/29–30 *otherwhyles ... rolles*: Cf. Virgil, *Eclogues* 3: 93, *Aeneid* 5: 84.

33/31 *lye ... woman*: Cf. Gen. 3: 15; *a wayte*: According to the *OED*, 'Many apparent examples of this word (WAIT) in texts of 14–16 c. really belong to the synonymous AWAIT *sb.*, which, like other words beginning with a prefix, was often written as two words. It is possible that the *a* was in the 16th c. sometimes apprehended by writers and readers as the indefinite article, but distinct evidence of this is wanting'.

34/8–9 *olde ... Adam*: Cf. 1 Cor. 15: 47.

34/9–11 Sidenote 2: Not in Lt.

34/13 *watched ... eyes*: Probably an allusion to Argus, the monster with a hundred eyes, which was sent by Hera to guard Io. Ovid, *Metamorphoses* 1: 625–7.

34/23 *gyue ... good chere*: cuticulam ... curamus ociosi (Being at leisure we pamper ourselves). Cf., *Curare cuticulam, Adagia*, II. iv. 75 (*OO, 2,* 546E).

34/26 *sallets*: A 'sallet' is a helmet without a crest and with the lower part curving outwards at the back (*OED, s.v.* 1.).

34/28–9 *bathed ... muskballes*: Not in Lt. See the Introduction, p. xliii; *pommaunders*: A 'pomander', is a ball of spices carried in a bag at the neck, waist or wrist (*OED, s.v.* 1.).

34/31 *who say*: om. *1533*, not in Lt.

34/34–6 *peace ... peace*: See above, 33/6–7 n.

35/1–2 *There ... persones*: Cf. Isa. 48: 22 and 57: 21.

35/5 *kepe batayle and fyght*: sholde fyght *1533, belligeremur*.

35/6–8 *we shal haue hym ... our double ennemy, bothe*: we shall haue him twyse our ennemy / ... bothe *1533, bis hostem sumus habituri, simul*.

35/7 *beynge*: yf he be *1533*, not in Lt.

35/8 *bycause*: bycause that *1533, quod*.

35/9–10 *(for ... agree)*: Cf. 2 Cor. 6: 14.

35/10 *also*: also that *1533, simul* (at the same time).

35/11–12 *and wickedly ... made*: but vniustly haue broken thappoyntment made bytwene hym and vs *1533, et ... ictum foedus nepharie soluimus*.

36/1 *the loue of hym*: loue *1533, amore*.

36/5–6 *frome . . . blode*: Cf. 1 Pet. 1: 18–19.

36/9–11 *Who so euer . . . abrode*: Cf. Luke 11: 23. *Luc. xj.*: Internal gloss taken from the Lt. sidenote.

36/15–16 *The rewarde . . . deth*: Rom. 6: 23.

36/18–19 *fyghtest . . . quarell*: *tam foedam toleras* (you endure so filthy [a death]).

36/21 *thrugh wretched and myserable*: for myserable *1533, misera*.

36/26 *how . . . fynyssh*: with what lusty stomackes fynysshe they *1533, alacribus studijs, quicquid . . . exhauriant*.

36/28 *they renne*: ronne they *1533, rapiantur* (they hastened away).

36/28–9 *wel . . . formest*: Not in Lt.

36/29 *how moche worth*: how smal *1533, quantula* (how small).

36/31 *Which is nothing els*: Veryly *1533, Nempe* (truly).

36/33 *gloryfyed*: praysed *1533, celebrentur*.

37/1–2 *to haue . . . bederoll*: Not in Lt.

37/7 *chefe ruler of our game*: *Agonothetes* (superintendent of public games).

37/8 *veryly*: om. *1533, Profecto*.

37/8–10 *mules . . . Virgil*: *tripodas . . . mulos . . . Achilles . . . Aeneas*. The Eng. translator has rearranged the terms of this chiasmus. Cf. Homer, *Iliad* 23: 260; Virgil, *Aeneid* 5: 110.

37/9 *tripodas*: According to the *OED* (*s.v.* A. 1.), TRIPOD means a three-legged vessel, often presented as a prize or votive offering. Its earliest recorded use in a Lt. text in England occurred in 1370; its first use in an Eng. text, c.1611 in Chapman's translation of the *Iliad* 18. 308.

37/10–11 *eye . . . man*: Cf. 1 Cor. 2: 9.

37/14 *afterward*: here after *1533, deinde*.

37/15 *How beit*: But *1533, Sed*; *and*: om. *1533*, not in Lt.

37/16 *euen*: om. *1533, et* (even).

37/19 *set before*: profred to *1533, proposita*.

37/22 *why*: Not in Lt.

37/25–6 Sidenote 1: Not in Lt.

37/35–38/2 *Achilles . . . Hectors*: Cf. Homer, *Iliad* 22: 395 ff.; *as Hectors was*: as Hectors *1533*, not in Lt.

38/2–3 *are togyther cast downe*: is cast downe *1533, pariter . . . demergitur* (together is plunged into).

38/10–13 Sidenote 1: Not in Lt.

38/12 *eyen*: eyes *1533*, *oculis*. *1534* habitually uses the more conservative plural form. See the Introduction, p. xlvii n. 1.

38/12–13 *and . . . therfore*: Not in Lt. This addition lessens the contrast and balance in the original: *quoniam nemo uidet, pauci credunt, paucissimi formidant* (since no one sees, few believe, very few fear).

38/14 *passeth*: dothe passe *1533*, *praestat*.

38/19 *for thy body*: to thy body *1533*, *corporis*.

38/19–20 *worde . . . soule*: Cf. Luke 4: 4.

39/1–3 *Whan . . . trouth*: Cf. Rom. 1: 21; *trouth*: vertue or trouth *1533*, *ueritas*.

39/10–11 *loue, and compassyon of thy neyghbour*: Doublets for 'charite'. See the Introduction, p. lii.

39/11 *god . . . charite*: Cf. 1 John 4: 7–8.

39/11–13 *For . . . it*: Cf. 1 Cor. 12: 26.

39/23–5 *There . . . aryseth*: Cf. Isa. 34: 3.

39/26 *paynted sepulcres*: Matt. 23: 27. Compare with Tyndale's 'paynted tombes'. See the Introduction, p. lii.

39/28–9 *Theyr . . . tonges*: Cf. Pss. 5: 11 and 13: 3.

39/29–30 *The bodyes . . . goost*: Cf. 1 Cor. 3: 17 and 6: 19.

39/29–31 Sidenote 3: Not in Lt.

39/32–3 Sidenote 4: Σῶμα . . . Σῆμα.

39/32–4 *It is called . . . soule*: Internal gloss on *Soma quasi Sima*. According to the Orphic doctrine, the human soul passed from one body (σῶμα) to another, that is, from one charnel-house (σῆμα) to another, until the ingrained taint of original sin was washed out and the purified soul was translated to the stars. Cf. Plato, *Gorgias* 493A and *Cratylus* 400C.

40/3–4 *corpse . . . dayes*: Cf. John 11: 39.

40/7–8 *the mouth . . . hert*: Cf. Matt. 12: 34–5.

40/11 *Mayster . . . lyfe*: Cf. John 6: 69.

40/13 *that soule*: the soule *1533*, *ea . . . anima*.

40/14 *so moche as*: not yet *1533*, *uel* (even).

40/16–17 *Good . . . agayn*: Cf. 3 Kgs. 17: 17–24, 4 Kgs. 4: 18–37.

40/33–4 *Yf . . . vs*: Cf. Rom. 8: 31.

41/3–6 *with hym . . . in vs also*: As Head of the Mystical Body, Christ triumphed over Satan, sin and death both for Himself and in principle for His members (cf. Eph. 5: 23 and Rom. 5: 17–18). Now the Christian soldier must actualize in his own life the victory over Satan made available to him by Christ's death and resurrection.

41/7–8 *thou . . . heed*: Cf. Phil. 4: 13, Eph. 4: 15.

41/8–10 Sidenote 2: Not in Lt.

41/14–15 *to answere . . . agayn*: Free translation of *ne benignitati illius desis ipse* (lest you are wanting in your duty to His kindness).

41/16 *his liberalite . . . meryte*: This passage calls to mind the Roman Catholic teaching on congruous merit, that which 'is based on the liberality of one who gives a reward' as distinct from condign merit, that which 'has a title arising from a concept of justice' (C. S. Sullivan, 'Merit', *New Catholic Encyclopedia*, 1967). It anticipates Erasmus's defence of the concept of congruous merit in *De Libero Arbitrio* (1524) and Luther's rejection of both concepts of merit in *De Servo Arbitrio* (1525). Cf. *Luther and Erasmus: Free Will and Salvation*, The Library of Christian Classics, Vol. 17, trans. E. Gordon Rupp and Philip S. Watson (Philadelphia, 1969), pp. 51, 311, 321.

41/20–1 *haue . . . worlde*: John 16: 33.

41/25–9 Sidenote 3: Not in Lt. Cf. Homer, *Odyssey* 12: 85–110. See the Introduction, p. xv.

41/34 *as that*: than that *1533, ut*.

42/9 *one . . . brede*: Cf. *Transversum digitum, Adagia*, I. v. 6 (*OO, 2*, 184F).

42/23–6 Sidenote 2: The Lt. reads *Allegoria septem uitiorum Capitalium* (Allegory of the seven capital sins).

42/25–6 *Cananei . . . Iebuzei*: Cf. Deut. 7: 1.

42/30–1 *Paule . . . stop*: 1 Thess. 5: 17. Cf. Tyndale's 'Praye continually'.

42/36–43/1 *These . . . helpe*: Horace, *Ars Poetica*, ll. 410–11. The original verses refer to the co-operation of art and nature in writing a good poem.

43/3–5 *To . . . passe*: Cf. Jas. 1: 6.

43/6–8 Sidenote 1: Not in Lt.

43/7–8 *ye knowe . . . aske*: Matt. 20: 22.

43/9 *communeth*: commeth *1533, sermones misceat*.

43/17–20 *Moyses . . . worse*: Cf. Exod. 17: 11.

43/23–5 *infantes . . . spyrite*: Cf. 1 Cor. 14: 20, Eph. 4: 13.

43/26–9 *Whan . . . hym*: Matt. 6: 7–8.

43/29–31 *Paule . . . knowlege*: Cf. 1 Cor. 14: 19; *to the Corinthes*: Internal gloss taken from the Lt. sidenote.

43/30 *wordes*: After this the Eng. omits *in spiritu, hoc est* (in the spirit, that is), an ambiguous reference to the gift of tongues. See the Introduction, p. xl.

43/31-2 *Moyses . . . me*: Exod. 14: 15.

44/2-7 Sidenote 1: Not in Lt. See the Introduction, pp. xliv–xlv, for a discussion of the Eng. translator's handling of *pietas*.

44/3-4 *lyfte . . . to the*: Cf. Ps. 120: 1.

44/10 *Amalachytes*: Cf. Exod. 17: 8–16.

44/11-12 *manna from heuen*: See below, 44/24–45/11.

44/12 *water . . . rocke*: Cf. Exod. 17: 6.

44/14-16 *Oh . . . trouble me*: Ps. 22: 5.

44/20 *easy*: *tolerabilem*.

44/24-45/11 *manna . . . this*: Cf. Exod. 16: 13–21.

44/27-8 *For . . . author*: Cf. 1 Tim. 3: 16.

44/30-1 *by this propertie . . . goddes lawe*: Not in Lt. See the Introduction, p. xliii.

44/33 *is*: om. *1533, est*.

45/4-5 *this . . . thereof*: John 6: 61.

45/9-10 *one tytle or pricke*: Cf. Matt. 5: 18. See the Introduction, p. lii.

45/13-14 *water of . . . vp*: Cf. Ps. 22: 2.

45/14-15 *yᵉ waters . . . waye*: Cf. Ecclus. 24: 40–1.

45/16-17 *mystical . . . ouer*: Cf. Ezek. 47: 1–6.

45/17-18 *welles . . . agayne*: Cf. Gen. 26: 18.

45/19-22 *.xij. . . . desert*: Cf. Exod. 15: 27.

45/20 *mansions*: According to the *OED* (*s.v.* 4.), a 'mansion' is the distance between two halting places on a journey.

45/21-2 *and made . . . desert*: Not in Lt.

45/23 *well . . . iourney*: Cf. John 4: 6.

45/24-6 Sidenote 1: Not in Lt. Cf. John 9: 1–17.

45/25-6 *water . . . fete*: Cf. John 13: 5.

45/35-6 *if . . . nyght*: Cf. Josh. 1: 8, Ps. 1: 2.

46/1 *no . . . night*: Cf. Ps. 90: 5–6.

46/3-11 *And . . . farther*: Cf. Augustine, *De Doctrina*, PL, xxxiv, 63.

46/4 *to begyn withall*: The first use of this phrase recorded in the *OED* (BEGIN 1. d.) occurred in 1531: Tyndale, *Expos. & Notes* (1849) 220, 'And to begin withal, they said *Confiteor*'.

46/6 *to a more perfyte thynge*: *ad hanc militiam* (to this warfare).

46/4–15 Sidenote 1: Not in Lt. Cf. Homer, *Odyssey* 12: 39–46.

46/10–11 *that is* . . . *farther*: This internal gloss gives an allegorical interpretation of the Sirens; see the Introduction, p. xliii.

46/11–13 *Basilius* . . . *people*: *Sermo de Legendis Libris Gentilium, PG*, xxxi, 563–90.

46/13–14 *Augustyn* . . . *muses*: *De Ordine, PL*, xxxii, 988.

46/15–16 *Ierom* . . . *warre*: *Epistola 70, PL*, xxii, 666.

46/16–17 *Cyprian* . . . *Egipcians*: Cited by Augustine, *De Doctrina, PL*, xxxiv, 63.

46/22–3 *verily* . . . *god*: Not in Lt.

46/22–4 *For* . . . *Ietro*: Cf. Exod. 18: 13–27.

46/28–30 *Ierom* . . . *scripture*: *Epistola 53, PL*, xxii, 544.

47/5 *or vttermost parte of his lyppes*: *summis labijs*, doublet for 'with the typ of his tonge' (47/4–5). See the Introduction, p. xliii.

47/10–11 *philosophers* . . . *secte*: The teaching of Plotinus (AD 205–70) on the union of the soul with the One through contemplation furthered the development of mystical theology. For St. Augustine, see below, 49/9–10 n. Although hostile to Christianity, Proclus (*c.* AD 410–85) greatly influenced later Christian writers.

47/14–19 *And* . . . *inhabyte*: Cf. *De Doctrina, PL*, xxxiv, 62.

47/17 *furthermore*: farthermore *1533, Deinde* (and then).

47/21–3 *For* . . . *clene*: Titus 1: 15.

47/21 *shal althyng*: all shall *1533, omnia* . . . *sunt*.

47/22–30 Sidenote 1: Not in Lt. Cf. Cant. 6: 7–8.

47/27–8 *thy best beloued* . . . *beautifull*: Cf. Cant. 2: 10.

47/28–31 *And* . . . *an israelyte*: Cf. Deut. 21: 10–13.

47/31–48/2 *Ozee* . . . *god*: Osee 1: 2–11.

47/31–48/6 Sidenote 2: Not in Lt. Deut. 21: 12. For an allegorical interpretation of this practice of tonsure, see the Introduction, p. xv.

48/3–4 *with lyght* . . . *breed*: *consperso* (with a cake of meal, i.e. unleavened bread); *season*: after this the Eng. omits *sed hic cibus temporarius erat* (but this food was temporary). See the Introduction, p. xl.

48/3–5 *The ebrewes* . . . *iourney*: Cf. Exod. 12: 34, 39.

48/7–10 Sidenote 1: The Lt. simply reads *Manna*.

48/10–12 *holy* . . . *mynde*: Cf. Augustine, *De Doctrina, PL*, xxxiv, 23, 36.

48/11–21 Sidenote 2: Not in Lt. Cf. 1 Par. 13: 10, 2 Kgs. 6: 6–7.

48/14 *manna* . . . *putrifye*: Cf. Exod. 16: 20.

48/16 *set*: set to *1533, admoliri* (to lay on [hands]).

48/16–19 *Oza . . . seruyce*: Cf. 2 Kgs. 6: 6–7.

48/20–1 *of no lesse . . . estemed*: *Oracula mera (ut sunt)* (pure oracles—as they are).

48/22–3 Sidenote 3: Not in Lt.

48/24 *in to*: to *1533*, not in Lt.

48/25 *wylt come*: shalte comme *1533, adieris*.

48/25–6 *if . . . mekely*: Cf. Augustine, *De Doctrina, PL*, xxxiv, 64.

48/26–7 *the pleasures . . . spouse*: Cf. Cant. 4.

48/27 8 *precyous . . . Salomon*: Cf. Cant. 3: 11.

49/1–4 *Thynke . . . scripture*: Cf. Augustine, *De Doctrina, PL*, xxxiv, 68–9.

49/4–6 *if . . . fulfilled*: Matt. 5: 18. As opposed to the *Enchiridion*'s 'perysshe . . . perissh', Tyndale translates *intereant . . . interiturus est* as 'perisshe . . . scape', but both the *Enchiridion* and Tyndale use the words 'iote' and 'tytle'.

49/5–6 *iote, or tytle*: According to the *OED*, Tyndale was the first to use the word 'jot' in 1526: *Matt.* v. 18, 'One iott or one tytle of the lawe shall not scape'. But *MED* quotes *jote* '*a.* 1500'. See the Introduction, p. lii.

49/9–10 *Origene . . . Augustyne*: Origen (*c*.185–*c*.254) emphasized the importance of the spiritual over the literal sense in scriptural exegesis. Ambrose (*c*.339–97) wrote commentaries on scripture, adopting the allegorical method of Origen. Jerome (*c*.345–420) revised the Old Latin New Testament according to the Greek and made a new translation of the Hebrew Old Testament into Latin. Christian Neoplatonism and the allegorical method of Origen were transmitted through Ambrose to Augustine (354–430).

49/13–14 *Paule . . . spirituall*: Cf. Rom. 7: 14.

49/17–18 *that were nigh . . . lyuyng also*: Not in Lt.

49/19 *mayster Dunce*: Duns Scotus.

49/19–20 Sidenote 3: The Lt. reads *Scotistae*. See above, 6/25 n.

49/23–4 *and the meke spyrite of Christ*: Quasi-doublet of 'ye holy guust' (*spiritusancto* [oic]).

49/33 *And . . . diuynes*: For an expression of Erasmus's aversion to *Neoterici*, however, see his letters to Thomas Grey, one of his pupils in Paris, and to John Colet (Allen, *1*, 192–3, 246).

50/1–2 *similitudes . . . redils*: Not in Lt.

50/4–6 *The wisdom . . . feblenes*: Cf. the *Paraclesis*: *Haec omnibus ex aequo sese accommodat, submittit se parvulis, ad illorum modulum sese attemperat, lacte illos alens, ferens, confovens, sustinens, omnia faciens, donec grandescamus in Christo* (*OO*, 5, 140A) ('This doctrine in an equal degree accommodates itself to all, lowers itself to the little ones, adjusts itself to their measure, nourishing them with milk, bearing, fostering, sustaining them, doing everything until we grow in Christ' (Olin, p. 96)).

50/6–9 *She . . . stomacke*: Cf. 1 Cor. 3: 1–2, Heb. 5: 12.

50/10 *the contrary wyse*: vpon the other side *1533*, *contra*.

50/24–6 Sidenote 2: Not in Lt.

50/25 *so: om. 1533, sic.*

50/26 *slacke*: slacked *1533*, *languere* (be inert).

50/27 *than*: but *1533*, *quam*.

50/30 *the flesshe*: the flesshe / that is to say / the lettre / or that ye se outwarde *1533*, *Caro*. See the Introduction, p. xlvi; *nothyng*: not *1533*, *non*; *spiryte*: spiryte within *1533*, *Spiritus*.

50/30–1 *the flesshe . . . lyf*: Cf. John 6: 64.

50/30–51/2 Sidenote 3: Not in Lt.

50/32 *the lettre . . . lyfe*: 2 Cor. 3: 6. The *Enchiridion* here resembles Tyndale's 'geveth lyfe'; *the lettre*: y^t the lettre *1533*, *litera*; *it is*: and it is *1533*, *est*; *that gyueth lyfe*: gyueth lyfe *1533*, *qui uiuificat*.

51/1–2 *we . . . carnall*: Cf. Rom. 7: 14.

51/2–3 *Spirituall . . . thynges*: Cf. 1 Cor. 2: 13.

51/3–5 *In . . . spiryte*: Cf. John 4: 20–4, Jas. 1: 17.

51/3–6 Sidenote 1: Not in Lt.

51/6–7 *that thynge . . . to do*: y^t they onely be able to do *1533*, *quod unum possunt [facere]* (which one thing they are able [to do]).

51/7–8 Sidenote 2: The Lt. reads *Similitudo Origenica* (An example from Origen). Cf. Origen, *Contra Celsum*, *PG*, xi, 703–6.

51/16–18 *Paule . . . gyftes*: Cf. 1 Cor. 12: 30–1.

51/17 *with theyr mouth*: *spiritu* (in the spirit). The Eng. refers to those who say the office in Lt. without understanding it rather than to those who have the gift of tongues; *or whiche speke*: whiche speketh *1533*, *uel qui . . . loquuntur*; *tonges*: tonges that thynge they vnderstande not *1533*, *linguis*.

51/18 *them*: them to leue theyr infancy / and *1533*, not in Lt.

51/19 *there be any that*: a man *1533*, *cui* (to anyone).

51/19–20 *the mynde*: a corrupte mynde *1533*, *animi*.

51/20 *at the leest of nature*: for lacke of capacite *1533*, *[uitio] naturae*.

51/21 *enforce to*: enforce *1533*, *conantur*.

51/22–3 *let not . . . eateth*[2]: Rom. 14: 3.

51/28–9 *the booke . . . openeth*: Cf. Apoc. 5: 1 and 3: 7.

51/29 *whiche*: the which *1533*, *Is qui*. Although typologically Christ is the 'key of Dauyd', the relative clause modifies 'he' (51/28) not 'key'.

52/1–2 *the father . . . them*: Matt. 11: 27.

52/3 *But . . . asyde*: Erasmus calls himself back from a digression in a variation on the phrase 'To turn one's style' (*OED*, STYLE I. 1. d.) meaning 'to change to another subject'.

52/6 *newe armure*: thy newe armure *1533*, *noua arma*.

52/7 *thy newe warre*: the newe warre *1533*, *nouae militiae tuae*.

52/10–12 *the bee . . . behynde*: Cf. Plutarch, *Moralia* 32E. For the contrasting activity of the spider, see below, 166/9–11 n.

52/14–15 *the philosophers . . . gentyles*: Internal gloss on *sua*.

52/17–18 *what so euer . . . Chrystes*: Augustine, *De Doctrina*, *PL*, xxxiv, 49.

52/19–20 *harneys . . . persed*: Cf. Homer, *Iliad* 18: 478 ff.

52/21–4 *Dauid . . . philistiens*: Cf. Cant. 4: 4.

52/24–5 *harneys . . . speketh*: Cf. Allen, *1*, 356–7. Sidenote 2: Not in Lt. Cf. Homer, *Iliad*, 1 and Virgil, *Aeneid*, 4.

52/30 *make*: maketh (singular) *1533*, *praeficiunt* (plural).

52/31–2 *wytte, facultyes, scyences, and craftes*: *artibus* (occupations; skills) is translated as 'facultyes' (*OED*, *s.v.* 8., arts, trades) and as 'craftes'; *ingenijs* (mental powers, abilities, geniuses) is translated as 'wytte' (*OED*, *s.v.* II. 5., genius, intellectual ability) and 'scyences' (*OED*, *s.v.* 3., particular branches of knowledge or study).

53/1–8 Sidenote 1: The Lt. reads *Allegoria Dauid*.

53/2–3 *yf . . . feare*: Horace, *Odes*, III. iii. 7–8.

53/3–13 *the harnes . . . broke*: Cf. 1 Kgs. 17: 38–40, 49.

53/8–9 *the fyue . . . knowlege*: Cf. 1 Cor. 14: 19.

53/10–24 Sidenote 2: Not in Lt.; *than*: then *1533*, not in Lt.; *Than*: then 1533, not in Lt.

53/13–14 *whan . . . scripture*: Cf. Matt. 4: 1–11.

53/16–21 *And . . . spere*: Wisd. 5: 18–21.

53/21–4 *he . . . zele*: Isa. 59: 17.

53/25–54/1 *armure . . . god*: Cf. 2 Cor. 10: 4–5.

54/1–8 *the armure . . . god*: Cf. Eph. 6: 13; 2 Cor. 6: 7, Eph. 6: 14–17.

54/8–9 *be . . . couered and fenced*: shall be . . . couered and fensed *1533*, *erit . . . tectus*.

54/10–13 *Who . . . sworde*: Rom. 8: 35.

54/15–21 *But . . . Iesu*: Rom. 8: 37–9.

54/18 *vertues*: virtutes *1533, uirtutes*.

54/22 *the wepons . . . lyght*: Rom. 13: 12.

54/22-3 *Paule . . . man*: Saul was taller than any other man in Israel (Cf. 1 Kgs. 10: 23). The Lt. name *Paulus* meaning 'small' was adopted by St. Paul during his first missionary journey, probably to signify his role as apostle to the gentiles.

54/23-4 *the refuse . . . worlde*: Cf. 1 Cor. 4: 13.

54/24 *Of suche armure therfore haboundaunce*: Of suche armure therfore haboundauntly *1533, Talis igitur armaturae uim*. In revising *1533, 1534* disregards proper Eng. word-order. See the Introduction, p. xlvii.

54/34 *of holy scripture*: Internal gloss. See the Introduction, p. xlii.

55/1 *the buckler of fayth*: See above, 54/1-8 n.

55/2 *easely*: be able to *1533, facile*.

55/3 *receyue*: haue *1533, accipias*.

55/10 *Where as*: but where as *1533, cum* (while).

55/20 *doctrynes*: conclusions *1533, dogmatum*.

55/20-1 *Chryst . . . not*: Cf. John 14: 27.

55/21-2 Sidenote 1: Not in Lt.

55/23-4 Sidenote 2: Not in Lt.

55/24 *and that*: om. *1533*, not in Lt.

55/25 *father*: parens. Tyndale never used the word 'parents' in his writings, but preferred 'father' or 'father and mother' (Mozley, p. 101). See the Introduction, p. lii.

55/27-56/2 Sidenote 3: Not in Lt. The Eng. sidenote erroneously identifies Socrates and Plato as Stoics.

55/27 *Stoikes*: Stoicism, founded by Zeno *c.*300 BC, advocated strength of character in individual and social ethics, resulting in *apatheia* or spiritual peace. Later Stoics included Cicero and Epictetus, both authors of handbooks on morality. See the Introduction, pp. xviii–xix.

56/1-2 *doth . . . malyce*: Cf. Wisd. 7: 30.

56/3 *Beliall*: Identified with Satan according to the rabbinical literature of the second century BC.

56/3-10 Sidenote 1, *Wyse man . . . wysdom*: Not in Lt.

56/6 *the very . . . father*: John 1: 9, cf. Heb. 1: 3.

56/8-10 *as he . . . wysdome*: Cf. 1 Cor. 1: 30.

56/10-14 *We . . . wysdom of god*: 1 Cor. 1: 23-4. Note especially the similarity between the *Enchiridion* and Tyndale's 'an occasion of fallinge'.

56/11-12 *an occasyon of stumblyng and fallyng*: an occasion of vnite *1533, scandalum*.

56/18–19 *and vnder the name of wysdome*: and vnder a fayned colour of honeste *1533*, doublet for 'false tytle'.

56/22–4 *If . . . god*: 1 Cor. 3: 18–19. For Erasmus's practice of direct quotation from the scriptures, see the Introduction, pp. xv–xvi. Sidenote 3: Not in Lt.

56/25 *for*: om. *1533, enim*.

56/25–9 *for . . . folyshnes*: 1 Cor. 1: 19–20. The *Enchiridion*'s 'subtile lawyer' reads better than Tyndale's 'scrybe'.

56/25–57/1 Sidenote 4: Not in Lt.

57/1–2 *these . . . men*: Cf. Matt. 15: 14.

57/1–7 Sidenote 1: The Lt. reads *Nomine Christiani, re Hostes* (Christians in name, Enemies in fact).

57/8–20 Sidenote 2: The Eng. greatly expands the Lt. *Hesiodus*.

57/14–15 *Paule . . . euyll*: Cf. Rom. 16: 19.

57/17 *Hesiodus*: Internal gloss taken from the Lt. sidenote. See above, 57/8–20 n.

57/18–19 *whiche . . . counseyle*: Hesiod, *Works and Days*, 296–7.

57/23–5 *He . . . scorne*: Ps. 2: 4.

57/25–6 *they . . . them*: Wisd. 4: 18.

57/29–58/1 *I . . . feared*: Prov. 1: 26.

58/1–2 *whan they . . . dreames*: whan they awaked out of theyr dreame *1533, experrecti*.

58/3–5 *These . . . honour*: Wisd. 5: 3–4.

58/3–7 Sidenote 1: Not in Lt.

58/6–7 *This . . . deuyll*: Jas. 3: 15.

58/7 *ennemy . . . destruction*: Phil. 3: 19.

58/8–10 Sidenote 2: Not in Lt.

58/13 *after custome*: after *1533, consuetudinem*.

58/15–16 *By whiche . . . length*: By which it is caused *1533, quo fit*.

58/19 *seconde deth*: Cf. Apoc. 20: 6.

58/22–6 *Al . . . thynges*: Wisd. 7: 11–12.

58/23 *to men*: mihi. Perhaps the compositor mistook a stray mark over 'me' for a nasal sign.

58/28–9 *For . . . rest*: Cf. Judg. 9: 16.

58/30 *his seuenfolde grace*: *septeno illo Chrismate*. Cf. Isa. 11: 2–3. Himelick (*Enchiridion*, p. 62) translates the phrase as 'sevenfold anointment'. In 1 John 2: 20, however, *chrisma* is used to mean 'spiritual grace'. Holborn (p. 40, l. 15) emends the Lt. text to *charismate* (grace).

T

58/32–59/1 *of a clere conscience*: Not in Lt.

59/1 *a ioye knowen*: whiche ioye is knowen *1533, gaudium . . . cognitum.*

59/4–6 *This . . . desyre*: Cf. Jas. 1: 5–6.

59/7–8 *dygge . . . erth*: Cf. Prov. 2: 4, Matt. 13: 44.

59/9 *knowe thy selfe*: A saying inscribed on the temple at Delphi, γνῶθι σεαυτόν. Cf. *Nosce teipsum, Adagia,* I. vi. 95 (*OO, 2,* 258D).

59/9–10 *Whiche . . . byleued*: Cf. Juvenal, *Satires* 11: 27.

59/11–12 *auctours . . . sentence*: The adage is variously ascribed to Socrates, Pythagoras, and Thales, and is referred to by Plato, *Phaedrus* 229E, and Ovid, *Art of Love* 2: 500.

59/14 *doctryne and teachynge*: conclusyon and doctryne *1533, dogmatis.*

59/17–19 *O thou . . . sorte*: Cant. 1: 7.

59/23–4 *Paule . . . heuen*: Cf. 2 Cor. 12: 2; *whom god so loued: cui contigerat* (to whom it happened).

59/24 *ye*: om. *1533, uel* (even).

59/24–5 *yet . . . hymself*: Cf. 1 Cor. 4: 3.

59/26–8 *If . . . no man*: Cf. 1 Cor. 2: 15.

59/29 *do . . . presume*: shold . . . presume *1533, confidimus* (indicative).

59/30 *vnprofytable sowdyour*: Cf. 'unprofitable servant', Matt. 25: 30, Luke 17: 10; *knoweth*: knewe *1533, habeantur cognitae* (present tense).

59/31–60/3 Sidenote 1: The Lt. reads *Gigantes e terra nati.*

59/33–60/1 *out of*[2] *. . . of vs*: Doublet for 'out of our owne flesshe'. See the Introduction, p. xliv.

60/2 *certeyn . . . erth*: Ovid, *Metamorphoses* 3: 101–30.

60/4 *and so harde . . . the other*: Not in Lt.

60/7 *Iosue*: Internal gloss taken from the Lt. sidenote.

60/7–8 *aungell of lyght*: 2 Cor. 11: 14.

60/8 *Art . . . enemyes parte*: Josh. 5: 13.

60/15–16 Sidenote 1: The Lt. differs: *Homo ex diuersissimis compactus* (Man made from very diverse parts).

60/17 *goodly*: numine (godly).

60/20 *as concernyng yᵉ soule*: In our myndes *1533, Secundum animam.*

60/20–5 *as concernyng . . . beest*: In his 'Letter to Martin Lypsius', an Augustinian canon and fellow editor, Erasmus takes exception to the criticism of this passage published by Edward Lee, then a little known cleric, later (1531) Archbishop of York (Allen, *3,* 329).

60/21 *receyuable of yᵉ diuyne nature*: celestial and of godly capacite *1533, diuinitatis . . . capaces.*

60/27 *the serpent*: Cf. Gen. 3.

60/27–61/15 Sidenote 4: Not in Lt.; *vpon*[1]: on *1533*, not in Lt. Cf. *Auribus lupum teneo, Adagia*, I. v. 25 (*OO, 2*, 190F). See the Introduction, p. xv.

61/7 *I . . . without the*: Ovid, *Amores*, III. xi. 39.

61/12 *On the other parte*: On the other party *1533, Contra*.

61/15 *ye thinges*: these thinges *1533, ea*.

61/17 *whiche*: of substaunce which *1533, quae*.

61/19 *in thynges of lyke nature*: with thinges of lyke nature *1533, similibus*.

61/20 *his contagyousnes*: contagiousnes of hym *1533, eius contagio*.

61/21 *be gone out of kynde*: hath gone out of kynde *1533, degenerarit*.

61/21–7 Sidenote 1: Not in Lt.

61/22–3 *Prometheus . . . mynde*: Cf. Horace, *Odes*, I. xvi. 13–16.

61/23 *mynglyng*: myxed *1533, admixta*.

61/24–6 *that is . . . creacyon*: that is to say / it spronge not in vs naturally / or nature gaue it not to vs in our creacion or natiuite *1533*, internal gloss.

61/26 *hath . . . corrupted*: hath . . . corrupte *1533, deprauauit*.

62/1 *in a maner*: Supplied by the Eng. translator to qualify what reads like a denial of free will.

62/3–4 *debate and parte takyng in it selfe*: debate and parte takyng among them selfe *1533, seditiosa*.

62/8 *as*: as that *1533, ut*.

62/21–2 Sidenote 2: In the Lt. text this sidenote comes after Sidenote 3, 62/29–30.

62/22–3 *or the fyrste example of honestye*: *honestatis Ideae*, doublet for 'the orygynall decree of nature'. Note *1534*'s apt translation of the Platonic Idea.

62/25 *stryue*: shall stryue *1533, contendit* (present or future tense); *senyours or eldermen*: senyours *1533, nutu maioribus*; cf. Plato, *Republic* 3, 412C2.

62/26 *despyse*: shall despyse *1533, negligunt* (present tense).

62/33 *father and mother*: *parentes*. See above, 55/25 n. and the Introduction, p. lii.

63/4 *affections or passyons*: Direct object of 'thynke and reken' (63/7). The Eng. follows the Lt. word-order here to the detriment of clarity.

63/10 *with prison and punyshment*: in preson / and with punyshment *1533, ergastulis*.

63/11 *may rendre*: rendre *1533*, *praestent* (subjunctive).

63/13 *may do no harme*: do no harme *1533*, *nihil ... damni dent* (subjunctive).

63/14–25 *yᵉ sones ... thynges*: Plato, *Timaeus* 69C–D.

63/26–8 *and ... perturbacions*: *Nec ignorauit in huiusmodi perturbationibus coercendis, uitae beatitudinem consistere*. The Eng. translator retains the litotes and the indirect discourse form of the Lt.

63/28 *that they shall lyue*: them for to lyue *1533*, *eos ... uicturos*.

63/28–31 *that they ... yᵉ same*: Plato, *Timaeus* 42B.

63/29 *that haue ouercomme*: whiche sholde haue ouercomme *1533*, *qui ... superassent* (subjunctive).

63/30 *that they shall*: them for to *1533*, not in Lt; *were*: sholde be *1533*, *fuissent* (subjunctive).

63/31 *for the soule*: to that soule *1533*, *animae*; *lyke vnto*: *quidem* (even). The Eng. qualifies what reads like an assertion of equality with God.

63/32 *for reason*: vnto reason *1533*, *rationi*.

63/32–64/1 *reason ... brayne*: Plato, *Timaeus* 44D.

63/32 *for a kyng*: vnto a kyng *1533*, *regi*.

64/1–2 Sidenote 1, *braynes*: brayne *1533*, *cerebro*.

64/2–3 *most farre ... beestes*: most farre ... a beest *1533*, *minime bruta* (in the least degree brutish).

64/4–6 *very thynne ... knowlege*: Plato, *Timaeus* 75C.

64/6 *no debate*: thrugh the shewyng of them no debate *1533*, *nihil tumultus*; *myght ryse*: sholde ryse *1533*, *cooriretur*.

64/7 *but that ... reporters*: whiche he *1533*, *ut illis quasi renunciantibus ... ille*.

64/7–8 *sholde ... perceyue it*: sholde not ... perceyue *1533*, *non ... persentisceret*.

64/8–19 *But ... agaynst hym*: Plato, *Timaeus* 70A.

64/9 *one*: one of them *1533*, *quaeque*.

64/15 *separated*: separate *1533*, *semouit*.

64/19–26 *power ... kynge*: Plato, *Timaeus* 70D–E.

64/27–8 *what rebellyon ... teche the*: Plato, *Timaeus* 91B–C.

65/3 *lyke a kyng or a ruler*: Internal gloss taken from the Lt. sidenote, which reads *Ratio tanquam rex* (Reason like a king).

65/8 *Homere ... egle*: Cf. *Iliad* 8: 247 and 24: 292–3; *syt*: set *1533*, *insidere* (to sit on). 'Confusion between *set* and *sit* arose as early as the beginning of the 14th c.' according to the *OED* (SET).

65/11–12 *golde² ... betokeneth wysdom*: For the analogy between the most precious metal and the most precious spiritual gift, cf. 'By gold is wisdom betokeneth, as Solomon said, "A desirable gold-treasure lieth in the wise man's mouth."' (Benjamin Thorpe, ed., *The Sermones Catholici, or Homilies of Ælfric in the Original Anglo-Saxon, with an English version* (1844; reprinted London, 1971), I, 117.)

65/16 *nothynge*: not *1533, ne quid*; *by meanes of*: by reason of *1533, per.*

65/21 *that is to saye, a ruler*: Internal gloss inserted perhaps for the sake of alliteration, 'ruler . . . robber' (65/21–2).

65/24 *Reason*: Internal gloss taken from the Lt. sidenote.

65/29 *moderacyon*: moderacyon discretly *1533, moderatione.*

65/30 *Stoici*: For the Stoics, see above, 55/27 n.

65/31 *Peripotetici*: Theophrastus, Aristotle's successor as head of the philosophical school, willed a 'peripatos' or 'covered walking place' to his associates as a home for their continued studies. Thus the name 'Peripatetics' gradually became a synonym for 'Aristotelians'. The quality of the school declined, however, as Aristotle's followers concentrated on empirical questions to the neglect of metaphysics.

66/1–12 *Stoici . . . ymaginacyons*: Cf. Diogenes Laertius, 'Zeno', *Lives of Eminent Philosophers* 7: 110–17.

66/2–3 *to teche . . . prynciples*: Not in Lt.

66/2–14 Sidenote 1: Not in Lt. The Eng. translator erroneously identifies Platonists with Stoics. See above, 55/27–56/2 Sidenote 3.

66/4 *be comme*: now be comme *1533, perueneris.*

66/10–12 *and with moche ado some which be more gentyll graunte . . . preuentyng*: ye and scarsely they graunte . . . more gentyl preuentyng *1533, uixque humaniores quidam . . . praeuertentes . . . concedunt* (and some only just more humane grant . . . anticipating).

66/13–18 *Peripotetici . . . other*: For a more exact statement of Aristotle's position on the morality of the passions, see *Nicomachean Ethics*, II. vi. 10–11.

66/15–67/10 Sidenote 2: Not in Lt.; *wele*: welth *1533*, not in Lt.

66/17 *maketh . . . a mater*: Not in Lt.

66/18–21 *Socrates . . . deth*: Plato, *Phaedo* 61A.

67/15 *complexion*: According to the *OED* (*s.v.* I. 1.), 'complexion' is the combination of the four humours of the body in a certain proportion.

67/16–25 *Socrates . . . fiersnes*: Plato, *Phaedrus* 246A, 253C–254E.

67/23–4 *swete apace*: *multum sudans* (sweating greatly). The first instance of 'apace' used to describe swift motion (*OED, s.v.* 1. b.) occurred in 1535: Coverdale, *Ps.* lviii. 6, 'Like water that runneth a pace'. Rather than gloss the phrase as 'sweat quickly', I suggest 'sweat profusely', remembering that the context refers to moral not physical effort.

67/25 *and sharpe spurres*: and with sharpe spurres *1533, calcaribusque.*

67/27 *not*: not that *1533, non.*

67/28 *to be stopped*: is stopped *1533, interclusam [esse].*

67/32 *that*[2]: so that *1533, ut.*

67/36 *reason*: Internal gloss.

68/3–4 *and this happeneth ... countrees*: Not in Lt.

68/10–11 *to be solytary ... chorlysshe*: Not in Lt.; *selfe mynded*: the first use of this word recorded in the *OED* occurred in 153[1] [The *OED* incorrectly dates *Answer to More* as 1530; the revised *STC* gives 1531.]: Tyndale, *Answ. More* III. xiii Wks. (1575) 315/1, 'Opiniatiue, selfe-mynded and obstinate'.

68/17–20 Sidenote 5, *yll dysease*: euyll dysease *1533, Morbus.*

68/18 *the disease*: one disease *1533, morbum.*

68/26 *against ... wall*: Cf. Jer. 1: 18 and 15: 20.

69/9 *Solempnes: tristior* (the sadder character). The first use of 'solemn' to describe a serious person which is recorded in the *OED* (*s.v.* 6. b.) occurred in 1580–3. *And he*: And *1533, Qui.*

69/11 *lyghter*: somwhat easyer *1533, leuioribus.*

69/15 Sidenote 2: Not in Lt.

69/17 *Secondly*: more ouer *1533, Deinde* (next).

69/22–3 *what so euer ... obteyne*: Plato, *Republic* 435C, 497D; *Greater Hippias* 304E; *Cratylus* 384B. Cf. *Difficilia quae pulchra, Adagia,* II. i. 12 (*OO, 2,* 410–11).

69/25–6 Sidenote 4: Not in Lt.

69/26–31 *nothyng ... flesshe*: Jerome, *Epistola 125, PL,* xxii, 1072.

69/33 *Now therfore*: Than now therfore *1533, modo.*

70/1 *conceyue thou*: conceyue *1533, concipe.*

70/10–11 *yea ... pleasaunt*: in conclusion with custome it shall be very pleasaunt *1533, consuetudine demum etiam iucundum* (at length with habit even pleasant).

70/12–14 *The waye ... quietnes*: Hesiod, *Works and Days,* ll. 290–2.

70/15 *shall there be*: is there *1533, erit.*

70/16 *the tamer*: hym that is ye tamer *1533, domitoris.*

71/1–18 Sidenote 1: Cf. Matt. 10: 34–5.

71/10–14 *This ... togyther*: Cf. Eph. 2: 14.

71/11 *hath made both one*: knyt two in one *1533, fecit utraque unum.*

71/21–4 *Walke ... flesshe*: Cf. Gal. 5: 16–17.

71/24 *that ... wolde*: Cf. Rom. 7: 18; *can not do: faciatis* (subjunctive in a result clause). The Eng. seems to deny free will.

71/25–72/1 *If . . . lyue*: Rom. 8: 13.

72/1–3 Sidenote 1: Not in Lt.

72/4 *I chastise . . . seruytude*: 1 Cor. 9: 27.

72/5–6 *If . . . lawe*: Gal. 5: 18.

72/6–8 *And . . . god*: Rom. 8: 15.

72/8–10 *I se . . . membres*: Rom. 7: 23.

72/11–12 *the vtter . . . by daye*: Cf. 2 Cor. 4: 16.

72/12–13 *Plato . . . man*: Cf. *Timaeus* 69C–D.

72/14 *eyther*: outher *1533, neque.* According to the *OED* (EITHER), *outher*, an early equivalent of 'either', became obsolete in literary English in the sixteenth century (cf. OUTHER).

72/15 *separated*: separate *1533, disiunctos.*

72/16 *must*: sholde *1533, sit.*

72/17–22 *The fyrst . . . celestyall*: 1 Cor. 15: 45–7.

72/21–2 *The seconde . . . celestyall*: The *Enchiridion* here is close both to Douai–Rheims and to Tyndale's 1526 NT: 'The seconde man is from heven, hevenly.' Tyndale's 1534 NT, however, reads 'the seconde man is the Lorde from heaven'.

72/18–19 *lyuynge soule . . . spiryte quyckenynge*: *animam uiuentem . . . animam uiuificantem.* Sidenote 3: Not in Lt.

72/24–30 *As . . . incorrupcion*: 1 Cor. 15: 48–50.

73/2–3 *Oh . . . deth*: Rom. 7: 24. The 1534 *Enchiridion* corresponds exactly with Tyndale's NT, whereas Douai–Rheims gives 'the body of this death' as in the Vulgate, *de corpore mortis huius. Oh wretched man*: O wretche *1533, Infelix . . . homo.*

73/2–19 Sidenote 1: Not in Lt.

73/5 *also*: om. *1533, et* (also).

73/5–7 *He . . . eternal*: Gal. 6: 8.

73/8–20 *twynnes . . . law*: Cf. Gen. 25: 22–34.

73/16–17 *the right . . . elder brother*: *ius . . . primogenitorum.* Tyndale's Pentateuch renders this long phrase as 'byrthrighte'. See the Introduction, p. liii.

73/18 *with a vyle prest and rewarde*: *uili . . . autoramento.* See 180/23 n. for a different Eng. translation of *autoramentum* (wages, hire, reward). The later editions, *STC* 10481 and 10486, misprint 'priest' to give this passage an anticlerical note which sounds strangely here if these two undated editions are, as I suggest, Marian publications. See the Introduction, pp. xxxviii–xxxix and the Appendix.

73/20 *of law*: Not in Lt. This addition underlines the contrast between 'law' and 'grace'. See the Introduction, p. xv.

73/21–5 *Bitwene . . . daunger*: Cf. Gen. 27: 41–5.

74/2 *Iacob . . . lorde*: Cf. Gen. 28: 13–16, 32: 24–30 and 35: 9–13.

74/4–5 *the elder . . . yᵉ yonger*: Gen. 25: 23.

74/5 *And Isaac the father*: but the father Isaac *1533, Pater uero.*

74/6–7 *thou Esau . . . necke*: Gen. 27: 40.

74/11 *Paule . . . husbande*: Cf. Eph. 5: 22.

74/12–13 *better . . . woman*: Ecclus. 42: 14.

74/13–17 *Eue . . . dede*: Cf. Gen. 3: 1–6.

74/15 *she . . . corrupted*: she is . . . corrupte *1533, ea corrupta.*

74/14–18 Sidenote 1: Not in Lt.

74/18–21 *I wyl . . . hele*: Gen. 3: 15. The *Enchiridion*, 'she shal trede downe thy heed / and thou shalte lay awayte to her hele', differs significantly from Tyndale's Pentateuch: 'And that seed shall tread the on the heed, and thou shalt tread hit on the hele'.

74/22 *weakened*: weyked *1533, fregit* (broke).

74/22–75/10 Sidenote 3: Not in Lt.

75/1–7 *sara . . . ioy*: Cf. Gen. 18: 10–14 and 21: 1–7.

75/3 *called*: calleth *1533, vocat* (present tense).

75/4–5 *she was . . . woxen barayn*: she was . . . bareyn *1533, illi desijssent muliebria.*

75/7–8 *be woxed olde and are weake*: haue wexed olde and are weyked *1533, consenuerunt* (have lost strength).

75/8 *yᵗ*: the *1533, illa.*

75/10 *as . . . feest*: Prov. 15: 15.

75/10–21 *And . . . voyce*: Cf. Gen. 21: 9–12.

75/11 *hath he*: hath *1533, habet.*

75/13 *yᵗ the childe*: yᵉ chylde *1533, filio.*

75/26–31 *For euen . . . weaknes*: Cf. 2 Cor. 12: 7–9.

75/28 *whan*: om. *1533*, not in Lt.; *the lorde*: om. *1533, dominum*; *yᵉ messenger*: yᵗ messenger *1533*, understood in Lt.

75/29 *answer*: answere of god *1533*, not in Lt.

76/2 *For*: om. *1533, enim.*

76/2–4 *For . . . himselfe*: 2 Cor. 4: 7.

76/7 *prayer . . . desyre*: prayer agayne / and desyre *1533, iteratis precibus implorandum esse.*

76/9–17 Sidenote 2: Not in Lt.

76/10 *we be admonysshed y^t*: om. *1533*, not in Lt.

76/12 *that*: om. *1533*, understood in Lt.; *is*: to be *1533*, *esse*.

76/12–14 *Hidra . . . woundes*: See above, 33/17 n. and the Introduction, p. xv.

76/15–16 *contynuall . . . althing*: Virgil, *Georgics* 1: 145–6.

76/18 *pull and drawe*: drawe *1533*, *urge*.

76/18–25 Sidenote 3, *must be holden downe*: must be holde down *1533*, *stringendus*; *Protheus is . . . compulsyon*: not in Lt.

76/19 *bynde fast*: bynde *1533*, *stringe*; *Protheus . . . bandes*: Cf. Homer, *Odyssey* 4: 385–424.

76/19–22 *whyle . . . ryuer*: Virgil, *Georgics* 4: 440–2.

76/20 *wonderful thinges*: maner monstres and affections of thynges *1533*, *miracula rerum*.

76/22 *and neuer leaue him*: om. *1533*, not in Lt.

77/1 *than*: there *1533*, *Tum* (then).

77/1–5 *than . . . fyre*: *Georgics* 4: 406–9.

77/1–11 Sidenote 1: Not in Lt. Cf. Virgil, *Georgics* 4: 315–558.

77/6–8 *The more . . . bandes*: *Georgics* 4: 411–12.

77/10–28 *Iacob . . . persone*: Cf. Gen. 32: 24–31.

77/12–18 Sidenote 2: The Eng. expands the Lt. considerably: *Constanter sicut Iacob relucteris. Praemium uictoriae.* (You should resist resolutely just as Jacob. The reward of victory.)

77/20 *Furthermore by touchyng the thigh*: Farthermore thrugh touchyng of ye thigh *1533*, *Deinde tacto femore*.

77/21 *wyddred*: wexed wyddred *1533*, *emarcuit*.

77/22–3 *God . . . fete*: Cf. 3 Kgs. 18: 21, 'How long do you halt between two sides [i.e. the Lord and Baal]?' (Douai–Rheims).

77/24 *also*: After this the Eng. omits: *et dum utrumque male conantur. [sic] in utroque claudicant* (and when they attempt both badly, they limp in both [cases]). See the Introduction, p. xl.

77/28–78/1 *After . . . concupysences*: Cf. Gal. 5: 24.

77/28 *After*: After that *1533*, *Vbi*; *thy flesshe*: thy flesshe or thy body *1533*, *carnem tuam*. 78/1 *it*: hym *1533*, *eam* i.e. *caro* (f.) 'flesh'.

78/3–4 *taste . . . swete*: Cf. Ps. 33: 9.

78/5 *Israell*: The etymology of 'Israel' is uncertain. Among the possible meanings are: 'God contends', 'God is strong', 'God shines forth', or 'God heals' (J. A. Pierce, 'Israel', *New Catholic Encyclopedia*, 1967); *not . . . or*: not . . . neyther *1533*, *non . . . non*.

78/5–8 *God . . . consolacion*: Cf. 3 Kgs. 19: 11–12.

78/5–14 Sidenote 2: Not in Lt.

78/10–11 *I . . . hole*: Gen. 32: 30. The *Enchiridion*, 'my soule is made hole', differs from Tyndale's Pentateuch, 'yet is my lyfe reserved'.

78/11–12 *Thou . . . se me*: Cf. Exod. 33: 20.

78/12 *me*: me / that is to say / no carnall man *1533*, *me*.

78/17 *were euen*: had ben and that *1533*, *Erant . . . uel*.

78/20–2 *Orygene . . . flesshe*: *Commentariorum in Epistolam . . . ad Romanos, PG*, xiv, 850, 856.

78/21 *makyng*: maketh *1533*, *facit*.

78/23–5 *That . . . Christ*: 1 Thess. 5: 23.

78/27–79/2 *my soule . . . please the*: Cf. Isa. 26: 9.

79/2–3 *let . . . god*: Cf. Dan. 3: 86.

79/4 *porcions*: peticions *1533*, *portionem*.

79/16 *as one*: is *1533*, *uelut*.

79/16–29 Sidenote 3: Not in Lt.

79/23–5 *Remembre . . . him*: 1 Cor. 6: 16–17.

79/28–80/4 *That . . . lyfe*: Prov. 2: 16–19. The Eng. incorrectly translates *ad eam* (to her) as 'in to hell' (80/3).

80/1 *hath forgotten*: hath forgete *1533*, *oblita est*.

80/5–9 *That . . . the man*: Prov. 6: 24–6.

80/11–19 *A folysshe . . . hell*: Prov. 9: 13–18.

80/21–2 *coulde . . . haue ben paynted*: could . . . haue be paynted *1533*, *fucariue poterant*. According to the *OED* (BE A. IV. 8.) 'The common literary form of the past participle in 14–15 c. was *be*, before the general acceptance of the northern *ben, bene*'.

80/25 *importunytie*: *improbitas* (depravity).

80/36 *imputed*: imputed / that is to saye / it dothe neyther good nor harme *1533*, *imputatur*.

81/3 *more playnly*: *pinguiore, quod aiunt Minerua* (more grossly, as they say, than Minerva). Cf. *Pingui Minerva, Adagia*, I. i. 37 (*OO*, *2*, 42A).

81/5–6 *art vnder . . . parentes*: doest reuerence to thy father and mother *1533*, *Vereris parentes*. 81/17 gives 'father' for *parente*. See above, 55/25 n. and the Introduction, p. lii.

81/26 *euen that*: That *1533*, *hoc*.

81/27 *what so euer that is*: that that thynge is *1533*, *quod est id*; *goth*: went *1533*, *accesserit* (future perfect tense).

/27 y^t *harlot the flesshe*: the harlot / that is to say the flesshe *1533*, *meretricem carnem*.

81/27–31 *If . . . spiryte*: Cf. 1 Cor. 6: 16.

81/30 *in to*: to *1533, in*.

81/33 *wenen*: weneth *1533, putant. 1534*'s plural form agrees with the Lt.

82/3 *disceyuen*: deceyueth *1533, Imponunt*. See above, 81/33 n.

82/4–5 *or hym . . . the lawe*: Doublet for 'felon'. See the Introduction, p. xliv.

82/8 *grefe or sorow*: grefe *1533, dolore*.

82/15 *haue amended*: amended *1533, emendatum. 1534* translates the perfect passive form more exactly while *1533* translates it more fluently.

82/16 *and also enioyne*: Also yf he enioyne *1533, et . . . irrogat*.

82/33–83/1 *Thou . . . fasteth not*: Cf. Rom. 14: 3.

83/4 *momblest vp*: mumblest in *1533, obmurmuras* (roar against).

83/13 *flesshwarde*: According to the *OED* (FLESH II. 11) 'fleshward' means in the direction of the flesh, the depraved nature of man in its conflict with the promptings of the Spirit. See the Glossary.

83/24 Sidenote 2: Not in Lt.

83/28–30 y^e *threde . . . Labirinthus*: Cf. Plutarch, 'Theseus', *Parallel Lives of Greeks and Romans*, 19 and Catullus, *Poems* 64: 112–15.

83/30–1 *whiche . . . maze*: Internal gloss. See the Introduction, p. xliii.

84/4–5 *departe . . . wayes*: Job 21: 14.

84/6 *rules*: rulers *1533, Canones*.

84/11 *yuels, the remanentes*: euyl thynges remaynyng *1533, mala, reliquias*.

84/14 *bothe . . . and also*: bothe partly . . . and also *1533, tum . . . tum*; the Eng. is a better translation of *cum . . . tum* (both . . . and especially) than of *tum . . . tum* (first . . . then).

84/15 *These yuels*: These *1533, Ea*.

84/18 *progenytours*: parentum. See above, 55/25 n. and the Introduction, p. lii.

84/18–20 *lyght . . . vpon vs*: Cf. Ps. 4: 7.

84/20 *shewed*: infuderat (poured out). The Eng. translates erroneously. Sidenote 1: Not in Lt.

85/1 *must be taken away*: must be take away *1533, tollenda*.

85/13 *the streyght way*: Cf. Matt. 7: 14.

85/15–16 *ones . . . backwarde*: Cf. Luke 9: 62; *thou shuldest loke backwarde*: sholdest loke backwarde *1533, respicias*.

85/16 *must reioyce*: sholdest reioyce *1533, exultes*.

85/16–17 *reioyce ... way*: Cf. Ps. 18: 6.

85/17–19 *euer ... apoynted*: Cf. Phil. 3: 13–14.

85/19–20 *yᵉ crowne ... contynue*: Cf. Jas. 1: 12.

85/30 *one iote*: See above, 49/5–6 n.

85/33 *were*: were but *1533, essent; some maner tales*: some maner of tales *1533, fabulae quaepiam*. *1533* uses the partitive genitive as does the Lt.

86/6 *On this wyse*: and on this wyse *1533, Sic*.

86/8 *these thinges*: the thinges *1533, eorum*.

86/10 *these are*: those thynges be true *1533*, not in Lt.

86/17–18 *whiche the dyuels*: the deuylles *1533, daemones*.

86/17–19 *whiche² ... feare*: Cf. Jas. 2: 19.

86/19–20 *vnto the equyte of nature*: *aequitati naturae*. The *OED* (EQUITY II. 3.) refers to the *naturalis aequitas* of the Roman jurists, the recourse to general principles of justice to correct or supplement the provisions of the law. Here Erasmus measures the teachings of Scripture against the natural law instead of vice versa.

86/24 *At the leestway ... passed*: ye of those thynges passed *1533, Vel ex praeteritis*.

86/24–5 *make ... come*: thou mayst easely coniecte what shall folowe *1533, futurorum coniecturam facito* (imperative mood). See the Introduction, p. xlvi.

86/25 *howe great*: great *1533, Quanta*.

86/31–2 *feruently ... fayth*: Cf. Luke 17: 5.

86/34 *but that he wolde departe*: that wolde not departe *1533, ut non resiliat*.

87/4 *gyuen vnto*: rewarded or recompensed to *1533, reddi* (to be given).

87/4–5 *hundred ... immortall*: Cf. Matt. 19: 29.

87/5 *conscyence*: conscyence presently *1533, conscientiae*.

87/11 *as he hath ... drinke*: *gladiatorio*.

87/12–13 *A slouthful ... not¹*: Prov. 13: 4.

87/13–15 *The kyngdom ... obtayne it*: Cf. Matt. 11: 12.

87/17–24 Sidenote 2: Not in Lt.

87/20–2 *Egypt ... pottes*: Cf. Exod. 16: 3.

87/22–88/1 *Sodoma ... perysshe*: Cf. Gen. 19: 15–17, 26.

87/24 *and she was turned*: she was turned *1533, et uersa est*.

87/25 *hath no leyser*: had no leyser *1533, non uacat; the regyon*: any region *1533, ulla ... regione*.

87/25–88/1 *is commaunded*: was commaunded *1533, iubetur* (present tense).

87/25–88/11 Sidenote 3: Not in Lt.

88/1 *onelesse*: oneles that *1533*, *nisi*; *perysshe*: to haue perysshed *1533*, *perire* (present infinitive).

88/2–3 *The prophete . . . Babylon*: Cf. Jer. 50: 8 and 51: 6.

88/9–10 *Oh . . . from the*: Cf. Luke 12: 20.

88/15 *chefe*: chefest *1533*, *utilissima*.

88/16–17 *beyng sure that Christ*: but be sure Chryst *1533*, *certus Christum*.

88/18 *Se*: set *1533*, *Aude* (dare).

88/18–19 *mistrust thyne owne selfe*: mystruste in thyne owne selfe *1533*, *tibi diffidere*.

88/21–3 *Commytte . . . vp*: Ps. 54: 23.

88/23–6 *The lorde . . . soule*: Ps. 22: 1–3.

88/27–8 *Thou . . . Belial*: Cf. Matt. 6: 24; 2 Cor. 6: 15.

88/28–9 *God . . . legges*: See above, 77/22–3.

88/29–31 *his stomake . . . luke warme*: Apoc. 3: 15–16. The *Enchiridion* and Douai–Rheims give 'luke warme' while Tyndale gives 'bitwene bothe'.

88/31 *God . . . soules*: e.g., Exod. 20: 5.

89/2 *by his dethe*: with deth *1533*, *morte sua*.

89/2–8 *There . . . walke*: Cf. Matt. 7: 13–14.

89/3 *folowyng ye affectyons*: obedyence of the affections *1533*, *obsequium affectuum* (the submission of the affections).

89/8–17 Sidenote 2: Not in Lt.

89/9–10 *sythe the worlde began*: synce the worlde began *1533*, *ab orbo condito*.

89/11 *Adrasta*: Adrasta / otherwyse called Nemesis or Rhamnusia / that is to say *1533*, *Adrestei*. The Greek goddess of divine vengeance, Nemesis had her best-known shrine at Rhamnus in Attica. Cf. Aeschylus, *Prometheus Bound*, l. 936; Plato, *Republic* 451A, and 'Adrastia Nemesis, Rhamnusia Nemesis', *Adagia*, II. vi. 38 (*OO*, *2*, 595D). See the Introduction, p. xlvi.

89/12 *must be crucyfied*: be crucified *1533*, *crucifigaris necesse est*; *crucyfied . . . worlde*: Cf. Gal. 6: 14.

89/14–19 *One . . . suche*: Cf. '. . . the folk cast [piety] back on those whom they call "ecclesiastics", as if they themselves had no traffic whatever with the church and their baptismal vows had not the slightest effect. The priests, in turn, that call themselves "secular", as if admitted to the world, not to Christ, roll this burden off upon the regulars; the regulars put it upon the monks; the monks that have more liberty upon those that are stricter, and both together upon the mendicants; the mendicants upon the Carthusians, among whom, and nowhere else, piety lies hidden ...' (*Folly*, p. 102).

89/18 *though I be a monke*: Not in Lt.

89/19 *sayth he*: om. *1533*, *inquit* (he says).

89/22 *than*: then *1533*, *ergo* (then).

89/25 Sidenote 4: Not in Lt.

89/27 *ambicion*: ambicyon / y^t is to say *1533*, *ambitionem*; *pleasures*: yf thou call ye worlde pleasures *1533*, *delitias*.

90/1 *so arte thou worldly*: yf thou be worldly *1533*, *si mundanus es*.

90/3–4 *who so euer . . . discyple*: Cf. Matt. 10: 38 and 16: 24.

90/4–10 *To dye . . . to the*: Cf. Rom. 6: 3–11.

90/10–22 *The humilite . . . monkes*: Cf. Thomas à Kempis, *De paucitate amatorum crucis christi*, *The Imitation of Christ*, *A Facsimile Reproduction of the First Edition printed at Augsburg in 1471–2*, ed. W. J. Knox Little (London, 1893), Bk. 2, Ch. 11.

90/16 *more wanton or nyce*: more a wanton thyng *1533*, *delicatius*.

90/17 *wyll take no payne with him*: wilt thou take no payne with hym *1533*, *nolis compati*.

90/23 Sidenote 2: Not in Lt.

90/27–8 *whether . . . plow men*: Horace, *Odes*, II. xiv. 11–12; *kynges or poore plow men*: knyghtes or plowe men *1533*, *reges*, *siue inopes . . . coloni*. *1534* agrees with both Horace and the Lt. *Enchiridion*. Assuming that *1533* is the translation Tyndale made for Sir John Walsh, Mozley suggests (p. 99) that Tyndale translated *reges* as 'knyghtes' to 'make the cap fit his master'. See the Introduction, pp. xlix–l.

90/31 *of a christen man*: of a chrysten mans lyuynge *1533*, *Christianismi*.

91/7–9 *all . . . Eneas*: Cf. Virgil, *Aeneid* 6: 282–95.

91/8 *in ye first entring of hel*: in ipsis Auerni faucibus.

91/9–15 Sidenote 1, *Eneas . . . Sybyl*: Not in Lt.

91/11 *begyle*: begiled *1533*, not in Lt.

91/17 *shalt . . . beare*: shal . . . beare *1533*, *sint . . . subeunda*. *1534* here uses the more original verb form.

91/18 *many thinges*: thynges ynough *1533*, *multa*.

91/24 *fauoure*: grace *1533*, *gratia*.

91/28–9 Sidenote 2: Not in Lt.

91/30 *mayst thou*: than mayste thou *1533*, *potes*.

92/2 *what is it that*: what is that *1533*, *quid*.

92/3 *fleynge* ... *fyre*: Horace, *Epistles*, I. i. 46.

92/6 *therof*: of it *1533*, not in Lt.

92/6–7 Sidenote 3: Not in Lt.

92/17–18 *tourmentynge* ... *care*: Not in Lt.

92/20 *lenger*: more *1533*, *diutius*.

92/21 *with* ... *labour*: the greuouser is the payne *1533*, *hoc laboretur molestius*.

92/24 *sharpe*: tedyous *1533*, *aspera*.

92/29 *whiche*: that they whiche *1533*, *qui*.

92/30–93/13 Sidenote 5: Not in Lt. The Eng. confuses Pentheus (see below, 93/11–12 n.) with Actaeon, a hunter who was changed into a stag and eaten by his own hounds because he gazed upon Diana bathing. Cf. Ovid, *Metamorphoses* 3: 138–252.

93/2 *moche*: so moche *1533*, *maxime*.

93/5–6 *the bytternesse* ... *hony*: Cf. Plautus, *The Casket Comedy* 1: 69–70.

93/9 *causen* ... *to be sharpe and bytter*: cause ... to be sharpe and bytter *1533*, *exasperant*. *1534* uses the older verb form. See the Introduction, p. xlvii.

93/11–12 *Ticius* ... *Pentheus*: For assaulting Leto, Tityus was punished in Hades by two vultures gnawing at his liver. Cf. *Odyssey* 11: 576–81. For Ixion, cf. Pindar, *Pythian Odes* 2: 21–49. For Tantalus, cf. *Odyssey* 11: 582–92. For Sisyphus, cf. *Odyssey* 11: 593–600. For Pentheus, cf. Euripides, *Bacchanals* and Ovid, *Metamorphoses* 3: 511–733.

93/13–14 *Whose also is that late confessyon*: of whome is also the late confessyon *1533*, *Quorum est et illa ... confessio*. ...

93/14–16 *We* ... *not*: Wisd. 5: 7.

93/16 *knewe not*: knowe not *1533*, *ignorauimus*. See the Introduction, p. xlvi.

93/19 *Pharao*: Cf. Exod. 1: 8–22. *Nabugodonosor*: For Nebuchadnezzar, cf. 4 Kgs 24: 1–2, 10–16 and 25: 1–21.

93/20–2 *take* ... *lyght*: Matt. 11: 29–30.

94/5 *than* ... *besynesse*: Not in Lt.

94/5–6 *more cherefull and more confortable*: more cherefull and more comfortable *1533*, *hilarius*. *1534* characteristically emends *1533* to the Latinate form of the word.

94/14 *but also*: but *1533*, *uerum etiam*.

94/16–17 *so soone vadynge and vanysshynge*: whiche so sone fade and vanysshe *1533*, *futilia*.

94/17 *self thynges*: very same thynges *1533*, *ipsis*.

94/22 *The marchaunt man, after he*: After that the merchaunt man *1533*, *Mercator posteaquam.*

94/25–6 Sidenote 1: Not in Lt.

94/26 *be it*: if it so be than *1533, si quidem* (if indeed).

94/27–8 *what other thynge* ... *hathe he at lengthe prepared*: at the later ende ... what other thynge hath he prepared *1533, quid tandem aliud* ... *parauit.*

94/28–9 *yf he kepe* ... *perpetuall tourment*: more than the mater of myserable care if he kepe his goodes / if he lese them a perpetuall tourment *1533, quam miserae solicitudinis materiam, ut seruet, cruciatum, si perdat.*

94/29–30 *But yf*: If *1533*, Sin.

94/30 *is made*: shulde be made *1533, fiat.* See the Introduction, p. xlvi.

95/1–2 *bothe* ... *and also*: partly ... besyde that *1533, et* ... *et* (both ... and).

95/4 *moche sorowe*: moche bothe sorowe *1533, dolore.*

95/4–5 *hathe enforced*: enforseth *1533, contendit* (present or perfect tense).

95/6–7 *Chryste* ... *he not*: Cf. Gal. 6: 7.

95/7 *mocketh he not*: neyther he mocketh any man *1533, nec irridet*; *also that thynge*: an other thynge *1533, et illud.*

95/8 *from the worlde*: out of the worlde *1533, a mundo.*

95/16–17 *that rychesse encreaseth*: these richesse encrease *1533, crescunt opes illae.*

95/16–18 *that rychesse* ... *awaye*: Cf. Matt. 6: 20.

95/17 *mothes*: the mouthes *1533, tineae* (larvae).

95/22–3 *wylte ronne through out*: shalte reken *1533, cucurreris.*

95/23–4 *nothynge of all*: nothynge not of all *1533, nihil.*

95/31 *these*: these thinges *1533, haec.*

95/31–2 *all* ... *heuen*: Cf. Luke 12: 31.

96/1 *god* ... *Salomon*: Cf. 3 Kgs. 3: 11–14.

96/2 *them that flye from her*: them that flyeth from her *1533, fugientes.*

96/3–4 *what so euer* ... *prosperous*: Cf. Rom. 8: 28.

96/6–7 *pleasure and conforte*: pleasure *1533, uoluptatem.*

96/7 *swete*: swetnesse *1533, dulcia* (sweet things).

96/19–22 *but thynke* ... *taught*: This passage reveals the ethical focus of Erasmus's Christology. Although the word 'Christ' occurs an extraordinary number of times in the *Enchiridion*, the reader is left with very little sense of Christ's personality. See the Introduction, p. xvi.

96/20 *symplicite, innocencye*: symplycite / or innocency *1533, simplicitatem*.

96/26–7 *Let . . . lyght*: Cf. Matt. 6: 22.

96/29 *eyther . . . or*: eyther . . . or els *1533, aut . . . aut* (either . . . or, either . . . or else).

96/30 *Hate*: Also that thou hate *1533, oderis*.

97/1–6 *what so euer . . . rewardes*: Cf. 1 Thess. 5: 9–10.

97/6–10 *But . . . hurtfull*: Cf. Matt. 6: 23.

97/12–15 *what so euer . . . iourney*: Cf. 'Principle and Foundation', *The Spiritual Exercises of St. Ignatius Loyola*, trans. Elder Mullan, S.J. (New York, 1914), p. 19.

97/14–15 Sidenote 1: Not in Lt.

97/15–31 *thre orders . . . marke*: Cf. Diogenes Laertius, 'Zeno', *Lives of Eminent Philosophers* 7: 101–7.

97/16 *in suche maner fylthy*: of suche maner fylthe *1533, ita . . . turpia*.

97/20 *if thou dyddest them not*: Not in Lt.

97/32–98/3 *The very . . . them*: Cf. Augustine, *De Doctrina, PL*, xxxiv, 55, 20.

98/1–2 *referring them to a better purpose*: Not in Lt.

98/2 *but . . . enioye*: and . . . to enioy *1533, frui*.

98/2–3 *settyng his herte in them*: putting his hole felycite in them *1533*, not in Lt. See the Introduction, p. xlviii.

98/7–9 Sidenote 1: Not in Lt. This sidenote defines 'Pietie' in terms of God rather than of neighbour. See the Introduction, pp. xliv–xlv.

98/13–14 *makest . . . restyng place*: makest thou a stop and taryeng *1533, consistis*.

98/19 *profyte . . . thyself*: in thy selfe enioye hym *1533, fruaris*.

98/23 *lyke a marchaunt venterer, bolde*: boldly as an aduenterous merchaunt *1533, tanquam audax mercator*. According to the *OED*, the phrase 'marchaunt venterer' means a merchant engaged in the organization and dispatch of trading expeditions overseas and the establishment of factories and trading stations in foreign countries. See the Glossary.

98/24–5 *apply . . . god*: See above, 46/16–17 n.

98/25–8 Sidenote 3, *loke . . . meaneth*: Not in Lt. See above, 46/3–48/5.

98/27 *Knowe thy selfe*: See above, 59/9 n.

98/28 *kepe the within thy lystes*: Doublet for 'passe not thy boundes' (98/27–8). See the Introduction, p. xliv.

U

98/28–30 *It . . . loue*: Cf. *melior est profecto humilis rusticus qui deo seruit quam superbus philosophus qui se neglecto cursum celi considerat*, The *Imitation of Christ, A Facsimile Reproduction of the First Edition printed at Augsburg in 1471–2*, ed. W. J. Knox Little (London, 1893), Bk. 1, Ch. 2.

98/29 *more loue*: more of loue *1533*, *amare magis* (to love more); *moche to knowe*: to haue more of knowlege *1533*, *magis sapere* (to know more).

98/30 *amonge*: amongest *1533, in.*

99/6–7 *Money is chaunced vnto the*: Money chaunsed vnto the *1533, Obuenit pecunia*. *1534* retains the pattern of using an inflexion of 'be' (*OED, s.v.* IV. 14. b.) to form the perfect tense of an intransitive verb when expressing a condition now attained rather than the action of reaching it.

99/8 *make . . . mammon*: Luke 16: 9. Both the *Enchiridion* and Tyndale's NT give 'wycked mammon', a phrase which also occurs in the title of Tyndale's tract, *The Parable of the Wicked Mammon* (Antwerp, 1528), *STC* 24454. See the Introduction, p. lii.

99/9 *of good mynde*: good mynde *1533, bonae mentis.*

99/9–16 Sidenote 2: Not in Lt. Cf. Diogenes Laertius, 'Crates of Thebes', *Lives of Eminent Philosophers* 6: 87.

99/11 *flynge*: flyeng *1533, praecipita* (cast down headlong).

99/21 *be thou the more diligent*: be more dylygent *1533, solicitior esto.*

99/22 *and not the more carelesse*: hauyng no lesse care than thou haddest before *1533, non securior* (not more careless); *this wyse thynkynge*: haue in mynde *1533, id cogitans.*

99/24–100/18 Sidenote 3: Not in Lt.

99/25–100/1 *Prometheus . . . boxe*: Cf. Hesiod, *Works and Days*, ll. 42–105.

100/14–15 *For . . . not*: Cf. 1 Cor. 7: 29, 31.

100/17 *hath pleased*: pleaseth *1533, placuit* (perfect tense).

100/17–18 *it hath . . . byleue*: Cf. 1 Cor. 1: 21, 25.

100/23–101/5 *Thou . . . god*: For Erasmus's own inability to fast, see his 'Letter to Arnold Bostius', a Carmelite of Ghent (Allen, 5, 202).

100/24 *fast*: selfe *1533, ieiunium.*

100/26 *wycked*: wanton *1533, Nequam* (wicked).

100/29 *Thyne eye . . . fawty*: Cf. Matt. 6: 23; *vicyous and fawty*: corrupt *1533, Vitiosus.*

101/2 *takest hede to*: prouydest for *1533, Curas*; *thy helth and lyuynge*: helth and good lyuing *1533, ualetudinem.*

101/5–102/7 *There . . . entent*: This passage was placed on the *Index*

Expurgatorius . . . (Antwerp, 1571) (Bataillon, p. 228 n.). Cf. 'And next to these come the folk who have arrived at the foolish but gratifying belief that if they gaze on a picture of Polyphemus-Christopher they will not die that day, or that whoever salutes in certain prescribed words an image of Barbara will come through a battle unharmed . . . Indeed, they have discovered another Hercules, and even another Hippolytus, in George . . .' (*Folly*, p. 56).

101/6 *Christofer*: According to a popular medieval belief, anyone who looked on an image of this saint was saved from harm that day. Images of Christopher were therefore placed in a conspicuous place opposite the church door.

101/10 *Rochus*: St. Roch (*c*.1350–*c*.1379) was believed to have stopped the plague in Ferrara in 1439.

101/12 *Barbara*: The patroness of those exposed to sudden death, St. Barbara was a popular subject for Flemish and Italian artists in the fifteenth and sixteenth centuries. *George*: The cult of St. George was introduced into the West by the Crusaders. For his legend and iconography, see the Introduction, p. xix.

101/13 *Apolyne*: St. Apollonia of Alexandria suffered during the persecution of Decius from a mob which broke her teeth.

101/14 *Iob*: Cf. Job 2: 4–8.

101/14–15 *he wolde be without*: he shulde be without *1533, careat*.

101/17 *Hieron*: saynt Hierom *1533, Hieroni*. For St. Jerome, see above, 49/9–10 n. Perhaps Erasmus intended St. Hieron, the missionary to the Frisians who was martyred by the Norsemen *c*.856. His cult was popular in Holland in the Late Middle Ages.

101/18–19 *after this maner*: after this same maner *1533, ad hunc modum*.

101/19–20 *feare, or coueyte*: fauour or els loue *1533, timemus uel cupimus*.

101/21 *also be dyuerse*: be dyuers *1533, et . . . diuersi sunt*; *to dyuerse nacyons*: in dyuers natures *1533, diuersis nationibus*.

101/23 *the almayns*: Internal gloss added to distinguish Erasmus's countrymen from the English.

101/24 *euery where*: in euery where *1533, passim*.

102/2 *ye tenth . . . Hercules*: A tithe of the gains in war and peace were offered to Hercules on the *Ara Maxima* in the cattle market at Rome.

102/3–4 Sidenote 1: Not in Lt. For Aesculapius, cf. Plato, *Phaedo*, 118A.

102/5 *Neptunus*: Bulls were sacrificed to Neptune, sometimes by being thrown alive into rivers. In Ionia and Thessaly bullfights were held in Neptune's (or Poseidon's) honour.

102/5–6 Sidenote 2: Not in Lt.

102/7–8 Sidenote 3: Not in Lt.

102/10 *he myght not fynde*: he shulde not fynde *1533*, *offendat* (subjunctive).

102/16 *godlynes made deuyllysshe and wycked*: honouryng of god dishonouryng of god *1533*, *pietas tua impia est.*

102/17 *our holy relygyous men*: our holy men *1533*, *Religiosulis.*

102/18–19 *whiche . . . god*: 1 Tim. 6: 5. Where the *Enchiridion* translates *pietatem* as 'honouring of god', Tyndale's NT gives 'godlines'. See the Introduction, p. liii.

102/20–1 *deceyue . . . Chryste*: Cf. Rom. 16: 18; *seruyng theyr owne belyes*: whyle they obey and serue their bely *1533*, *uentri suo seruientes.*

102/23 *these*: those *1533*, *haec* (these).

102/23–4 *of a certayne . . . supersticyon*: with certayne . . . superstycion *1533*, *quadam superstitione.*

102/27 *whiche*: whiche thynges *1533*, not in Lt.

102/30 *vtterly*: om. *1533*, *omnino.*

103/1 *those*: those thynged [*sic*] *1533*, not in Lt.

103/3 *theyr lyues helth*: helth *1533*, *incolumen uitam.*

103/4 *so that*: if *1533*, *si*; *that lyfe*: it *1533*, *eam uitam.*

103/5 *them*: it *1533*, not in Lt.

103/8–10 *whether we lyue . . . dye*: Cf. Rom. 14: 8.

103/10–11 *desyre . . . Christ*: Cf. Phil. 1: 23.

103/13–14 *bycause . . . heed*: Cf. Acts 5: 41.

103/13 *bycause*: y^t *1533*, *quod*; *be accompted*: might be accompted *1533*, *habeantur.*

103/13–14 *euen after this maner to be made*: whiche euen in this worlde shulde be *1533*, *qui uel hoc modo . . . conformentur. 1533* misread *mundo* for *modo.*

103/15 *maner thynges*: maner of thynges *1533*, *istiusmodi.*

103/16 *suffre and permyt*: suffre *1533*, *Tolero.*

103/17 *I . . . waye*: Cf. 1 Cor. 12: 31.

103/17–22 Sidenote 1: Not in Lt. For this definition of 'Piety', see the Introduction, p. xlv.

103/22 *pietie*: seruynge and honourynge god *1533*, *pietatis.*

103/25 *pietie*: pity / that is to saye the honouryng of god *1533*, *pietatem.* For a discussion of the gloss, see the Introduction, p. xlv.

103/26–8 *from thynges . . . inuysyble*: Cf. Augustine, *De Trinitate*, *PL*, xlii, 1061.

104/2 *or els*: or *1533*, *siue*; *thereof*: of it *1533*, not in Lt.

104/7 *intellygyble*: According to the *OED* (*s.v.* 3.), 'intelligible' means capable of being apprehended only by the understanding (not by the senses).

104/9 *circles*: cyrcle *1533, sphaeras*.

104/10 *them*: them as the foure elementes *1533, his*.

104/15 *sencyble powers*: sencyble powers / that is to say to the fyue wyttes *1533, sensibus*.

104/16 *eyther*: *om. 1533, uel*.

104/17 *more profytable*: most profytable *1533, utilius*.

104/18–19 *to the angelyke worlde*: to the angelyke worlde / that is to say to the soule of man *1533, illi* (to that).

104/20 *mynde*: mynde / that is to say god *1533, mens*.

104/22 *in the visyble worlde ... in the inuysyble worlde*: *illic ... in illo* (in that matter ... in that). The Eng. helpfully clarifies the Lt. pronouns.

104/31 *this grosser*: the grosse parte of this *1533, in hoc crassiore*.

105/5 *pietye*: pity / to honour god *1533, pietatis*. See the Introduction, p. xlv.

105/11–17 Sidenote 2, *The glory ... Chryste*: Not in Lt.

105/13–15 *he whiche ... Chryste*: 2 Cor. 4: 6.

105/20 *the sonne ... vnto the*: Mal. 4: 2.

105/21 *the thynges inuysyble*: thinges inuysible whiche thou seest not *1533, res inuisibiles*.

105/22 *so excellent, so pure and so perfyte*: so excellent, so pure, so perfyte *1533, adeo non ... nullas* (of so great account); *the visyble thynges*: thinges whiche be sene *1533, eae quae uidentur*.

105/24–5 *these outwarde and corporal thynges*: this outwarde corporall thinges *1533, in corporeis rebus*.

105/26 *shal be mete ... moche more*: shalbe a gret deale meter *1533, conueniet ... longe magis*.

105/27 *same*: same thynge *1533, idem*.

106/4–5 *lyke pleasyng lyke*: as lyke vnto lyke *1533, similis simili*. *Simile gaudet simili, Adagia*, I. ii. 21 (*OO, 2*, 79E).

106/8 *felt*: fylthy *1533, sentitur*.

106/18–23 *so ... body*: See Plato, *Phaedo* 63E–64A, 80D–81A.

106/22 *loue*: louyng *1533, amorem*.

106/23–4 *Neyther ... vs*: Cf., e.g., Matt. 10: 38.

106/23 *that*: the *1533, illa*.

106/24–5 *neyther ... heed*: e.g. Rom. 6: 3–8, 2 Tim. 2: 11.

106/26-7 *for . . . kylled*: Ps. 43: 23.

106/28-9 *seke . . . erthe*: Col. 3: 2.

106/29 *perceyuance*: The first use of this word (PERCEIVANCE) recorded in the *OED* occurred in 1534: Tyndale, Eph. 1: 8, 'Which grace he shed on us aboundantly in all wisdome and perceavaunce [1526 prudency, 1611 BIBLE prudence].'

106/30 *meaneth . . . thynge*: By this phrase, not found in Lt., the Eng. translator introduces Erasmus's explanation of the quotation from Colossians; *or is*: it *1533*, not in Lt.

106/32-3 *the lesse fealynge we haue*: *quanto magis . . . desipuerimus* (as we act the more foolishly).

107/18 *to yᵉ body*: of the body *1533*, *corporis*.

107/18-19 *a moche more redy*: moche more and redy *1533*, *multo prae-sentius*.

107/19-21 *for feare . . . forsaken the*: Not in Lt.

107/23 *comme*: shulde come *1533*, *ueniat*.

107/24-5 *Go . . . fyre*: Matt. 25: 41.

107/33-108/15 Sidenote 2, *Sylenus be . . . inwarde*: Not in Lt.

108/8 *must be obserued*: must be obserued and kepte *1533*, *obseruandum*.

108/11 *loke*: shuldest loke *1533*, *spectes* (subjunctive).

108/14-15 *Silenus . . . thynges*: Cf. Plato, *Symposium* 215B-217A; *Sileni Alcibiadis, Adagia*, III. iii. 1 (*OO, 2*, 770C); cf. '. . . all human affairs, like the Sileni of Alcibiades, have two aspects, each quite different from the other . . .' (*Folly*, p. 36).

108/15-25 *For . . . outwardly*: Cf. Augustine, *De Doctrina, PL*, xxxiv, 68-9.

108/16-22 *the ymage . . . shortly*: Cf. Gen. 2: 7-21, Gen. 3: 1-8 and 22-4.

108/17 *Eue*: and Eue *1533*, *Euam*; *taken*: plucked *1533*, *subductam* (pulled up, removed).

108/18 *the eatynge of the tree forbydden*: howe they were forbyd the tree of knowlege of good and yuell *1533*, *interdictum, ne de ligno ederent*.

108/22 *shortly*: The Eng. mistranslates *breviter* (briefly), which ought to read 'in short' and begin the next sentence.

108/23 *sholdest rede*: rede *1533*, *legeris*. Since the perfect subjunctive indicates completed action, *legeris* is correctly translated in 108/22 and 23 but not in 108/15, 'shalte rede'.

108/26 *haddest songe*: shuldest synge *1533*, *cantaueris* (subjunctive). See the Introduction, p. xlvi.

108/26–8 *the ymage . . . cley*: For the creation of man out of clay, cf. Ovid, *Metamorphoses* 1: 82–8. For Prometheus's theft of fire, cf. Hesiod, *Works and Days*, 50 ff.; *Theogony*, 565 ff. and Aeschylus, *Prometheus Bound*, 107 ff. For Prometheus and Pandora's box, see above, 99/25–100/1 n.

108/27 *deceyte*: subtyltie *1533*, *dolo* (deceit).

108/28 *gaue*: to gyue *1533*, *animasse*.

108/28–109/5 Sidenote 1, *A great . . . lyghtnynge*: Not in Lt.

109/10–14 Sidenote 1: The Lt. has only *Pocula Circes*.

109/11 *agaynst nature*: *inuita Minerua*. Festugière explains this phrase as 'malgré les dispositions naturelles' (p. 145 n. 2.).

109/11–14 *If . . . beestes*: Cf. *Odyssey* 10: 282–320.

109/14–16 *If . . . vse them*: For Tantalus, see above, 93/11–12 n.

109/16–17 *The stone . . . myserable*: For Sisyphus, see above, 93/11–12 n.

109/17–19 *If . . . infatygable*: For the labours of Hercules, see Apollodorus, *The Library*, trans. Sir James George Frazer (London, 1939), *1*, 185–237.

109/21–4 *the infantes . . . fraude*: Cf. Gen. 25: 22–34 and 27: 1–29. 109/23 *a messe of potage*: According to the *OED*, this phrase (see MESS *sb.* I. 2.) was 'proverbially current in allusions to the story of Esau's sale of his birthright (Gen. xxv: 29–34)'. The *OED* notes its use in 1526: *Pilg. Perf.* (W. de W., 1531), I, xi. 30; in the Bibles of 1537 and 1539, and in the Geneva Bible of 1560.

109/24–5 *Golye . . . Dauid*: Cf. 1 Kgs. 17: 49.

109/25 *the heare . . . shauen*: Cf. Judges 16: 19.

109/28–9 *the history of Titus Liuius*: Livy's *Ab Urbe Condita Libri* presented the history of Rome from 753 to 9 BC. Using the materials and form of the earlier annals, Livy emphasized Republican integrity and freedom as the heritage of Augustan Rome.

109/29 *so that*: so *1533*, *modo* (provided that).

109/30 *in that historye*: in the one / that is to say Titus Liuyus *1533*, *in illa*; *are*: be *1533*, *insunt*; *may amende*: wolde amende *1533*, *emendent*.

110/1 *are*: be *1533*, not in Lt.

110/1–9 *in the other . . . spiryte*: Cf. Augustine, *De Doctrina*, *PL*, xxxiv, 77–8.

110/3 *may hurt*: shulde hurte *1533*, *officiant* (may hinder).

110/3–4 *theft . . . homicide*: Cf. 2 Kgs. 11: 2–27.

110/4–5 *The vehement loue of Sampson*: om. *1533*, *Sampson perdite amans*. Cf. Judges 16: 1–19.

110/3–5 Sidenote 1: Not in Lt.

110/6 *were conceyued*: conceyued *1533*, not in Lt. *1534* gives the passive form and meaning of *conceive* (*OED*, 3. *pass.*, to be made pregnant). Cf. 1563–87: Foxe *A. & M.* (1596) 1341/1, 'The Queene was conceived and quicke with child.' For Lot's daughters, cf. Gen. 19: 30–6.

110/7 *euery where despised, but*: dispysed *1533*, *ubique contempta*.

110/9–10 *Manna . . . mouth*: Cf. Wisd. 16: 21.

110/12–14 *Dionisius . . . god*: The *De Divinis Nominibus* of Pseudo-Dionysius discusses the Godhead under the aspects of Good, Unity and Trinity, Beauty, Love, Being, Life, Wisdom, Intelligence and Reason. See Dionysius the Areopagite, *On the Divine Names and The Mystical Theology*, trans. C. E. Rolt, Translations of Christian Literature, Series I: Greek Texts, No. 1 (New York, 1920).

110/14–16 *Augustyne . . . man*: Augustine wrote Books One to Three of the *De Doctrina Christiana* in AD 396 as an introduction to scriptural interpretation, emphasizing the allegorical method. In AD 426 he added Book Four, adapting Ciceronian rhetoric for the Christian preachers of the Scriptures.

110/15–16 *the doctryne of a christen man*: The Eng. title parallels that of Tyndale's *Obedience of a Christian Man* (Antwerp, 1528), *STC* 24446.

110/17 *allegoryes*: allegorye *1533*, *allegoriarum*; *Origene*: See above, 49/9–10 n. Sidenote 3, *Allegoryes*: Allegory *1533*, *allegorias*.

110/20 *dreamyngly and vnfruytfully: frigide* (lifelessly). The subject-matter and diction of this phrase are the same as the first usage recorded in the *OED* (*s.v.* DREAMINGLY): 1545, Coverdale, *Writ. & Transl.* (1844) 511, 'Allegories handled, not dreamingly or unfruitfully.'

110/24 *bycause*: that *1533*, *quod*.

110/25 *colde*: weake *1533*, *frigere*.

110/25–6 *kendled with the fyre of eloquence*: fortyfyed with strengthe of eloquence *1533*, *eloquentiae uiribus . . . condiatur*.

110/28 *for so moche as*: for *1533*, *quod*; *contented*: content *1533*, *contenti*.

111/2 *Pictagoras*: Pythagoras (*fl.* 530 BC) founded a quasi-religious community in southern Italy which aimed at purification of soul in order to escape transmigration.

111/2–6 *Augustyne . . . scripture*: Cf. *De Civitate Dei*, PL, xli, 229–33.

111/4 *of open and clere: figuratum* (adorned with figures of speech).

111/5 *we haue sayd*: I haue sayde before *1533*, *diximus*.

111/10 *and*: whiche men *1533*, *qui*.

111/15 *contencyons*: contencion *1533*, *concertationem*; *of argumentes*: scholasticam (Scholastic).

111/19 *the letter which kylleth*: Cf. 2 Cor. 3: 6.

111/21–2 *the vayle ... Moyses*: Cf. 2 Cor. 3: 13–16.

111/22–4 *Paule ... obscurely*: Cf. 1 Cor. 13: 12.

111/23 *seeth*: saythe *1533, uidet*; *speculum and*: *speculum 1533, speculum, et*; *that is through*: not the thynge selfe and clerely / but the ymage or symylitude of the very thynge as it were in *1533*, internal gloss.

111/24 *And*: and as *1533, Et ut.*

111/25–6 *The flesshe ... lyfe*: John 6: 64.

111/26 *I ... durst not haue sayd*: I ... wolde haue ben afrayde to haue sayd *1533, Mihi ... religio fuisset dicere* (It would have been a responsibility for me to say). See the Introduction, p. xlviii.

111/27 *had ben*: shold haue ben *1533, fuerat futurum*; *for me to say*: to saye *1533*, not in Lt.

111/30–112/1 *it is ... spiryte*: Cf. Rom. 8: 13; 2 Cor. 3: 6.

112/1–2 *vnto this thynge*: in this thynge *1533, hoc.*

112/11 *Esaias*: Cf. Isa. 40: 6–8.

112/15 *fruytes ... nombreth*: Cf. Gal. 5: 22–3.

112/15–16 Sidenote 1: Not in Lt.

112/16 *casteth of*: counseyleth from her *1533, dissuadet* (advises against).

112/18–19 *pullyng ... pytte*: Cf. Luke 14: 5.

112/19 *restoringe ... blynde*: Cf. Mark 8: 22–6.

112/19–20 *rubbynge ... corne*: Cf. Luke 6: 1–4.

112/20 *vnwasshen handes*: Cf. Matt. 15: 20; *the feestes of synners*: Cf. Matt. 9: 10–13.

112/21 *parable ... publycane*: Cf. Luke 18: 10–14; *fastynges*: Cf. Matt. 6: 16–18.

112/21–2 *the carnall bretherne*: Cf. Rom. 9: 3–5.

112/22–3 *the reioysynge ... Abraham*: Cf. Matt. 3: 9.

112/23 *offryng ... temple*: Cf. Matt. 5: 23–4.

112/24 *prayynge*: Cf. Matt. 6: 5–6; *dilatyng their philateirs*: delatyng of theyr philateirs *1533, in philacterijs dilatatis*. Cf. Matt. 23: 5. 'Phylacteries' are four texts of Scripture (Deut. vi. 4–9 and xi. 13–21, Ex. xiii. 1–10 and 11–16) written in Hebrew letters on vellum and contained in a small leather box, worn by Jews during morning prayer on all days except the sabbath, as a reminder of the obligation to keep the law (cf. *OED*, PHYLACTERY 1.).

112/23–7 Sidenote 2: Not in Lt.

112/26–7 *in the syght of man ... in the syght of god*: The internal glosses add antithesis.

112/27–31 *byleue . . . verite*: John 4: 21, 23, 24.

112/34–5 *at the maryage . . . spiryte*: Cf. John 2: 1–10; Gregory the Great, *Homiliarum in Ezeckielem Prophetam*, *PL*, lxxvi, 831.

113/4–5 *he dispysed . . . spirytually*: Cf. 1 Cor. 11: 27–9.

113/6–8 *the flesshe . . . lyfe*: Cf. John 6: 64.

113/9 *agnus dei*: *cruce aerea* (a copper cross). An agnus dei is an oval piece of wax impressed with the image of Christ as the Paschal Lamb on the obverse and with the pope's coat of arms on the reverse. It is worn suspended from the neck as a protection against the devil, sickness, and sudden death.

113/16–17 *art not ones moued with . . . no no more than if they*: Not in Lt.

113/21–3 *one . . . churche*: Cf. 1 Cor. 6: 15–17.

113/30–4 *Many . . . agayne*: Cf. 'I don't condemn their custom [of attending daily Mass], of course, especially when they have plenty of leisure or are persons who spend the whole day in worldly occupations. I simply disapprove of those who persuade themselves superstitiously that the day will be unlucky unless they begin it with Mass and who go straight from church to trade or moneymaking or court where, if their business succeeds—whether by hook or crook—they attribute success to the Mass' ('The Whole Duty of Youth', *Colloquies*, pp. 36–7).

113/32–4 Sidenote 2: Not in Lt.

114/1 *pite*: pite / that is to say of pure lyfe or seruyce of god *1533, pietatis*. See the Introduction, p. xlv.

114/4–5 *discusse . . . bosome*: *Excute te intus in sinu.* Cf. Vulgate: *Insuper excussi sinum meum*, 2 Esdras 5: 13 and Cicero, *Epistulae ad Quintum Fratrem* II. xiii. 1, *in sinu est*.

114/18 *stayned*: inquinate *1533, inquinatus* (dirty).

114/18–19 *The body*: Thy body *1533, caro*.

114/21–2 *But if . . . lyfe*: Cf. Rom. 6: 4.

114/25 *the mynde*: thy mynde *1533, animo*.

114/27 *that is to vnderstande*: that is to be vnderstande *1533, puta* (for example). The *OED* notes that 'understand' as a past participle form was common till about 1575.

114/29 *woldest counterfayte*: sholdest counterfayte *1533, imiteris* (subjunctive).

114/30 *dyddest labour*: woldest labour *1533, labores* (subjunctive).

115/1 *Fraunces*: For St. Francis, see above, 9/1 n.

115/3–4 *stubburne and selfe wylled . . . wyse in thyne owne opinyon*: Not in Lt.

115/6 *fylthy lucre*: See above, 12/28 n. and the Introduction, p. lii.

115/8 *with ... yuell*: Cf. Rom. 12: 21.

115/9 *thousande*: *centum*.

115/10–13 *Thou ... a lyue*: Cf.

'Phaedrus: A Franciscan tunic was spread over him ... A cowl was placed at his head ...

Marcolphus: A new kind of death!

Phaedrus: But they swear the devil has no jurisdiction over those who die thus. So, they say, St. Martin and St. Francis, among others, died.

Marcolphus: But *their* liues correspond to this kind of death.'

('The Funeral', *Colloquies*, p. 368)

115/14 *of pure life*: pure lyfe *1533*, *pietatis*. Sidenote 1: Not in Lt.

115/15 *is fette*: shewynge how thou sholdest honour god in euery thynge is fette *1533*, *petitur*; *commodyously*: commodyously in suche maner / that in no wyse thou canst be deceyued *1533*, *comodissime*.

115/18 *euery one ... laboure to*: euery saynt loke thou *1533*, *singulorum ... stude*.

115/18–19 *one vyce ... one vertue*: all vyces / vyce by vyce / so that thou sacryfyse to euery saynt syngularly some one vyce syngularly / or else study to enbrace and counterfayte some one syngular vertue in euery saynt / suche as thou perceyuest to haue reigned moost chefely in euery saynt / syngularly of them whiche thou worshyppest so specyally *1533*, *singula uitia ..., aut singulas uirtutes amplecti*. See the Introduction, p. xxxvii.

115/19 *If this be done inwardly*: If this shall comme to passe *1533*, *Hoc si accesserit*; 'inwardly' is supplied by the translator to balance 'outwardly' (115/20).

115/25–6 *preposterous and out of ordre*: preposterous and out of ordre / and accordynge to the commune prouerbe / the carte set before the horse *1533*, *praepostera*. See the Introduction, p. xlvi.

116/7 *vnfaythfull*: *fideles*, emended by the Eng. translator probably to contrast with 'faythfull' (116/8). Sidenote 1: Not in Lt.

116/10 *mayst lerne*: myghtest lerne *1533*, *discas* (present tense).

116/14–15 Sidenote 3: Not in Lt. Apelles was a fourth-century BC Greek painter who did a portrait of Alexander the Great wielding the thunderbolts of Zeus. His most famous painting was that of Venus rising from the sea.

116/16 *wordes*: oracyon *1533*, *oratione* (language).

116/19 *vnlykenesse*: vnlyke thynge *1533*, *dissimilitudinis*.

116/21 *deducted and deryued*: deducte and deryuate *1533*, *ductam*.

116/23–4 *the worde ... hert*: Cf. John 1: 1, 18.

116/31 *alienate, straunger and farther of*: The doublets define 'alienate'; see the Glossary.

117/1 *rauysshed*: rapte *1533*, not in Lt.

117/8–12 *ye iewes . . . Christ*: Cf. Luke 22: 47–54.

117/12–13 *ye flesshe . . . at all*: Cf. John 6: 64.

117/13–16 *that . . . also*: Cf. Augustine, *Sermo 215*, *PL*, xxxviii, 1074.

117/16 *While thapostels*: The apostles *1533*, *Apostoli donec*.

117/23–5 *after . . . faythe*: Cf. Mark 16: 14.

117/25 Compare the *Enchiridion*'s 'cast in their tethes' with Tyndale's 'cast in their tethe'. For Tyndale, see the Introduction, p. lii. According to the *OED*, 'A double plural *teeths* was formerly (and is still *dial.*) used in speaking of a number of persons. . . .' See also the Glossary.

117/27–8 *except . . . departe*: John 16: 7.

117/30–1 *y^t is to say, the loue and honour of god*: Internal gloss on 'pyte'.

117/31 *flessh*: his humanite *1533*, *carne*.

117/33–4 *Though . . . not so*: 2 Cor. 5: 16.

118/1 *ascended . . . spiryt*: Cf. 1 Cor. 12: 31.

118/6 *euen for this cause*: yea for this causeth *1533*, *uel hoc . . . adfert* (euen causes this).

118/7 *pyte*: godly loue or holynes *1533*, *pietati*.

118/10 *ther are none . . . cured*: none are . . . cured *1533*, *nulla . . . corriguntur*.

118/11 *thynken*: thynketh (singular) *1533*, *credit* (believes).

118/15–16 *lokyng . . . aduauntage*: Cf. Rom. 16: 18.

118/23–4 *yonge . . . man*: Cf. 1 Cor. 3: 1–2, Eph. 4: 13.

118/29–30 *in stede of inuysible*: *ob visibilia* (in return for visible things). Himelick translates the phrase, 'for the sake of material considerations' (*Enchiridion*, p. 114).

118/30–135/16 *and^1 . . . scylence*: This passage was placed on the *Index Expurgatorius* . . . (Antwerp, 1571) (Bataillon, p. 258 n.).

118/33 *to be withdrawen*: that thou be withdrawen *1533*, *auocari*.

119/1–2 *to fall in to a certayne iewysshnesse*: fall in to certeyn supersticion of ceremonyes lyke vnto the iewes *1533*, *in Iudaismum quendam recidere*. See the Introduction, p. xlvi.

119/7–9 *to call . . . spirytuall*: e.g. cf. Gal. 2: 14–16.

119/14–15 *If . . . seasoned*: Matt. 5: 13.

119/21–3 Sidenote 3: Not in Lt. St. Paul the Hermit fled to the Lower Thebiad during the persecution of Decius (AD 250), and remained in the Egyptian desert until his death *c.*341. St. Antony (250–356) distributed his wealth to the poor and embraced a solitary life first at home and then in the Egyptian desert. 119/20–2 *To these . . . Antonyes*: Cf. 'And now I am sure you perceive how much is owed to me by this class of men [preachers], who with their ceremonials and silly pedantries and bawling exercise a kind of despotism over mortal men, and believe themselves to be Pauls and Anthonies' (*Folly*, p. 93).

119/24–5 Sidenote 4: Not in Lt.

119/24–6 *after . . . them selfe*: Terence, *The Brothers* 1: 98–9.

120/5–6 *Thou shalte . . . thynges*: Not in Lt.

120/13 *shuldest be*: sholdest be but *1533, sis*.

120/13–14 *doynge seruyce . . . onely*: obseruyng onely vnfruytfull tradicyons and ceremonyes of the inuencyons of man *1533, mutis tantum elementis seruiens*. See below, 134/18–19 n. and the Introduction, p. xlvi.

120/14–15 *that . . . worlde*: Cf. Matt. 6: 1; *worlde 1533*: worde *1534, homines*; *if*: and yf *1533, si*.

120/15–16 *But . . . flesshe*: Rom. 8: 4.

120/16–23 *fruytes . . . chastyte*: Cf. Gal. 5: 22–3.

120/26 *this*: this to saye *1533, hoc*.

120/26–9 *I am . . . dedes*: Luke 18: 11–12.

120/27 *a weke*: in a weke *1533, in Sabbato*.

120/28 *humbly*: humble *1533, humilem* (adjective).

120/30 *is it I pray the*: These words, not in Lt., add vividness to the rhetorical address.

120/33–4 *whiche . . . god*: Cf. Matt. 15: 3.

120/34 *woldest transgresse*: sholdest transgresse *1533, transgrederis*.

121/2–17 *No . . . god*: Rom. 8: 1–8.

121/2 *graffed*: According to the *OED*, Tyndale was the first to use this sense (GRAFT 1. b., inserted with the result of producing a vital union) in 1531: *Exp. I John* ii (1538), 23, 'All they that are grafted into Christe to follow hys doctrine.'

121/5–6 *that thing . . . flesshe*: y^t which the lawe weyked by reason of the flesshe coude not performe or make good *1533, quod impossibile erat legi, que infirmabatur per carnem*.

121/13 *The wysdome*: for wysdom *1533, prudentia*.

121/23 *what*: that *1533*, *quod*; *wysdome of the flesshe*: Cf. 2 Cor. 1: 12.

121/24 *that they turned*: they turned it *1533*, *detorquent*.

121/24–5 *as they call it*: that they call *1533*, *quam uocant*.

121/25 *eyther other*: Only use of this sense recorded in *OED* (EITHER A. I. 1. d.) is by Tyndale: 15[30], *Lev*. Prol., 'For which cause either other of them were ordained'; *set vp their creestes*: Cf. Juvenal, *Satires* 4: 70.

121/27 *excellently vnlerned and ignorant*: starke fooles *1533*, *egregie indocti*. See the Introduction, p. xlvii. *But*: More ouer *1533*, *Caeterum* (moreover, but).

121/27–8 *to lyue in the spiryt*: Cf. Gal. 5: 25.

121/29–122/1 *as diligently . . . Tully*: Erasmus writes here against a defective knowledge of Cicero's language; later in the *Ciceronianus* (1528) he attacks an exclusive imitation of Cicero's style and vocabulary.

121/30 *manfully*: maliciously *1533*, *fortiter* (stoutly).

122/5–7 *Thou . . . Christ*: Cf. *Scopae dissolutae*. *Scopas dissoluere, Adagia*, I. v. 95 n. 1 (*OO, 2*, 218A).

122/10–16 *Let . . . god*: Col. 2: 18–19.

122/14–15 *body . . . ioyntes*: body by couples and ioyntes mynystred vp and compacte *1533*, *corpus per nexus et coniunctiones sumministratum, et constructum*; *couples*: The only instance which the *OED* gives for this usage (ligaments) is also a translation of Col. ii. 19 from Coverdale's New Testament of 1535.

122/19–22 *Yf . . . worlde*: Col. 2: 20.

122/23 *he sayth*: saith *1533*, *inquit*.

122/23–6 *yf . . . erth*: Col. 3: 1–2.

122/28 *Whether*: whether y^t *1533*, *num*.

122/31–3 *Mortifye . . . ydols*: Col. 3: 5. Sidenote 1: Not in Lt.

122/34 *after*: after that *1533*, *post*.

122/34–5 *Now . . . malyce*: Col. 3: 8.

122/35–123/2 *spoylyng . . . hym*[2]: Col. 3: 9–10.

123/3 *he . . . erth*: Cf. 1 Cor. 15: 47.

123/4 *whose . . . heuen*: Cf. Phil. 3: 20.

123/10 *as with ceremonyes*: as ceremonyes *1533*, *tanquam . . . ceremonijs*.

123/13–15 *Aboue . . . body*: Col. 3: 14–15. The *Enchiridion* gives 'charite' for Tyndale's 'love'. See the Introduction, p. lii.

123/14 *an ouercommer*: a victor *1533*, not in Lt.

123/21 *workes*: worke *1533*, *operum* (plural).

123/23–31 *The dedes . . . suche lyke*: Gal. 5: 19–21. This heavily glossed passage is a far cry from the spare translation in Tyndale: 'The dedes of the flesshe are manyfest, whiche are these, advoutrie, fornicacion, vnclennes, wantannes, ydolatrye, witchecraft, hatred, variaunce, zele, wrath, stryfe, sedicion, sectes, envyinge, murther, dronkennes, glottony, and soche lyke. . . .'

123/25 *vnshamefastnes*: to be shameles *1533*, *impudicitia* (incontinence).

123/31–2 *yf . . . spiryt*: Gal. 5: 25.

123/32–3 *declaryng and vtteryng*: *indicans*. According to the *OED* (UTTER II. 8), this sense was first used by Tyndale in 1526: *Mark* iii. 12, 'He streyghtly charged them that they shulde not vtter him.'

123/33–124/1 *let . . . an other*: Gal. 5: 26.

124/1 *The tree . . . fruite*: Cf. Matt. 7: 16.

124/1–2 *As vnto this that*: That *1533*, *Quod*.

124/5 *thy spiryte*: the spiryte *1533*, *spiritus*.

124/16–17 *taken . . . handes*: *interceptam*.

124/17 *for whiche*: for *1533*, *ob* (because of).

124/18 *father*: *parentem*, see above, 55/25 n. and the Introduction, p. lii.

124/19 *emulacyon and disdayne*: emulacion (whiche may be called indignacion or disdayne) *1533*, *emulationes*. See the Introduction, p. xlvi.

124/27 Sidenote 1: For 'Monkes' the Lt. reads *Orat ne offendantur monachi hoc sermone*. (He pleads that monks will not be offended by this discussion.)

124/33 *perteynen*: perteyneth *1533*, *pertinent*; the plural form of *1534* agrees with the Lt.

124/36–125/1 *But . . . the better*: Livy, XXI. iv. 1.

125/5 *certeyn dedes*: a labour *1533*, *labore*.

125/9–10 *sure and careless*: suertye and careles *1533*, *oscitantium* (yawning).

125/12–14 Sidenote 1: Not in Lt.

125/12 *those*: suche thynges *1533*, *ea* (these).

125/14–15 *euer . . . bondage*: Cf. Gal. 3: 23–4. The *Enchiridion* gives 'tuters or scholemaisters' as compared with Tyndale's 'scolemaster' and Douai–Rheims' 'pedagogue'. See the Introduction, p. lii.

125/15 *lyberty of the spiryte*: Cf. 2 Cor. 3: 17.

125/16 *large . . . charite*: Cf. Eph. 4: 13.

125/17–18 *stande . . . bondage*: Gal. 5: 1.

125/18–19 *and so was the lawe*: the lawe was *1533*, *Itaque lex . . . fuit*.

125/18–23 *and so was . . . Iesu*: Gal. 3: 24–6.

125/20 *myght be iustifyed*: sholde be iustyfyed *1533, iustificemur*.

125/23–31 *and we . . . god*: Gal. 4: 3–7.

125/32–4 *Bretherne . . . an other*: Gal. 5: 13–15. Compare the *Enchiridion's* 'charite' with Tyndale's 'love'. See the Introduction, p. lii.

126/2–4 *Ye . . . father*: Rom. 8: 15.

126/3 *the spiryte*[1] *. . . but*: The Eng. translator supplies the words missing from the scriptural quotation: *spiritum servitutis iterum in timore sed accepistis.*

126/4 *dade father*: *Abba pater*. Tyndale's NT gives 'Abba father'.

126/6–8 *Exercyse . . . thynges*: 1 Tim. 4: 7–8. The *Enchiridion* gives 'pietie' where Tyndale gives 'godlines'. See the Introduction, p. liii.

126/8–9 *God . . . lybertye*: 2 Cor. 3: 17.

126/10 *places*: places / whan *1533, locum*.

126/11 *mought be despysed*: sholde be despysed *1533, contemnatur*.

126/16 *stampeth in to vs*: mengleth with other sayinges *1533, inculcat* (tramples in, mixes in). See the Introduction, p. xlvii.

126/18 *This . . . Moyses*: Cf. Deut. 6: 5.

126/19 *This . . . gospell*: Cf. Matt. 22: 37; *iterateth*: According to the *OED* (*s.v.* 2), the first use of this sense, 'asserts repeatedly' occurred in 1533: *Supper of the Lord*, attributed to Tyndale, Wks. (Parker Soc.) III. 245, 'I am here compelled to inculk and iterate it with so many words.'

126/21–2 Sidenote 1: Not in Lt.

126/21–5 *After . . . an other*: Cf. John 13: 34–5 and 15: 12–13.

126/25–6 *What . . . an other*: Cf. 1 John 4: 7.

126/28–9 *he . . . aungelles*: Cf. 1 Cor. 13: 1–2.

126/32–3 *lady psalters, or saynt Katherynes knottes*: *preculas*; *lady psalters*: the long rosary of 150 Hail Marys. See J. B. Trapp, 'A double "mise en point" ', *Moreana*, 11 (1966), 48–50; *saynt Katherynes knottes*: Devotion to St. Catherine of Alexandria (d. 305) as one of the Fourteen Holy Helpers (*Vierzehnheiligen*) reached its culmination in the fifteenth century, though I have been unable to discover exactly what 'saynt Katherynes knottes' were.

126/34 *charite . . . neyghbour*: Cf. 1 Cor. 8: 1.

126/34–127/1 *compte . . . Chryst*: Cf. Rom. 12: 5.

127/1–2 *reioyse . . . owne*: Cf. 1 Cor. 12: 26.

127/3–5 *Yf . . . ignoraunt*: Cf. 2 Tim. 2: 24.

127/5–7 *lyfte . . . nedy*: Cf. 1 Thess. 5: 14.

127/20–3 Sidenote 2: Not in Lt.

127/23–5 *he wolde . . . apostles*: Cf. Augustine, *Regula ad servos Dei*, *PL*, xxxii, 1377–84.

127/33–5 Sidenote 4: Not in Lt. See above, 41/25–9 n.

127/35–128/3 *Paule . . . Christ*: Cf. Gal. 4: 31. Tyndale's NT omits the rest of this verse as given in the Vulgate: *qua libertate nos christus liberavit.*

128/3 *so be*: om. *1533, sed.*

128/3–4 *He . . . lawfully*: Cf. 1 Tim. 1: 8.

128/8 *to put . . . in them*: Not in Lt.

128/9–10 *The apostle . . . Abraham*: Cf. Rom. 4: 1–3.

128/10–18 Sidenote 2: Not in Lt.

128/13 *Neomenye*: The Jewish festival held at the beginning of the lunar month. Cf. 'Neomenia, the first day of the new moon next after the equinoctial . . .' ('Letter to John Harris', *St. Thomas More: Selected Letters*, p. 186).

128/17 *sore agreued*: agreued *1533, stomachantem* (angry, irritated, vexed).

128/17–129/1 *For . . . you*: Isa. 1: 11–15.

128/18 *your victimes*: victimes *1533, uictimarum uestrarum.*

128/19–22 Sidenote 3: Not in Lt.

128/23–5 Sidenote 4: Not in Lt.

128/24 *suffre*: suffre any more *1533, feram* (endure).

128/26 *kalendas*: The first day of any month in the Roman calendar (*OED*, CALENDS 1.).

128/26–7 Sidenote 5: Not in Lt.

128/28–129/1 Sidenote 6: Not in Lt.

128/28–129/1 *from you*: After this the Eng. omits *et cum multiplicaueritis orationes uestras, non exaudiam uos* (and when you multiply your prayers, I will not listen to you). See the Introduction, p. xl.

129/5 *prayers*: prayers / whiche they call dayly seruyce *1533, precum.* Sidenote 1: Not in Lt.

129/17–31 *Me . . . god*: Isa. 58: 2–5.

129/20–1 Sidenote 2: Present in Lt., *1534*; om. *1533.*

129/23 (*answereth the prophete*): Internal gloss. See the Introduction, p. xliii.

129/29 *bowe*: bowe downe *1533, contorquere.*

129/29–30 *cast vpon*: strawe vndernethe *1533, sternere* (strew).

X

130/2 *what*: that *1533*, *quid*; *wasshen*: wasshed *1533*, *Lauamini*.

130/3 *sayth*: sayd *1533*, *inquit* (present tense).

130/2–4 *Be . . . syght*: Isa. 1: 16.

130/6–8 *The eyes . . . eares*: Cf. Matt. 6: 4, Isa. 11: 3.

130/8–9 *God . . . inwarde*: Cf. Matt. 25: 1–12.

130/9–10 *He . . . maister*: Cf. Matt. 7: 21. Tyndale also has 'Master, Master' as compared with Douai–Rheims' 'Lord, Lord'.

130/13–15 *Seke . . . wydowe*: Isa. 1: 17.

130/16–23 *Is . . . flesshe*: Isa. 58: 6–7.

130/17 *whiche*: om. *1533*, *quod*; *Teare and cancell*: loose or cancell *1533*, *Dissolue*. Sidenote 2: Not in Lt.

130/21 *them whiche haue no place of habytacion*: them whiche hath no place of habytacion *1533*, *uagos* (wanderers).

130/29–30 *leest . . . dyed*: 1 Cor. 8: 11.

130/34–5 *God . . . sacryfyce*: Cf. John 4: 24.

131/3–4 *If . . . mynde*: See *Disticha Catonis*, eds. Marcus Boas and Henricus Johannes Botschuyver (Amsterdam, 1952), 1 : 1; *se thou honoure*: se that thou honour *1533*, *tibi . . . sit . . . colendus*.

131/5 *though he be*: beyng eyther *1533*, *uel*.

131/6 *without degre of schole*: *minutum* (insignificant).

131/8 *The sentence*: The intellectyon of the sentence *1533*, *Ea*.

131/8–9 *lyke . . . lyke*: See above, 106/4–5 n.; *in lyke*: with lyke *1533*, *similibus*.

131/11–12 *without doute a mynde*: veryly mynde *1533*, *quidem* [*mens*].

131/14 *thynkest*: thynkest that *1533*, *putas*; *to be a*: is *1533*, understood in Lt.

131/14–15 *but . . . spyrite*: Ps. 50: 19.

131/15–16 *And . . . calues*: Cf. Isa. 1: 11.

131/16–17 *yet . . . humble*: See above, 131/14–15 n.

131/15–17 Sidenote 1: The Eng. 'Inwarde thynges . . .' mistranslates the Lt. *Exteris rebus*. . . .

131/18–19 *that that thyng be not away*: that thyng not to be away *1533*, not in Lt.

131/22 *the inner man*: thy inner maner *1533*, *interioris hominis*.

131/22–3 *the vestymentes . . . snowe*: Cf. Ps. 50: 9; *be also whyte as snowe*: be white as snowe also agreable to the same *1533*, *sint et . . . candida, sicut nix*.

131/25 *that is nothyng worthe*: that is nothynge worthy *1533*, *nihil agitur*.

131/28–31 *Thou . . . also*: Cf. Matt. 15: 17–20.

131/32 *coddes, draffe*: coddes of beenes / peson *1533*, *siliquis* (husks).

131/32–3 *glutteth . . . swyne*: Cf. Luke 15: 16.

132/2–4 *whose . . . Egypt*: Cf. Ezek. 8: 7–9.

132/5–6 Sidenote 1: Not in Lt.

132/9–10 *With . . . cursest*: Cf. Ps. 61: 5.

132/13–14 *Except . . . wepe*: Cf. Jer. 13: 17.

132/15 *they whiche se may not se*: whan they se they shulde not se *1533*, *uidentes non uideant*. 132/15–16 *they whiche here maye not here*: whan they here they shulde not here *1533*, *audientes non audiant*. For the reference cf. Matt. 13: 13, Luke 8: 10.

132/16–17 *with . . . perceyue*: Isa. 6: 9, Jer. 5: 21.

132/19–22 *This . . . hemmes*: Cf. Ps. 44: 11, 14.

132/20 *Dauyd commaundeth*: is commaunded *1533*, *iubetur a Dauid*.

132/21 *beautye and godlynesse*: beautye and goodlynesse *1533*, *decor*.

132/23–4 *outwarde . . . inwarde*: Supplied by the Eng. translator to emphasize the contrast of ideas.

132/25–32 *Is . . . buryeng*: Cf. 'This man leaves wife and children at home and sets out on a pilgrimage to Jerusalem, Rome, or the shrine of St. James, where he has no particular business' (*Folly*, p. 70).

133/1–3 *Thou . . . wexe*: Cf. 'Then what shall I say of the people who so happily fool themselves with forged pardons for sins, measuring out time to be spent in purgatory as if with an hour-glass, and figuring its centuries, years, months, days, and hours as if from a mathematical table, beyond possibility of error?' (*Folly*, p. 56).

133/2 *to be washen awaye*: to be wasshed away *1533*, *elui*.

133/2–3 *with a lytell . . . wexe*: Not in Lt.

133/8–9 *Swete . . . swete*: Cf. Isa. 5: 20.

133/13–14 *Magdaleyne . . . her*: Cf. Luke 7: 47.

133/20 *worlde 1533*: worde *1534*, *mundi*.

133/27 *and to the thynges whiche be*: to thinges *1533*, *et ea quae . . . sunt*.

133/28 *as men . . . payne*: Not in Lt.; *these*: those *1533*, *isti* (those).

133/29 *not feble . . . chyldren*: Cf. Prov. 22: 15.

133/29–30 *dry . . . lyfe*: Cf. Ezek. 37: 1–3.

133/33-4 Sidenote 3: Not in Lt.

134/2 *him*: them *1533, eos*.

134/5 *Philautia*: Cf. φιλαυτίαν, *Adagia*, I. iii. 92 (*OO*, 2, 147C); *Folly*, pp. 13, 29, 30, 59, 61, 73. *Philautia*: According to the *OED*, Tyndale was the first to use this word (PHILAUTY) in 152[8]: *Obed. Chr. Man* Pref., *Wks.* (1537) 103, 'They will say yet more shamefully, that no man can vnderstand the Scriptures without Philautia, that is to say Philosophy.'

134/7-8 *that we . . . iniquite*: Cf. Isa. 59: 4.

134/10-11 *I . . . knowlege*: Rom. 10: 2.

134/11 *acording to*: after *1533, secundum*.

134/12 *thend . . . Christ*[1]: Rom. 10: 4.

134/12-13 *Christ*[2] *. . . spyrit*: Cf. John 4: 24.

134/13 *he . . . charyte*: Cf. 1 John 4: 8. For the use of 'charyte' see the Introduction, p. lii.

134/15-17 *Therfore . . . thurste*: Isa. 5: 13.

134/18 *elementes*: lawe *1533, elementis*. 134/18-19 *seruauntes . . . worlde*: Cf. Gal. 4: 3, Col. 2: 20. Tyndale's 1526 NT has 'ordinacions' and Tyndale's 1534 NT has 'ordinaunces' for the *Enchiridion*'s 'elementes and princyples'.

134/23-4 *Bycause . . . loues*: Cf. John 6: 9-13.

134/27-8 *Moyses . . . rocke*: Cf. Exod. 17: 6.

134/28 *rocke*: rocke of stone *1533, petra*.

134/28-30 *neyther . . . Christ*: Cf. John 7: 38.

134/29 *flowe, issue, or spring*: floweth / issueth / or springeth (singular) *1533, fluunt*.

134/30 *this surely was spoken*: that was spoken verely *1533, Hoc autem dictum est*.

134/33 *thou mayste . . . waxe bygge*: myghtest . . . waxe bygge *1533, grandis . . . euadas* (present subjunctive).

134/33-4 *enbrasyng*: enbrace *1533, amplexus* (embrace).

134/34 *mynde . . . grounde with*: and crepe not alwaye on the grounde with the *1533, ne uelis cum immundis animalibus humi reptare*.

135/1-3 *those . . . mynde*: Cf. Plato, *Phaedrus* 251A-B.

135/3 *mynde*: mynde of men *1533, animis*; *by certayne steppes*: with certayne steppes *1533, gradibus quibusdam*. 135/3-4 *steppes . . . Iacob*: Cf. Gen. 28: 12.

135/3-5 Sidenote 1, *flee*: flye *1533, euolandum* (fly). According to the *OED*, confusion between 'flee' and 'fly' has occurred since the Old English period (see *OED*, FLEE).

135/7–9 *Who so euer . . . hym*: Cf. Jas. 4: 8.

135/9–16 *And . . . scylence*: Cf. Pseudo-Dionysius, *De Mystica Theologia*, *PG*, iii, 998–9. This passage, I believe, is the most spiritually exalted one in the entire *Enchiridion*.

135/10–12 Sidenote 2: Not in Lt.

135/12–15 Sidenote 3: Not in Lt.

135/12 *this lyght*: his lyght *1533*, *luce sua*; *lyght inaccessyble*: 1 Tim. 6: 16. Cf. Tyndale's 1526 NT, 'light that no man can obtayne' and Tyndale's 1534 NT, 'light that no man can attayne'.

136/2 *he gothe bosydes*: goth besydes *1533*, *discedit*; *ronneth*: rometh *1533*, *currit*.

136/4 *bookes . . . comen welthe*: *politia* (*The Republic*).

136/4–7 *denyeth . . . honesty*: Cf. Plato, *Republic* 484C–D, 506A, 519C.

136/8 *synke*: shulde synke *1533*, *insidere* (to sink).

136/9 *Therfore*: For that consyderacion therfore *1533*, *Quare*.

136/20–1 *and kysses of the parentes*: whyles the father and mother kysse them *1533*, *et parentum oscula*. See above, 55/25 n. and the Introduction, p. lii.

136/23–5 *bycause . . . poured in*: Quintilian, *Institutio Oratoria*, I. viii. 4.

136/26 *yonge sucklynges*: lytle bodyes *1533*, *infantilibus*. See the Introduction, p. xlvii.

136/27 *home*: whom *1533*, *domi*.

136/31 *here*: let them here *1533*, not in Lt.

136/31–137/1 *alas . . . lefte alone*: alas that euer she was borne / seyng that she is but a wretche a woman loste or cast awaye *1533*, *se miseram ac destitutam*.

137/7 *towe catcheth fyre*: thou catchest fyre *1533*, *ignem uicinum naptha* (petroleum near fire).

137/10 *of*: from *1533*, *ex*; *be planted*: myght be planted *1533*, *inserantur*.

137/12 *coulde be shake*: coulde be shaken *1533*, *queant conuelli*. *1534* omits *1533*'s nasal sign.

137/15 *worthy . . . not to be counterfayted*: worthy . . . not to be counterfayte *1533*, *non imitatione dignos*. *1533* follows the Old French original more closely than *1534*. (See *OED*, COUNTERFEIT *a.* and *pa. pple.*)

137/17 *thoughe . . . Arystotle*: Cf. *Nicomachean Ethics*, VI. xiii. 3 and VII. ii. 1–2.

137/17–19 *vertue . . . fledde*: Cf. Plato, *Protagoras* 352C, 357D–E.

137/21–4 *But . . . onely*: Cf. Cicero, *De Oratore* 3: 213, *Brutus* 142, *Orator* 56.

137/25–7 *Socrates . . . opinyons*: See above, 137/17–19 n.

137/27 *brother*: Not in Lt. The direct address adds warmth to the voice of the speaker.

137/29 *money*: many *1533, pecuniam.*

137/30 *eyther*: to eyther *1533, utrique. 1533* correctly translates the Latin dative case.

138/1 *whiche*: that which *1533, quod.*

138/9–10 *in to the substaunce of the body*: Not in Lt.

138/21 *the worst thinges haue pleased*: the worste hath pleased *1533, placuerint* (plural).

138/24–5 *This . . . kynges | this . . . men*: The Eng. reverses the order of the Lt. clauses, putting 'kynges' before 'great men'.

138/26 *trewly be no rascals*: veryly ben no comen people *1533, profecto uulgus non sunt.* See the Introduction, p. xlvii.

138/27–139/19 Sidenote 2: Not in Lt.

139/1–4 *Who so euer . . . thynges*: Cf. '. . . what difference is there between those who in Plato's cave look admiringly at the shadows and simulacra of various things, desiring nothing, quite well satisfied with themselves, as against the wise man who emerges from the cave and sees realities?' (*Folly*, p. 64, referring to *Republic* 514A–515C).

139/4–6 *Shulde . . . stone*: Cf. *Lesbia regula, Adagia,* I. v. 93 (*OO, 2,* 217C).

139/15–16 *It . . . heuen*: Cf. Luke 12: 32; *as vnto . . . due*: as vnto whome doutlesse is due onely *1533, cui soli debetur.*

139/16–17 *Strayte . . . lyfe*: Cf. Matt. 7: 14.

139/18–19 *whether . . . or*: *utrum . . . an.* According to the *OED* (*s.v.* B. II. 3.), 'whether' is used to introduce a disjunctive dependent question expressing choice, usually with a correlative.

139/20 *paterns*: patrons *1533*, internal gloss on 'tables'. See the Glossary for 'paterns' and 'patron'.

139/23–4 *it shall . . . euery thynge*: *unumquodque in exemplum uocare conueniet.* A clearer Eng. translation would read, '. . . it shall be meet that thou consider everything as an example.'

139/26–7 *as moche as concerneth*: as appertaynyng to *1533, quantum . . . attinet.*

139/29–30 *y^t fayth . . . nothynge*: Cf. Jas. 2: 14; *y^t*: om. *1533*, understood in Lt.

139/31–3 Sidenote 2: Not in Lt.

COMMENTARY 271

140/1–2 Sidenote 1: Not in Lt.

140/1–3 *forsoth . . . beautye*: Horace, *Epistles*, I. vi. 36–7.

140/4–5 *noblenes . . . strawe*: Horace, *Satires*, II. v. 8.

140/5 *now*: om. *1533, iam.*

140/6–7 *Oh . . . vertue*: Horace, *Epistles*, I. i. 53–4. Lt. *nummos* (cash) is more vivid than Eng. 'money'.

140/12 *in other*: in other men suffrynge them vnpunysshed *1533, in alijs.*

140/15 *In tyme past*: In tyme paste against *1533, Olim in.*

140/15–16 Sidenote 2, *The lybertie of olde tyme*: *Antiqua Comaedia scite notatis uitijs plausum uulgi meruit* (When vices were skilfully censured, ancient comedy deserved the applause of the common people).

140/18 *and that by authorite*: ye with authoryte *1533, de plaustris* (from the wagons). Cf. *De Plaustro loqui, Adagia*, I. vii. 73 (*OO, 2*, 290F). This proverb refers to the licence allowed to the writers of Old Comedy to attack on the stage leading citizens and even the gods; the adage was extended to include any open attack. Wagon processions formed part of the vintage celebration and were associated with early Greek comedy.

140/24 *nobles and estates*: *proceribus* (nobles). Since 'estates' is a doublet for 'nobles', the class referred to here is probably the Second Estate, barons and knights (*OED*, ESTATE 6.).

140/24–141/6 *The athenes . . . comme*: Cf. Seneca, *Epistulae Morales* 115: 14–16.

140/24–5 *in theyr commune house . . . enterludes*: *theatra*. 'Interludes' (cf. 1.4) were dramatic presentations, usually of a light or humorous character, inserted between the acts of the mystery-plays and moralities or between the courses of a banquet at a manor house (*OED, s.v.* 1.).

140/26–141/15 Sidenote 3: Not in Lt.

140/26 *a certeyn tragedy of Euripides*: Danaë, Frag. 324 (Richard M. Gummere, ed., *Epistulae Morales, 3*, 328 n.).

141/3–4 *had not the poete . . . desyred*: except the poete . . . had desired *1533, ni . . . Poeta . . . iussisset.*

141/5 *of money*: at money *1533, auri.*

141/6 *in the gentyles, hystoryes*: in the hystories of gentyles *1533, apud illos exempla* (among them examples).

141/16–20 *Phocion . . . Cato*: Phocion (*c.*402–318 BC) refused to accept the hundred talents sent him by Alexander the Great after a peace embassy and requested instead the release of four Greek prisoners. Cf. Plutarch, 'Phocion', *Parallel Lives of Greeks and Romans*, 18. The Eng. sidenote erroneously connects the anecdote of the gifts with Philip of Macedonia.

When arranging for the ransom of Roman prisoners in 280 BC, Fabricius Luscinus resisted the bribes of King Pyrrhus, much to the admiration of the latter.

After the sack of Rome by the Gauls (389 BC), Marcus Furius Camillus (d. 365 BC) rallied the citizens to drive out the invaders and rebuild the capital, thus earning for himself the title of 'Second Founder of Rome'.

When two of his own sons were convicted of plotting to restore Tarquinius to the throne, Lucius Junius Brutus sentenced them to death and witnessed their execution.

For Pythagoras, see above, 111/2 n.

Socrates (469–399 BC) was noted for his powers of physical endurance and his indifference to comfort and luxury.

It is not clear which Cato the text refers to and the Eng. translator does not give us a sidenote here. Marcus Porcius Cato (234–149 BC) bitterly opposed the debilitating influence of Hellenistic culture on Roman life. Marcus Porcius Cato Uticensis (95–46 BC), great-grandson of the elder Cato, earned a reputation for uncompromising honesty as Roman tribune, conqueror of Cyprus and governor of Utica in North Africa.

141/16–142/8 Sidenote 1: Not in Lt.

141/23–142/2 *Holy . . . mariage*: Cf. Augustine, *Confessions, PL*, xxxii, 693–4 and 731–2.

141/24 *he hym selfe*: he of hym selfe *1533, ipse de se*.

142/5 *Or yf*: or els if *1533, Aut si*.

142/6 *asse amonge apes*: Cf. *Asinus inter simias, Adagia*, I. v. 41 (*OO, 2*, 198E).

142/11 *more worthy*: more *1533, magis* (more).

142/15 *dyd not . . . appertayne*: as it . . . pertayned not *1533, aut non . . . pertineat*.

142/19 *worthy to be nombred*: to be nombred *1533, ponendum*.

142/22 *the wyse . . . worlde*: Cf. Luke 16: 8.

142/29 *they thynke*: thynke *1533, iudicent*.

142/30–143/4 Sidenote 4: Not in Lt.

143/1 *Democritus*: Democritus (*c.*460–*c.*370 BC) is known as 'the Laughing Philosopher' because of his response to human folly. Cf. Juvenal, *Satires* 10: 33–4 and 47–53.

143/3 *graffed . . . him*: Cf. Rom. 11: 17.

143/3–4 *to be one . . . god*: Cf. 1 Cor. 12: 12 and 6: 17.

143/5–6 *that thou . . . god*: Cf. 1 John 3: 1. The Eng. translator puts the Lt. clauses in a more climactic order with 'art called' followed by 'art so in dede'.

143/8–9 *Dauyd . . . god*: Cf. Ps. 83: 11.

143/9–10 *Take . . . worlde*: Cf. 1 Cor. 1: 27–8.

143/9 *chose*: choseth *1533*, *elegerit*. *1534* gives the correct sequence of tenses with the perfect subjunctive.

143/10–11 *In Adam . . . degre*: Cf. 1 Cor. 15: 47; *be all borne*: all are borne *1533*, *omnes . . . nascimur*.

143/11 *In . . . one*: Cf. Rom. 12: 5; *be all one*: are all one thyng neyther hygh ne lowe of degre one more than another *1533*, *omnes unum sumus*.

143/17–19 *not ryche . . . hym selfe*: Cf. Gen. 13: 2, 14: 14–16 and 22: 12.

143/21–2 *ye are . . . do*: John 8: 44.

143/22–3 Sidenote 2: Not in Lt.

143/23–5 *Not . . . Abraham*: Cf. Rom. 9: 6–7.

143/27–8 *Chryst . . . heuen*: Cf. Matt. 7: 21.

143/31–2 *who so euer . . . father*: Cf. John 8: 44.

143/32–3 *excepte . . . lye*: Cf. John 14: 6.

143/33–4 *the sone . . . Chryst*: Cf. Rom. 8: 16–17.

144/1 *let them loke*: let them take hede *1533*, *ipsi uiderint*.

144/2 *yet moost honourable*: the most honourable *1533*, *sed tamen illustrissima*.

144/4 *whiche . . . body*: Cf. Gal. 6: 14, 17.

144/11–12 *whiche . . . goodes*: Cf. Matt. 13: 46.

144/13–14 *whiche . . . rychesse*: Cf. Prov. 8: 11, Ecclus. 1: 26.

144/15 *golde . . . fyre*: Cf. Apoc. 3: 18.

144/16 *wonder*: wondreth *1533*, *miratur*. *1533* treats the subject, 'the commune people', as singular; *1534*, as plural.

144/17 *lyuelode*: *praedia* (farms). Himelick translates *praedia* as 'real estate' (*Enchiridion*, p. 138). See the Glossary.

144/18–19 *thornes . . . gospell*: Cf. Matt. 13: 7.

144/20–1 *they . . . can folowe*: can folow *1533*, *possunt . . . sequi*.

144/21 *the strayte waye*: Cf. Matt. 7: 14.

144/24 *Mydas or Cresus*: For Midas, cf. Ovid, *Metamorphoses* 11: 100–45. For Croesus, the last king of Lydia (*c*.560–546 BC), cf. Herodotus, *1*, 30, 32.

144/24–5 Sidenote 4: Not in Lt.

144/25 *manfully*: vtterly *1533*, *fortiter*.

144/26–7 *He . . . lackyng*: Cf. Matt. 6: 33.

144/27–9 *He . . . pleasaunt*: Cf. Matt. 4: 4.

144/29 y^t *hath . . . him*: Cf. Rom. 13: 14.

145/3 *are*: is *1533*, *sunt*. See the Introduction, p. xlvi.

145/6 *laughter of Aiax*: After losing the arms of Achilles to Odysseus, Ajax slaughtered a flock of sheep, thinking they were his enemies. Madly laughing at his delusion of triumph, he slew himself in shame when he came to his senses. Cf. Sophocles, *Ajax*; *Ajacis risus*, *Adagia*, I. vii. 46 (*OO*, *2*, 280E).

145/6–26 Sidenote 1: Not in Lt.

145/14 *Who*: whiche *1533*, *Quo. Who . . . sauerly*: Cf. Ps. 33: 9.

145/14–15 *milesij sibarite . . . epicuryens*: Miletus, chief of the Ionian cities in south-west Asia Minor, had close contacts with Sybaris until the latter's destruction in 510 BC. Cf. *Fuere quondam strenui Milesij*, *Adagia*, I. ix. 49 (*OO*, *2*, 351F). A city of Magna Graecia on the Gulf of Tarentum, Sybaris became proverbially wealthy by monopolizing the Etruscan trade. The Eng. translator mistakenly assumes that *milesij sibarite* refers to one group of people rather than two. See 145/S. 1. Epicurean ethics taught that pleasure is the beginning and end of the good life. Although Epicurus (*c*.341–*c*.270 BC) held that pleasure should be sought in moderation, his philosophy was popularly misunderstood to advocate sensuality and luxury. See also Thompson, ed., 'Introduction to the Epicurean', *Colloquies*, pp. 535–7.

145/24 *gestynges*: According to the *OED*, Tyndale was the first to use this word in 1526: Eph. v. 4, 'Nether folishe talkyng, nether gestinge' (see *OED*, JESTING).

145/24–9 *If thou . . . ye other*: Cf. 'Beware, then, of thinking any Lucullus dines more enjoyably off the partridges, pheasants, doves, hares, wrasses, sheat-fish, or morays served to him than does a godly man off black bread, herbs, or legumes, with water or small beer or well-diluted wine for his drink' ('The Epicurean', *Colloquies*, p. 548).

145/27 *frutes*: *leguminibus Pythagoricis*. Cf. *Attic Nights of Aulus Gellius*, IV. xi. 4–5. For Pythagoras, see above, 111/2 n.

146/3 *call*: calleth *1533*, *appellat*. See 144/16 n.

146/6–7 *how be it forsothe, he loueth not hymself*: yet loueth he not hym selfe verily *1533*, *quanquam ne se quidem amat*. See the Introduction, p. xlvii.

146/7–8 *For . . . first*: Cf., e.g., Matt. 19: 19.

146/13 *flaterynges*: flateryng *1533*, *blanditijs*.

146/17–18 *father and mother*: *parentes*, see above, 55/25 n. and the Introduction, p. lii.

146/22 *other thynge*: other *1533*, *aliud*.

146/25–6 *wynketh or sheweth fauour*: wynke or fauoure them *1533*, *uel conniuet, uel etiam fauet*.

146/26 *do synne*: sinne *1533*; 146/27 *may synne*: might synne *1533*, *peccent* (present subjunctive).

146/29–30 *And shal I . . . loke vpon your . . . your*: I wyll . . . vysyte their . . . their *1533*, *Et non uisitabo . . . super . . . uestras . . . uestras.*

146/29–31 *And . . . adultery*: Osee 4: 14.

146/30–1 *doughters in lawe*: The Eng. *Enchiridion* correctly translates the Lt.'s *nurus*. The Vulgate gives *sponsas* and Douai–Rheims, 'spouses'.

146/32 *vysyte*: loke vpon *1533*, *Visitabo.*

146/32–3 *I . . . theym*: Ps. 88: 33–1.

146/33 *wyll not scater*: wyl not take *1533*, *non dispergam.*

147/1 *all . . . Chryst*: Cf. 2 Cor. 5: 17.

147/3 *is*: be *1533*, *est.*

147/12 *wyckednesse*: *imbecillitatem* (weakness).

147/14 *al be it, it is*: though it be *1533*, *Quanquam . . . est.*

147/21–4 *If . . . hym selfe*: Cf. Plato, *Gorgias* 508E and John Chrysostom, *Expositio in Psalmum 139, PG,* lv, 420.

147/23–4 *this . . . he*: the one . . . the other *1533*, *hic . . . ille.*

147/29 *fyrst*: om. *1533*, *prius.*

147/30 *more greuous*: moche more greuous *1533*, *multo atrocius.*

147/33–4 *reioyseth . . . Chryst*: Cf. Phil. 4: 13; *reioyseth he not*: reioyseth *1533*, *nonne gloriatur.*

147/35 *fyerse*: beyng fyerse *1533*, *ferox.*

148/2 *Contrary wyse*: On the other syde *1533*, *Contra.* See the Introduction, p. xlviii.

148/3 *receyuynge*: whan he hath receyued *1533*, *acceptam.*

148/5 *But yet*: ye but *1533*, *Immo.*

148/5–6 *farder . . . stomacke*: more contrary to the greatnesse of the mynde *1533*, *alienius a magnitudine animi.*

148/6 7 *to be puffed . . . quietnes*: to be put asyde from the quyet *1533*, *dimoueri a statu* (to be removed from the equilibrium). See the Introduction, p. xlvii.

148/7 *mynde*: spyrite *1533*, *mentis.*

148/10 *dyddest ouercomme*: shuldest ouercome *1533*, *superaris* (indicative).

148/11 *stomacke*: mynde *1533*, *animo.*

148/12–13 *to despyse . . . good*: Cf. Matt. 5: 44.

148/14 *scaleth*: scale *1533*, *superet* (subjunctive).

148/17 *can*: coulde *1533*, *possit* (present subjunctive); *hert*: mynde *1533*, *animum*; *can*: coulde *1533*, *possit* is understood here.

148/18 *harme*: After this the Eng. omits *bene mereri, de male merentibus* (to deserve well of those who deserve ill). See the Introduction, p. xl.

148/18–19 *praye . . . hym*: Cf. Luke 6: 28.

148/27 *forsothe . . . hysse at it*: yᵉ all the worlde repreue / refuse / and disalowe it *1533*, *sane, uel uniuersus mundus explodat, exibiletque*. See the Introduction, p. xlvii.

148/29 *all mortall men*: what soeuer is in the worlde *1533*, *quicquid est mortalium*; *alowe it*: alowe *1533*, *applaudat*.

149/1 *it*: om. *1533*, not in Lt.

149/4 *politykly*: om. *1533*, not in Lt.

149/8–9 *Thus . . . father*: Cf. John 8: 44.

149/9 *But . . . verite*: Cf. John 14: 6.

149/9–10 *Foole . . . from the*: Luke 12: 20.

149/10–13 *He had . . . more*: Cf. Luke 12: 16–19.

149/14 *to syt abrode*: *incubaret*. According to the *OED* (sɪᴛ B. 10. b.) the phrase means to take up the posture necessary for hatching eggs.

149/15–16 *dragon . . . flece*: Cf. Ovid, *Metamorphoses* 7: 149–51.

149/16 *men*: *ferae* (wild beasts).

149/19–21 *to gape . . . ysope*: For the fable, see *Caxton's Aesop*, ed. R. T. Lenaghan (Cambridge, Mass., 1967), p. 77. See the Introduction, p. xv.

149/20–4 Sidenote 2, *as . . . water*: Not in Lt.

149/24–5 *To refuse . . . aduauntage*: Terence, *The Brothers* 2: 216.

149/28–9 *shadowisshe lyfe*: presente lyfe whiche is but a shadow *1533*, *umbraticae uitae*.

149/29–30 *notwithstandynge . . . susteyned*: namely whan god (if we byleue yᵉ gospel) wyll minyster althing necessary for this lyfe / if we haue confydence in hym *1533*, *quod tamen fuerat suppeditandum a deo*; *god . . . susteyned*: Cf. Matt. 6: 31–3; *sufficyently . . . susteyned*: Not in Lt.

149/31 *prouyde nothyng at all*: make no prouysion atall *1533*, *nihil consulere*.

150/1 *lede alway*: lede away *1533*, *semper . . . exigamus*.

150/4–5 Sidenote 1, *To herken . . . rebuked*: The Lt. gives a different emphasis: *Solertem et sapientem mundus uocat* (The world calls it clever and wise).

150/7 *the danes and the scytes*: *Dacae . . . et Scythae*. The Dacians, not 'Danes' as the Eng. mistranslates, inhabited the area that corresponds to modern Rumania; the Scythians, the area that corresponds approximately to the Ukraine.

150/9 *who so euer*: who euer *1533, qui.*

150/21 *if thou shalte smell*: *si sagax* (if you are keen-scented; i.e. clever).

150/23 *I wyll whorle agayne*: I wyll horle agayne *1533, retorquebo* (twist back, bend back). According to the *OED* (WHIRL 6.) *whirl* and *hurl* were occasionally confused with each other. See the Glossary.

150/27–9 *they . . . lyght*: Cf. Isa. 5: 20.

150/30 *whiche notwithstandyng*: Notwithstandyng *1533, Verum.*

150/30–1 *at one tyme*: euen at ones *1533, simul* (at once, at the same time).

150/31 *defye . . . vnto them*: defye them and set no store of them / leest thou sholdest be mynded to be lyke them *1533, contemnere, ne similis illorum esse uelis.*

150/32 *that thou mayst desyre to*: them so that thou woldest fayne *1533, ut . . . cupias.*

150/33–151/2 *than . . . wept for*: Cf. Augustine, *Sermo* 175, *PL*, xxxviii, 945–6.

151/2–3 *Be . . . conformable*: Be . . . confirmable *1533, conformari.* According to the *OED* (CONFORM, v.), 'In 14–16 c. there was considerable confusion between *conform* and *confirm.* . . .'

151/2–5 *Be . . . perfyte*: Rom. 12: 2.

151/9 *Thou . . . also*: Cf. John 12: 36, Eph. 5: 8. *Thou . . . also, suffre*: but suffre thou . . . also *1533, Tu . . . sine.*

151/9–10 *suffre . . . their deed*: Matt. 8: 22; *their deed*: theyr deed bodies *1533, mortuos suos.*

151/10–11 *lette . . . dyche*: Cf. Matt. 15: 14; *lette*: and let *1533*, understood in Lt.

151/13 *ensample Christ*: ensample of Chryste *1533, exemplari . . . Christo.*

151/14–15 *Thou . . . lyght*: Cf. John 11: 9.

151/15 *if this lyght shyne . . . thou*: the lyght shynynge . . . yf thou *1533, Hoc perlucente, si. . . .*

151/15–30 Sidenote 1: Not in Lt.

151/23 *Euripus*: The narrowest part of the channel between the island of Euboea and the mainland of Greece, where the current frequently changes direction in response to the tides. Cf. *Euripus homo, Adagia,* I. ix. 62 (*OO, 2,* 357A); *Bragmanyes . . . Stoikes*: Brahmins form the priestly caste among the Hindus (*OED*). Cf. also the virtuous pagans of the 'yle of Bragman', who allegedly warded off an attack of Alexander the Great with this description of their Utopian simplicity of life: '. . . wee haue no ricchess ne none wee coueyten, and alle the godes of our contree ben in comoun . . . And instede of tresour of gold and syluer wee maken oure tresoure of accord and pees and for to loue euery man other' (*Mandeville's Travels,* ed. M. C. Seymour (Oxford, 1967), p. 212). See the similar description of the simple, pacificist and egalitarian lifestyle of the Brahmins in *Alexander and Dindimus: or, The Letters of Alexander to Dindimus, King of the Brahmans, with the Replies of Dindimus; being a second fragment of the alliterative romance of Alisaunder; translated from the Latin, about A.D. 1340–50; re-edited from the unique ms. in the Bodleian Library, Oxford.* By the Revd. Walter W. Skeat . . . EETS ES 31 (London, 1878), ll. 290–2, 349–50, 377–8, 429–33. Following Diogenes of Sinope (*c.*410–*c.*320 BC), Cynics advocated extreme individualism and indifference to material possessions. For the Stoics, see above, 55/27 n.

151/24 *dogmies and doctryne*: pryncyples *1533, dogmata.*

152/5–6 *neyther . . . himselfe*: Cf. 2 Cor. 5: 15.

152/11–13 *whiche . . . redemptyon*: Cf. 1 John 4: 10, Rom. 5: 10.

152/14–15 *may hate*: shall hate *1533, oderit* (hortatory subjunctive).

152/21 *maye perysshe*: perysshe *1533, pereat.*

152/22 *whome*: suche as *1533, quem; made . . . saued*: hathe made hym selfe to be / but let the man be saued *1533, ipse se fecit, sed ut seruetur homo.*

152/24 *and*: but *1533, et.*

152/24–5 *Neyther . . . not*: Cf. Matt. 5: 44.

152/28–9 *To wepe . . . ioyen*: Cf. Rom. 12: 15.

152/29 *take*: rather take *1533, ferat.*

153/1–2 *I know not . . . whyte*: Cf. Catullus 93.2.

153/5 *what thynges*: can those thynges whiche *1533, quae.*

153/5–6 *to the . . . recompensed*: for yᵉ which wolde his kyndnes done to the / sholde be recompensed *1533, tibi . . . qui suam in te beneficentiam . . . uoluit retaliari.*

153/9 *the lorde*: our lorde *1533, domino; coheyre in Chryste*: Cf. Rom. 8: 17.

153/10 *a membre . . . body*: Cf. Eph. 4: 25.

153/12–15 *one body . . . vs*: Eph. 4: 4–6.

153/15 *euerywhere*: The Eng. lessens the anaphora by not translating *per omnia* as 'through all'.

153/17 *circumstaunces of rethoricyens*: In developing the subject matter of an oration, rhetoricians could elaborate on the time, place, manner, cause and occasion of an action (*OED*, CIRCUMSTANCE I. 2.).

153/17–18 *some valure*: no lytel valure *1533, nonnihil* (something).

153/22–3 *In Christ . . . thing*: Cf. Gal. 3: 28.

153/23–4 *this one thyng*: this *1533, Hoc unum.*

153/24 *it is ynough*: let this suffyse the *1533, satis sit.*

153/25-7 *What soeuer . . . heed*: Cf. 1 Cor. 12: 26.

153/27 *We . . . an other*: Eph. 4: 25.

153/28-9 *The heed . . . god*: Cf. 1 Cor. 11: 3.

154/1 *lyke with lyke*: Cf. *Æqualis aequalem delectat*, *Adagia*, I. ii. 20 (*OO*, *2*, 78D). See also 106/4-5 n.; *y*^{t}: the other *1533*, *illud*.

154/1-2 *vnlykenesse . . . hate*: This proverb is not found in the *Adagia*, although *Similitudo mater amoris* is. Cf. *Adagia*, I. ii. 21 (*OO*, *2*, 79E); *vnlykenesse*: dyuersite *1533*, *Dissimilitudo*.

154/13 *monke*: After this the Eng. omits *Minor Coletao* (Franciscan to Coletan). See the Introduction, p. xl. For the Franciscans, see above, 'gray freres', 9/1 n. The Coletans were Franciscan Observants in Northern France and Belgium, a group reformed by the abbess St. Colette (1381-1447).

154/14 *Carmelytes*: This group was formed by religious men and pilgrims after the establishment of the Crusaders' kingdom in the Holy Land in the twelfth century. *Iacobytes*: A name originally applied to the French Dominicans because their first house (1217) was located near the church of St. Jacques (cf. *OED*, JACOBIN A. 1.). For the Dominicans, see above, 'blacke freres', 8/32 n.

154/16 *Where . . . enemy*: Cf. Matt. 5: 44; *her*: his *1533*, not in Lt. The antecedent, however, is *charitas* (f.).

154/22 *that . . . body*: Cf. Rom. 12: 5; *the heed*: our heed *1533*, *capite*.

154/22-3 *endued . . . spiryte*: Cf. Eph. 4: 4.

154/25-6 *perceyue and vnderstande*: perceyue *1533*, *intelligamus*.

154/26 *our selfe to haue receyued*: y^t we our selfe haue receyued *1533*, *nos ipsos accepisse*.

154/28-9 *neyther shulde any man study*: and that we myght vnderstande how no man ought to study *1533*, *Neque quisquam . . . studeat*; *study*: *studeat* (desire).

155/2-27 *As . . . an other*: 1 Cor. 12: 12-25, 27.

155/17-19 *moche rather . . . more necessary*: moche more necessary *1533*, *multo magis . . . necessariora*.

155/21 *vnhonest*: Out of the two examples of this sense (uncomely) given in the *OED* (*s.v.* 1. b., 1382, 1398), the first renders the same scripture passage as does the English *Enchiridion*, 1382: Wyclif 1 *Cor*. xii. 23, 'And tho membris that ben vnhonest, han more honeste.'

155/24-5 *scisme . . . stryfe*: diuision / debate or stryfe *1533*, *schisma*; *diuisyon, debate or stryfe*: doublets for 'scisme'. See the Introduction, p. xliv.

155/26 *indifferently*: The Eng. *Enchiridion* and Tyndale's NT both give 'indifferently' (equally) where Douai-Rheims gives 'mutually'.

155/28 *For as we (saythe he)* ... *haue*: saying ... we haue *1533*, *Sicut enim (inquit)* ... *habemus*.

155/28–32 *For* ... *vs*: Rom. 12: 4–6.

155/30–1 *And* ... *an other*: but syngularly we be membres eche one of another *1533*, *singuli autem alter alterius membra*.

155/32 *doynge trouthe*: workyng verite *1533*, *Veritatem* ... *facientes*.

155/32–156/2 *doynge* ... *charyte*: Eph. 4: 15–16. For the use of 'charyte' where Tyndale's NT uses 'love' see the Introduction, p. lii.

155/33 *by all maner thynges*: in all maner thynges *1533*, *per omnia*.

155/34 *the hole*: all the *1533*, *totum*.

155/35 *mynistryng one*: wherby one parte mynystreth *1533*, *subministrationis*.

156/1 *acte* ... *measure*: operacion and vertue whiche spryngeth of the heed and capacite of euery membre / in receyuynge *1533*, *operationem in mensuram uniuscuiusque membri*.

156/1–2 Sidenote 1, *to the profite of the soule*: ad omnium utilitatem (to the profit of all [the members of the Mystical Body]).

156/3–4 *beare* ... *burden*: Cf. Gal. 6: 2.

156/4 *bycause* ... *another*: Eph. 4: 25.

156/11 *other*: other men *1533*, *aliorum*; *grynneth*: According to the *OED* (*s.v.* 1. a.), 'grin' here means to draw back the lips and display the teeth as an indication of pain.

156/19 *myne*: myne owne *1533*, *meum*.

156/34 *may not punysshe*: punisshe not *1533*, *non puniunt* (indicative).

157/2–12 *I* ... *iniust*: Matt. 5: 39–41, 44, 45.

157/3 *(sayth Christ there)*: Internal gloss. See the Introduction, p. xliii.

157/19–20 *If* ... *haue*: Matt. 5: 46.

157/20 *this thynge*: these thinges (yᵗ is to saye / to loue them that loueth the) *1533*, *istud*.

157/21 *myschefe*: an euyll thynge *1533*, *scelus*.

157/22 *Here thou*: Here *1533*, *Audi*.

157/23 *the great counsaylour and interpretour*: bothe a great wyse man and connynge and an interpretour also *1533*, *magnum* ... *et consultum, et interpretem*.

157/24–33 *Blysse* ... *goodnesse*: Rom. 12: 14, 17–21.

157/32 *heed*: heed / that is to say / thou shalt make hym to loue feruently *1533*, *caput*.

158/5 *it is* ... *suffre*: For the opposite point of view, see Plato, *Gorgias* 509C–D.

158/22–3 *The greater* ... *thy selfe*: Cf. Matt. 20: 26 and 23: 11.

158/28–30 *The more* ... *lorde*: Cf. Luke 12: 48.

158/31–159/1 *Byleuest* ... *men*: This passage was placed on the *Index Expurgatorius* ... (Antwerp, 1571) (Bataillon, p. 336 n.).

158/31 *propriete*: proprete or impropriacyon *1533, proprietatem.*

159/1 *pertayne*: perteyne indifferently *1533, pertinet.*

159/6 *beare* ... *no*: beare not ... no *1533, Non gero.*

159/7 *shepherd*: *Pastor*; *Let vs graunt*: Let vs graunt you *1533, Demus*; *thou are not*: art not thou *1533, non es?*

159/8 *loke*: consyder *1533, uideris.*

159/15–16 *sayeng* ... *that thou art*: Not in Lt. See the Introduction, p. xliii.

159/16–17 Sidenote 1: Not in Lt.

159/17 *voyce*: voyce or pronouncynge *1533, uoce.*

159/19–21 Sidenote 2: Not in Lt.

159/24 *to their glory and prayse*: prayse in them self *1533, gloriae*; *prayse*: After this the Eng. omits *id genus plurima facinora* (this kind of grievous crimes). See the Introduction, p. xl.

160/10–11 Sidenote 2, *A prety* ... *offycers*: *Praedonum Praedo* (Robber of robbers).

160/15–16 *No man* ... *in an offyce*: Cf. Plato, *Republic* 347C, 520D–E.

160/18 *enchaunt*: do enchaunt *1533, incantent* (subjunctive).

160/28 *forthwith*: streyghtwaye *1533, protinus.*

160/30 *se thou thynke not*: se that thou thynke not *1533, ne* ... *putaris.*

160/31 *but*: but se thou *1533, Immo.*

161/2 *greate outragyous excesse*: great outrage or excesse *1533, flagitium.*

161/3 *the rychesse of the commune people*: the comen peoples *1533, plebeis.*

161/5 *the maners of the commune people*: the comen peoples *1533, popularibus.*

161/14–15 *thy frendes* ... *authorite*: *tuos.* See the Introduction, p. xlii.

161/15 *open not*: set not open *1533, ne* ... *explices.*

162/14 *myscheuously*: *flagitiose* (shamefully). None of the senses in the *OED* render the Lt. exactly.

162/16 *commune*: publyke *1533, Publicam.*

162/17 *that which is commune*: comen maters *1533, publico.*

162/31 *els*: om. *1533, si.*

163/1 *a ferre better thynge*: ferre better *1533*, *longe melius*.

163/1–2 Sidenote 1: Not in Lt.

163/7–8 *He . . . worlde*: Cf. John 18: 36.

163/9 *But . . . them*: Cf. Matt. 20: 25.

163/10–12 *he whiche . . . lorde*: Cf. Matt. 20: 26.

163/13–15 Sidenote 3: Not in Lt.

163/16–19 *Chryste . . . Chryste*: Cf. Matt. 23: 8–10.

163/19 *whiche . . . all*: Cf. Eph. 4: 15.

163/19–20 *shepherde*: *pastor*. Sidenote 4: Not in Lt.

163/28–9 *a certayne worlde*: Erasmus protests against the attitude which defines 'world' as lay life in opposition to clerical (*OED*, WORLD I. 4.) rather than an exclusive concern with temporal and mundane affairs (cf. Ibid. I. 2.) which every Christian is called to rise above.

163/32 *Augustyne, Ambrose, and Hierome*: See above, 49/9–10 n.

164/1 *straungers . . . fayth*: Cf. Eph. 2: 12; *ennemyes . . . Chryst*: Phil. 3: 18.

164/5 *delusyons*: delyces *1533*, *praestigijs* (illusions).

164/7–8 *This . . . lyght*: Cf. John 1: 9–10.

164/8–9 *This . . . myschefe*: Cf. 1 John 5: 19.

164/11 *put vpon hym Christ*: Cf. Rom. 13: 14; *Christ . . . charite*: Cf. 1 John 4: 8. See the Introduction, p. lii.

164/12–13 *From . . . hym*: Cf. John 15: 19.

164/18 *corrupting . . . god*: Cf. 2 Cor. 2: 17 and 4: 2.

164/19–21 *wresten . . . scripture*: See above, 139/4–6 n.

164/25 *al . . . god*: Cf. Rom. 13: 1.

164/25–6 *his combe ryseth*: See above, 121/25 n.

164/29–30 *the same . . . therof*: Cf. Luke 16: 2.

164/31 *forbyd . . . ones*: Cf. Matt. 10: 10, Luke 3: 11.

165/2–3 *that . . . an other mans*: Cf. St. Thomas Aquinas, *Summa Theologiae*, IIa–IIae, q. 26, art. 4.

165/12 *it*: om. *1533*, *id*, doublet for 'that'.

165/13–14 *Adulterers . . . Dauyd*: Cf. 2 Kgs. 11.

165/15 *ryche Abraham*: Cf. Gen. 13: 2.

165/18 *quenes . . . Salomon*: Cf. 3 Kgs. 11: 3; *and*: om. *1533*, *et*; *They . . . god*: Cf. Phil. 3: 19.

165/19 *dronkennesse of Noe*: Cf. Gen. 9: 21.

165/21 *Loth . . . doughters*: Cf. Gen. 19: 30–6.

165/26 *I do not gaynsaye them*: I do not agaynst saye them *1533, non reclamo*.

165/28 *folowe . . . repentaunce*: Cf. 2 Kgs. 12.

165/29–31 *Mary Magdaleyne . . . Iesu*: Cf. Luke 7: 37–8 and 44–7.

165/31–2 *Thou . . . Paule*: Cf. 1 Cor. 15: 9, Gal. 1: 13. Tyndale's NT gives 'congregacion' for 'churche'. For More's objection to this usage, see the Introduction, p. liii.

165/32–3 *thou . . . Peter*: Cf. Matt. 26: 69–75, Luke 22: 54–61.

165/33–5 *stretche . . . Paule*: According to an ancient tradition, St. Paul was beheaded on the Ostian Road, a short distance south-west of Rome.

165/35 *feare . . . Peter*: St. Peter was crucified at Rome *c.* AD 65 during the persecution of Nero. Cf. Tertullian, *Adversus Gnosticos Scorpiace, PL*, ii, 175.

166/9–11 *spyders . . . our selues*: I have been unable to find a classical source for Erasmus's figure of the spider. In the Elizabethan period, however, the figure was a commonplace. See, for example, Thomas Nashe, 'The Returne of Pasquill', *The Works of Thomas Nashe*, ed. Ronald B. McKerrow, I. 93. ll. 28–9 and 'Notes', ibid. IV. 61. See also, 'bee', 52/10–12 n. The *locus classicus* for the fable of the spider and the bee is Jonathan Swift, 'The Battle of the Books' in *A Tale of a Tub . . .*, ed. A. C. Guthkelch and D. Nichol Smith, 2nd edn. (Oxford, 1958), pp. 228–33.

166/11–12 *What . . . thy god?*: According to the *OED*, 'what' (*s.v.* A. I. 3.) is used in rhetorical questions to imply an emphatic contrary assertion.

166/12–14 *Bycause . . . multyplye*: See above, 165/15 n. The Lt. *Enchiridion* gives *foeturae* (young) for 'catell' as does Tyndale's Pentateuch.

166/17 Sidenote 3: Not in Lt. 166/17–18 *the rychesse of Cresus, whiche*: rychesse as moche as euer kyng Cresus had (whose exceding great ryches is come into a comen prouerbe) whiche rychesse ones gotten *1533, Croesi opes . . . quas*. For Croesus, see above, 144/24 n.

166/20 *depe in the grounde*: *domi* (at home).

166/23–4 *without . . . slayne*: Cf. Gen. 22: 1–12.

166/28–9 Sidenote 4: Not in Lt.

166/32–167/6 *The symple . . . them*: Cf. Gen. 19: 25–36.

167/3 *large and wastfull*: *uasto*. For *uasto*, the Eng. gives both the literal definition 'wastfull' and the transferred meaning 'large'.

167/7 (*growe and multyply*): Gen. 1: 22; Tyndale's Pentateuch also gives 'Growe'.

167/13–15 *Dauyd . . . hym*: See above, 165/13–14 n.

167/16 *streyghtwaye*: According to the *OED* (2.), Tyndale was the first to use this sense in 1526: *Matt*. iv. 20, 'They strayght waye lefte there nettes.' *John* xxi. 3, They . . . entred into a shippe strayght waye.' *Rom*. ix. 7, 'Nether are they all children strayght way be cause they are the seede of Abraham.'

167/18–19 *Peter . . . wyll*: See above, 165/32–3 n., 165/35 n.

167/20 *thynkest thou*: thynkest thou than *1533*, not in Lt; *to forswere*: for that cause / to forsweare *1533*, *de causa peierare*.

167/21–3 *Paule . . . waye*: Cf. Acts 9: 1–20, 1 Tim. 1: 13.

167/26–8 *Mathewe . . . tollage*: Cf. Matt. 9: 9.

167/32–3 *saynt Augustyne . . . concubynes*: See above, 141/23–142/2 n.

168/22–3 *by this folisshnes . . . byleue*: Cf. 1 Cor. 1: 21.

168/24 *he is . . . Chryste*: *misere desipit, qui Christum non sapit* (he is woefully a fool, who does not know Christ). The Eng. translator changes the Lt. for the sake of contrast with the previous clause.

168/26–7 *currishnes*: *Cynicum*. Diogenes, the first Cynic, acquired the epithet 'the Dog' (ὁ κύων) because of his neglect of manners. See also, 151/23 n.

168/32–3 *But . . . Chryst*: Cf. 1 Cor. 9: 22.

169/12–13 *we may drawe*: we drawe *1533*, *consistamus* (subjunctive).

169/18 *may bryng*: bringeth *1533*, *adducat* (subjunctive).

169/19 *eyther*: eyther other *1533*, *Vtrumque*.

169/25–7 *Fabius . . . best*: Cf. Quintilian, *Institutio Oratoria*, XII. xi. 30.

170/2 *more receyuable*: more capax *1533*, *capacior*. *1533* adds the sidenote, 'Capax apte to receyue', which *1534* omits.

170/7 *playne or lystes*: *stadio*.

170/7–14 *Of the whiche . . . honestye*: Jerome (*Adversus Jovinianum*, PL, xxiii, 282–8) lists many examples of chaste pagan women, of whom the most famous is probably the Roman matron Lucretia.

170/31 *must be warned and exhorted*: sholde be warned and exhorted *1533*, *sunt admonendi*.

170/32 *this is . . . synne*: the very nature and properte of synne were thus *1533*, *ut hanc esse peccati naturam*.

171/5 *bytwene thre wayes*: Cf. *In trivio sum, Adagia*, I. ii. 48 (*OO, 2*, 89D).

171/8–10 Sidenote 1: The Lt. gives a different emphasis: *A politica uirtute gradus est ad salutem* (From civic virtue it is a step to salvation). Cf. Plato, *Phaedo* 82A–B.

171/15–27 *IF . . . sathan*: Cf. Pico, 'Duodecima regula: propterea quod tentaris, ne credas te a deo derelictum aut deo parum gratum esse: aut parum iustum & perfectum. memor sis quod postquam Paulus vidit diuinam essentiam, patiebatur tentationem carnis: qua permittebat deus eum tentari: ne de superbia tentaretur: in quo etiam homo debet aduertere quod Paulus qui erat vas electionis & raptus usque ad tertium caelum: tamen erat in periculo ne de suis virtutibus superbiret: sicut ipse dicit de se ne magnitudo rcuclationum extolleret me datus est mihi stimulus carnis meae qui me colaphizet. Quare super omnes tentationes homo debet maxime se munire contra tentationem superbia: quia radix omnium malorum superbia est: contra quod unicum remedium est: cogitare semper quod deus se humiliauit pro nobis usque ad crucem: & mors nos vel inuitos eousque nos humiliabit ut simus esca vermium.' The Twelve Rules and Twelve Weapons are quoted from Pico, fo. 111ᵛ–12. For a discussion of the possible influence of Pico on Erasmus, see the Introduction, pp. xxi–xxii.

171/19–22 bycause . . . sone: Cf. Heb. 12: 6–8.

171/25 to be admytted and receyued vnto: to be admitted or let in euen in to *1533*, admitti.

171/25–7 Paule . . . sathan: Cf. 2 Cor. 12: 2–7.

171/27–8 Iob . . . Frauncys: Cf. Job 1–2. St. Jerome spent two ycars as a hermit in the desert of Chalcis, where he was plagued by ill-health and sexual fantasies. Cf. *Epistola 22, PL*, xxii, 398–99. During his three-year sojourn as a hermit in a cave near Subiaco, St. Benedict was tempted to abandon his solitary life by the memory of a woman he had once seen. Cf. Gregory the Great, *Vita S. Benedicti, PL*, lxvi, 132. Brother Leo of Assisi recounts that St. Francis suffered from a two-year long spiritual temptation at St. Mary of the Angels. Cf. *The Mirror of Perfection*, trans. Robert Steele (London, 1938), pp. 145–6.

172/1–2 god . . . endure: Cf. 1 Cor. 10: 13; shall cause: shal make *1533*, faciet.

172/7–8 (for . . . deuour): Cf. 1 Pet. 5: 8.

172/7–9 Sidenote 2, Let . . . be hold downe: Let . . . be holden down *1533*, suprimatur. The *OED* gives both 'hold' (A. 3. δ.) and 'holden' (A. 3. β.) as pa. pple. forms.

172/9–15 as soone as . . . greate: Cf. Pico, 'Decima regula: ut in tentationibus semper in principio occurras & allidas paruulos babylonis ad petram. Petra autem est Christus: quia sero medicina paratur.'

172/10–11 to trede . . . serpent: Cf. Gen. 3: 15.

172/12–15 Sidenote 3: Not in Lt.

172/13–14 to dasshe . . . stone: Cf. Ps. 136: 9.

172/14–15 stone . . . Chryst: Cf. 1 Cor. 10: 4. Cf. Augustine, *Enarratio in Psalmum 136, PL*, xxxvii, 1773–4.

172/23 *as . . . before*: See above, 45/35–46/3.

173/2–4 Sidenote 1: Not in Lt., *feare*[1]: *1533*, fayry *1534*. This sidenote refers to 'nyght feare' (173/6).

173/5–6 Sidenote 2: Not in Lt.

173/6–7 *not . . . myddaye*: Cf. Ps. 90: 5–6.

173/9–10 *thou . . . Chryste*: Cf. Phil. 4: 13.

173/11 *euen the very lowest*: euen vnto the very lowest *1533*, *etiam infimis*.

173/11–12 *Haue . . . worlde*: John 16: 33.

173/12–17 *Agayn . . . all togyder*: Cf. Pico, 'Septima regula: . . . ut si opus suum bonum aliquod tibi offert: ut inde in vanam gloriam incidas: tu illud statim non ut opus tuum: sed ut beneficium dei cogitans humilias te & iudicas parum gratum te esse deo de beneficijs eius.'

173/18–20 *What . . . it*: 1 Cor. 4: 7.

173/21–4 *yf . . . onely*: Cf. Pico, 'Quinta regula: quod in illis duodecim armis nec in quocumque alio humano remedio confidas: sed in sola virtute Iesu christi qui dixit: confidite ego vici mundum: & alibi: Princeps mundi huius eijcitur foras: quare & nos sola eius virtute confidamus: & mundum posse vincere: & diabolum superare: Et ideo debemus semper petere eius auxilium per orationem & sanctorum suorum.'

173/23 *thy heed Chryst*: Cf. Eph. 4: 15.

173/28–174/5 *WHan . . . vertue*: Cf. Pico, 'Septima regula: ut non solum non vincaris a diabolo quum te tentat: se ut vincas ipsum: & hoc est quando non solum non peccas: sed ex ea re unde te tentauerat occasionem sumis alicuius boni . . . .'

174/5–7 *Hercules . . . displeasure*: See above, 109/17–19 n.

174/24–9 *BVt . . . agayn*: Cf. Pico, 'Octaua regula: ut quum pugnas: pugnes quasi vincendo deinde perpetuam pacem habiturus: quia forte hoc tibi dabit deus ex gratia sua: & diabolus amplius non redibit confusus de tua victoria . . . .'

174/26 *may be*: may be veryly *1533*, *potest*.

174/30–2 *Neyther . . . mynisshed*: Cf. Origen, *Contra Celsum*, *PG*, xi, 1582–3.

175/1–6 *But . . . body*: Cf. Pico, 'Octaua regula: . . . sed quum vicisti geras te quasi mox pugnaturus ut in pugna semper victoriae: & in victoria semper sis memor pugnae.'

175/7 *I . . . standynge*: Cf. Isa. 21: 8, Hab. 2: 1.

175/14 *abhorreth*: abhorre *1533*, *execrantur* (plural form as in *1533*).

175/17 *single fornicacion*: *simplicem fornicationem*, fornication as opposed to adultery.

175/22–3 Sidenote 3: Not in Lt.

176/4–5 *After . . . Hesiodus*: Cf. Hesiod, *Works and Days*, 361–2.

176/8–27 *Se . . . temptacyon*: Cf. Pico, 'Vndecima regula: recordare quod licet in ipso conflictu tentationis arma videatur pugna: tamen longe dulcius est vincere tentationem quam ire ad peccatum ad quod te inclina & in hoc multi decipiuntur: quia non comparant dulcedinem victoriae dulcedini peccati. Sed comparant pugnam voluptati: & tamen homo qui milies expertus est quid sit: cedere tentationi deberet semel saltem experiri quid sit vincere tentationem.'

177/4 *softe without resistence*: *muliebrior*.

177/21 *vertue*: strengthe *1533*, *uirtutis*.

177/24 *A man . . . agayne*: Cf. *Attic Nights of Aulus Gellius*, XVII. xxi. 31 and *Vir fugiens, & denuo pugnabit, Adagia*, I. x. 40 (*OO*, *2*, 379C).

177/25 *Dauid*: See above, 165/13–14 n., 167/13–15 n.; *Salomon*: see above, 165/18 n.

177/26 *Peter*: See above, 165/32–3 n., 165/35 n., 167/18–19 n.; *Paule*: see above, 165/31–2 n., 165/33–5 n., 167/21–3 n.

177/33 *pite*: vertuous lyuynge *1533*, *pietatis*.

178/8 *a refresshyng . . . labour*: Cf. Matt. 11 : 28.

178/9 *This alone, is*: This is a thynge *1533*, *Haec est una*.

178/20–1 *the mylke . . . Christ*: Cf. 1 Cor. 3 : 2.

178/21–2 *But . . . therof*: Cf. Cant. 7 : 8; *ye date tree*: the date tree / that is to saye the tre of vyctorie *1533*, *palmam*. The internal gloss in *1533* becomes Sidenote 3 in *1534*.

178/26 *not onely*: onely *1533*, *non solum*.

178/27 *if . . . in vs*: Cf. Rom. 8 : 9.

178/30 *Not withstandyng that*: Not withstandynge *1533*, *Verum*.

178/30–1 *with ye more profyte*: the more profyte *1533*, *quo maiore fructu*.

178/32 *shalbe houefull*: 'houefull' is not given in the *OED*, although 'behoveful' (advantageous) is.

179/2–27 *Suche . . . heed*: Cf. Pico, 'Quarta regula: recordetur non solum esse aegreferondam hanc pugnam: sed optandam etiam si nullum inde nobis praemium perueniret *1557* [peruenire, *1504*]: solum ut conformemur christo deo & domino nostro: & quotiens resistendo alicui tentationi: alicui ex sensibus tuis vim facis cogita cuinam parti crucis christi conformis reddaris: ut quando gulae resistens gustum affligis: recordare illum felle potatum & aceto. Quando manus retrahis a rapina alicuius rei quae tibi placet cogita manus illius pro te ligno crucis affixas: & si resistis superbiae recordare illum qui cum in forma dei esset, pro te formam dei esset pro te formam serui accepisse: & humiliatum usque ad mortem crucis: & cum de ira tentaris recordare illum qui deus erat: & omnium hominum iustissimus cum se tamen videret quasi latronem &

illudi: & conspui: & flagellari: & opprobrijs omnibus affici: & cum latronibus deputari: nullum tamen unquam aut irae aut indignationis signum ostendit: sed patientissime omnia ferens omnibus mansuetissime respondebat: & sic discurrendo per singula inuenies *1557* [inuenias, *1504*] nullam esse passionem quae te Christo aliqua ex parte *1557* [patte, *1504*] conformem non efficiat.' (The emendations are taken from Ioannes Picus Mirandula, *Opera Omnia* (Basel, 1557), pp. 332–4.)

179/3 *crucifyeng*: certifyeng *1533, crucifigendis*; *of euery one of thyne affectyons*: of euery thyne affectyons *1533, singulis affectibus tuis*.

179/5 *any maner*: any *1533, omnino*.

179/9 *oh*: om. *1533, o*. Sidenote 2: Not in Lt.

179/9–11 *howe . . . sake*: Cf. Phil. 2: 6–8.

179/14–15 *he . . . eysell*: Cf. Matt. 27: 34, 48.

179/19–20 *lyke . . . mouthe*: Cf. Isa. 53: 7.

179/22 *and yet . . . sake*: Cf. 2 Cor. 8: 9.

179/22–3 *that . . . heed*: Cf. Matt. 8: 20.

180/1 *atones*: According to the *OED* (*s.v.* 6.), Tyndale was the first to use this sense (immediately) in 1531: *Exp. & Notes* (1849) 179, 'The apostles were clear-eyed, and espied antichrist at once.'

180/8–17 *shall . . . deite*: Cf. Pico, The Eighth Weapon, *Hominis dignitas & natura*.

180/10–11 *with . . . bought*: Cf. 1 Cor. 6: 20.

180/15 *a membre of Christe*: Cf. Eph. 5: 30. 180/15–16 *a membre of the churche*: Cf. Col, 1: 18. Tyndale's NT gives 'congregacion' for 'churche'. See the Introduction, p. liii.

180/16 *our bodyes . . . holy goost*: Cf. 1 Cor. 3: 16, 6: 19.

180/22–3 *Synne . . . serpent*: Cf. Gen. 3: 15.

180/23 *prest wages*: prest wagest *1533, autoramentum*. The *OED* gives only the analogous form 'prest-money'. See 73/18 n. for a different Eng. translation of *autoramentum* (wages, hire, reward).

180/33–4 *compare . . . dyuell*: Cf. 'Meditation on the Two Standards', *The Spiritual Exercises of St. Ignatius Loyola*, trans. Elder Mullan, S.J. (New York, 1914), pp. 74–6.

181/2 *called . . . god*: Cf. John 15: 14.

181/3 *inherytaunce . . . god*: Cf. Gal. 4: 7.

181/3–4 *By . . . dyuell*: Cf. John 8: 34.

181/5–6 *origynall patron and trewe ensample*: Idaea. See above, 62/22–3 n.

181/12 *lybertie and fredom*: liberalitate (generosity).

181/14–16 *With . . . thyselfe*: Cf. Luke 15: 20.

181/15–16 *and whan . . . thyselfe*: *resipiscentem*, doublet for 'amended'. See the Introduction, p. xliv.

181/26 *and make my selfe bonde*: The doublet defines 'mancypate'. See the Glossary.

181/33–182/5 *ANd . . . soules*: Cf. Pico, The Seventh Weapon, *Aeternum praemium: aeterna poena.*

182/9–15 *vertue . . . it*: Cf. Pico, The Ninth Weapon, *Pax bonae mentis.*

182/12–13 *of whiche*: whiche *1533, quod.*

182/13 *haue a taste*: haue tasted *1533, degustaril.*

182/14 *nothyng*: nor nothynge *1533, nihil.*

182/18–19 *That . . . gospell*: Cf. Matt. 19: 29.

182/21 *or*: nor *1533, neque.*

182/21–3 *whiche . . . hym*: Cf. 1 Cor. 2: 9.

182/23–4 *hym in this lyfe / forsothe*: hym / and verily in this lyfe *1533, nimirum in hac uita.*

182/24–30 *forsothe . . . synne*: This passage was placed on the *Index Expurgatorius . . .* (Antwerp, 1571) (Bataillon, p. 378 n.).

182/24–5 *the worme . . . not*: Cf. Isa. 66: 24, Mark 9: 45.

182/26–7 *Neyther . . . gospell*: Cf. Luke 16: 19–24.

182/26–30 *Neyther . . . synne*: Cf. 'Letter to Beda' (Allen, 6, 105).

182/28–9 *them . . . thynges*: See above, 93/11–12 n.

183/2–8 *MOre ouer . . . for euer*: Cf. Pico, The Fourth Weapon, *Vita somnus & umbra*, and The Fifth Weapon, *Mors instans & improuisa.*

183/2–5 *howe . . . vnware*: Perhaps a reminiscence of the Dance of Death, a popular motif in fifteenth-century preaching, literature and art. The woodcut series of Hans Holbein the Younger, depicting Death's power over every rank of society from fool and beggar to pope and emperor, marks the culmination of the tradition.

183/10–16 *impenytency . . . lyfe*: Cf. Pico, The Sixth Weapon, *Suspitio impoenitentiae.*

183/14–15 *and be cleane . . . agayne*: Not in Lt.

183/15–16 *specially . . . iniquyte*: Cf. Isa. 5: 18.

183/16 *lynes*: lyues *1533, funiculos* (cords).

183/17–19 *Slypper . . . laboure*: Cf. *Aeneid* 6: 126, 128, 129.

183/18–19 *spirytuall lyght*: *superas . . . auras* (the light of day). The Eng. translator gives an allegorical interpretation of Aeneas' return to daylight.

183/19–20 *Therfore . . . euen*: Therfore at the leestway *1533, Proinde uel* (Therefore especially).

183/20 *admonisshed*: being monisshed *1533, admonitus.*

183/20–184/15 Sidenote 1: Not in Lt.

183/20–2 *Esopes . . . agayne*: Cf. *Caxton's Aesop*, ed. R. T. Lenaghan (Cambridge, Mass., 1967), p. 167.

184/1–2 *Remedyes . . . vyces*: In Chapters 32 through 38, Erasmus seems to undertake a discussion of the Seven Deadly Sins, but he breaks off after treating only four of them: lust, avarice, ambicion and wrath. Gluttony, envy and sloth are omitted. For this incomplete presentation, see the Introduction, p. xiv, and for the tradition, see Morton W. Bloomfield, *The Seven Deadly Sins* (East Lansing, Mich., 1952).

184/21–3 Sidenote 2: Not in Lt.

184/22 *hony*: of hony *1533, mellis.*

184/26–7 *to prophane and vnhalowe*: to prophane and pollute *1533, Prophanare*; *to prophane . . . temple*: Cf. 1 Cor. 3: 16–17.

184/27–8 *Christ . . . bloode*: Cf. Heb. 13: 12.

184/32 *than*: that *1533, quam.*

185/13 *age . . . wretched*: Cf., 'And yet you see them [amorous old men] still enjoying life so much and trying to be young so hard that one of them dyes his white hair, another covers his baldness with a wig, another enjoys the use of borrowed teeth, probably taken from the jaw of a pig; another is perishing miserably for love of some girl, and outdoes any adolescent in his amorous absurdities' (*Folly*, pp. 41–2).

185/16–17 *deuoure . . . wetyngly*: Cf. *Semper tibi pendeat hamus, Adagia*, I. ix. 46 (*OO*, 2, 350–1).

185/21–7 *corage . . . yet be able to do*: Cf. Pico, The Twelfth Weapon, *Testimonia martyrum & exempla sanctorum.*

185/24–5 *thou . . . shuldest . . . be able*: thou . . . shulde . . . be able *1533, possis.*

185/30–1 *she . . . angels*: Cf. Ambrose, *De Virginibus, PL*, xvi, 202.

185/32 *flyeth backe*: fleeth backe *1533, resilit* (leaps back, springs back). See above, 135/3–5 n.

186/18 *father and mother*: *parentes*, see above, 55/25 n. and the Introduction, p. lii.

186/25–6 *this . . . shadowe*: Cf. Wisd. 2: 2, 5. Cf. *Homo bulla, Adagia*, II. iii. 48 (*OO*, 2, 500A).

187/2–3 *that . . . fyre*: Cf. Matt. 25: 41.

187/6–9 Sidenote 1: Not in Lt.

187/16–17 *crucyfyest . . . god*: Cf. Heb. 6: 6.

187/18 *yᵉ rule aboue rehersed*: See above, 181/9–16.

187/19–21 *call ... at all*: Cf. Rom. 5: 8–9.

187/22 *no*: om. *1533*, *nulla*.

187/24–7 Sidenote 3, *Venus ... loue²*: *Duae Veneres inter se comparentur* (The two Venuses compared); *Cupido ... loue⁴*: Not in Lt.

187/25 *of hyghest goodnesse*: of infynyte goodnesse *1533*, *summi boni*.

187/26 *pleasure and beautye*: pleasures and beautye *1533*, *pulchri*; *those*: these *1533*, *illas*.

187/26–8 *Compare ... pastyme*: Cf. Plato, *Symposium* 180D–E.

187/9–30 Sidenote 4: Not in Lt.

187/31–188/1 *thy good ... thynkest*: Cf. Heb. 1: 14 and Jerome, *Commentariorum in Evangelium Matthaei*, *PL*, xxvi, 135.

188/1–2 *god ... open*: Cf. Prov. 24: 12.

188/2–3 *whiche ... erth*: Cf. Dan. 3: 55.

188/3–7 *And ... man*: Cf. '. . . how is it that men aren't ashamed to do in the sight of God and in the presence of the holy angels what they would be ashamed to do before men?' ('The Young Man and the Harlot', *Colloquies*, p. 155).

188/4 *harde by*: According to the *OED* (HARD BY A), Tyndale was the first to use this phrase in 1526: Acts xxvii. 7, 'We saled harde by the costes off Candy.'

188/7–8 *I wolde ... thynke*: I woldest thou shouldest thynke *1533*, *Puta*. See the Introduction, p. xlvi.

188/9–11 Sidenote 1: Not in Lt.

188/22–8 *that ... monstrous*: See above, 185/13 n.

188/25–6 *are ... become*: are *1533*, *sint*.

188/26 *were*: haue ben *1533*, *fuerint*.

189/1 *also*: om. *1533*, *et*.

189/11–13 *to be made ... hoore*: Cf. 1 Cor. 6: 15–16.

189/17–18 *vnto other ... the same*: Not in Lt.

189/18–19 *remembre ... vndefyled*: Cf. Heb. 13: 4.

189/20–1 *thy wedlocke ... beareth*: Cf. Eph. 5: 23–5, 32. Tyndale's NT gives 'congregacion' for 'churche'. See the Introduction, p. liii.

189/22 *clene bareyn*: *minimum*.

189/32–3 Sidenote 6: Not in Lt.

189/32 *those*: those his *1533*, *illis*.

190/1 *leueth*: leueth behynde her *1533*, *relinquit*.

190/5–11 *If ... age*: See above, 185/13 n.

190/6 *to beholde thy selfe withall*: Not in Lt. See the Introduction, p. xliii.

190/8 *muste be bridled*: to be brydeled *1533*, *est . . . coercenda.*

190/10 *mockyng stocke*: First use of this phrase recorded in *OED* (*s.v.* 1. b.) is by Tyndale in 1526: 2 *Pet.* ii. 13, 'Off you they make a mockyng-stoke.'

190/15–25 Sidenote 5: Not in Lt.

190/24 *is y*ᵉ *tyme*: it is tyme *1533*, *tempus est.*

190/25 *Abysac*: Cf. 3 Kgs. 1: 1–4.

190/27 *in her enbrasynges kepe thou*: with the enbrasynges of her kepe the *1533*, *huius amplexibus . . . confoue.*

191/7–8 *he . . . perisshe*: Cf. Ecclus. 3: 27.

191/8 *in them to perisshe*: to perisshe therin *1533*, *in illo pereat.*

191/9 *Syrenes*: For the Sirens, see Homer, *Odyssey* 12: 39–54, 165–91.

191/17 *If*: yf *1533*, It *1534*, *Si*; *flye*: flee *1533*, *fugeris*. See above, 135/3–5 n.

191/22 *often*: ofte *1533*, *frequenter.*

191/29 *was created*: wast created *1533*, *creatus es.*

192/5 *beyng*: be *1533*, not in Lt.

192/7–8 *whiche . . . naught*: For the subordination of material to intellectual and moral goods by pagan philosophers, cf. Plato, *Alcibiades I*, 134B and Aristotle, *Politics* 1323A–B. For the Stoics, see above, 55/27 n. and below, 193/28–30 n. For the Cynics, see above, 151/23 n.

192/14–24 Sidenote 2: The Eng. expands the Lt.: *Opiniones euangelicae de cura pecuniae.*

192/22 *these thinges*: the same *1533*, *ista.*

192/24–7 *the parable . . . counterfayte*: Cf. Matt. 6: 26–34, Luke 12: 24–31.

192/27–9 *the same . . . discyples*: Cf. Matt. 10: 10, Luke 10: 4.

192/29–32 *he commaundeth . . . vs*: Cf. Matt. 6: 33, Luke 12: 31.

193/6 *euerywhyt*: According to the *OED* (WHIT 2. a.), Tyndale was the first to use this sense (completely) in 1526: John vii. 23, 'Disdayne ye at me: because I made a man every whit whoale on the saboth daye?' Ibid. xiii. 10, 'He that is wesshed nedeth not but to wesshe his fete, but is clene every whit.' Sidenote 1: Not in Lt.

193/16–17 *that . . . serue hym*: Not in Lt.

193/18 *Nestor*: The Polonius of the *Iliad*, Nestor is described as over sixty years old by Homer (*Iliad* 1: 247–52) and over two hundred years old by Ovid (*Metamorphoses* 12: 187–8).

193/18–19 Sidenote 2: Not in Lt. The Eng. translator presumably

COMMENTARY 293

expanded Ovid's *nunc tertia [centum] vivitur aetas* into a full 'thre hundred yeres'.

193/19–20 *but . . . whiche*: but veryly I wolde not say that he were a very good christen man / that *1533, bene Christianum equidem non dixerim, qui. . . .*

193/23 *fedeth . . . sparowes*: Cf. Matt. 10: 29.

193/28–30 *And . . . mynde*: Cf. Epictetus, *Discourses*, I. i. 7–13 and III. xxiv. 68–9.

194/3–4 *No trewly*: The Eng. translator supplies an answer to the preceding series of rhetorical questions.

194/11–13 Sidenote 2: Not in Lt.

194/28–31 *He . . . alyue*: For legacy-hunters, cf. Pliny, *Letters* 2: 20 and Lucian, 'Pluto and Hermes', *Dialogues of the Dead*, 15.

194/31 *y^t wyll tell*: yt he wyll tell *1533, a quo . . . audiat.*

195/2–3 *to themselues*: for themselues *1533, ad suum compendium* (to their advantage).

195/15 *Christ . . . thornes*: Cf. Matt. 13: 22; *very*: yea *1533, et* (also, even).

195/21 *flatter thou thy selfe*: flatter thy selfe *1533, tibi . . . blandiare.*

195/23 *verite saythe*: Cf. John 14: 6.

195/23–5 *it is . . . heuen*: e.g. Matt. 19: 24.

195/26–7 *A ryche . . . man*: Jerome, *Epistola 120, PL*, xxii, 984. Cf. *Dives aut iniquus est, aut iniqui haeres, Adagia*, I. ix. 47 (*OO, 2*, 351A).

195/31–2 *the vyce . . . Paule*: Cf. Eph. 5: 5, Col. 3: 5.

195/31–196/2 Sidenote 3, *Mammon . . . couetousnes*: Not in Lt.

196/1–2 *neyther . . . also*: Cf. Matt. 6: 24.

196/19–20 *This . . . be*: Luke 12: 20.

196/22 *ye pouerty . . . mother*: Cf. Luke 2: 7; *Christes mother*: Internal gloss. See the Introduction, p. xliii.

196/22–3 *the pouerty of thapostels*: Cf. 2 Cor. 11: 27.

196/23 *of Christ*: Cf. Matt. 8: 20.

196/24–6 *Ve . . . worlde*: Cf. Luke 6: 24.

196/32–197/3 *honour . . . Christ*: Cf. John 5: 41 and 6: 15.

197/5–7 *to be praysed . . . dede*: Cf. 2 Cor. 10: 17–18.

197/22 *he dothe it, or for feare*: eyther he doth it for feare *1533, aut metu facit.*

197/23 *or for profyte*: or bycause thou woldest do hym a good turne *1533, aut ut prosis* (or that you may be useful).

197/25 *iudgeth*: supposed *1533, iudicat.* See the Introduction, p. xlvi.

197/26 *is gyuen vnto*: is gyuen *1533, debeatur*.

197/27 *gyue dylygence*: *cura* (trouble yourself about). Although this phrase is not recorded in the *OED* (*s.v.* 1. e.), an analogous phrase, 'To put diligence', is.

197/29 *thyne honoure*: the honour y^t is offred the *1533, honorem tuum*; *thou art in dette*: thou arte bounde *1533, debes*.

197/31 *to ascrybe vnto thy selfe*: ascrybe to thyne owne selfe *1533, tibi arrogare*.

198/12–15 *Remembre . . . prece*: Cf. Horace, *Beatus ille*, Epode 2.

198/14 *also separated*: seperate *1533, et . . . semotae*.

198/17 *What difficultye*: and what diffycultie *1533, Quam difficile*.

198/19 *on hygh*: an hyghe *1533, ex alto*.

198/24–6 *who so euer . . . grace*: Cf. Luke 14: 11.

198/24–7 Sidenote 3: Not in Lt.

198/29–30 *How . . . hym*: Cf. John 6: 15.

198/31 *whan . . . asse*: Cf. Matt. 21: 7.

198/32 *clothed . . . thorne*: Cf., e.g., Matt. 27: 28–9.

198/33 *vngloryous . . . dethe*: Cf. Phil. 2: 8.

198/33–4 *But . . . gloryfyed*: Cf. Acts 3: 13.

198/34–199/1 *Let . . . Chryste*: Cf. Gal. 6: 14.

199/1–2 *whome . . . protection*: Cf. 1 Cor. 1: 30; *welth, sauyng, defence and protection*: Doublets for 'helthe'. See the Introduction, p. xliv.

199/8 *thou . . . thyselfe*: See above, 59/9, 11–12 n.

199/9–11 *what so euer great . . . thy good*: Cf. Jas. 1: 17.

199/32 *bryngeth . . . playne*: Cf. Isa. 40: 4.

199/32–3 *whiche . . . pryde*: Cf. 2 Pet. 2: 4.

200/1 *though . . . sort*: though they seme somwhat as they were tryfles *1533, licet leuiora*.

200/5 *to set . . . fethers*: Cf. Juvenal, *Satires* 4: 70. See also above, 121/25 n.

200/9–10 *forgetfull . . . afore the*: Cf. Phil. 3: 13.

200/18–20 *the pecocke . . . abate*: I have been unable to find a classical source for the peacock's low opinion of himself; however, a fifteenth-century bestiary notes: 'Natura pauonis talis est quod in tantum se exaltat sua pulcritudine: quod desiderat volare et ire et iacere: sed postquam respicit suos pedes turpissimos: ita fortiter contristatur: quod non uolat alte sed manet tristis et dolens' (*De Pauone, Libellus de Natura Animalium*, ed. J. I. Davis (London, 1958)).

200/25 *knytteth*: kutteth *1533, adglutinet*.

200/28 *bubble*: burble *1533*, *bulla* (bubble). According to the *OED* (*Bubble*, v.), 'The Eng. *bubble* can hardly be separated from the earlier BURBLE, common in the same sense from 1300.'

201/2–3 *For . . . vengeaunce*: Cf. Juvenal, *Satires* 13: 189–92. By translating *muliebre* as 'chyldysshe', the Eng. translator weakens the allusion to Juvenal's *quod vindicta | nemo magis gaudet quam femina* (ll. 191–2).

201/29 *woldest consyder*: shuldest consyder *1533*, *consyderes*.

201/30 *yf he wolde not*: onlesse he wyll hym selfe *1533*, *si nolit*.

201/34 *whiche thynge*: whiche *1533*, *quod*.

202/19 *howe often*: how ofte *1533*, *quoties*.

202/22–9 *if . . . made*: Cf. Matt. 18: 23–35.

202/29–31 *To . . . large*: 'This man leaves wife and children at home and sets out on a pilgrimage to Jerusalem, Rome, or the shrine of St. James, where he has no particular business' (*Folly*, p. 70). See also above, 22/10–13 n.

202/32–5 *there . . . brother*: Cf. Matt. 5: 23–4.

202/37–203/1 *forgyue . . . offences*: See above, 202/22–9 n.

203/3–5 *What . . . enemy*: Cf. Rom. 5: 8–9.

203/6–7 *howe . . . shamefull*: Cf. Luke 18: 32–3.

203/8–9 *the heed . . . body*: Cf. Eph. 4: 15–16.

203/9 *membre of Christ*: Cf. 1 Cor. 6: 15.

203/11 *Ye*: Euen so *1533*, *Ita*; *were thou worthy*: were not thou vnworthy *1533*, *ne tu dignus eras*.

203/11–13 *In . . . iustyce*: See above, 202/22–9 n.

203/14–15 *whan . . . him*: Cf. Luke 23: 34.

203/15–16 *Is . . . brother*: Cf. Matt. 5: 39.

203/17–19 *not . . . seruaunt*: See above, 202/22–9 n.

203/23 *call and prouoke*: call in *1533*, *inuito*.

203/25 *ease it*: After this, the Eng. omits *si resarcire, resarci* (if [thou canst] repair it, repair it). See the Introduction, p. xl.

204/23 *blacke colour*: Black choler; an excess of black bile was formerly believed to be the cause of melancholy (*OED*, CHOLER 4.).

204/29–30 *whiche ought to be in euery man*: Not in Lt.

204/32–3 *To . . . kyndnesse*: Cf. Rom. 12: 21.

205/8–10 *how large . . . sayle*: Cf. Virgil, *Georgics* 4: 117.

205/10 *truly*: certayne *1533*, *Neque*.

205/11 *mynde or purpose*: mynde / purpose / or intencyon *1533*, *propositi*.

205/13–15 Sidenote 2: Not in Lt.

205/31–207/26 *Though . . . pleasaunt*: This section of the *Enchiridion* originally served as the conclusion of Erasmus's 'Letter to John the German'. See the Introduction, p. xvii.

206/4–5 Sidenote 1: The Eng. omits the explicit mention of Erasmus's motive in writing the *Enchiridion*: *ne in monachatum aliquem uanum illiceretur* (lest he be inveigled into a vain monastic life).

206/3–17 *A thynge . . . loue*: This passage was attacked by Zuñiga, *Erasmi . . . Blasphemiae et Impietates* (Rome, 1522) and defended by Erasmus in *Apologia ad Blasphemias Jac. Stunicae* (*OO, 9*, 364–5). A passage in Erasmus's response (*Rursus adducens locum ex Enchiridio . . . idem admonent quod ego*) was placed on the *Index librorum expurgatorum* (Madrid, 1584) (Bataillon, pp. 410–11 n.).

206/7–8 *walke . . . man*: Cf. Matt. 23: 15.

206/11–12 *euen . . . chrystendome*: *quasi extra cucullum Christianismus non sit*. Perhaps there is a reminiscence here of the medieval proverb: *Cucullus non facit monachum*. Cf. *Measure for Measure*, V. i. 257: '*Cucullus non facit monachum*: honest in nothing, but in his clothes.'

206/12–13 Sidenote 2: Not in Lt.

206/15–16 *bondage . . . the iewes*: *Iudaismum*. See above, 119/1–2 n.

206/17 *The ordre of monkshyp is not pytie*: Erasmus defended this controversial statement in his 'Letter to Beda' (Allen, *6*, 105) and his 'Letter to Robert Aldridge' (Allen, *7*, 139).

206/28 *holy prophete Chryst*: *Prophetas sanctos, Christum*.

206/30–1 *to be redde . . . daye*: Cf. Horace, *Ars Poetica*, l. 269.

206/35–6 *Origene, Ambrose and Augustyne*: See above, 49/9–10 n.

207/10 *recorded*: were mynded *1533*, *praemeditatos* (considered beforehand).

207/10–12 *to adorne . . . countrees*: See above, 46/16–17 n.

207/19 *father*: *parentem*. See above, 55/25 n. and the Introduction, p. lii.

207/22–4 *that thou . . . man*: Cf. Eph. 4: 13.

207/25 *to my hert*: in my hert *1533*, *animo . . . meo*.

207/26 *saynt Andomers*: The town of St. Omer in the Pas de Calais was founded around the Abbey of St. Bertin, where Erasmus was lodging when he completed the original version of the *Enchiridion*. St. Omer was later famous as the home of the Jesuit College for English recusants (1593–1762).

207/32 *Wynkyn . . . Byddell*: For Wynkyn de Worde and John Byddell, see the Introduction, p. xxxvi and n. 1.

APPENDIX

Substantive Variants from the later Sixteenth-century Editions

Page 10

5 *popes*] *1534*, bysshop of Romes *1538*, *1541*, *1544 A*, *1544 B*, *1548*; poope of Romes *Marian A, Marian B, 1576*.

9 *pope*] *1534*, bysshoppe of Rome *1538*, *1541*, *1544 A*, *1544 B*, *1548*; Poope of Rome *Marian A, Marian B, 1576*.

Page 11

18 *pope*] *1534*, bysshop of Rome *1538*, *1541*, *1544 A*, *1544 B*, *1548*, *Marian A, Marian B, 1576*.

Page 13

24 *pope*] *1534*, byshope *1538*.

24 *great prynces | of the pope of Rome | ye*] *1534*, gret and myghtye prynces, yea and *1541*, *1544 A*, *1544 B*, *1548*, *Marian A, Marian B, 1576*.

25 *popes*] *1534*, byshop of Romes *1538*.

25-7 *But . . . techer.*] *1534*, *om. 1541*, *1544 A*, *1544 B*, *1548*, *Marian A, Marian B, 1576*.

27–30 *There . . . prosperite.*] *1534*. But there is no man that dothe more or better seruyce vnto Princes, or that deserueth more thanke at theyr handes, than he doth, whiche endeuours him selfe all that he can that the people maye obedyently do their dutyes to god and their Prince, and vertuously encrease in welthe and prosperyty and so to liue in vnity togither. *1541*, *1544 A*, *1544 B*, *1548*, *Marian A, Marian B, 1576*.

Page 14

25 *preestes | bysshops | cardynalles | popes |*] *1534*, priestes, and bysshops that truly prech gods worde *1541*, *1544 A*, *1544 B*, *1548*, *Marian A, Marian B, 1576*.

25 *popes*] bisshops of Rome *1538*.

Page 19

30 *chefe pastour nexte vnto Chryste*] *1534*, pastour and folower of Chryste *1541*, *1544 A*, *1544 B*, *1548*, *Marian A, Marian B, 1576*.

Page 21

3 *pope*] *1534*, bysshop of Rome *1538*, *1541*, *1544 A*, *1544 B*, *1548*;
Pope of Rome *Marian A*, *Marian B*, *1576*.

Page 22

8 *popes*] *1534*, bysshop of Romes *1538*.

9 *popes*] *1534*, bysshop of Romes *1538*.

8–9 *yet . . . pardons*] *1534*, (whiche is all togyther vayne) yet he condempneth not all thynges *1541*, *1544 A*, *1544 B*, *1548*, *Marian A*,
Marian B, *1576*.

Page 90

Sidenote 2: *Monkes*] *1534*, *om.* *1541*, *1544 A*, *1544 B*, *1548*. *Not om.*
Marian A, *Marian B*, *1576*.

22 *monkes*] *1534*, relygious *1541*, *1544 A*, *1544 B*, *1548*. *Not emended*
in Marian A, *Marian B*, *1576*.

Page 113

16 *sayest masse*] *1534*, herest seruice *1576*.

19–20 *enforcest to be*] *1534*, expressest *1576*.

26 *sayest masse*] *1534*, hearest yᵉ communion *1576*.

31 *masses they haue ben at*] *1534*, times they haue ben at seruice *1576*.

Page 114

Sidenote 1: *masse*] *1534*, effecte of the Communion *1576*.

7 *aulter*] *1534*, table *1576*.

7 *masse*] *1534*, yᵉ effecte of the Communion *1576*.

Page 124

Sidenote 1: *Monkes.*] *1534*, *om.* *1541*, *1544 A*, *1544 B*, *1548*. *Not om.*
Marian A, *Marian B*, *1576*.

27 *monkes or*] *1534*, *om.* *1541*, *1544 A*, *1544 B*, *1548*. *Not om.*
Marian A, *Marian B*, *1576*.

Page 125

3 *monkes*] *1534*, religion *1541*, *1544 A*, *1544 B*, *1548*. *Not emended*
in Marian A, *Marian B*, *1576*.

6 *monkes*] *1534*, religion *1541*, *1544 A*, *1544 B*, *1548*. *Not emended in*
Marian A, *Marian B*, *1576*.

Page 138

26 *popes*] *1534*, prestes *1541*, *1544 A*, *1544 B*, *1548*. *Not emended in*
Marian A, *Marian B*, *1576*.

Page 154

13 *monke*] *1534*, bysshop *1541, 1544 A, 1544 B, 1548. Not emended in Marian A, Marian B, 1576.*

Page 163

14 *popes and bysshops*] *1534*, bysshops of Rome, and other bysshops *1538*; bysshops, and preestes *1541, 1544 A, 1544 B, 1548. Not emended in Marian A, Marian B, 1576.*

31 *monkes*] *1534*, relygyous *1541, 1544 A, 1544 B, 1548. Not emended in Marian A, Marian B, 1576.*

Page 177

26 *Peter . . . apostle*] *1534*, Peter and Paule ye apostles and capteyns of the churche *1538, 1541, 1544 A, 1544 B, 1548. Not emended in Marian A, Marian B, 1576.*

Page 193

Sidenote 1: *Fryers*] *1534, om. 1541, 1544 A, 1544 B, 1548. Not om. Marian A, Marian B, 1576.*

Page 206

Sidenote 3: *The order of monkes.*] *1534, om. 1541, 1544 A. Not om. 1544 B, 1548, Marian A, Marian B, 1576.*

Press-Variants in the 1534 *Enchiridion*

	Folger	University Microfilm of British Library	Rylands
Title-page	Ro = / terdame, and	Ro = / terdame, and	Ro= / terodame,
51/S.1	eve (for eye*, *1533*)	eve	eve
53/S.2	pynacle*	pynacle	pvnacle
106/6	peace*	peace	peacs
158/1	thou.	thou.	thou,*
165/25	Chryst.*	Chryst.	Chryst
195/23	y^e	y^t*	y^e

* indicates variant used in Text.

GLOSSARY

THIS glossary of the 1534 English translation of Erasmus's *Enchiridion militis Christiani*, based on the *Oxford English Dictionary*, contains words whose meanings and forms are not easily recognizable. In cases of ambiguity the original Latin has been consulted to ascertain the correct meaning. No attempt has been made to record such normal sixteenth-century variants as *a* for *o*, *c* for *k*, *d* for *th*, *en* for *in*, *i* for *j*, *in* for *vn* and *vn* for *in*, *n* for *m*, *t* for *d*, *u* for *o*, *u* for *v*, and *v* for *u*, *y* for *i*, etc., except in cases where such spellings might cause undue difficulty for the reader. Unusual or irregular spellings of proper names (e.g., *arestew*) have been recorded. In general, only the first occurrence of a word has been noted, with *etc.* indicating a later use in the text. In listing page and line numbers in the Glossary, precedence has been given to the occurrence of a word in the main body of the text over its occurrence in a sidenote. If the word occurs only in a sidenote, however, it has been duly marked (e.g. '*appropried* . . . 68/S.4'). Words with unusual meanings or grammatical forms found only in the *1533* text are also recorded (e.g. '*burble* . . . 200/28—*1533 Variant*'). In order to demonstrate the English *Enchiridion*'s highly innovative use of language, the nearly one hundred words, phrases, senses, and forms which antedate the *OED*'s examples are noted in the Glossary (e.g. '*agreyng* . . . *First use of this word recorded in* OED, *1540*.'). As evidence for linking this translation to William Tyndale, the approximately fifteen usages first found in his known works have also been indicated (e.g., '*atones* . . . 180/1 etc. *See n. for first use by Tyndale*.'). The abbreviation *See n.* refers the reader to the Commentary.

A

abrode *adv. See* **syt.**

abyde *v.* endure, bear 128/27

accept *pp.* accepted 84/34

accombred *pp.* encumbered 54/33

accompt *v.*, *accompt for* reckon, estimate 62/30; *pp.* accounted 24/29 *etc.*

accomptes *n. pl.* the rendering of a reckoning of responsibility 160/27

accordyngly *adv.* properly 61/5–6

acordynge *adj.* proper 202/10

acquyteth *v. pr. 3 sg.* repays, requites 148/1

acrased *ppl. a.* diseased 38/26

adamante *n.* alleged rock of surpassing hardness 11/14

adressed *pp.* redressed 164/21

aduenture *v. imp.* venture, dare 88/19

aduertysed *pp.* admonished 62/18

adulters *n. pl.* adulterers 121/26 *etc.*

aduste *ppl. a.* scorched 4/26

aduysement *n.* consultation 75/11; reflection 121/19

affectes *n. pl.* appetites 11/21; inward dispositions 18/30

affections *n. pl.* passions 12/27 *etc.*

affectuously *adv.* lovingly 126/23

afore *prep.* before 139/20

afore tyme *adv.* previously 5/35

after *adv.* afterwards 26/28 *etc.*

after *prep.* according to 6/4

agayne *adv.* besides 73/11 *etc.*

agaynst *prep.* towards 135/11

agreyng (to) *ppl. a.* in conformity with 6/13. *First use of this word recorded in* OED, *1540*.

a knowen *pp.* informed 162/9

aliaunce *n.* kinship, consanguinity 153/19

alienate *ppl. a.* alien 116/31. *First use of this sense recorded in* OED (*A. 2.*) *1599*.

almayns *n. pl.* Germans 101/23

aloes *n. pl.* aloes 184/22

alowe *adv.* below 64/22

alowe *v.* laud, praise, commend 20/23 *etc.*; *pp.* approved 5/16

amende *v. imperative* reform, convert 158/5; *pp.* 82/15

an hongred *ppl. a.* overcome with hunger 144/27–8 *etc.*

anone *adv.* at once 21/10 *etc.*

answered *v. pa.* spoke in reply to an opinion 137/21

anywhyt *adv. phr. See* **whyt.**

apace *adv.* (*Meaning not in* OED) profusely 67/24. *See* 67/23–4 *n.*

a parte *adv.* aside 136/15

aperteyneth *v. pr. 3 sg.* pertains 89/22–3

aplye *v.* conform 158/24

apparayle *n.* dress, attire 27/5

appert *adj.* open 140/9 *etc.*

appose *v.* question 125/6

appoynted *pp.* equipped 34/18 *etc.*

appropried *ppl. a.* attributed as proper to 68/S.4

approued *pp.* proved by experience, tried 86/13

apte *adj.* fit, prepared, ready 185/32

arbytrement *n.* absolute decision, direction or control 62/17

arestew *n.* Aristaeus 77/S.1. *See* 77/1–11 *n.*

aryght *adv.* justly, correctly 197/28

assayed *pp.* examined for the sake of information 47/3 *etc.*

assured *ppl. a.* made sure 136/14

assymuleth *v. pr. 3 sg.* makes like 184/15. *First use of this word recorded in* OED, *1547.*

astonyed *ppl. a.* astonished 117/1

athenes *n. pl.* Athenians 140/24

atones *adv.* immediately 180/1 *etc. See n. for first use by Tyndale.*

attempte *v.* seek to influence 10/20. *First use of this sense recorded in* OED (*II.* 7.) a. *1547.*

attendaunce *n.* attention 171/7 8

auauntage *n.* resulting benefit 8/6

auoyded *pp.* cleared out 14/12

authorite *n.* authorization 140/18. *See n.*

awaye *adv. awaye with* bear 88/29

awayt *n.* ambush 33/12 *etc. See* **wayte.**

B

bandes *n. pl.* fetters 76/19

bankettynge *vbl. n.* carousal 34/24.

First use of this word recorded in OED, *1535.*

banne *v.* curse 35/22

barbarous *adj.* foreign 47/28

be *pp.* been 80/22—*1533 Variant etc. See* 80/21–2 *n.*

beames *n. pl.* rays 141/21.

beare . . . in hande *v.* assure 91/6; *pp.* abuse with false pretence 101/8

beastly, beestly *adj.* animal, natural, 'carnal' 62/32. *Last use of this sense recorded in* OED (*1.*) *1526*; resembling a beast in conduct 119/28

becke *n.* gesture notifying a command 25/6 *etc.; pl.* nods 80/7

bederoll *n.* list of names 37/2

bedlem *adj.* mad 57/4

begyle *v.* overreach with guile 157/2

behest *n.* promise 42/S.2

behoueth *v. pr. 3 sg.* is incumbent (upon), proper or due 4/18

belly *n.* womb 73/10 *etc.*

belongeth *v. pr. 3 sg.* pertains 90/8 *etc.*

benefycence *n.* active kindness 173/17 *etc.*

bestowed *v. pa.* conferred as a gift 36/9. *First use of this sense recorded in* OED (*6.*) *1580.*

besyde *prep.* other than 71/5

besydes *prep.* in addition to 99/20. *First use of this sense recorded in* OED (*B.* 2.) *1535.*

besyeth *v. pr. 3 sg.* disturbs 75/23

besyly *adv.* carefully 189/25

besynes, besynesse *n.* anxiety 10/10 *etc.;* difficulty 61/29 *etc.;* activity 87/19 *etc.*

betokeneth *v. pr. 3 sg.* is a type or emblem of 32/S.1 *etc.*

blissed, blyssed *ppl. a.* blessed, enjoying the bliss of heaven 37/11 *etc.*

blyssest *v. pr. 2 sg.* bless 132/9 *etc.*

bolde *v. imperative* embolden 185/22 *etc.*

bonde *adj.* in a state of serfdom or slavery 63/10 *etc.*

bordes *n. pl.* supply of daily provisions 145/27

boulte *v.* examine by sifting 7/12

bounde *ppl. a.* under obligations of duty, gratitude 67/33 *etc.*

bourded v. pa. jested 5/30
bourdyngly adv. jestingly 5/29
bowe v. bend 139/7
brable v. dispute obstinately 12/30
Bragmanyes n. pl. Brahmins 151/23 etc. See n.
brede n., *fynger brede* (OED *brede*) Variant of 'finger-breadth' the width of a finger used as a measure 42/9; *nayle brede* the smallest amount 136/1. First use of this phrase recorded in OED (I. 3. a.) 1639.
brenne v. burn 40/36; pr. p. 33/16 etc.
breueness n. abbreviation, shortening 11/S.1. See 11/5–7 n.
breuyer n. Variant of 'breviary' (?) summary, epitome 4/22. First use of 'breviary' recorded in OED, 1547.
bukler n. shield 54/5 etc.
burble n. bubble 200/28—1533 Variant. See n.
burgynge pr. p. (for this form see OED *burge*) burgeoning, sprouting 205/17
but conj. unless 4/17 etc.; yet 158/14
but and yf conj. but if 197/28
by and by adv. phr. straightway 145/18–19
byleue n. assent of the mind 136/17. First use of this sense recorded in OED (2.) 1533.

C

caduke adj. transitory 94/16 etc.
call n. caul 128/S.2
call v. consider 139/23. See 139/23–4 n.
cam adj. See **clene cam**.
cankred ppl. a. corroded 4/26 etc. First use of this sense recorded in OED (2.) 1570.
canuasse v. subject to attack or assault 92/17. Only use of this sense recorded in OED (2. b.) 1599.
capacyte n. ability to take in impressions 120/6
capax adj. able and ready to take or receive 79/S.3. See also 170/2—1533 Variant and n.
carayn n. carrion 195/1
carefull adj. sorrowful 91/18
carenly adv. like carrion 184/32.

First use of this word recorded in OED, 1547–64.
case n., *in good case* well off 39/8
cast pp., *cast downe* (This sense not in OED) degraded 63/6
caste v., *caste a comptes* reckon accounts 193/24
cates n. pl. choice foods 44/14. First use of this sense recorded in OED (2.) 1578.
cauelacion n. frivolous fault-finding 20/S.5. First use of this sense recorded in OED (1. b.) c. 1540.
cause v. be the cause of 172/2
causes n. pl., *in lyghter causes* in cases of smaller consequence 124/15
cautel n. caution 38/7 etc.
cecyle n. Sicily 41/S.3
certes adv. certainly 37/14
chalenge v. lay claim to 27/6
chaunce n. fortune 10/3 etc.; pl. mishaps 6/6
chaunceth v. pr. 3 sg. happens 14/18 etc.; pp. come about by chance 99/7. See 99/6–7 n.
checke n. bitter reproach 148/1 etc.
cherefull adj. gladdening 94/5
choppe n., *at one choppe* at one stroke 193/6. First use of this phrase recorded in OED (I. 4. c.) 1581.
chorlysshe adj. ungracious 68/11
christendom n. Christianity 26/20 etc.
Chrystwarde adv. used as a n., *vnto Christwarde* toward Christ 57/5 etc. See OED -ward 6. b.
cicuta n. common hemlock 107/18 etc.
circumstaunces n. pl. 153/17. See n.
ciuyle adj. civilized 99/S.3. First use of this sense recorded in OED (8.) 1553.
claryfyed ppl. a made pure or clear 17/34
clawen v. fawn upon 165/13
clene adv. entirely 22/1 etc.
clene cam adv. phr. cross from the purpose 22/1–2. See n. First use of this phrase recorded in OED (Cam B.) 1579.
clerke n. scholar 3/10
clerkly adv. scholarly 5/20 etc.
coaction n. coercion 27/31

codde *n.* husk 45/3 *etc.*

cognisaunces *n. pl.* emblems 144/1

cogytacyons *n. pl.* reflections 86/30

colour¹ *n.* outward appearance 75/16

colour² *n.* choler 204/23. *See n.*

coloure *v.* embellish, set off in rhetorical colours 111/9. *Only use of this sense recorded in* OED (*2.*) c. *1300.*

coloured *ppl. a.* specious 151/16 *etc.*

combrance *n.* distress 60/S.4

combred *v. pa.* hampered 53/5 *etc.*

combrous *adj.* troublesome 8/25 *etc.*

comen *adj.* common 8/16 *etc.*

comfort(e) *n.* encouragement 36/23 *etc.*; refreshment 45/13

comforted *pp.* encouraged 85/13

comly *adj.* seemly 163/S.1

commaunde *v.* commend 29/13. *Last use of this sense recorded in* OED (*IV. 17.*) c. *1500.*

comme *v., comme of* come along! 147/11

comment *n.* commentary 206/33

commeth *v. pr. 3 sg.* converses 43/9 —*1533 Variant*

commodious *adj.* profitable 91/12

commodyously *adv.* profitably 115/15

commodites *n. pl.* material advantages 91/4 *etc.*

communaltie *n.* commonwealth 62/3 *etc.*; the common people collectively 119/9 *etc.*

commune *adj.* public 160/3 *etc.*

communycacyon *n.* conversation 39/21

comon *v.* converse 28/31

compact *ppl. a.* composed of 60/15; firmly put together 155/34

comparacions *n. pl.* comparisons 47/9 *etc.*

compare *v.* vie with 158/11

compasse *v.* ponder 32/13; *pr. 3 sg.* reaches 92/S.5, goes round 172/8

compendyous *adj.* succinct 32/2 *etc.*; expeditious, direct 169/13–14

compendyously *adv.* concisely 32/9 *etc.*

complexion *n.* 67/15 *etc. See n.*

composicions *n. pl.* 13/21. *See n. First use of this sense recorded in* OED (*III. 25.*) *1570.*

compounde *adj.* composite 135/7

compte *v.* consider (a thing) to be (so and so) 126/34 *etc.*

conceyte *n.* one's own private opinion 49/15 *etc.*; favourable opinion 95/29

conceyue *v. imp.* form a purpose in the mind 70/1; *were conceyued, pp.* made pregnant 110/6. *See n.*

conformed *pp.* made like 179/27

confortable *adj.* encouraging 94/6. *See* 94/5–6 *n.*

conforte *n., to be of good conforte* to keep one's courage 40/S.1

conforte *v. imperative* encourage 177/23

confusyon *n.* ruin, destruction 102/15

confyrmable *adj.* conformable 103/14 *etc.*

connyng *adj.* skilful 77/1 *etc.*

connyng *n.* erudition 97/28

conscience *n.* inward knowledge 141/14

consecrate *pp.* consecrated 35/14 *etc.*

contagyous *adj.* morally injurious 67/5

contagyousnes *n.* infectiousness 61/20 *etc.*

contynue *v.* persevere 85/20

conuenyent *adj.* appropriate 29/2 *etc.*

conuersacion *n.* mode or course of life 46/13 *etc.*; the action of having dealings with others 75/14 *etc.*; said figuratively of one's spiritual being 123/4

conuersaunt *adj.* dwelling habitually 142/13

conueyaunce *n.* conducting 83/28

copled *pp.* linked, joined 182/34

corage *v. imperative* encourage 185/22

corresyes *n. pl.* things that fret or cause care 151/21. *For this form see* OED (*Corsie*)

corrupte *ppl. a.* infected 64/17

corruptous *adj.* (*Not in* OED) capable of corrupting 20/19

cosyn *n.* a thing having affinity of nature to another 193/9

couenant *n.* mutual agreement 4/4

couert *n.* that which serves for concealment 25/11—*1533 Variant*

counted *pp.* considered 6/8 *etc.*

countenaunce *n., out of countenaunce* disconcerted, abashed 171/32

counterfayte v. imitate 43/28 etc.;
pa. portrayed 86/16; counterfeyted,
pp. imitated 57/9

couples n. pl. ligaments 122/15. Only
use of this sense recorded in OED (I.
2. trans. a.) 1535. See 122/14–15 n.

cowardfull adj. (Not in OED)
cowardly 37/30

craft(e) n. art 32/10 etc., skill 70/15
etc.; trick 77/S.1; pl. expedients
170/10

credence n. trustworthiness 74/2 etc.

croked adj. twisted 10/30

crokes n. pl. convolutions 7/27. See
7/27–8 n.

crudelite n. cruelty 69/13–14

currishnes n. cynicism 168/26–7.
First use of this word recorded in
OED, 1542. See 151/23 n., 168/
26–7 n.

cursed ppl. a., cursed spekyng male-
diction, cursing 68/7

custody n. safekeeping 84/14 etc.

customable adj. customary 34/9 etc.

customably adv. habitually 122/30

D

dade n. dad, father 125/30

damaske adj., damaske . . . waters
rose-water distilled from Damask
roses 34/28

damoyselles n. pl. damsels, maids-
in-waiting 47/S.1

dampne v. condemn 66/6 etc.

dastarde n. despicable coward 148/4

dasynge vbl. n. stupefaction 58/15.
First use of this word recorded in
OED, a. 1535.

daunger n., within his daunger at his
mercy 73/25; in daunger to liable
to 63/17

daungered pp. endangered, exposed
199/19

deale n., not . . . one deale not one bit
169/12. See also some deale.

deducted ppl. a. deduced, derived
116/21

dedycate ppl. a. devoted 43/14;
v. pa. 127/11

defaute n. fault, offence 24/19 etc.

defende v. maintain 16/29 etc.; repel
156/30

defye v. renounce 133/18 etc.

degree n. social or official rank 138/28

delectable adj. delightful 83/12

delectacyon n. delight 46/10 etc.

delue v. turn up with a spade 12/21
etc.

delyces n. pl. sensual or worldly
pleasures 164/5—1533 Variant

departed pp. divided 16/26

descryued v. pa. described 93/12

desyrousnesse n. eagerness 9/14.
First use of this word recorded in
OED, 1571.

dette ppl. a. owing 15/33

deyntyes n. pl. pleasures, joys 145/11

deyntyest adj. superlative choicest
145/8

diffyne v. state the nature or proper-
ties of 7/13

dilated pp. set forth at length 45/33

dilatyng vbl. n. widening 112/24

disalowe v. disapprove of 46/3;
pr. p. 15/30

discense n. descent 183/17

disdaynfull adj. scornful 145/28.
First use of this word recorded in
OED, a. 1542.

disgysynges vbl. n. pl. masks or
masquerades 140/25

dishonested pp. dishonoured 207/14

dishonesty n. dishonour 197/9 etc.

dissymule v. overlook, ignore 15/29
etc.

disworshyp n. dishonour 185/16

diuersitye n. distinction 68/29 etc.

diuyne adj. religious 6/30

diuynes n. pl. theologians 6/35 etc.

diuynite n. theology 6/30 etc.

do v. emphatic 7/15. See n. First use
of this form recorded in OED (B.
25. c.) 1581.

dogmies n. pl. (This form not found
in OED) tenets 151/24. First use
of word (Dogma) recorded in OED,
a. 1600.

domage n. harm 99/10 etc.

dotypol n. blockhead 190/11–12

douteth v. pr. 3 sg. is in doubt or
uncertainty 81/25 etc.

doutlesse adj. indubitable 139/29

draffe n. refuse, hog's wash 131/32

dreamyngly adv. lifelessly (Meaning
not in OED) 110/20. First use of

this word recorded in OED, *1545.*
See n.
drenches *n. pl.* potions 109/S.1
Dunces *n. poss.* Duns Scotus's 6/25.
See n.
dureth *v. pr. 3 sg.* lasts 204/4
durst *v. pa.* dared 59/25
dusked *pp.* dimmed 84/18
dylate *v.* enlarge, expatiate 111/9
dylygence *n., gyue dylygence (Phrase not* in OED) exert yourself 197/27
See n.
dyuell *n.* devil 181/17

E

easement *n.* alleviation 92/20 *etc.*
easye *adj.* indolent, careless 171/18.
First use of this sense recorded in OED (7.) *1649.*
echone *pron.* each one 4/19
effecte *n.* 11/24. *See n.*
effectuous *adj.* effectual 9/26 *etc.*
eiecte *pp.* expelled 108/21
eldermen *n. pl.* members of the governing class 62/25
elected *ppl. a. absol.* those chosen for eternal salvation 56/12 *etc. First use of this sense recorded in* OED (*I. b.*) *1548.*
election *n.* deliberate choice 84/24 *etc.*
enarracyon *n.* exposition 206/33.
First use of this word recorded in OED, *1563–87.*
encrease *v.* augment, enlarge 111/9
endeuer, endeuoyre *refl. v.* exert oneself 8/10, 6/18 *etc.; pr. 3 sg.* endeavours 13/29
endeuoyre *n., do his endeuoyre* exert himself to the uttermost 176/28
endued *pp.* possessed (of a certain quality) 5/18 *etc.*
endyted *ppl. a.* inspired 145/9
enforce *refl. v.* exert 12/8 *etc.*; strive 50/28; *enforsynge, refl. pr. p.* exerting 6/5
enforcement *n.* effort 51/27 *etc. First use of this sense recorded in* OED (2.) *1547–64.*
ensample *n.* pattern or model of conduct 47/24 *etc.*
ensewed *pp.* imitated 66/5 *etc.*

enterludes *n. pl.* interludes 140/25.
See 140/24–5 *n.*
entreate *v.* deal with 120/7; *pr. 2 sg.* 158/31; *pr. 3 sg.* handles (a subject) 6/25 *etc.*
entremedleth *v. pr. 3 sg.* concerns himself 6/31–2 *etc.*
equyte *n., equyte of nature* 86/19–20.
See n.
erbage *n.* herbaceous growth or vegetation 58/31
erecte *ppl. a.* elated with pride 199/31.
Only use of this sense recorded in OED (*II. 6.*) *1631.*
ernest *n.* pledge 182/20
errant *adj., errant theues* public, notorious robbers 161/11
eschewed *pp.* avoided 13/32 *etc.*
estate *n.* status 138/28; moral condition 180/29; *pl.* Second Estate, i.e., barons and knights 140/24.
See n.
estymacion *n.* worth in the opinion of others 12/2 *etc.*
ethneys, ethnicy, Ethnykes, ethnytes (*Only third variant spelling given in* OED) *n. pl.* Gentiles, heathen, pagans 43/26, 70/25, 170/6, 120/3
euangyles *n. pl.* gospels 12/S.1
euen *n.* eve of a holy day 29/16
euen, euyn *adv.* even 6/8 *etc.*
euer among *adv. phr.* (*Meaning not in* OED) repeatedly 64/30
euerywhyt *adv. phr. See* **whyt.**
euyll *adv., euyll at ease* ill at ease 38/28
euyll fauoured *adj.* ill-looking 101/3 *etc.*
exagerate *v.* dwell on the greatness of (faults) 22/25. *First use of this sense recorded in* OED (2.) *1564.*
exasperate *pp.* provoked to anger 17/22. *First use of this sense recorded in* OED (4.) *1534.*
excepte *conj.* unless 101/7
expedyent *adj.* conducive to a definite purpose 76/9
expert(e) *adj.* skilful 34/18 *etc.*; experienced 142/8
exposicyon *n.* explanation, interpretation 121/S.1
expouned *ppl. a.* explained 45/32

extreme *adj.*, *extreme iudgement* Last Judgment 186/S.2

extymulate *pp.* incited 19/10. *First use of this word recorded in OED, 1603.*

eyen *n. pl.* eyes 17/16 *etc. See the Introduction, p. xlvii, n. 1.*

eysell *n.* vinegar 179/15

eyther *pron.* each of the two 137/30. *See* 137/29–30 *n.*; *eyther other* both 121/25. *See n. for only use by Tyndale.*

F

face *n.* effrontery 9/18 *etc. First use of this sense recorded in OED (7.) 1537.*

facounde *adj.* facund, eloquent 154/12

facoundiousnes *n.* (*Not in* OED) eloquence 97/27

facoundyous *adj.* eloquent 57/17 *etc.*

facte *n.* deed 7/16 *etc. First use of this sense recorded in OED (1. a.) 1545.*

faculty *n.* occupation, profession 8/S.1; *pl.* arts, trades 52/31. *See* 52/31–2 *n.*

fame *n.* reputation 24/25

fantasyes *n. pl.* spectral apparitions 91/S.1

fardel(l) *n.* burden 193/12; *pl.* baggage 144/20 *etc.*

farderforth *adv.* for some distance further 184/18

farre forth, ferforth *adv.*, far 204/10; *so farre forth as* to the extent that 14/28 *etc.*; to the specified extent and no more 139/24

farthermore *adv.* furthermore 47/17 —*1533 Variant*

fassyon *n.* manner 7/22 *etc.*

fassyoned *pp.* formed 18/7

faute *n.* culpability 48/13

fawnynge vpon *pr. p.* flattering 22/19

fayne *adj.* obliged 49/1

fayne *adv.* gladly 204/7

fayners *n. pl.* contrivers of a fiction 52/30 *etc.*

fayneth *v. pr. 3 sg.* pretends 42/11; *pa.* represented in fiction 19/5 *etc.*; *pp.* fabled 52/26

faynynge *vbl. n.* dissembling 20/9 *etc.*

feared *ppl. a.* frightened 41/28 *etc.*

feders *n. pl.* shepherds 11/11. *First use of this sense recorded in OED (4.) 1611.*

felowe *n.* man 62/8

felyshyp *n.* fellowship, companionship 117/17

fende *n.* fiend, devil 180/8

fenseth *v. pr. 3 sg.* fortifies 42/33

ferforth *See* farre forth.

feruent *adj.* ardent 58/11 *etc.*

fesauntes *n. pl.* pheasants 145/26

fet(te) *pp.* fetched 52/20 *etc.*; derived 135/25

flesshwarde *adv.* used as *n.* to thy flesshwarde 83/12–13. Cf. 83/13 *n.* Only use recorded in OED, 1647. but cf. OED -ward 6. b.

fley *v.* flay, strip the hide off 19/31

flood *n.* flowing in of the tide 151/S.1

flumatyke *adj.* phlegmatic 68/9–10

fondnesse *n.* foolishness 149/19

for *prep.* with a view to 84/14

forbeare *v.* endure 119/30

foresaid *adj.* aforesaid 103/24

forgete *pp.* forgotten 80/1—*1533 Variant etc.*

formalytes *n. pl.* 8/26. *See* 8/25–6 *n.*

formest *adv.* most forward in position 36/29

forsothe *adv.* truly 22/8 *etc.*

forsweare *v.* perjure 186/20

forsworne *ppl. a.* perjured 36/4

forthwith *adv.* at once 25/14 *etc.*

forthwithall *adv.* immediately 58/31

fortune *n.* chance, luck 41/11 *etc.*

fortune *v.* happen 15/18 *etc.*

fourme *n.* model 135/26

frantik *adj.* insane 204/3

frenesse *n.* generosity 120/22

fret *pp.* eaten 4/27

frowarde *adj.* refractory 84/21 *etc.*

frowardly *adv.* perversely 65/20

fugytyue *adj.* fleeting 7/9

full *adj.* replete 128/18

furbyssher *n.* one who removes rust from armour 4/25

fyerse *adj.* violent like a wild beast 147/35

fygures *n. pl.* 10/30 *etc.*

fygureth *v. pr. 3 sg.* represents typically 72/S.4 *etc.*

fyled *pp.* corrupted 168/8
fylthy *adj.* disgraceful, contemptible 36/12 *etc. See also* **lucre.**
fynde *v.* support 100/22 *etc.*
fynyssheth *v. pr. 3 sg.* brings to completion 126/19

G

gape for *v. pr. 1 pl.* are eager to obtain 9/23
garnysshed *v. pa.* decorated 46/17 *etc.*
gaynsaye *v.* contradict 165/26
gendred *ppl. a.* engendered 60/2
generacion *n.* offspring 74/20 *etc.*; breed 176/1–2
gentyll *adj.* noble 37/23 *etc.*
gentylnesse *n.* condition of being noble in respect of birth 61/21
gestes *n. pl.* guests 80/19
gestynges *vbl. n. pl.* jokings 145/24. *See n. for first use by Tyndale.*
glutteth *v. pr. 3 sg.* feeds to repletion 131/32
gorgyous *adj.* showy 140/16
gorgyousnesse *n.* splendour 9/15. *First use of this word recorded in* OED, *1549.*
graffeth *v. pr. 3 sg.* implants 185/6; *pp.* grafted 121/2 *etc. See n. for first use by Tyndale.*
graue *v.* impress deeply 136/12; *pp.* 65/25 *etc.*
greces *n. pl.* stairs 112/3
greues *n. pl.* griefs 199/18
grosheed *n.* dullard 142/7. *First use of this word recorded in* OED, *1580.*
grosse *adj.* dull, stupid 117/18
grounde *n.* foundation 56/4
grounded *pp.* set on a firm basis 70/3
groundly *adv.* thoroughly 91/10
grudge *v.* trouble the conscience 189/31; *pr. 3 sg.* grumbles 38/10 *etc.*
grudgyng *vbl. n.* grumbling 61/30
grynneth *v. pr. 3 sg.* 156/11. *See n.*
guerdon *n.* reward 36/S.2
gule *n.* gluttony 205/26
gyrdle *n., vnder her gyrdle* under her control 186/24
gyueth backe *v. pr. 3 sg.* falls back, retreats 37/21. *First use of this sense*

recorded *in* OED (*XVI. 55. b.*) *1548.*

H

habergyon *n.* habergeon 53/22 *etc.*
halte *v.* limp 77/21 *etc.*
hange of *v.* depend confidently on 28/19 *etc. See* 28/19–20 *n.*
hanger *n.* short sword, originally hung from the belt 54/37
hansom *adj.* ready at hand 3/3 *etc. See n. for first use by Tyndale.*
hapned *pp.* befallen, happened 67/26
happe *v.* come to pass 94/26
happely *adv.* happily 32/15; perhaps 37/1 *etc.*
harde by *prep.* close by 188/3. *See n. for first use by Tyndale.*
hardy *adj.* daring 66/17
hardynes *n.* daring 68/13
harneys *n.* the body armour of a foot-soldier 4/26 *etc.*
hastyng *pr. p.* hurrying 87/17
haunte *n.* society 198/15
he *pron.* it 38/29 *etc.*
heare *n.* hair 109/25
helth *n.* salvation 53/22 *etc.*
hertles *adj.* destitute of courage 37/31 *etc.*; foolish 80/16
hertyly *adv.* sincerely 178/28
hest *n.* determination 61/14
his *poss. pron.* its 6/16 *etc.*
hoke *n.* hook 129/29 *etc.*
holding *ppl. a.* grasping 69/6
hole *adj.* healthy 145/19
holpen *pp.* helped 7/8
homely *adj.* plain 111/10
homlynesse *n.* plainness 44/29
honest *adj.* upright 46/20; honourable 63/3 *etc.*; comely 155/22
honestie, *n.* honour gained 38/23 *etc.*; integrity 62/23 *etc.*
honestly *adv.* in a becoming manner 61/28
honestynge *vbl. n.* (*Not in* OED) adorning 98/25
hoore *adj.* grey or white with age 168/2 *etc.*
horle *v.* utter (words) with vehemence 150/23—*1533 Variant. See* **whorle.** *First use of this sense recorded in* OED (5.) *1667.*

hote *adj.* angry 69/1
houefull *adj.* (*Not in* OED) advantageous 178/32. *See n.*
humanite *n.* kindness 169/7
husbande *n.*, *good husbande* thrifty manager 69/7
hye mynded *adj.* arrogant 115/2
hyest *adj.* highest 145/11
hym *pron.* it 92/S.5
hym selfe *reflex. pron.* itself 164/9

I

ieopard *v.* venture 148/14
ieopardous *adj.* dangerous 68/28
iestyng *vbl. n.* jesting 5/29
impenytency *n.* obduracy 183/10
impropriacyon *n.* appropriation 158/31—*1533 Variant. First use of this sense recorded in* OED (*2.*) *1611.*
inaccessyble *adj.* that cannot be reached 135/12. *First use of this word recorded in* OED, *1555.*
incircumcised *ppl. a.* uncircumcised 52/23
incogytable *adj.* inconceivable 135/13
incommodytees *n. pl.* inconveniences, disadvantages 92/9 *etc.*
incontynent *adv.* straightway 118/12
indifferent, indyfferent *adj.* neutral 80/31 *etc.*; equal, identical 92/11 *etc. First use of this sense recorded in* OED (*II.* 9.) *1547*; impartial 141/18
indifferently *adv.* equally 32/25 *etc.*
induce *v.* initiate, instruct 111/15. *Last use of this sense recorded in* OED (*3. a.*) *1511–12*; *pp.* moved 169/2
indurate *adj.* obstinate 63/23
infatygable *adj.* indefatigable 109/19
infecte *pp.* tainted with moral corruption 119/3
inflate *ppl. a.* puffed up 122/12–13
inquynate *pp.* corrupted 170/3. *First use of this word recorded in* OED, *1542.*
in sonder *adv.* asunder, into separate parts 16/26
instantes *n. pl.* 8/25. *See* 8/25–6 *n.*
instructe *ppl. a.* educated 6/28
instygate *pp.* stimulated 205/21.

First use of the word recorded in OED, *1542.*
instytute *ppl. a.* established 119/17
intellygyble *adj.* 104/7 *etc. See n.*
interpretate *pp.* interpreted 196/24
inwarde *adj.* internal 128/19
inwarde *adv.* mentally or spiritually 107/S.2
ioconde *adj.* cheerful 87/S.1
iote *n.* jot 49/5 *etc. See* 49/5–6 *n. for first use by Tyndale; see also* **tytle.**
iowels *n. pl.* jewels 48/27
iterateth *v. pr. 3 sg.* asserts repeatedly 126/19 *etc. See n. for first use by Tyndale*; *pr. p.* repeating (an action) 187/16. *First use of this sense recorded in* OED (*1.*) *1533.*
iudgement *n.* opinion 188/18
iust *v.* join battle 42/3

K

kalendas *n.* 128/26 *etc. See n.*
Katherynes knottes *n. pl.* 126/33. *See* 126/32–3 *n.*
knappisshnes *n.* abruptness 158/1. *First use of this word recorded in* OED, *1617.*
knowen *pp.* apprised 83/5
knowlegeth *v. pr. 3 sg.* recognizes as true 143/27
kynde *n.* class 20/3; sex 68/15; *gone out of kynde* degenerated 61/21, *growe out of kynde* degenerate 79/22. *First use of this phrase recorded in* OED (*I. 3. d.*) a. *1547.*
kynrede *n.*, *in a maner of kynrede* as it were cognate 135/20

L

lacedemonyes *n. pl.* Lacedemonians, Spartans 141/22
ladeth *v. pr. 3 sg.* burdens 53/4 *etc. First use of this sense recorded in* OED (*I. 1. c.*) *1538*; lade, *pp.* 64/4
ladynge *pr. p.* loading 158/6
lady psalters *n. pl.* 126/32. *See* 126/32–3 *n.*
laude *n.* praise 96/6
laude *v.* praise 79/3
laye *v.*, *laye . . . at* attack 174/1
layser, leyser *n.* leisure 7/23 *etc.*

leest *conj.* lest 17/8 *etc.*

leest *n.* defect 51/20 cf. OED *last sb.*³; (*last recorded use* c. *1380*)

leestway *n.*, *at the leestway* at least 86/24 *etc.*

lese *v.* lose 4/16 *etc.*

let *v. absol.* hinder 117/26; *letteth pr. 3 sg.* 63/20

lethargy *n.* prolonged and unnatural sleep 133/31

leude, lewde *adj.* vile 39/21; wicked 48/18, 20/26 *etc.*

leuer *comp. adj.* more acceptable 94/10 *etc.*; *to haue leuer* to hold it preferable 92/27

leuer *comp. adv.* more willingly 25/4 *etc.*

leyser *n. See* **layser.**

list, lyst *v.* wish 53/24 *etc.*; *impers. with dat.* 147/14

logycyner *n.* (*Not in* OED) *Variant of 'logicianer'* logician 154/10. *First use of this word recorded in* OED, *1548.*

luckely *adv.* happily 6/17

lucre *n.* profit 18/16 *etc.*; *fylthy lucre* dishonourable gain 12/28, 115/6, 166/27. *See* 12/28 *n. for first use by Tyndale.*

lure *n.*, *made to the lure* brought under control 186/3–4

lust *n.* desire 21/28

lustely *adv.* vigorously, energetically 70/4 *etc.*

lusty *adj.* vigorous 36/26 *etc.*

lycour *n.* liquid 13/7 *etc.*

lyghteth *v. pr. 3 sg.* lessens 124/22

lyghtly *adv.* easily 196/5

lyke *quasi-trans. v. with dat.* please 5/21

lyking *vbl. n.* healthy condition 192/16

lystes *n. pl.* limits 98/28; space enclosed for tournaments 170/7

lyuelode *n.* property yielding an income 144/17

lyuely *adj.* living 12/7 *etc.*

M

magnyfycall *adj.* of language: exalted 27/9. *First use of this sense recorded in* OED (*4.*) *1572.*

malepertly *adv.* presumptuously 48/29

malifycence *n.* evil-doing 181/S.1. *First use of this word recorded in* OED, *1598.*

maliuolence *n.* ill-will 153/18

mancypate *v.* enslave 181/26. *First use of this sense recorded in* OED (*2.*) *1574.*

maner *n.* kind, sort; with ellipsis of 'of' 6/9 *etc.*; *in a maner* as it were 8/2; *on that maner wyse* in that way 67/32; *pl.* morals 5/32 *etc.*

mansions *n. pl.* 45/20. *See n.*

manuell *n.* hand weapon, handbook 4/22 *etc. See n.*

marchaunt venterer *n. phr.* 98/23. *See n. First use of this noun phrase recorded in* OED, *1550.*

margaryte *n.* pearl as the type of something precious 144/11

marke *n.* target 14/23 *etc.*

mary *n.* marrow 134/26

maystry *v.* master 62/20. *Last use of this word* (*Maistrie*) *recorded in* OED c. *1532.*

mean(e) *adj.* inferior 16/S.3; intermediate in time 17/28 *etc.*; middle 41/24; intermediate in quality 81/2 *etc.*; moderate 93/1 *etc.*; moderate in degree of excellence 198/12; *in the meane season* meanwhile 17/36 *etc.*; *in the meane space* meanwhile 83/4

meanly *adv.* moderately well 179/33; *not . . . meanly* in no slight degree 172/24. *First use of this phrase recorded in* OED (*2. b.*) *1590.*

measurably *adv.* in moderation 46/7 *etc.*

measure *n.* moderation, temperance 120/23 *etc.*

meate *n.* food 38/19 *etc.*

meate bordes *n. pl.* dining tables 37/9

meddle, medell *v.* busy oneself 16/30 *etc.*; have sexual intercourse 159/S.1

mede *n.* recompense 36/14

meked *pp.* humbled 129/22

messe *n.* a portion of pulpy food 109/23 *etc. See also* **potage** *and n.*

mete *adj.* proper 9/30 *etc.*; suitable 52/5

milesij *n. pl.* inhabitants of Miletus 145/14 *etc. See* 145/14–15 *n.*

mischeuous *adj.* entailing harm 74/17 *etc.*

mistrusted *v. pa.* had doubts about 7/13 *etc.*

mo *adj.* more 13/34 *etc.*

mocions *n. pl.* desires, impulses, inclinations 64/31 *etc.*

mocke *n.* derisive speech 140/6; *pl.* 6/22 *etc.*

mockyng stocke *n. phr.* laughing stock 190/10. *See n. for first use by Tyndale.*

mol(l)yfyeth *v. pr. 3 sg.* renders soft 104/28–9; *pp.* softened in disposition 11/15

momblest *v. pr. 2 sg., momblest vp* utter in indistinct tones 83/4. *First use of this phrase recorded in* OED, *1538.*

momentany *adj.* transitory 87/1 *etc.*

monysshed *pp.* admonished 19/11 *etc.*

more *adj.* greater 150/29 *etc.*

mortyferous *adj.* death-dealing 186/ 36. *First use of this word recorded in* OED, *1535.*

moste *adj.* greatest 11/25 *etc.*

motyon *n.* suggestion 202/7

mought *v. Variant of 'mote'* must 126/11

muskballes *n. pl.* receptacles for the perfume musk 34/29

myndes *n. pl.* moral dispositions 9/36

mynysshe *v.* reduce 19/17 *etc.*; *pp.* lessened 144/30–1

mynyster *v. imp.* manage 99/7 *etc.*

myschefe *n.* wickedness 63/20 *etc.*

myscheuously *adv.* shamefully 162/14. *See n.*

mysdemynge *pr. p.* thinking evil of 120/9

mysdoyng *vbl. n.* wrongdoing 202/22

mysentreated *v. pa.* ill-treated 74/S.3

myslyke *v.* offend 5/15

mystrust *n.* suspicion, distrust 151/28–9 *etc.*

N

name *n.* appellation 144/17 *etc.*

naturall *adj., naturall foole* a simpleton by birth 91/21

naughty *adj.* bad, inferior 12/24 *etc. See n. for first use by Tyndale.*

naughtynesse *n.* the state of being bad, faulty, or defective in some respect 13/6 *etc. First use of this sense recorded in* OED (*2.*) *1550.*

ne *conj.* nor 49/32

nedely *adv.* of necessity 38/6 *etc.*

nedes *adv.* necessarily 86/6

Neomenye *n.* 128/13 *etc. See n.*

nere *adv.* closely 7/18

nere nother *pron.* neither of two things 109/29–30

nexte *adj.* nearest 14/25

nominals *n. pl.* Nominalists 9/4. *See* 9/3–4 *n.*

nones *pron., for the nones* on purpose 8/4 *etc.*

noryses *n. pl.* wet nurses 136/20

notable *adj.* conspicuous 24/1

nothyng *adv.* in no way 90/6 *etc.*

nouysses *n. pl.* novices 25/31

noye *v.* affect injuriously 20/16

noyous *adj.* troublesome 66/8

noysaunces *n. pl.* troubles 33/15 *etc.*

noysome *adj.* harmful 147/15 *etc.*

nyce *adj.* foolish 90/16

nyggardes *n. pl.* misers 140/16 *etc.*

nyggishnes *n.* stinginess 68/14 *etc First use of this word recorded in* OED, *1562.*

nyggysshe *adj.* stingy 174/13. *First use of this word recorded in* OED, *1542.*

nygh *adj.* near 64/16 *etc.*

nygh *adv.* nearly 68/31

O

obduracyon *n.* hardening in sin 183/10

obiecte *v.* attribute to anyone as a fault or crime 159/19

obprobryous *adj.* shameful 159/27

often *adj.* frequent 51/27

one *adj., at one tyme* at the same time 150/30–1

ones *adv.* at some future time 6/19

operacyon *n.* exertion of energy 38/25

oppressed *pp.* suppressed 179/25
opynyon *n.* estimation, reputation 141/9. *First use of this sense recorded in* OED (6.) *1551*.
or *conj.* ere 172/15 *etc.*
or . . . or *conj.* either . . . or 197/22–3
ordynate *adj.* regulated 44/S.1
ordynaunce *n.* warlike provision 8/13 *etc.*
orysons *n. pl.* prayers 124/2
other *pron. pl.* other things or persons of the kind mentioned 22/4 *etc.*
otherwhyles *adv.* sometimes 33/29 *etc.*
ouerhyp *v.* pass over 141/15
ouer ragyng *adv.* exceedingly 22/28
ouer ronne *v.* outrun, surpass 28/6
outher *adv.* either 72/14—*1533 Variant. See n.*
outward *adv.* externally 107/S.2

P

pall *n.* cloak 198/32
parcyall *adj.* prejudiced 154/15
parell *n.* peril 7/5
part taker *n.* sharer 79/15
parte *n.* function, duty 9/S.3; *on our parte* on our side 60/8 *etc.*
parte takyng *vbl. n.* the action of taking sides in a dispute 62/3. *First use of this sense recorded in* OED (2.) *1548*.
partye *n.* side in a dispute 9/2
passe *v.* care, take any heed 4/2. *First use of this sense followed by inf. recorded in* OED (X. 23. c.) *1549–62*; *pr. 3 sg.* surpasses 38/14 *etc.*
passynge *adv.* surpassingly, pre-eminently 110/27
pastymes *n. pl.* sports 34/10 *etc.*
paterns *n. pl.* models deserving imitation 139/20. *First use of this spelling recorded in* OED (1. β.) *1548*.
patron *n. Earlier spelling of 'pattern'* archetype 11/20 *etc.*
pauilyon *n.* tent 34/13 *etc.*
peased *pp.* quieted, calmed 204/16
pece *n.* a part of a whole 6/20
pecemeale *adv., by pecemeale (adv. phr.)* separately 7/12. *First use of this phrase in* OED (1. b.) *1545.*

pelfare *n.* (*Not in* OED) huckstering 13/22. *See n.*
peraduenture *adv.* perhaps 6/2 *etc.*
perces *n. pl.* Persians 141/22
perceyuaunce *n.* mental perception 106/29. *See n. for first use by Tyndale.*
perchaunce *adv.* perhaps 133/1
perfyt(e)nesse *n.* perfection in a religious sense 18/S.2 *etc.*
persed *pp.* pierced 52/20 *etc.*
perseuerant *adj.* lasting 204/5
perseuerantly *adv.* perseveringly 78/7
pertayneth *v. pr. 3 sg.* belongs 90/6
pertynacy *adj.* persistency 21/23 *etc.*
peson *n. pl.* peas 131/32—*1533 Variant*
pestyferous *adj.* morally pernicious 172/11
petie *v.* pity 6/1
peuysshnesse *n.* foolishness 184/24
philateirs *n. pl.* phylacteries 112/24 *etc. See n.*
phrenesy *n.* frenzy, delirium 23/21
piete, pietie, pietye *n.* (*Third variant spelling not given in* OED) devotion to religious duties 102/S.4, 98/7 *etc.*, 105/5. *First use of this sense recorded in* OED (II. 2.) *1604*; piety, dutifulness to superiors 103/S.1. *First use of this sense recorded in* OED (II. 3.) *1579. See the Introduction, pp. xliv–xlv.*
pite, pitie, pyte, pytie *n.* piety 38/30 *etc.*, 82/S.4 *etc.*, 118/7 *etc.*, 44/5 *etc. See the Introduction, pp. xliv–xlv.*
plenteous *adj.* copious 111/8
plenty *n.* abundance 59/11
plesauntly *adv.* pleasingly 135/12
polityke *adj.* sagacious in political affairs 150/3 *etc.*
politykly *adv.* prudently, with skilful management 149/4
poll *v. See* pyll.
pollers *n. pl.* plunderers 11/12
pollyng *vbl. n.* plundering 9/16
polycy *n.* prudent action 66/18
pommaunders *n. pl.* 34/28. *See 34/28–9 n.*
pope holy *adj.* hypocritical 58/S.1
porpas *n.* porpoise 145/26
potage *n.* soup of any kind 109/23 *etc. See also* messe *and n.*

potycaries *n. pl.* apothecaries 6/36

power *n.* faculty of the body 64/19 *etc.*

poynarde *n.* dagger 4/22. *First use of this word recorded in* OED, *1588.*

poynte *n.* condition, state 141/5; *poyntes of warre* warlike exercises 34/29

poyson *adj.* poisonous 172/11

praye *n.* booty 36/22

prece *n.* crowding 198/15

prece *v.* push 169/26

preposterous *adj.* foolish 21/30. *First use of this sense recorded in* OED (*2.*) *1542*; inverted in position or order 115/25. *First use of this sense recorded in* OED (*1.*) *1552.*

prescript *adj.* appointed 9/8

presente *adj.* immediately accessible 7/8 *etc. First use of this sense recorded in* OED (*5.*) *1539.*

presently *adv.* promptly 42/1; at the present time 86/9 *etc.*

prest, prest wages *n., n. phr.* payment in advance 73/18, 180/23. *See n.*

pretende *v.* claim 10/24–5

preuented *v. pa.* deprived 73/11 *etc. First use of this sense recorded in* OED (*II. 6.*) *1549*; *pr. p.* acting before 66/12

preuy, priuy *adj.* private 17/17 *etc.*; hidden 42/17

preuytees *n. pl.* secrets 52/1

price *n. See* pryce.

pricke *n.* dot 45/10

primate *n.* chief, leader 10/12

principates *n. pl.* principalities 54/17–18

priuely *adv.* secretly 74/23 *etc.*

probacion *n.* demonstration, proof 123/16 *etc.*

promyssyon *n., lande of promyssyon* Promised Land 32/S.2 *etc.*

propertie *n.* proprietorship 152/10 *etc.*

prophanat *pp.* profaned 132/3

propone *v.* propose for consideration 19/1

propounde *v.* propose for consideration 19/1—*1533 Variant. First use of this word recorded in* OED, *1537.*

propre *adj.* one's own 11/27

propriete *n.* ownership 158/31

proueth *v. pr. 3 sg.* learns by experience 92/5; *pa.* made trial of 91/20 *etc.*

prouidid *ppl. a.* prepared, ready 99/S.3. *First use of this sense recorded in* OED (*2.*) *1579.*

prouoked *pp.* stimulated 6/11 *etc.*

pryce *n.* value 80/7 *etc.*; *of pryce* of great value 95/18; *had in price* valued highly 139/33–4 *with inf.* 161/19–20

prycked *pp.* incited, provoked 174/12

purchasynge *vbl. n.* obtaining 91/24

put *v.* thrust, push 129/14. *Last use of this sense recorded in* OED (*B. I. 1.*) *c. 1440.*

pykequarelles *n. pl.* quarrelsome persons 20/32 *etc. See n. for first use by Tyndale.*

pyll *v., pyll and poll* ruin by extortions 15/10 *etc. See n. for first use by Tyndale.*

pyllers *n. pl.* robbers 11/12

pystels *n. pl.* epistles 10/22

pytcheth *v. pr. 3 sg.* makes fast with stakes, as a net or the like 186/26. *First use of this sense recorded in* OED (*B. 3.*) *1545.*

Q

queene *n.* strumpet 186/8; *quenes, pl.* 121/22

quick, quicke, quycke *adj.* full of acute reasoning 6/27; full of vigour, energy 10/8 *etc.*; lively 37/22; living 39/12 *etc.*

quickeneth *v. pr. 3 sg.* gives or restores life 50/31 *etc.*; *pp.* stimulated 37/30

quiddites *n. pl.* quiddities 8/26. *First use of this sense recorded in* OED (*1.*) *1569. See* 8/25–6 *n.*

quiteth *v. pr. 3 sg.* acquits (himself of a task) 37/20

quycknesse *n.* briskness 43/17 *etc.*

quyetnesse *n.* tranquillity 93/1

quyte *v.* requite, reward 37/6 *etc.*

R

racke *n.* frame to hold fodder 64/24

rage *n.* violent passion 67/36

rascall, raskal *adj.* belonging to the rabble 138/28, 63/7

raskall *n.* rabble 85/29; *rascals, pl.* unprincipled fellows 138/26. *First use of this sense recorded in OED (3.) 1586.*

rather *adv., the rather* the more readily 50/17; all the more quickly 67/26

rauysshed *pp.* transported in spirit 106/14 *etc.*

reals *n. pl.* Realists 9/3. *See 9/3–4 n.*

reboundeth *v. pr. 3 sg.* redounds 153/26 *etc.*

rebukefull *adj.* of a rebuking character 140/17

receyuable *adj.* capable of receiving 60/21 *etc.*

rechelesse *adj.* careless 41/27 *etc.*

recompenseth *v. pr. 3 sg.* makes compensation for 68/18 *etc.; pp.* repaid 137/3 *etc.*

recorde *v.* ponder 178/31

redils *n. pl.* riddles, mysteries 50/2

redounde *v.* return 154/31

reed *adj.* red 73/13 *etc.*

refrayne *v.* restrain 200/26; *pr. p.* 63/27

regenerate *ppl. a.* spiritually reborn 143/2

reiecte *pp.* rejected, cast away 171/23

rehersall *n.* recounting 141/16

reken *v. imperative* regard, consider 63/7

relygyon *n.* the monastic life 26/31 *etc.;* a particular religious rule 127/S.2

renne *v.* run 36/28 *etc.*

repent *refl. v.* affect oneself with contrition for something done 6/3 *etc.*

replenysshed *ppl. a.* fully or abundantly stocked 3/5

reprehended *pp.* reprimanded 23/16 *etc.*

reproued *ppl. a.* reprobate 188/18. *Last use in OED (1.) 1523.*

repugnynge *pr. p., repugnynge agaynst* striving against 72/9 *etc.*

requyrest, *v. pr. 2 sg.* dost request 32/22 *etc.;* requireth *pr. 3 sg.* demands 94/14 *etc.;*

resydue *n.* remainder 65/27

reuers *n. pl.* plunderers 161/11

reuyle *v.* subject to contumely or abuse 8/30

reysed *pp., reysed vp* caused to appear, especially by means of incantations 9/7

right, *adv.* very 9/26 *etc.*

roborate *pp.* confirmed 137/11

rolled *pp.* considered 179/21

rolles *n. pl. (Meaning not in OED)* coils 33/30

rowme *n.* office, function 6230/; position 98/30 *etc.*

rowte *v.* snore 34/21

rude *adj.* uneducated 7/33; inexperienced 71/1

rufflyng *ppl. a.* swaggering, arrogant 10/15

rufflynge, ruffeling *vbl. n.* disturbance 11/31 *etc.*

ryght *n.* justice 130/14

ryot *n.* extravagance 140/S.3

ryottours *n. pl.* revellers 145/15

ryueled *adj.* wrinkled 185/4

S

sacerdotes *n. pl.* priests 15/S.1 *etc. Only instance of this word recorded in OED, 1685.*

sadnesse *n.* gravity 142/22

sal(l)et *n.* 53/22; *pl.* 34/26 *etc. See n.*

sarazyns *n. pl.* Saracens 159/19

sauegarde *n.* safety 57/13

sauerly *adv.* with appreciation 145/14

sauour *v.* relish 4/6 *etc.;* have some of the characteristics (of) 10/26 *etc. First use of this sense recorded in OED (I. 4. a.) 1548; pr. 3 sg.* tastes well 145/3.1

scape *v.* escape 183/18

scarse *adv.* scarcely, barely 119/30 *etc.*

science *n.* knowledge acquired by study 98/S.2; *scyences, pl.* particular branches of knowledge or study 52/32. *See 52/31–2 n.*

sclaunder *n.* slander, calumny 7/11 *etc.*

sclaunderous *adj.* shameful 140/17–18

sclaundred *pp.* slandered, defamed 156/26

sclaundryng *vbl. n.* utterance of slanders 20/10 *etc.*

scrippe *n.* small bag, wallet 192/28

scripture *n.* inscription 15/32

scytes *n. pl.* Scythians 150/7. *See n.*

se *v., to se vnto* to do what is needful for 146/4

seace *v.* cease 57/21 *etc.*

selfe mynded *ppl. a.* obstinate in one's opinion 68/10–11. *See n. for first use by Tyndale.*

semblable *adj.* like, similar 178/24

sensyble *adj.* endowed with the faculty of sensation 71/6 *etc.*

sensybly *adv.* consciously 78/19

sentence *n.* maxim 20/S.2; opinion 21/3 *etc.*

seperate *pp.* separated, disunited 61/2

set *v., set by* esteem 169/23; *pp.* 192/19; *set of, pp.* put off, repulsed 175/11

shadowisshe *adj.* insubstantial 149/28–9. *First use of this sense recorded in* OED (*2. b.*) *1561.*

shake *pp.* weakened in belief 137/12. *See n.*

shap *n.* shape, form 48/25

shewed *pp.* displayed (light) 84/20

shitteth *v. pr. 3 sg. See* **shyt.**

shrewde *adj.* abusive 148/1 *etc. First use of this sense recorded in* OED (*12. b.*) *1538;* evil-disposed 199/13

shyrle *adj.* shrill 43/34

shyt *v.* shut 16/17 *etc.; shyt forth, pp.* expelled 16/17–18

sibarite *n. pl.* inhabitants of Sybaris 145/14 *etc. See* 145/14–15 *n.*

singularly *adv.* in a special manner 115/2

skolde *v.* brawl 8/32 *etc.*

skylleth *v. impers. pr. 3 sg.* matters 180/4

sleest *v. pr. 2 sg.* slay, destroy with sin 23/12 *etc.*

sleper *adj.* asleep 42/5

slyp(p)er *adj.* deceitful 33/28 *etc.;* slippery 183/17 *etc.*

smothe *adj.* bland 130/8. *First use of this sense applied to persons recorded in* OED (*6. b. (b).*) *1592.*

smytte *pp.* stricken strongly in feeling 171/32

so that *conj.* provided that 16/1

sodayn *adj.* impromptu 135/18. *First use of this sense recorded in* OED (*7.*) *1591.*

solempnely *adv.* solemnly, formally 27/24

solempnes *n.* the quality of being serious 69/9. *First use of this sense recorded in* OED (*Solemn 6. b.*) *1580–3. See n.*

soleyn *adj.* averse to society 68/11

some deale *adv.* somewhat 44/34 *etc.*

somme *n.* sum, whole 11/1

somthynge *adv.* somewhat 22/31 *etc.*

soole *adj.* sole, one and only 4/20

sore *adv.* sorely, greatly 4/27 *etc.*

sorowe *v.* regret 204/19

sorte *n.* group of animals 59/19

souke *v.* suck, extract 46/19

sowseth *v. pr. 3 sg.* immerses 185/8

spewe, spue *v.* vomit 120/8 *etc.;* reject with loathing 128/16

spoylyng *pr. p.* divesting oneself (of sins) 122/35

spyll *v.* destroy 156/9

squyre *n.* square, tool for measuring right angles 139/6

stable *v.* live in a stable 64/24

stablysshed *pp.* established, ordained permanently 14/17

stampeth *v. pr. 3 sg.* impresses permanently (on the mind) 126/16. *First use of this sense recorded in* OED (*III. 8. f.*) *1662.*

starke *adj.* sheer 199/26

stay *v.* support 40/35 *etc.*

stede *n.* place 18/23 *etc.*

stere(d) *pp.* stirred 172/26 *etc.*

sterres *n. pl.* stars 104/10

Stoicy *n. pl.* Stoics 55/S.3. *See* 55/27 *n.*

stomacke *n.* disposition 37/23 *etc.;* digestive organ 38/23

stoutly *adv.* vigorously 149/3

straunge *adj.* foreign 80/6 *etc.*

strayte *adj.* strict 81/11 *etc.;* so narrow as to make transit difficult 139/16; severe 198/20

straytly *adv.* strictly 25/18 *etc.*

straytnes *n.* distress 54/11; strictness 186/S.2

strength *v.* strengthen 48/7; **streng-**
thyng *pr. p.* strengthening 4/8
streyghtwaye *adv.* immediately
167/16. *See n. for first use by Tyn-*
dale.
strokest *v. pr. 2 sg.*, *strokest . . . thyne*
owne heed flatter yourself 167/26
stryues *n. pl.* disputes 15/20
study *n.* desire 6/11 *etc.*; *pl.* occupations, pursuits 34/10 *etc.*
study *v.*, *study for* be solicitous for
167/12
stutteth *v. pr. 3 sg.* stutters 50/4
styfly *adv.* stubbornly 151/26 *etc.*
subgestyon *n.* suggestion 172/S.3.
Only examples of this word (*Sub-*
jestion) *recorded in* OED, *1556 and*
1596.
subtyle *adj.* fine 104/28
subuerted *ppl. a.* overturned 62/23
etc.
sudorye *n.* a cloth for wiping off
sweat; handkerchief 116/32
suffysed *pp.* satisfied 196/13
summularies *n. pl.* 6/35. *See n.*
Only use of this sense recorded in
OED (*1.*) *1581.*
sure *adj.* safe, secure 113/9
suspecte *adj.*, *haue . . . suspecte* be
suspicious of 34/20 *etc. Last use of*
this phrase recorded in OED (*A. b.*)
a. *1533.*
suttell *adj.* subtle, wily 54/35
swage *v. imperative* assuage, reduce
115/4 *etc.*; *pp.* assuaged, mitigated
93/4
swalowe *n.* whirlpool 41/S.3
swarue *v.* turn away 165/25
swete *v.*, *swete apace* sweat profusely
67/23-4. *See n.*
sycke *adj.* deeply affected by repug-
nance 128/27. *First use of this sense*
recorded in OED (*A. 4. (d).*) *1590.*
symonyake *n.* simoniac 160/1
etc.
syngular *quasi-adv.* especially 32/8
etc.
syngulerly *adv.* specially 82/18 *etc.*
synke *n.* a gathering-place of vice
55/26
syt *v.*, *to syt abrode* 149/14. *See n.*
sythe *conj.* since the time that
89/9.

T

table *n.* a board on which a picture
is painted 60/12 *etc.*
take *pp.* taken 85/1—*1533 Variant*
etc.; *take vp* adopted 140/13
taste *n.*, *out of taste* not able to distinguish flavours 69/19. *First use of*
this phrase recorded in OED (*II. 4.*
b.) a. *1541.*
tasted *pp.* experienced 145/14
temper *n.*, *out of temper* out of proper
condition 38/18
tempred *pp.* regulated 155/22
tethes *n.* (*double plural*), *cast in their*
tethes brought up in reproach against
them 117/25 *etc. See n. First use*
of this phrase recorded in OED (*III.*
4. d.) *1535.*
than *adv.* then, at that time 142/1;
now and than occasionally 201/23
therhence *adv.* from there 183/18
therwith *adv.* with that as an instru-
ment 174/1
tho *demons. adj.* those 151/4 *etc.*
thorowe *adv.* through, from surface
to surface 132/3
thyderwarde *adv.* towards that
place 87/17
thynke *v. imperative* judge, consider
63/7; *pr. 3 sg.* supposes 147/11
tollage *n.* payment of toll or tribute
167/28
toppes *n. pl.* heads 45/15 *etc. First*
use of this sense recorded in OED
(*II. 3. c.*) *1624.*
toure *n.* tower 42/32 *etc.*
tournynge *ppl. a.* revolving 108/20-1.
First use of this sense recorded in
OED (*1.*) *1558.*
towe *n.* fibre of flax 137/7
toys *n. pl.* jokes 69/10. *First use of this*
sense recorded in OED (*I. 3.*) *1542.*
translate *v.* convey to heaven, said
of the death of the righteous 55/7
trauaylfull *adj.* (Not in OED) labo-
rious 69/23
trespace *n.* sin 79/6
tripodas *n. pl.* 37/9. *See n.*
tropes *n. pl.* 10/31. *See n. for first*
use by Tyndale. First use of this
word recorded in OED, *1533.*
troublous *adj.* painful 11/31 *etc.*

trowyng *pr. p.* believing 138/6
trumpe *n.* trumpet 129/15
tryacle *n.* treacle, antidote 48/13
trye *v.* ascertain the truth by test 10/20
turned *pp.*, *turned and wynded* turned this way and that 67/19
tykleth *v. pr. 3 sg.* arouses as by tickling 82/22
tytle *n.* alleged right 36/12; any minute point of a letter 45/9 *etc.*; *iote, or tytle* a minute amount 49/5–6. *See n.*

V

vadynge *pr. p.* fading, perishing 94/16
valure *n.* value, worth 20/31 *etc.*
valyauntnes *n.* valour 148/6
vary *v.* differ 142/16
vauntage *n.* profit 37/3
vayne *n.* 10/28. *See n.*; *pl.* 12/7 *etc.*
Ve *interj.* an exclamation of lament 196/24
very *adj.* true 13/14 *etc.*; *comp.* 146/3
veryly *adv.* truly 6/5 *etc.*
vesture *n.* garment 24/1 *etc.*
veyles *n. pl.* 26/1. *See n.*
violate *pp.* violated, subjected to injury 118/11
viser *n.* an outward appearance under which something different is hidden 18/13
vnclenly *adj.* morally or spiritually impure 64/31 *etc.*
vnderset *pp.* supported 85/8 *etc.*; *inf.* 168/12
vnderstande *pp.* understood 33/32 *etc.*
vndiscrete *adj.* injudicious 137/16
vnegall *adj.* unequal 181/33
vnexperte *adj.* inexperienced 149/23
vnfaynedly *adv.* without feigning, sincerely 152/24
vnfortunatly *adv.* unhappily 185/21. *First use of this word recorded in OED, 1548.*
vngracyousnesse *n.* wickedness, reprobacy 23/13 *etc.*
vnhardy *adj.* not courageous 34/31
vnhonest *adj.* uncomely 155/21. *Only examples of this sense re-*

corded *in* OED (*1. b.*) *1382* and *1398. See n.*
vnite *n.* unity 153/16 *etc.*
vniuersite *n.* the whole aggregate of persons 145/15
vnkynde *adj.* lacking in natural gratitude 35/10 *etc.*; unnaturally cruel 80/31 *etc.*; lacking in filial affection or respect 81/21
vnkyndely *adv.* ungratefully 181/25
vnkyndnes *n.* ingratitude 199/24
vnlyberal *adj.* illiberal, base, mean 202/17. *Only use of this word recorded in OED, 1570.*
vnneth *adv.* scarcely 129/16
vnsauery *adj.* tasteless 45/3 *etc.*
vnshamefastnes *n.* immodesty 22/31 *etc.*
vnshamefull *adj.* shameless 188/25
vnspecable *adj.* ineffable 48/24
vnsyttynge *ppl. a.* unbecoming, unfitting 197/31
vnto *prep.* until 77/11
vnware *adj.* unexpectedly 33/26 *etc.*
vnyt *pp.* united 60/22
vouched saufe *pp.* deigned 52/2
voyde *v.* keep clear of 38/7
vse *n.* accustomed practice 120/4
vse *v.* follow (a manner or course of life) 7/25 *etc.*
vtter *adj.* outward 45/2 *etc.*
vttermost *adj.* utmost, extreme 33/1–2 *etc.*; outermost 47/5
vtteryng *pr. p.* setting forth the character of 123/33. *See 123/32–3 n. for first use by Tyndale.*
vysyte *v.* punish 146/32
vytayles *n. pl.* victuals 100/25

W

walter *v.* roll to and fro 34/26 *etc.*
wanton *adj.* self-indulgent, luxurious 90/16. *First use of this sense recorded in* OED (*A. 4.*) *1538*; insolent in triumph or prosperity 141/11 *etc.*
warde *suffix* having a specified direction 97/7. *Cf. Chrystwarde* 57/5 and *flesshwarde* 83/13
ware *adj.* conscious 58/25; prudent 149/7 *etc.*
waster *n.* cudgel 67/24

watche *n.* watching as a devotional exercise 101/1 *etc.*

waye *n. a greate waye* to a great extent 95/26. *First use of this sense recorded in* OED (*II. 8. c.*) *1601.*

wayte *n., a wayte* ambush 33/31. *See n.*

wayted *v. pa., wayted on* escorted 48/S.2

waywardnes *n.* intractability 68/14

weaketh *v. pr. 3 sg.* weakens 84/32

wel fauouredly *adv.* handsomely 111/S.2

welth *n.* well-being 146/21

wenches *n. pl.* young women 166/32 *etc.*

wenen *v.* believe 81/33 *etc.; pr. p.* 138/6

werre *n.* war 4/24

wete *v. See* wyte.

wetyngly *adv.* knowingly 81/23 *etc.*

wexe *v.* wax, grow 17/26 *etc.; woxen, pp.* become, turned 11/16 *etc.*

weyeth *v. pr. 3 sg.* sinks through its own heaviness 62/28

whan *conj.* since 116/18

what *interrog. pron.* 166/11. *See* 166/11–12 *n.*

wherwith *rel. adv.* whereby 106/3

wher(e)withall *interrog. adv.* with what 119/14–15. *First use of this form recorded in* OED (*I. 1.*) *1535; rel. adv.* whereby 79/7 *etc. First use of this form recorded in* OED (*II. 2.*) *1578.*

whether *adj.* whichever of the two 79/19 *etc.; interrog. pron.* whither, to what purpose 101/7; *whether . . . or* 139/18–19. *See n.*

whome *rel. pron.* which 170/9

whorle *v.* throw or cast with violence, confused with *hurl* 150/23. *See* horle

whyle *n., one whyle (adv. phr.)* on one occasion 106/3; *an other whyle (adv. phr.)* on another occasion 106/4

whyles *conj.* while, during the time that 7/14

whyt *n., anywhyt (adv. phr.)* in the least degree 194/2; *euerywhyt (adv. phr.)* completely 193/6. *See n. for first use by Tyndale*; *one whyt (adv. phr.)* in the least degree 142/21

wise *n., on this wise* in this way 49/1 *etc.*

withal *prep.* substituted for 'with', *prep. in postposition* 67/35 *etc.*

withall *adv.* therewith 5/24; *to begyn withall* 46/4. *See n. for first use by Tyndale.*

withdrawe *v.* draw away, deflect 170/20

withinforth *adv.* everywhere within 93/9 *etc.*

without *prep.* outside 18/9 *etc.*

withoutforth *adv.* everywhere without 93/8 *etc.*

wolde *v. pa.* wished 7/26 *etc.*

wonderer of *n.* one who has a profound admiration for 141/5. *First use of this word recorded in* OED, *1573.*

wonderfull *adj.* such as to excite astonishment 68/24 *etc.*

wondryng *vbl. n.* marvelling 161/12

worde *n.* (*Variant spelling of 'worlde'—1534*) society at large 120/15. *First use of this sense recorded in* OED (III. 15.) *1603;* the cosmos 133/20

wordly *adj.* (*Variant spelling of 'worldly'—1533*) secular 28/18

worlde *n., it is a worlde* it is a marvel 24/4

wormes *n. pl.* insects 147/15

worshipful *adj.* honourable 142/20 *etc.*

woxen *pp. See* wexe.

wrake *n.* wreck 101/17

wraste *v.* turn 12/26

wrastle *v.* wrestle 35/28 *etc.*

wreke *n.* revenge 31/23 *etc.*

wresten *v.* turn from the true or proper signification 164/19

wring, wrynge *v.* distress, rack 179/20; twist (a writing, words) 12/26

writhen *pp.* diverted (to a person) 28/18

wronge *adj.* false 144/17

wrought *pp.* rendered 75/31

wrye *v.* deviate 165/25; *pr. 3 sg.* turns aside 136/1 *etc.*

wydder *v.* wither, pine 134/26; *pa.* withered, shrivelled 77/21 *etc.*

wyfe *n.* woman 75/18

wylde *adj.* self-willed 141/11

wyll *n.* desire 11/28 *etc.*

wyn *v.* overcome 9/21

wynche *v.* recoil from 11/30. *See n.*

wynded *pp. See* turned.

wynke *v.* 'shut one's eyes' to something wrong 15/31

wynnyng *vbl. n.* gain, profit 101/16

wyt(te) *n.* the faculty of thinking 8/24 *etc.*; genius, intellectual ability 52/31. *See* 52/31–2 *n.*; mind 151/3; *pl.* the faculties of perception 71/6

wyte, wete *v., that is to wyte* that is to say 40/10 *etc.*

Y

ymagerye *n.* images collectively 139/20

ymagynacions *n. pl.* ideas 8/25

ymagyneth *v. pr. 3 sg.* plots 42/12

yonglynges *n. pl.* beginners, novices 178/21

yuell *adv.* ill, wrongfully 71/14 *etc.* severely 179/20

yuels *n. pl.* evils 182/16

LIST OF PROPER NAMES

(The names of tribes, countries, and nations have been omitted unless they were deemed to be of interest or difficulty; the references are selective).

CORRIGENDA

p. xxii, l. 28: *delete* [?]
p. xxiii, l. 3: *for* in two *read* two in
p. xxiii, l. 5: *for* editions *read* edition
p. xlvi, l. 28: *for* 188/6 *read* 188/7
p. 37, variants, l. 1: *for* 14–15 *read* 15
p. 40, sidenote 1: *for* 27–9 *read* 26–8
p. 40, variants, l. 1: *for* 9 *read* 8; *for* 14 *read* 13; l. 2: *for* 15 *read* 14; *for* 32
read 31
p. 158, l. 1: *for* knappishsnes *read* knappisshnes
p. 196, sidenote 3: *transfer to next page and delete* l. 32–p. 197,

EARLY ENGLISH TEXT SOCIETY

LIST OF PUBLICATIONS
1864–1981

NOVEMBER 1981

Orders from non-members of the Society should be placed with a bookseller. Orders from booksellers for volumes in part 1 of this list should be sent to Oxford University Press, Saxon Way West, Corby, Northants. NN18 9ES. Orders from booksellers for volumes in part 2 of this list should be sent to the following addresses: orders for E.E.T.S. reprints to Oxford University Press, Saxon Way West, Corby, Northants. NN18 9ES; orders for Kraus reprints from North America to Kraus Reprint Co., Route 100, Millwood, N.Y. 10546, U.S.A., from other countries to Kraus Reprint Co., FL 9491 Nendeln, Liechtenstein.

EARLY ENGLISH TEXT SOCIETY

The Early English Text Society was founded in 1864 by Frederick James Furnivall, with the help of Richard Morris, Walter Skeat and others, to bring the mass of unprinted Early English literature within the reach of students and to provide sound texts from which the New English Dictionary could quote. In 1867 an Extra Series was started of texts already printed but not in satisfactory or readily obtainable editions. In 1921 the Extra Series was discontinued and all publications were subsequently listed and numbered as part of the Original Series. In 1970 the first of a new Supplementary Series was published; unlike the Extra Series, volumes in this series will be issued only occasionally, as funds allow and as suitable texts become available.

In the first part of this list are shown the books published by the Society since 1938, Original Series 210 onwards and the Supplementary Series. A large number of the earlier books were reprinted by the Society in the period 1950 to 1970. In order to make the rest available, the Society has come to an agreement with the Kraus Reprint Co. who reprint as necessary the volumes in the Original Series 1–209 and in the Extra Series. In this way all the volumes published by the Society are once again in print.

Membership of the Society is open to libraries and to individuals interested in the study of medieval English literature. The subscription to the Society for 1981 is £12·00 (or for U.S. members $25.00, Canadian members Can. $30.00), due in advance on 1 January, and should be paid by cheque, postal order or money order made out to 'The Early English Text Society', and sent to Mrs. Rachel Hands, Assistant Executive Secretary, Early English Text Society, 35 Beechcroft Road, Oxford. Payment of this subscription entitles the member to receive the new book(s) in the Original Series for the year. The books in the Supplementary Series do not form part of the issue sent to members in return for the payment of their annual subscription, though they are available to members at a reduced price; a notice about each volume is sent to members in advance of publication.

Private members of the Society (but not libraries) may select in place of the annual issue past volumes from the Society's list chosen from the Original Series 210 to date or from the Supplementary Series. The value of such texts allowed against one annual subscription is £16·00, and all these transactions must be made through the Executive Secretary. Members of the Society may purchase copies of books O.S. 210 to date for their own use at a discount of 25% of the listed prices; private members (but not libraries) may purchase earlier publications at a similar discount. All such orders must be sent to the Assistant Executive Secretary.

Details of books, the cost of membership and its privileges, are revised from time to time. The prices of books are subject to alteration without notice. This list is brought up to date annually, and the current edition should be consulted.

November 1981

ORIGINAL SERIES 1938-1980

O.S. 210 **Sir Gawain and the Green Knight,** re-ed. I. Gollancz, with intro- £3·25
ductory essays by Mabel Day and M. S. Serjeantson. 1940 *(for*
1938), *reprinted* 1966.

211 **The Dicts and Sayings of the Philosophers:** translations made by £8·75
Stephen Scrope, William Worcester and anonymous translator,
ed. C. F. Bühler. 1941 *(for* 1939), *reprinted* 1961.

212 **The Book of Margery Kempe,** Vol. I, Text *(all published),* ed. S. B. £8·25
Meech, with notes and appendices by S. B. Meech and H. E. Allen.
1940 *(for* 1939), *reprinted* 1961.

213 **Ælfric's De Temporibus Anni,** ed. H. Henel. 1942 *(for* 1940), *re-* £4·75
printed 1970.

214 **Forty-Six Lives translated from Boccaccio's De Claris Mulieribus** £6·00
by Henry Parker, Lord Morley, ed. H. G. Wright. 1943 *(for* 1940),
reprinted 1970.

215, 220 **Charles of Orleans: The English Poems,** Vol. I, ed. R. Steele £7·25
(1941), Vol. II, ed. R. Steele and Mabel Day (1946 *for* 1944);
reprinted as one volume with bibliographical supplement 1970.

216 **The Latin Text of the Ancrene Riwle,** from Merton College MS. 44 £5·00
and British Museum MS. Cotton Vitellius E. vii, ed. C. D'Evelyn.
1944 *(for* 1941), *reprinted* 1957.

217 **The Book of Vices and Virtues:** A Fourteenth-Century English £8·75
Translation of the *Somme le Roi* of Lorens d'Orléans, ed. W. Nelson
Francis. 1942, *reprinted* 1968.

218 **The Cloud of Unknowing and The Book of Privy Counselling;** ed. £5·75
Phyllis Hodgson. 1944 *(for* 1943), *corrected reprint* 1981.

219 **The French Text of the Ancrene Riwle,** British Museum MS. Cotton £6·00
Vitellius F. vii, ed. J. A. Herbert. 1944 *(for* 1943), *reprinted* 1967.

220 **Charles of Orleans : The English Poems,** Vol. II; *see above* O.S. 215.

221 **The Romance of Sir Degrevant,** ed. L. F. Casson. 1949 *(for* 1944), £5·75
reprinted 1970.

222 **The Lyfe of Syr Thomas More, by Ro. Ba.,** ed. E. V. Hitchcock and £7·25
P. E. Hallett, with notes and appendices by A. W. Reed. 1950 *(for*
1945), *reprinted* 1974.

223 **The Tretyse of Loue,** ed. J. H. Fisher. 1951 *(for* 1945), *reprinted* £4·75
1970.

224 **Athelston : a Middle English Romance,** ed. A. McI. Trounce. 1951 £4·75
(for 1946), *reprinted* 1957.

225 **The English Text of the Ancrene Riwle,** British Museum MS. Cotton £5·75
Nero A. xiv, ed. Mabel Day. 1952 *(for* 1946), *reprinted* 1957.

226 **Respublica :** an interlude for Christmas 1553 attributed to Nicholas £3·50
Udall, re-ed. W. W. Greg. 1952 *(for* 1946), *reprinted* 1969.

227 **Kyng Alisaunder,** Vol. I, Text, ed. G. V. Smithers. 1952 *(for* 1947), £8·75
reprinted 1961.

O.S. 228	The Metrical Life of St. Robert of Knaresborough, together with the other Middle English pieces in British Museum MS. Egerton 3143, ed. Joyce Bazire. 1953 (*for* 1947), *reprinted* 1968.	£4·75
229	The English Text of the Ancrene Riwle, Gonville and Caius College MS. 234/120, ed. R. M. Wilson with an introduction by N. R. Ker. 1954 (*for* 1948), *reprinted* 1957.	£4·25
230	The Life of St. George by Alexander Barclay, ed. W. Nelson. 1955 (*for* 1948), *reprinted* 1960.	£4·50
231	Deonise Hid Diuinite and other treatises related to *The Cloud of Unknowing*, ed. Phyllis Hodgson. 1955 (*for* 1949), *reprinted with corrections* 1958.	£5·75
232	The English Text of the Ancrene Riwle, British Museum MS. Royal 8 C. i, ed. A. C. Baugh. 1956 (*for* 1949), *reprinted* 1959.	£3·50
233	The Bibliotheca Historica of Diodorus Siculus translated by John Skelton, Vol. I, Text, ed. F. M. Salter and H. L. R. Edwards. 1956 (*for* 1950), *reprinted* 1968.	£9·00
234	Paris and Vienne translated from the French and printed by William Caxton, ed. MacEdward Leach. 1957 (*for* 1951), *reprinted* 1970.	£4·75
235	The South English Legendary, Corpus Christi College Cambridge MS. 145 and British Museum MS. Harley 2277, with variants from Bodley MS. Ashmole 43 and British Museum MS. Cotton Julius D. ix, ed. C. D'Evelyn and A. J. Mill. Vol. I, Text, 1959 (*for* 1957), *reprinted* 1967.	£7·25
236	The South English Legendary, Vol. II, Text, ed. C. D'Evelyn and A. J. Mill. 1956 (*for* 1952), *reprinted* 1967.	£7·25
237	Kyng Alisaunder, Vol. II, Introduction, commentary and glossary, ed. G. V. Smithers. 1957 (*for* 1953), *reprinted with corrections* 1969.	£5·75
238	The Phonetic Writings of Robert Robinson, ed. E. J. Dobson. 1957 (*for* 1953), *reprinted* 1968.	£3·50
239	The Bibliotheca Historica of Diodorus Siculus translated by John Skelton, Vol. II, Introduction, notes and glossary, ed. F. M. Salter and H. L. R. Edwards. 1957 (*for* 1954), *reprinted* 1971.	£3·50
240	The French Text of the Ancrene Riwle, Trinity College Cambridge MS. R. 14. 7, with variants from Paris Bibliothèque Nationale MS. fonds fr. 6276 and Bodley MS. 90, ed. W. H. Trethewey. 1958 (*for* 1954), *reprinted* 1971.	£6·00
241	þe Wohunge of Ure Lauerd and other pieces, ed. W. Meredith Thompson. 1958 (*for* 1955), *reprinted with corrections* 1970.	£5·00
242	The Salisbury Psalter, ed. Celia Sisam and Kenneth Sisam. 1959 (*for* 1955–6), *reprinted* 1969.	£9·75
243	The Life and Death of Cardinal Wolsey by George Cavendish, ed. R. S. Sylvester. 1959 (*for* 1957), *reprinted* 1961.	£5·00
244	The South English Legendary, Vol. III, Introduction and glossary, ed. C. D'Evelyn. 1959 (*for* 1957), *reprinted* 1969.	£3·50
245	Beowulf: facsimile of British Museum MS. Cotton Vitellius A. xv, with a transliteration and notes by J. Zupitza, a new reproduction of the manuscript with an introductory note by Norman Davis. 1959 (*for* 1958), *reprinted* 1981.	£11·25
246	The Parlement of the Thre Ages, ed. M. Y. Offord. 1959, *reprinted* 1967.	£4·50

O.S. 270	Fifteenth Century Translations of Alain Chartier's Le Traite de l'Esperance and Le Quadrilogue Invectif, Vol. I, Text, ed. Margaret S. Blayney. 1974.	£7·00
271	The Minor Poems of Stephen Hawes, ed. Florence Gluck and Alice B. Morgan. 1974.	£6·00
272	Thomas Norton's The Ordinal of Alchemy, ed. John Reidy. 1975.	£6·50
273	The Cely Letters, 1472–1488, ed. Alison Hanham. 1975.	£8·00
274	The English Text of the Ancrene Riwle, Magdalene College Cambridge MS Pepys 2498, ed. A. Zettersten. 1976.	£6·00
275	Dives and Pauper, Text Vol. I, ed. Priscilla H. Barnum. 1976.	£8·00
276	Secretum Secretorum, Vol. I, Text, ed. M. A. Manzalaoui. 1977.	£15·00
277	Laȝamon's Brut, Vol. II. Text (lines 8021–end), ed. G. L. Brook and R. F. Leslie. 1978.	£15·00
278	The Ayenbite of Inwyt, Vol. II, Introduction, Notes and Glossary, ed. Pamela Gradon. 1979.	£8·00
279	Of Arthour and of Merlin, Vol. II, Introduction, Notes and Glossary, ed. O. D. Macrae-Gibson. 1979.	£7·00
280	Dives and Pauper, Text Vol. I, Part 2, ed. Priscilla H. Barnum. 1980.	£8·00
281	Fifteenth Century Translations of Alain Chartier's Le Traite de l'Esperance and Le Quadrilogue Invectif, Vol. II, Introduction, Notes and Glossary, ed. Margaret S. Blayney. 1980.	£8·00
282	Erasmus Enchiridion Militis Christiani, an English Version, ed. Anne M. O'Donnell. 1981.	£16·00

SUPPLEMENTARY SERIES

S.S. 1	Non-Cycle Plays and Fragments, ed. Norman Davis with an appendix on the Shrewsbury Music by F. Ll. Harrison. 1970.	£7·00
2	The Book of the Knight of the Tower translated by William Caxton, ed. M. Y. Offord. 1971.	£6·00
3	The Chester Mystery Cycle, Vol. I, Text, ed. R. M. Lumiansky and David Mills. 1974.	£10·00
4	The Winchester Malory, a facsimile with introduction by N. R. Ker. 1976.	£57·00
5	Ælfric's Catholic Homilies, Series II, Text, ed. Malcolm Godden. 1979.	£17·00
6	The Old English Orosius, ed. Janet Bately. 1980.	£17·00
7	Seinte Katerine, ed. S. R. T. O. d'Ardenne and E. J. Dobson. 1981.	£17·00

FORTHCOMING VOLUMES

O.S. 283	The Digby Plays, ed. Donald C. Baker, J. L. Murphy and L. B. Hall. (1982)	£11·00
284	Hali Meiðhad, ed. Bella Millett. (1982)	£6·00
285	John Capgrave's Abbreuiacion of Cronicles, ed. Peter J. Lucas.	
	The Old English Herbarium and Medicina de Quadrupedibus, ed. H. J. de Vriend.	
	Aelred of Rievaulx's De Institutione Inclusarum : Two Middle English Translations, ed. J. Ayto and A. Barratt.	

LIST 2

ORIGINAL SERIES 1864–1938

O.S. 1 Early English Alliterative Poems . . . from MS. Cotton Nero A. x, £5·50
ed. R. Morris. 1864, *revised* 1869, *reprinted* 1965.

2 Arthur, ed. F. J. Furnivall. 1864, *reprinted* 1965. *Paper.* £1·50

3 William Lauder Ane conpendious and breue tractate concernyng ye £2·25
Office and Dewtie of Kyngis, ed. F. Hall. 1864, *reprinted* 1965.
Also available reprinted as one volume with O.S. 41 $11.25
William Lauder The Minor Poems, ed. F. J. Furnivall. 1870, *reprinted*
Kraus 1973.

4 Sir Gawayne and the Green Knight, ed. R. Morris. 1864. Superseded
by O.S. 210.

5 Alexander Hume of the Orthographie and Congruitie of the Britan £2·25
Tongue, ed. H. B. Wheatley. 1865, *reprinted* 1965. *Paper.*

6 The Romans of Lancelot of the Laik, re-ed. W. W. Skeat. 1865, *re-* £4·75
printed 1965. *Paper.*

7 The Story of Genesis and Exodus, ed. R. Morris. 1865, *reprinted* $17.50
Kraus 1973.

8 Morte Arthure [alliterative version from Thornton MS.], ed. E. Brock. £3·25
1865, *reprinted* 1967.

9 Francis Thynne Animadversions uppon Chaucer's Workes . . . 1598, £6·00
ed. G. H. Kingsley. 1865, *revised* F. J. Furnivall 1875, *reprinted* 1965.

10, 112 Merlin, ed. H. B. Wheatley, Vol. I 1865, Vol. IV with essays $41.25
by J. S. S. Glennie and W. E. Mead 1899; *reprinted as one volume*
Kraus 1973. (See O.S. 21, 36 for other parts.)

11, 19, 35, 37 The Works of Sir David Lyndesay, Vol. I 1865; Vol. II $35.00
1866 The Monarch and other Poems, ed. J. Small; Vol. III 1868 The
Historie of . . . Squyer William Meldrum etc., ed. F. Hall; Vol. IV
Ane Satyre of the Thrie Estaits and Minor Poems, ed. F. Hall.
Reprinted as one volume Kraus 1973. (See O.S. 47 for last part.)

12 Adam of Cobsam The Wright's Chaste Wife, ed. F. J. Furnivall. 1865, £1·50
reprinted 1965. (See also O.S. 84.)

13 Seinte Marherete, ed. O. Cockayne. 1866. Superseded by O.S. 193.

14 King Horn, Floriz and Blauncheflur, The Assumption of our Lady, £5·75
ed. J. R. Lumby. 1866, *revised* G. H. McKnight 1901, *reprinted* 1962.

15 Political, Religious and Love Poems, from Lambeth MS. 306 and £7·25
other sources, ed. F. J. Furnivall. 1866, *reprinted* 1962.

16 The Book of Quinte Essence . . . Sloane MS. 73 c. 1460–70, ed. F. J. £1·50
Furnivall. 1866, *reprinted* 1965. *Paper.*

17 William Langland Parallel Extracts from 45 MSS. of Piers Plowman, $10.00
ed. W. W. Skeat. 1866, *reprinted* Kraus 1973.

18 Hali Meidenhad, ed. O. Cockayne. 1866, *revised* F. J. Furnivall 1922 $7.50
(*for* 1920), *reprinted* Kraus 1973.

19 Sir David Lyndesay The Monarch and other Poems, Vol. II. See
above, O.S. 11.

20 Richard Rolle de Hampole English Prose Treatises, ed. G. G. Perry. $5.00
1866, *reprinted* Kraus 1973. *Paper.*

21, 36 Merlin, ed. H. B. Wheatley. Vol. II 1866, Vol. III 1869; *reprinted* $38.75
as one volume Kraus 1973.

22 The Romans of Partenay or of Lusignen, ed. W. W. Skeat. 1866, $20.00
reprinted Kraus 1973.

O.S. 23   **Dan Michel Ayenbite of Inwyt**, ed. R. Morris. 1866, *revised* P. Gradon,   £6·00
        reprinted 1965.

24   **Hymns to the Virgin and Christ** ... and other religious poems, ed. F. J. $10.00
      Furnivall. 1867, *reprinted* Kraus 1973.

25   **The Stacions of Rome, The Pilgrims Sea-Voyage** etc., ed. F. J. Furni- $5.00
      vall. 1867, *reprinted* Kraus 1973. *Paper.*

26   **Religious Pieces in Prose and Verse** from R. Thornton's MS., ed. G. G $26.00
      Perry. 1867, *reprinted* Kraus 1973.

27   **Peter Levins Manipulus Vocabulorum**, ed. H. B. Wheatley. 1867, $25.00
      reprinted Kraus 1973.

28   **William Langland The Vision of Piers Plowman**, ed. W. W. Skeat.   £4·50
      Vol. I Text A 1867, *reprinted* 1968. (See O.S. 38, 54, 67, and 81 for
      other parts.)

29, 34   **Old English Homilies of the 12th and 13th Centuries**, ed. R. Morris. $22.50
      Vol. I. i 1867, Vol. I. ii 1868; *reprinted as one volume* Kraus 1973. (See
      O.S. 53 for Vol. II.)

30   **Pierce the Ploughmans Crede** etc., ed. W. W. Skeat. 1867, *reprinted* $6.25
      Kraus 1973. *Paper.*

31   **John Myrc Instructions for Parish Priests**, ed. E. Peacock. 1868, *re-* $12.00
      printed Kraus 1973.

32   **Early English Meals and Manners**: The Babees Book etc., ed. F. J. $32.50
      Furnivall. 1868, *reprinted* Kraus 1973.

33   **The Book of the Knight of La Tour-Landry** (from MS. Harley 1764), $17.50
      ed. T. Wright. 1868, *reprinted* Kraus 1973.

34   **Old English Homilies of the 12th and 13th Centuries**, Vol. I. ii. See
      above, O.S. 29.

35   **Sir David Lyndesay The Historie of** ... Squyer William Meldrum etc.,   £2·25
      ed. F. Hall. 1868, *reprinted* 1965. *Also available reprinted as one*
      volume with O.S. 11, 19, and 37. See above, O.S. 11.

36   **Merlin**, Vol. III 1869. See above, O.S. 21.

37   **Sir David Lyndesay Ane Satyre** ... Vol. IV. See above, O.S. 11.

38   **William Langland The Vision of Piers Plowman**, ed. W. W. Skeat.   £4·75
      Vol. II Text B 1869, *reprinted* 1972. (See O.S. 28, 54, 67, and 81 for
      other parts.)

39, 56   **The Gest Hystoriale of the Destruction of Troy**, ed. G. A. Panton   £12·00
      and D. Donaldson. Vol. I 1869, Vol. II 1874; *reprinted as one volume*
      1968.

40   **English Gilds** etc., ed. Toulmin Smith, L. Toulmin Smith and L.   £11·25
      Brentano. 1870, *reprinted* 1963.

41   **William Lauder The Minor Poems**. See above, O.S. 3.

42   **Bernardus De Cura Rei Famuliaris**, with some early Scottish   £2·25
      Prophecies etc., ed. J. R. Lumby. 1870, *reprinted* 1965. *Paper.*

43   **Ratis Raving**, and other Moral and Religious Pieces in prose and verse, $10.00
      ed. J. R. Lumby. 1870, *reprinted* Kraus 1973.

44   **Joseph of Arimathie**: the Romance of the Seint Graal, an alliterative $10.00
      poem, ed. W. W. Skeat. 1871, *reprinted* Kraus 1973.

45   **King Alfred's West-Saxon Version of Gregory's Pastoral Care**, ed. H. $21.25
      Sweet. Vol. I 1871, reprinted with corrections and an additional note
      by N. R. Ker 1958, *reprinted* Kraus 1973. (See O.S. 50 for Vol. II.)

46   **Legends of the Holy Rood**, Symbols of the Passion and Cross-Poems, $17.50
      ed. R. Morris. 1871, *reprinted* Kraus 1973.

47   **Sir David Lyndesay The Minor Poems**, ed. J. A. H. Murray. 1871, $15.00
      reprinted Kraus 1973. (See O.S. 11, 19, 35, 37 for other parts.)

48   **The Times' Whistle**, and other poems; by R. C., ed. J. M. Cowper. $15.00
      1871, *reprinted* Kraus 1973.

O.S. 49 **An Old English Miscellany**: a Bestiary, Kentish Sermons, Proverbs of $21.25
Alfred and Religious Poems of the 13th Century, ed. R. Morris. 1872,
reprinted Kraus 1973.

50 **King Alfred's West-Saxon Version of Gregory's Pastoral Care**, ed. H. $16.25
Sweet. Vol. II 1871, reprinted with corrections by N. R. Ker 1958,
reprinted Kraus 1973. (See O.S. 45 for Vol. I.)

51 **þe Liflade of St. Juliana**, ed. O. Cockayne and E. Brock. 1872, *re-* £4·00
printed 1957. (See O.S. 248 for more recent edition.)

52 **Palladius On Husbandrie**, ed. B. Lodge. Vol. I 1872, *reprinted* Kraus $15.00
1973. (See O.S. 72 for Vol. II.)

53 **Old English Homilies of the 12th Century** etc., ed. R. Morris. Vol. II $30.00
1873, *reprinted* Kraus 1973. (See O.S. 29, 34 for Vol. 1.)

54 **William Langland The Vision of Piers Plowman**, ed. W. W. Skeat. £6·00
Vol. III Text C 1873, *reprinted* 1978. (See O.S. 28, 38, 67, and 81 for
other parts.)

55, 70 **Generydes**, a romance, ed. W. A. Wright. Vol. I 1873, Vol. II $17.50
1878; *reprinted as one volume* Kraus 1973.

56 **The Gest Hystoriale of the Destruction of Troy.** Vol. II. See above,
O.S. 39.

57 **Cursor Mundi**, ed. R. Morris. Vol. I Text ll. 1–4954, 1874, *reprinted* £4·50
1961. (See O.S. 59, 62, 66, 68, 99, and 101 for other parts.) *Paper.*

58, 63, 73 **The Blickling Homilies**, ed. R. Morris. Vol. I 1874, Vol. II £8·25
1876, Vol. III 1880; *reprinted as one volume* 1967.

59 **Cursor Mundi**, ed. R. Morris. Vol. II ll. 4955–12558, 1875, *reprinted* £5·75
1966. (See O.S. 57, 62, 66, 68, 99, and 101 for other parts.) *Paper.*

60 **Meditations on the Supper of our Lord**, and the Hours of the Passion, $5.00
translated by Robert Manning of Brunne, ed. J. M. Cowper. 1875,
reprinted Kraus 1973. *Paper.*

61 **The Romance and Prophecies of Thomas of Erceldoune**, ed. J. A. H. $8.75
Murray. 1875, *reprinted* Kraus 1973.

62 **Cursor Mundi**, ed. R. Morris. Vol. III ll. 12559–19300, 1876, *reprinted* £4·50
1966. (See O.S. 57, 59, 66, 68, 99, and 101 for other parts.) *Paper.*

63 **The Blickling Homilies**, Vol. II. See above, O.S. 58.

64 **Francis Thynne's Emblemes and Epigrames**, ed. F. J. Furnivall. 1876, $8.75
reprinted Kraus 1973.

65 **Be Domes Dæge, De Die Judicii**: an Old English version of the Latin £3·50
poem ascribed to Bede, ed. J. R. Lumby. 1876, *reprinted* 1964.

66 **Cursor Mundi**, ed. R. Morris. Vol. IV ll. 19301–23836, 1877, *reprinted* £4·50
1966. (See O.S. 57, 59, 62, 68, 99, and 101 for other parts.) *Paper.*

67 **William Langland The Vision of Piers Plowman**, ed. W. W. Skeat. $32.50
Vol. IV. 1 Notes, 1877, *reprinted* Kraus 1973. (See O.S. 28, 38, 54,
and 81 for other parts.)

68 **Cursor Mundi**, ed. R. Morris. Vol. V ll. 23827–end, 1878, *reprinted* £4·50
1966. (See O.S. 57, 59, 62, 66, 99, and 101 for other parts.) *Paper.*

69 **Adam Davy's 5 Dreams about Edward II** etc. from Bodleian MS. Laud $8.75
Misc. 622, ed. F. J. Furnivall. 1878, *reprinted* Kraus 1973.

70 **Generydes**, a romance, Vol. II. See above, O.S. 55.

71 **The Lay Folks Mass Book**, ed. T. F. Simmons. 1879, *reprinted* 1968. £10·00

72 **Palladius On Husbandrie**, ed. B. Lodge and S. J. Herrtage. Vol. II £4·75
1879. (See O.S. 52 for Vol. I.) *Paper.*
Also available reprinted as one volume with O.S. 52.

73 **The Blickling Homilies**, Vol. III. See above, O.S. 58.

74 **The English Works of Wyclif** hitherto unprinted, ed. F. D. Matthew. $40.00
1880, *reprinted* Kraus 1973.

75 **Catholicon Anglicum**, an English–Latin Wordbook 1483, ed. S. J. H. $31.25
Herrtage and H. B. Wheatley. 1881, *reprinted* Kraus 1973.

O.S. 76, 82   Ælfric's Lives of Saints, ed. W. W. Skeat. Vol. I. i 1881, Vol. I. ii   £7·00
1885; *reprinted as one volume* 1966. (See O.S. 94 and 114 for other parts.)

77   Beowulf, autotypes of Cotton MS. Vitellius A. xv. 1882. Superseded by O.S. 245.

78   The Fifty Earliest English Wills . . . 1387–1439, ed. F. J. Furnivall.   £5·75
1882, *reprinted* 1964.

79   King Alfred's Orosius, ed. H. Sweet. Vol. I Old English Text and Latin $18.75
Original (*all published*) 1883, *reprinted* Kraus 1974.

80   The Life of Saint Katherine, from Royal MS. 17 A. xxvii etc., ed. $17.50
E. Einenkel. 1884, *reprinted* Kraus 1973.

81   William Langland The Vision of Piers Plowman, ed. W. W. Skeat. $45.00
Vol. IV. 2 General Preface and indexes. 1884, *reprinted* Kraus 1973.
(See O.S. 28, 38, 54, and 67 for other parts.)

82   Ælfric's Lives of Saints, Vol. I. ii. See above, O.S. 76.

83   The Oldest English Texts, ed. H. Sweet. 1885, *reprinted* 1966.   £12·00

84   [Adam of Cobsam] Additional Analogs to The Wright's Chaste Wife,
ed. W. A. Clouston. 1886, *reprinted* Kraus 1973. (See also O.S. 12.)

85   The Three Kings of Cologne, ed. C. Horstmann. 1886, *reprinted* Kraus $21.25
1973.

86   The Lives of Women Saints etc., ed. C. Horstmann. 1886, *reprinted* $17.50
Kraus 1973.

87   The Early South-English Legendary, from Bodleian MS. Laud Misc. $36.25
108, ed. C. Horstmann. 1887, *reprinted* Kraus 1973.

88   Henry Bradshaw The Life of Saint Werburge of Chester, ed. C. Horst- $17.50
mann. 1887, *reprinted* Kraus 1973.

89   Vices and Virtues [from British Museum MS. Stowe 240], ed. F.   £4·50
Holthausen. Vol. I Text and translation. 1888, *reprinted* 1967. (See
O.S. 159 for Vol. II.)   *Paper.*

90   The Rule of S. Benet, Latin and Anglo-Saxon interlinear version, ed. $18.00
H. Logeman. 1888, *reprinted* Kraus 1973.

91   Two Fifteenth-Century Cookery-Books, ed. T. Austin. 1888, *reprinted* $18.00
Kraus 1981.

92   Eadwine's Canterbury Psalter, ed. F. Harsley. Vol. II Text and notes $18.75
(*all published*) 1889, *reprinted* Kraus 1973.

93   Defensor's Liber Scintillarum, ed. E. W. Rhodes. 1889, *reprinted* $17.50
Kraus 1973.

94, 114   Ælfric's Lives of Saints, ed. W. W. Skeat. Vol. II. i 1890, Vol. II.   £7·00
ii 1900; *reprinted as one volume* 1966. (See O.S. 76, 82 for other parts.)

95   The Old English Version of Bede's Ecclesiastical History of the English $28.75
People, ed. T. Miller. Vol. I. i 1890, *reprinted* Kraus 1976.

96   The Old English Version of Bede's Ecclesiastical History of the English $28.75
People, ed. T. Miller. Vol. I ii 1891, *reprinted* Kraus 1976. (See
O.S. 110, 111 for other parts.)

97   The Earliest Complete English Prose Psalter, ed. K. D. Bülbring. $15.00
Vol. I (*all published*) 1891, *reprinted* Kraus 1973.

98   The Minor Poems of the Vernon MS., ed. C. Horstmann. Vol. I 1892, $28.75
reprinted Kraus 1973. (See O.S. 117 for Vol. II.)

99   Cursor Mundi, ed. R. Morris. Vol. VI Preface etc. 1892, *reprinted*   £4·00
1962. (See O.S. 57, 59, 62, 66, 68, and 101 for other parts.)

100   John Capgrave The Life of St. Katharine of Alexandria, ed. C. Horst- $32.50
mann, forewords by F. J. Furnivall. 1893, *reprinted* Kraus 1973. *Paper.*

101   Cursor Mundi, ed. R. Morris. Vol. VII Essay on manuscripts and   £4·00
dialect by H. Hupe. 1893, *reprinted* 1962. (See O.S. 57, 59, 62, 66, 68,
and 99 for other parts.)   *Paper.*

102   Lanfrank's Science of Cirurgie, ed. R. von Fleischhacker. Vol. I Text $22.50
(*all published*) 1894, *reprinted* Kraus 1973.

O.S. 103   **History of the Holy Rood-tree**, with notes on the orthography of the $10.00
Ormulum etc., ed. A. S. Napier. 1894, *reprinted* Kraus 1973.

104   **The Exeter Book**, ed. I. Gollancz. Vol. I Poems I–VIII. 1895, $20.00
reprinted Kraus 1973. (See O.S. 194 for Vol. II.)

105, 109   **The Prymer or Lay Folks' Prayer Book**, ed. H. Littlehales. Vol. I $18.00
1895, Vol. II 1897; *reprinted as one volume* Kraus 1973.

106   **Richard Rolle The Fire of Love and The Mending of Life** . . . translated $20.00
by Richard Misyn, ed. R. Harvey. 1896, *reprinted* Kraus 1973.

107   **The English Conquest of Ireland**, A.D. 1166–1185, ed. F. J. Furnivall. $12.50
Vol. I Text (*all published*) 1896, *reprinted* Kraus 1973.

108   **Child-Marriages, Divorces and Ratifications** etc. in the Diocese of $22.50
Chester 1561–6 etc., ed. F. J. Furnivall. 1894 (*for* 1897), *reprinted*
Kraus 1973.

109   **The Prymer or Lay Folks' Prayer Book**, Vol. II. See above, O.S. 105.

110   **The Old English Version of Bede's Ecclesiastical History of the**   £6·00
English People, ed. T. Miller. Vol. II. i 1898, *reprinted* 1963.

111   **The Old English Version of Bede's Ecclesiastical History of the**   £6·00
English People, ed. T. Miller. Vol. II. ii 1898, *reprinted* 1963. (See
O.S. 95, 96 for other parts.)

112   **Merlin**, Vol. IV. See above, O.S. 10.

113   **Queen Elizabeth's Englishings of Boethius, Plutarch and Horace**, $18.00
ed. C. Pemberton. 1899, *reprinted* Kraus 1973.

114   **Ælfric's Lives of Saints**, Vol. II. ii. See above, O.S. 94.

115   **Jacob's Well**, ed. A. Brandeis. Vol. I (*all published*) 1900, *reprinted* $21.25
Kraus 1973.

116   **An Old English Martyrology**, re-ed. G. Herzfeld. 1900, *reprinted* $28.00
Kraus 1973.

117   **The Minor Poems of the Vernon MS.**, ed. F. J. Furnivall. Vol. II $22.50
1901, *reprinted* Kraus 1973. (See O.S. 98 for Vol. I.)

118   **The Lay Folks' Catechism**, ed. T. F. Simmons and H. E. Nolloth. $11.25
1901, *reprinted* Kraus 1973.

119, 123   **Robert of Brunne's Handlyng Synne** [and its French original], $26.25
ed. F. J. Furnivall. Vol. I 1901, Vol. II 1903; *reprinted as one volume*
Kraus 1973.

120   **Three Middle-English Versions of the Rule of St. Benet** and two $18.75
contemporary rituals for the ordination of nuns, ed. E. A. Kock.
1902, *reprinted* Kraus 1973.

121, 122   **The Laud Troy Book**, Bodleian MS. Land Misc. 595, ed. J. E. $36.25
Wülfing. Vol. I 1902, Vol. II 1903, *reprinted as one volume* Kraus
1973.

123   **Robert of Brunne's Handlyng Synne**, Vol. II. See above, O.S. 119.

124   **Twenty-Six Political and other Poems** . . . from Bodleian MSS. Digby $16.25
102 and Douce 322, ed. J. Kail. Vol. I (*all published*) 1904, *reprinted*
Kraus 1973.

125, 128   **The Medieval Records of a London City Church** (St. Mary at $37.50
Hill), 1420–1559, ed. H. Littlehales. Vol. I 1904, Vol. II 1905;
reprinted as one volume Kraus 1973.

126, 127   **An Alphabet of Tales**, an English 15th-century translation of the $36.25
Alphabetum Narrationum, ed. M. M. Banks. Vol. I 1904, Vol. II
1905; *reprinted as one volume* Kraus 1973.

128   **The Medieval Records of a London City Church**, Vol. II. See above,
O.S. 125.

129   **The English Register of Godstow Nunnery** . . . *c.* 1450, ed. A. Clark. $26.25
Vol. I 1905, *reprinted* Kraus 1971.

130, 142   **The English Register of Godstow Nunnery** . . . *c.* 1450, ed. A. Clark. $32.50
Vol. II 1906, Vol. III 1911; *reprinted as one volume* Kraus 1971.

O.S. 182	Speculum Christiani, ed. G. Holmstedt. 1933 (*for* 1929), *reprinted* Kraus 1971.	$31.25
183	The Northern Passion (Supplement), ed. W. Heuser and F. A. Foster. 1930, *reprinted* Kraus 1971. (See O.S. 145, 147 for other parts.)	$10.00
184	John Audelay The Poems, ed. E. K. Whiting. 1931 (*for* 1930), *reprinted* Kraus 1971.	$20.00
185	Henry Lovelich's Merlin, ed. E. A. Kock. Vol. III. 1932 (*for* 1930), *reprinted* Kraus 1971. (See E.S. 93 and 112 for other parts.)	$20.00
186	Nicholas Harpsfield The Life and Death of Sr. Thomas More, ed. E. V. Hitchcock and R. W. Chambers. 1932 (*for* 1931), *reprinted* 1963.	£11·75
187	John Stanbridge The Vulgaria and Robert Whittinton The Vulgaria, ed. B. White. 1932 (*for* 1931), *reprinted* Kraus 1971.	$12.50
188	The Siege of Jerusalem, from Bodleian MS. Laud Misc. 656, ed. E. Kölbing and M. Day. 1932 (*for* 1931), *reprinted* Kraus 1971.	$10.00
189	Christine de Pisan The Book of Fayttes of Armes and of Chyualrye, translated by William Caxton, ed. A. T. P. Byles. 1932, *reprinted* Kraus 1971.	$20.00
190	English Mediaeval Lapidaries, ed. J. Evans and M. S. Serjeantson. 1933 (*for* 1932), *reprinted* 1960.	£5·75
191	The Seven Sages of Rome (Southern Version), ed. K. Brunner. 1933 (*for* 1932), *reprinted* Kraus 1971.	$16.25
191A	R. W. Chambers: On the Continuity of English Prose from Alfred to More and his School (an extract from the introduction to O.S. 186). 1932, *reprinted* 1966.	£3·00
192	John Lydgate The Minor Poems, ed. H. N. MacCracken. Vol. II Secular Poems. 1934 (*for* 1933), *reprinted* 1961. (See E.S. 107 for Vol. I.)	£8·50
193	Seinte Marherete, from MS. Bodley 34 and British Museum MS. Royal 17 A. xxvii, re-ed. F. M. Mack. 1934 (*for* 1933), *reprinted* 1958.	£5·75
194	The Exeter Book, ed. W. S. Mackie. Vol. II Poems IX–XXXII. 1934 (*for* 1933), *reprinted* Kraus 1973. (See O.S. 104 for Vol. I.)	$17.50
195	The Quatrefoil of Love, ed. I. Gollancz and M. M. Weale. 1935 (*for* 1934), *reprinted* Kraus 1971. *Paper.*	$6.25
196	An Anonymous Short English Metrical Chronicle, ed. E. Zettl. 1935 (*for* 1934), *reprinted* Kraus 1971.	$17.50
197	William Roper The Lyfe of Sir Thomas Moore, knighte, ed. E. V. Hitchcock. 1935 (*for* 1934), *reprinted* Kraus, 1976.	$23.75
198	Firumbras and Otuel and Roland, ed. M. I. O'Sullivan. 1935 (*for* 1934), *reprinted* Kraus 1971.	$17.50
199	Mum and the Sothsegger, ed. M. Day and R. Steele. 1936 (*for* 1934), *reprinted* Kraus 1971.	$11.25
200	Speculum Sacerdotale, ed. E. H. Weatherly. 1936 (*for* 1935), *reprinted* Kraus 1971.	$18.75
201	Knyghthode and Bataile, ed. R. Dyboski and Z. M. Arend. 1936 (*for* 1935), *reprinted* Kraus 1971.	$17.50
202	John Palsgrave The Comedy of Acolastus, ed. P. L. Carver. 1937 (*for* 1935), *reprinted* Kraus 1971.	$17.50
203	Amis and Amiloun, ed. MacEdward Leach. 1937 (*for* 1935), *reprinted* 1960.	£5·75
204	Valentine and Orson, translated from the French by Henry Watson, ed. A. Dickson. 1937 (*for* 1936), *reprinted* Kraus 1971.	$25.00
205	Early English Versions of the Tales of Guiscardo and Ghismonda and Titus and Gisippus from the Decameron, ed. H. G. Wright. 1937 (*for* 1936), *reprinted* Kraus 1971.	$20.00
206	Osbern Bokenham Legendys of Hooly Wummen, ed. M. S. Serjeantson. 1938 (*for* 1936), *reprinted* Kraus 1971.	$20.00

O.S. 207 The Liber de Diversis Medicinis in the Thornton Manuscript, ed. £4·75
M. S. Ogden. 1938 (*for* 1936), *revised reprint* 1969.

208 The Parker Chronicle and Laws (Corpus Christi College, Cambridge £16·50
MS. 173); a facsimile, ed. R. Flower and H. Smith. 1941 (*for* 1937),
reprinted 1973.

209 Middle English Sermons, from British Museum MS. Royal 18 B. $30.00
xxiii, ed. W. O. Ross. 1940 (*for* 1938), *reprinted* Kraus 1981.

EXTRA SERIES 1867–1920

E.S. 1 The Romance of William of Palerne, ed. W. W. Skeat. 1867, *reprinted* $35.00
Kraus 1973.

2 On Early English Pronunciation, by A. J. Ellis. Part I. 1867, *reprinted* $15.00
Kraus 1973. (See E.S. 7, 14, 23, and 56 for other parts.)

3 Caxton's Book of Curtesye, with two manuscript copies of the treatise, $8.00
ed. F. J. Furnivall. 1868, *reprinted* Kraus 1973. *Paper.*

4 The Lay of Havelok the Dane, ed. W. W. Skeat. 1868, *reprinted* Kraus $20.00
1973.

5 Chaucer's Translation of Boethius's 'De Consolatione Philosophiæ', ed. £4·50
R. Morris. 1868, *reprinted* 1969.

6 The Romance of the Cheuelere Assigne, re-ed. H. H. Gibbs. 1868, $5.00
reprinted Kraus 1973. *Paper.*

7 On Early English Pronunciation, by A. J. Ellis. Part II. 1869, *reprinted* $15.00
Kraus 1973. (See E.S. 2, 14, 23, and 56 for other parts.)

8 Queene Elizabethes Achademy etc., ed. F. J. Furnivall, with essays on $20.00
early Italian and German Books of Courtesy by W. M. Rossetti and
E. Oswald. 1869, *reprinted* Kraus 1973.

9 The Fraternitye of Vacabondes by John Awdeley, Harman's Caveat, $8.75
Haben's Sermon etc., ed. E. Viles and F. J. Furnivall. 1869, *reprinted*
Kraus 1973.

10 Andrew Borde's Introduction of Knowledge and Dyetary of Helth, with $35.00
Barnes's Defence of the Berde, ed. F. J. Furnivall. 1870, *reprinted*
Kraus 1973.

11, 55 The Bruce by John Barbour, ed. W. W. Skeat. Vol. I 1870, Vol. IV £7·25
1889; *reprinted as one volume* 1968. (See E.S. 21, 29, for other parts.)

12, 32 England in the Reign of King Henry VIII, Vol. I Dialogue between $40.00
Cardinal Pole and Thomas Lupset, ed. J. M. Cowper (1871), Vol. II
Starkey's Life and Letters, ed. S. J. Herrtage (1878); *reprinted as one
volume* Kraus 1973.

13 Simon Fish A Supplicacyon for the Beggers, re-ed. F. J. Furnivall, $12.00
A Supplycacion to . . . Henry VIII, A Supplication of the Poore
Commons and The Decaye of England by the great multitude of shepe,
ed. J. M. Cowper. 1871, *reprinted* Kraus 1973.

14 On Early English Pronunciation, by A. J. Ellis. Part III. 1871, *re-* $25.00
printed Kraus 1973. (See E.S. 2, 7, 23, and 56 for other parts.)

15 The Select Works of Robert Crowley, ed. J. M. Cowper. 1872, *re-* $15.00
printed Kraus 1973.

16 Geoffrey Chaucer A Treatise on the Astrolabe, ed. W. W. Skeat. 1872, £4·50
reprinted 1968.

17, 18 The Complaynt of Scotlande, re-ed. J. A. H. Murray. Vol. I 1872, $35.00
Vol. II 1873; *reprinted as one volume* Kraus 1973.

19 The Myroure of oure Ladye, ed. J. H. Blunt. 1873, *reprinted* Kraus $40.00
1973.

20, 24 The History of the Holy Grail by Henry Lovelich, ed. F. J. Furnivall. $45.00
Vol. I 1874, Vol. II 1875; *reprinted as one volume* Kraus 1973. (See
E.S. 28, 30, and 95 for other parts.)

E.S. 21, 29   **The Bruce by John Barbour**, ed. W. W. Skeat. Vol. II 1874, Vol. £10·00
III 1877; *reprinted as one volume* 1968. (See E.S. 11, 55 for other part.)

22   **Henry Brinklow's Complaynt of Roderyck Mors**, The Lamentacyon of a $10.00
Christen agaynst the Cytye of London by Roderigo Mors, ed. J. M.
Cowper. 1874, *reprinted* Kraus 1973.

23   **On Early English Pronunciation**, by A. J. Ellis. Part IV. 1874, *re-* $30.00
printed Kraus 1973. (See E.S. 2, 7, 14, and 56 for other parts.)

24   The History of the Holy Grail by Henry Lovelich, Vol. II. See above,
E.S. 20.

25, 26   **The Romance of Guy of Warwick**, the second or 15th-century £8·50
version, ed. J. Zupitza. Vol. I 1875, Vol. II 1876; reprinted as one
volume 1966.

27   **John Fisher The English Works**, ed. J. E. B. Mayor. Vol. I (*all pub-* $30.00
lished) 1876, *reprinted* Kraus 1973.

28, 30, 95   **The History of the Holy Grail by Henry Lovelich**, ed. F. J. $26.25
Furnivall. Vol. III 1877; Vol. IV 1878; Vol. V The Legend of the Holy
Grail, its Sources, Character and Development by D. Kempe 1905;
reprinted as one volume Kraus 1973. (See E.S. 20, 24 for other parts.)

29   The Bruce by John Barbour, Vol. III. See above, E.S. 21.

30   The History of the Holy Grail by Henry Lovelich, Vol. IV. See above,
E.S. 28.

31   **The Alliterative Romance of Alexander and Dindimus**, re-ed. W. W. $8.75
Skeat. 1878, *reprinted* Kraus 1973.

32   **England in the Reign of King Henry VIII**, Vol. II. See above, E.S. 12.

33   **The Early English Versions of the Gesta Romanorum**, ed. S. J. H. £11·25
Herrtage. 1879, *reprinted* 1962.

34   The English Charlemagne Romances I: Sir Ferumbras, ed. S. J. H. £6·00
Herrtage. 1879, *reprinted* 1966.

35   The English Charlemagne Romances II: **The Sege of Melayne, The** $20.00
Romance of Duke Rowland and Sir Otuell of Spayne, ed. S. J. H.
Herrtage. 1880, *reprinted* Kraus 1973.

36, 37   The English Charlemagne Romances III and IV: **The Lyf of** £6·00
Charles the Grete, translated by William Caxton, ed. S. J. H. Herrtage.
Vol. I 1880, Vol. II 1881; *reprinted as one volume* 1967.

38   The English Charlemagne Romances V: **The Romance of the Sowdone** £5·75
of Babylone, re-ed. E. Hausknecht. 1881, *reprinted* 1969.

39   The English Charlemagne Romances VI: **The Taill of Rauf Coilyear,** £4·75
with the fragments of Roland and Vernagu and Otuel, re-ed. S. J. H.
Herrtage. 1882, *reprinted* 1969.

40, 41   The English Charlemagne Romances VII and VIII: **The Boke of** $60.00
Duke Huon of Burdeux translated by Lord Berners, ed. S. L. Lee. Vol. I
1882, Vol. II 1883; *reprinted as one volume* Kraus 1973. (See E.S. 43,
50 for other parts.)

42, 49, 59   **The Romance of Guy of Warwick**, from the Auchinleck MS. £11·50
and the Caius MS., ed. J. Zupitza. Vol. I 1883, Vol. II 1887, Vol. III
1891; *reprinted as one volume* 1966.

43, 50   The English Charlemagne Romances IX and XII: **The Boke of** $25.00
Duke Huon of Burdeux translated by Lord Berners, ed. S. L. Lee.
Vol. III 1884, Vol. IV 1887; *reprinted as one volume* Kraus 1973.

44   The English Charlemagne Romances X: **The Foure Sonnes of Aymon,** $21.25
translated by William Caxton, ed. O. Richardson. Vol. I 1884, *re-*
printed Kraus 1973.

45   The English Charlemagne Romances XI: **The Foure Sonnes of Aymon,** $35.00
translated by William Caxton, ed. O. Richardson. Vol. II 1885, *re-*
printed Kraus 1973.

46, 48, 65   **The Romance of Sir Beues of Hamtoun**, ed. E. Kölbing. Vol. I $31.25
1885, Vol. II 1886, Vol. III 1894; *reprinted as one volume* Kraus 1973.

E.S. 77, 83, 92   The Pilgrimage of the Life of Man, translated by John Lydgate $53.75
from the French by Guillaume de Deguileville, Vol. I ed. F. J.
Furnivall (1899), Vol. II ed. F. J. Furnivall (1901), Vol. III introduction, notes, glossary, etc. by K. B. Locock (1904); *reprinted as one
volume* Kraus 1973.

78   Thomas Robinson The Life and Death of Mary Magdalene, ed. H. O.   £3·50
Sommer. 1899. *Paper.*

79   Dialogues in French and English by William Caxton, ed. H. Bradley. $6.25
1900, *reprinted* Kraus 1973. *Paper.*

80   Lydgate's Two Nightingale Poems, ed. O. Glauning. 1900, *reprinted* $8.75
Kraus 1973.

80A Selections from Barbour's Bruce (Books I–X), ed. W. W. Skeat, $35.00
1900, *reprinted* Kraus 1973.

81   The English Works of John Gower, ed. G. C. Macaulay. Vol. I   £7·00
Confessio Amantis Prologue–Bk. V. 1970. 1900, *reprinted* 1978.

82   The English Works of John Gower, ed. G. C. Macaulay. Vol. II   £7·00
Confessio Amantis V. 1971–VIII, *In Praise of Peace.* 1901, *reprinted*
1978.

83   The Pilgrimage of the Life of Man, Vol. II. See above, E.S. 77.

84   Lydgate's Reson and Sensuallyte, ed. E. Sieper. Vol. I Manuscripts,   £5·75
Text, and Glossary. 1901, *reprinted* 1965. (See E.S. 89 for Part II.)

85   The Poems of Alexander Scott, ed. A. K. Donald. 1902, *reprinted* $10.00
Kraus 1973.

86   The Poems of William of Shoreham, ed. M. Konrath. Vol. I (*all* $26.00
published) 1902, *reprinted* Kraus 1973.

87   Two Coventry Corpus Christi Plays, re-ed. H. Craig. 1902; *second*   £3·50
edition 1957, *reprinted* 1967.

88   Le Morte Arthur, a romance in stanzas, re-ed. J. D. Bruce. 1903, $11.25
reprinted Kraus 1973.

89   Lydgate's Reson and Sensuallyte, ed. E. Sieper. Vol. II Studies and   £4·00
Notes. 1903, *reprinted* 1965. (See E.S. 84 for Part I.)

90   English Fragments from Latin Medieval Service-Books, ed. H. Little- $5.00
hales. 1903, *reprinted* Kraus 1973. *Paper.*

91   The Macro Plays, ed. F. J. Furnivall and A. W. Pollard. 1904. Superseded by O.S. 262.

92   The Pilgrimage of the Life of Man, Vol. III. See above, E.S. 77.

93   Henry Lovelich's Merlin, ed. E. A. Kock. Vol. I 1904, *reprinted* Kraus $27.50
1973. (See E.S. 112 and O.S. 185 for other parts.)

94   Respublica, ed. L. A. Magnus. 1905. Superseded by O.S. 226.

95   The History of the Holy Grail by Henry Lovelich, Vol. V. See above,
E.S. 28.

96   Mirk's Festial, ed. T. Erbe. Vol. I (*all published*) 1905, *reprinted* Kraus $26.00
1973.

97   Lydgate's Troy Book, ed. H. Bergen. Vol. I Prologue, Books I and II, $27.50
1906, *reprinted* Kraus 1973. (See E.S. 103, 106, and 126 for other
parts.)

98   John Skelton Magnyfycence, ed. R. L. Ramsay. 1908 (*for* 1906), $30.00
reprinted Kraus 1976.

99   The Romance of Emaré, ed. E. Rickert. 1908 (*for* 1906), *reprinted*   £3·50
1958.

100 The Middle English Harrowing of Hell and Gospel of Nicodemus, $17.50
ed. W. H. Hulme. 1908 (*for* 1907), *reprinted* Kraus 1976.

101 Songs, Carols and other Miscellaneous Poems from Balliol MS. 354, $25.00
Richard Hill's Commonplace-book, ed. R. Dyboski. 1908 (*for* 1907),
reprinted Kraus 1973.

E.S. 102 **The Promptorium Parvulorum**: the First English–Latin Dictionary, $36.25
ed. A. L. Mayhew. 1908, *reprinted* Kraus 1973.

103, 106 **Lydgate's Troy Book**, ed. H. Bergen. Vol. II, Book III, 1908; $45.00
Vol. III, Books IV and V, 1910; *reprinted as one volume* Kraus 1973.
(See E.S. 97, 126 for other parts.)

104 **The Non-Cycle Mystery Plays**, ed. O. Waterhouse. 1909. Superseded by S.S. 1.

105 **The Tale of Beryn**, with a Prologue of the Merry Adventure of the $25.00
Pardoner with a Tapster at Canterbury, ed. F. J. Furnivall and W. G.
Stone. 1909, *reprinted* Kraus 1973.

106 **Lydgate's Troy Book**, Vol. III. See above, E.S. 103.

107 **John Lydgate The Minor Poems**, ed. H. N. MacCracken. Vol. 1 £8·25
Religious Poems. 1911 (*for* 1910), *reprinted* 1961. (See O.S. 192 for
Vol. II.)

108 **Lydgate's Siege of Thebes**, ed. A. Erdmann. Vol. I Text. 1911. £5·25
reprinted 1960. (See E.S. 125 for Vol. II.)

109 **The Middle English Versions of Partonope of Blois**, ed. A. T. Bödtker. $45.00
1912 (*for* 1911), *reprinted* Kraus 1973.

110 **Caxton's Mirrour of the World**, ed. O. H. Prior. 1913 (*for* 1912), $22.50
reprinted Kraus 1978.

111 **Raoul Le Fevre The History of Jason**, translated by William Caxton, $15.00
ed. J. Munro. 1913 (*for* 1912), *reprinted* Kraus 1973.

112 **Henry Lovelich's Merlin**, ed. E. A. Kock. Vol. II 1913, *reprinted* £5·00
1961. (See E.S. 93 and O.S. 185 for other parts.) *Paper.*

113 **Poems by Sir John Salusbury and Robert Chester**, ed. Carleton Brown. $11.25
1914 (*for* 1913), *reprinted* Kraus 1973.

114 **The Gild of St. Mary, Lichfield**: Ordinances and other documents, $9.00
ed. F. J. Furnivall. 1920 (*for* 1914), *reprinted* Kraus 1973. *Paper.*

115 **The Chester Plays**, ed. Dr. Matthews. Vol. II 1916 (*for* 1914), *reprinted* 1967. £3·75

116 **The Pauline Epistles in MS.** Parker 32, Corpus Christi College, $35.00
Cambridge, ed. M. J. Powell. 1916 (*for* 1915), *reprinted* Kraus 1973.

117 **The Life of Fisher**, ed. R. Bayne. 1921 (*for* 1915), *reprinted* Kraus $10.00
1973.

118 **The Earliest Arithmetics in English**, ed. R. Steele. 1922 (*for* 1916), $7.50
reprinted Kraus 1973.

119 **The Owl and the Nightingale**, ed. J. H. G. Grattan and G. F. H. $12.00
Sykes. 1935 (*for* 1915), *reprinted* Kraus 1973.

120 **Ludus Coventriæ**, or The Plaie called Corpus Christi, Cotton MS. £7·00
Vespasian D. viii, ed. K. S. Block. 1922 (*for* 1917), *reprinted* 1961.

121 **Lydgate's Fall of Princes**, ed. H. Bergen. Vol. I 1924 (*for* 1918), £7·25
reprinted 1967.

122 **Lydgate's Fall of Princes**, ed. H. Bergen. Vol. II 1924 (*for* 1918), £7·25
reprinted 1967.

123 **Lydgate's Fall of Princes**, ed. H. Bergen. Vol. III 1924 (*for* 1919), £7·25
reprinted 1967.

124 **Lydgate's Fall of Princes**, ed. H. Bergen. Vol. IV 1927 (*for* 1919), £10·00
reprinted 1967.

125 **Lydgate's Siege of Thebes**, ed. A. Erdmann and E. Ekwall. Vol. II $22.00
Introduction, Notes, Glossary etc. 1930 (*for* 1920), *reprinted* Kraus
1973.

126 **Lydgate's Troy Book**, ed. H. Bergen. Vol. IV 1935 (*for* 1920), *reprinted* Kraus 1973. (See E.S. 97, 103, and 106 for other parts.) $50.00